HTML5 and CSS3
Complete
ILLUSTRATED

Second Edition

© VikaSuh/Shutterstock.com

Sasha Vodnik

 CENGAGE

Australia • Brazil • Mexico • Singapore • United Kingdom • United States

HTML5 and CSS3—Illustrated Complete
Second Edition
Sasha Vodnik

Product Director: Kathleen McMahon

Product Team Manager: Kristin McNary

Senior Product Manager: Jim Gish

Senior Director of Development: Marah Bellegarde

Product Development Manager: Leigh Hefferon

Senior Content Developer: Marjorie Hunt

Product Assistant: Abigail Pufpaff

Marketing Director: Michele McTighe

Senior Marketing Manager: Eric La Scola

Manufacturing Planner: Fola Orekoya

Developmental Editor: Pamela Conrad

Full Service Project Management: GEX Publishing Services

Proofreader: Gail Marks

Indexer: Alexandra Nickerson

QA Manuscript Reviewers: Danielle Shaw, Jeff Schwartz, and John Freitas

Cover Designer: GEX Publishing Services

Cover Artist: GEX Publishing Services

Cover image: © VikaSuh/Shutterstock.com

Composition: GEX Publishing Services

For product information and technology assistance, contact us at
Cengage Customer & Sales Support, 1-800-354-9706
or support.cengage.com.
For permission to use material from this text or product, submit all requests online at **www.cengage.com/permissions.**

Library of Congress Control Number: 2015945493
ISBN: 978-1-305-39404-9

Cengage
20 Channel Street
Boston, MA 02210
USA

Cengage is a leading provider of customized learning solutions with employees residing in nearly 40 different countries and sales in more than 125 countries around the world. Find your local representative at: **www.cengage.com.**

Cengage products are represented in Canada by Nelson Education, Ltd.

To learn more about Cengage platforms and services, register or access your online learning solution, or purchase materials for your course, visit **www.cengage.com.**

The websites featured in this book are fictional. Names, characters, businesses, places, are either the products of the author's imagination or used in a fictitious manner. Any resemblance to actual websites, places, or people is purely coincidental.

Trademarks:
Some of the product names and company names used in this book have been used for identification purposes only and may be trademarks or registered trademarks of their respective manufacturers and sellers.

Printed at CLDPC, USA, 10-20

Brief Contents

Contents

Appendix

Preface

Welcome to *HTML5 and CSS3—Illustrated Complete Second Edition*. This book has a unique design: Each skill is presented on two facing pages, with steps on the left and screens on the right. The layout makes it easy to learn a skill without having to read a lot of text and flip pages to see an illustration.

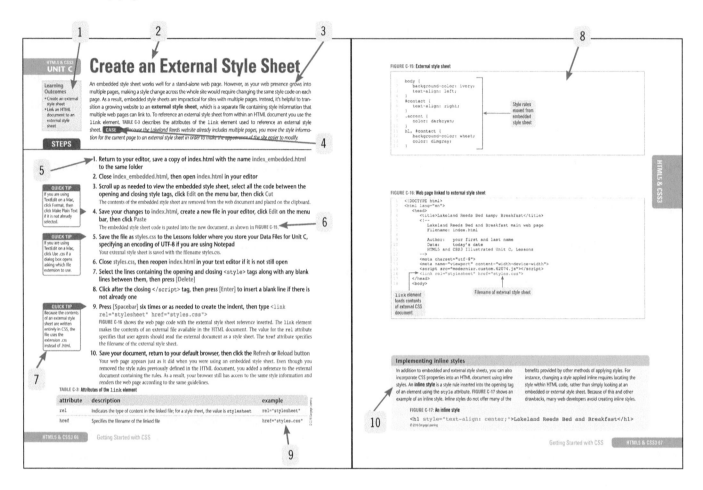

1 New! Learning Outcomes box lists measurable learning goals for which a student is accountable in that lesson.

2 Each two-page lesson focuses on a single skill.

3 Introduction briefly explains why the lesson skill is important.

4 A case scenario motivates the steps and puts learning in context.

5 Step-by-step instructions and brief explanations guide students through each hands-on lesson activity.

6 New! Figure references are now in red bold to help students refer back and forth between the steps and screenshots.

7 Tips and troubleshooting advice, right where you need it—next to the step itself.

8 New! Larger screen shots with green callouts and code students type shown in red.

9 Tables provide summaries of helpful information such as element and property syntax.

10 Clues to Use yellow boxes provide useful information related to the lesson skill.

This book is an ideal learning tool for a wide range of learners—the "rookies" will find the clean design easy to follow and focused with only essential information presented, and the "hotshots" will appreciate being able to move quickly through the lessons to find the information they need without reading a lot of text. The design also makes this book a great reference after the course is over! See the illustration on the left to learn more about the pedagogical and design elements of a typical lesson.

What's New in this Edition

- **Coverage** — This book covers basic to advanced concepts and skills for developing web pages and websites using HTML5 and CSS3. This new edition is fully updated with many enhancements, including new coverage of responsive design, teaching how to build sites that can be accessed by any device; and debugging using browser tools; it also now integrates mobile design and testing throughout.

- **New! Learning Outcomes** — Each lesson displays a green Learning Outcomes box that lists skills-based or knowledge-based learning goals for which students are accountable. Each Learning Outcome maps to a variety of learning activities and assessments.

- **New! Updated Design** — This edition features many new design Improvements to engage students — including larger lesson screenshots with green callouts and code students type formatted in red.

- **New! Independent Challenge 4: Explore** — This new case-based assessment activity allows students to explore new skills and use creativity to solve a problem or create a project.

Assignments

This book includes a wide variety of high-quality assignments you can use for practice and assessment. Assignments include

- **Concepts Review** — Multiple choice, matching, and screen identification questions.

- **Skills Review** — Step-by-step, hands-on review of every skill covered in the unit.

- **Independent Challenges 1-3** — Case projects requiring critical thinking and application of the unit skills. The Independent Challenges increase in difficulty. The first one in each unit provides the most hand-holding; the subsequent ones provide less guidance and require more critical thinking and independent problem solving.

- **Independent Challenge 4: Explore** — Case projects that let students explore new skills that are related to the core skills covered in the unit and are often more open ended, allowing students to use creativity to complete the assignment.

- **Visual Workshop** — Critical thinking exercises that require students to create a project by looking at a completed solution; they must apply the skills they've learned in the unit and use critical thinking skills to create the project from scratch.

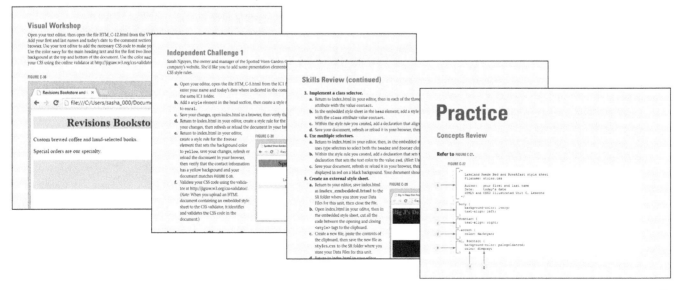

Instructor Resources

This book comes with a wide array of high-quality technology-based, teaching tools to help you teach and to help students learn. The following teaching tools are available for download at our Instructor Companion Site. Simply search for this text at *login.cengage.com*. An instructor login is required.

- **New! Learning Outcomes Map** — A grid for each unit shows the learning activities and assessments that map to each learning outcome in that unit.
- **Instructor's Manual** — Available as an electronic file, the Instructor's Manual includes lecture notes with teaching tips for each unit.
- **Data Files for Students** — To complete most units, students need Data Files, which are included as an Instructor Resource. Students can also download Data Files on cengagebrain.com.
- **Sample Syllabus** — Prepare and customize your course easily using this sample course outline.
- **PowerPoint Presentations** — Each unit has a corresponding PowerPoint presentation covering the skills and topics in that unit.
- **Figure Files** — The figures in the text are provided on the Instructor Resources site to help you illustrate key topics or concepts.

- **Solution Files** — Solution Files are files that contain the finished project that students create or modify in the lessons or end-of-unit material.
- **Solutions Document** — This document outlines the solutions for the end-of-unit Concepts Review, Skills Review, Independent Challenges and Visual Workshops.
- **Test Banks** — Cengage Learning Testing Powered by Cognero is a full-featured, online assessment system that allows instructors to create tests from publisher-provided content as well as write new questions. With the test generator, you can
  - Create tests from publisher-provided question sets.
  - Edit publisher questions.
  - Write your own questions.
  - Tag questions with learning objectives, rubrics, and other meta-information.
  - Print tests or deliver them online through a learning management system.

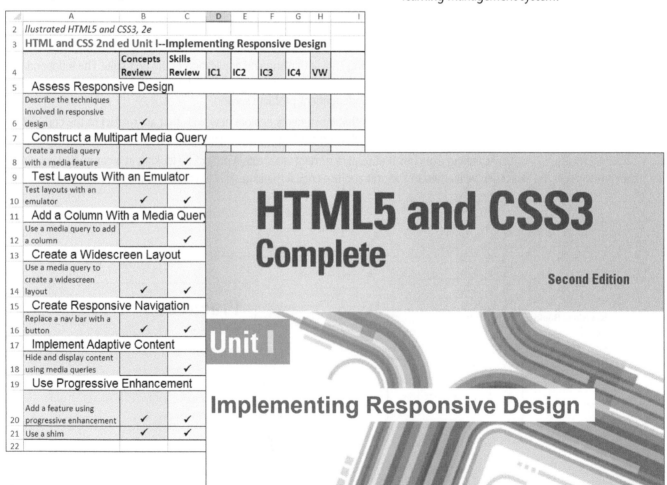

Before You Begin

1. Download Data Files

To complete many of the lessons and end-of-unit assignments, you need to use the Data Files that were created specifically for this book. All Data Files are available as part of the Instructor Resources. You can also download Data Files for free at cengagebrain.com. (For detailed instructions, go to www.cengage.com/ct/studentdownload.)

2. Verify System Requirements

To complete the lessons in this book, you need 2 types of applications: an editor and one or more browsers. You can use a plain text editor such as Notepad (part of Windows) or TextEdit (part of Mac OS X), but a code editor is recommended. Free code editors include Aptana Studio 3 (Win/Mac), KomodoEdit (Win/Mac), Notepad++ (Win), and TextWrangler (Mac). You can complete the lessons with a single desktop browser, but real world web development requires testing on a wide variety of browsers and devices. If possible, you should secure access to all of the following desktop browsers: Chrome (Win and Mac), Firefox (Win and Mac), Internet Explorer (Win), and Edge (Win). In addition, if possible, you should make arrangements to test using Safari on iOS (iPhone or iPod Touch) and Chrome on Android.

3. Review These Figure Notes

Figures showing code include line numbers. If your editor shows line numbers, they may not exactly match those shown in the figures; instead, use the line numbers in the figures as a rough guide for orienting yourself in your data files. In figures showing newly entered code, that code is displayed in red for easy identification. If your code editor highlights code in one or more colors, this will not match the color shown in the figures.

Acknowledgements

Thanks to the many people who have helped make this book a reality. Jim Gish was consistently encouraging and made sure the resources were available for a top-notch revision. Marjorie Hunt wrangled the schedule and kept her eye on the big picture so I could focus on the details. Pam Conrad went the extra mile as developmental editor to ensure the explanations were clear, the steps all worked as intended, and all the i's were dotted and the t's crossed. The great people at GEX Publishing Services laid everything out on the page and made it look great. Jeff Schwartz, Danielle Shaw, and John Freitas meticulously tested all the steps and let me know what needed fixing before the book went out the door. John McKelvy/mackjackstudio.com and Kenji Oshima/coachkenji.com created the logos and layout prototypes for the fictitious businesses in the lessons and practice projects. Roland McGrath generously provided recent Android devices for testing.

Finally, thanks to my parents, Jim and Diana Vodnik, for helping me to see learning as both an adventure and a priority. And thanks to my husband, Jason Bucy, for his love, support, and help in navigating the balancing act that's a fundamental part of an author's life.

Feedback and Questions

The author welcomes feedback and questions about this book from instructors and students. You can contact Sasha Vodnik on Twitter at *@sashavodnik*.

CENGAGE**brain**.com

Buy. Rent. Access.

Access Student Data Files, CourseMate,
and other study tools on **cengagebrain.com**.

For detailed instructions visit
http://solutions.cengage.com/ctdownloads/.

Store your Data Files on a USB drive for maximum efficiency in
organizing and working with the files.

Macintosh users should use a program to expand WinZip or PKZip archives.
Ask your instructor or lab coordinator for assistance.

Getting Started with HTML

CASE You've been hired by Lakeland Reeds Bed and Breakfast to build a website. You can create your own web pages like those found on the World Wide Web using just your computer and a text editor. In this unit, you'll learn about planning and wireframing a website, creating the head and body sections of a web page, adding web page text, and testing your web page in desktop and mobile browsers.

Unit Objectives

After completing this unit, you will be able to:

- Define a project plan
- Create wireframes and a storyboard
- Create an HTML document
- Set up the document head and body
- Add text to a web page

- Add a comment to a web document
- Preview your web page on a desktop computer
- Configure web server software
- Preview your web page on mobile devices

Files You Will Need

L	0 files	IC3	0 files
SR	0 files	IC4	0 files
IC1	0 files	VW	0 files
IC2	0 files		

©VikaSuh/Shutterstock.com

Define a Project Plan

Learning
Outcomes
• Identify questions
  to ask a potential
  client
• Use a project plan
  to summarize
  client responses

People and organizations around the world share information using the **World Wide Web**, or **web** for short. You can make your own information available on the web by creating **web pages**, which are documents formatted to be accessible on the web, and then publishing them as **websites**, which are available to anyone with web access. Whether you intend to make a single web page or a large set of interrelated web pages, making information accessible on the web starts with careful planning. Whether you're brainstorming for a personal site or meeting with a client regarding a site you've been hired to create, your first step is to create a **project plan**, which is also known as a **design document**. A project plan summarizes your client's parameters for the site, including audience, budget, and timeline. **CASE** *You held a planning meeting with Phillip Blaine, owner of Lakeland Reeds, to discuss the components he would like included in his new website.* **FIGURE A-1** *shows the project plan you developed based on client responses at this meeting.*

DETAILS

Important questions to consider when planning a website include the following:

- **What are the goals and objectives of the website?**

  In order to understand the goals and objectives for the site, you want to ask your client a variety of questions. For example, "What is the mission of the organization? Why do you want a website? What are the short-term goals of the website? What are the long-term goals of the website? What do you hope to gain by having a web presence? Who is your target audience? Do your objectives support the needs of your target audience?" The more thorough you are in asking questions of the client, the better prepared you will be to design the website.

- **Who is the target audience?**

  It can be helpful to know the target audience for a website when choosing a layout and design. Websites should look different based upon who will be visiting the site and why they are interested in the content. Some potential questions to ask about the target audience might be, "Who are the typical members of your audience? What is the mix of genders? What is the age range? What professions are they in? What is the average education level? Why will people visit this website? Will your desktop visitors be using Microsoft Windows, Apple OS X, or another operating system? Which web browsers will they use to view the website? How common is mobile device use among your audience members? Which types of mobile devices do they use?" While your client may not have ready answers to all of these questions, getting even a few answers can help prepare you for the design phase.

- **What type of website is it?**

  Identifying the type of website the owner wants can help to focus the scope of the project. A website usually has one of a small number of main functions: providing a web presence that serves as an online informational brochure, providing important information for special interest groups and nonprofit organizations, showcasing examples of different types of works and designs commonly used by web design individuals and agencies, providing multiple levels of information with page templates, extracting information from databases, or conducting the sale of products or services and other business transactions through the Internet. It is important to clearly define what the site will include, as well as what the site won't include.

- **What is the budget for the project?**

  Every website design project should include a budget that is presented to the client prior to completing any work. The budget should be included in the project plan, which becomes part of the contract.

- **What is the timeline for the project?**

  You should always provide the website owner with a timeline that includes the delivery date of the final website, along with various implementation milestones along the way. The timeline should always identify who is responsible for which tasks.

Project plan for Lakeland Reeds Bed and Breakfast

Objectives:
- Make general info about the facility and contact info available online
- Enable prospective guests to view the accommodations and grounds
- Allow prospective guests to book a stay online

Target audience:
- 35+
- Live in southern Canada and the upper Midwest U.S.
- Want to "get away from it all"
- Not sure about technical details of users, but it's assumed most will have some web experience

Site type:
- Billboard (while the client wants some e-commerce functionality, they will accomplish this by linking to another site that takes reservations; thus, no advanced functionality is required for this site)

Budget:
- Hien is preparing a few detailed options for the client; this section will be updated when the budget is finalized and the contract is signed

Timeline:

Milestone	Date	Who's responsible
Design mockup submitted for approval	April 1, 2018	Project manager
Draft site published to testing server	April 15, 2018	Project manager
Feedback received from client	April 22, 2018	Phillip Blaine
Client feedback incorporated	May 1, 2018	Project manager
Final feedback from client	May 8, 2018	Phillip Blaine
Final feedback incorporated	May 22, 2018	Project manager
Final signoff from client	June 5, 2018	Phillip Blaine
Site goes live	June 5, 2018	Project manager

Client contact info:

Phillip Blaine

Lakeland Reeds Bed and Breakfast

45 Marsh Grass Ln.

Marble, MN 55764

(218) 555-5253

HTML5 & CSS3

Deciding how much to charge

Estimating the amount of time a project will take can be difficult, especially for new web designers. If you work for a web design agency, the budget will typically be developed by your supervisors. If you are a freelance web designer, you must place a value on your time that takes many things into consideration, such as the cost of computer equipment and software, supplying your own insurance, advertising, and other expenses. There really is no set hourly or project fee in this industry, as it varies dramatically depending upon the geographic market, competition, and experience level of the web designer. New web designers often barter, or trade, their skills for products or services offered by a website owner as a means of building a portfolio.

Learning
Outcomes
• Define wireframes
  and storyboards
• Identify wireframe
  and storyboard
  components

Create Wireframes and a Storyboard

When you create a web page or a website, it can be helpful to start by getting a clear idea of what you're trying to build. Web designers typically accomplish this by creating a **wireframe**, which is a sketch that outlines the components of each web page and their place in the layout. A designer usually creates one wireframe for each web page or web page type. For a website containing multiple pages, they also create a **storyboard**, which illustrates links among the pages. When there is a web design team working on a project, the people responsible for art or design often create the wireframes and storyboard, and then they hand off these documents to the developers, who use these documents to create a web page or website. **CASE** ▶ *You work with Karl Dixon, one of your colleagues in the art department, to create a wireframe and a storyboard for the Lakeland Reeds website based on the project plan.*

DETAILS

When you create a wireframe and a storyboard for a website, be sure to include these main steps:

• **Identify components to include**

  Before you start sketching, it's important to get a firm handle on all the elements that the website you're working on must include. A good place to start is your project plan, which should include a thorough inventory of items that must be part of the website; for instance, an existing logo and color scheme that a client already uses in all of its printed materials. You should augment this list with any other essential design elements based on your understanding of the site's target audience and functionality; for example, most multipage websites need a standardized navigation section that provides links to each of the pages.

QUICK TIP
Many common web
page designs use
columns that are
about one third the
width of the page to
approximate
traditional aesthetic
proportions.

• **Sketch possible layouts and then select one**

  The next step is to place the elements in a layout that's functional, usable, and, ideally, aesthetically pleasing. This step is often the job of a graphic designer; however, it's a skill that many web developers without artistic backgrounds have obtained with study and practice. Whoever does this step, it often involves a series of sketches that either lays out a set of choices or progressively fine-tunes a theme. For a simple website, a single layout should suffice for all the site's pages; however, if some pages have requirements that are best served by distinct layouts, these layouts need to be finalized in this step as well. The wireframe in **FIGURE A-2** shows the layout for the main page of the Lakeland Reeds website.

• **Map the relationships among web pages**

  Any time you're creating a website or a single web page with links to other websites, it's helpful to map out the relationships between pages. This map is a crucial tool when you create the navigation system for the website. The storyboard in **FIGURE A-3** lists the pages of the Lakeland Reeds website and illustrates the relationships among them, as well as links to external pages.

FIGURE A-2: Wireframe for Lakeland Reeds main web page

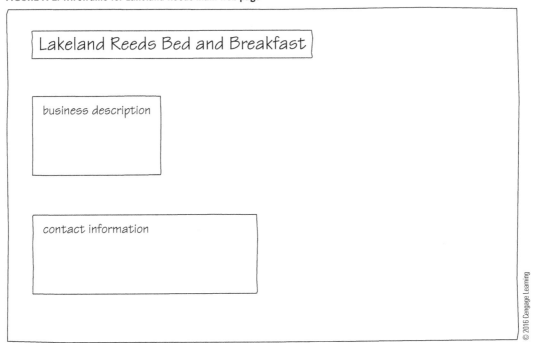

FIGURE A-3: Storyboard for Lakeland Reeds website

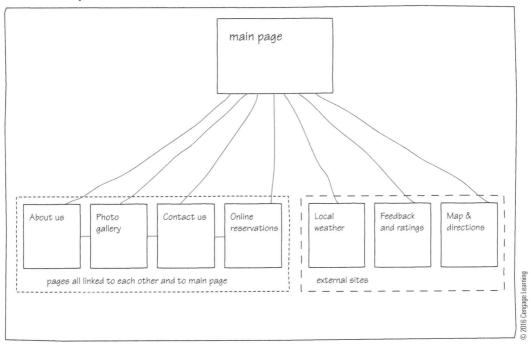

Creating a website from a template

An alternative to creating a layout for your website is to download a **template**, which is a generic layout that includes a color scheme and element positions but which uses placeholder images and text. Some templates are available to download and use for free, while others must be purchased from the designer. A web developer can simply replace the placeholder items with elements specific to the website being developed. While a template is not as specifically tailored to the companies or topics of the websites where it is used, it can save time in the web development process and can be an invaluable tool when a site needs to be up right away.

Create an HTML Document

Learning
Outcomes
• Enter a DOCTYPE
declaration
• Add basic tags to
an HTML
document
• Save an HTML
document

Web pages are written in **Hypertext Markup Language (HTML)**, which is a standardized format for specifying the structure of a web page. An HTML document consists solely of text. As a result, you can create a web page in a text editor such as Notepad, which is included with Windows, or TextEdit, which is part of Mac OS X. To create a web page, you enter text that you want to display on the page along with HTML codes known as **tags**, which specify how a browser should treat each item in the document. An HTML tag always starts with an opening angle bracket (<) and ends with a closing angle bracket (>). The text between the angle brackets specifies the HTML element type being applied to the selection. While most tags occur in pairs, some tags, known as **one-sided tags**, are used by themselves. In addition, every document starts with a **DOCTYPE declaration**, which is text that resembles a tag and provides information about the programming language used to write the page. **CASE** *You create the basic structure of the main page for the Lakeland Reeds website.*

STEPS

QUICK TIP
To write HTML in
TextEdit on a Mac,
you need to change
two program
preferences. Press
[command][,] to
open the Preferences
dialog box. On the
New Document tab,
click Plain text. On
the Open and Save
tab, uncheck Add
".txt" extension to
plain text files.

1. **Start your text editor**
   A new, blank document opens.

2. **Type** `<!DOCTYPE html>`**, then press** [Enter]
   This DOCTYPE declaration lets browsers know that the document contents are written in HTML.

3. **Type** `<html>`**, press** [Enter] **twice, then type** `</html>`**, as shown in** FIGURE A-4
   A tag pair assigns meaning to a web page **element**, which is a specific component of the page, such as a paragraph or a heading. You place the **opening tag** at the start of the element you are marking and the **closing tag** at the end. A closing tag is the same as its corresponding opening tag except that the opening angle bracket is followed by a slash (/). The `html` tag pair marks the beginning and the end of the web page.

4. **Click** File**, then click** Save
   The Save As dialog box opens.

TROUBLE
If you don't have the
empty folder
structure for storing
this unit's files, create
a Lessons folder
within the drive and
folder where you
store your Data Files
for Unit A, then save
your file to the
Lessons folder.

5. **Navigate to the drive and folder where you store your Data Files for Unit A, then open the** Lessons **folder**

6. **In the** File name **box (Windows) or** Save As **box (Mac), type** index.html
   The standard name for the main page of a website is "index." The .htm or .html extension signifies that a file is written in HTML.

7. **If you are using Notepad in Windows, click the** Save as type list arrow**, then click** All Files (*.*)

8. **If you are using TextEdit on a Mac, click the** If no extension is provided, use ".txt" box **to uncheck it**

9. **Click** Save
   The index.html file is saved to your storage location.

Using other web page creation software

Many other programs are available that allow you to create web pages visually by clicking buttons and using drag-and-drop to place items on a page. However, creating your first web pages by entering HTML directly—sometimes referred to as **hand-coding**—is one of the best ways to become familiar with HTML and the underlying structure of a web page. Many professional developers use a **code editor**, which is a text editor that is optimized for writing code in a programming language. FIGURE A-5 shows the web page in Notepad++, a free code editor available for Windows, and points out some features common to code editors. Other popular free code editors include Aptana Studio 3 (Win and Mac), Komodo Edit (Win and Mac), and TextWrangler (Mac).

FIGURE A-4: The basic structure of the web page

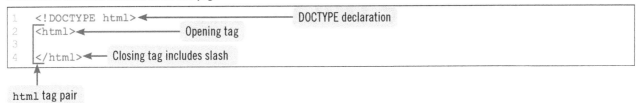

FIGURE A-5: The basic structure of the web page in Notepad++

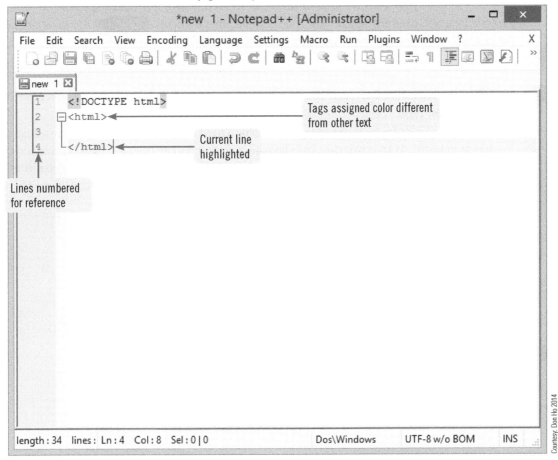

Understanding the difference between HTML and XHTML

Extensible Hypertext Markup Language (XHTML) is a version of HTML that conforms to the rules of Extensible Markup Language (XML). Although most modern web documents are written in HTML, some organizations require XML-compatible code, and therefore use XHTML instead of HTML. HTML and XHTML have only a handful of differences, and utilities are available that can automatically convert code from one to the other. In general, HTML syntax is less strict than XHTML code, and some aspects of code that you can omit in HTML are required in XHTML code. Except where otherwise stated, all the code you write in this book will conform to the rules of HTML.

Learning Outcomes
- Define element nesting
- Add a head section to an HTML document
- Add a body section to an HTML document

Set Up the Document Head and Body

Within the `html` tag pair for a web page, the document contents are divided into two sections. The **head section** contains elements that specify information about the web page but are not displayed in the browser window, such as the page title that appears in a browser tab. The contents of the **body section** are visible in the main window of a web browser and include elements like headings and paragraphs. Both the `head` and `body` tag pairs are located within, or **nested** within, the `html` tag pair. Most elements in the code for a web page are nested within one or more other elements. **CASE** *As you continue creating the structure for the Lakeland Reeds web page, you add the head and body sections to the page.*

STEPS

QUICK TIP
To read more about any HTML tag used in this book, see Appendix A.

1. **Click the blank line between the opening and closing `html` tags, press [Spacebar] three times, then type** `<head>`

   This is the opening tag for the head tag pair. Adding a fixed number of spaces before a nested tag makes it appear indented. As your web page code becomes longer and more complex, these indentations make it easier to identify the beginning and end of an element at a glance. For the code you enter in this book, you'll use three spaces for each indent level. **FIGURE A-6** shows HTML code with several layers of nested tags that are formatted with indentations.

2. **Press [Enter] twice, press [Spacebar] three times, then type** `</head>`

   This creates the closing tag for the head tag pair.

3. **Press [Enter], press [Spacebar] three times, then type** `<body>`

   This creates the opening tag for the body tag pair.

4. **Press [Enter] twice, press [Spacebar] three times, then type** `</body>`

   This creates the closing tag for the body tag pair.

QUICK TIP
To save your work without using the menus, you can press [Ctrl][S] (Windows) or [command][S] (Mac).

5. **Save your work**

   FIGURE A-7 shows the completed web page structure including the head and body sections.

FIGURE A-6: HTML code containing multiple layers of nested elements

```
1    <!DOCTYPE html>
2    <html>
3        <head>
4            <title>Comparing HTML and XHTML</title>
5        </head>
6        <body>
7            <p>HTML vs. XHTML</p>
8            <table>
9                <tr>
10                   <th>Aspect</th>
11                   <th>HTML</th>
12                   <th>XHTML</th>
13               </tr>
14               <tr>
15                   <td>Tag nesting</td>
16                   <td>Tags may be closed out of order</td>
17                   <td>Tags must be closed in the order opened</td>
18               </tr>
19               <tr>
20                   <td>Tag case</td>
21                   <td>Tags may be written in upper or lower case</td>
22                   <td>Tags must be written in lower case</td>
23               </tr>
24           </table>
25       </body>
26   </html>
```

Indentations indicate sections of code visually

FIGURE A-7: Completed web page structure

```
1    <!DOCTYPE html>
2    <html>
3        <head>
4                        ←── Head section
5        </head>
6        <body>
7                        ←── Body section
8        </body>
9    </html>
```

Describing nesting relationships

An element nested within another element is called a **child element** of the enclosing element, and the enclosing element is known as the **parent element**. In the code shown in **FIGURE A-6**, the head element is both a child of the html element and the parent of the title element. In addition, the html element is the **grandparent** element of the title element, which can be referred to as a **grandchild element** of the html element. Two elements that are both children of the same parent element are known as **sibling elements**. The head element and the body element are sibling elements, because they are both children of the html element.

Add Text to a Web Page

Learning
Outcomes
• Add a `title`
  element
• Add an `h1` element
• Add paragraphs
  with the `p` element

Because an HTML document is simply a plain text document that includes HTML codes, entering text for your web pages is as simple as typing it. You add the appropriate HTML tags to specify the element type for each text item on the page as you type that text. **CASE** ▶ *You enter the page title that will appear in the tab or title bar of a viewer's browser, along with the basic information about Lakeland Reeds.* FIGURE A-8 *shows an updated wireframe of the main Lakeland Reeds web page that includes the specific text content.*

STEPS

TROUBLE
If your code editor indents automatically, you may not need to add spaces. Just be sure that your insertion point is indented six spaces before entering the `title` element.

1. **Click the blank line above the closing `</head>` tag, press [Spacebar] six times, then type** `<title>Lakeland Reeds Bed and Breakfast</title>`

   The `title` element specifies text that appears in the tab or title bar of the web browser opening the page. This element is part of the document's head section because the text does not appear in the main browser window. This line is indented six spaces because it is nested within the `head` element, which is nested within the `html` element.

2. **Click the blank line between the opening and closing `<body>` tags, press [Spacebar] six times, then type** `<h1>Lakeland Reeds Bed and Breakfast</h1>`

   The `h1` element represents the highest-level heading on the page. TABLE A-1 compares this element to the 5 other heading elements in HTML.

TROUBLE
If you're using Notepad and can't see all the text in the window at once, click Format on the Menu bar, then click Word Wrap.

3. **Press [Enter], press [Spacebar] six times, then type** `<p>A country getaway perfect for fishing, boating, biking, or just watching the day go by.</p>`

   The `p` element marks a paragraph of text.

4. **Press [Enter], press [Spacebar] six times, then type** `<p>(218) 555-5253</p>`

   Your document should look like the one shown in FIGURE A-9. Not all editors wrap text in the same way, so your editor may show line 9 starting at the far left, rather than indenting it. This does not affect the meaning of the code, however.

5. **Save your work**

Understanding the complementary roles of HTML and CSS

Browsers generally display the content of HTML elements such as `h1` and `p` in ways that visually distinguish the content. However, at its core, HTML is intended to indicate only the meanings of elements such as headings and paragraphs in a web page, but not to tell web browsers how the elements should appear. Instead, HTML has a companion language, **Cascading Style Sheets (CSS)**, which is designed for describing the appearance of items. As you write HTML, you should keep in mind that your only goal in marking content with HTML elements is to describe to browsers and to user agents the type of content a page includes. When you learn to write CSS code, you'll use that language to specify visual display properties such as fonts, colors, borders, and placement within a browser window.

FIGURE A-8: Updated wireframe

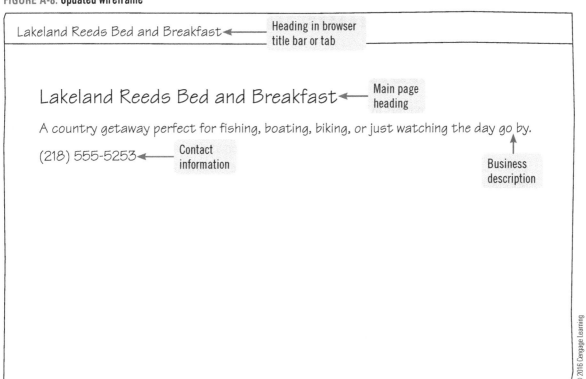

Lakeland Reeds Bed and Breakfast — Heading in browser title bar or tab

Lakeland Reeds Bed and Breakfast — Main page heading

A country getaway perfect for fishing, boating, biking, or just watching the day go by. — Business description

(218) 555-5253 — Contact information

FIGURE A-9: `title`, `h1`, and `p` elements entered

```
1   <!DOCTYPE html>
2   <html>
3      <head>
4         <title>Lakeland Reeds Bed and Breakfast</title>
5      </head>
6      <body>
7         <h1>Lakeland Reeds Bed and Breakfast</h1>
8         <p>A country getaway perfect for fishing, boating, biking, or just watching the day
9         go by.</p>
10        <p>(218) 555-5253</p>
11     </body>
12   </html>
```

title element

h1 element

p element for business description

p element for contact information

TABLE A-1: HTML heading elements

element	sample code	default rendering in browsers
h1	`<h1>Heading 1</h1>`	**Heading 1**
h2	`<h2>Heading 2</h2>`	**Heading 2**
h3	`<h3>Heading 3</h3>`	**Heading 3**
h4	`<h4>Heading 4</h4>`	**Heading 4**
h5	`<h5>Heading 5</h5>`	**Heading 5**
h6	`<h6>Heading 6</h6>`	**Heading 6**

Add a Comment to a Web Document

Learning Outcomes
- Add comment tags
- Add comment text

In addition to marking text that appears on your web pages, you can create text elements in your web page code that browsers ignore. These elements, known as **comments**, are not rendered by browsers and are viewable only by team members or other developers who examine the HTML code of your web pages. Comments can be especially helpful when you are creating or adding on to a large, complex web document or website, or when other web developers will be working with your code—now or in the future. Common uses for comments include explaining what a particular section of HTML does or pointing out the beginning and end of parts of a web page containing numerous HTML elements. The comment tag pair begins with <!-- and ends with -->. **CASE** *You add a comment to the head section of your document describing its content, listing yourself as the author, and indicating the date it was last modified.*

STEPS

1. **Click at the end of the line containing the** `title` **element, then press** [Enter]

2. **Press** [Spacebar] **six times, then type** <!--

3. **Press** [Enter] **twice, press** [Spacebar] **six times, then type** -->
   FIGURE A-10 shows the comment tags entered in your document. The contents of your comment go between the opening <!-- and closing --> tags. **TABLE A-2** describes the tags used to create a comment element, along with tags for all the other elements you've created in this unit.

4. **Click the blank line between the opening and closing comment tags, press** [Spacebar] **nine times, type** Lakeland Reeds Bed and Breakfast main web page, **then press** [Enter]

5. **Press** [Spacebar] **nine times, type** Filename: index.html, **then press** [Enter] **twice**
   You can include blank lines within a comment to improve readability.

QUICK TIP
Adding extra spaces after the colon lines up your name with the filename in the previous line of text, making the information easier to read.

6. **Press** [Spacebar] **nine times, type** Author:, **press** [Spacebar] **three times, type your first and last name, then press** [Enter]

7. **Press** [Spacebar] **nine times, type** Date:, **press** [Spacebar] **five times, type today's date, then press** [Enter]

8. **Press** [Spacebar] **nine times, then type** HTML5 and CSS3 Illustrated Unit A, Lessons
   Your completed comment should match the one shown in **FIGURE A-11**.

9. **Save your work**

Understanding single-line and multi-line comments

An HTML comment can be either single-line or multi-line. A **single-line comment** includes the opening tag, comment text, and closing tag on a single line. For instance, the following comment is a single-line comment:

<!-- This page last updated 5/26/2018 -->

By contrast, a **multi-line comment** occupies multiple lines. In a multi-line comment, the opening and closing tags are often on their own lines, and the content may occupy one or more additional lines, like the comment you created in the steps in this lesson. The choice to use a single-line comment or a multi-line comment is generally based on the amount of comment text you want to add to your document. A single-line comment makes sense for a word or phrase, while using a multi-line comment can make it easier to read a longer comment by breaking it up over multiple lines.

FIGURE A-10: Comment tags added to an HTML document

```
1   <!DOCTYPE html>
2   <html>
3       <head>
4           <title>Lakeland Reeds Bed and Breakfast</title>
5           <!--                        Opening comment tag
6
7           -->                         Closing comment tag
8       </head>
9       <body>
10          <h1>Lakeland Reeds Bed and Breakfast</h1>
11          <p>A country getaway perfect for fishing, boating, biking, or just watching the day
12          go by.</p>
13          <p>(218) 555-5253</p>
14      </body>
15  </html>
```

FIGURE A-11: Comment text added to an HTML document

```
1   <!DOCTYPE html>
2   <html>
3       <head>
4           <title>Lakeland Reeds Bed and Breakfast</title>
5           <!--
6               Lakeland Reeds Bed and Breakfast main web page     Comment text
7               Filename: index.html                               entered between
8                                                                  opening and closing
9               Author:   Faduma Egal                              comment tags
10              Date:     9/26/2018
11              HTML5 and CSS3 Illustrated Unit A, Lessons
12          -->
13      </head>
14      <body>
15          <h1>Lakeland Reeds Bed and Breakfast</h1>
16          <p>A country getaway perfect for fishing, boating, biking, or just watching the day
17          go by.</p>
18          <p>(218) 555-5253</p>
19      </body>
20  </html>
```

TABLE A-2: Basic web page elements

element	function	code sample
comment	adds text viewable only by team members or other developers who examine the HTML code of your web pages	`<!-- This page last updated 5/26/2018 -->`

html	marks the beginning and the end of the web page	`<html>`
		`  web page contents`
		`</html>`

head	contains elements that are not part of the web page shown in the browser window	`<head>`
		`  head contents, such as title and meta elements`
		`</head>`

title	specifies text that appears in the title bar of the web browser opening the page	`<title>Lakeland Reeds</title>`

body	includes contents that are visible in the main window of a web browser	`<body>`
		`  body contents, such as p and h1 elements`
		`</body>`

p	marks a paragraph of text	`<p>Escape to the lake!</p>`
h1	represents the highest-level heading on the page	`<h1>Lakeland Reeds</h1>`

Preview Your Web Page on a Desktop Computer

Learning
Outcomes
• Open an HTML
document in a
web browser
• Compare how
HTML documents
are rendered by
different browsers

An important step in the process of creating a web page is to **preview** it, which involves opening it in one or more browsers and examining the result. When a web page isn't interpreted as expected by a browser, you can research the problem and make corrections to the code before publishing the page. In addition, because different browsers can interpret the same page with slight differences, it's good practice to test your pages with multiple browsers. While many desktop browsers and versions exist, a good place to start is the current versions of Google Chrome, Mozilla Firefox, and Microsoft Internet Explorer (IE). **CASE** ▸ *You preview your Lakeland Reeds web page in the three most commonly used desktop web browsers.*

STEPS

TROUBLE
If your web page
does not match
FIGURE A-12 return
to your editor,
compare your code
to **FIGURE A-11**,
edit as necessary,
save the file, then
repeat Step 1 to
preview your edited
web page.

1. **Navigate to the drive and folder where you store your Data Files for Unit A using your file manager, open the** Lessons folder, **then double-click** index.html

   The web page opens in your system's default web browser. FIGURE A-12 shows the file open in Chrome.

2. **Return to your file manager, right-click (Windows) or press [control] and click (Mac)** index.html, **point to** Open with, **then click another browser name in the list**

   The web page opens in another browser.

3. **Note any differences between the two browsers in the way the page is displayed**

   Often differences in the way each browser displays, or **renders**, a web page are subtle, such as slight variations in the space between lines. FIGURE A-13 shows a web page displayed in different browsers.

4. **Repeat Steps 2 and 3 until you have viewed your page in the current versions of Chrome, Firefox, and Internet Explorer**

Understanding the effect of browser extensions on page rendering

Modern browsers are highly customizable, allowing users to install new features and modify default settings. One common way of customizing a browser is to install an **extension**, which is a small application that changes the way web pages are rendered or integrates features with the content of a web page. Some of the most common extensions stop video or audio from loading and playing automatically on a web page, or enable web developers to examine or change the code of a web document. Some extensions may highlight or underline text or add icons to web page text rendered in the browser window. It's important to understand that these changes are not part of the web page code you're opening, but they are added by extensions. For instance, if you have an extension installed for an Internet calling service such as Skype, you may see formatting changes to any phone number displayed on a web page you open. Extensions can be disabled, which stops them from functioning but keeps them installed on your system. As you're testing web documents that you create, you should disable any extensions installed on each browser you're using. You can find instructions to disable extensions on each major browser by using a search engine to perform a search on the words "disable extensions" and the name of the browser.

FIGURE A-12: Web page in Google Chrome

Contents of `title` element displayed in tab

Contents of `h1` element displayed as larger text

Browser displays `p` elements as standard text

Location of file; your path will differ

FIGURE A-13: HTML document rendered in different browsers

Slight differences in text appearance

title text displayed in different places

Chrome

Firefox

Internet Explorer

Understanding why browsers display web pages differently

The display of web pages in HTML5 starts with the specifications maintained by groups such as the **World Wide Web Consortium (W3C)**, an organization that helps build consensus around changes and additions to the language, and publishes descriptions of the current standards. The standards list and describe all the available elements, along with parameters for how browsers should handle them. Browsers are built around software known as **rendering engines** that translate web page elements into visual, auditory, or tactile representations based on these standards. Because the standards require some interpretation, no two engines render the same HTML code in exactly the same way. In addition, the creators of rendering engines do not always implement all of the current standards in their software. Because the audience for your web pages will almost always be using a number of different browsers, it's important to test your code in a variety of popular desktop browsers and on multiple desktop operating systems (such as Windows 8, Windows 7, and Mac OS X).

Configure Web Server Software

Learning
Outcomes
• Describe the role
of web server
software in
website testing
• Enable the web
server in a code
editor

Testing a web page includes previewing it on some devices other than your desktop computer, such as mobile devices. Because you can't directly open a file from your desktop computer on another device, many developers install software known as web server software on their desktop computers. **Web server software** makes web documents available over a network to other computers, which are known as **clients**. Many code editors, such as Dreamweaver, include their own web server software, which you simply need to turn on in the application's settings in order to use it. **CASE** ▸ *To prepare for testing your web page on mobile devices, you configure the web server software built into Aptana Studio 3, which is a free code editor for both Windows and Mac that you can download from aptana.com.*

STEPS

Note: The following steps use Aptana Studio 3, which is a free code editor for both Windows and Mac, and which integrates by default with Firefox. If you're using a different code editor with a built-in web server, use the editor's documentation to enable its web server, then proceed to the next lesson.

1. **Open Aptana Studio 3, click** Window **(Win) or** Aptana Studio 3 **(Mac) on the menu bar, then click** Preferences

2. **Double-click** Aptana Studio **on the left side of the Preferences dialog box, double-click** Web Servers **in the list that opens, then click** Built-in
   The Built-in Web Server Preferences are displayed as shown in **FIGURE A-14**.

QUICK TIP
The IP address
127.0.0.1 is a
special value that's
accessible only
on the current
computer. Any other
value in the list will
also be accessible to
other devices on the
same network.

3. **If the value for IP Address is 127.0.0.1, click the** IP Address **arrow**
   A list of possible IP addresses is displayed as shown in **FIGURE A-15**.

4. **Click any value other than 127.0.0.1 on the IP Address menu**

5. **Click** Apply, **then click** OK

Understanding web servers

Creating and saving a web page on your computer is not sufficient to make it available to all web users. Every web page accessible on the web is located on a **web server**, which is a computer that is running web server software and that is always connected to the Internet. Although someone who's technologically proficient can configure a personal web server in their home or business, most public websites are made available on dedicated web servers that are maintained by teams of professionals and connected to the Internet with high-capacity connections. Many companies run web servers and sell space on them for a monthly fee. When you create a web page that you want to make publicly available on the web, you must first secure space on a web server and upload your files to that web server.

FIGURE A-14: Aptana Studio 3 Built-in Web Server Preferences

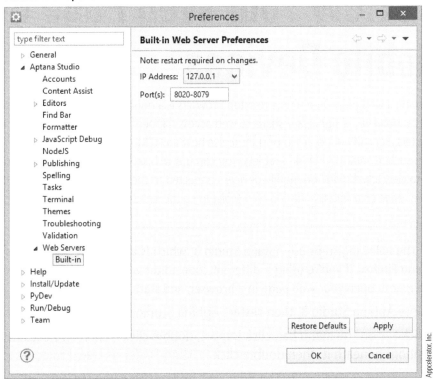

FIGURE A-15: Aptana Studio 3 IP Address options

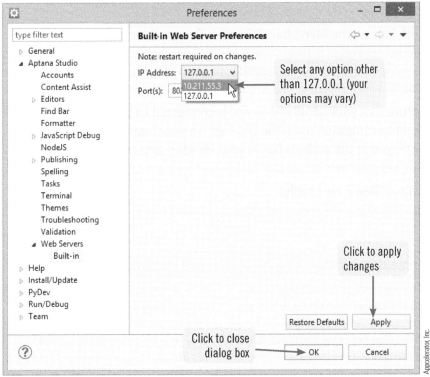

Preview Your Web Page on Mobile Devices

Learning
Outcomes
• Explain the impor-
tance of testing
web pages on
mobile devices
• View an HTML
document on
mobile devices

Previewing a web page on multiple desktop browsers is a good start for getting an idea of how it will look for users. However, a significant share of web access happens on mobile devices rather than on desktop computers. For this reason, it's important to see how an HTML document is rendered on web browsers on devices such as smartphones and tablets. You can use web server software running on your desktop computer to view a web page on mobile devices connected to the same wireless network. **CASE** *You test your web page on a smartphone and on a tablet using the web server built into Aptana Studio 3.*

STEPS

Note: The following steps use Aptana Studio 3, which is a free code editor for both Windows and Mac, and Firefox. If you're using a different code editor with a built-in web server, use the editor's web server to open your web page in a browser, and start with Step 7.

1. **Close Aptana Studio 3, then restart Aptana Studio 3**

2. **Click File on the menu bar, click Import, double-click General if necessary to view the options beneath it, then double-click Existing Folder as New Project**

QUICK TIP
All files and folders
within the folder
you specify as
a project are
accessible using
the web server.

3. **Click Browse, navigate to the drive and folder where you store your Data Files for this unit, click OK (Win) or Open (Mac), then click Finish**

4. **Click Window on the menu bar, point to Show View, then click Project Explorer**
   The Project Explorer pane is displayed, with the location of your data files listed.

5. **Click the triangle ▷ to the left of the folder containing your Data Files for this unit in the Project Explorer pane, click the triangle ▷ next to the Lessons folder, then double-click index.html**
   Your web page opens in Aptana Studio 3.

QUICK TIP
You can copy the
address from the
Address bar, paste it
in an email, and
email yourself the
address. Next,
access your email on
your mobile device,
then click the
address to open it in
the browser on your
mobile device.

6. **Click Run on the Menu bar, then click Run on the menu that opens**
   Your web page opens in Firefox. Notice the address in the Address bar shown in FIGURE A-16. Because you are accessing the web page via the Aptana Studio 3 web server, the address starts with a series of numbers, which is the numerical address of your web server. The numerical address varies from computer to computer.

7. **Ensure that your handheld device is connected to the same wireless network as your desktop computer, open the browser on your handheld device, enter the address displayed in the address bar in your desktop browser, then touch the Go button**
   Your web page opens in your handheld device's browser. FIGURE A-17 shows the page on a smartphone.

8. **Repeat Step 7 on a tablet**
   Your web page opens in your tablet's browser. FIGURE A-18 shows the page on a tablet.

Testing web documents on mobile devices

As people increasingly access the web using mobile devices, it's important to test your content on the mobile devices used by your audience. Most users accessing the web on a mobile device use either Safari (on Apple iOS devices such as the iPhone and iPad) or Chrome (on Google Android devices such as Nexus and Galaxy series phones and tablets). Although it's unlikely that you'll physically own every device that your audience may use to access your content, you can start by testing on any mobile devices you have. In addition, by sharing devices with fellow students and colleagues, you may be able to access many of the most common devices.

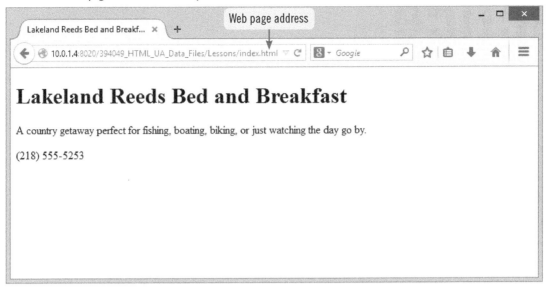

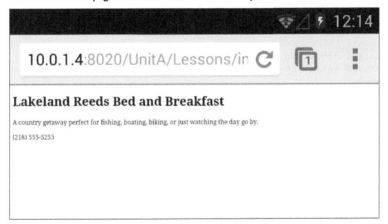

HTML5 & CSS3

Practice

Concepts Review

Refer to FIGURE A-19 **to answer the following questions.**

FIGURE A-19

```
 1  <!DOCTYPE html>
 2  <html>
 3    <head>
 4      <title>Lakeland Reeds Bed and Breakfast</title>
 5      <!--
 6          Lakeland Reeds Bed and Breakfast main web page
 7          Filename: index.html
 8
 9          Author:   Faduma Egal
10          Date:     9/26/2018
11          HTML5 and CSS3 Illustrated Unit A, Lessons
12      -->
13    </head>
14    <body>
15      <h1>Lakeland Reeds Bed and Breakfast</h1>
16      <p>A country getaway perfect for fishing, boating, biking, or just watching the day
17      go by.</p>
18      <p>(218) 555-5253</p>
19    </body>
20  </html>
```

a → 1
b → 8
c → 16
g → 4
f → 9
e → 15
d → 18

1. Which item creates a comment?
2. Which item marks the body section?
3. Which item marks text that is displayed in the browser tab?
4. Which item marks the head section?
5. Which item specifies a paragraph of text?
6. Which item indicates that the document is written in HTML?
7. Which item marks a top-level heading?

Match each term with the statement that best describes it.

8. nested
9. preview
10. wireframe
11. tags

a. a sketch that outlines the components of each web page and their places in the layout
b. to open a web document in one or more browsers and examine the result
c. when a tag pair is located within another tag pair
d. HTML codes that specify how a browser should treat each item in a web document

Select the best answer from the list of choices.

12. The process of identifying the goals and objectives, as well as the target audience, of the website is summed up in the _____ .

    a. web server
    b. wireframe
    c. project plan
    d. storyboard

13. A text editor that's optimized for writing code in a programming language is known as a _____ .

    a. hand coder
    b. code editor
    c. web browser
    d. visual editor

14. What code in an HTML document lets browsers know that the document contents are written in HTML?

    a. `title` element
    b. `head` element
    c. `body` element
    d. DOCTYPE declaration

15. Which type of tag do you place at the end of an element?

    a. deprecated
    b. closing
    c. one-sided
    d. opening

16. A _____ makes web documents available over a network to other computers.

    a. browser
    b. DOCTYPE declaration
    c. web server
    d. client

Skills Review

1. **Create an HTML document.**
   a. Open a new document in your text editor.
   b. Enter a DOCTYPE declaration.
   c. Enter tags to create the `html` element.
   d. Save the file as **index.html** to the Review folder in the drive and folder where you store your Data Files for this unit.

2. **Set up the document head and body.**
   a. Enter tags to create the document's head section.
   b. Enter tags to create the document's body section.
   c. Save your work.

3. **Add text to a web page.**
   a. Within the head section, add a `title` element containing the text **Big J's Deep Dish Pizza**.
   b. Within the body section, add an `h1` element containing the text **Big J's Deep Dish Pizza**.
   c. Below the `h1` element and within the body section, enter a `p` element containing the text **Authentic Chicago-style deep dish pizza—eat in, carry out, or call for delivery**.
   d. Below the existing `p` element, add another `p` element containing the text **(416) 555-3337**.
   e. Save your work.

4. **Add a comment to a web page.**
   a. Within the head section, add tags to create a comment.
   b. Within the comment, enter the following text:
   Big J's Deep Dish Pizza main web page
   Filename: index.html
   Author: your first and last name
   Date: today's date
   HTML5 and CSS3 Illustrated Unit A, Skills Review
   c. Save your work.

Skills Review (continued)

5. Preview your web page on a desktop computer.

a. Open index.html from the Review folder in your Data Files folder for this unit using your default browser. Compare your screen to FIGURE A-20

b. Repeat Step 5a using other browsers until you have viewed the document in current versions of Chrome, Firefox, and Internet Explorer.

FIGURE A-20

Big J's Deep Dish Pizza

Authentic Chicago-style deep dish pizza--eat in, carry out, or call for delivery.

(416) 555-3337

6. Preview your web page on mobile devices.

a. Open index.html from the Review folder in your Data Files folder for this unit using Aptana Studio 3 or another code editor with a built-in web server.

b. Use your code editor to open index.html in a desktop browser using the built-in web server.

c. Use the web address displayed in the desktop browser to open index.html on a smartphone, then repeat to open index.html on a tablet.

Independent Challenge 1

Spotted Wren Garden Center, a local garden shop and plant store, has hired you to create a website for its business. Sarah Nguyen, the shop's owner and manager, would like you to create a web presence as a new avenue of marketing, as well as a means to keep regular customers up to date on seasonal specials and new products.

a. Open a new document in your text editor, then create a DOCTYPE declaration by typing **<!DOCTYPE html>**

b. Type **<html>** and **</html>** on separate lines to create the html element.

c. Within the html element, type <head> and </head> on separate lines to create the head element.

d. After the head tags, type <body> and </body> on separate lines to create the body element.

e. Save the file as **index.html** to the UnitA/IC1 folder.

f. Within the head section, add a title element containing the text **Spotted Wren Garden Center**. (*Hint*: Type <title> as the opening tag and </title> as the closing tag.)

g. Within the body section, add an h1 element containing the text **Spotted Wren Garden Center**. (*Hint*: Type <h1> as the opening tag and </h1> as the closing tag.)

h. Below the h1 element and within the body section, enter a p element containing the text **For your year-round garden and yard needs, with a focus on the unusual and hard to find.** (*Hint*: Type <p> as the opening tab and </p> as the closing tag.)

i. Below the existing p element, add another p element containing the text **(402) 555-9736**. (*Hint*: Be sure to use the opening and closing tags for the p element.)

j. Within the head section, add a comment using <!-- as the opening tag and --> as the closing tag that contains the following text:

Spotted Wren Garden Center main web page

Filename: index.html

Author: your first and last name

Date: today's date

HTML5 and CSS3 Illustrated

Unit A, Independent Challenge 1

FIGURE A-21

Spotted Wren Garden Center

For your year-round garden and yard needs, with a focus on the unusual and hard to find.

(402) 555-9736

k. Save your work.

l. Open index.html from the IC1 folder in your Data Files folder for this unit using your default browser. Compare your screen to FIGURE A-21. Repeat using other browsers until you have viewed the document in current versions of Chrome, Firefox, and Internet Explorer.

m. Use a code editor with a built-in web server to view index.html on a smartphone and on a tablet.

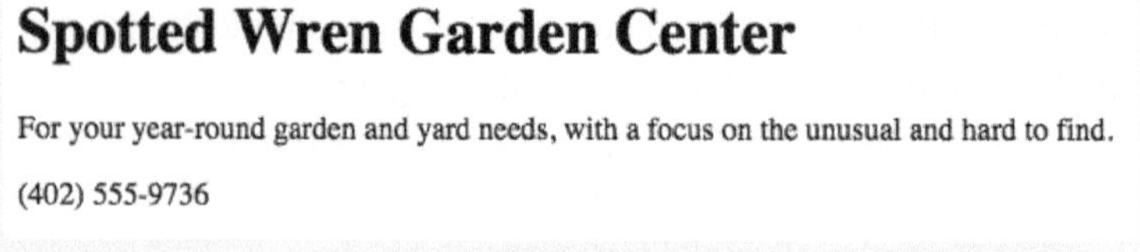

Independent Challenge 2

To help build your web design skills, you have volunteered to create a website for the Murfreesboro Regional Soccer League (MRSL). The league organizes recreational leagues every summer and fall for local, nonprofessional soccer players to get exercise and have fun. You start your work on the site by creating a web page with a basic description of the league along with contact information.

a. Open a new document in your text editor, then create a DOCTYPE declaration.

b. Enter tags to create the `html` element.

c. Within the `html` element, enter tags to create the `head` and `body` elements.

d. Save the file as **index.html** to the UnitA/IC2 folder.

e. Within the head section, add a `title` element containing the text **Murfreesboro Regional Soccer League**.

f. Within the body section, add an `h1` element containing the text **Murfreesboro Regional Soccer League**.

g. Below the `h1` element and within the body section, enter a `p` element containing the text **Get exercise, have fun, and build your soccer skills playing with us. Teams for beginners as well as experienced players.**

h. Below the existing `p` element, add another `p` element containing the text **(615) 555-2255**.

i. Within the head section, add a comment containing the following text:
Murfreesboro Regional Soccer League main web page
Filename: index.html
Author: your first and last name
Date: today's date
HTML5 and CSS3 Illustrated Unit A, Independent Challenge 2

j. Save your work.

k. Open index.html from the IC2 folder in your Data Files folder for this unit using your default browser. Compare your screen to **FIGURE A-22**. Repeat using other browsers until you have viewed the document in current versions of Chrome, Firefox, and Internet Explorer.

l. Use a code editor with a built-in web server to view index.html on a smartphone and on a tablet.

FIGURE A-22

Murfreesboro Regional Soccer League

Get exercise, have fun, and build your soccer skills playing with us. Teams for beginners as well as experienced players.

(615) 555-2255

Independent Challenge 3

In your new job creating sites for a web design firm, you've been assigned a new client, Hotel Natoma. The hotel's business manager, Diego Merckx, wants to use the web to showcase the facility and its amenities.

a. Open a new document in your text editor, then create a DOCTYPE declaration.

b. Enter tags to create the `html` element.

c. Within the `html` element, enter tags to create the `head` and `body` elements.

d. Save the file as **index.html** to the UnitA/IC3 folder.

e. Within the head section, add a `title` element containing the text **Hotel Natoma**.

f. Within the body section, add an `h1` element containing the text **Hotel Natoma**.

Independent Challenge 3 (continued)

g. Below the h1 element and within the body section, enter a p element containing the text **A low-impact, Earth-friendly home base in the center of everything San Francisco has to offer**.

h. Below the existing p element, add another p element containing the text **(415) 555-8378**.

i. Within the head section, add a comment containing the following text:
Hotel Natoma main web page
Filename: index.html
Author: your first and last name
Date: today's date
HTML5 and CSS3 Illustrated Unit A, Independent Challenge 3

j. Save your work.

k. Open index.html from the UnitA/IC3 folder using your default browser. Compare your screen to FIGURE A-23. Repeat using other browsers until you have viewed the document in current versions of Chrome, Firefox, and Internet Explorer.

l. Use a code editor with a built-in web server to view index.html on a smartphone and on a tablet.

FIGURE A-23

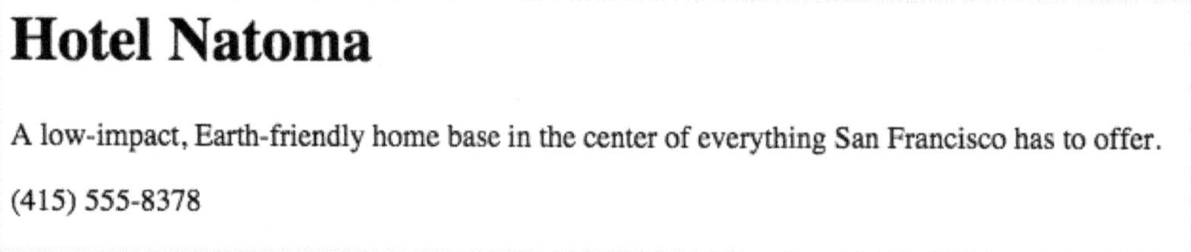

Hotel Natoma

A low-impact, Earth-friendly home base in the center of everything San Francisco has to offer.

(415) 555-8378

Independent Challenge 4: Explore

You've been hired to create a website for Eating Well in Season (EWIS), a business in Glover, Vermont, that delivers produce from local farms to its customers. You'll start by creating a basic web page that describes the business and provides contact information.

a. Draw a wireframe for the main web page of the EWIS website. Include title and heading elements containing the name of the business. Below the main heading, include three subheadings: Meals, Sources, and Scheduling. Include a paragraph of text below each subheading. At the bottom of the page, include contact information.

b. Open a new document in your text editor, then add a DOCTYPE declaration and all structuring elements necessary to create the sections of an HTML document. Save the file as **index.html** to the Unit A/IC4 folder.

c. Add a title element containing the text **Eating Well in Season**.

d. Within the body section, add an h1 element containing the text **Eating Well in Season**.

e. Below the h1 heading, use an <h2></h2> tag pair to create a subheading containing the text **Meals**. Below the h2 heading, add a paragraph containing the text **Meals prepared fresh daily using local ingredients**. Add a second h2 heading containing the text **Sources**, and a paragraph below it containing the text **Produce and meats supplied by New England farmers and gardeners**. Add a third h2 heading containing the text **Scheduling**, and a paragraph below it containing the text **Deliveries on your schedule, any time of the afternoon or evening**.

f. Below the final paragraph, add a paragraph containing the text **(802) 525-3947**.

g. Within the head section, add single-line comments containing the name of the business, the filename, your first and last name, today's date, and the text **HTML5 and CSS3 Illustrated Unit A, Independent Challenge 4**.

Independent Challenge 4: Explore (continued)

h. Save your work.

i. Open index.html from the IC4 folder in the Data Files folder for this unit using your default browser. Compare your screen to **FIGURE A-24**. Repeat using other browsers until you have viewed the document in current versions of Chrome, Firefox, and Internet Explorer.

j. Use a code editor with a built-in web server to view index.html on a smartphone running Apple iOS, on a smartphone running Google Android, on a tablet running Apple iOS, and on a tablet running Google Android. (*Hint*: Ask classmates, friends, and family members about using their devices to preview your document.)

FIGURE A-24

Eating Well in Season

Meals

Meals prepared fresh daily using local ingredients.

Sources

Produce and meats supplied by New England farmers and gardeners.

Schedule

Deliveries on your schedule, any time of the afternoon or evening.

(802) 525-3947

Visual Workshop

Use a text editor to create the web page shown in FIGURE A-25. Include a comment that contains the business name, filename, your first and last name, today's date, and the text **HTML5 and CSS3 Illustrated Unit A, Visual Workshop**. When you are finished, save the file as **index.html** to the UnitA/VW folder. Preview the web page in all three major desktop browsers, as well as on a smartphone and a tablet.

FIGURE A-25

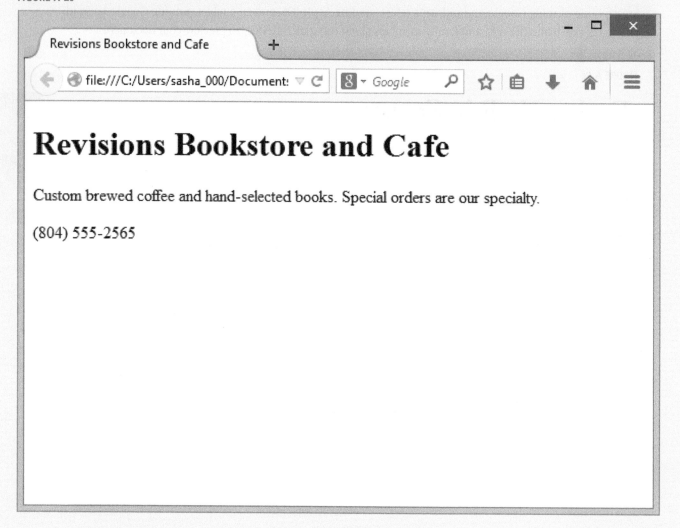

Getting Started with HTML

Structuring Content in a Web Document

CASE You are building a web page for Lakeland Reeds Bed and Breakfast that contains basic information about the business. In this unit, you will use HTML elements and attributes to structure the page contents, incorporate information for browsers, and validate and debug your work.

Unit Objectives

After completing this unit, you will be able to:

- Evaluate web accessibility standards
- Incorporate attributes
- Implement the `div` element
- Add HTML5 semantic elements
- Use special characters

- Specify the viewport
- Debug your HTML code
- Validate your HTML code
- Create an XHTML document

Files You Will Need

L	3 files	IC3	3 files
SR	3 files	IC4	2 files
IC1	2 files	VW	2 files
IC2	3 files		

For specific filenames, see Filenames_B.pdf in the Unit B Data Files folder.

Learning
Outcomes
• Identify guidelines
  for creating
  accessible web
  pages

Evaluate Web Accessibility Standards

Once you make a web page publicly available on the Internet, users can access it using a wide variety of **user agents**, which are programs and devices that interpret web documents. Many web users view pages with the default settings in modern desktop and mobile browsers such as Google Chrome, Apple Safari, Mozilla Firefox, and Microsoft Internet Explorer (IE). Some users with disabilities may use custom browser settings, or even specialized software or hardware, to access the web. While laws in many countries spell out mandatory accessibility standards for government websites, building a high level of accessibility into any web pages you create widens the potential audience for your work, as illustrated in FIGURE B-1. Thus, as a web developer, it's important that you understand and implement web accessibility standards as you create your web pages in order to make them adaptable to the needs of different users and the capabilities of different user agents. A widely used reference for implementing web accessibility is the **Web Content Accessibility Guidelines (WCAG)** maintained by the World Wide Web Consortium (W3C). **CASE** ▶ *To help ensure that the Lakeland Reeds website is widely accessible, you review the main tenets of web accessibility standards.*

DETAILS

The WCAG describes techniques for helping your web content meet the following goals as broadly as possible:

- **Perceivable**

  All your web page content needs to be accessible in whatever format a given user needs to access it. This includes ensuring that any information that you convey visually is also available by non-visual means, such as text descriptions for images and videos. Many people with visual impairments access the web using devices called **screen readers** that read aloud web page content, such as text and descriptions that a user selects. In addition, any audio content should be accompanied by transcripts or written descriptions, which can substitute for many users with auditory impairments.

- **Operable**

  Users interface with computers in different ways. While many users scroll web pages and click links using a mouse, ensuring that no elements of your web pages rely on the use of a mouse makes your web pages more accessible to people with some physical impairments. Web pages need to allow users to explore and read the web page content at the users' pace. Web pages should allow scrolling or self-updating features to be paused, stopped, or hidden. Designs should not include elements known to cause seizures, such as certain frequencies of flashing. Finally, navigation within the site and to external pages should be clearly indicated, easy to understand, and, ideally, redundant.

- **Understandable**

  The language that a web page is written in should be indicated, and ways for users to understand any specialized vocabulary used in the web page should be included. Links should not make unexpected or drastic changes to the way a web page is displayed; some warning should be given if clicking a link will result in a non-standard change. When possible, forms that accept user input should include means for identifying common errors and allowing users to correct them.

- **Robust**

  Web pages should be coded according to web standards, ensuring that they can be accessed by the widest possible variety of programs and devices.

Be sure you understand and use these techniques when designing web pages in order to maximize accessibility.

Revisions Bookstore and Cafe

Custom brewed coffee and hand-selected books.

Special orders are our specialty.

Learn about our <u>store history</u>, look at our <u>upcoming events</u>, and see <u>where we're located</u>.

412 N. 25th St.
Richmond, VA 23223
(804) 555-2565

Background darkened for improved text contrast

Navigation bar added to facilitate moving around site and to make site organization viewable at a glance

Revisions Bookstore and Cafe

<u>Home</u> | <u>Store History</u> | <u>Upcoming Events</u> | <u>Location</u>

Custom brewed coffee and hand-selected books.

Special orders are our specialty.

412 N. 25th St.
Richmond, VA 23223
(804) 555-2565

Understanding your role in web accessibility

In addition to a web developer's work creating a site, other factors significantly influence web accessibility. The developers of user agents make decisions that affect how their software and devices interact with web content, which impacts whether users can access content in specific ways. In addition, some web content is produced using software that automates the web development process, and the accessibility choices of the makers of these packages affects the accessibility of the content produced using them. Thus, while web developers have a crucial role to play in building and maintaining a web page that's available to everyone, it can be useful to see your role as part of a larger team and to recognize when you run against a limitation that can't easily be fixed.

Incorporate Attributes

Learning
Outcomes
• Add an attribute
name
• Add an attribute
value

Many, but not all, HTML elements allow you to set attributes. An **attribute** is additional code within an opening element tag that specifies information about that element. To use an attribute, you provide two pieces of information: an attribute name and the value you are assigning to the attribute. Within an element's opening tag and following the tag name, you insert a space, followed by the attribute name, an equal sign (=), and the attribute value enclosed in quotes. **CASE** *You add attributes to two elements in your document to give browsers information about the document's content.*

STEPS

1. **In your editor, open the HTM_B-1.html file from the Lessons folder where you store your Data Files for this unit**

2. **Below the `title` element, insert the comment shown in FIGURE B-2, substituting your name and today's date where indicated**

3. **Save a copy of the file to the Lessons folder with the name aboutus.html**

   As shown in **FIGURE B-2**, the body section of the document contains an h1 element, an h2 element, and two p elements.

4. **Open aboutus.html in a browser**

   The document is displayed with a large heading, a smaller heading, and two paragraphs of text.

5. **Return to your editor, then click just to the left of the closing > in the opening <html> tag**

6. **Press [Spacebar], then type `lang="en"`**

   The `lang` attribute specifies the language in which a document's content is written. The value en specifies English as the language. **TABLE B-1** lists the `lang` values for several other languages. **FIGURE B-3** shows the `lang` attribute and value inserted in the opening <html> tag.

7. **Click after the closing comment tag (-->), press [Enter], then press [Spacebar] six times or as needed to create the indent**

   Because you want the new element nested within two other elements (html and head), you indent six spaces—three for each level of indentation.

8. **Type `<meta charset="utf-8">`**

   FIGURE B-4 shows the meta element and the charset attribute and value in the head section of the document. The meta element enables you to pass information about a web page to user agents that open it. The charset attribute specifies the **character encoding**, which is the system user agents should employ to translate the electronic information representing the page into human-recognizable symbols, such as letters and numbers.

9. **Save your document, return to your browser, then click the Refresh or Reload button to view the changes to your web document**

   The appearance of the page in the browser does not change. In general, meta elements and attributes of the html element do not change how a document is rendered.

FIGURE B-2: Starting code for About Us page

```
1   <!DOCTYPE html>
2   <html>
3      <head>
4         <title>Lakeland Reeds Bed and Breakfast - About Us</title>
5         <!--
6            Lakeland Reeds Bed and Breakfast
7            Filename: aboutus.html
8
9            Author:   your first and last name
10           Date:     today's date
11           HTML5 and CSS3 Illustrated Unit B, Lessons
12        -->
13     </head>
14     <body>
15        <h1>Lakeland Reeds Bed and Breakfast</h1>
16        <h2>About Us</h2>
17        <p>Lakeland Reeds is an ideal place to unplug from your daily routine. We're here
18        to help you get the most out of your time with us, from canoes and life vests for a
19        day out on the lake, to DVDs and popcorn for a quiet evening in. We look forward to
20        welcoming you!</p>
21        <p>45 Marsh Grass Ln. - Marble, MN 55764 - (218) 555-5253</p>
22     </body>
23   </html>
```

Comment → (lines 5–12)
h1 element (line 15)
h2 element (line 16)
First p element (lines 17–20)
Second p element (line 21)

FIGURE B-3: `lang` attribute inserted in opening `<html>` tag

```
1   <!DOCTYPE html>
2   <html lang="en">
3      <head>
4         <title>Lakeland Reeds Bed and Breakfast - About Us</title>
            keland Reeds Bed and Breakfast
            lename: aboutus.html
```

Attribute name
Attribute value enclosed in quotes
Attribute placed within opening `<html>` tag

FIGURE B-4: `meta` element with `charset` attribute

```
1   <!DOCTYPE html>
2   <html lang="en">
3      <head>
4         <title>Lakeland Reeds Bed and Breakfast - About Us</title>
5         <!--
            Lakeland Reeds Bed and Breakfast
            Filename: aboutus.html

            Author:   Faduma Egal
10          Date:     10/13/18
11          HTML5 and CSS3 Illustrated Unit B, Lessons
12        -->
13        <meta charset="utf-8">
14     </head>
           iy>
           <h1>Lakeland Reeds Bed and Breakfast</h1>
           <h2>About Us</h2>
```

meta element added to head section
closing tag for head section
Attribute name
Attribute value enclosed in quotes

TABLE B-1: Basic `lang` attribute values

lang value	language	lang value	language	lang value	language
ar	Arabic	fr	French	pt	Portugese
de	German	he	Hebrew	ru	Russian
el	Greek	hi	Hindi	sa	Sanskrit
en	English	it	Italian	ur	Urdu
es	Spanish	ja	Japanese	zh	Chinese

Implement the `div` Element

**Learning
Outcomes**
• Use the HTML `div`
  element
• Add a parent
  element to
  existing elements

To create the basic structure of a web page, you use the `html`, `head`, and `body` elements. In addition, you can add content to the body section with elements such as `h1` and `p`. It can be useful to group content within the body section to help keep the code organized, especially in larger web documents. The `div` element is used as a parent element for other elements on your page that function together. For instance, you could use a `div` element to mark a heading element and its related paragraph elements as a group. **CASE** ▶ *The code for the Lakeland Reeds About Us page includes content specific to this page. You organize the code by adding a `div` element enclosing the content specific to this page, which includes the h2 heading and the first p element.*

STEPS

1. **Return to aboutus.html in your editor, click after the closing </h1> tag, then press [Enter] to add a new line**

2. **Press [Spacebar] six times or as needed to create an indent that matches the indent for the preceding </h1> tag, then type <div>**
   The `<div>` tag is the opening tag for the `div` element and should be indented 3 spaces more than the opening `<body>` tag.

3. **Click after the first closing </p> tag, then press [Enter]**

4. **Press [Spacebar] six times or as needed to create an indent that matches the indent for the opening <div> tag, then type </div>**
   The `div` element contains both the `h2` element and the first `p` element between its opening and closing tags.

5. **Click before the opening <h2> tag, press [Spacebar] three times or as needed to create an indent, click before the first opening <p> tag, then press [Spacebar] three times or as needed to create an indent**
   Because you are adding a parent element, you increase the indentation of tags for child elements to keep your code readable. Compare your code to **FIGURE B-5**, which shows the code containing the new `div` element.

6. **Save your document, return to your browser, then refresh or reload aboutus.html in your browser**
   As shown in **FIGURE B-6**, the appearance of the page in the browser does not change. Because the `div` element is used for structuring code, adding the `div` element to the document does not change the way the document is rendered. The document looks the same after the `div` element is added as it did before.

Writing for the web

Many users want a process of finding and consuming web content that is dynamic and fast-paced. When you write content for the web, you should keep this in mind. Web content should generally be brief and scannable. A user should be able to get the gist of what your page contains with a quick glance. This allows users to quickly decide to stay on the page if the page contains the information they're looking for, or to navigate elsewhere and keep looking. You can make content scannable by including a short, descriptive heading at the top, and by breaking the content itself into sections with headings. After writing the actual content, it can be useful to revise it with the goal of removing half the words. This helps focus your writing and reduces the content of your web page to the essentials, which makes it easier for web users to scan and read.

After you publish content online, it's crucial to keep it up to date—out of date information makes your website's content seem unreliable. You can minimize the amount of regular updating you need to do by reducing or eliminating relative references to dates (such as "5 years ago" or "in 18 months") or labeling specific dates as being in the future (such as "The building will be completed in 2013.")

FIGURE B-5: Code containing new `div` element

```
1    <!DOCTYPE html>
2    <html lang="en">
3        <head>
4            <title>Lakeland Reeds Bed and Breakfast - About Us</title>
             <!--
                 Lakeland Reeds Bed and Breakfast
                 Filename: aboutus.html

                 Author:   your first and last name
                 Date:     today's date
                 HTML5 and CSS3 Illustrated Unit B, Lessons
             -->
13           <meta charset="utf-8">
14       </head>
15       <body>
16           <h1>Lakeland Reeds Bed and Breakfast</h1>
17           <div>
18               <h2>About Us</h2>
19               <p>Lakeland Reeds is an ideal place to unplug from your daily routine. We're
20               here to help you get the most out of your time with us, from canoes and life
21               vests for a day out on the lake, to DVDs and popcorn for a quiet evening in. We
22               look forward to welcoming you!</p>
23           </div>
24           <p>45 Marsh Grass Ln. - Marble, MN 55764 - (218) 555-5253</p>
25       </body>
26   </html>
```

Children of new `div` element indented three additional spaces

Opening `<div>` tag added

Closing `</div>` tag added

FIGURE B-6: About Us page in a browser

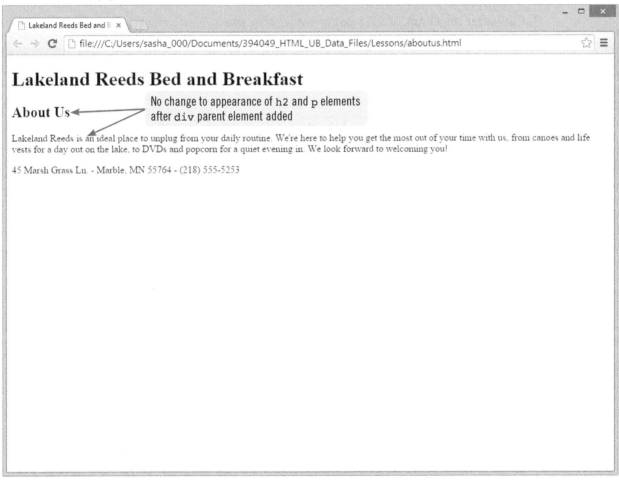

file:///C:/Users/sasha_000/Documents/394049_HTML_UB_Data_Files/Lessons/aboutus.html

Lakeland Reeds Bed and Breakfast

About Us

No change to appearance of `h2` and `p` elements after `div` parent element added

Lakeland Reeds is an ideal place to unplug from your daily routine. We're here to help you get the most out of your time with us, from canoes and life vests for a day out on the lake, to DVDs and popcorn for a quiet evening in. We look forward to welcoming you!

45 Marsh Grass Ln. - Marble, MN 55764 - (218) 555-5253

Add HTML5 Semantic Elements

Learning Outcomes
• Use the HTML5 header, article, and footer elements
• Make semantic elements work for IE8 users.

All HTML elements have **semantic** value—that is, they indicate the meaning of their content. For instance, the h1 element marks text as a top-level heading, and the p element marks a paragraph of text. The div element has limited semantic meaning—it groups elements but adds no information about what type of information it contains. However, the most recent version of HTML, known as **HTML5**, includes a number of grouping elements, known as **semantic elements** that indicate the role of their content. Search engines can use this semantic information to provide more accurate search results. This means that using semantic elements can make it easier for people using a search engine to find information about your business or organization. TABLE B-2 lists several semantic elements. Because older versions of Internet Explorer can't interpret semantic elements, you also include a script element in the head section, which instructs older browsers how to interpret the semantic elements. The script element references code in an external file that browsers can use to help them interpret the elements. **CASE** *You add the* header *and* footer *elements to indicate the content at the start and end of the page, and you add a* script *element referencing a file that makes it possible for users of older versions of Internet Explorer to view the document.* FIGURE B-7 *shows a wireframe of the About Us page with each section marked.*

STEPS

1. **Return to aboutus.html in your editor**

2. **Click after the opening <body> tag, press [Enter], press [Spacebar] six times or as needed to create the indent, then type** <header>
   The header element marks content that occurs at the start of a document.

3. **Click after the closing </h1> tag, press [Enter], press [Spacebar] six times or as needed to create the indent, then type** </header>
   A header element is added as the parent element of the h1 element.

4. **Click just before the opening <h1> tag, then press [Spacebar] three times or as needed to create the indent**

5. **Click after the closing </div> tag, press [Enter], press [Spacebar] six times or as needed to create the indent, then type** <footer>

6. **Click after the second closing </p> tag, press [Enter], press [Spacebar] six times or as needed to create the indent, then type** </footer>
   A footer element is added as the parent element of the second p element.

7. **Click just before the second opening <p> tag, then press [Spacebar] three times or as needed to create the indent**

8. **In the head section, click after the <meta> tag, press [Enter], press [Spacebar] six times or as needed to create the indent, then type**
   `<script src="modernizr.custom.62074.js"></script>`
   A script element references an external script file whose name is specified as the src attribute value. FIGURE B-8 shows the completed code.

9. **Save your document, return to your browser, then refresh or reload aboutus.html**
   Like the div element, semantic elements do not change the page's display in a browser.

10. **If you have access to Internet Explorer 8 or an earlier version of Internet Explorer, use it to open aboutus.html**
    Because of the script element you added to the document's head section, the document is displayed correctly in older versions of Internet Explorer.

FIGURE B-7: Wireframe for Lakeland Reeds About Us page

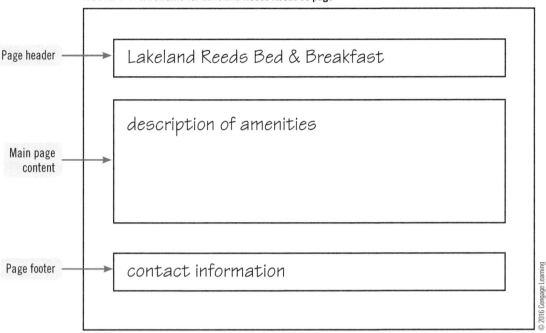

Page header → | Lakeland Reeds Bed & Breakfast

Main page content → | description of amenities

Page footer → | contact information

© 2016 Cengage Learning

FIGURE B-8: Code with semantic elements and `script` element

```
10              Date:      today's date
11              HTML5 and CSS3 Illustrated Unit B,
12          -->
13          <meta charset="utf-8">
14          <script src="modernizr.custom.62074.js"></script>
15      </head>
16      <body>
17          <header>
18              <h1>Lakeland Reeds Bed and Breakfast</h1>
19          </header>
20          <div>
21              <h2>About Us</h2>
22              <p>Lakeland Reeds is an ideal place to unplug from your daily routine. We're
23              elp you get the most out of your time with us, from canoes and life
24              a day out on the lake, to DVDs and popcorn for a quiet evening in. We
25              ard to welcoming you!</p>
26          </div>
27          <footer>
28              <p>45 Marsh Grass Ln. - Marble, MN 55764 - (218) 555-5253</p>
29          </footer>
30      </body>
31  </html>
```

Attribute value enclosed in quotes

script element added for IE8 compatibility

Attribute name

header element added as parent of h1 element

footer element added as parent of second p element

TABLE B-2: Selected HTML5 semantic elements

element	intended use
article	stand-alone piece of work, such as a single entry in a blog
aside	part of a page that's tangential to the main page content, such as a sidebar or pull quote
footer	information about a section or document that usually appears at the end, such as contact information, attributions, and/or footnotes
header	information about a section or document that usually appears at the beginning, such as a heading, logo, and/or table of contents
nav	main elements of site and page navigation
section	section of content focused on a common theme, such as a chapter of a larger work

© 2016 Cengage Learning

Use Special Characters

Most text is added to web pages simply by typing it. However, a handful of common characters, such as the & symbol, run the risk of being misinterpreted by user agents as computer instructions rather than as plain text. In addition, many characters, such as bullet symbols, do not appear as keys on standard keyboards. **Character references**, which are specially formatted codes that represent characters in the HTML document character set, are used when these characters are needed on a web page. Character references always begin with an ampersand (&) and end with a semicolon (;). The rest of the code consists of either a pound sign (#) followed by numbers or an English language abbreviation for the associated character name. Every character has a number code, known as a **numeric character reference**, but only a few commonly used characters also have an abbreviation-based alternative, known as a **named character reference**. Character references exist for all characters you can type; however, the only characters for which it's important to use the codes are those listed in TABLE B-3. **CASE** ▶ *You replace the word* and *in the name of the business with an ampersand symbol (&) in both the main page heading and the* title *element to match the appearance of the organization name on signs and other branded materials. You also replace each hyphen (-) in the footer with a bullet character (•).*

STEPS

1. Return to aboutus.html in your editor, then locate the title element

2. Delete the word and in the name Lakeland Reeds Bed and Breakfast, type &, then be sure there is a space before and after the character reference

3. Locate the h1 element

4. Delete the word and in the name Lakeland Reeds Bed and Breakfast, type &, then be sure there is a space before and after the character reference

5. Delete the first hyphen (-) within the footer element, type •, then be sure there is a space before and after the character reference

6. Delete the second hyphen (-) within the footer element, type •, then be sure there is a space before and after the character reference

   FIGURE B-9 shows the special characters inserted in the code for the web page.

7. Save your work, then refresh or reload aboutus.html in your browser

   As shown in FIGURE B-10, the word *and* in the browser title bar and in the main web page heading is replaced with the ampersand (&) symbol, and each hyphen in the final line of text is replaced with the bullet (•) character.

Finding codes for other characters

UTF-8 is the most commonly used character encoding on the web today. This encoding supports character references for thousands of characters. These symbols may include characters in different writing systems and international currency symbols, as well as icons and pictograms for a variety of themes. You can go to unicode.org/charts or fileformat.info to browse supported characters by subject. Note that not all symbols are displayed in every browser or operating system. This is because browsers and operating systems use different default fonts, and a given font may contain character descriptions for some, but not all, UTF-8 characters. For this reason, it's important to test a page containing a less-common special character in all browsers that you anticipate your audience will use to view the page. This lets you confirm that the character is recognized and displayed when the page is rendered in a browser, or make adjustments if the character is not recognized.

FIGURE B-9: Codes for special characters inserted in web page

```
1   <!DOCTYPE html>
2   <html lang="en">
3      <head>
4         <title>Lakeland Reeds Bed &amp; Breakfast - About Us</title>
5         <!--
6            Lakeland Reeds Bed and Breakfast
7            Filename: aboutus.html
8
9            Author:   your first and last name
10           Date:     today's date
11           HTML5 and CSS3 Illustrated Unit B, Lessons
12        -->
13        <meta charset="utf-8">
14        <script src="modernizr.custom.62074.js"></script>
15     </head>
16     <body>
17        <header>
18           <h1>Lakeland Reeds Bed &amp; Breakfast</h1>
19        </header>
20        <div>
21           <h2>About Us</h2>
22           <p>Lakeland Reeds is an ideal place to unplug from your daily routine. We're
23           here to help you get the most out of your time with us, from canoes and life
24           vests for a day out on the lake, to DVDs and popcorn for a quiet evening in. We
25           look forward to welcoming you!</p>
26        </div>
27        <footer>
28           <p>45 Marsh Grass Ln. &#8226; Marble, MN 55764 &#8226; (218) 555-5253</p>
29        </footer>
30     </body>
31  </html>
```

Named character references for the ampersand (&) character

Numeric character references for the bullet (•) character

HTML5 & CSS3

FIGURE B-10: About Us page incorporating special characters

Ampersand symbols inserted in `title` and `h1` elements using named character references

Bullet characters inserted in `footer` element using numeric character references

TABLE B-3: Important character references

character	character name	numeric character reference	named character reference
&	ampersand	&#38;	&amp;
'	apostrophe	&#39;	' (does not work in older versions of Internet Explorer)
>	greater-than sign	&#62;	&gt;
<	less-than sign	&#60;	&lt;
"	quotation mark	&#34;	&quot;

Specify the Viewport

Learning Outcomes
- Add viewport meta element
- Set content attribute value

When the browser on a mobile device opens a web page, it needs to figure out how the document should be displayed on its small screen. Some web pages can scale to fit any browser, no matter the screen size. For other web pages, though, displaying the whole page at once would make its content too small to read. For this reason, most mobile browsers by default display only a portion of the page but at a legible size. These browsers display the page as if looking through an imaginary window, which is known as the **viewport**. To instruct browsers to display a page at the width of the browser window without zooming in, you change the browser's viewport settings using a `viewport meta` **element**, which is a meta element with the name attribute set to a value of viewport. As part of the `viewport meta` element, you also include a second attribute, content, whose value specifies one or more pairs of properties and values. TABLE B-4 lists viewport properties. To scale the page to fit the browser window, you use a content value of width=device-width. **CASE** *You add a* viewport meta *element to the About Us page to ensure that it is displayed at the width of the browser window on mobile devices.*

STEPS

TROUBLE
Consult the documentation for your web server if necessary.

1. **Using your web server, open** aboutus.html **on a smartphone or other handheld mobile device**

   As shown in FIGURE B-11, most mobile devices zoom the web page, displaying it as if viewing only a portion of a much larger screen and cutting off some of the content. To see all of the content at once would require zooming out, at which point most content would be illegible.

2. **Return to** aboutus.html **in your editor**

3. **In the head section, click after the** <meta> **tag, press [Enter], then press [Spacebar] six times or as needed to create the indent**

QUICK TIP
Even though the meta element supports many content value options for viewport, you usually only need to use the value that sets the width to device-width as you did in this step.

4. **Type** <meta name="viewport" content="width=device-width">

   FIGURE B-12 shows the viewport meta element added to the document. This viewport meta element instructs browsers to assume that the width of the content matches the width of the device.

5. **Save your changes, then refresh or reload aboutus.html on your mobile device**

   The viewport meta element you entered causes most mobile browsers to wrap the document contents to the browser window, making all the content of this page legible without scrolling left and right, as shown in FIGURE B-13.

TABLE B-4: **viewport** attribute properties

property	description	allowable values
width	The width of the viewport	device-width or a value in pixels
height	The height of the viewport	device-height or a value in pixels
initial-scale	The scale of the viewport when the document opens	a number representing the scale, with 1.0 equal to 100%
minimum-scale	The lower limit on the scale of the viewport	a number representing the scale, with 1.0 equal to 100%
maximum-scale	The upper limit on the scale of the viewport	a number representing the scale, with 1.0 equal to 100%
user-scalable	Whether a user is allowed to zoom the page or not	yes or no

FIGURE B-11: Web page without a `meta` viewport element on a mobile device

FIGURE B-12: `meta viewport` element added to document

```
1   <!DOCTYPE html>
2   <html lang="en">
3       <head>
4           <title>Lakeland Reeds Bed &amp; Breakfast - About Us</title>
5           <!--
6               Lakeland Reeds Bed and Breakfast
7               Filename: aboutus.html
8
9               Author:   your first and last name
10              Date:     today's date
11              HTML5 and CSS3 Illustrated Unit B, Lessons
12          -->
13          <meta charset="utf-8">
14          <meta name="viewport" content="width=device-width">
15          <script src="modernizr.custom.62074.js"></script>
16      </head>
```

FIGURE B-13: Web page with a `meta viewport` element on a mobile device

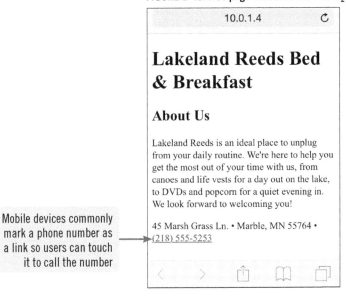

Mobile devices commonly mark a phone number as a link so users can touch it to call the number

Debug your HTML Code

Learning
Outcomes
• Identify bugs
  based on coding
  errors
• Correct coding
  errors

Even the most careful developer writes code from time to time that doesn't work. A problem that results from incorrectly written code is known as a **bug**, and the process of finding and removing bugs from code is called **debugging**. Simply viewing a document in one or more browsers can sometimes help illuminate bugs and narrow down where in the code the errors causing the problems might be located. **TABLE B-5** lists some common bugs in HTML code along with what often causes them. **CASE** ▶ *You practice debugging by introducing errors in the code for the About Us page, viewing the document in a desktop browser, and then examining the effects of the errors.*

STEPS

1. **Return to** aboutus.html **in your editor**

2. **Delete the opening** <h1> **tag within the** header **element**

3. **Delete the** & **at the start of the first character reference within the** footer **element**
   FIGURE B-14 shows the code with the two errors introduced.

4. **Save your changes, then refresh or reload aboutus.html in a browser**
   As shown in **FIGURE B-15**, the text of the first heading is no longer large, and the first bullet in the footer is replaced by the text of the character code that follows the &.

5. **Return to** aboutus.html **in your editor, click just before the word** Lakeland **within the** header **element, then type** <h1>

6. **Save your changes, then refresh or reload aboutus.html in a browser**
   The first heading is now displayed in larger text than the second heading, as it was previously.

7. **Return to** aboutus.html **in your editor, click just before the first** # **within the** footer **element, then type** &
   Your code should match **FIGURE B-16**.

8. **Save your changes, then refresh or reload aboutus.html in a browser**
   The first bullet character is once again displayed in the footer. Your web page should once again match **FIGURE B-10**.

TABLE B-5: Common bugs and causes

bug	common causes
Element appearance different than expected	Missing tags around content
	Element enclosed by tags for a different element
	Opening tag missing
	Closing > omitted from a tag
Special character not displayed correctly	Invalid character code specified
	& omitted from start of character code
	Code for a different character specified

FIGURE B-14: Errors introduced into aboutus.html

```
17      <body>
18          <header>
19              ──►Lakeland Reeds Bed &amp; Breakfast</h1>
20          </header>
21          <div>
22              <h2>About Us</h2>
                <p>Lakeland Reeds is an ideal place to unplug from your daily routine. We're
                here to help you get the most out of your time with us, from canoes and life
                vests for a day out on the lake, to DVDs and popcorn for a quiet evening in. We
26              look forward to welcoming you!</p>
27          </div>
28          <footer>
29              <p>45 Marsh Grass Ln. #8226; Marble, MN 55764 &#8226; (218) 555-5253</p>
30          </footer>
31      </body>
32  </html>
```

Opening `<h1>` tag removed

Opening & deleted from character code

Opening & still part of character code

FIGURE B-15: Web page with errors in browser

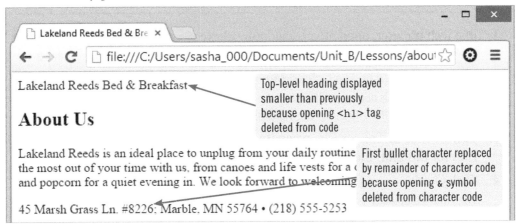

Top-level heading displayed smaller than previously because opening `<h1>` tag deleted from code

First bullet character replaced by remainder of character code because opening & symbol deleted from character code

FIGURE B-16: Web page code after debugging

```
1   <!DOCTYPE html>
2   <html lang="en">
3       <head>
4           <title>Lakeland Reeds Bed &amp; Breakfast - About Us</title>
5           <!--
6               Lakeland Reeds Bed and Breakfast
7               Filename: aboutus.html
8
9               Author:    your first and last name
10              Date:      today's date
11              HTML5 and CSS3 Illustrated Unit B, Lessons
12          -->
13          <meta charset="utf-8">
14          <meta name="viewport" content="width=device-width">
15          <script src="modernizr.custom.62074.js"></script>
16      </head>
17      <body>
18          <header>
19              <h1>Lakeland Reeds Bed &amp; Breakfast</h1>
20          </header>
21          <div>
22              <h2>About Us</h2>
23              <p>Lakeland Reeds is an ideal place to unplug from your daily routine. We're
24              here to help you get the most out of your time with us, from canoes and life
25              vests for a day out on the lake, to DVDs and popcorn for a quiet evening in. We
26              look forward to welcoming you!</p>
27          </div>
28          <footer>
29              <p>45 Marsh Grass Ln. &#8226; Marble, MN 55764 &#8226; (218) 555-5253</p>
30          </footer>
31      </body>
32  </html>
```

Validate your HTML Code

Previewing web pages in a variety of browsers can be useful for spotting problems with code and making sure that web pages display as expected for users. Another tool is **validation**, which is an automated process of comparing code you've written against the HTML5 coding standards. When previewing a page reveals an error in your code that is difficult to track down, validation can sometimes be useful in identifying the specific source of the problem. In addition, sometimes a user agent can interpret a web page as expected in spite of code that doesn't conform to specifications. In this case, validating code and correcting errors can help to ensure that the code will continue to work with future versions of both user agents and HTML standards, which may not continue to deal seamlessly with erroneous coding. The W3C offers a free online validator for web documents at validator.w3.org. **CASE** ▶ *Before sharing your work with your contacts at Lakeland Reeds, you validate your code.*

STEPS

1. **In a web browser, open** http://validator.w3.org
   The web page opens for the validation service provided by the W3C, as shown in **FIGURE B-17**.

2. **Click the** Validate by File Upload tab
   Because your page is not yet published on the Internet, you'll upload your file directly to the w3.org website for validation. **FIGURE B-18** shows the Validate by File Upload tab active.

3. **Click** Browse **or** Choose File, **navigate to the Lessons folder where you store your Data Files for this unit, then double-click** aboutus.html

QUICK TIP
Errors listed by the
validator always
specify the line and
character ("column")
numbers where it
encountered the error.
This is sometimes, but
not always, the
location of the code
you need to fix.

4. **Click** Check
   The browser uploads your document to the w3.org website and the result page opens, as shown in **FIGURE B-19**.

5. **Scroll down to read the validation results, including any notes or warnings**
   Notes and warnings provide additional information about aspects of your document that you may want to change. However, they do not prevent your document from validating. **TABLE B-6** lists and explains some common validation errors as well as two common validation warnings.

6. **If your document does not successfully validate as HTML5, return to your text editor, compare your document to** FIGURE B-12 **and make any necessary changes, save your work, then repeat Steps 1–4 to revalidate your file**

TABLE B-6: Common validation errors and warnings

error message	common cause
"End tag for body seen, but there were unclosed elements."	
"End of file seen when expecting text or an end tag."	You entered the opening tag for an element but left out its closing tag.
"Unclosed element *element*."	
"End of file reached when inside an attribute value. Ignoring tag."	You forgot the closing quotes (") after an attribute value.
"Named character reference was not terminated by a semicolon. (Or & should have been escaped as &.)"	
	You forgot the closing semicolon (;) after a character reference.
"Character reference was not terminated by a semicolon."	

warning message	explanation
"Using experimental feature: *HTML5 Conformance Checker*."	The w3.org validator does not consider its HTML5 validation service 100% accurate because the language is constantly being updated.
"Byte-Order Mark found in a UTF-8 file."	Your editor saved your document based on a standard that is not universally supported by older editors or browsers.

FIGURE B-17: W3C Markup Validation Service web page

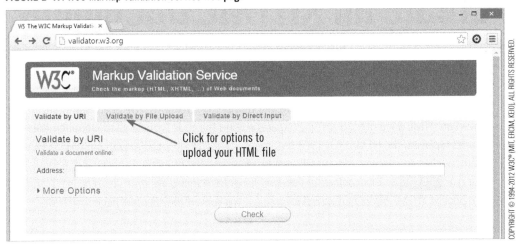

FIGURE B-18: Validate by File Upload tab

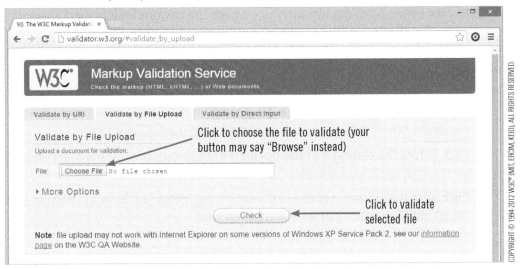

FIGURE B-19: Validation results for aboutus.html

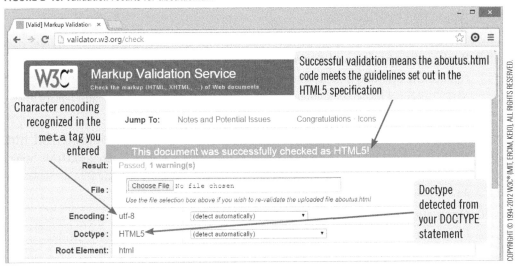

Create an XHTML Document

Learning
Outcomes
• Create a document
  that conforms to
  XHTML rules
• Validate an
  XHTML document

Today, most web pages are written in HTML. However, some web pages are written in **Extensible Hypertext Markup Language (XHTML)**, which is a version of HTML that conforms to the rules of another language known as **Extensible Markup Language (XML)**. The way HTML and XHTML are written is very similar. However, XHTML requires additional code in a number of situations, which are summarized in TABLE B-7. To convert an HTML document to XHTML requires editing the code to meet all the requirements of XHTML. This includes replacing the HTML DOCTYPE statement, `<!DOCTYPE html>`, with an XHTML DOCTYPE. Another common change involves closing all empty elements by placing a space and a slash (/) before the closing >. **CASE** ▸ *Your contacts at Lakeland Reeds think they'd like their site to be in HTML, but they'd like to see a page in XHTML before making a final decision. You convert the About Us page to XHTML.*

STEPS

1. **Return to aboutus.html in your editor, save a copy of the file to the Lessons folder with the name aboutusXHTML.html, then in the comment in the head section, change the filename listed to aboutusXHTML.html**

2. **In your editor, open the file doctype.txt from the Lessons folder, select the entire contents of the file, then press [Ctrl][C] (Win) or [command][C] (Mac) to copy it to the Clipboard**
   The doctype.txt file contains the XHTML 1.0 Transitional DOCTYPE declaration.

3. **Return to aboutusXHTML.html in your editor, delete the entire DOCTYPE statement, then press [Ctrl][V] (Win) or [command][V] (Mac) to paste the XHTML DOCTYPE you copied to the Clipboard into the document**
   The HTML5 DOCTYPE is replaced with the XHTML 1.0 Transitional DOCTYPE.

4. **Click before the closing > of the opening `<html>` tag, press [Spacebar], then type**
   `xmlns="http://www.w3.org/1999/xhtml"`

5. **Click after the closing > of the first `<meta>` tag, press [Backspace] (Win) or [delete] (Mac) until the entire tag is deleted, then type**
   `<meta http-equiv="Content-Type" content="text/html; charset=utf-8" />`
   This is the XHTML statement to specify encoding, which is more complex than its HTML5 equivalent.

6. **Click just before the closing > for the second `<meta>` tag, press [Spacebar], then type /**
   Adding a / before the closing > of a one-sided tag is necessary to close that element in XHTML.

7. **Click just before the closing > for the opening `<script>` tag, press [Spacebar], then type `type="text/javascript"`**
   Unlike HTML5, XHTML does not assume a default value for the language of a `script` element.

8. **Replace the opening and closing `<header>` tags with opening and closing `<div>` tags, then replace the opening and closing `<footer>` tags with opening and closing `<div>` tags**
   XHTML does not include definitions for HTML5 semantic elements, so you must replace them with generic `div` elements. Your document should match FIGURE B-20.

9. **Save your changes, then use the W3C validator to validate aboutusXHTML.html**
   FIGURE B-21 shows the validation results page for successful validation of aboutusXHTML.html. *Note:* If your document does not successfully validate, return to your text editor, compare your document to FIGURE B-20 and make any necessary changes, save your work, then revalidate your file.

10. **Open aboutusXHTML.html in a browser**
    Browsers render the XHTML version of the document the same as the HTML5 version.

FIGURE B-20: About Us document converted to XHTML

```
1   <!DOCTYPE html PUBLIC "-//W3C//DTD XHTML 1.0 Transitional//EN"
2      "http://www.w3.org/TR/xhtml1/DTD/xhtml1-transitional.dtd">
3   <html lang="en" xmlns="http://www.w3.org/1999/xhtml">
4      <head>
5         <title>Lakeland Reeds Bed &amp; Breakfast - About Us</title>
            eland Reeds Bed and Breakfast
            ename: aboutus.html
            hor:    your first and last name
            e:      today's date
            HTML5 and CSS3 Illustrated Unit B, Lessons
         -->
14        <meta http-equiv="Content-Type" content="text/html; charset=utf-8" />
15        <meta name="viewport" content="width=device-width" />
16        <script src="modernizr.custom.62074.js" type="text/javascript"></script>
17     </head>
18     <body>
19        <div>
20           <h1>Lakeland Reeds Bed &amp; Breakfast</h1>
21        </div>
22        <div>
23           <h2>A
24           <p>La        an ideal place to unplug from your daily routine. We're
             here       the most out of your time with us, from canoes and life
             vests      n the lake, to DVDs and popcorn for a quiet evening in. We
             look       ming you!</p>
28        </div>
29        <div>
30           <p>45 Marsh Grass Ln. &#8226; Marble, MN 55764 &#8226; (218) 555-5253</p>
31        </div>
32     </body>
33  </html>
```

HTML5 DOCTYPE statement replaced with XHTML Transitional version

xmlns attribute and value in quotes added to opening <html> tag

meta element specifying character encoding replaced with XHTML version

Space and closing / added to one-sided tag

type attribute and value in quotes added to script element

header and footer tag pairs replaced by div tag pairs

HTML5 & CSS3

FIGURE B-21: Validation results for aboutusXHTML.html

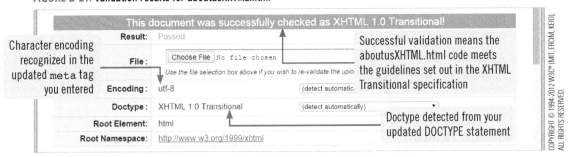

Character encoding recognized in the updated meta tag you entered

Successful validation means the aboutusXHTML.html code meets the guidelines set out in the XHTML Transitional specification

Doctype detected from your updated DOCTYPE statement

TABLE B-7: Differences between HTML and XHTML

aspect	HTML	XHTML
Tag nesting	Tags may be closed out of order	Tags must be closed in the order opened
Tag case	Tags may be written in upper or lower case	Tags must be written in lower case
Tag closure	Closing tags may be omitted for some elements	All opening tags must be matched with closing tags
Attribute-value pairs	Certain attribute names may be specified without values	Values required for all attributes
One-sided tags	One-sided tags do not need to be closed	One-sided tags must be closed
script and style elements	Element content requires no special formatting	Element content must be marked with code identifying it as CDATA
Attribute values	Values may be enclosed within quotes	Values must be enclosed within quotes
id and name attributes	Either attribute may be used	id attribute may be used, but name attribute prohibited
Character codes for certain special characters	Codes recommended	Codes required

Practice

Concepts Review

Refer to FIGURE B-22 **to answer the following questions.**

FIGURE B-22

```
1   <!DOCTYPE html>
2   <html lang="en">
3      <head>
4         <title>Lakeland Reeds Bed &amp; Breakfast - About Us</title>
5         <!--
6            Lakeland Reeds Bed and Breakfast
7            Filename: aboutus.html
8
9            Author:   your first and last name
10           Date:     today's date
11           HTML5 and CSS3 Illustrated Unit B, Lessons
12        -->
13        <meta charset="utf-8">
14        <meta name="viewport" content="width=device-width">
15        <script src="modernizr.custom.62074.js"></script>
16     </head>
17     <body>
18        <header>
19           <h1>Lakeland Reeds Bed &amp; Breakfast</h1>
20        </header>
21        <div>
22           <h2>About Us</h2>
23           <p>Lakeland Reeds is an ideal place to unplug from your daily routine. We're
24              here to help you get the most out of your time with us, from canoes and life
25              vests for a day out on the lake, to DVDs and popcorn for a quiet evening in. We
26              look forward to welcoming you!</p>
27        </div>
28        <footer>
29           <p>45 Marsh Grass Ln. &#8226; Marble, MN 55764 &#8226; (218) 555-5253</p>
30        </footer>
31     </body>
32  </html>
```

a → (line 2)
f ↓ (line 4)
b → (line 13)
c → (line 15)
d → (line 19)
e ↑ (line 29)

1. **Which item is a semantic element?**
2. **Which item tells mobile browsers how to display the document?**
3. **Which item is a named character reference?**
4. **Which item is an attribute name and value?**
5. **Which item is a numeric character reference?**
6. **Which item specifies the character encoding for the document?**

Match each term with the statement that best describes it.

7. WCAG
8. attribute
9. character reference
10. viewport meta element
11. debugging
12. validation
13. XHTML

a. the process of finding and removing incorrectly written code

b. a version of HTML that complies with the rules of XML

c. an automated process of comparing code you've written against the HTML5 coding standards

d. a specially formatted code that represents a character in the HTML document character set

e. code you can use to instruct mobile browsers to display a page at the width of the browser window without zooming in

f. additional code within an opening tag that specifies information about an element

g. a widely used reference for implementing web accessibility

Select the best answer from the list of choices.

14. According to WCAG, to make your web pages _____ you should ensure that no elements rely on the use of a mouse.

    a. perceivable   **c.** understandable

    b. operable   **d.** robust

15. Where are an attribute's name and value placed in your code?

    a. In the DOCTYPE   **c.** In an element's closing tag

    b. In an element's opening tag   **d.** In an external file

16. The `header` and `footer` elements are known as _____ elements.

    a. presentational   **c.** semantic

    b. structural   **d.** mandatory

17. Character references always begin with an ampersand (&) and end with a _____.

    a. quote (")   **c.** colon (:)

    b. hyphen (-)   **d.** semicolon (;)

18. Simply viewing your document in one or more browsers can sometimes help you recognize _____.

    a. bugs   **c.** attributes

    b. semantic elements   **d.** character references

Skills Review

1. **Incorporate attributes.**

    a. In your editor, open the HTM_B-2.html file from the SR folder where you store your Data Files for this unit, then save it as **history.html**.

    b. Below the `title` element, insert the following comment, substituting your name and today's date where indicated:

    `<!--`

        Big J's Deep Dish Pizza History web page

        Filename: history.html

        Author: your name

        Date: today's date

        HTML5 and CSS3 Illustrated Unit B, Skills Review

    `-->`

    c. Preview history.html in a browser.

    d. Return to your editor, then in the opening `<html>` tag, insert the attribute and value **lang="en"**.

    e. Below the comment add a `meta` element with an attribute and value that specifies the character encoding as utf-8.

    f. Save your document, then view the revised document in a browser.

2. **Implement the `div` element.**

    a. Return to history.html in your editor.

    b. Add a `div` element as the parent element of the h2 element and the first two p elements.

    c. Indent all three child elements of the new `div` element.

    d. Save your document, then view the revised document in a browser.

3. **Add HTML5 semantic elements.**

    a. Return to history.html in your editor.

    b. Add a `header` element as the parent element of the h1 element.

    c. Add a `footer` element as the parent element of the last p element.

    d. Indent the child elements of the new `header` and `footer` elements.

    e. Below the `<meta>` tag in the head section, add the following `script` element:

    `<script src="modernizr.custom.62074.js"></script>`

Skills Review (continued)

f. Save your document, then view the revised document in a browser.

g. If you have access to Internet Explorer 8 or an earlier version of Internet Explorer, use it to open history.html.

4. Use special characters.

a. Return to history.html in your editor.

b. In the content of the `title` element, replace the apostrophe (') with `&#39;`.

c. In the content of the `h1` element, replace the apostrophe (') with `&#39;`.

d. In the `footer` element, replace each instance of a hyphen (-) with `&#8226;`.

e. Save your document, then view the revised document in a browser. Your document should match **FIGURE B-23**.

5. Specify the viewport.

a. Using your web server, open history.html on a smartphone or other handheld mobile device.

b. Return to history.html in your editor.

c. In the head section, below the <meta> tag, enter the following `viewport` meta tag:

`<meta name="viewport"`
`content="width=device-width">`

d. Save your changes, then view the revised document on your mobile device. Your document should match **FIGURE B-24**.

6. Debug your HTML code.

a. Return to history.html in your editor.

b. Within the `div` element, delete the opening <h2> tag.

c. Within the `footer` element, delete the & at the start of the second character reference.

d. Save your changes, refresh or reload history.html in a browser, then identify the rendering errors.

e. Return to history.html in your editor, click just before the word History within the div element, then type <h2>.

f. Save your changes, then refresh or reload history.html in a browser.

g. Return to history.html in your editor, click just before the second # within the footer element, then type &.

h. Save your changes, refresh or reload history.html in a browser, then verify that no errors remain.

7. Validate your HTML code.

a. In a web browser, open http://validator.w3.org.

b. Use the Validate by File Upload tab to upload and validate history.html from the SR folder where you store your Data Files for this unit.

c. Scroll down to read the validation results, including any notes or warnings.

d. If your document does not successfully validate as HTML5, examine the error messages, return to your text editor, make any necessary changes, save your work, then revalidate your file

8. Create an XHTML document.

a. Return to history.html in your editor, save a copy of history.html to the SR folder with the name **historyXHTML. html**, then in the comment in the head section, change the filename listed to **historyXHTML.html**.

b. Delete the DOCTYPE, open doctype.txt from the SR folder, copy the contents of the file, then paste it at the start of historyXHTML.html.

FIGURE B-23

FIGURE B-24

Skills Review (continued)

c. In the opening `<html>` tag, add the attribute and value **xmlns="http://www.w3.org/1999/xhtml"**.

d. Replace the meta tag that specifies the character encoding for the document with **<meta http-equiv= "Content-Type" content="text/html; charset=utf-8" />**.

e. Add a closing / to the viewport `<meta>` tag.

f. Within the opening `<script>` tag, add the attribute and value **type="text/javascript"**.

f. Replace the `header` and `footer` elements with `div` elements.

g. Use http://validator.w3.org to validate historyXHTML.html.

h. Open historyXHTML.html in a browser and verify that its appearance matches that of history.html.

Independent Challenge 1

Spotted Wren Garden Center, a local garden shop and plant store, has hired you to create a website for their business. Sarah Nguyen, the shop's owner and manager, would like you to create a web presence as a new avenue of marketing, as well as a means to keep regular customers up to date on seasonal specials and new products. You continue building the site by structuring a page listing the store's summer hours.

a. In your editor, open the HTM_B-3.html file from the IC1 folder where you store your Data Files for this unit, then save it as **hours.html**.

b. In the head section, insert a comment containing the text **Spotted Wren Garden Center Summer Hours web page**, the filename **hours.html**, your first and last name, today's date, and the text **HTML5 and CSS3 Illustrated Unit B, Independent Challenge 1**, then save the file.

c. Preview hours.html in a browser.

d. Return to hours.html in your text editor, add an attribute specifying that the document contents are in English, then add an element that specifies the character encoding as utf-8. (*Hint:* Use the `charset meta` element.)

e. Add a `header` element as the parent of the h1 element and the first p element, then add a `div` element as the parent of the h2 element and the next seven p elements (*Note:* This includes all but the last p element).

f. Add a `footer` element as the parent of the final p element, then indent all child elements of the newly added `header`, `div`, and `footer` elements.

g. Add the following `script` element in the head section of your document:

<script src="modernizr.custom.62074.js"></script>

h. Replace the hyphen (-) in each p element within the `div` element with the named character reference **–**, then replace each hyphen within the `footer` element with the numeric character reference **•**. (*Hint:* Be sure your named character reference starts with **&** and ends with a semicolon (**;**).)

i. Save your changes and preview the document in a browser. Your document should match **FIGURE B-25**.

j. Add the following viewport `meta` tag to your document:

<meta name="viewport" content="width=device-width">

k. Save your changes and view the document on a handheld device such as a smartphone. Your document should match **FIGURE B-26**.

FIGURE B-25

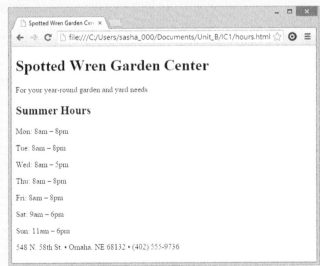

Independent Challenge 1 (continued)

l. Make intentional coding errors by deleting the third opening `<p>` tag within the `div` element and deleting the `&` at the start of the named character reference in the last p element within the `div` element, save your changes, view the document in a browser, then examine the results of the errors you introduced.

m. Fix the errors you introduced and use your browser to verify that the page is once again rendered as it was before. (*Hint*: Add back the opening `<p>` tag and the `&` as noted in step l.)

n. Use http://validator.w3.org to validate your document. If necessary, fix any errors in your document until it validates.

Independent Challenge 2

To help build your web design skills, you have volunteered to create a website for the Murfreesboro Regional Soccer League (MRSL). The league organizes recreational leagues every summer and fall for local, nonprofessional soccer players to get exercise and have fun. You continue working on the site by adding structure to the page that provides information for prospective participants.

a. In your editor, open the HTM_B-4.html file from the IC2 folder where you store your Data Files for this unit, then save it as **started.html**.

b. In the head section, insert a comment containing the text **Murfreesboro Regional Soccer League Getting Started web page**, the filename **started.html**, your first and last name, today's date, and the text **HTML5 and CSS3 Illustrated Unit B, Independent Challenge 2**, then save the file.

c. Preview started.html in a browser.

d. Add an attribute specifying that the document contents are in English in the opening `html` tag, then add a `meta` element after the closing comment tag that specifies the character encoding as **utf-8**.

e. Add a `header` element as the parent of the h1 element and the first p element. Add a `div` element as the parent of the next two p elements. Add a `footer` element as the parent of the final p element. Indent all child elements of the newly added `header`, `div`, and `footer` elements.

f. Add the following `script` element in the head section of your document:
`<script src="modernizr.custom.62074.js"></script>`

g. Within the `footer` element, replace each hyphen with the numeric character reference **•**. Save your changes and preview the document in a browser. Your document should match FIGURE B-27.

h. Add the following `viewport` `meta` tag to your document:
`<meta name="viewport" content="width=device-width">`

i. Save your changes and view the document on a handheld device such as a smartphone. Your document should match FIGURE B-28.

j. Introduce errors into your code by deleting one of the opening `<p>` tags and deleting the `#` within one of the character references. Save your changes, view the document in a browser, then identify the errors you introduced. Fix the errors you introduced and verify that the page is once again rendered as it was before.

FIGURE B-27

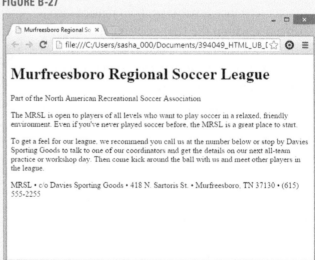

Structuring Content in a Web Document

Independent Challenge 2 (continued)

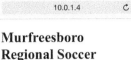

k. Use http://validator.w3.org to validate your document. If necessary, fix any errors in your document until it validates.

l. Save a copy of your document as **startedXHTML.html** to the IC2 folder, changing the filename listed in the comment in the head section, then replace the DOCTYPE with the contents of doctype.txt in the IC2 folder.

m. In the opening <html> tag, add the attribute and value **xmlns=http://www. w3.org/1999/xhtml**, then replace the meta element that specifies the character encoding for the document with **<meta http-equiv= "Content-Type" content="text/html; charset=utf-8" />**.

n. Add a closing / to the viewport <meta> tag, then in the opening <script> tag add **type="text/javascript"**.

o. Replace the header and footer elements with div elements.

p. Use http://validator.w3.org to validate startedXHTML.html. If necessary, fix any errors in your document until it validates.

> **Murfreesboro Regional Soccer League**
>
> Part of the North American Recreational Soccer Association
>
> The MRSL is open to players of all levels who want to play soccer in a relaxed, friendly environment. Even if you've never played soccer before, the MRSL is a great place to start.
>
> To get a feel for our league, we recommend you call us at the number below or stop by Davies Sporting Goods to talk to one of our coordinators and get the details on our next all-team practice or workshop day. Then come kick around the ball with us and meet other players in the league.
>
> MRSL • c/o Davies Sporting Goods • 418 N. Sartoris St. • Murfreesboro, TN 37130 • (615) 555-2255

Independent Challenge 3

In your new job creating sites for a web design firm, you've been assigned Hotel Natoma as a client. The hotel's business manager, Diego Merckx, wants to use the web to showcase the facility and its amenities. As you continue your work on the site, you work with the structure of the code for the page listing attractions near the hotel.

a. In your editor, open the HTM_B-5.html file from the IC3 folder where you store your Data Files for this unit, then save it as **nearby.html**.

b. In the head section, insert a comment containing the text **Hotel Natoma What's Nearby web page**, the filename **nearby.html**, your first and last name, today's date, and the text **HTML5 and CSS3 Illustrated Unit B, Independent Challenge 3**. Save the file, then preview it in a browser.

c. Add an attribute specifying that the document contents are in English. Add an element that specifies the character encoding as utf-8.

d. Add a header element as the parent of the h1 element. Add a div element as the parent of the h2 element and the next six p elements. Add a footer element as the parent of the final p element. Indent all child elements of the newly added header, div, and footer elements.

FIGURE B-29

e. Add the following script element in the head section of your document:
<script src="modernizr.cus-tom.62074.js"></script>

f. Within the title element and the h2 element, replace the apostrophe with the numeric character reference **'**. Within the footer element, replace each pipe character (|) with the numeric character reference **•**. Save your changes and preview the document in a browser. Your document should match **FIGURE B-29**.

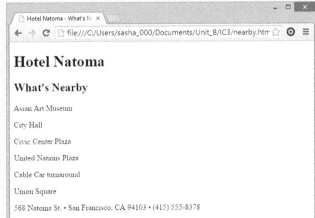

Independent Challenge 3 (continued)

FIGURE B-30

g. Add the following viewport `meta` tag to your document:

`<meta name="viewport" content="width=device-width">`

Save your changes and view the document on a handheld device such as a smartphone. Your document should match **FIGURE B-30**.

h. Introduce errors into your code by deleting one of the opening `<p>` tags, deleting the # within one of the character references, and deleting the & within a different character reference. Save your changes, view the document in a browser, then identify the errors you introduced. Without fixing the errors you introduced, use http://validator.w3.org to validate your document. Examine the error messages generated by the validator, then use the messages to track down and fix the errors in your document. Fix all errors in your document until it validates. Preview the document in a browser, then verify that the page is once again rendered as it was in **FIGURE B-29**.

i. Save a copy of your document as **nearbyXHTML.html** to the IC3 folder, changing the filename listed in the comment in the head section. Replace the DOCTYPE with the contents of doctype.txt in the IC3 folder. Without making any other changes to the document, use http://validator.w3.org to validate startedXHTML.html. Examine the error messages generated by the validator, then make the following changes one at a time, validating after each change, and noticing the differences in the error message list after each change:

- In the opening `<html>` tag, add the attribute and value **xmlns="http://www.w3.org/1999/xhtml"**.
- Replace the `meta` element that specifies the character encoding for the document with **<meta http-equiv="Content-Type" content="text/html; charset=utf-8" />**.
- Add a closing / to the `viewport` `<meta>` tag.
- In the opening `<script>` tag, add the attribute and value **type="text/javascript"**.
- Replace the `header` and `footer` elements with `div` elements.

Independent Challenge 4—Explore

You've been hired to create a website for Eating Well in Season (EWIS), a business in Glover, Vermont, that delivers produce from local farms to its customers. You'll continue your work on the site by enhancing the structure of a page that explains delivery options.

a. In your editor, open the HTM_B-6.html file from the IC4 folder where you store your Data Files for this unit, then save it as **delivery.html**.

b. In the head section, insert a comment containing the text **Eating Well in Season Delivery Options web page**, the filename **delivery.html**, your first and last name, today's date, and the text **HTML5 and CSS3 Illustrated Unit B, Independent Challenge 4**. Save the file.

c. The document's code contains two errors. Using the debugging tools you learned in this unit, locate and fix the errors.

d. Add an attribute specifying that the document contents are in English. Add an element that specifies the character encoding as utf-8.

e. Add a `header` element as the parent of the h1 element. Use **TABLE B-2** to choose an appropriate semantic element to use as the parent of the h2 element and the next two p elements. Add a `footer` element as the parent of the final p element. Indent all child elements of the three newly added semantic elements.

f. Add the following `script` element in the head section of your document:

`<script src="modernizr.custom.62074.js"></script>`

g. Browse the characters at fileformat.info for an appropriate character to replace the asterisks (*) in the footer element. (*Hint*: Many of the punctuation characters at http://www.fileformat.info/info/unicode/block/ general_punctuation/list.htm are suited to the task. When you identify an appropriate character, click the link on the same line starting with U, then on the page that opens, locate the value labeled "HTML Entity (decimal)".) Use the value for your new symbol to replace the * three times in the footer. Save your changes and preview the document in current versions of all three modern browsers on both Windows and Mac (Chrome for Windows and Mac, Firefox for Windows and Mac, and Internet Explorer for Windows), noting any differences between them. If the character does not display consistently among browsers, choose a different character and test it, repeating until you identify a character that all three browsers display consistently under both operating systems. **FIGURE B-31** shows one possibility.

h. Add the following viewport `meta` tag to your document:

FIGURE B-31

**<meta name="viewport"
content="width=device-width">**
Save your changes and view the document on a handheld device such as a smartphone. Your document should resemble **FIGURE B-32**.

i. If you are using a code editor, introduce some errors by deleting one of the opening <p> tags and deleting the # symbol within one of the character references. Notice any changes to the formatting of the code in your editor after you introduce the errors, such as underlining or changes in color. Use the documentation for your code editor to identify whether it includes features that suggest fixes to detected coding errors. Fix the errors you introduced and verify that the page is once again rendered as shown in **FIGURE B-31**.

FIGURE B-32

j. If you are using a code editor, use the editor's documentation to learn whether it can validate HTML documents. If so, use your editor to validate your document. If not, use http://validator.w3.org to validate your file. If necessary, fix any errors in your document until it validates.

Visual Workshop

In your editor, open the HTM_B-7.html file from the VW folder where you store your Data Files for this unit, then save it as **events.html**. In the head section, insert a comment containing a description of the page content, the filename **events.html**, your first and last name, today's date, and the text **HTML5 and CSS3 Illustrated Unit B, Visual Workshop**. Structure the web page to specify the following: the document contents are in English; the character encoding is utf-8; the main heading is the page header; the second-level heading and the four events are the main page content; and the contact information is the page footer. Ensure that Internet Explorer 8 correctly parses the page. Replace the word "and" in the browser tab and the main page heading with a character reference for the ampersand (&) symbol. Replace each hyphen in the contact information with a bullet character (•). The structured page should match FIGURE B-33. Also add code to ensure that smartphone browsers display the page as shown in FIGURE B-34. Validate your document, then if necessary, fix any errors until it validates successfully.

FIGURE B-33

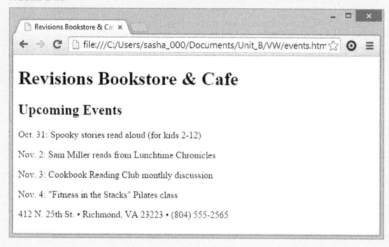

FIGURE B-34

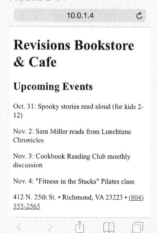

Getting Started with CSS

CASE As you continue your work on the Lakeland Reeds Bed & Breakfast website, your supervisor, Faduma Egal, has asked you to change the appearance of some web page content. In this unit, you learn about Cascading Style Sheets (CSS) and you use CSS code to style your web documents.

Unit Objectives

After completing this unit, you will be able to:

- Assess style rules
- Create an embedded style sheet
- Implement an ID selector
- Implement a class selector
- Use multiple selectors

- Create an external style sheet
- Link to an external style sheet
- Add a comment to a style sheet
- Debug and validate CSS code

Files You Will Need

L	3 files	IC3	3 files
SR	3 files	IC4	3 files
IC1	2 files	VW	2 files
IC2	3 files		

For specific filenames, see Filenames_C.pdf in the Unit C Data Files folder.

Assess Style Rules

Cascading Style Sheets (CSS) is a language used to specify how web page elements should be rendered in a browser. CSS is a separate language from HTML but the two languages are complementary—HTML code specifies the content of each web page element, and CSS code indicates how that content should be displayed. Because CSS is a separate language, it uses its own syntax. You create CSS code for an HTML document by writing **style rules**, which are lines or blocks of CSS code that specify the presentation of web page elements. The most recent version of CSS is known as **CSS3**. While CSS3 supports some features not available in previous versions, it uses the same syntax as previous versions. **CASE** ▸ *As you prepare to integrate CSS into the Lakeland Reeds website, you review style rule structure and syntax.*

DETAILS

CSS code builds on a few basic concepts:

• **Properties**

A CSS **property** is an aspect of the appearance of a web page element that can be modified. For instance, you can change the background color or text alignment of an element. CSS property names do not include spaces but they may include hyphens to make them more readable. For instance, to change text alignment, you use the `text-align` property. **TABLE C-1** lists CSS properties that you will use in this unit.

• **Declarations**

The basic building block of CSS code is the **declaration**, which is a combination of a property name and a value. When you specify a property name in CSS code, it is followed by a colon, the value, and a semicolon. Allowable values are specific to each property and vary widely, including keywords such as `center` and numerical values expressed in percentages or units of measurement. In addition, some properties take multiple values, separated by spaces. The following declaration specifies the `text-align` property and sets its value to `center`:

```
text-align: center;
```

The space after the colon is not required. However, because this space does not change the meaning of the code, it's common practice to include it to make the code easier to read at a glance.

• **Selectors**

To associate declarations with a web page element, you use **selectors**, which identify the HTML element or elements to which the declarations apply. CSS supports several different types of selectors. The most general selectors are the names of HTML elements, such as `h1` or `p`, which are known as **type selectors**. Type selectors apply associated declarations to every instance of the specified element in a web document. They also apply the declarations to all descendant elements of selected elements, a process known as **inheritance**. To apply declarations to all p elements in a document and their descendant elements, you would use the following selector:

```
p
```

You can specify multiple type selectors for a single set of declarations by separating the type selectors with commas. For instance, the following type selector applies declarations to all p elements and their descendants in a document, as well as to all h1 elements and their descendants in that document:

```
p, h1
```

• **Style rules**

You create a style rule by combining a selector and one or more declarations. The declarations are enclosed within curly braces (`{ }`). For readability purposes, each declaration is usually entered on its own line. In addition, the opening curly brace is placed after the selector, and the closing curly brace is placed on its own line after the final declaration. For instance, the style rule shown in **FIGURE C-1** centers text within all p elements and their descendants and also applies a background color of `ivory` to these elements and their descendants. You may also see style rules written on a single line, as shown in **FIGURE C-2**.

FIGURE C-1: A style rule

FIGURE C-2: A style rule entered on a single line

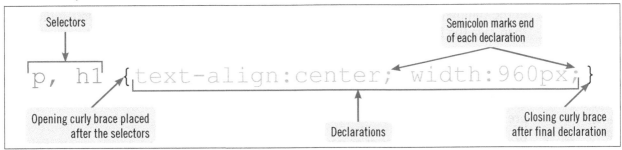

TABLE C-1: CSS properties and values

property	affects	allowable values	example
background-color	an element's fill color, behind any content such as text	name from a list of supported colors, or code using one of several systems for specifying color using numeric values	background-color: ivory;
color	an element's foreground color; for elements containing text, this is the text color	name from a list of supported colors, or code using one of several systems for specifying color using numeric values	color: wheat;
text-align	the horizonal alignment of text within the element that contains it	left, right, center, justify, inherit (same value as enclosing element)	text-align: center;

Spacing your CSS code

Web page rendering engines recognize declarations after a selector as starting after an opening curly brace ({) and ending with the closing curly brace (}). As long as a semicolon follows each value, any number of spaces, tabs, and new lines can occur within a set of declarations. As a result, the appearance of CSS code can vary widely. Most developers prefer to give each declaration its own line, often indented beneath its selector, as shown in **FIGURE C-1**, to make the code easier to read. Others prefer to keep all declarations

on the same line as the selector, as shown in **FIGURE C-2**, to keep their code compact and make it obvious which pairs are associated with which selector. While the code shown in this book uses the format shown in **FIGURE C-1**, don't be surprised to see the single-line format shown in **FIGURE C-2**—as well as other variations—in other examples of CSS that you may encounter. While you may be required to follow a given code format by an employer or a client, such formatting is most often a matter of personal taste.

© 2016 Cengage Learning

Create an Embedded Style Sheet

Learning Outcomes
- Add an embedded style sheet to an HTML document
- Create a style rule using a type selector

To affect the presentation of elements in a single web page, you can create an **embedded style sheet**, which consists of CSS style rules entered in the head element of an HTML document. When you add the CSS style rules to the head element, you indicate to user agents that your style rules are written in CSS by nesting them within an HTML style element. **CASE** ▶ *You specify the background color for the body element and center the h1 text of the main web page for Lakeland Reeds B&B by adding an embedded style sheet to the document.*

STEPS

1. **Open your editor, open the** HTM_C-1.html **file from the Lessons folder where you store your Data Files for Unit C, then save the file as** index.html **to the same location**

2. **In the comment in the head section, enter your name and today's date where indicated, then save the file**

3. **Open** index.html **in your browser**
   The web page contains a level 1 heading and three paragraphs, as shown in FIGURE C-3.

TROUBLE
Because some code editors indent automatically, you may not need to press [Spacebar] to indent. As you work through this unit, use the figures to check for and match indenting.

4. **Return to your editor, click at the end of the line containing the** script **element, then press [Enter]**

5. **Press [Spacebar] six times or as needed to create the indent, type** <style>**, press [Enter] twice, press [Spacebar] six times or as needed to create the indent, then type** </style>

6. **Click the blank line between the opening and closing style tags, press [Spacebar] nine times or as needed to create the indent, type** body {**, press [Enter] twice, press [Spacebar] nine times or as needed to create the indent, then type** }
   You enter CSS code between the opening and closing tags for the style element. Styles specified for the body element are inherited by all elements in the web document.

QUICK TIP
Styles applied to an element also apply to any elements nested within that element. This means that declarations assigned to the body element apply to all elements on the page.

7. **Click the blank line between the opening and closing curly braces, press [Spacebar] twelve times or as needed to create the indent, type** background-color: ivory;**, press [Enter], press [Spacebar] twelve times or as needed to create the indent, then type** text-align: left;
   The background-color property sets the color behind page content, and the text-align property determines the horizontal alignment of text. This style rule sets the background color of the entire page (the body element) to ivory, and left-aligns all text within the body element. Compare your document to FIGURE C-4.

QUICK TIP
If the background color in your web document is white instead of ivory, verify that you entered each declaration between the opening and closing curly braces, and that each value ends with a semicolon.

8. **Save your document, return to your default browser, then click the** Refresh **or** Reload **button to view changes to your web document**
   As FIGURE C-5 shows, the background of the entire document is now ivory. Because major browsers left-align text by default, the text alignment is unchanged from FIGURE C-3.

FIGURE C-3: Default appearance of index.html in a browser

h1 element → **Lakeland Reeds Bed & Breakfast**

A country getaway perfect for fishing, boating, biking, or just watching the day go by.

p elements → Reserve your perfect weekend today.

45 Marsh Grass Ln. :: Marble, MN 55764 :: (218) 555-5253

FIGURE C-4: Embedded style sheet added to HTML document

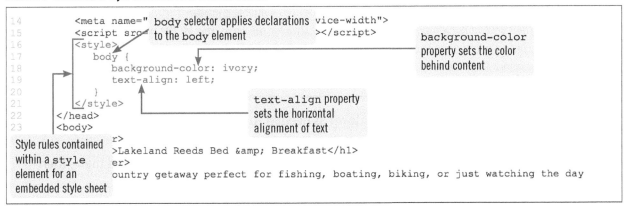

```
14        <meta name=" body selector applies declarations vice-width">
15        <script src       to the body element      ></script>
16        <style>                                                          background-color
17            body {                                                       property sets the color
18                background-color: ivory;                                 behind content
19                text-align: left;
20            }                                    text-align property
21        </style>                                 sets the horizontal
22      </head>                                    alignment of text
23      <body>
                r>
                >Lakeland Reeds Bed &amp; Breakfast</h1>
                er>
                ountry getaway perfect for fishing, boating, biking, or just watching the day
```

Style rules contained within a `style` element for an embedded style sheet

FIGURE C-5: Web page styled by embedded style sheet

Lakeland Reeds Bed & Breakfast

A country getaway perfect for fishing, boating, biking, or just watching the day go by.

Reserve your perfect weekend today.

45 Marsh Grass Ln. :: Marble, MN 55764 :: (218) 555-5253

All web page text left-aligned ←

→ Background color for entire document changed to ivory

Understanding the `type` attribute of the `style` element

XHTML and older versions of HTML require an attribute in the opening `<style>` tag to specify the language of the code the element contains. When style sheets were first developed, this attribute was incorporated into web standards to allow for multiple style languages to be used with web pages. To specify that a style sheet contained CSS code, you would use the value `text/css` for the `type` attribute, as in the following opening tag:

```
<style type="text/css">
```

CSS has emerged as the standard for providing style information for web documents. For this reason, when parsing an HTML5 document, modern browsers assume that the contents of a `style` element are written in CSS. Therefore, you do not need to specify the `type` attribute when using the HTML5 DOCTYPE (`<DOCTYPE html>`).

Implement an ID Selector

Learning
Outcomes
• Add an id
  attribute to an
  HTML element
• Create a style rule
  using an ID
  selector

Sometimes instead of affecting the presentation of all the elements of a certain type, you want to make changes that affect only a single element. For instance, maybe a certain p element requires a different alignment from all the other p elements in a document. HTML allows you to add the id attribute to the opening tag for an element to give the element a unique identifier. You can then create a special type of selector known as an **ID selector** to create CSS code that applies to that element alone. An ID selector is simply a pound sign (#) followed by the value of the id attribute for the element, as shown in FIGURE C-6. The declarations in a style rule that uses an ID selector apply only to the element with the specified id attribute value. Although all descendant elements of a selected element inherit the same declarations, creating a style rule for a descendant element with different values for the same properties overrides the inherited values. For instance, setting a value for the text-align property using the p selector would override a text-align value set using the body selector. Likewise, setting this property using an id selector on a p element would override the inherited value. **CASE** ▶ *The main Lakeland Reeds web page contains several paragraph elements. The visual style for the page calls for the paragraph element containing the contact information to be right-aligned. You use an id attribute and ID selector to change the alignment of the contact information.*

STEPS

1. **Return to your editor, scroll down as needed to the p element within the footer element**

2. **In the opening <p> tag, position the insertion point between the p and the >, then press [Spacebar]**

3. **Type** id="contact"
   The paragraph containing the contact information is assigned the unique id value contact.

4. **Scroll up as needed to the embedded style sheet, click after the closing curly brace for the body style rule, press [Enter], then press [Spacebar] nine times or as needed to create the indent**

5. **Type** #contact {, **then press [Enter]**

6. **Press [Spacebar] twelve times or as needed to create the indent, type** text-align: right;, **then press [Enter]**
   The default value of text-align is left, which aligns the left edges of each line of text in an element. Specifying a value of right lines up the right edges of the text instead and aligns them with the right edge of the enclosing element.

7. **Press [Spacebar] nine times or as needed to create the indent, then type }**
   Your completed code should match FIGURE C-7.

8. **Save your document, return to your default browser, then click the Refresh or Reload button to view changes to your web document**
   As FIGURE C-8 shows, the contact information at the bottom of the page is right-aligned.

FIGURE C-6: **A style rule using an ID selector**

The pound sign indicates this is an ID selector ➔

```
#contact {
    text-align: right;
}
```

This ID selector applies to the element with the `id` attribute value `contact`

© 2016 Cengage Learning

FIGURE C-7: `id` **attribute and style rule with ID selector added**

```
16          <style>
17              body {
18                  background-color: ivory;
19                  text-align: left;
20              }
21              #contact {
22                  text-align: right;
23              }
24          </style>
25      </head>
26      <body>
27          <header>
28              <h1>Lakeland Reeds Bed &amp; Breakfast</h1>
29          </header>
30          <p>A country getaway perfect for fishing, boating, biking, or just watching the day
31          go by.</p>
32          <p>Reserve your perfect weekend today.</p>
33          <footer>
34              <p id="contact">45 Marsh Grass Ln. :: Marble, MN 55764 :: (218) 555-5253</p>
35          </footer>
36      </body>
37  </html>
```

New style rule using an ID selector ➔ (line 21)

`id` attribute with value of `contact` added to opening `<p>` tag

FIGURE C-8: `p` **element right-aligned using ID selector**

`p` element with `id` attribute value `contact` right-aligned

Implement a Class Selector

Learning
Outcomes
• Add a class
  attribute to an
  HTML element
• Create a style rule
  using a class
  selector

Sometimes you want to apply a style rule to multiple elements in a web document without adding an additional layer of HTML code. While the `id` attribute limits a given value to a single instance in a web page, you can create a selector that applies to any number of elements on a page using the HTML `class` attribute, which does not have this limit. A **class selector** creates a style rule based on values assigned to elements using the HTML `class` attribute. This allows you to apply a style rule to an unlimited number of separate elements. As FIGURE C-9 shows, a class selector consists of a period followed by a class attribute value. **CASE** ▶ *The next step in implementing the visual design for the Lakeland Reeds web page is to change the text color of the two paragraphs that appear before the contact information. You add a `class` attribute to the two elements containing these paragraphs and then add a style rule using a class selector and the `color` property to modify their presentation.*

STEPS

QUICK TIP
Developers generally
use class names that
describe the goal of
the formatting, such
as accent, rather
than describing the
content, like blue.

1. **Return to your text editor, scroll down if necessary to the opening tag for the first `p` element, position the insertion point between the `p` and the `>`, press [Spacebar], then type** `class="accent"`

2. **In the opening tag for the second `p` element, position the insertion point between the `p` and the `>`, press [Spacebar], then type** `class="accent"`
   The first two `p` elements are both assigned the class value `accent`.

3. **Scroll up as needed to view the embedded style sheet, click after the closing curly brace for the `#contact` style rule, press [Enter], then press [Spacebar] nine times or as needed to create the indent**

4. **Type** `.accent {` **, then press [Enter]**

5. **Press [Spacebar] twelve times or as needed to create the indent, type** `color: darkcyan;`, **then press [Enter]**
   The `color` property sets the color of text in an element that contains text.

6. **Press [Spacebar] nine times or as needed to create the indent, then type** `}`
   Compare your completed code to FIGURE C-10.

7. **Save your document, return to your default browser, then click the Refresh or Reload button to view changes to your web document**
   As FIGURE C-11 shows, the text of the first two `p` elements in the document is bluish rather than black.

Inserting multiple attributes

There is no limit to the number of attributes you can include in a single HTML element. Thus, you can apply multiple style rules to a single element using any combination of a single `id` attribute value and one or more `class` attribute values. For example, you might assign a `class` value to certain paragraphs in a web page, along with an `id` value for a selected paragraph in the section to add extra elements to its style. The code for the opening tag might look as follows:

```
<p class="feature" id="topfeature">
```
This code assigns the `class` value `feature` and the `id` value `topfeature` to the `p` element. If multiple rules applied to the same element specify values for the same attribute, the value from the last rule in the style sheet is applied. This means it's important to take care with the order of rules in your style sheets. If your pages do not appear as you expect, verify that the order of rules is correct.

FIGURE C-9: A style rule using a class selector

The period indicates this is a class selector → .accent {
    color: darkcyan;
}

This class selector applies to all elements with the `class` attribute value accent

© 2016 Cengage Learning

FIGURE C-10: `class` attributes and style rule with class selector added

```
16          <style>
17              body {
18                  background-color: ivory;
19                  text-align: left;
20              }
21              #contact {
22                  text-align: right;
23              }
24              .accent {
25                  color: darkcyan;
26              }
27          </style>
28      </head>
29      <body>
30          <header>
31              <h1>Lakeland Reeds Bed &amp; Breakfast</h1>
32          </header>
33          <p class="accent">A country getaway perfect for fishing, boating, biking, or just
34          watching the day go by.</p>
35          <p class="accent">Reserve your perfect weekend today.</p>
36          <footer>
37              <p id="contact">45 Marsh Grass Ln. :: Marble, MN 55764 :: (218) 555-5253</p>
```

New style rule using a class selector

`class` attribute with value of accent added to opening `<p>` tags for two elements

FIGURE C-11: Text color of `p` elements changed using a class selector

Text color changed for `p` elements with `class` attribute value accent

Deciding whether to use an ID or class selector

The fact that only one element in a web document can have a given `id` attribute value can cause problems, especially in large documents. If you inadvertently add the same `id` attribute value to multiple elements on a page, the results in the browser may not be what you expected. In addition, changes to your HTML code may expose problems that weren't previously apparent and that are caused by duplicate `id` values. For this reason, many designers avoid using ID selectors at all, preferring to do all element-specific styling with the `class` attribute. The same `class` attribute value can be assigned to one element or to multiple elements, which provides designers with more flexibility. In addition, the `class` attribute accepts multiple values, separated by spaces, so there's no danger of running out of class values for an element.

HTML5 & CSS3

Use Multiple Selectors

Sometimes you want to assign the same CSS properties to the HTML elements specified by multiple selectors. While you could create a style rule and duplicate it for each selector, an easier way is to add multiple selectors to a single rule. To do this, you simply enter the selectors with a comma after each one except the last. Adding a space after each comma is optional, but it helps make the code easier to read. After the final selector, you type an opening curly brace and enter declarations as you would for any other style rule. For example, the style rule in **FIGURE C-12** applies a background color of `wheat` and a text color of `dimgray` to all `h1` elements as well as to the element with the `id` attribute value `contact`. CSS supports many other selectors, and **TABLE C-2** describes some of the most commonly used. **CASE** ▶ *The page design calls for the background of the `h1` element and the element with the ID `contact` to be set to the color wheat, and the text color of both to be `dimgray`. You use a single style rule to apply these declarations to both elements.*

STEPS

1. **Return to your text editor, click after the closing curly brace for the** body **style rule, then press** [Enter]

2. **Press** [Spacebar] **nine times or as needed to create the indent, type** `h1, #contact {`, **then press** [Enter]

QUICK TIP ▶
For more information about color names that you can use in HTML documents, see www.w3.org/TR/css3-color/#svg-color.

3. **Press** [Spacebar] **twelve times or as needed to create the indent, type** `background-color: wheat;`, **then press** [Enter]

4. **Press** [Spacebar] **twelve times or as needed to create the indent, type** `color: dimgray;`, **then press** [Enter]

5. **Press** [Spacebar] **nine times or as needed to create the indent, then type** `}`

   Compare your completed code to **FIGURE C-13**.

6. **Save your document, return to your default browser, then click the** Refresh **or** Reload **button to view changes to your web document**

   As **FIGURE C-14** shows, the header element and the contact information are formatted with a tan (`wheat`) background color and a dark gray (`dimgray`) text color.

TABLE C-2: Commonly used CSS selectors

selector	description	example	selects
Descendant	Specifies a series of nested elements and selects the final, most deeply nested element	`article div p`	Each p element nested within a `div` element that is itself nested within an `article` element
Direct child	Selects an element that is a child (but not grandchild, etc.) of another specified element	`div > p`	Each p element whose parent element is a `div` element
Direct next sibling	Selects an element that is a sibling of another specified element and *directly* follows that element	`h1 + p`	Each p element that is a sibling of an `h1` element and *directly* follows that `h1` element
Next sibling	Selects an element that is a sibling of another specified element and follows that element (potentially with other siblings between them)	`h1 ~ p`	Each p element that is a sibling of an `h1` element and follows that `h1` element

FIGURE C-12: A style rule that uses multiple selectors

Multiple selectors specified

```
h1, #contact {
    background-color: wheat;
    color: dimgray;
}
```

Selectors separated by a comma

© 2016 Cengage Learning

FIGURE C-13: Style rule with multiple selectors added

```
16          <style>
17              body {
18                  background-color: ivory;
19                  text-align: left;
20              }
21              #contact {
22                  text-align: right;
23              }
24              .accent {
25                  color: darkcyan;
26              }
27              h1, #contact {
28                  background-color: wheat;
29                  color: dimgray;
30              }
31          </style>
```

New style rule using multiple selectors

FIGURE C-14: Text and background colors of two elements changed using multiple selectors

Lakeland Reeds Bed & Br ×

file:///C:/Users/sasha_000/Documents/394049_HTML_UC_Data_

Lakeland Reeds Bed & Breakfast ←

A country getaway perfect for fishing, boating, biking, or just watching the day go by.

Reserve your perfect weekend today.

45 Marsh Grass Ln. :: Marble, MN 55764 :: (218) 555-5253

Text and background color changed for h1 element and element with id attribute value contact

Create an External Style Sheet

Learning
Outcomes
• Create an external
  style sheet
• Link an HTML
  document to an
  external style
  sheet

An embedded style sheet works well for a stand-alone web page. However, as your web presence grows into multiple pages, making a style change across the whole site would require changing the same style code on each page. As a result, embedded style sheets are impractical for sites with multiple pages. Instead, it's helpful to transition a growing website to an **external style sheet**, which is a separate file containing style information that multiple web pages can link to. To reference an external style sheet from within an HTML document you use the link element. **TABLE C-3** describes the attributes of the link element used to reference an external style sheet. **CASE** ▶ *Because the Lakeland Reeds website already includes multiple pages, you move the style information for the current page to an external style sheet in order to make the appearance of the site easier to modify.*

STEPS

1. **Return to your editor, save a copy of index.html with the name** index_embedded.html **to the same folder**

2. **Close** index_embedded.html, **then open** index.html **in your editor**

QUICK TIP

If you are using TextEdit on a Mac, click Format, then click Make Plain Text if it is not already selected.

3. **Scroll up as needed to view the embedded style sheet, select all the code between the opening and closing style tags, click** Edit **on the menu bar, then click** Cut
   The contents of the embedded style sheet are removed from the web document and placed on the clipboard.

4. **Save your changes to** index.html, **create a new file in your editor, click** Edit **on the menu bar, then click** Paste
   The embedded style sheet code is pasted into the new document, as shown in **FIGURE C-15**.

QUICK TIP

If you are using TextEdit on a Mac, click Use .css if a dialog box opens asking which file extension to use.

5. **Save the file as** styles.css **to the Lessons folder where you store your Data Files for Unit C, specifying an encoding of UTF-8 if you are using Notepad**
   Your external style sheet is saved with the filename styles.css.

6. **Close** styles.css, **then reopen** index.html **in your text editor if it is not still open**

7. **Select the lines containing the opening and closing** <style> **tags along with any blank lines between them, then press** [Delete]

8. **Click after the closing** </script> **tag, then press** [Enter] **to insert a blank line if there is not already one**

QUICK TIP

Because the contents of an external style sheet are written entirely in CSS, the file uses the extension .css instead of .html.

9. **Press** [Spacebar] **six times or as needed to create the indent, then type** <link rel="stylesheet" href="styles.css">
   FIGURE C-16 shows the web page code with the external style sheet reference inserted. The link element makes the contents of an external file available in the HTML document. The value for the rel attribute specifies that user agents should read the external document as a style sheet. The href attribute specifies the filename of the external style sheet.

10. **Save your document, return to your default browser, then click the** Refresh **or** Reload **button**
    Your web page appears just as it did when you were using an embedded style sheet. Even though you removed the style rules previously defined in the HTML document, you added a reference to the external document containing the rules. As a result, your browser still has access to the same style information and renders the web page according to the same guidelines.

TABLE C-3: Attributes of the link element

attribute	description	example
rel	Indicates the type of content in the linked file; for a style sheet, the value is stylesheet	rel="stylesheet"
href	Specifies the filename of the linked file	href="styles.css"

© 2016 Cengage Learning

FIGURE C-15: External style sheet

```
1   body {
2       background-color: ivory;
3       text-align: left;
4   }
5   #contact {
6       text-align: right;
7   }
8   .accent {
9       color: darkcyan;
10  }
11  h1, #contact {
12      background-color: wheat;
13      color: dimgray;
14  }
```

Style rules moved from embedded style sheet

FIGURE C-16: Web page linked to external style sheet

```
1   <!DOCTYPE html>
2   <html lang="en">
3       <head>
4           <title>Lakeland Reeds Bed &amp; Breakfast</title>
5           <!--
6               Lakeland Reeds Bed and Breakfast main web page
7               Filename: index.html
8
9               Author:    your first and last name
10              Date:      today's date
11              HTML5 and CSS3 Illustrated Unit C, Lessons
12          -->
13          <meta charset="utf-8">
14          <meta name="viewport" content="width=device-width">
15          <script src="modernizr.custom.62074.js"></script>
16          <link rel="stylesheet" href="styles.css">
17      </head>
18      <body>
```

link element loads contents of external CSS document

Filename of external style sheet

Implementing inline styles

In addition to embedded and external style sheets, you can also incorporate CSS properties into an HTML document using inline styles. An **inline style** is a style rule inserted into the opening tag of an element using the `style` attribute. **FIGURE C-17** shows an example of an inline style. Inline styles do not offer many of the benefits provided by other methods of applying styles. For instance, changing a style applied inline requires locating the style within HTML code, rather than simply looking at an embedded or external style sheet. Because of this and other drawbacks, many web developers avoid creating inline styles.

FIGURE C-17: An inline style

```
<h1 style="text-align: center;">Lakeland Reeds Bed and Breakfast</h1>
```

© 2016 Cengage Learning

Link to an External Style Sheet

Learning
Outcomes
• Link multiple
HTML documents
to an external style
sheet

Once you create an external style sheet for a website, you can apply the style rules it contains to every page on the site simply by adding a `link` element referencing the style sheet file to each HTML document. If you later decide to make changes to the appearance of your website, any change you make to the external style sheet is reflected immediately on all the pages that link to it. FIGURE C-18 illustrates the relationship between the HTML documents that make up a website and an external style sheet. **CASE** *The class and id attributes that correspond to the code you added to the main web page have been added to the Lakeland Reeds B&B About Us page. You add a link in the About Us document to the external style sheet file you created in order to apply the style rules from the external style sheet to the About Us page as well.*

STEPS

QUICK TIP
If you are using
TextEdit on a Mac,
click the Ignore Rich
Text Commands
check box in the
Open dialog box
to select it for any
HTML file you open.

1. **Return to your text editor, open the file** HTM C-2.html **from the Lessons folder where you store your Data Files for Unit C, then save it as** aboutus.html

   The file contains multiple elements with the `class` attribute value of `accent` and an element with an `id` attribute value of `contact`.

2. **In the comment within the head section, enter your name and today's date where indicated, then save your changes**

3. **Open** aboutus.html **in your browser**

   All the page elements are left-aligned and all text is black on a white background, resembling the appearance of the main Lakeland Reeds page at the beginning of the unit.

4. **Return to your editor, click at the end of the line containing the** script **element, then press [Enter]**

5. **Press [Spacebar] six times or as needed to create the indent, then type** `<link rel="stylesheet" href="styles.css">`

   This is the same `link` element you inserted into index.html. FIGURE C-19 shows the completed code.

6. **Save your document, return to your default browser, then click the** Refresh **or** Reload **button to view the changes to the About Us page**

   The browser now renders the web page with a layout similar to the main page of the website.

7. **Return to your editor, open** styles.css, **then in the** h1, **#contact style rule, change the value for the** background-color **property from** wheat **to** palegoldenrod

8. **Save your document, return to your default browser, then click the** Refresh **or** Reload **button to view the changes to the About Us page**

   As FIGURE C-20 shows, the background of the main heading and the contact information is now a different shade.

9. **Reopen** index.html **in your default browser**

   As shown in FIGURE C-20, the changes in the main page match the changes in the About Us page because the presentation of both documents is based on the external style sheet in styles.css.

FIGURE C-18: Relationship between web pages and external style sheet

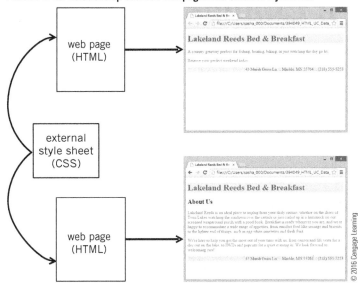

© 2016 Cengage Learning

FIGURE C-19: About Us page with link to external style sheet

```
15          <script src="modernizr.custom.62074.js"></script>
16          <link rel="stylesheet" href="styles.css">

            d Reeds Bed &amp; Breakfast</h1>
21          </header>
22          <h2>About Us</h2>
23          <p class="accent">Lakeland Reeds is an ideal place to unplug from your daily
24          routine, whether on the shore of Twin Lakes watching the sundown over the cattails
25          or just curled up in a hammock on our screened wraparound porch with a good book.
26          Breakfast is ready whenever you are, and we're happy to accommodate a wide range of
27          appetites, from comfort food like sausage and biscuits to the lighter end of
28          things, such as egg white omelettes and fresh fruit.</p>
29          <p class="accent">We're here to help you get the most out of your time with us,
30          from canoes and life vests for a day out on the lake, to DVDs and popcorn for a
31          quiet evening in. We look forward to welcoming you!</p>
32          <footer>
33             <p id="contact">45 Marsh Grass Ln. :: Marble, MN 55764 :: (218) 555-5253</p>
34          </footer>
35       </body>
36    </html>
```

Every document linking to an external style sheet uses the same code for the `link` element

Document contains class and ID values corresponding to selectors in external style sheet

FIGURE C-20: Multiple pages styled with a single style sheet

Corresponding p elements in both pages are rendered with the same styles

Add a Comment to a Style Sheet

Learning Outcomes
• Add CSS comment characters to a style sheet
• Add text to a CSS comment

Just as comments are useful in providing information for yourself and other developers in an HTML file, it can also be helpful to include comments in an external CSS file. CSS uses a different syntax than HTML for creating comments. In CSS, /* marks the start of a comment, and */ marks the end. Just like with HTML, CSS comments can be just a single like or can span multiple lines. Anything entered between the starting and ending comment characters is ignored by browsers. **CASE** ▶ *You add documentation to your external style sheet by adding a comment to the start of the file.*

STEPS

1. **Return to** styles.css **in your editor**

2. **Insert a blank line before the code** body {

QUICK TIP
Just as with HTML comments, you can enter the opening and closing characters for a CSS comment on the same line, with content between them.

3. **On the blank line you inserted, type** /*, **press [Enter] twice, then type** */
   Anything you enter between the opening and closing comment characters is ignored by browsers.

4. **Between the opening and closing comment characters, enter the following text, substituting your first and last name and today's date where indicated:**

```
Lakeland Reeds Bed and Breakfast style sheet
Filename: styles.css


Author:    your first and last name
Date:      today's date
HTML5 and CSS3 Illustrated Unit C, Lessons
```
   FIGURE C-21 shows the completed style sheet, including the comment.

5. **Save your document, return to** aboutus.html **in your default browser, then click the** Refresh **or** Reload button
   As **FIGURE C-22** shows, the appearance of the page is unchanged, and the comment text you entered is not displayed in the browser window.

6. **Return to** index.html **in your browser, then click the** Refresh **or** Reload button
   Just like the About Us page, the appearance of the main web page is unaffected by the CSS comment.

Organizing CSS code

As a style sheet grows, it's important to keep it organized so you can quickly find style rules you want to edit. One of the most common methods of organization in CSS is to mirror the structure of the HTML document(s) to which the style sheet is applied. For instance, a style rule for the body element, which affects the entire document, would go at the start of a style sheet, followed by style rules for sections of the document in order, with style rules for specific elements occurring after the style rule for the section in which they're contained. Some developers also include a CSS comment at the start of each section in the style sheet to make it easier to figure out what part of the style sheet you're in while reading it. For instance, before styles for the

footer element and elements nested within it, you might include a comment such as

```
/* footer section */
```

Sometimes it makes sense to style content in two different parts of the document with a single style rule—for instance, to apply similar styles to all p elements, or to both the header and footer sections. It generally makes sense to place a global style rule, such as a rule for all p elements, near the top of the style sheet. For style rules that apply to multiple separate parts of the document, you can use the same placement, or you may decide to break up the style rule so the styles for each part of the page are located in their own parts of the style sheet.

FIGURE C-21: Comment added to external style sheet

```
 1    /*
 2        Lakeland Reeds Bed and Breakfast style sheet
 3        Filename: styles.css
 4
 5        Author:   your first and last name
 6        Date:     today's date
 7        HTML5 and CSS3 Illustrated Unit C, Lessons
 8    */
 9
10    body {
11        background-color: ivory;
12        text-align: left;
13    }
```

CSS start comment characters

CSS end comment characters

FIGURE C-22: Web page appearance unchanged by addition of CSS comment

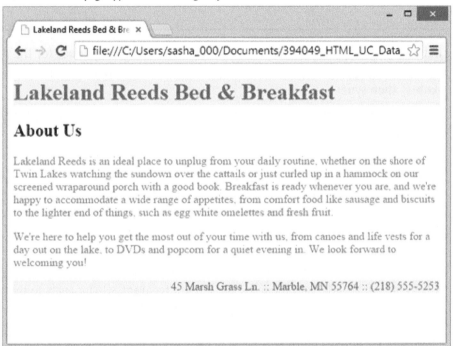

HTML5 & CSS3

Viewing CSS comments in code editors

As with other parts of HTML and CSS code, many code editors automatically generate the closing comment characters for a CSS comment after you enter the opening characters, and they may automatically indent any lines between the opening and closing characters. In addition, some editors apply other informal standards to make CSS comments easier to view and read. One of these standards is to include an asterisk (*) at the start of every line between the opening and closing characters, aligned with the asterisk that starts the comment, as shown in **FIGURE C-23**. This creates the appearance of a vertical line in the code that indicates the size of the comment section at a glance. In addition, some code editors indent the closing comment characters

a single space, which aligns the * in the closing characters with the preceding line of asterisks. Because no characters within a CSS comment are parsed by browsers—including spaces and asterisks—these formatting choices have no effect on the website.

FIGURE C-23: CSS comment lines preceded by asterisks

```
 1    /*
 2     * Lakeland Reeds Bed and Breakfast style sheet
 3     * Filename: styles.css
 4     *
 5     * Author:    Faduma Egal
 6     * Date:      6/23/2018
 7     * HTML5 and CSS3 Illustrated Unit C, Lessons
 8     */
```

Debug and Validate CSS Code

Learning
Outcomes
• Use browser
developer tools
to view CSS
declarations and
disable a CSS
declaration
• Validate a CSS
document

When multiple style rules select the same element and specify different values for the same property, CSS standards include rules for determining which declaration applies to the element. These rules calculate a selector's **specificity**, which is its priority relative to other selectors. The declaration whose selector has the highest specificity is applied to an element. FIGURE C-24 illustrates the specificity rankings of basic selectors. If two selectors have the same specificity, the one that appears last in the style sheet is applied. If your CSS code does not affect the appearance of elements in browsers as you expect, you can use utilities known as **developer tools** that are built into all modern browsers to debug your code. These tools let you inspect the CSS properties and values for each element in a document and view which declarations are applied to an element. You can also validate your CSS code. **CASE** *You use browser tools to examine the style rules applied to the elements on the main Lakeland Reeds web page, and you upload your external style sheet to a CSS validator to verify that it complies with the rules of CSS.*

STEPS

1. **Return to** styles.css **in your editor, click after the closing curly brace for the final style rule, press [Enter], type** p { **, press [Enter], press [Spacebar] 3 times, type** color: red; **, press [Enter], then type** }

2. **Save your changes to** styles.css **, return to** index.html **in your browser, then click your browser's** Refresh **or** Reload button

   The text color of the three p elements on the page remains unchanged.

3. **Right-click the contact information, then click** Inspect element

   On the left side of the browser tools, a hierarchical view of the HTML code for the page is displayed with the p element containing the contact information highlighted. On the right, each style rule is listed, with its declarations color coded, as shown in FIGURE C-25.

4. **Scroll down the list of style rules as needed to the** p **style rule**

   Notice that the color declaration in the p style rule is crossed out or displayed in faded text, indicating that it has not been applied. Both the p selector and the #contact selector apply to the selected element. Because the #contact selector has greater specificity, the dimgray value specified using that selector overrides the red value assigned using the p selector.

5. **Find the** h1, #contact **style rule, move the mouse pointer over the** color **property name until a check box is displayed to its left, then click the** check box **to uncheck it**

   Browser tools enable you to toggle or edit property values to see the effect in the browser. When you remove the color declaration associated with the #contact selector, the color declaration for the p selector is applied to the selected element because it has the highest specificity, and the contact information turns red. Note that the other p elements do not turn red because they are styled by the .accent style rule, which has higher specificity than the p style rule.

6. **Click the** Refresh **or** Reload button**, then scroll down to the** body **style rule**

   The browser reloads the saved style sheet, returning the contact information to its original gray color.

7. **In your browser, click the** Close Developer Tools button ⊠ **in the top-right corner of the developer tools, click the** Address Bar **, type** jigsaw.w3.org/css-validator **, then press [Enter]**

   The web page for the CSS validation service provided by the W3C opens, as shown in FIGURE C-26.

8. **Click the** By file upload tab **, click** Browse **or** Choose File **, navigate to the Lessons folder where you store your Data Files for this unit, double-click** styles.css **, then click** Check

   The browser uploads your style sheet to the w3.org website and the result page opens.

9. **Scroll down to read the validation results, including any notes or warnings**

FIGURE C-24: Specificity rankings of basic CSS selectors

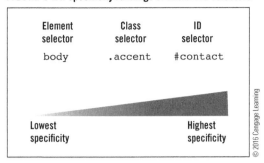

FIGURE C-25: Developer tools in Chrome

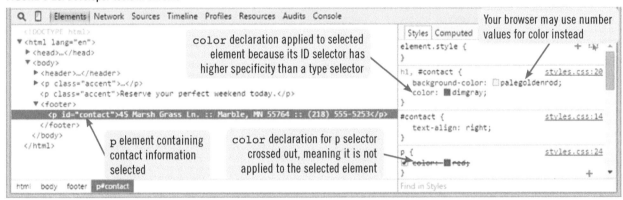

FIGURE C-26: W3C CSS Validation Service page

Choosing between different possible selectors

Sometimes when creating a style rule, you'll find that you have a choice between two or more different selectors that could perform the same task. For instance, if you want to style all the elements within the footer element, you could use the footer type selector, or you could add a class attribute to each nested element and use a class selector for your style rule instead. In general, web developers aim to use the simplest selectors possible. In addition, using selectors, such as type selectors, that don't require additional HTML coding is generally preferred over using ID or class selectors when practical. Finally, it's important to consider the roles of inheritance and specificity when writing a style rule; in some cases, two selectors may appear as if they'll perform the same task, but due to interactions with other style rules, only one of the selectors is suited to the job. Writing CSS and checking the results of your style rules in browsers is one of the best ways to develop a feel for which selector is the best candidate in a given situation.

Practice

Concepts Review

Refer to FIGURE C-27.

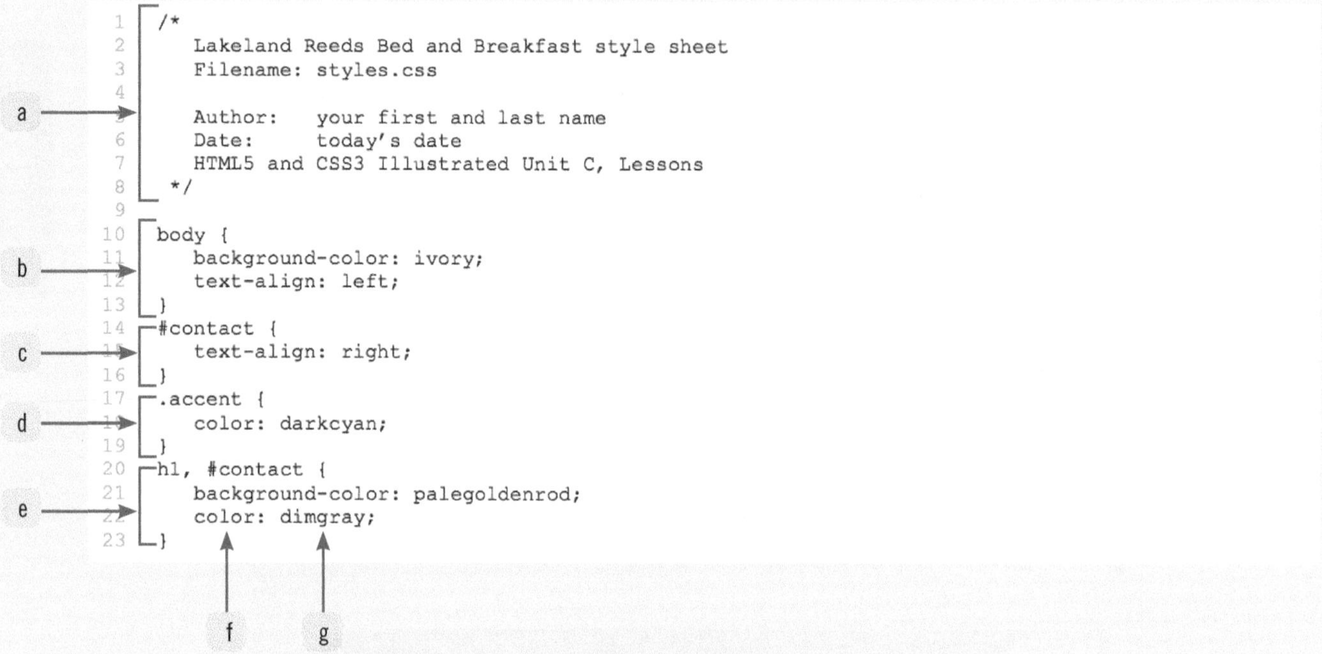

FIGURE C-27

```
1  /*
2       Lakeland Reeds Bed and Breakfast style sheet
3       Filename: styles.css
4
a  ━━━▶5    Author:   your first and last name
6       Date:     today's date
7       HTML5 and CSS3 Illustrated Unit C, Lessons
8  */
9
10 body {
11     background-color: ivory;
b  ━━━▶12    text-align: left;
13 }
14 #contact {
c  ━━━▶15    text-align: right;
16 }
17 .accent {
d  ━━━▶18    color: darkcyan;
19 }
20 h1, #contact {
21     background-color: palegoldenrod;
e  ━━━▶22    color: dimgray;
23 }
```

      f   g

1. **Which style rule uses multiple selectors?**
2. **Which style rule uses an HTML id attribute value as the selector?**
3. **Which style rule uses an HTML class attribute value as the selector?**
4. **Which style rule uses the name of an HTML element as the selector?**
5. **Which item is a CSS property name?**
6. **Which item is ignored by a user agent?**
7. **Which item is the value assigned to a CSS property?**

Match each term with the statement that best describes it.

8. **type selector**
9. **ID selector**
10. **class selector**
11. **style rule**
12. **declaration**
13. **embedded style sheet**
14. **external style sheet**

a. a line or block of CSS code that specifies the presentation of web page elements

b. a selector that applies the specified declarations only to the element with the specified ID

c. the most general kind of selector, which is the name of an HTML element

d. a selector that creates a style rule based on values assigned to elements using the HTML class attribute

e. CSS code that specifies a CSS property to apply to the selector(s) and the value to assign to the property

f. a separate file containing style information that multiple web pages can link to

g. CSS code entered in the head section of an HTML document

Select the best answer from the list of choices.

15. **Which part of a style rule identifies the HTML element or elements to which the style rule applies?**
    a. property
    b. selector
    c. value
    d. the code between the opening and closing curly braces

16. **A style rule ends with which of the following?**
    a. */
    b. }
    c. ;
    d. </style>

17. **A CSS comment ends with which of the following?**
    a. */
    b. :
    c. ;
    d. </style>

18. **A declaration ends with which of the following?**
    a. :
    b. }
    c. ;
    d. </style>

19. **An embedded style sheet ends with which of the following?**
    a. */
    b. :
    c. ;
    d. </style>

20. **Which is the most straightforward solution for affecting the presentation of a single web page?**
    a. external style sheet
    b. embedded style sheet
    c. inline styles
    d. multiple selectors

21. **Which of the following enables you to modify the presentation of multiple web pages with a single change?**
    a. external style sheet
    b. embedded style sheet
    c. inline styles
    d. multiple selectors

22. **Which of the following is a class selector?**
    a. text-align: left
    b. #logo
    c. .pullquote
    d. footer

Skills Review

1. **Create an embedded style sheet.**
   a. Open the file HTM_C-3.html in your editor from the SR folder where you store your Data Files for this unit, enter your name and today's date in the comment section where indicated, then save the file as **index.html** to the same SR folder.
   b. Preview index.html in your browser.
   c. Return to index.html in your editor, then within the head section and below the script element, add the opening and closing tags for a style element.
   d. Within the style element, add a style rule that uses a type selector to select the article element.
   e. Within the style rule you created, add a declaration that aligns text in the center.
   f. Save your document, refresh or reload it in your browser, then verify that the paragraphs beginning with "Eat in..." and "Voted..." are center-aligned.

2. **Implement an ID selector.**
   a. Return to index.html in your editor, then in the first p element, which contains the text "Authentic Chicago-style pies," add an id attribute with the value tagline.
   b. In the embedded style sheet in the head element, add a style rule that uses an ID selector to select the element with the id attribute value tagline.
   c. Within the style rule you created, add a declaration that aligns text on the right.
   d. Save your document, refresh or reload it in your browser, then verify that the paragraph below the heading is right-aligned.

Skills Review (continued)

3. Implement a class selector.

a. Return to index.html in your editor, then in each of the three p elements within the footer element, add a class attribute with the value contact.

b. In the embedded style sheet in the head element, add a style rule that uses a class selector to select the elements with the class attribute value contact.

c. Within the style rule you created, add a declaration that aligns text on the right.

d. Save your document, refresh or reload it in your browser, then verify that the contact information is right-aligned.

4. Use multiple selectors.

a. Return to index.html in your editor, then, in the embedded style sheet in the head element, add a style rule that uses type selectors to select both the header and footer elements.

b. Within the style rule you created, add a declaration that sets the background color to the value black, and a second declaration that sets the text color to the value red. (*Hint:* Use the color property to set the text color.)

c. Save your document, refresh or reload it in your browser, then verify that the header and the footer contents are displayed in red on a black background. Your document should match FIGURE C-28.

5. Create an external style sheet.

a. Return to your editor, save index.html as **index_embedded.html** to the SR folder where you store your Data Files for this unit, then close the file.

b. Open index.html in your editor, then in the embedded style sheet, cut all the code between the opening and closing <style> tags to the clipboard.

c. Create a new file, paste the contents of the clipboard, then save the new file as **styles.css** to the SR folder where you store your Data Files for this unit.

d. Return to index.html in your editor, then delete the lines containing the opening and closing <style> tags along with any blank lines between them.

e. Below the script element, insert a link element that points to styles.css.

FIGURE C-28

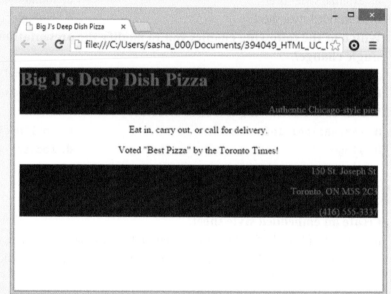

f. Save your document, refresh or reload it in your browser, then verify that its appearance still matches FIGURE C-28.

6. Link to an external style sheet.

a. Return to your editor, open the file HTM_C-4.html from the SR folder where you store your Data Files for this unit, enter your name and today's date in the comment section where indicated, then save the file as **history.html** to the same SR folder.

b. Preview history.html in your browser.

c. Return to your editor, then insert a link element below the script element that points to styles.css.

d. Save the document, reload history.html in your default browser, then verify that the page is displayed using the styles in the external style sheet.

e. Return to styles.css in your editor, change the value for text alignment in the style rule for the article element so the text is left-aligned, then save styles.css.

Skills Review (continued)

f. Refresh or reload history.html in your browser, then verify that its appearance matches **FIGURE C-29**.

g. Refresh or reload index.html in your browser, then verify that the main paragraphs are now left-aligned.

7. Add a comment to a style sheet.

a. Return to styles.css in your editor, then add opening and closing characters for a CSS comment on separate lines before the first style.

b. Between the comment tags, add the following comment text, substituting your name and today's date where indicated:

```
Big J's Deep Dish Pizza
style sheet
Filename: styles.css
Author:    your first and
           last name
Date:      today's date
HTML5 and CSS3 Illustrated
Unit C, Skills Review
```

c. Save your changes to styles.css, refresh or reload index.html and history.html in your browser, then verify that the appearance of both documents is unaffected.

8. Debug and validate CSS code.

a. Return to styles.css in your editor, add a declaration that aligns text in the center within the style rule for the `header` and `footer` elements.

b. Save your changes, refresh or reload index.html in your browser, then verify that only the main header is center-aligned.

c. Use your browser's developer tools to inspect the styles applied to the contact information at the bottom of the document.

d. In the style rule for the `contact` class in the browser developer tools, uncheck the declaration that sets the text alignment to right, then notice the effect on the footer text.

e. Refresh or reload the page in the browser, then notice the effect on the alignment of the contact information.

f. Close the developer tools, then open http://jigsaw.w3.org/css-validator/.

g. Upload styles.css, check it against the standards for CSS, review the validation results, then fix any errors that are identified.

FIGURE C-29

Independent Challenge 1

Sarah Nguyen, the owner and manager of the Spotted Wren Garden Center, is happy with your work so far on the company's website. She'd like you to add some presentation elements to the web page you created, so you incorporate some CSS style rules.

a. Open your editor, open the file HTM_C-5.html from the IC1 folder where you store your Data Files for this unit, enter your name and today's date where indicated in the comment section, then save the file as **index.html** to the same IC1 folder.

b. Add a `style` element in the head section, then create a style rule for the `h1` element that sets the background color to `coral`.

c. Save your changes, open index.html in a browser, then verify that the heading is displayed with a background color.

d. Return to index.html in your editor, create a style rule for the `h1` and `p` elements that aligns text in the center, save your changes, then refresh or reload the document in your browser and verify that all text content is centered.

e. Return to index.html in your editor, create a style rule for the `footer` element that sets the background color to `yellow`, save your changes, refresh or reload the document in your browser, then verify that the contact information has a yellow background and your document matches **FIGURE C-30**.

f. Validate your CSS code using the validator at http://jigsaw.w3.org/css-validator/. (*Note*: When you upload an HTML document containing an embedded style sheet to the CSS validator, it identifies and validates the CSS code in the document.)

FIGURE C-30

Independent Challenge 2

As you continue developing the website for the Murfreesboro Regional Soccer League, you decide to add presentation features to the web pages. You've created two web pages for the site, so you create an external style sheet.

a. Open your editor, open the file HTM_C-6.html from the IC2 folder where you store your Data Files for this unit, enter your name and today's date where indicated in the comment section, then save the file as **index.html** to the same IC2 folder.

b. Add a `style` element in the head section, then create a style rule for the `h1` element that sets the background color to `orangered`.

c. Save your changes, open index.html in a browser, then verify that the heading is displayed with a background color.

d. Return to index.html in your editor, create a style rule for the `h1` and `article` elements that aligns text in the center, save your changes, then refresh or reload the document in your browser and verify that all content except the contact information is centered. (*Note*: The contact information is not centered because those p elements are part of the `footer` element and not the body text.)

e. Return to index.html in your editor, create a style rule for the `footer` element that sets the background color to `green` and the text color to `white`, save your changes, then refresh or reload the document in your browser and verify that the contact information is displayed as white text on a green background.

Independent Challenge 2 (continued)

f. Return to index.html in your editor, add class attributes with the value contact to the two p elements in the footer section, create a style rule that right-aligns the text in these paragraphs, save your changes, refresh or reload the document in your browser, then verify that your document matches FIGURE C-31.

g. Save index.html as index_embedded.html, close the file, then reopen index.html.

h. Cut the CSS code from your embedded style sheet to the Clipboard, create a new file, paste the CSS code into it, then save the new file as **styles.css** to the IC2 folder where you store your Data Files for this unit.

i. In index.html, delete the style element, add an element that links to the styles.css file you created, save your changes, refresh or reload index.html in your browser, then verify that the document still matches FIGURE C-31.

j. Return to styles.css in your editor, add a comment at the start of the document that includes the text **Murfreesboro Regional Soccer League style sheet**, the filename, your first and last name, today's date, and the text **HTML5 and CSS3 Illustrated Unit C, Independent Challenge 2**, then save your changes.

k. Open the file HTM_C-7.html in your editor from the IC2 folder, enter your name and today's date where indicated in the comment section, then save the file as **started.html** to the same folder.

l. Add an element that links to the styles.css file, save your changes, open started.html in a browser, then verify that the document matches FIGURE C-32.

m. Validate your CSS code using the validator at http://jigsaw.w3.org/css-validator/.

FIGURE C-31

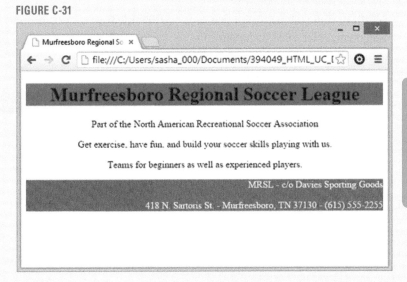

FIGURE C-32

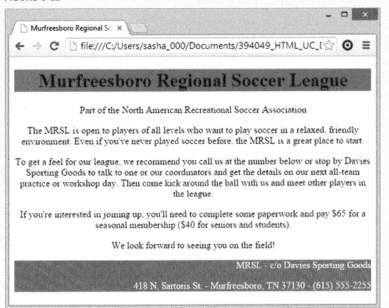

Independent Challenge 3

As you continue your work on the website for Hotel Natoma, you incorporate a color scheme and basic text alignment using CSS.

a. Open your text editor, open the file HTM_C-8.html from the IC3 folder where you store your Data Files for this unit, enter your name and today's date where indicated in the comment section, then save the file as **index.html** to the same IC3 folder. Repeat for HTM_C-9.html, saving it as **nearby.html**.

b. Preview both files in a browser.

c. Return to your editor, create a new document, enter a CSS comment containing the text **Hotel Natoma style sheet**, the filename **styles. css**, your first and last names, today's date, and the text **HTML5 and CSS3 Illustrated Unit C, Independent Challenge 3**, then save the document with the name **styles.css** to the IC3 folder.

d. Create style rules to apply the following presentation details, adding HTML attributes to both web documents when necessary:

- set the background color of h1 elements to `darkgreen` and the text color to `white`

- set the text color of h2 elements to `darkgreen`

- center-align h2 elements and all p elements except the contact information, which should be right-aligned (*Hint*: Use a general selector for all p elements, then create a more specific selector for just the elements containing the contact information.)

- set the background color of the `footer` element to `darkseagreen`

e. Save your work, add a link to your external style sheet to both index.html and nearby.html, then save your changes.

f. Preview index.html and nearby.html in a web browser. Compare index.html to FIGURE C-33 and nearby.html to FIGURE C-34, making corrections to your code as needed.

g. Validate your CSS code using the validator at http://jigsaw.w3.org/css-validator/.

FIGURE C-33

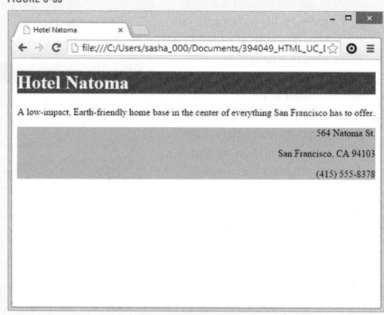

FIGURE C-34

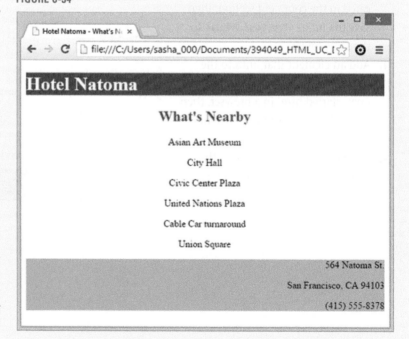

Independent Challenge 4—Explore

You've been hired to create a website for Eating Well in Season (EWIS), a business in Glover, Vermont, that delivers produce from local farms to its customers. Another team member has created a style sheet for the site but has been unable to resolve some errors in the code. You continue your work on the site by linking to and debugging the style sheet, incorporating a color scheme, and aligning the page content.

a. Open your text editor, open the file HTM_C-10.html from the IC4 folder where you store your Data Files for this unit, enter your name and today's date where indicated in the comment section, then save the file as **index. html** to the same IC4 folder. Repeat for HTM_C-11.css, saving it as **styles.css**. Preview index.html in a browser.

b. Return to styles.css in your browser, enter a CSS comment containing the text **Eating Well in Season style sheet**, the filename **styles.css**, your first and last names, today's date, and the text **HTML5 and CSS3 Illustrated Unit C, Independent Challenge 4**, then save your changes.

c. Create style rules to apply the following presentation details, adding HTML attributes to the web document when necessary:
   - set the background color of the `header` and `footer` elements to `olive` and the text color to `floralwhite`
   - set the text color of the h1 element and of the p element in the `footer` element containing the text Eating Well in Season to `khaki` (*Hint*: You will need to add a `class` or `id` attribute to this p element.)
   - set the background color of the h2 elements to `khaki`

d. Save your changes to styles.css, link index.html to the external style sheet, save your changes to index.html, then preview the document in a browser.

e. Using the debugging methods you learned in this unit, edit your CSS as necessary until your document matches FIGURE C-35. (*Hint*: Debugging may include making changes to both the CSS and HTML code.)

f. Validate your CSS code using the validator at http://jigsaw.w3.org/css-validator/.

FIGURE C-35

HTML5 & CSS3

Visual Workshop

Open your text editor, then open the file HTM_C-12.html from the VW folder where you store your Data Files for this unit. Add your first and last names and today's date to the comment section, save the file as **index.html**, then preview it in a browser. Use your text editor to add the necessary CSS code to make your web page match the one shown in FIGURE C-36. Use the color `navy` for the main heading text and for the first two lines of the address. Use the color `lightblue` for the background at the top and bottom of the document. Use the color `maroon` as the text color for the phone number. Validate your CSS using the online validator at http://jigsaw.w3.org/css-validator/.

FIGURE C-36

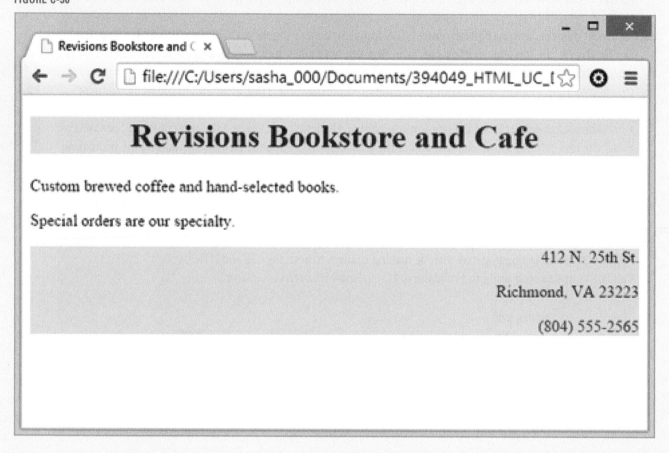

Laying Out Elements With CSS

CASE As you continue building a website for Lakeland Reeds Bed & Breakfast, you want to more precisely influence where elements are positioned in a browser window and in relation to each other. In this unit, you practice using CSS properties that give you control over web page layout.

Unit Objectives

After completing this unit, you will be able to:

- Assess the CSS box model
- Set element width and borders
- Set margins and padding
- Align elements with `float`
- Control page flow with `clear`

- Implement fixed positioning
- Implement relative positioning
- Control stacking order
- Implement absolute positioning

Files You Will Need

L	4 files	IC3	3 files
SR	3 files	IC4	3 files
IC1	3 files	VW	3 files
IC2	3 files		

For specific filenames, see Filenames_D.pdf in the Unit D Data Files folder.

Assess the CSS Box Model

Learning
Outcomes
• Describe the
components of the
CSS box model

CSS represents the characteristics of every web page element using the **box model**, which treats each element as a rectangular box having several global properties. The properties most significant to the box model are described in TABLE D-1. **CASE** *Before you enhance the layout of the Lakeland Reeds About Us page, you familiarize yourself with the CSS box model.*

DETAILS

A few concepts are important for using box model properties effectively:

QUICK TIP

A declaration of border: 0; means that the border for the affected element is not visible and takes up no space.

• **Distinguishing between padding, border, and margin**

The padding, border, and margin properties all create space around the contents of a web page element; it's important to understand the relationship of these components to each other in order to create the results you want. Of these three aspects of the box model, **border**, which represents a line around an element formatted with the width, style, and color that you specify, is the only one that can be seen in a web browser. A border serves as a reference point for the other two properties, as illustrated in FIGURE D-1. **Padding** is the space inside a border between the border and the element content, while **margin** is the space outside the border between the border and adjacent or parent elements.

QUICK TIP

Relative units are useful when you want to calculate the size of document content based on other elements, while absolute units are best for elements that need to keep specific dimensions.

• **Understanding CSS units of measure**

You specify a number as the value of the padding, margin, and width properties. In addition, the border property takes a number as one of the three components of its value. All of these numbers must be accompanied by the abbreviation for a unit of measure. CSS supports many units of measure, but the four most commonly used are ems (em), percent (%), pixels (px), and rems (rem), which are described in TABLE D-2. Ems, percent, and rems are **relative units**, meaning that they are calculated based on the sizes of other elements on a web page. Pixels are **absolute units**, meaning that they represent a specific length or height that doesn't change.

QUICK TIP

To calculate an element's total vertical space, you add the height value to the padding, border, and margin values.

• **Calculating box size**

Positive values for padding, border, and margin all increase the amount of space on a web page that an element occupies. However, an element's width and height values (and their min- and max- variants) do not include these properties. When you specify an element's width value or height value, it applies only to the element content. Any values you specify for padding, border, or margin are added to the width value or height value when a browser calculates the space occupied by an element. To determine how much horizontal room an element will occupy, you add the width value to the padding, border, and margin values, as FIGURE D-2 illustrates. There is one exception to this rule: when the bottom margin of one element is adjacent to the top margin of another element, the margins combine, or **collapse**, into a single margin equal to the greater of the two values.

TABLE D-1: Box model properties

property	description	example*
border	a visible border around an element specified with a thickness value, a style keyword, and a color name or value	border: 1px solid black;
padding	the space inside a border between the border and the element content	padding: 5%;
margin	the space outside a border between the border and adjacent or parent elements	margin: 10px;
width	the horizontal size of an element's content, excluding border, padding, and margin	width: 25%;
min-width	the minimum horizontal size of an element's content, excluding border, padding, and margin	min-width: 320px;
max-width	the maximum horizontal size of an element's content, excluding border, padding, and margin	max-width: 1000px;
height	the vertical size of an element's content, excluding border, padding, and margin	height: 5rem;
min-height	the minimum vertical size of an element's content, excluding border, padding, and margin	min-height: 2em;
max-height	the maximum vertical size of an element's content, excluding border, padding, and margin	max-height: 5em;

*Values in CSS units, with a % value based on width of parent element

FIGURE D-1: The CSS box model

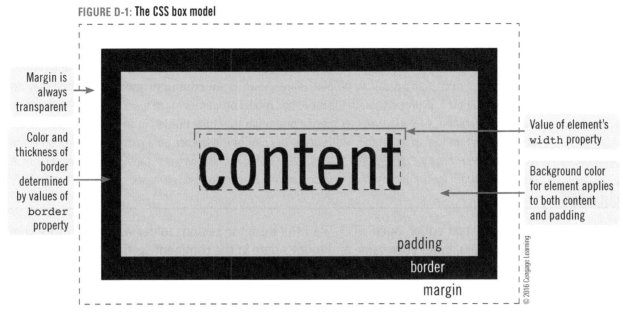

Margin is always transparent

Color and thickness of border determined by values of `border` property

Value of element's `width` property

Background color for element applies to both content and padding

content

padding
border
margin

© 2016 Cengage Learning

FIGURE D-2: Calculating web page space occupied by an element

```
p {
    width: 10em;
    padding: 0.5em;
    border: 0.25em solid black;
    margin: 1em;
}
```

left and right margin

left and right padding

1em + 0.25em + 0.5em + 10em + 0.5em + 0.25em + 1em = 13.5em

width

Total horizontal space occupied

left and right border

© 2016 Cengage Learning

TABLE D-2: Commonly used CSS units of measure

abbreviation	unit	description	example
em	em	A multiple of the computed font size for the current element, where 1em represents 100% of this size	`padding: 1.4em;`
%	percent	A percentage of another value for the current element or an ancestor element; each CSS property that takes a value in % specifies what value the % calculation is based on	`margin: 10%;`
px	pixel	A unit equal to approximately 1/96 inch or 0.26 millimeter	`padding: 10px;`
rem	rem	A multiple of the computed font size for the `html` element, where 1rem represents 100% of this size	`margin: 0.25rem;`

© 2016 Cengage Learning

Set Element Width and Borders

Learning
Outcomes
• Set the width of
  an element
• Use shorthand and
  specific properties
  to set element
  borders

To set box properties for web page elements, you create declarations that assign values to the properties. The `margin`, `border`, and `padding` properties are known as **shorthand properties** because they assign values to multiple CSS properties—in this case, box model properties for all four sides of an element—with a single declaration. CSS also supports specific properties to set the border, or padding of a particular side of an element, as well as to set the width, style, or color of the border on a particular side of an element, as described in TABLE D-3. **CASE** ▸ *You start your changes to the layout of the About Us page by specifying a minimum width for the document content and adding borders to some elements.*

STEPS

QUICK TIP
The h1 content
includes the
tag, which is a
single-sided tag that
creates a line break.

1. **In your text editor, open HTM_D-1.html from the Lessons folder where you store your Data Files, enter your name and today's date in the comment section, save the file as aboutus.html, then repeat for the file HTM_D-2.css, saving the file as styles.css**

TROUBLE
As you enter code,
refer to the figures as
needed to help you
verify the placement
of the code you are
typing.

2. **Examine the structure of the HTML document and the styles in the style sheet, then open aboutus.html in a browser**

   The content is grouped within `header`, `article`, `aside`, and `footer` elements. All the content sections are enclosed in a `div` element with the `class` attribute value `container`. The style sheet contains comments identifying the section of the page that each rule or rules apply to.

3. **In styles.css, add the declaration** `max-width: 640px;` **in the** `.container` **rule before the existing declaration**

   This declaration limits the width of the document content, making it easier to read on larger screens.

QUICK TIP
In a style rule that
uses multiple type
selectors, it's
common to list the
selectors in
alphabetical order.

4. **Below the first comment in the document, add a new line containing the comment** `/* reset styles */`, **type** `article, body, div, footer, header, h1, h2, p {` **below the comment, press [Enter] twice, then type** `}`

   This style rule uses multiple type selectors to select all the elements containing text in aboutus.html.

5. **Within the style rule you created in Step 4, type** `border: 0;`

   This removes the border from all elements displayed in the browser window. This type of style rule is known as a **reset rule** because it resets one or more common properties (the border, in this example) of multiple elements to a common baseline, ensuring that default values that may be different between browsers do not cause a web page to be displayed inconsistently. When you set the value of a CSS property to 0, there's no need to specify units.

6. **Below the `aside` style rule in the** `/* sidebar */` **section of the style sheet, type** `aside p {` **on a new line, press [Enter] twice, then type** `}`

7. **Within the style rule you created in Step 6, type** `border-bottom: 1px solid black;` **on a new line, press [Enter], then type** `border-top: 1px solid black;`

   FIGURE D-3 shows the changes to the style sheet.

8. **Save your work, then reload aboutus.html in your browser**

   The document content is now exactly 640px wide and surrounded by a border. In addition, each paragraph in the `aside` element has a horizontal border above and below it.

TROUBLE
If you're using IE
and your document
does not match
FIGURE D-4, click
the Settings button
(IE11) or click Tools
on the menu bar
(IE10), click
Compatibility View
settings, uncheck
"Display intranet
sites in Compatibility
View," click Close,
then refresh
the page.

9. **Right-click the text** What a weekend!, **click Inspect Element, then in the developer tools, click Computed (Chrome), Box Model (Firefox), or Layout (IE)**

   The developer tools illustrate the box model values for the selected p element, as shown in FIGURE D-4.

10. **Open aboutus.html on a handheld device such as a smartphone**

   The page is displayed at a narrower width to fit the device. This is because you set the width using `max-width`, allowing browsers to display the page at a narrower width when appropriate.

FIGURE D-3: width and border declarations added to style sheet

```
10    /* reset styles */
11    article, body, div, footer, header, h1, h2, p {
12        border: 0;
13    }
14
15    /* body and page container */
16    .container {
17        max-width: 640px;
18        background-color: beige;
19    }
```

Using max-width allows content to be displayed at a narrower width on smaller screens; note that declarations for box model properties are listed first within a style rule by convention

```
30    /* sidebar */
31    aside {
32        background-color: goldenrod;
33    }
34    aside p {
35        border-bottom: 1px solid black;
36        border-top: 1px solid black;
37    }
```

Declarations add top and bottom borders to aside p element without adding left or right borders

FIGURE D-4: Width and border properties applied to About Us page

Maximum width of element with container class value set to 640px

br element adds a line break within the h1 element, splitting the content into two lines

1px black border added to top and bottom of p element within aside element

Illustration of box model values in Chrome developer tools

p element within aside element selected in browser tools

Browser default value for margin; your browser may also add a default value for padding

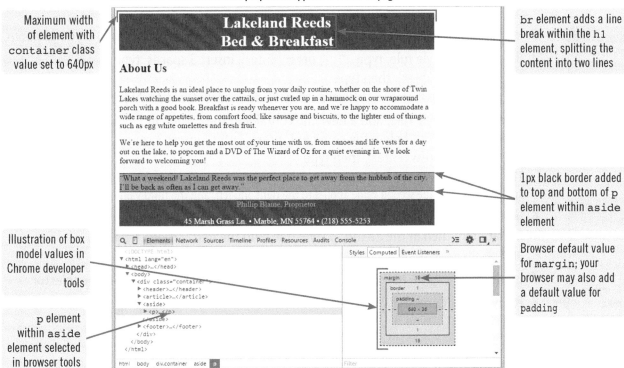

TABLE D-3: Specific properties for components of box model

component	properties	description	values
border	border-*side*-width	thickness of a visible border	a border thickness, such as 1px
	border-*side*-style	style of a visible border	dashed, solid, or another keyword
	border-*side*-color	color of a visible border	a color name or value, such as black
padding	padding-*side*	space between border and content	a value in a CSS unit, such as 5%
margin	margin-*side*	space between border and adjacent elements	a value in a CSS unit, such as 1.2em

Set Margins and Padding

You can assign different margin and padding values to different sides of an element by providing multiple values for the margin and padding shorthand properties, with a space separating each value, as described in **TABLE D-4**. In addition to numbers, the margin property supports the value auto. If you assign the value auto to the left and right margins of an element, the element is centered horizontally within its parent element. **CASE** ▶ *You continue your changes to the layout of the About Us page by specifying margins and padding.*

STEPS

1. **Return to** styles.css **in your editor, within the style rule below the** /* reset styles */ **comment, add the declarations** padding: 0; **and** margin: 0; **on separate lines**
   These declarations expand your reset style rule to set the margin and padding to 0 on all sides of all elements.

2. **In the** .container **style rule, add the declaration** margin: 0 auto; **below the** max-width **declaration**
   The declaration sets the left and right margins to auto, centering the element horizontally within the browser window.

3. **In the** h1 **style rule, add the declaration** padding: 0.4em; **before the existing declarations**

4. **Below the** h1 **style rule, type** h2 { **, press [Enter], insert 3 spaces, type** padding: 0.4em 0.6em; **, press [Enter], then type** }
   The declaration sets the top and bottom padding to 0.4em and the left and right padding to 0.6em.

5. **Below the** h2 **style rule, add a new line containing the comment** /* main content */, **type** article p { **below the comment, press [Enter], insert 3 spaces, type** padding: 0 1em 1em; **, press [Enter], then type** }
   This style rule uses 3 values to set padding for all p elements within the article element. The first value applies to the top, the second value applies to the right and left, and the third value applies to the bottom.

6. **In the** aside **style rule, add the declaration** padding: 1em 0; **before the existing declaration, then in the** aside p **style rule, add the declarations** padding: 0.4em 0; **and** margin: 0 0.6em; **on separate lines**

7. **In the** footer **style rule, add the declaration** padding: 0.6em; **below the selector**

8. **Below the** footer **style rule, add a new line containing** footer p { **, press [Enter], insert 3 spaces, type** margin: 0.4em; **, press [Enter], then type** }
   Your updated style sheet should match **FIGURE D-5**.

9. **Save your work, then reload** aboutus.html **in your browser**
   The document layout is updated to include the margins and padding you specified as shown in **FIGURE D-6**.

10. **Right-click the text** What a weekend!, **click** Inspect Element, **then in the developer tools, click** Computed (Chrome), Box Model (Firefox), **or** Layout (IE)
    The box model illustration in the developer tools is updated to include the margin and padding you specified for p elements within the aside element.

FIGURE D-5: padding and margin declarations added to style sheet

```
10    /* reset styles */
11    article, body, div, footer, header, h1, h2, p {
12        border: 0;
13        padding: 0;
14        margin: 0;
15    }
16
17    /* body and page container */
18    .container {
19        max-width: 640px;
20        margin: 0 auto;
21        background-color: beige;
22    }
23
24    /* headings */
25    header {
26        background-color: darkgreen;
27    }
28    h1 {
29        padding: 0.4em;
30        color: white;
31        text-align: center;
32    }
33    h2 {
34        padding: 0.4em 0.6em;
35    }
36
37    /* main content */
38    article p {
39        padding: 0 1em 1em;
40    }
41
42    /* sidebar */
43    aside {
44        padding: 1em 0;
45        background-color: goldenrod;
46    }
47    aside p {
48        border-bottom: 1px solid black;
49        border-top: 1px solid black;
50        padding: 0.4em 0;
51        margin: 0 0.6em;
52    }
53
54    /* footer section */
55    footer {
56        padding: 0.6em;
57        color: white;
58        background-color: darkgreen;
59        text-align: center;
60    }
61    footer p {
62        margin: 0.4em;
63    }
64    footer p.accent {
65        color: goldenrod;
66    }
```

Code continued with line 42 in figure to the right   Code continued from figure on the left

FIGURE D-6: padding and margin properties applied to About Us page

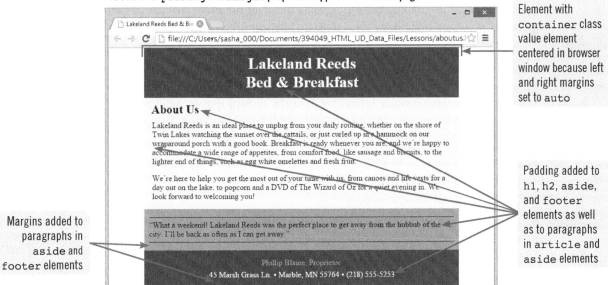

Element with container class value element centered in browser window because left and right margins set to auto

Padding added to h1, h2, aside, and footer elements as well as to paragraphs in article and aside elements

Margins added to paragraphs in aside and footer elements

TABLE D-4: Interpretation of different numbers of values for the margin and padding shorthand properties

# of values	values apply to	example
four	top, right, bottom, left	margin: 0 5% 5% 0;
three	top, left/right, bottom	padding: 0 2em 1em;
two	top/bottom, left/right	margin: 0 10px;
one (shorthand property)	top/left/bottom/right	padding: 5%;

Align Elements with `float`

Learning
Outcomes
• Float elements on
a web page

By default, a browser renders elements in a web document in the order they appear, with most elements displayed below the element that precedes them. This default arrangement of elements is known as **normal flow**. In some cases, though, you want the elements that follow an element to wrap around it, rather than being stacked below it. To do so, you use the CSS `float` property. The `left` and `right` values of the `float` property align the element horizontally with the left or right edge of the parent element, respectively, and allow elements that follow to fill in the remaining horizontal space. FIGURE D-7 illustrates the effect of the `float` property on web page elements. **CASE** ▶ *The design of the About Us page calls for the aside element to be displayed as a sidebar along the right edge of the page, and the main content to be displayed to its left. You resize the `aside` and `article` elements so they fit side-by-side within the container element, and you use the `float` property to display them next to each other.*

STEPS

1. **Return to styles.css in your editor, enter** `article {` **on a new line below the** `/* main content */` **comment, press [Enter] twice, then type** `}`

2. **In the `article` style rule, add the declaration** `width: 70%;`
   A percentage value for `width` is calculated based on the width of the parent element, which in this case is the element with the `class` value `container`. Using a percentage value for the `article` width allows it to scale if the document is displayed at a narrower width on a small screen. Setting the width to 70% leaves the remaining 30% of the parent width for the content of the `aside` element.

3. **In the `article` style rule, add the declaration** `float: right;`
   The `article` element comes before the `aside` element in the HTML document. Assigning it a `float` value of `right` aligns it with the right edge of the parent element, which is the element with the `class` value `container`, and lets the remaining elements, including the `aside` element, flow around it on the left side.

4. **Save your changes, then reload aboutus.html in your browser**
   The `article` element is narrower and displayed on the right side of the browser window, and the `aside` and `footer` elements are displayed to its left. However, because the `article` element is removed from the normal flow and has no background color specified, the background colors and borders of the `aside` and `footer` elements are visible behind the `article` element text. In addition, the content of the `article` element is no longer taken into account when determining the length of its parent element, so the `article` element content extends below the bottom border of the parent element.

5. **Return to styles.css in your editor, then in the `aside` style rule, add the declaration** `width: 30%;` **before the** `padding` **declaration**
   FIGURE D-8 shows the updated code.

6. **Save your changes, then reload aboutus.html in your browser**
   The narrower `aside` element fits next to the `article` element content and its background color and margins do not extend across the page.

7. **Right-click the text** About Us, **click** Inspect Element, **then in the developer tools, move the mouse pointer over the opening** `<article>` **tag**
   The element is highlighted. Notice that it is only as wide as the area it occupies in the browser window, which is 70% of the width of its parent element, as shown in FIGURE D-9.

8. **Move the mouse pointer over the tags for the `aside`, `footer`, and `header` elements in the developer tools**
   Each element is highlighted in the browser window. The dimensions of the `aside` element reflect the `width` value you specified, while the `header` and `footer` elements extend the full width available within the parent element.

FIGURE D-7: Using the `float` property

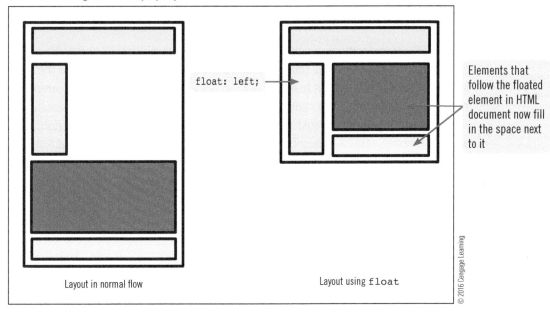

float: left;

Elements that follow the floated element in HTML document now fill in the space next to it

Layout in normal flow

Layout using `float`

© 2016 Cengage Learning

FIGURE D-8: Updated code for floating main content

```
37    /* main content */
38    article {
39        width: 70%;
40        float: right;
41    }
42    article p {
43        padding: 0 1em 1em;
44    }
45
46    /* sidebar */
47    aside {
48        width: 30%;
49        padding: 1em 0;
50        background-color: goldenrod;
51    }
```

FIGURE D-9: About Us page with floated `article` element

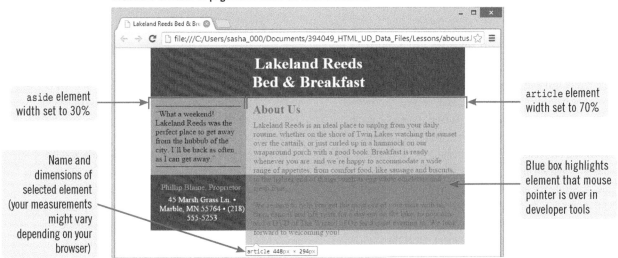

aside element width set to 30%

Name and dimensions of selected element (your measurements might vary depending on your browser)

article element width set to 70%

Blue box highlights element that mouse pointer is over in developer tools

Control Page Flow with `clear`

Learning
Outcomes
• Clear a float on a
  web page

The CSS `float` property gives you basic control over how web page elements are rendered in relation to each other. However, in some situations, using `float` is not enough to create the layout you want. For instance, sometimes you want to ensure that text or another object follows a floated element, rather than running alongside it. You can control the flow of web page elements more precisely with the CSS `clear` property, which prevents floated elements from being displayed to the left, right, or on either side of another element. TABLE D-5 describes the effects of common `clear` values, and FIGURE D-10 illustrates the effect of specifying a `clear` value for an element. **CASE** *You use the* `clear` *property to ensure that the footer element is displayed below the* `aside` *element.*

STEPS

1. **Return to** styles.css **in your editor**

2. **In the** `footer` **style rule, add the declaration** `clear: right;` **below the existing declarations**

   Specifying the value `right` for the `clear` property prevents a floated element from being displayed to the right of the current element. FIGURE D-11 shows the `clear` property inserted in the style sheet.

3. **Save your work**

4. **Reload aboutus.html in your browser**

   As FIGURE D-12 shows, the `footer` element is now displayed below the `aside` element.

TABLE D-5: **Values of the clear property**

value	description
left	element is displayed at next location in the document where no element is floated to the left
right	element is displayed at next location in the document where no element is floated to the right
both	element is displayed at next location in the document where no element is floated either to the left or to the right
none	element is displayed at next available location in the document, regardless of surrounding floated elements

© 2016 Cengage Learning

Creating multicolumn layouts with `float`

Some of the most widely used layouts in print media involve columns of text and graphics running parallel to each other down the page. You can use the `float` property to create a basic version of this arrangement, known as a multicolumn layout. To build a two-column layout, you float an element containing one column of content, and either allow the other column to remain in the normal flow, or float it on the other side. To create the appearance of even columns, the column with more content should be floated and assigned a distinct background color, and the other column should use the background color of the parent element rather than specifying

its own. To create a three-column layout, you float an element that will serve as one column on the left, float another element on the right, and allow the element that will be the middle column to remain the normal flow.

Remember that a floated element must come before an element that runs alongside it in your HTML code, and it's important not to change the order of elements in HTML simply for presentational purposes. If the semantic order of your HTML code doesn't lend itself to creating the desired layout using the `float` property, you should instead consider using the `position` property, which is covered later in this unit.

FIGURE D-10: Using the `clear` property

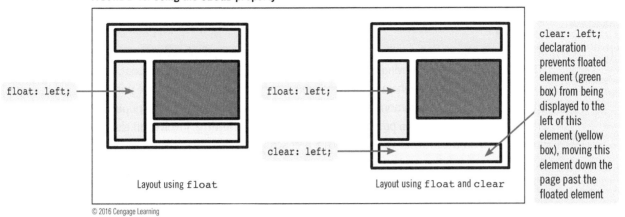

float: left;

clear: left;

float: left;

clear: left; declaration prevents floated element (green box) from being displayed to the left of this element (yellow box), moving this element down the page past the floated element

Layout using `float`

Layout using `float` and `clear`

© 2016 Cengage Learning

FIGURE D-11: Updated code including `clear` property

```
59    /* footer section */
60    footer {
61        padding: 0.6em;
62        color: white;
63        background-color: darkgreen;
64        text-align: center;
65        clear: right;
66    }
```

FIGURE D-12: About Us page with footer using `clear` property

Footer element displayed in normal flow after right margin is clear of floated elements

Dealing with floated content that's longer than its parent element

An element's content can extend below the bottom of its container element, especially when the content of a floated element is longer than other elements on a page. When a floated element is followed by another element in the normal flow, the `clear` property can be useful in extending the formatting of the parent element to all the content within it. However, in some cases the order of elements in HTML code does not lend itself to this layout. In these cases, you can add the declaration `overflow: auto;` to the parent element to extend it horizontally to give the appearance of the floated element still being in the normal flow.

In some browsers, this declaration results in a scroll bar being displayed on the right side of the parent element, which some designers find unsightly. Other approaches to solving this same problem that use more advanced CSS tools are in wide use. One popular method, known as a clearfix, is detailed at http://css-tricks.com/snippets/css/clear-fix/.

Implement Fixed Positioning

So far, your layouts have been limited to web page elements being displayed in the order they appear in your HTML documents, or by moving elements outside the normal flow using the `float` property. CSS also lets you specify more precisely where an element should be positioned on a web page using the `position` property. **TABLE D-6** describes commonly used values for the `position` property. One popular effect that developers create with the `position` property, known as **fixed positioning**, involves an element remaining in the same position in the browser window while a user scrolls the remaining page content. To implement fixed positioning, you use the `position` property with a value of `fixed`. You then specify either a horizontal position using the `left` or `right` property, or a vertical position using the `top` or `bottom` property, or both a horizontal and vertical position. **TABLE D-7** describes the properties used in fixed positioning and their values. **FIGURE D-13** illustrates how fixed positioning affects the flow of elements in a web page. **CASE** *You anticipate other pages in the Lakeland Reeds website will include so much information that users will need to scroll; you'd like the main heading to stay on the page as they do so. You use fixed positioning to do this.*

STEPS

1. **Return to** styles.css **in your text editor**

2. **Below the** `/* headings */` **comment and in the** `header` **style rule, add the declarations** `width: 100%;`, `max-width: 640px;`, **and** `position: fixed;`
   Fixed positioning removes the element from the normal flow, and it is sized relative to the browser window. Setting the `width` to 100% ensures that the `header` width is not limited to the width of its content, and setting the `max-width` to 640px gives the element the same maximum width as the remaining page content. Setting `top` to 0 specifies that the element should stay at the top of the browser window. **FIGURE D-14** shows the new rule in the style sheet.

3. **Save your work, open** HTM_D-3.html **from the Lessons folder, enter your name and today's date in the comment section, then save the file as** longpage.html
   The longpage.html file contains filler text meant to simulate a page with a lot of content. This filler text is known as **lorem ipsum**. A long document makes it easier to see the effect of fixed positioning.

4. **Open** longpage.html **in your browser**
   The page includes all the same elements as the aboutus.html file. The main heading is displayed in the same location on the page, but the `aside` and `article` content have moved up the page and are partially hidden by the heading. This is because an element with fixed positioning is removed from the normal flow. Because you did not specify a `top`, `bottom`, `left`, or `right` value for the header, it is displayed in its default position.

5. **Scroll down to the bottom of the page**
   As you scroll, the main header remains in the same place at the top of the page, and the text flows behind it, as shown in **FIGURE D-15**.

TABLE D-6: Commonly used values of the `position` **property**

value	description
absolute	element is removed from the normal flow and positioned relative to the nearest ancestor element that has a position value other than `static`
fixed	element is removed from the normal flow and positioned relative to the browser window, and remains in this position even as a user scrolls through the document
relative	element remains in the normal flow and is positioned relative to its default position
static (default)	element is displayed in its default position in the normal flow

FIGURE D-13: Implementing fixed positioning

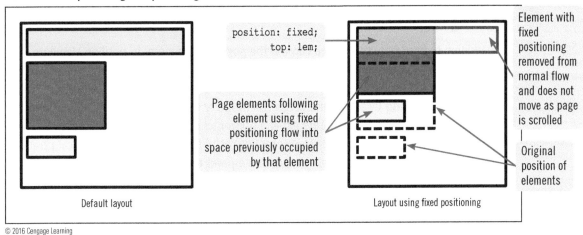

```
position: fixed;
     top: 1em;
```

Page elements following element using fixed positioning flow into space previously occupied by that element

Element with fixed positioning removed from normal flow and does not move as page is scrolled

Original position of elements

Default layout

Layout using fixed positioning

FIGURE D-14: header style rule added to style sheet

```
24   /* headings */
25   header {
26       width: 100%;
27       max-width: 640px;
28       position: fixed;
29       background-color: darkgreen;
30   }
```

FIGURE D-15: Test page showing header element using fixed positioning

header element remains in the same place within the browser window as you scroll down the page

article text moves behind the header element as you scroll

Lorem ipsum text fills the article element to simulate a long web page

TABLE D-7: CSS properties and values used in fixed positioning

property	value	description
position	fixed	Removes element from normal flow, positions it relative to the browser window, and keeps it in this position even as a user scrolls through the document
top, bottom	*value* in ems, pixels, or another supported unit, or *percent* of the height of the browser window	Moves the element the specified distance down from the top edge (top) or up from the bottom edge (bottom) of the browser window; the default value, 0, leaves the element in its original vertical position
left, right	*value* in ems, pixels, or another supported unit, or *percent* of the width of the browser window	Moves the element the specified distance right from the left edge (left) or left from the right edge (right) of the browser window; the default value, 0, leaves the element in its original horizontal position

Implement Relative Positioning

In addition to fixed positioning, you can use the `position` property to position elements in other ways. One of these, known as **relative positioning**, allows you to make adjustments to the default position of an element while preserving the space allotted to the element in the normal flow. You implement **relative positioning** by setting the `position` property to `relative`. You specify how far to move the element from its default location using either a horizontal position with the `left` or `right` property, or a vertical position with the `top` or `bottom` property, or both a horizontal and vertical position. **TABLE D-8** describes the properties used in relative positioning and their values. **FIGURE D-16** illustrates how relative positioning affects the flow of elements in a web page. **CASE ▶** *With the header removed from the page flow, the remaining page content flows up and is overlapped by the* `header` *element. You use relative positioning on the* `article`, `aside`, *and* `footer` *elements to move them down to recreate the previous layout of the page, while preserving the fixed positioning of the header.*

STEPS

1. **Return to** *styles.css* **in your editor**

QUICK TIP
While horizontal and
vertical positions can
sometimes be
calculated, it's often
a process of trial and
error to arrive at the
correct values.

2. **In the** `.container` **rule, add the declarations** `position: relative;` **and** `top: 6.2em;` **after the existing declarations**

   The value of 6.2em for the element's `top` value moves it down from the top of the parent element exactly the height of the `header` element. **FIGURE D-17** shows the updated code.

3. **Save your work, refresh longpage.html in your browser, then scroll to the top of the page if necessary**

   As a result of the relative positioning you applied, the page content that follows the header is now displayed below the `header` element as it was previously, as shown in **FIGURE D-18**.

4. **Scroll to the bottom of the page.**

TABLE D-8: CSS properties and values used in relative positioning

property	value	description
position	relative	Moves element relative to its original position but preserves the space reserved for the element in the normal flow
top, bottom	**value** in ems, pixels, or another supported unit, or **percent** of the height of the browser window	Moves the element the specified distance down from the top edge (`top`) or up from the bottom edge (`bottom`) of the closest ancestor element that is also positioned; the default value, 0, leaves the element in its original vertical position
left, right	**value** in ems, pixels, or another supported unit, or **percent** of the width of the browser window	Moves the element the specified distance from the left edge (`left`) or from the right edge (`right`) of the closest ancestor element that is also positioned; the default value, 0, leaves the element in its original horizontal position

© 2016 Cengage Learning

Maintaining accessibility with positioning

When you alter the layout of your web pages using positioning, it's important to plan for non-visual user agents, as well as devices with smaller screens, to make sure your page content still flows logically. User agents that don't process positioning continue to render all content from top to bottom in the document. Thus, your HTML code should contain elements in the order users will encounter them. In addition, you can help all user agents understand the content of your pages and present it appropriately by using semantic elements to indicate the content of different columns; for instance, `aside` for a sidebar, `article` for main page content, and `footer` for the page footer.

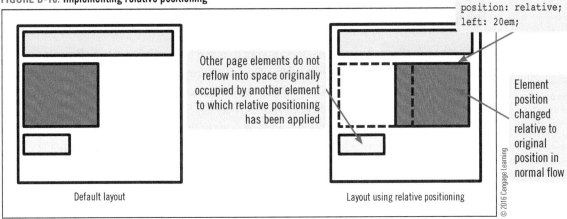

position: relative;
left: 20em;

Other page elements do not reflow into space originally occupied by another element to which relative positioning has been applied

Element position changed relative to original position in normal flow

Default layout

Layout using relative positioning

© 2016 Cengage Learning

FIGURE D-17: Styles for relative positioning added to style sheet

```
17    /* body and page container */
18    .container {
19        max-width: 640px;
20        margin: 0 auto;
21        background-color: beige;
22        position: relative;
23        top: 6.2em;
24    }
```

FIGURE D-18: Test page with relatively positioned element

Top of container element is below header element as a result of relative positioning

HTML5 & CSS3

Control Stacking Order

One of the side effects of using positioning in your layouts is the possibility of two elements occupying the same space on a web page. Elements with either a fixed or relative position can be moved to positions occupied by other elements, or two positioned elements can be moved to the same place. While it requires careful planning to ensure that a positioned element doesn't unintentionally obscure the view of another element, the ability to overlap, or **stack**, elements introduces additional possibilities for creative layouts. A positioned element is placed in a new **layer**, which is a new level displayed on top of the normal flow. As FIGURE D-19 illustrates, the arrangement of layers is similar to placing clear sheets of plastic over a sheet of paper. By default, positioned elements are stacked based on their order in the HTML code, with the first element at the bottom and subsequent elements stacked on top. You can change the stacking order of positioned elements by assigning values for the z-index property of one or more elements. Values can be positive or negative, and an element with a larger z-index value is displayed on top of an element with a smaller value. **CASE** ▶ *You explore the effect of stacking order on the* header *element and the container using the* z-index *property.*

STEPS

1. **Return to** styles.css **in your editor**

QUICK TIP
Values for the
z-index property
can be any number,
including a negative
number. Stacking
order is based solely
on which element
has a larger
z-index value.

2. **In the** header **style rule, add the declaration** z-index: -1; **below the existing declarations**

   FIGURE D-20 shows the declaration inserted in the style sheet.

3. **Save your changes to** styles.css

4. **Reload** longpage.html **in your browser, scroll to the top of the page if necessary, then scroll down the page**

   The header element, which includes the main heading text, is now covered by the aside and article content in the stacking order, as shown in FIGURE D-21.

5. **Return to** styles.css **in your editor**

6. **In the** header **style rule, add** /* **before the declaration** z-index: -1; **, then add** */ **after the declaration**

   You do not want the container element to be displayed above the header element, so you remove the z-index declaration. Formatting the declaration as a comment preserves it in your code while ensuring that user agents ignore it when rendering documents.

7. **Save your changes to** styles.css

8. **Reload longpage.html in your browser, scroll to the top of the page if necessary, then scroll down the page**

   The header element once again remains above the aside and article content in the stacking order.

Understanding stacking context

Controlling stacking order with the z-index property is straightforward in many cases. However, in some situations, it's important to understand some of the finer details of the property in order to achieve the results you want. The z-index property determines stacking order based on a **stacking context**, which is the element containing elements to be stacked. When stacking sections of a page, stacking order works pretty predictably, as all elements share a stacking context—the html element. However, when both a parent and child element are positioned, you cannot use the z-index property to stack the child element above another element on the page. This is because the stacking context for this child element is its parent element, rather than the html element containing all page contents. You can learn more about the details of stacking context and strategies for working with it at developer.mozilla.org/en-US/docs/Web/Guide/CSS/Understanding_z_index.

Element with the lowest z-index value is stacked below other positioned elements

z-index: 1;

z-index: 3;

z-index: 2;

Element with the highest z-index value is stacked on top of other positioned elements

© 2016 Cengage Learning

FIGURE D-20: z-index declaration added to header style rule

```
26    /* headings */
27    header {
28        width: 100%;
29        max-width: 640px;
30        position: fixed;
31        background-color: darkgreen;
32        z-index: -1;
33    }
```

FIGURE D-21: Test page with z-index value added to header element

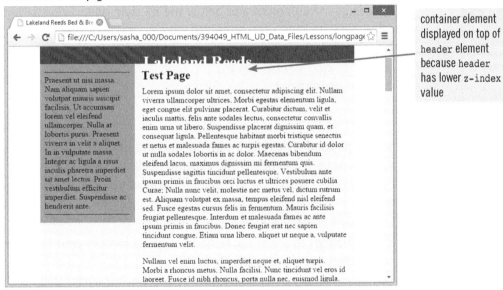

container element displayed on top of header element because header has lower z-index value

Evaluating website layout types

By default, web page content occupies the entire width of a user's browser window. When most users accessed the web with a desktop computer, designers often used a **static layout**, which specifies a fixed width for the web page content. However, a static layout that's sized appropriately for a desktop computer often doesn't fit on the screen of a smaller device such as a smartphone. Designers for some websites find that setting a fixed width and expecting users to scroll and/or zoom to view the entire page is still their best option. However, many other sites have replaced static layouts with **fluid layouts**—also known as **liquid layouts**—in which the content size is constrained with the min-width and max-width properties and the columns are sized using percentages. A liquid layout fills the width of whatever window it's displayed in, up to the maximum width limit. This allows designers to take advantage of larger screens on desktop computers while still making the entire width of the site viewable on a handheld device.

Implement Absolute Positioning

Another type of CSS positioning is **absolute positioning**, which takes an element out of the normal flow and positions it in a location you specify. The top, right, bottom, and left properties specify the new location of an absolutely positioned element relative to the closest ancestor element that is also positioned. TABLE D-9 describes the properties used in absolute positioning and their values. FIGURE D-22 illustrates how absolute positioning affects the flow of elements in a web page. **CASE** ▶ *The owners of Lakeland Reeds would like you to add and position a text placeholder for a logo. You add a new p element for the logo text and use absolute positioning to position it next to the existing main heading text.*

STEPS

1. **Return to** longpage.html **in your text editor, then below the** h1 **element and before the closing** </header> **tag, enter the following code on a new line:**
   `<p class="logo">&#8466;&#8475;</p>`
   This code creates a new p element with the class attribute value logo, as shown in FIGURE D-23.

2. **Save your changes to** longpage.html, **then reload longpage.html in your browser**
   The cursive characters L and R are displayed in the bottom left corner of the header element, increasing the height of the header element so it overlaps some of the content below it.

3. **Return to** styles.css **in your editor, then enter the following style rule below the** /* headings */ **comment and below the** h2 **style rule:**
   ```
   p.logo {
       padding: 0.2em;
       border: 2px solid beige;
       color: goldenrod;
   }
   ```
   This style rule sets the padding, border, and color for the element with the logo class.

QUICK TIP
If you want to position an element in relation to an ancestor element that is not positioned, you can add the declaration position: relative; to the ancestor element. Without top, right, bottom, and left values, the ancestor element remains in its original position but serves as the reference point for absolutely positioning its descendant element.

4. **Within the** p.logo **style rule, insert the declarations** position: absolute;, top: 2em;, **and** left: 2em; **below the existing declarations, as shown in** FIGURE D-24
   These declarations set the position of the element to absolute, and position it 2em from the top and left of the nearest positioned ancestor element. Because the parent element, which is the header element, has a position value of fixed, the top and left values are calculated in relation to the header element.

5. **Save your changes to** styles.css, **reload longpage.html in your browser, then scroll up to the top of the page if necessary**
   The logo placeholder text is displayed next to the main heading and the space reserved for it in the normal flow is removed, as shown in FIGURE D-25.

6. **Load** longpage.html **on a smartphone, then scroll the page and verify that the layout is displayed as expected.**

7. **Validate your HTML and CSS code**

Creating a Cohesive Website

All the pages on a website should be visually similar enough that users can tell that they're on the same site. Visual design, including a color scheme and logo, plays an important role. In addition, page elements, such as headings and sidebars, should appear in a consistent place on every page. Your website designs should also make use of elements that are standard on most other websites, making your website instantly familiar to even first-time visitors. Thus, an important part of creating a new web design is exploring other websites sharing similar audiences or topics to get a clear understanding of the standard elements that users may expect to see.

FIGURE D-22: Implementing absolute positioning

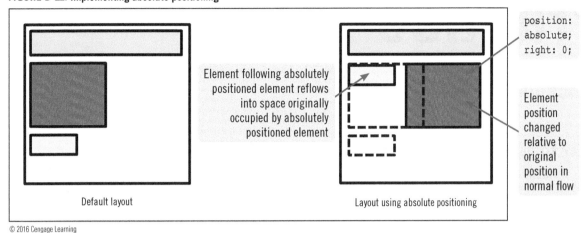

Default layout

Layout using absolute positioning

Element following absolutely positioned element reflows into space originally occupied by absolutely positioned element

position: absolute; right: 0;

Element position changed relative to original position in normal flow

© 2016 Cengage Learning

FIGURE D-23: Logo placeholder element added to longpage.html

```
20          <header>
21              <h1>Lakeland Reeds<br>Bed &amp; Breakfast</h1>
22              <p class="logo">&#8466;&#8475;</p>
23          </header>
```

code for cursive capital L

code for cursive capital R

FIGURE D-24: Style rule to absolutely position element with `logo` class value

```
39      h2 {
40          padding: 0.4em 0.6em;
41      }
42      p.logo {
43          padding: 0.2em;
44          border: 2px solid beige;
45          color: goldenrod;
46          position: absolute;
47          top: 2em;
48          left: 2em;
49      }
```

FIGURE D-25: Logo placeholder absolutely positioned

Logo placeholder text placed next to main heading using absolute positioning

TABLE D-9: CSS properties and values used in absolute positioning

property	value	description
position	absolute	Removes element from normal flow and positions it relative to the closest ancestor element that is also positioned
top, bottom	*value* in ems, pixels, or another supported unit, or *percent* of the height of the browser window	Moves the element the specified distance down from the top edge (top) or up from the bottom edge (bottom) of the closest ancestor element that is also positioned; the default value, 0, leaves the element in its original vertical position
left, right	*value* in ems, pixels, or another supported unit, or *percent* of the width of the browser window	Moves the element the specified distance right from the left edge (left) or left from the right edge (right) of the closest ancestor element that is also positioned; the default value, 0, leaves the element in its original horizontal position

© 2016 Cengage Learning

Practice

Concepts Review

Refer to FIGURE D-26 **to answer the questions that follow.**

FIGURE D-26

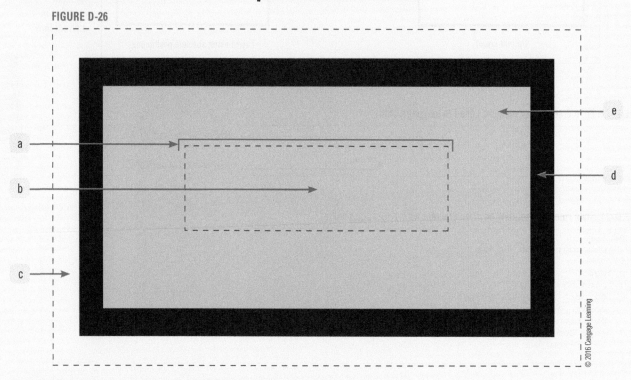

© 2016 Cengage Learning

1. Which item represents the element border?
2. Which item represents the element content?
3. Which item represents the element width?
4. Which item represents the element padding?
5. Which item represents the element margin?

Match each term with the statement that best describes it.

6. relative positioning
7. absolute positioning
8. fixed positioning
9. lorem ipsum
10. layer

a. a new level of content displayed on top of the normal flow
b. effect in which an element remains in the same position in the browser window while a user scrolls the remaining page content
c. standard filler text used for print layouts
d. lets you make adjustments to the default position of an element while preserving the space allotted to the element in the normal flow
e. takes an element out of the normal flow and allows other elements to flow into the space it would have occupied

Select the best answer from the list of choices.

11. **Which property do you use to align an element horizontally with the left or right edge of its parent element?**
    a. position
    b. z-index
    c. float
    d. clear

12. **Which property do you use to precisely specify the location of an element on a web page?**
    a. position
    b. z-index
    c. float
    d. clear

13. **Which property do you use to control the stacking order of positioned elements?**
    a. position
    b. z-index
    c. float
    d. clear

14. **Which property creates space that is unaffected by an element's background color?**
    a. width
    b. padding
    c. margin
    d. border

15. **Which declaration sets an element's padding to 0 on top, 1em on the right and left, and 2.5em on the bottom?**
    a. padding: 0 1em 1em 2.5em;
    b. padding: 1em 2.5em;
    c. padding: 0 2.5em 1em;
    d. padding: 0 1em 2.5em;

Skills Review

1. **Set element width and borders.**
   a. In your editor, open HTM_D-4.html from the SR folder where you store your Data Files for this unit, enter your first and last name and today's date in the comment section, save the file as **index.html**, then repeat for HTM_D-5.css, saving it as **styles.css**.
   b. Below the first comment section in styles.css, add a comment containing the text **reset styles**, then create a style rule that applies to the article, body, div, footer, header, h1, h2, h3, and p elements and sets all border widths to 0.
   c. Set the maximum width of the element with the class value container to 640px.
   d. Set the width of the div element within the header element to 70% and set 3px solid red borders on all sides.
   e. Add 3px solid black borders to all sides of p elements within the header element.
   f. Create a style rule that selects the p element nested in the header element with the class value established, set its width to 25%, then repeat for the p element nested in the header element with the class value award and for the p element nested in the header element with the class value options.
   g. Set the width of the p element nested in the header element with the class value phone to 50%, then set 3px solid red borders on all sides.
   h. Set the width of the article element to 65%.
   i. Add 3px solid black borders on all sides of the footer element.
   j. Save your changes, preview index.html in a browser, then verify that all the properties you set were applied successfully.

2. **Set margins and padding.**
   a. Return to styles.css in your editor, then in the style rule below the reset styles comment, add declarations that set padding and margins to 0.
   b. Set the top and bottom margins of the element with the class value container to 0 and the left and right margins to auto, then repeat for the p element within the header element with the class value options and for the article element. (*Hint*: You can set all four values with a single declaration.)
   c. For the div element within the header element, set the top margin to 0, the bottom margin to 0.6em, and the left and right margins to auto.
   d. Set padding for all p elements nested in the header element to 6px on all sides.

e. For the p element within the header element with the class value phone, set the top and bottom margins to 0.4em and the left and right margins to auto.

f. Set the padding for the article element to 5em on top and 1em on all other sides, and for the footer element to 0.5em on all sides.

g. Set margins for the h3 element to 1em on top, 0 on the right and left sides, and 0.4em on the bottom.

h. Create a style rule for p elements nested in the article element, then set the bottom margin of these elements to 0.5em.

i. Create a style rule for p elements with the class value myo nested within the article element, then set the left margin of these elements to 1em.

j. Create a style rule for p elements with the class value list nested within the article element, then set the left margin of these elements to 2em.

k. Save your changes, refresh or reload index.html in your browser, then verify that all the properties you set were applied successfully. Refer to **FIGURE D-27** as needed to compare your results to the completed document.

3. Align elements with float and control page flow with clear.

a. Return to styles.css in your editor, float the p element with the class value established nested within the header element to the left, then float the p element with the class value award nested within the header element to the right.

b. Set the p element with the class value phone nested within the header element to clear floats on both margins.

c. Save your changes, refresh or reload index.html in your browser, then verify that all the properties you set were applied successfully.

4. Implement fixed positioning.

a. Return to styles.css in your editor, set the width of the header element to 100% and set its maximum width to 640px.

b. Give the header element a fixed position at the top of the browser window. (*Hint*: Set the top property to 0.)

c. Save your changes, refresh or reload index.html in your browser, scroll down the page, then verify that the properties you set were applied successfully. (*Hint*: Reduce the height of your browser window if necessary to check the scrolling behavior of the document.)

5. Implement relative positioning.

a. Return to styles.css in your editor, then relatively position the element with the class value container, setting its position to be 11em lower than its starting position.

b. Save your changes, refresh or reload index.html in your browser, then verify that all the properties you set were applied successfully.

6. Control stacking order.

a. Return to styles.css in your editor, then stack the header element below the container element. (*Hint*: Use -1 as the stacking value.)

b. Save your changes, refresh or reload index.html in your browser, scroll down to the bottom of the page, then verify that the header is displayed behind the scrolling content.

FIGURE D-27

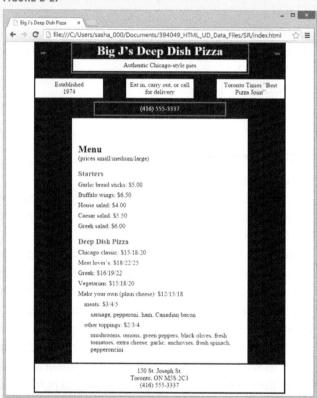

Skills Review (continued)

c. Return to styles.css in your editor, then mark the declaration you added in Step a as a comment.

d. Save your changes, refresh or reload index.html in your browser, scroll down to the bottom of the page, then verify that the header content remains on top of the scrolling content.

7. Implement absolute positioning.

a. Return to index.html in your editor, add a p element with the class value pointright containing the character code ☛ just before the closing </header> tag, then add another p element below it with the class value pointleft and containing the character code ☚.

b. Save your changes to index.html, then in styles.css, create style rules for the two elements you created in the previous step, setting the character color to red and the background color to black.

c. Absolutely position the two elements you created in Step a, setting the element with the class value pointright 0.4em from the top of the parent element and 0.4em from its left side, and setting the element with the class value pointleft 0.4em from the top of the parent element and 0.4em from its right side.

d. Save your changes, reload index.html in your browser, then verify that pointing finger icons are shown in the top left and right corners of the header. Your completed document should match FIGURE D-27.

e. Open index.html on a smartphone and verify that the layout is displayed as expected.

f. Validate your HTML and CSS code.

Independent Challenge 1

Sarah Nguyen, the owner of the Spotted Wren Garden Center, has asked you to enhance the layout of the website you created for the store. You start by implementing the new layout on the main page.

a. In your editor, open HTM_D-6.html from the IC1 folder where you store your Data Files for this unit, enter your first and last name and today's date in the comment section, save the file as **index.html**, then repeat for HTM_D-7.css, saving it as **styles.css**.

b. In styles.css, create a reset styles comment, then add a style rule under the comment that sets border, margin, and padding to 0 for the article, body, div, footer, header, h1, h2, h3, and p elements.

c. Below the reset styles style rule, create a global styles section, set the bottom margin of h2 and h3 elements to 0.4em, then set the top and bottom margins of p elements to 0.4em.

d. Set a bottom border on the header element of 3px solid red, then use the same settings for the top border of the footer element and the left border of the article element.

e. Set the maximum width of the element with the class value container to 640px, then set the width of the article element to 52% and create a style rule to set the aside element to 38%.

f. Float the aside element to the left and the article element to the right, then set the footer element to be displayed only when the left and right margins are clear of floated elements.

g. Set the left and right margins of the element with the class value container to auto.

h. Add 0.5em padding to the header and footer elements, and 2% padding to the article and aside elements.

i. Create a style rule for p elements within the article element, then set the left margin of these elements to 1em.

j. Save your changes to styles.css, open index.html in a browser, then compare your document to FIGURE D-28.

k. Open index.html on a smartphone and verify that the layout is displayed as expected.

l. Validate your HTML and CSS code.

FIGURE D-28

Independent Challenge 2

As you continue your volunteer work creating a website for the Murfreesboro Regional Soccer League, you incorporate some of the layout properties and techniques you've learned to enhance the appearance of the organization's main web page.

a. In your editor, open HTM_D-8.html from the IC2 folder where you store your Data Files for this unit, enter your first and last name and today's date in the comment section, save the file as **index.html**, then repeat for HTM_D-9.css, saving it as **styles.css**.

b. In styles.css, create a reset styles comment, then add a style rule that sets border, margin, and padding to 0 for the article, aside, body, div, footer, header, h1, h2, and p elements.

c. Create a body and page container comment, add a style rule for the element with the class value container below the comment, then set the maximum width of the element to 640px.

d. Create a main content comment, create a style rule for the article element, then set the width of the element to 55%

e. Set the width of the aside element to 35%.

f. Float the aside element to the left and the article element to the right, then set the footer element to be displayed only when the left and right margins are clear of floated elements.

g. Set the margins of the element with the class value container so the element is centered horizontally in the browser window.

h. Add 0.5em padding to the header and footer elements, 2% padding to the aside element, and 3% padding to the article element.

i. Create a style rule for the h2 element within the aside element, then set the bottom margin to 0.4em.

j. Create a style rule for p elements within the aside element, then set the top and bottom margins to 0.4em.

k. Create a style rule for p elements with the class value description within the aside element, then set the left margin to 1em.

l. Add a 3px solid black border around the element with the class value container.

m. Save your changes to styles.css, open index.html in a browser, then compare your document to **FIGURE D-29**.

n. Open index.html on a smartphone and verify that the layout is displayed as expected.

o. Validate your HTML and CSS code.

FIGURE D-29

Independent Challenge 3

You've been working with Diego Merckx, the manager of Hotel Natoma, to develop a new layout for the website. You style a page of museum listings with the new layout.

a. In your editor, open HTM_D-10.html from the IC3 folder where you store your Data Files for this unit, enter your first and last name and today's date in the comment section, save the file as **museums.html**, then repeat for HTM_D-11.css, saving it as **styles.css**.

b. In styles.css, create a reset styles comment, then add a style rule that sets border, margin, and padding to 0 for the article, body, div, footer, header, h1, h2, and p elements.

c. Set the maximum width of the element with the class value container to 800px, then set its margins so the element is centered horizontally in the browser window.

d. Set the width of the article element to 60%, then set its margins so its content is horizontally centered between the left and right edges of its parent element.

Independent Challenge 3 (continued)

e. Add 3px solid black borders to the left and right sides of the element with the `class` value `container`, and to the top and bottom of the `header` and `footer` elements.

f. Add 10px padding to the header and footer elements and 15px padding to the article element.

g. Apply fixed positioning to the `header` element 0 px from the top of the browser window, then specify a maximum width of 780px and a width of 100%.

h. Apply 4em of padding to the top of the element with the `class` value `container`, then save styles.css.

i. In museums.html, add 2 p elements as children of the `header` element, each containing the character code `&#9728;`, one with the `class` value `logoleft`, and the other with the `class` value `logoright`, then save museums.html.

j. In styles.css, create a style rule for the p elements nested in the `header` element, then set the text color for the elements to `linen`.

k. Create a style rule for the p element with the `class` value `logoleft` nested in the `header` element, absolutely position the element, then set the element 1em from the top and 3em from the left of the positioned ancestor element.

l. Create a style rule for the p element with the `class` value `logoright` nested in the `header` element, absolutely position the element, then set the element 1em from the top and 3em from the right of the positioned ancestor element.

m. Save your changes to styles.css, open museums.html in a browser, then compare your document to **FIGURE D-30**.

n. Reduce the height of your browser window if necessary so not all page contents are visible, scroll down the page, then verify that the `header` element remains fixed at the top of the window and the remaining text scrolls under it.

o. Open museums.html on a smartphone and verify that the layout is displayed as expected.

p. Validate your HTML and CSS code.

FIGURE D-30

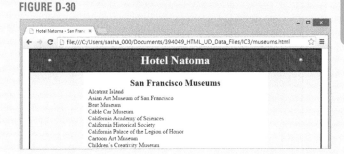

Independent Challenge 4—Explore

As you continue your work building the website for your client Eating Well in Season, you've developed a new visual layout for the site. You'll use positioning to apply the new layout to the main page of the site.

a. In your editor, open HTM_D-12.html from the IC4 folder where you store your Data Files for this unit, enter your first and last name and today's date in the comment section, save the file as **index.html**, then repeat for HTM_D-13.css, saving it as **styles.css**.

b. Add reset styles that set margins, padding, and border to 0 for all elements in use on the page.

c. Create a style rule for the element with the `class` value `container`, set the maximum width of the element to 800px, then center it in the browser window.

d. Set the width of the `article` element to 62.5%, create a style rule for the `aside` element, set its width to 37.5%, then use absolute positioning to display it against the top and right of the element with the `class` value `positioncontainer`. (*Hint:* You can use a `position` value of `relative` to make the parent element the positioning context without changing its location in the layout.)

e. Set margins and padding for page elements until your document matches **FIGURE D-31** in a browser.

f. Open index.html on a smartphone and verify that the layout is displayed as expected.

g. Validate your HTML and CSS code.

FIGURE D-31

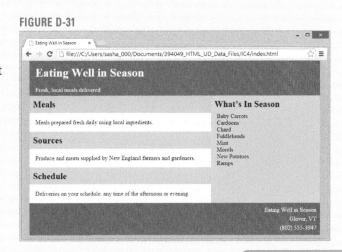

Visual Workshop

In your editor, open the file HTM_D-14.html from the VW folder where you store your Data Files for this unit, enter your first and last name and today's date in the comment section, save the file as **index.html**, then repeat for HTM_D-15.css, saving it as **styles.css**. Edit styles.css to create the layout shown in FIGURE D-32. When you are finished, open index.html in a browser and on a smartphone and verify that the layout is displayed as expected, then validate your HTML and CSS code.

FIGURE D-32

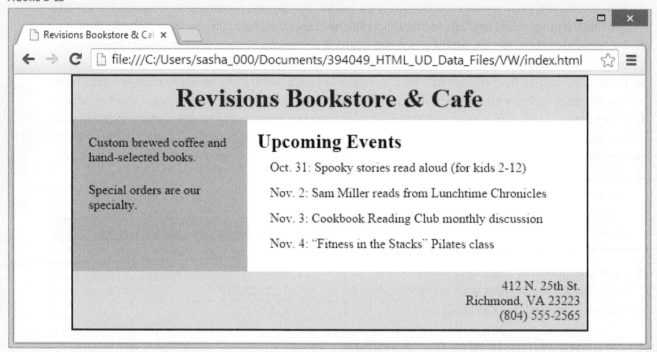

Formatting Text with CSS

CASE You can use CSS to change the font, size, and color of text, and you can style text with bold, italic, and other variations. As you continue your work on the Lakeland Reeds Bed & Breakfast website, you customize the appearance of text in the web pages.

Unit Objectives

After completing this unit, you will be able to:

- Assess web fonts
- Declare a font family
- Use a custom font
- Declare font size and line height
- Implement bold and italics

- Style pseudo-elements
- Specify hex and RGB colors
- Add shadows
- Create a media query

Files You Will Need

L	3 files	IC3	3 files
SR	3 files	IC4	3 files
IC1	3 files	VW	3 files
IC2	3 files		

For specific filenames, see Filenames_E.pdf in the Unit E Data Files folder.

Assess Web Fonts

When you create a document in a word processing program such as Microsoft Word, you can format text with any font installed on your computer. When you create a web document in an editor, you can likewise use CSS to format web page text with different fonts. However, when you style web page text with CSS, you are limited by the fonts available on your *users'* machines. This limitation makes it a challenge to ensure that your web pages appear consistently on different devices. **CASE** ▸ *One of your colleagues has created a mock-up of the Lakeland Reeds Bed & Breakfast About Us web page with text formatting. As you prepare to incorporate the fonts and other text characteristics into the web page, you review strategies for working with fonts in web pages.*

DETAILS

Strategies for implementing fonts consistently on the web include the following:

• **Specifying multiple font families**

You specify the font family for the text of an element using the CSS font-family property. The value consists of names of one or more **font families**, which are collections of single typefaces and their variants. For example, the Arial font family contains characters in the standard Arial typeface, including italic and bold versions of those characters. Every operating system has some font families installed by default, but different operating systems often have different fonts installed, meaning that not every browser or user agent has a given font available for rendering. To bridge this discrepancy, CSS enables you to use a font stack as the value of the font-family property. A **font stack** is a list of font families in order of preference, separated by commas. For example,

`font-family: Tahoma, Arial;`

specifies that a user agent should display the text of associated elements in the Tahoma font, but if that's not available, the user agent should use Arial instead, as shown in **FIGURE E-1**. **TABLE E-1** lists some font stacks. Note that you surround any font family name containing a space with quotes (for instance, `"Times New Roman"`).

• **Specifying a generic font family**

CSS also defines five **generic font families**, which are groupings of font families according to shared characteristics. Two generic font families are based on whether a font incorporates **serifs**, which are small finishing strokes at the ends of lines making up each character. A font that uses these strokes is known as a **serif font**, while a font without these strokes is called a **sans-serif font**. Serif and sans-serif fonts are the most commonly used fonts both online and in print. **TABLE E-2** shows examples of all five generic font families.

You add the name of a generic font family to the end of a font stack to provide guidance to user agents when your other font family choices are not available. For example,

`font-family: Tahoma, Arial, sans-serif;`

instructs user agents without access to either Tahoma or Arial to use the default sans-serif font on the user's system instead. In general, all font stacks should end with a generic font family.

• **Implementing custom fonts**

User agents can also download and apply **custom fonts** or **downloadable fonts** that are not installed on a user's computer. Many companies that create and license fonts also enable you to link to fonts on their web servers. To do so, you add a link element to your HTML file using a URL provided by the font host as the value for the href attribute. The URL links to a font-specific style sheet on a web server run by the font provider, which provides the necessary CSS code to make the font available to style elements on your site. Because web server issues can prevent a font from downloading correctly, you should always use a font stack when you use a custom font.

FIGURE E-1: Fonts applied from a font stack

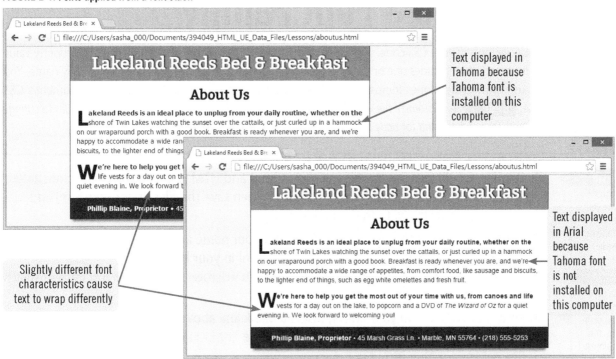

Text displayed in Tahoma because Tahoma font is installed on this computer

Text displayed in Arial because Tahoma font is not installed on this computer

Slightly different font characteristics cause text to wrap differently

TABLE E-1: Commonly used font stacks

font type	font stack
wide sans-serif	`Verdana, Geneva, sans-serif`
narrow sans-serif	`Tahoma, Arial, Helvetica, sans-serif`
wide serif	`Georgia, Palatino, "Palatino Linotype", serif`
narrow serif	`"Times New Roman", Times, serif`
monospace	`"Courier New", Courier, monospace`

© 2016 Cengage Learning

TABLE E-2: Generic font families

generic font family	examples	characteristics	best for
Serif	Times New Roman Georgia	Finishing strokes at the end of each line making up a character	Headings on computer screens and other backlit displays
Sans-serif	Arial Tahoma	Lack of serifs	Paragraphs of text on computer screens and other backlit displays
Monospace	Courier New Lucida Console	Each character uses the same amount of horizontal space	Code samples
Cursive	*Monotype Corsiva* Comic Sans	Flowing strokes that simulate handwritten text	Decorative purposes only, not main web page text, as font families in these groups can be difficult to read
Fantasy	Papyrus **Impact**	Exaggerated style	

© 2016 Cengage Learning

Declare a Font Family

To specify fonts in your CSS code, you use the `font-family` property. The `font-family` property value is a font stack that includes one or more font family names and ends with a generic font family name. You can use browser developer tools to test a font stack without permanently changing a document's CSS code. **CASE** *To customize the website and enhance the readability of text, you create style rules to change the fonts for headings and for body text for the Lakeland Reeds Bed & Breakfast website.*

STEPS

QUICK TIP
Throughout this unit, compare your code to the figures to confirm indents and placement.

QUICK TIP
Tahoma was developed for enhanced readability on computer screens. It is installed on almost every Windows and Mac system, but it is not installed on most mobile devices.

QUICK TIP
Be sure to place the comma after the closing quote in `"Times New Roman"`, not before.

TROUBLE
If you don't see a difference in the display of the paragraphs, your system may not have the Tahoma font installed.

1. **Open your editor, open the files HTM_E-1.html and HTM_E-2.css from the Lessons folder where you store your Data Files for this unit, then save the files as aboutus.html and styles.css, respectively, to the same location**

2. **In the comment at the top of each file, enter your name and today's date where indicated, save the files, then open aboutus.html in your browser**
   FIGURE E-2 shows the current appearance of the About Us web page. Note that your text may wrap differently than shown in the figure.

3. **Return to styles.css in your editor, insert a blank line above the closing curly brace for the body style rule, indent as needed, then type** `font-family: Tahoma, Arial, Helvetica, sans-serif;`
   This declaration specifies the default font for all text within the body element. User agents without access to the first choice, Tahoma, should look next for Arial, then, if necessary, for Helvetica. If none of these are available, the text should be displayed in the user agent's default sans-serif font.

4. **Insert a blank line above the closing curly brace for the h1, h2 style rule, indent as needed, then type** `font-family: "Times New Roman", Times, serif;`
   This declaration overrides the default font family you set for the body element. The font name Times New Roman is enclosed in quotes because the name is more than one word. **FIGURE E-3** shows the completed code.

5. **Save your changes to styles.css, then refresh or reload aboutus.html in your browser**
   As **FIGURE E-4** shows, the headings are displayed in Times New Roman or another serif font, and the remaining body text is displayed in Tahoma or another sans-serif font. If the Tahoma font is not installed on your computer, the appearance of body text of your web page may differ from **FIGURE E-4**.

6. **Right-click (Win) or press [control] and click (Mac) the paragraph that begins "We're here," then click Inspect Element**
   The developer tools are displayed.

7. **On the right side of the developer tools pane, click Styles (IE and Chrome) or Rules (Firefox), then scroll down the list of style rules in the right pane to the body rule**

8. **Click the value of the `font-family` property as many times as necessary until it is highlighted in blue, click after the comma following Tahoma to position the insertion point, press [Backspace] (Win) or [delete] (Mac) until the word Tahoma is deleted, then press [Enter]**
   The font Tahoma is removed from the font stack, and the browser displays the body text in Arial instead.

9. **Repeat Step 8 for each of the remaining font families until only `sans-serif` is left**
   Testing all the fonts in your font stack ensures that your layout appears as expected no matter which of the fonts a system uses. Remember that any changes you make to a document's code in browser developer tools are only temporary, and are discarded the next time you refresh or reload the page.

10. **Click the h2 element on the left side of the developer tools pane, scroll as needed on the right side to view the h1, h2 rule, then repeat Steps 8 and 9 to test all fonts in the font stack for the headings**

FIGURE E-2: The About Us web page

Lakeland Reeds Bed & Breakfast

About Us

Lakeland Reeds is an ideal place to unplug from your daily routine, whether on the shore of Twin Lakes watching the sunset over the cattails, or just curled up in a hammock on our wraparound porch with a good book. Breakfast is ready whenever you are, and we're happy to accommodate a wide range of appetites, from comfort food, like sausage and biscuits, to the lighter end of things, such as egg white omelettes and fresh fruit.

We're here to help you get the most out of your time with us, from canoes and life vests for a day out on the lake, to popcorn and a DVD of The Wizard of Oz for a quiet evening in. We look forward to welcoming you!

Phillip Blaine, Proprietor • 45 Marsh Grass Ln. • Marble, MN 55764 • (218) 555-5253

FIGURE E-3: Style sheet containing `font-family` declarations

```
17    /* body */
18    body {
19        max-width: 640px;
20        margin: 0 auto;
21        border-left: 1px solid black;
22        border-right: 1px solid black;
23        background-color: aliceblue;
24        font-family: Tahoma, Arial, Helvetica, sans-serif;
25    }
26
27    /* headings */
28    h1, h2 {
29        padding: 0.4em;
30        text-align: center;
31        font-family: "Times New Roman", Times, serif;
32    }
```

FIGURE E-4: About Us page with updated fonts

h1 and h2 text displayed in Times New Roman

Remaining body text displayed in Tahoma

Lakeland Reeds Bed & Breakfast

About Us

Lakeland Reeds is an ideal place to unplug from your daily routine, whether on the shore of Twin Lakes watching the sunset over the cattails, or just curled up in a hammock on our wraparound porch with a good book. Breakfast is ready whenever you are, and we're happy to accommodate a wide range of appetites, from comfort food, like sausage and biscuits, to the lighter end of things, such as egg white omelettes and fresh fruit.

We're here to help you get the most out of your time with us, from canoes and life vests for a day out on the lake, to popcorn and a DVD of The Wizard of Oz for a quiet evening in. We look forward to welcoming you!

Phillip Blaine, Proprietor • 45 Marsh Grass Ln. • Marble, MN 55764 • (218) 555-5253

Choosing fonts

When deciding which fonts to use for a website, it's important not to use too many fonts, which can make a page chaotic and make it hard for users to understand the relationships among the page contents. A common practice for a basic web page is to start with just two fonts: one serif font and one sans-serif font. The rule of thumb for web design is serif fonts for headings and sans-serif fonts for paragraphs. You can use your browser's developer tools to identify the fonts used by sites you visit.

Use a Custom font

Learning
Outcomes
• Locate a custom
  font online
• Add a link
  element for a
  custom font
• Add a custom font
  to a font stack

Limiting the fonts in your web pages to those installed on users' devices can result in layouts that don't display uniformly and can greatly reduce your font options. To create a more uniform appearance and open a wider set of font possibilities in your layouts, you can incorporate custom fonts. **CASE** *You've identified a more modern serif font, which is hosted by Google, to use for the headings on the Lakeland Reeds website. You download the code to link to the font definition from the Google Fonts website and add the new font to your font stack for headings.*

STEPS

1. **In your browser, open** google.com/fonts

   Google makes a collection of custom fonts available for free use. This web page allows you to browse fonts, as shown in **FIGURE E-5**, and generates the appropriate `link` element for any font you decide to use.

2. **In the search box, type** Bitter

   A preview of the Bitter font is displayed.

3. **Click** Add to Collection, **then at the bottom of the window click** Use

   The Almost done! page opens. To minimize the amount of font data your users have to download, Google defaults to providing only the normal version of a font. You can use the check boxes on this page to make other versions of the font available as well, such as the italic and bold versions.

4. **Scroll down the page to the text** *3. Add this code to your website,* **click the** `link element` **below the text to select it, then press** [Ctrl][C] **(Win) or** [command][C] **(Mac) to copy the code**

   This element links to a stylesheet containing all the CSS code you need to use the selected font on your website.

5. **Return to** aboutus.html **in your editor, insert a new line below the** `script` **element in the head section, indent as needed, then press** [Ctrl][V] **(Win) or** [command][V] **(Mac) to paste the code**

   The link element is added to the head section, as shown in **FIGURE E-6**.

6. **Save your changes, then return to** styles.css **in your editor**

7. **In the** h1, h2 **style rule, click after the colon for the** `font-family` **declaration, press** [Spacebar], **then type** Bitter,

   Adding the link element to the HTML file makes the font available to your website, but you must reference it in a `font-family` declaration to implement it in your layout. **FIGURE E-7** shows the updated style sheet code.

8. **Save your changes, then open** aboutus.html **in your browser**

   As **FIGURE E-8** shows, the h1 and h2 headings are now displayed using the downloaded Bitter font.

QUICK TIP
Viewing a style sheet
was not supported
by IE at the time this
book was written.

9. **In the developer tools, open the downloaded style sheet using the steps for your browser:**

   • **Chrome: Click** Sources, **on the left side double-click** fonts.googleapis.com, **then click** css?family=Bitter

   • **Firefox: Click** Style Editor (Firefox), **then on the left side click** css 1 rule

   The downloaded style sheet containing an `@font-face` rule is displayed on the right side of the browser tools.

FIGURE E-5: Google Fonts web page

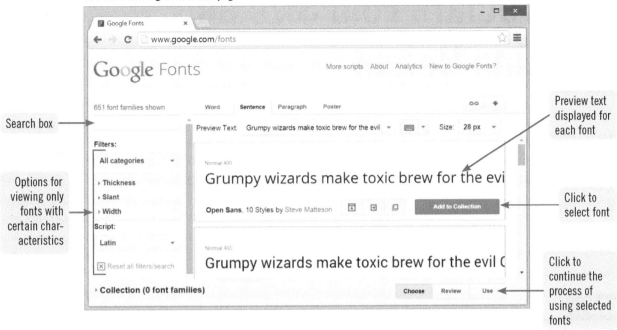

Search box

Options for viewing only fonts with certain characteristics

Preview text displayed for each font

Click to select font

Click to continue the process of using selected fonts

FIGURE E-6: `link` element added to aboutus.html

```
15        <script src="modernizr.custom.62074.js"></script>
16        <link href='http://fonts.googleapis.com/css?family=Bitter' rel='stylesheet'
17        type='text/css'>
18        <link rel="stylesheet" href="styles.css">
```

link element copied from Google Fonts website

href value references an address on a web server

link element for font placed before link element for website style sheet

FIGURE E-7: Bitter font added to start of font stack

```
28    h1, h2 {
29        padding: 0.4em;
30        text-align: center;
31        font-family: Bitter, "Times New Roman", Times, serif;
32    }
```

FIGURE E-8: Headings displayed with downloaded font

h1 and h2 headings displayed using Bitter font

Learning
Outcomes
• Set font size
• Set line height

Declare Font Size and Line Height

You can specify the font size of an element using the CSS `font-size` property. This property changes the font size of any web page element that includes text. You can specify `font-size` values in many different units, including ems, rems, and pixels. Recall that an em is a multiple of the font size inherited from an element's parent. A rem—which is an abbreviation for root em—is specifically a multiple of the font size of the `html` element. Developers commonly use pixels (px) to set a default size for the `html` element, and then set font sizes throughout the page in ems or rems. This technique enables you to adjust the sizes of all fonts on a page if necessary while maintaining the proportions between them. In addition to setting an element's font size, you can also use the `line-height` property to set the minimum amount of vertical space each line occupies. The design of each font family includes blank space above and below every line of text; you can use the `line-height` property to increase this space. **CASE** ▸ *You create a reset rule to set the base font size for the document. You also specify font sizes and line heights for the* p, h1, *and* h2 *elements.*

STEPS

1. **Return to styles.css in your editor, in the reset styles section and above the existing style rule, type** `html {`**, press [Enter], indent as needed, type** `font-size: 12px;`**, press [Enter], then type** `}`

   This rule sets the font size for the `html` element—the root font size for the document—to 12px.

2. **Save your changes, then refresh or reload aboutus.html in your browser**

   The font sizes for all elements are smaller, as shown in **FIGURE E-9**. The p elements inherit the new font size of 12px from the `html` element. The headings remain larger than the other text because browsers size headings in proportion to the root font size.

3. **Return to styles.css in your editor, type** `p {` **below the existing style rule in the body section, press [Enter], indent as needed, type** `font-size: 1.2em;`**, press [Enter], then type** `}`

   This rule sets the font size for all p elements to 1.2 times the inherited font size (12px × 1.2 = 14.4px).

4. **Before the closing curly brace for the h1 style rule, add a new line, indent as needed, then type** `font-size: 3em;`

   This sets the font size for the h1 element to 3 times the inherited font size, or 36px.

5. **Below the h1 style rule, type** `h2 {`**, press [Enter], indent as needed, type** `font-size: 2.4em;`**, press [Enter], then type** `}`

   This sets the font size for the h2 element to 2.4 times the inherited font size, or 28.8px.

6. **Save your changes, then refresh or reload aboutus.html in your browser**

   The font size of all elements increases, with the headings slightly larger than their default sizes, and the body text slightly smaller.

7. **Return to styles.css in your editor, before the closing curly brace for the p style rule, add a new line, indent as needed, then type** `line-height: 1.4em;`

   This declaration sets the line height for all p elements to 1.4 times the font size of the element itself. For many font families, the default line height is 1.2em, so this rule slightly increases the vertical space for lines of text, which results in more space between lines of text. Your style sheet should match **FIGURE E-10**.

8. **Save your changes, then refresh or reload aboutus.html in your browser**

   The spacing between lines of text in the article section is increased as a result of the `line-height` declaration, as shown in **FIGURE E-11**.

FIGURE E-9: About Us page after setting root font size

Font sizes of
all elements
reduced based
on smaller
inherited
font size

FIGURE E-10: Style sheet including `font-size` and `line-height` declarations

```
10   /* reset styles */
11   html {
12       font-size: 12px;
13   }
14   article, body, div, footer, header, h1, h2, p {

29   p {
30       font-size: 1.2em;
31       line-height: 1.4em;
32   }

40   h1 {
41       color: ivory;
42       background-color: darkgoldenrod;
43       font-size: 3em;
44   }
45   h2 {
46       font-size: 2.4em;
47   }
```

FIGURE E-11: About Us page with new font sizes and line heights

Font sizes of all elements
increased based on
`font-size` declarations

Space between lines of text
in p elements increased as
a result of `line-height`
declaration

Using white space

Graphic designers refer to empty space in a layout as **white space**. In general, every visual design needs some white space. Empty space in a design helps make it clear where one element ends and another begins. In addition, you can create specific visual effects by varying the amount of white space in a design. You can use the `padding` property to create white space around an element that shares that element's background color, and you can use the `margin` property to create white space that uses the background color of the parent element.

Implement Bold and Italics

Learning
Outcomes
• Create a span
  element
• Format text in
  bold
• Format text in
  italics

CSS enables you to modify web page text in a number of ways. Two of the most common are making text bold and italic. You can make text bold using the `font-weight` property, and you can make text italic using the `font-style` property. TABLE E-3 summarizes the CSS properties related to fonts that you've learned so far in this unit and describes the syntax for the `font` shorthand property. Bold and italic styles are often applied to words or phrases, rather than to entire paragraphs or pages, so you often need a way to indicate the section of a paragraph to format. You can use the `span` element for this purpose. The `span` element is a generic element, like `div`; however, it allows you to isolate a specific section of a larger element. All of the elements you have worked with so far are **block-level elements**, which are boxes occupying the full length of their parent elements and rendered with a line break before and after. The `span` element is an **inline element**, meaning that it does not expand to fill the space of its parent and is not rendered with line breaks before or after. **CASE** *You use the* `font-weight` *property to apply bold to the name of the owner in the contact information. You also use the* `font-style` *property to italicize the title of the DVD in the second paragraph.*

STEPS

1. **Return to** aboutus.html **in your editor, place the insertion point just to the left of the** *P* **in the name** *Phillip Blaine* **at the start of the text in the** `footer` **element, then type** `<span class="accent">`

2. **Place the insertion point just to the right of the** *r* **at the end of the word** *Proprietor*, **then type** `</span>`

   The phrase Phillip Blaine, Proprietor is enclosed within the <span> tags. This creates an inline element that you can style separately from the surrounding content.

3. **Save your changes, return to** styles.css **in your editor, type** `.accent {` **in the footer section below the final style rule, press** [Enter], **indent as needed, type** `font-weight: bold;`, **press** [Enter], **then type** `}`

   This rule formats the element with the `class` value `accent`, which is the `span` element you just created, as bold text.

4. **Save your changes, return to** aboutus.html **in your text editor, place the insertion point just to the left of the** *T* **at the start of the name** *The Wizard of Oz* **near the end of the second** `p` **element, then type** `<span class="title">`

5. **Place the insertion point just to the right of the** *z* **at the end of the word** *Oz*, **type** `</span>`, **then save your changes**

   Compare your code to FIGURE E-12.

6. **Return to** styles.css **in your text editor, type** `.title {` **in the main content section below the final style rule, press** [Enter], **indent as needed, type** `font-style: italic;`, **press** [Enter], **then type** `}`

   This rule formats the element with the `class` value `title` as italic text. Your completed style sheet should match FIGURE E-13.

7. **Save your changes, then refresh aboutus.html in your browser**

   The movie title *The Wizard of Oz* is displayed in italics, and the text Phillip Blaine, Proprietor in the footer appears in bold, as shown in FIGURE E-14.

FIGURE E-12: span elements added to text

Owner's name enclosed within `<span>` tags with class value accent

```
<p>We&rsquo;re here to help you get the most out of your time w
canoes and life vests for a day out on the lake, to popcorn and
<span class="title">The Wizard of Oz</span> for a quiet evening
forward to welcoming you!</p>
</article>
<footer>
    <p><span class="accent">Phillip Blaine, Proprietor</span> &bull; 45 Marsh Grass
    Ln. &bull; Marble, MN 55764 &bull; (218) 555-5253</p>
40    </footer>
```

Movie title enclosed within `<span>` tags with class value title

FIGURE E-13: .title and .accent rules added to style sheet

```
53    article p {
54        padding: 0 1em 1em;
55    }
56    .title {
57        font-style: italic;
58    }
59
60    /* footer section */
67    footer p {
68        margin: 0.4em;
69    }
70    .accent {
71        font-weight: bold;
72    }
```

FIGURE E-14: Text formatted in bold and italics

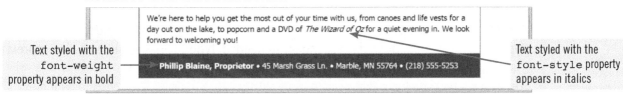

Text styled with the `font-weight` property appears in bold

Text styled with the `font-style` property appears in italics

We're here to help you get the most out of your time with us, from canoes and life vests for a day out on the lake, to popcorn and a DVD of *The Wizard of Oz* for a quiet evening in. We look forward to welcoming you!

Phillip Blaine, Proprietor • 45 Marsh Grass Ln. • Marble, MN 55764 • (218) 555-5253

TABLE E-3: Font properties

property	description	example
font-style	Provides access to a font family's italic or oblique style	`font-style: italic;`
font-variant	Provides access to a font family's small caps style	`font-variant: small-caps;`
font-weight	Sets the weight of text using keywords or values including normal, bold, or a multiple of 100 up to 900, where 100 is lightest and 900 is heaviest	`font-weight: bold;`
font-size	Changes an element's font size to a value specified in an applicable unit, including px, %, rem, or em	`font-size: 2em;`
line-height	Specifies the height of each line containing text in an applicable unit, including px, %, rem, or em	`line-height: 1.4em;`
font-family	Specifies one or more font families and/or a generic font, separated by commas; font family names composed of multiple words must be surrounded by quotes	`font-family: "Times New Roman", Times, serif;`
font	Shorthand property that can set all 6 preceding properties in a single declaration, using the syntax [font-style] [font-variant] [font-weight] font-size [/line-height] font-family; at minimum, both font-size and font-family values must be specified, and all values within square brackets are optional	`font: italic small-caps bold 2em/1.4em "Times New Roman", Times, serif`

Style Pseudo-Elements

Learning Outcomes
- Style the first line of a paragraph as a pseudo-element
- Style the first letter of a paragraph as a pseudo-element

As an alternative to the span element, CSS supports another means of selecting specific parts of a block element. A **pseudo-element** is a selector that identifies a specific part of an element and lets you style the selection as if it were its own element. To use a pseudo-element, you begin your selector with a standard selector that identifies the element you wish to style a portion of. You then add a colon (:) followed by the name of the pseudo-element. TABLE E-4 describes five commonly used pseudo-elements. **CASE** *You implement the* :first-letter *and* :first-line *pseudo-elements to enhance the appearance of the paragraphs in the* article *element.*

STEPS

1. **Return to** styles.css **in your editor**

2. **In the main content section and below the closing curly brace for the** article p **style rule, insert a new line, then type** article p:first-line {

   The selector starts with the descendant selector article p. The :first-line pseudo-element is added to the end, resulting in a style rule that modifies the first line of each p element within the article element.

3. **Press [Enter], indent as needed, type** font-weight: bold;, **press [Enter], then type** }

4. **Save your changes, then refresh or reload aboutus.html in your browser**

   As **FIGURE E-15** shows, the entire first line of each paragraph within the article element is displayed in bold.

5. **Return to** styles.css **in your editor, in the main content section and below the closing curly brace for the** article p:first-line **style rule, insert a new line, then type** article p:first-letter {

6. **Press [Enter], indent as needed, type** font-size: 3em;, **press [Enter], indent as needed, type** float: left;, **press [Enter], indent as needed, type** line-height: 0.9em;, **press [Enter], then type** }

   The :first-letter selector allows you to create a **drop cap**, a common visual effect in print media in which the first letter of a paragraph or section is enlarged and drops below the first line of text. You use the float property to make the text that follows the enlarged letter flow around it. Setting the line height for a drop cap is commonly necessary to integrate the letter optimally with the remaining paragraph text. Your code should match **FIGURE E-16**.

7. **Save your changes, then refresh or reload aboutus.html in your browser**

   As **FIGURE E-17** shows, the first letter of each paragraph within the article element is enlarged, and multiple lines of text run to its right.

TABLE E-4: CSS pseudo-elements

pseudo-element	effect	properties commonly used with
:first-line	styles the first line of text in the current element	font-family, font-size, font-weight
:first-letter	styles the first letter of text in the current element	font-family, font-size, line-height
:before	inserts specified content before the content of the current element	content
:after	inserts specified content after the content of the current element	content
:selection	styles web page content selected by user	background-color, color

© 2016 Cengage Learning

FIGURE E-15: `:first-line` pseudo-elements styled in paragraphs

Font weight for entire first line of each paragraph set to bold

FIGURE E-16: Style rules using pseudo-elements added to style sheet

```
49   /* main content */
50   article {
51       background-color: ivory;
52   }
53   article p {
54       padding: 0 1em 1em;
55   }
56   article p:first-line {
57       font-weight: bold;
58   }
59   article p:first-letter {
60       font-size: 3em;
61       float: left;
62       line-height: 0.9em;
63   }
64   .title {
65       font-style: italic;
66   }
```

FIGURE E-17: `:first-letter` pseudo-elements styled in paragraphs

First letter of each line is styled as a drop cap

Specify Hex and RGB Colors

Learning
Outcomes
• Specify a color
using the hexa-
decimal system
• Specify a color
using the RGB
system

You've already practiced setting the color and background color of text using color names. CSS also allows you to specify a color using several other common systems, as described in TABLE E-5. In the **hexadecimal system**—also known as the **hex system**—the value starts with a pound sign (#), followed by six characters, which may include the numbers 0–9 and the letters a–f. The first two characters specify the red value, the middle two characters indicate the green value, and the final pair of characters represents the blue value. The **RGB system** uses a set of comma-separated values known as an **RGB triplet**. Each value ranges from 0–255 or 0–100%, which represent the amounts of red, green, and blue in the color. **CASE** ▶ *You'll specify new colors using hexadecimal and RGB color codes.*

STEPS

1. **Return to** styles.css **in your text editor**

2. **In the** body **style rule, delete the value** aliceblue **in the** background-color **declaration, then replace it with the value** #dee9f9

   This hexadecimal value specifies a light blue color that's slightly different than the aliceblue shade.

3. **In the** h1 **style rule, delete the value** darkgoldenrod **in the** background-color **declaration, then replace it with the value** rgb(184,148,77)

   This RGB value specifies a different medium brown color than the previous one.

QUICK TIP
In addition to
background-
color, hex and RGB
colors can be used as
values for color,
margin-color, or
any other property
that takes a color as
its value.

4. **In the** footer **style rule, delete the value** saddlebrown **in the** background-color **declaration, then replace it with the value** rgb(52,24,15)

   Compare your updated style sheet to FIGURE E-18.

5. **Save your work, then refresh or reload aboutus.html in your browser**

   The background color surrounding the content changes as well as the background colors for the h1 and footer elements, as shown in FIGURE E-19.

TABLE E-5: **CSS color systems**

system	format	support
name	*name* where *name* is a name from the CSS3 list of 147 colors	all browsers
hexadecimal	#*rrggbb* or #*rgb* where *rr* (or *r*) is the red value, *gg* (or *g*) is the green value, and *bb* (or *b*) is the blue value in hexadecimal absolute value (00–FF or 0–F)	all browsers
RGB	rgb(*rrr*,*ggg*,*bbb*) where *rrr* is the red value, *ggg* is the green value, and *bbb* is the blue value in absolute value (0–255) or percent (0%–100%)	all browsers
RGBa	rgba(*rrr*,*ggg*,*bbb*,*a*) same as RGB but where *a* is a decimal value representing the alpha (transparency); 0 is fully transparent and 1 is fully opaque	modern browsers (not IE8)
HSL	hsl(*hhh*,*sss*%,*lll*%) where *hhh* is the hue value in degrees (0–360), *sss* is the saturation value in percent (0%–100%), and *lll* is the light value in percent (0%–100%)	modern browsers (not IE8)
HSLa	hsla(*hhh*,*sss*,*lll*,*a*) same as HSL but where *a* is a decimal value representing the alpha (transparency); 0 is fully transparent and 1 is fully opaque	modern browsers (not IE8)

FIGURE E-18: Color names replaced with hex and RGB colors

```
20    /* body */
21    body {
22        max-width: 640px;
23        margin: 0 auto;
24        border-left: 1px solid black;
25        border-right: 1px solid black;
26        background-color: #dee9f9;
27        font-family: Tahoma, Arial, Helvetica, sans-serif;
28    }
```

Hex value where first two characters specify the red value, next two the green value, and last two the blue value

```
34    /* headings */
35    h1, h2 {
36        padding: 0.4em;
37        text-align: center;
38        font-family: Bitter, "Times New Roman", Times, serif;
39    }
40    h1 {
41        color: ivory;
42        background-color: rgb(184,148,77);
43        font-size: 3em;
44    }
```

RGB value where the first number specifies the red value, the next one the green value, and the last one the blue value

```
68    /* footer section */
69    footer {
70        padding: 0.6em;
71        color: ivory;
72        background-color: rgb(52,24,15);
73        text-align: center;
74    }
```

OK to use different color schemes in the same style sheet

FIGURE E-19: About Us page with updated colors

Background colors of h1, body, and footer elements changed

Your colors may differ but you should still notice a difference from the colors displayed on your screen before refreshing

Understanding hexadecimal values

The two RGB color systems—using a triplet of RGB values or using hexadecimal values—allow you to specify the same 16.7 million colors. Each value in an RGB triplet can range from 0 to 255, giving you 256 possible values (1–255, plus the value 0). Hexadecimal values provide the same range using only two characters. The standard decimal numbering system allows 10 possibilities for each digit: the numbers 0–9. Hexadecimal (from roots meaning "six" and "ten") offers 16 possibilities for each character: the numbers 0–9 plus the letters A–F.

Many common colors are represented in hexadecimal notation with repeating pairs of characters (such as #00DDFF). CSS supports shortening these values to three characters, with the assumption that any three-character hexadecimal value represents the color created by doubling each character. For example, a user agent would interpret the hexadecimal value #0DF as #00DDFF.

Add Shadows

Learning
Outcomes
• Add a shadow to
  text
• Add a shadow to a
  box element

CSS includes the `text-shadow` and `box-shadow` properties, which automate the creation of shadows for text and box elements, respectively. Each property can take the same basic values for horizontal offset, vertical offset, blur, and shadow color. In addition, box-shadow supports a couple of additional options. **TABLE E-6** and **FIGURE E-20** detail how each value affects the appearance of a shadow for each property. You can add multiple shadows to an element to create more complex effects by separating the values for each shadow with a comma. **CASE** ▶ *You enhance the main heading by adding a text shadow, using the background color of the* `footer` *element for contrast. You also add a box shadow to the body to give the page the appearance of being raised above its background.*

STEPS

Many websites such as css3gen.com allow you to create text and box shadows visually using a set of controls, which then generates the code you need based on your selections.

1. **Return to styles.css in your editor**

2. **Just above the closing curly brace for the `h1` style rule, add a new line, indent as needed, then type** `text-shadow: 2px -1px 2px rgb(52,24,15);`
   This code creates a text shadow with a positive horizontal offset (placing the shadow to the right of the text), a negative vertical offset (placing the shadow above the text), a blur radius, and a shadow color that matches the dark brown color used as the background for the `footer` element.

3. **Just above the closing curly brace for the `body` style rule, add a new line, indent as needed, then type** `box-shadow: 0 10px 6px -6px #777;`
   This code creates a box shadow with no horizontal offset, a positive vertical offset (placing the shadow below the box), a blur radius, a negative spread distance that reduces how far the shadow spreads, and a gray shadow color. Your code should match **FIGURE E-21**.

4. **Save your work, then refresh or reload aboutus.html in your browser**
   The main heading text has a dark shadow above it and to its right. In addition, the `body` element has a shadow below it that moves away from both the left and right edges due to the negative value you specified for spread distance. Compare your screen to **FIGURE E-22**.

TABLE E-6: Syntax of the `text-shadow` and `box-shadow` properties

property	value	affects	notes
text-shadow and box-shadow	horizontal offset	location of shadow horizontally behind text or box	Required value; must be the first number in the list; positive value offsets shadow to the right, and negative value offsets shadow to the left
	vertical offset	location of shadow vertically behind text or box	Required value; must be the second number in the list; positive value offsets the shadow down, and negative value offsets the shadow up
	blur radius	blurriness of shadow	Optional value; must be positive; must be third number in list; value of 0 creates a shadow with a sharp edge
	color	color of shadow behind text or box	Optional value; may appear before or after numerical settings
box-shadow only	spread distance	expansion or contraction of shadow	Optional value; must be the fourth number in the list; positive value expands shadow by the specified value, and negative value contracts the shadow
	inset	whether shadow is displayed outside or inside of border	Optional `inset` keyword makes the shadow display inside the element border; may appear before or after other settings

FIGURE E-20: `text-shadow` and `box-shadow` examples

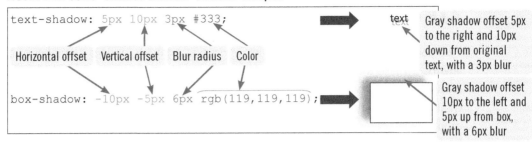

FIGURE E-21: Code for text shadow and box shadow

```
20   /* body */
21   body {
22       max-width: 640px;
23       margin: 0 auto;
24       border-left: 1px solid black;
25       border-right: 1px solid black;
26       background-color: #dee9f9;
27       font-family: Tahoma, Arial, Helvetica, sans-serif;
28       box-shadow: 0 10px 6px -6px #777;
29   }
30   p {
```
```
41   h1 {
42       color: ivory;
43       background-color: rgb(184,148,77);
44       font-size: 3em;
45       text-shadow: 2px -1px 2px rgb(52,24,15);
46   }
```

FIGURE E-22: About Us page with text shadow and box shadow

Picking a color scheme

Although hex and RGB values make over 16 million colors available for use on your web pages, it's best not to try to use all of them at once. In fact, visual designs often use only two or three colors that complement each other.

In any color scheme, the colors are not used equally—generally, one or two of the colors are reserved as accent colors. Many free tools are available to help you create color schemes. You can use a website such as paletton.com to identify complementary colors and create a color scheme. You can also install the free Adobe Color app on a mobile device to automatically generate a color scheme using your camera.

Create a Media Query

Learning Outcomes
• Create a media query
• View a print preview of a web page

Web pages can be accessed on computer screens, as printouts, and via a number of other types of user agents. Because these destinations can vary widely in factors like size, resolution, and contrast, styling created for one output is not always ideal on others. To accommodate these differences, CSS allows you to create a subset of styles within a style sheet and specify which type of device should use them. To create a group of rules for a specific device, you create a **media query**, which starts with the keyword @media, lists one or more values for media type, and then specifies style rules specific to this media, enclosed within curly braces. TABLE E-7 describes the available media type values. For printed output, CSS also supports the @page **rule**, which is used in a way that is similar to a selector and which enables you to set properties that apply to a printed page. The @page rule is commonly used to specify margins for printed output. Recall that if a style sheet contains two declarations with the same specificity that apply to the same element, the last one is applied. For this reason, you should place media queries after the general style rules in your style sheets. **CASE** *You create a media query for printed output.*

STEPS

1. **Return to** styles.css **in your editor**

2. **Below the closing curly brace for the final style rule, add two blank lines, then add the comment** /* print styles */

3. **Below the comment you added, add a new line, type** @media print {, **press** [Enter], **then indent as needed**

   The print value specifies that the associated style rules are for rendering the output on a printer.

4. **Enter the style rules, the closing curly brace for the media query, and the** @page **rule as shown in** FIGURE E-23.

   The first style rule sets the color of all text to black and the background of each section to white in order to ensure the content is legible on a black and white printer. The second rule allows the body element to occupy the entire width of the page and removes the borders. The media query surrounds all of the style rules it contains in a set of curly braces, and the style rules in the media query are indented. The @page rule, which is specifically for printed output, sets the printed margins to 1 inch on all sides.

5. **Save your work, then refresh or reload** aboutus.html **in your browser**

   The browser continues to apply the default styles, so the appearance doesn't change.

6. **Open a print preview of the page using the steps for your browser:**
   - **Chrome and Firefox (Win): Click** ☰, **then click** Print
   - **Firefox (Mac): Click** ☰, **click** Print, **click the** PDF arrow, **then click** Open PDF in Preview
   - **Internet Explorer: Click** ⚙, **point to** Print, **then click** Print preview

   A preview of the printed page is displayed, showing the text in black with a white background and no border. FIGURE E-24 shows the preview in Chrome.

TABLE E-7: Media type values for media queries

media type	intended use
all	All devices
print	Printed output and print preview on a screen
screen	Computer screen
speech	Screen reader

FIGURE E-23: Media query for printed output added to style sheet

```
84    /* print styles */
85    @media print {
86       body, h1, article, footer {
87          color: #000;
88          background-color: #fff;
89       }
90       body {
91          max-width: 100%;
92          border: 0;
93       }
94    }
95    @page {
96       margin: 1in;
97    }
```

Style rules indented within curly braces for media query

FIGURE E-24: Print preview of About Us web page in Chrome

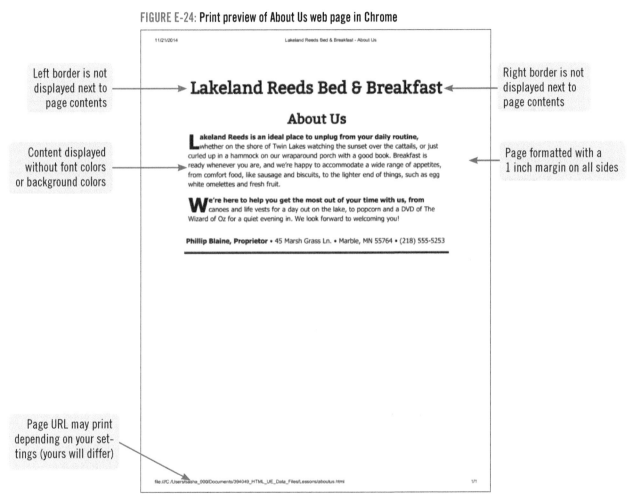

Left border is not displayed next to page contents

Right border is not displayed next to page contents

Content displayed without font colors or background colors

Page formatted with a 1 inch margin on all sides

Page URL may print depending on your settings (yours will differ)

Creating media-specific styles using other methods

In addition to creating a media query within a style sheet, you can incorporate styles targeted at specific media in your web documents in different ways. One option is to place the media-specific styles in their own style sheet document, link that style sheet to the HTML file using a separate link element, and then use the media attribute to specify the appropriate media type(s). Especially on a larger website where the style sheets consist of hundreds or thousands of lines of code, dividing up style sheets in this manner can help keep the styles organized, and can allow different team members to work on different documents simultaneously without interfering with each other's work. Note that if you use multiple link elements, the general style sheet should come first in the HTML code, followed by the media-specific styles so that the general styles do not override the media-specific styles when rendered by a user agent.

Practice

Concepts Review

Refer to FIGURE E-25 **to answer the questions that follow.**

FIGURE E-25

1. Which item is styled using the `font-style` **property?**
2. Which item is styled using a pseudo-element and the `font-weight` **property?**
3. Which item is styled using a `span` **element and the** `font-weight` **property?**
4. Which item is styled using a custom font?
5. Which item is styled using the `box-shadow` **property?**

Match each term with the statement that best describes it.

6. **generic font family**
7. **inline element**
8. **RGB system**
9. **block-level element**
10. **font stack**
11. **hexadecimal system**
12. **media query**

a. a system for specifying color on a web page in which you provide red, green, and blue values represented with numbers 0–9 and letters a–f

b. an element that does not expand to fill the space of its parent and that is not rendered with line breaks before or after

c. a system for specifying color on a web page in which you provide red, green, and blue values represented as one-, two-, or three-digit numbers

d. a grouping of font families according to shared characteristics

e. a variation of a style rule that you use to create a group of rules for a specific device

f. a list of font families in order of preference, separated by commas

g. an element rendered as a box occupying the full length of its parent element, with a line break before and after

Select the best answer from the list of choices.

13. You set the amount of vertical space a line of text occupies using the CSS _____ property.
   - **a.** `font-weight`
   - **b.** `font-style`
   - **c.** `line-height`
   - **d.** `font-family`

14. You format web page text as bold using the CSS _____ property.
   - **a.** `font-family`
   - **b.** `font-weight`
   - **c.** `font-style`
   - **d.** `font-size`

15. You specify the size of web page text using the CSS _____ property.
   - **a.** `font-size`
   - **b.** `line-height`
   - **c.** `font-family`
   - **d.** `font-weight`

16. You format web page text as italic using the CSS _____ property.
   - **a.** `font-size`
   - **b.** `line-height`
   - **c.** `font-family`
   - **d.** `font-style`

17. The _____ element is a generic element that allows you to isolate a specific section of a larger element.
   - **a.** `div`
   - **b.** `span`
   - **c.** `p`
   - **d.** `h1`

18. `sans-serif` is an example of a(n) _____.
   - **a.** font stack
   - **b.** inline element
   - **c.** font family
   - **d.** generic font family

19. `:first-line` is an example of a(n) _____.
   - **a.** font family
   - **b.** media query
   - **c.** pseudo-element
   - **d.** `@page` rule

Skills Review

1. **Declare a font family.**
   - **a.** In your editor, open the file HTM_E-3.html from the SR folder where you store your Data Files for this unit, save it as **history.html**, then repeat to save the file HTM_E-4.css as **styles.css**.
   - **b.** Within the comment section at the top of each file, enter your first and last names and today's date, then save your changes.
   - **c.** Preview history.html in your browser.
   - **d.** Return to styles.css in your editor, in the body and container section (the code following the body and container comment), create a rule for the p element, then add a declaration to style the text with the font stack Arial, Helvetica, sans-serif.
   - **e.** Save your changes, then refresh or reload history.html in your browser and verify that all p elements are styled with the appropriate font.
   - **f.** Use the developer tools in your browser to test the layout with each font family in the font stack.

2. **Use a custom font.**
   - **a.** In your browser, open google.com/fonts.
   - **b.** Search on the font name Playfair, then add the font Playfair Display to your collection. (*Hint:* Do not select Playfair Display SC.)
   - **c.** Click Use, select the Normal 400 and Ultra-Bold 900 styles, then copy the generated link element.
   - **d.** Return to history.html in your editor, paste the link element into the head section before the link element for styles.css, then save your changes.

Skills Review (continued)

    e. Return to styles.css in your editor, then in the h1, h2 style rule, add a declaration to style the text with the font stack Playfair Display, Times New Roman, Times, serif. (*Hint*: Remember to use quotation marks around a font name that consists of multiple words, and be sure that the commas separating font names are outside of the quotes.)

    f. Save your changes, then refresh or reload history.html in your browser and verify that the h1 and h2 elements are styled with the appropriate font.

    g. Use the developer tools in your browser to test the layout with each font family in the font stack for the h1 and h2 elements.

3. Declare font size and line height.

    a. Return to styles.css in your editor, then, at the top of the reset styles section, create a style rule for the html element that sets the font size to 12px.

    b. Set the font size for p elements to 1.6em and line height to 1.4em.

    c. Set the font size for h1 elements to 4em and the font size for h2 elements to 2.8em

    d. Save your changes, then refresh or reload history.html in your browser and verify that the p, h1, and h2 elements are styled with the appropriate font size and line height.

4. Implement bold and italics.

    a. Return to history.html in your text editor, then create a span element with the class value title containing the text Toronto Times in the second paragraph in the article element.

    b. Create a span element with the class value accent containing the text (416) 555-3337 in the footer element, then save your changes.

    c. Return to styles.css in your text editor, add a declaration to set the font weight for the h1 element to 900.

    d. Add a declaration to set the font weight for the element with the class value contrastbox to bold, then add a declaration to set the font weight for the element with the class value accent to bold.

    e. Add a declaration to set the font style for the element with the class value title to italic, then save your changes.

    f. Save your changes, then refresh or reload history.html in your browser and verify that the appropriate elements are styled with bold and with italics.

5. Style pseudo-elements.

    a. Return to styles.css in your editor, then, in the main content section, create a style rule to select the first letter of the paragraph element with the class value firstparagraph within the article element.

    b. Add declarations to the new style rule that set its font size to 3em, its line height to 0.9em, and float it to the left.

    c. Save your changes, then refresh or reload history.html in your browser and verify that the first letter of the first paragraph after the h2 heading is displayed as a drop cap.

6. Specify hex and RGB colors.

    a. Return to styles.css in your editor.

    b. Set the background color of the body element to #ddd, the background color of the element with the class value container to rgb(255,204,102), and the background color of the article element to #fff.

    c. Set the background color of the element with the class value contrastbox to #ddd, and add a 1px solid border using the color #777.

    d. Save your changes, then refresh or reload history.html in your browser and verify that the page is styled with the appropriate background and border colors.

Skills Review (continued)

7. Add shadows.

   a. Return to styles.css in your editor.

   b. Add a text shadow to the h2 element with 2px horizontal offset, -1px vertical offset, 2px blur radius, and a color of rgb(255,204,102).

   c. Add a box shadow to the element with the `class` value `contrastbox` with 3px horizontal and vertical offset, 0 blur radius, and a color of #777.

   d. Save your changes, then refresh or reload history.html in your browser and verify that the appropriate elements have been styled with the text shadow and box shadow you specified. Your document should match **FIGURE E-26**.

8. Create a media query.

   a. Return to styles.css in your editor.

   b. At the bottom of the document, add a comment containing the text **print styles** and then create a media query for print devices.

   c. Within the media query, add the following style rules:

     • a style rule for the body, h2, and `article` elements that sets text color to #000 and background-color to #fff.

     • a style rule for the body element that sets its maximum width to 100%.

   d. Below the media query, create a style rule for printed pages that sets all margins to 1in. (*Hint*: Use the @page selector.)

   e. Save your changes, refresh or reload history.html, open a print preview of your document, then verify it matches the one shown in **FIGURE E-27**.

FIGURE E-26

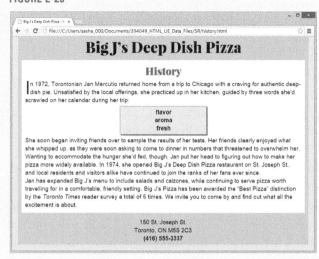

FIGURE E-27

Formatting Text with CSS   **131**

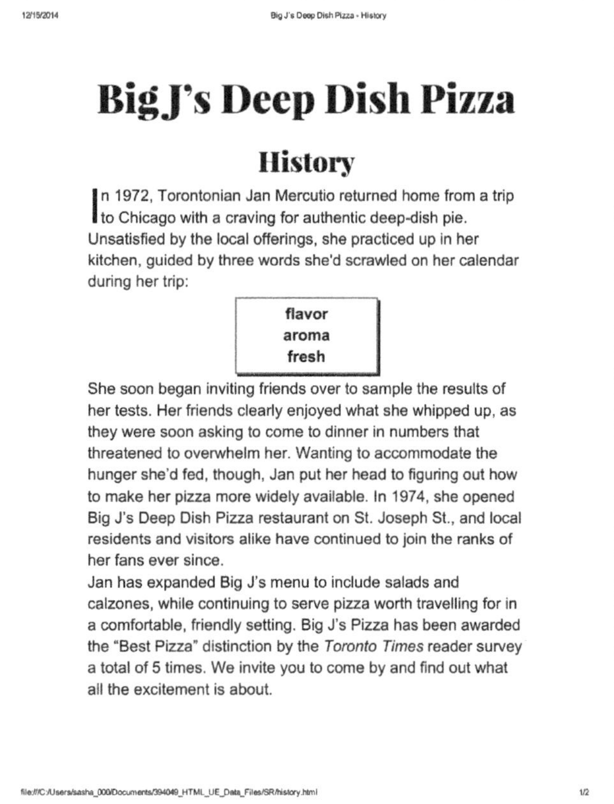

Independent Challenge 1

Sarah Nguyen, the owner and manager of the Spotted Wren Garden Center, is happy with your work so far on the company's website. She'd like you to begin to personalize the site by using a new font, styling the text, and incorporating a new set of colors.

a. In your editor, open HTM_E-5.html from the IC1 folder where you store your Data Files for this unit, save it as **hours.html**, open HTM_E-6.css, then save it as **styles.css**.

b. In the first comment section in each file, add your first and last names and today's date where indicated, then save your changes to both files.

c. Use google.com/fonts to locate the font named Lato, choose the Normal 400 and Bold 700 styles, then copy the `link` element for the font's stylesheet to the Clipboard

d. Return to hours.html in your editor, paste the `link` element just before the `link` element for your stylesheet, then save your changes.

e. Return to styles.css in your editor, then in the body and page container section (the code following the body and page container comment), create a style rule for the `body` element that uses Lato as the font family and falls back to Arial, then Helvetica, and finally to the default sans-serif font, and sets a background color of `#fff`.

f. In the reset styles section, create a style rule that specifies a font size of 12px for the `html` element.

g. In the global styles section, set the font size for the `p` element to 1.2em.

h. In the header section, create a style rule for the `h1` element that sets the font size to 3em and the font weight to `bold`.

i. In the main content section, set the font size for the `h2` element to 2.4em and the font weight to `bold`.

j. Return to hours.html in your editor, in the `article` element enclose each day of the week and the colon that follows it in a `span` element, then save your changes.

k. Return to styles.css in your editor, then in the main content section, set the font weight for `span` elements nested in `p` elements within the `article` element to `bold` and set their text color to `green`.

l. In the header section, specify a text color of #f15a24 for the `p` element nested within the `header` element.

m. In the body and page container section, set the background color of the element with the `class` value `container` using the following RGB values: red: 106, green: 194, blue: 56.

n. In the main content section, set the background color of the `article` element to `#fff`.

FIGURE E-28

o. In the page and body container section, add a box shadow to the element with the `class` value `container` that has 0 horizontal and vertical offsets, 10px of blur, and uses the color #000.

p. Preview your web page in a browser and compare your screen to **FIGURE E-28**.

q. Validate both your HTML and CSS documents.

r. Use the developer tools in your browser to test the layout with each font family in the font stack for the `body` element.

Independent Challenge 2

As you continue developing the website for the Murfreesboro Regional Soccer League, you incorporate font styling and colors into the site.

a. In your editor, open HTM_E-7.html from the IC2 folder where you store your Data Files for this unit, save it as **index.html**, open HTM_E-8.css, then save it as **styles.css**.

b. In the first comment section in each file, add your first and last names and today's date where indicated, then save your changes to both files.

c. In the reset styles section (the code following the reset styles comment), create a style rule that specifies a font size of 14px for the `html` element.

d. In the body and page container section, set the font family for the `body` element to Arial, specifying Helvetica as a fallback and sans-serif as the generic font.

e. In the body and page container section, create a style rule that sets the font size for p elements to 1.2em.

f. In the header section, set the background color of the `header` element to the color with the following RGB values: red: 140, green: 198, blue: 63.

g. In the header section, create a style rule for the `h1` element that sets the font size to 2em, the line height to 1.4em, the font family to Georgia with Times New Roman and Times as fallbacks and serif as the generic font, and creates a text shadow with 0 horizontal and vertical offsets, 10px of blur, and a color of ivory.

h. In the header section, create a style rule for p elements nested in the `header` element that sets the font style to italic.

i. In the main content section, create a style rule for the first line of the p element with the `class` value `firstparagraph` nested within the `article` element that sets the font weight to bold.

j. In the sidebar section, set the background color of the `aside` element to the value #c8f098.

k. In the sidebar section, set the font family for the h2 element nested in the `aside` element to Georgia, with Times New Roman and Times as fallbacks and a generic font of serif, and set the font size to 1.6em.

l. In the sidebar section, set the font weight of p elements with the `class` value `accent` nested in the `aside` element to bold.

m. In the footer section, create a style rule for p elements with the `class` value `accent` nested in the `footer` element that sets the font weight to bold.

n. Save your changes, open index.html in a browser, then compare your document to **FIGURE E-29**.

o. Use the developer tools in your browser to test the layout with each font family in the font stack for the `body` and `h1` elements.

FIGURE E-29

Independent Challenge 2 (continued)

p. Return to styles.css in your editor, add a comment at the bottom of the style sheet containing the text **print styles**, then use a media query to specify the following styles for printed output:

- For the aside, body, footer, and header elements and the element with the class value container, set the text color to #000, the background color to #fff, and the border to 0.
- For the body element, set the maximum width to 100%.
- For the header element, add a 2px solid black bottom border.
- For the aside element, add a 2px solid black left border.
- For the footer element, add a 2px solid black top border.

q. Below the media query, create a style rule that specifies 1in margins on all sides of a printed page.

r. Save your changes, refresh or reload index.html in your browser, display a print preview of the document, then compare your preview to FIGURE E-30.

FIGURE E-30

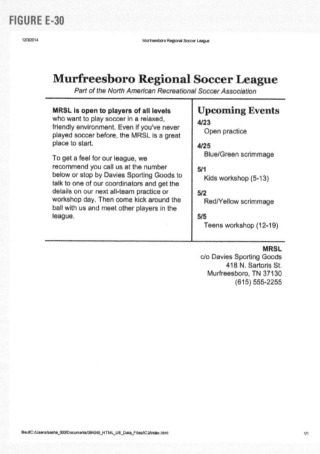

Independent Challenge 3

As you continue your work on the website for Hotel Natoma, you incorporate fonts and colors using CSS.

a. In your editor, open HTM_E-9.html from the IC3 folder where you store your Data Files for this unit, save it as **nearby.html**, open HTM_E-10.css, then save it as **styles.css**.

b. In the first comment section in each file, add your first and last names and today's date where indicated, then save your changes to both files.

c. Use google.com/fonts to locate the font named Krona One, choose the Normal 400 style, then copy the link element for the font's stylesheet to the Clipboard

d. Return to nearby.html in your editor, paste the link element just before the link element for your stylesheet, then save your changes.

e. Return to styles.css in your editor, then in the header section (the code following the header section comment), create a style rule for the h1 element that uses Krona One as the font family and falls back to Arial, then Helvetica, and finally to the default sans-serif font. Repeat in the aside section for the h2 element nested within the aside element.

f. In the style rule for the h1 element, set the font size to 2.4em, the line height to 1.6em, and the font weight to 400.

g. In the style rule for the h2 element nested within the aside element, set the font size to 1.6em, the line height to 2em, and the font weight to 400.

Independent Challenge 3 (continued)

h. In the reset styles section, create a style rule that specifies a font size of 14px for the `html` element.

i. In the body and page container section, create a style rule that sets the font family for the `body` element to Arial, with a fallback of Helvetica and a generic font of sans-serif. Also create a style rule for the `p` element that sets the font size to 1.4em.

j. In the main content section, set the font size for the `p` element within the `article` element to 2.1em and the line height to 1.4em.

k. In the header section, set the background color of the `header` element using the following RGB values: red: 8, green: 32, blue: 8, repeat in the footer section for the `footer` element, then in the sidebar section set the background color for the `aside` element using the following RGB values: red: 147, green: 173, blue: 120.

l. In the header section, create a style rule for the first letter of the `h1` element that sets the text color using the following RGB values: red: 8, green: 32, blue: 8, and sets the background color using the following RGB values: red: 147, green: 173, blue: 120.

m. In the sidebar section, create a style rule for the first letter of each `p` element nested within the `aside` element that creates a text shadow with 1px horizontal offset, -1px vertical offset, 2px blur, and a color of `linen`.

n. In the body and page container section, add a box shadow to the element with the `class` value `container` with 0 horizontal offset, 10px vertical offset, 6px blur, -6px spread, and a color of #777.

o. Save your changes, open nearby.html in a browser, then compare your document with **FIGURE E-31**.

p. Use the developer tools in your browser to test the layout with each font family in the font stack for the `body`, `h1` and `h2` elements.

q. Return to styles.css in your editor, add a comment at the bottom of the style sheet containing the text **print styles**, then use a media query to specify the following styles for printed output:

- For the `article`, `aside`, `body`, `footer`, and `header` elements, set the text color to #000 and the background color to #fff.
- For the `body` element, set the maximum width to 100%.

r. Below the media query, create a style rule that specifies 1in margins on all sides of a printed page.

s. Save your changes, refresh or reload nearby.html in your browser, display a print preview of the document, then compare your preview to **FIGURE E-32**.

FIGURE E-31

FIGURE E-32

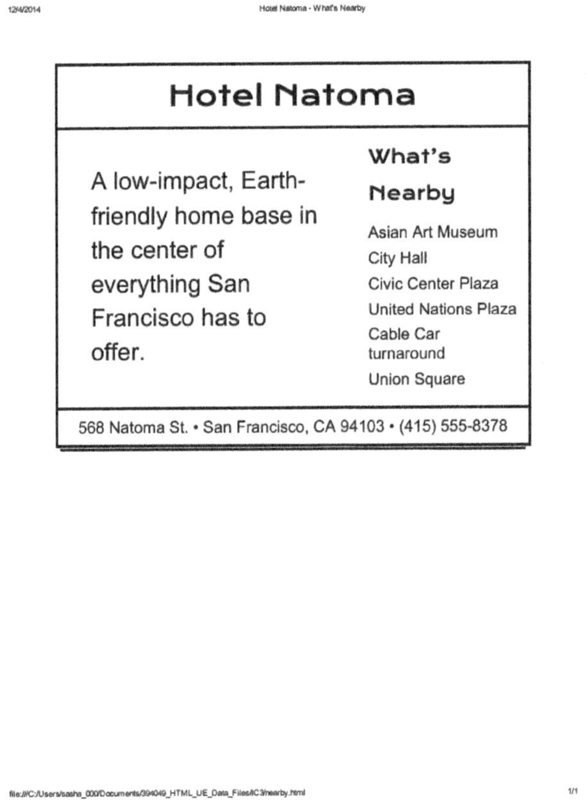

Independent Challenge 4 – Explore

As you continue your work creating the website for Eating Well in Season, a local food delivery company, you customize the design's fonts and colors.

a. In your editor, open HTM_E-11.html from the IC4 folder where you store your Data Files for this unit, save it as **index.html**, open HTM_E-12.css, then save it as **styles.css**.

b. In the first comment section in each file, add your first and last names and today's date where indicated, then save your changes to both files.

c. Use google.com/fonts to locate the font named Alegreya Sans, choose the Normal 400 style, then copy the `link` element for the font's stylesheet to the Clipboard

d. Return to index.html in your editor, paste the `link` element just before the `link` element for your stylesheet, then save your changes.

e. Return to styles.css in your editor, then in the body and page container section (the code following the body and page container comment), create a style rule that sets the font family for the `body` element to Alegreya Sans with a fallback to Arial, then Helvetica, and finally to the default sans-serif font. Also set the background color for the `body` element using the following RGB values: red: 170, green: 189, blue: 126.

f. In the body and page container section, create a style rule for the `p` element that uses the `font` shortcut property to set the font size to 1.6em and the font family to Verdana with a fallback to Geneva and a generic font of sans-serif.

g. In the reset styles section, create a style rule that specifies a font size of 12px for the `html` element.

h. In the body and page container section, specify a background color for the element with the `class` value `container` using the following HSL values: hue: 53 degrees, saturation: 91%, light: 61%. (*Hint*: Use the syntax for the HSL color system rather than the RGB color system, and be sure to include the `%` symbol after the second and third values.) In the header section, use the same color as the text color for the `h1` element nested in the `header` element.

i. In the header section, set the background color for the `header` element using the following RGB values: red: 161, green: 127, blue: 67.

j. In the header section, set the font weight of the `h1` element nested in the `header` element to normal, the font size to 4.6em, and the line height to 0.8em.

k. In the main content section, set the text color for `h2` elements nested in the `article` element using the following RGB values: red: 152, green: 192, blue: 61. Also set the font size to 2.8em and the font weight to `normal`.

l. In the sidebar section, set the font size for the `h2` element nested in the `aside` element to 2.8em, the line height to 0.8em, and the font weight to `normal`.

m. Return to index.html in your editor, in the `footer` element enclose each instance of the `&bull;` character code in a `span` element, then save your changes.

n. Return to styles.css in your editor, then in the footer section, add a style rule for `span` elements nested in the `footer` element that sets the font color using the following RGB values: red: 161, green: 127, blue: 67.

o. In the body and page container section, create an inset box shadow for the element with the `class` value `container` using 0 horizontal offset, 0 vertical offset, 3px blur, 5px spread, and the RGB values red: 170, green: 189, and blue: 126. (*Hint*: Add the keyword `inset` to the property value to create an inset shadow.) Repeat for the `header` element in the header section and for the `footer` element in the footer section.

Independent Challenge 4 – Explore (continued)

p. In the main content section, create an inset box shadow for the article element using 5px horizontal offset, 0 vertical offset, 3px blur, and the RGB values red: 170, green: 189, and blue: 126. (*Hint*: Add the keyword `inset` to the property value to create an inset shadow.)

q. Save your changes, open index.html in a browser, then compare your document with **FIGURE E-33**.

r. Use the developer tools in your browser to test the layout with each font family in the font stack for the body and p elements.

s. Return to styles.css in your editor, add a comment at the bottom of the style sheet containing the text **print styles**, then use a media query to specify the following styles for printed output:

FIGURE E-33

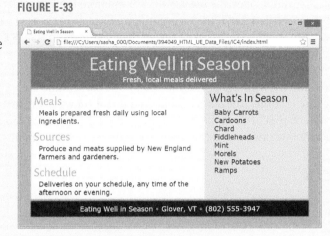

- For the article, article h2, aside, body, .container, footer, header, header h1, and header p selectors, set the text color to #000, the background color to #fff, and the box shadow to none.
- For the body element, set the maximum width to 100%.

t. Below the media query, create a style rule that specifies 1in margins on all sides of a printed page.

u. Save your changes, refresh or reload index.html in your browser, display a print preview of the document, then compare your preview to **FIGURE E-34**.

FIGURE E-34

12/5/2014   Eating Well in Season

Eating Well in Season
Fresh, local meals delivered

Meals
Meals prepared fresh daily using local ingredients.

Sources
Produce and meats supplied by New England farmers and gardeners.

Schedule
Deliveries on your schedule, any time of the afternoon or evening.

What's In Season

Baby Carrots
Cardoons
Chard
Fiddleheads
Mint
Morels
New Potatoes
Ramps

Eating Well in Season • Glover, VT • (802) 555-3947

file:///C:/Users/sasha_000/Documents/394049_HTML_UE_Data_Files/IC4/index.html   1/1

Visual Workshop

In your text editor, open the file HTM E-13.html from the VW folder where you store your Data Files for this unit, save the file as **events.html**, then repeat to save HTM_E-14.css as **styles.css**. Preview events.html in a browser. Use your text editor to style the web page to match the one shown in FIGURE E-35. Specify a font stack starting with Verdana as the default font family for the body element. Use the ultra-bold style of the downloadable Google wide serif font Playfair Display for the h1 and h2 headings. Use the RGB triplet 189,204,212 for the background color of the header and footer sections, and the RGB triplet 198,156,109 for the background color of the article element containing the Upcoming Events list. Be sure to format the dates in bold. Add text shadows to the first letters of the h1 and h2 headings, as well as to the first letter of each p element in the sidebar using the RGB triplet 198,156,109. Add a box shadow around the upcoming events list and another one around the parent element of the page contents.

FIGURE E-35

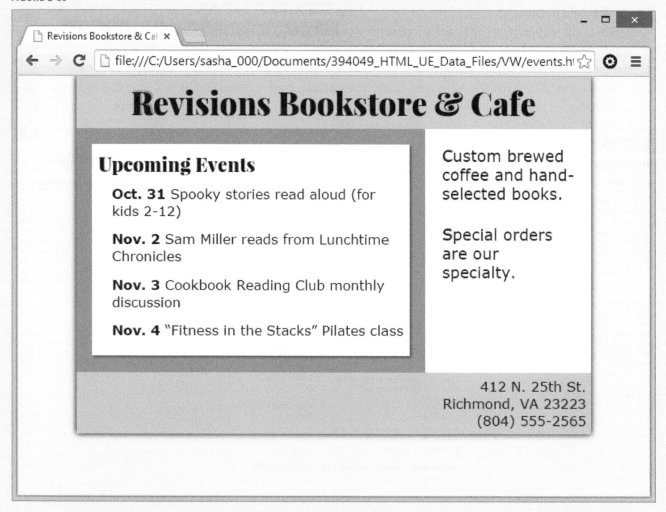

Inserting and Working with Links

CASE Now that you have created a basic set of web pages for Lakeland Reeds Bed & Breakfast, you integrate them together as a website by creating links between the pages. You also link to relevant information available on another website.

Unit Objectives

After completing this unit, you will be able to:

- Understand links
- Create relative links
- Create absolute links
- Change CSS display type
- Style links with a pseudo-class
- Style multiple link states
- Open links in new tabs
- Link within a document
- Aid navigational accessibility

Files You Will Need

L	7 files	IC3	4 files
SR	6 files	IC4	5 files
IC1	5 files	VW	5 files
IC2	5 files		

For specific filenames, see Filenames_F.pdf in the Unit F Data Files folder.

Understand Links

Learning
Outcomes
• Describe how
to link web
documents
• Identify the
components of
a URL

DETAILS

While a website is made up of a collection of web pages, another important element sets a website apart from a simple group of pages: linking. A **hyperlink**, more commonly known as a **link**, is text or another web page element that users can select to move to related content in the same page or in another document. Links let you widen the scope of a web page from a stand-alone source of information to an integral part of a set of options available on a website. In turn, links enable you to integrate the contents of a website with anything available on the web. **CASE** *As you prepare to incorporate links into the Lakeland Reeds B&B website, you review how to create and organize web page links.*

Use the following techniques to implement links effectively:

• **Creating links**

To create a link, you enclose the text or other element you want to serve as a link within an a element using the <a></a> tag pair. You use the href attribute to specify the filename of the location, web page, or other document to link to, which is known as the **target document**. TABLE F-1 explains the most common values for the href attribute. When a user agent encounters an a element, it enables users to interact with the element to open the linked document; for example, in a browser, users most commonly click linked text or images to follow links.

Visual browsers apply colors to linked text to indicate that it is a link and to convey a user's interactions with the link at a glance. By convention, an unclicked link is blue, a link that is in the process of being clicked by a user is red, and a link to a web page or document that has already been viewed by a user is purple. However, because CSS allows you to customize these colors, it's uncommon to see this color combination on the web today.

• **Organizing links**

Virtually every website includes a set of links for moving between web pages on the site. This design element is known as a **navigation bar** or **nav bar**, and usually occurs near the top of a web page, as shown in FIGURE F-1, or along one of the sides. A navigation bar should maintain the same location and appearance on every page on a website in order to give users a reliable way to move between pages. Some larger websites include a second set of links at the bottom of each page for information that most users may need only occasionally, such as the site's privacy policy or contact information.

When a web page is longer than an average user's screen, it can be useful to create an additional page-specific navigation bar that scrolls the user's screen to a section of the current page.

QUICK TIP
While several other
protocols are in use
on the Internet, the
web uses only http
and https.

• **Referencing web resources**

Every web page and other document available on the web can be referred to using a **uniform resource locator (URL)**, also known as a **web address**, which is a standard format for specifying how and where to access a resource on the Internet. As shown in FIGURE F-2, a URL consists of three parts: the scheme, the server name, and the path. The **scheme** is the way that computers ask for and communicate about the requested document. Web servers make documents available using the **Hypertext Transfer Protocol (http)** or **Hypertext Transfer Protocol Secure (https)** schemes. The **server name**, such as course.com or mail.google.com, identifies the general location of the target document on the web. The **path** is the sequence of folders in which the target document is stored on the server. A path may end with a filename such as compatibility.html, like the first URL in FIGURE F-2. The filename at the end of the URL is the name of the document a user agent should open in response to a user selecting the link. However, some URLs, such as the second one shown in FIGURE F-2, terminate instead with a series of variable names and values that a program on the web server uses to generate content dynamically. For instance, a link to a specific location on a map website includes information in the URL that enables the website to show the desired spot.

FIGURE F-1: A navigation bar

Navigation bar
provides a
consistent set
of links for
moving around
within the site

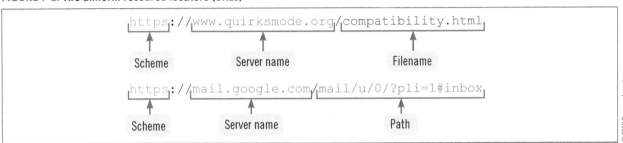

FIGURE F-2: Two uniform resource locators (URLs)

https://www.quirksmode.org/compatibility.html

Scheme   Server name   Filename

https://mail.google.com/mail/u/0/?pli=1#inbox

Scheme   Server name   Path

TABLE F-1: Possible values for the `href` attribute

value	description	example
filename	the filename of a web page or other document located in the same directory as the current page	`history.html`
path and filename	the path and filename of a web page in a different location on the same server	`/docs/register.pdf`
URL	scheme, server name, and, optionally, path for a resource located on another server	`https://mail.google.com/mail/?shva=1#inbox`
id **value**	named location within the current web document, preceded by a pound sign (#); can also be appended to a filename or URL	`#section3`

Creating links to documents other than web pages

Most web page links are to other web pages. However, sometimes it's useful to create a link to another type of document, such as a PDF file or a CSV file. You can specify any type of computer-readable document as the value for an `href` attribute. Although you can link to documents in almost any format from your web pages, it's important to keep in mind that HTML documents are the only ones that your users are guaranteed to be able to access. To be able to access documents in other formats, users' computers must have programs installed that interpret these files. The PDF format has become an unofficial web standard for documents that require a specific printed format, such as forms that must be filled out by hand and/or signed, and you can rely on most of your users

having the capability to view and print PDFs. You should make documents in other formats available based on the likely computer configurations of your target audience. For instance, on a website by and for users of a highly specialized type of software, you'd be safe in making files in that software format available; however, on a site for the general public, it's unlikely that most users would be able to access such files.

Keep in mind that web-focused formats such as HTML and PDF minimize file sizes as much as possible, meaning that documents usually download quickly. If you are making a document available in another format, pay attention to the file size and take any steps available to reduce the size.

Create Relative Links

Learning
Outcomes
• Create a relative
link to a web page
• Create a relative
link to a
non-HTML
document

You can use an a element to link to other documents in two basic ways. When you enter a URL as the href value, you create an **absolute link**, which is the full and complete address for the target document on the web. In some situations, however, it makes more sense to create a **relative link**, which gives only the path and filename information necessary to locate the target document based on the location of the current web page. Because web pages on a small website almost always share the same folder on a web server, it's most efficient to create relative links when creating a nav bar. **CASE** ▷ *You create a nav bar for the Lakeland Reeds B&B website and use relative links to reference the other pages on the site.*

STEPS

1. **In your text editor, open HTM_F-1.html from the Lessons folder where you store your Data Files for this unit, save it as index.html, then repeat to save HTM_F-2.html as aboutus.html, HTM_F-3.html as rooms.html, HTM_F-4.html as reserve.html, and HTM_F-5.css as styles.css**

2. **In the comment at the top of each file, enter your name and today's date where indicated, then save the files**

QUICK TIP
Because a web page
can contain multiple
nav elements, you
should include a
class value for
each nav element
that indicates its role.

3. **In reserve.html, add a new line beneath the header element, indent the same number of spaces, type <nav class="sitenavigation">, press [Enter] twice, then type </nav>**
   You use the nav element to create a nav bar.

4. **On the blank line between the opening and closing <nav> tags, indent three additional spaces, type <p>Home<p>, then press [Enter]**

5. **Repeat Step 4 to add the following p elements on separate lines:** <p>About Us</p>, <p>Rooms</p>, <p>Reservations</p>, <p>Local Weather</p>, <p>Directions</p>
   FIGURE F-3 shows the nav and p elements added to your code.

6. **Place the insertion point just to the left of the word *Home*, type <a href="index.html">, move the insertion point just after the word *Home*, then type </a>**
   The href value index.html is a relative link to the main page of the website.

QUICK TIP
If a user selects a link
to the current page,
the user agent
simply reloads the
page. It's important
to include this link
on the nav bar for
use on other pages
on the website.

7. **Repeat Step 6 to add a elements to the text for the following three links:**

   <a href="aboutus.html">**About Us**</a>

   <a href="rooms.html">**Rooms**</a>

   <a href="reserve.html">**Reservations**</a>

8. **In the last p element within the article element, place the insertion point to the left of the word *Read*, type <a href="weddings.pdf">, move the insertion point just after event., then type </a>**
   You make files in other formats available as well by using links. **FIGURE F-4** shows the completed code.

9. **Save your changes, then open reserve.html in a browser**
   FIGURE F-5 shows the main Reservations web page containing the nav bar and the linked body text. The width and float are set by a rule in styles.css using the nav.sitenavigation selector.

10. **Click About Us on the nav bar**
    The About Us web page opens.

11. **Click your browser's Back button to return to reserve.html, then click the link that begins Read about reserving...**

FIGURE F-3: `nav` element and link text added to index.html

```
23    <header>
24        <h1>Lakeland Reeds Bed &amp; Breakfast</h1>
25    </header>
26    <nav class="sitenavigation">
27        <p>Home</p>
28        <p>About Us</p>
29        <p>Rooms</p>
30        <p>Reservations</p>
31        <p>Local Weather</p>
32        <p>Directions</p>
33    </nav>
34    <article>
```

Each p element within the nav element contains the text for a link

FIGURE F-4: Navigation bar code with relative links

```
27    <nav class="sitenavigation">
28        <p><a href="index.html">Home</a></p>
29        <p><a href="aboutus.html">About Us</a></p>
30        <p><a href="rooms.html">Rooms</a></p>
31        <p><a href="reserve.html">Reservations</a></p>
32        <p>Local Weather</p>
33        <p>Directions</p>
34    </nav>
35    <article>
36        <h2 id="main">Reserva
37        <p>We're happy to take reservations up to a year in advance by phone, fax, or
38        email.</p>
39        <p>Feel free to contact us with any queries about Lakeland Reeds, or about
40        planning your trip.</p>
41        <p><a href="weddings.pdf">Read about reserving Lakeland Reeds for a wedding
42        or other special event.</a> (PDF)</p>
43    </article>
```

href attribute value specifies target document of link

Link target can be a document in a format other than HTML

Opening and closing <a> tags added around text for each link

FIGURE F-5: Web page displaying links

Linked text appears in blue by default

Links to documents you have opened (such as the current page) appear in purple by default

Unlinked text appears in the default text color for p elements

Navigation bar

When link to document clicked, target file is displayed in browser or downloaded and saved (depending on browser configuration)

Creating effective link text

You can create a link on any text on a web page. However, keeping a few rules in mind can enhance your site's accessibility and usability. Above all, link text should describe the target document. In a nav bar, a word or two that summarizes the content is usually sufficient. When you're inserting a link within a paragraph, a few words or a phrase may make more sense. For instance, instead of linking a phrase such as *click here*, creating a link on text such as *read more about your local watershed* helps users verify they're accessing the information they want. Users of screen readers may also check the link text on a web page as a means of scanning the page; using descriptive text increases accessibility in this instance.

Create Absolute Links

Learning
Outcomes
• Add an absolute
  link to a web
  document

Providing entire URLs in a elements isn't necessary for links to other pages on the same web server. However, when you want to link to information on another website, you must use absolute links, which include the full and complete address for the target document on the web. **CASE** ▸ *Phillip Blaine, the owner of Lakeland Reeds B&B, wants to include a link to an online weather forecast for the town where Lakeland Reeds is located. He'd also like the page to incorporate a link that enables users to easily generate customized driving directions to the establishment. You add absolute links targeting external websites to the last two items on the nav bar.*

STEPS

1. **In your browser, open a site that provides current weather conditions, such as wunderground.com or weather.com, type** Marble, MN **in the location search box, then press** [Enter]

   The website displays current weather conditions in Marble, MN, along with a forecast.

2. **Select the URL in the browser Address box, then copy it to the Clipboard**

   On wunderground.com, you can click the Share button, then click the Short Link box to display a shortened URL.

QUICK TIP
If a URL you paste
contains the &
symbol, replace each
occurrence with
& to ensure
your code validates.

3. **Return to** reserve.html **in your editor, place the insertion point just to the left of the phrase** *Local Weather* **within the** nav **element, type** `<a href="`**, paste the contents of the Clipboard, type** `">`**, place the insertion point just after the phrase** *Local Weather***, type** `</a>`**, then save your changes**

   The href value is an absolute link consisting of the entire URL for the target web page.

4. **Return to your web browser, open a site that provides driving directions, such as maps.google.com or mapquest.com**

5. **Type** Marble, MN **in the Search box, click the** Search button**, then click the** Directions **or** Get Directions button **when the map showing Marble, MN is displayed**

   A web page opens with a destination of Marble, MN, selected. If your home address doesn't appear automatically, you may be prompted to enter a starting point.

6. **Select the URL in the browser Address box, then copy it to the Clipboard**

TROUBLE
If the URL in the
address bar contains
no text after the
server name, explore
the page for a way to
create a link contain-
ing the information
you've entered, such
as the "Share or
embed map" option
under Settings on
maps.google.com or
the Link/Embed link
on mapquest.com,
and verify that the link
text begins with http.

7. **Return to** reserve.html **in your editor, place the insertion point just to the left of the word** *Directions* **within the** nav **element, type** `<a href="`**, paste the contents of the Clipboard, type** `">`**, place the insertion point just after the word** *Directions***, then type** `</a>`

   FIGURE F-6 shows the completed code for the two absolute links, using short links for both href values. In Google Maps, you can click the Settings button, click Share or Embed Map, then click the Short URL box to display a shortened URL like the one shown in the figure.

8. **Save your work, open** reserve.html **in your browser, then test the** Local Weather **and** Directions **links**

   FIGURE F-7 shows the completed nav bar.

9. **Return to** reserve.html **in your text editor, select the entire code for the** nav **bar, including the opening and closing** <nav> **tags, copy the code to the Clipboard, paste it below the** header **element in index.html, aboutus.html, and rooms.html, then save each document**

10. **In your web browser, use the links on the reserve.html nav bar to open the other pages in the website, then verify that all the links work on each page**

    Notice that the nav bar is longer than the article element on index.html. You'll adjust the layout in the next lesson to address this issue.

FIGURE F-6: Absolute links added to nav bar code

```
26    <nav class="sitenavigation">
        <p><a href="index.html">Home</a></p>
        <p><a href="aboutus.html">About Us</a></p>
        <p><a href="rooms.html">Rooms</a></p>
        <p><a href="reserve.html">Reservations</a></p>
        <p><a href="http://wxug.us/1hn14">Local Weather</a></p>
32      <p><a href="https://goo.gl/maps/bwf5R">Directions</a></p>
33    </nav>
```

Absolute link contains the entire URL for the target document

Short links used in place of full URLs (your URLs may differ)

FIGURE F-7: Nav bar with absolute links

Understanding mailto links

In addition to creating links that target web pages and other documents, you can construct a link that creates a new email to a specified recipient. Instead of beginning with `http://`, these links start with `mailto:` and are often referred to as **mailto links**. Despite their usefulness, mailto links present both usability and security issues and are not widely used by themselves. When a mailto link is activated, it's up to the user agent to identify which program should complete the request. This program is known as the default mail client. On some systems, the default mail client is a program; on other systems, a web-based email system is the default. This situation, especially on a shared computer, can mean that accessing the link creates unpredictable results, including failure to create the email, accompanied by an error message. In addition, because a mailto link includes a real email address and is publicly available on the Internet, these links are prime targets for

programs known as **email harvesters**, which continually explore web pages looking for email addresses that can then be targeted for spam emails.

If communication from your users is important, a few alternatives have replaced mailto links. Using more advanced HTML elements, you can create a form where users can enter comments and contact information, and then submit it to you without your email address or the sender's being exposed on the web. You can also create a personal or organizational social network feed and make it available on your website, inviting users to direct feedback or questions to you through that network instead of via email. If including a mailto link is a priority for a client, you can incorporate JavaScript code into your page that makes it harder for email harvesters to access the email address.

Change CSS `display` Type

The main nav bar for a website is usually displayed in one of two places: vertically along the left side of the page, or horizontally at or near the top of the page. It's easiest to work with and style link text when each link is a separate block-level element, allowing you to style it with padding, border, and/or margins. However, by default a block-level element is rendered with a line break before and after. You can change how an element is rendered by changing its display type using the CSS `display` property. **TABLE F-2** describes commonly used `display` property values. **CASE** ▶ *Your contacts at Lakeland Reeds like the nav bar you've created, but they would prefer the links to be displayed horizontally below the header. You set the `display` property to `inline-block` and change other properties to implement this new layout.*

STEPS

1. **Return to styles.css in your text editor, scroll to the `nav.sitenavigation` style rule in the site navigation section as needed, type `/*` before the `width` declaration and `*/` after it, then repeat for the `float` and `padding` declarations**

   Enclosing a declaration within comment characters is known as **commenting out** code. When you comment out a declaration, user agents won't apply it to your documents. However, the code is preserved in your style sheet in case you want to use it or refer to it later.

2. **Scroll to the main content section, repeat Step 1 to comment out the `width` and `float` declarations in the `article` style rule, then scroll to the footer section and repeat Step 1 to comment out the `clear` declaration in the `footer` style rule**

3. **Below the `nav.sitenavigation` style rule, add a new style rule with the selector `nav.sitenavigation p`, then add the declarations `display: inline-block;` and `margin: 0.5em;`**

   Setting the `display` property to `inline-block` means that each p element within your site navigation bar is displayed without line breaks before and after it. Setting a margin creates space between the p elements, which are now displayed next to each other in a row.

4. **In the `nav.sitenavigation` rule, add the declaration `text-align: center;`**

   Because inline-block elements do not occupy 100% of the width of their parent elements, the `text-align` value of the parent element determines how they are aligned, just like it determines how words are aligned within a parent element. Your code should match **FIGURE F-8**.

5. **Save your changes, then refresh or reload reserve.html in your browser**

   As **FIGURE F-9** shows, the nav bar is now displayed horizontally below the header element, and the `article` element occupies the full width of the container.

6. **Use the nav bar links to view all the pages on the site and verify that the layout changes have been applied to all documents**

7. **Return to styles.css in your editor, then in the media query at the end of the document, create a new style rule below the h2 rule with the selector `nav` and the declaration `display: none;`**

   Because nav elements are not functional in a printout, you set the `display` value to none to hide them in printed output. **FIGURE F-10** shows the code added to the media query.

8. **Save your changes, refresh or reload reserve.html in your browser, then open a print preview**

   The page is formatted for printing without the site nav bar, and the page is laid out as if the nav bar was not part of the document.

FIGURE F-8: Style sheet with changes for new layout

```
47   /* site navigation bar */
48   nav.sitenavigation {
49   /*    width: 19%; */
50   /*    padding: 3%; */
51   /*    float: left; */
52       color: #34180f;
53       text-align: center;
54   }
55   nav.sitenavigation p {
56       display: inline-block;
57       margin: 0.5em;
58   }
59
60   /* main content */
61   article {
62   /*    width: 69%; */
63       padding: 0 3% lem;
64       background-color: ivory;
65   /*    float: right; */
66   }
```

text-align property affects the alignment of child inline-block elements as well as text

display value for p elements within the site nav bar set to inline-block

Unneeded declarations commented out

```
87   /* footer section */
88   footer {
89       padding: 0.6em;
90       background-color: #34180f;
91       color: ivory;
92       text-align: center
93   /*    clear: both; */
94   }
```

FIGURE F-9: Nav bar orientation changed to horizontal

Navigation bar displayed horizontally rather than vertically

p elements centered within parent element

FIGURE F-10: Code added to style sheet to exclude `nav` elements from printed output

```
175       h2 {
176           font-size: 2.2em;
177       }
178       nav {
179           display: none;
180       }
181   }
182   @page {
```

TABLE F-2: Commonly used values of the `display` property

value	rendered as	line breaks before and after?	box model support
block	box occupying the full width of its parent element	yes	all properties
inline	content that does not expand to the full width of its parent	no	margin-left, margin-right
inline-block	box that does not expand to the full width of its parent	yes	all properties
none	document rendered as if element does not exist		

Style Links with a Pseudo-Class

In addition to creating basic styles for a elements, you can create CSS styles to change the format of a link in response to a user's interaction with the link. To do so, you use a **pseudo-class**, which is a categorization of a web page element based on a relationship or condition of the element at a given moment, rather than on a static attribute value. The word *pseudo* means *like* or *similar to*, so the term *pseudo-class* means *like a class*, referencing its similarity to the class attribute. A pseudo-class is analogous to a class value being assigned temporarily to an element only when the element meets certain criteria. One of the most useful pseudo-classes is the :hover pseudo-class, which applies to an element when a user moves the mouse pointer over the element. The a element is the only HTML element that supports the :hover pseudo-class. Often used to change the appearance of a link before a user clicks it, :hover provides visual confirmation that the user is about to click the desired link. **CASE** ➤ *You use the :hover pseudo-class for the links in the site navigation bar to change the color of link text when a user moves the mouse pointer over a link.*

STEPS

1. **Return to** styles.css **in your text editor**

2. **In the site navigation bar section, below the** nav.sitenavigation p **style rule, add a style rule with the selector** nav.sitenavigation a:hover
   You specify the :hover pseudo-class after the a selector, with no space in between.

3. **Within the new style rule, add the declaration** color: ivory;
   This declaration changes the font color to ivory when a user's mouse pointer is over an a element within the site nav bar. **FIGURE F-11** shows the new style rule.

4. **Save your changes, then refresh or reload reserve.html in your browser**

5. **Move your mouse pointer over the** Home link **on the nav bar**
   As **FIGURE F-12** shows, the link text appears ivory when the mouse pointer is over it. In addition, the mouse pointer becomes a pointing hand when positioned over a link.

6. **Move your mouse pointer to a blank area of the web page**
   The link text returns to its default color.

7. **Repeat Steps 5 and 6 to test the remaining links on the nav bar**

Styling the :hover pseudo-class

You can style the :hover pseudo-class using any property that is valid for an a element. However, it's best to avoid changing the values of properties for the :hover pseudo-class that affect the line height of text, such as line-height, font-size, or font-weight. Changing any of these properties can affect the page layout—for instance, it can cause the elements below a nav bar to move down temporarily because the height of the nav bar increases to accommodate the new value while the mouse pointer is over a link. Instead, properties such as color, background-color, and text-shadow are commonly used to

affect the appearance of links while the mouse pointer is over them but without affecting the overall layout.

Note that because the a element is an inline element, you cannot set box model properties including width, padding, border, or margin unless you first change its display type. However, if you set the display type of a elements to inline-block or block, you can then work with their box model properties. This is an especially useful technique when changing the background color of links with the :hover pseudo-class because it can be useful to create padding around the link text.

FIGURE F-11: Style rule for `:hover` pseudo-class

```
56   nav.sitenavigation p {
57      display: inline-block;
58      margin: 0.5em;
59   }
60   nav.sitenavigation a:hover {
61      color: ivory;
62   }
63
64   /* main content */
65   article {
```

Style rule for `:hover`
pseudo-class of links
in site nav bar

FIGURE F-12: Text color changed by `:hover` style rule

Style rule for
`:hover`
pseudo-class
applied when
mouse pointer
is over link

Mouse pointer
becomes a
pointing hand
when over a
link

Understanding the difference between pseudo-elements and pseudo-classes

Both pseudo-elements and pseudo-classes are CSS selectors that you specify with a colon preceding them. However, there are a number of differences between these two features. You use a pseudo-element to work with part of an element, such as the first letter. As long as the base element exists in your HTML code, a style rule that uses a pseudo-element selector is always applied to the page. By contrast, you use a pseudo-class to style an element based on the status of user interaction with it. This means that styling for a pseudo-class can be applied to a web page at certain times and not at others—for example, only when the mouse pointer or focus is on a link. You can

think of a pseudo-element as a way to create or carve out an element using CSS; likewise, a pseudo-class is a way to assign a class value to an element based on its state.

Starting with CSS3, the language has standardized on using a single colon before a pseudo-class (such as `:focus`) and two colons before a pseudo-element (such as `::first-letter`) to distinguish between the two in code. However, older browsers do not recognize the double-colon versions of pseudo-elements, so it's best to continue to use a single colon for both features until older browsers, such as IE8, are no longer in wide use.

Style Multiple Link States

In addition to :hover, links have four other states that you can style with pseudo-classes—:link, :visited, :focus, and :active. TABLE F-3 summarizes the 5 pseudo-classes for links. While you are not required to use all five pseudo-classes for a link, you must specify any you do use in the order shown in the table (though :hover and :focus can be swapped or specified for the same rule). **CASE** ▶ *You implement additional pseudo-classes for the Lakeland Reeds nav bar to maximize contrast within the site's color scheme.*

STEPS

1. **Return to** styles.css **in your text editor, scroll to the** /* body */ **comment, then, after the** p **style rule, create a style rule with the selector** a:link **containing the declaration** color: black;

   The :link pseudo-class applies only when the other four do not. This style rule sets the text color to black for unfollowed links on any part of a page.

2. **Below the rule you just entered, create a style rule with the selector** a:visited **containing the declaration** color: #888;

   This style rule sets the text color to dark gray for a link that has been followed.

3. **Below the rule you just entered, create a style rule with the selector** a:active **containing the declarations** position: relative;, top: 1px;, **and** left: 1px;

   This style rule positions a link that is in the process of being clicked slightly down and to the right, creating a visual illusion of movement, similar to a physical button being pressed.

4. **Below the** /* site navigation bar */ **comment and above the** nav.sitenavigation a:hover **style rule, create a style rule with the selector** nav.sitenavigation a:link **containing the declarations** text-decoration: none; **and** color: #34180f;

   This style rule sets the default appearance of a elements within the site nav bar, removing the default underline for link text and setting the text color to dark brown.

5. **Below the rule you just entered, create a style rule with the selector** nav.sitenavigation a:visited **containing the declaration** color: #744f42;

   This style rule sets the text color of followed links within the site nav bar to a medium brown.

6. **In the** nav.sitenavigation a:hover **style rule, add the selector** nav.sitenavigation a:focus

   Adding the :focus pseudo-class to this selector ensures that the color change rollover effect is also applied when users navigate the page using a keyboard. FIGURE F-13 shows the code for the additional pseudo-elements.

7. **Save your changes, return to your web browser, then clear your browsing history**

   The option varies among browsers but is commonly listed under privacy or safety settings.

8. **Refresh or reload** reserve.html **in your browser, then move your mouse pointer over the** Home link **on the nav bar**

   The link text appears ivory when the mouse pointer is over it, as it did previously. The link for the current page, which is open in the browser, is a medium brown based on the :visited style rule for the nav bar.

9. **Press and hold the mouse button**

   The link text moves slightly down and to the right, creating an illusion that simulates a physical key being pressed, as shown in FIGURE F-14.

10. **Release the mouse button, then let the target page load**

    The Home and Reservations links appear medium brown, indicating you've visited those pages.

QUICK TIP
You don't need to specify styles for the :active pseudo-class for the site nav bar because it does not require different styling than the default settings.

QUICK TIP
Although the :link and :visited pseudo-classes are rendered on all devices, styles for the :focus and :active pseudo-classes, like those for :hover, are generally not rendered when interacting with a touchscreen.

FIGURE F-13: Global pseudo-class styles and styles for site nav bar added to style sheet

```
31  p {
32      font-size: 1.4em;
33      line-height: 1.6em;
34  }
35  a:link {
36      color: black;
37  }
38  a:visited {
39      color: #888;
40  }
41  a:active {
42      position: relative;
43      top: 1px;
44      left: 1px;
45  }
46
47  /* header section */
```

```
67  nav.sitenavigation p {
68      display: inline-block;
69      margin: 0.5em;
70  }
71  nav.sitenavigation a:link {
72      text-decoration: none;
73      color: #34180f;
74  }
75  nav.sitenavigation a:visited {
76      color: #744f42;
77  }
78  nav.sitenavigation a:hover, nav.sitenavigation a:focus {
79      color: ivory;
80  }
```

FIGURE F-14: Links styled using multiple pseudo-classes

Link text offset down and to the right while being clicked based on style for :active pseudo-class

Unvisited link in article element formatted based on default style for :link pseudo-class

After clearing browser history, link text for unvisited pages displayed in dark brown based on style for :link pseudo-class

Link text for current page displayed in medium brown based on style for :visited pseudo-class

TABLE F-3: Pseudo-class states for linked elements

pseudo-class	provides styles for
:link	link that has not been visited, does not currently have the focus or the mouse pointer over it, and is not being clicked
:visited	link that has already been viewed
:focus	link that currently has the focus regardless of how it was selected, including via keyboard navigation
:hover	link that the mouse pointer is currently over
:active	link that is currently being clicked

Open Links in New Tabs

By default, a link opens a new web page in the same tab as the source page. This enables users to revisit previous pages using the back buttons in their browsers. In certain situations, however, you want a link to open a web page in a new tab. For instance, some websites open target pages for links to external sites in new tabs so users can have both sites open at once. Opening a link in a new window or tab from a web page containing a lot of information allows a user to easily and quickly return to their place on the original page when they're done with the linked information. You can control where a link target opens by including the `target` attribute of the a element. A value of `_blank` specifies that the target page should open in a new tab. **TABLE F-4** details the commonly used values for the `target` attribute. **CASE** *In consultation with your contacts at Lakeland Reeds, you've decided that the Local Weather and Directions link targets should open in new tabs. You add the* `target` *attribute to these links.*

STEPS

1. Return to reserve.html in your editor

2. Within the `nav` element, position the insertion point before the closing > in the opening <a> tag for the Local Weather link

3. Press [Spacebar], then type `target="_blank"`

4. Position the insertion point before the closing > in the opening <a> tag for the Directions link

5. Press [Spacebar], type `target="_blank"`, then save your changes

   FIGURE F-15 shows the web page code with the `target` attributes added.

6. Refresh or reload reserve.html in your browser, then click the Local Weather link

   The web page displaying the current weather opens in a new tab, as shown in **FIGURE F-16**.

7. Close the browser tab displaying the weather information, click the reserve.html tab if it is not the active tab, then click the Directions link

   Like the weather page, the web page displaying directions opens in a new tab.

8. Close the browser tab displaying directions, then return to reserve.html in your editor

9. Select the entire code for the nav bar, including the opening and closing <nav> tags, copy the code to the Clipboard, use it to replace the existing `nav` elements in index.html, aboutus.html, and rooms.html, then save your work on each document

TABLE F-4: Common values of the `target` property of the a element

value	description
`_blank`	Opens target document in a new tab
`_self`	Opens target document in same tab as source document (default value)

FIGURE F-15: `target` attribute added to external links

```
26        <nav class="sitenavigation">
27            <p><a href="index.html">Home</a></p>
28            <p><a href="aboutus.html">About Us</a></p>
29            <p><a href="rooms.html">Rooms</a></p>
30            <p><a href="reserve.html">Reservations</a></p>
31            <p><a href="http://wxug.us/1hn14" target="_blank">Local Weather</a></p>
32            <p><a href="https://goo.gl/maps/bwf5R" target="_blank">Directions</a></p>
33        </nav>
```

target attribute value set to _blank for both links to external sites

FIGURE F-16: Link target opened in new tab

Source page still open on original tab

Short link opens full original URL

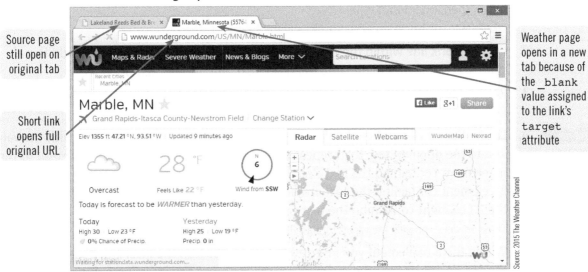

Weather page opens in a new tab because of the _blank value assigned to the link's `target` attribute

Source: 2015 The Weather Channel

Using short links

Especially long external links can clutter your web page code. To make your code easier to read, you can use **short links**, which are generated URLs that use especially short domain names and specially crafted paths to represent large, unwieldy links as short, manageable URLs. Many popular websites allow you to share links to their content using custom short links with domain names specific to the company. For instance, Google generates short links that use the goo.gl domain name, and the New York Times uses the domain nyti.ms for its short links. Even without access to a custom domain, you can generate your own short links using a web-based service such as bit.ly or tinyurl.com. To use these services, you start by copying the full URL of the web page you want to link to, then navigating to the website of whichever link shortener you choose. Next, you paste your long link into the text box

for that purpose, then click the associated button, which is often labeled "shorten" or something similar. The service processes your link and returns a new short link that starts with the link shortener's name. You then copy the new link to the Clipboard and paste it into your web page.

One drawback of using short links in your website is that users are unable to tell from inspecting the URL what domain the link targets, which could be unsettling to some people. Short links make more sense on websites for large, well-established businesses and organizations and for websites that target people likely to have experience using such links. You may want to consider avoiding using short links on a website for a person or organization that's not well known, or on a site that targets more security-focused users.

Link Within a Document

Learning
Outcomes
• Create links to
  elements within a
  web page

You can link to locations within the current web page using the same elements and attributes as other links you've created. However, instead of linking to URLs or filenames, you link to elements within the current document that have specific values for the id attribute. To reference an id value using the href attribute of the a element, you simply precede the id value with a pound sign (#). Because this symbol is also known as a hash mark, links to id values are known as **hash links**. **CASE** *You add an id value to the h3 element for each room heading on the Rooms page, then add a second nav bar to the page containing a hash link to each room heading.*

STEPS

1. **Return to** rooms.html **in your editor, add a blank line before the** h3 **element containing the text** *Sun Room*, **indent and type** `<nav class="pagenavigation">`, **press** [Enter] **twice, then indent and type** `</nav>`

   Like the site nav bar, you use the nav element for the page nav bar.

2. **On the blank line within the** nav **element you created in Step 1, indent 3 additional spaces, create a** p **element containing the text** Sun Room, **then press** [Enter]

3. **Repeat Step 2 to add three additional** p **elements to the nav bar containing the text** Reed Room, Treehouse, **and** Garden Room

QUICK TIP

Another common use of hash links involves adding an id value to a page's main heading, then creating links to that heading at the bottom of each section of the page, allowing users to easily return to the top of the page.

4. **Locate the** h3 **element containing the text** *Sun Room*, **add an** id **attribute with the value** sun **to the opening tag, then repeat to add an** id **attribute with the value** reed **to the** h3 **element containing the text** *Reed Room*, **an** id **attribute with the value** tree **to the** h3 **element containing the text** *Treehouse*, **and an** id **attribute with the value** garden **to the** h3 **element containing the text** *Garden Room*

   These id values provide the values for hash links to the headings.

5. **Within the** nav **element you inserted in Step 1, position the insertion point to the left of the phrase** *Sun Room*, **type** `<a href="#sun">`, **move the insertion point to the right of the phrase** *Sun Room*, **then type** `</a>`

6. **Repeat Step 5 to create the following three links, as shown in** FIGURE F-17:

   ```
   <p><a href="#reed">Reed Room</a></p>

   <p><a href="#tree">Treehouse</a></p>

   <p><a href="#garden">Garden Room</a></p>
   ```

TROUBLE

If the web page is not long enough to place the element with the target id value at the top of the window, the element may remain in the middle or at the bottom of the window.

7. **Save your work, return to** styles.css **in your editor, then below the** `/* main content */` **comment and after the** `.title` **rule, enter the style rules shown in** FIGURE F-18

   The first two new style rules shown in FIGURE F-18 style the nav element with the class value pagenavigation and p elements within that nav element. The final three new style rules set properties for the :link, :visited, :hover, and :focus pseudo-classes for links within the new nav element.

8. **Save your work, open** rooms.html **in your browser, click the** Sun Room **link in the page nav bar, scroll back up, then repeat to test the remaining links in the page nav bar**

Linking to id values in other documents

You can combine a relative or absolute link with a hash value to link to a specific element in a different document. When specifying the href value for the link, simply enter the URL or filename for the target document, add a pound sign (#) to the end, then add the id value. When the target page opens in a user's browser, the page scrolls to the element with the specified id value.

FIGURE F-17: Completed code for page `nav` **bar**

```
34              <article>
35                  <h2>Rooms</h2>
36                  <p>All rooms include down comforters, air conditioning, and DVD players, and
37                  each can accommodate an additional twin fold-out bed.</p>
38                  <nav class="pagenavigation">
39                      <p><a href="#sun">Sun Room</a></p>
40                      <p><a href="#reed">Reed Room</a></p>
41                      <p><a href="#tree">Treehouse</a></p>
42                      <p><a href="#garden">Garden Room</a></p>
43                  </nav>
44                  <h3 id="sun">Sun Room</h3>
45                  <p>With windows on three sides, the sunlight in this second-floor room
46                  supports a large selection of houseplants.</p>
47                  <p>1 queen bed.</p>
48                  <h3 id="reed">Reed Room</h3>
49                  <p>This first-floor room looks out over the reeds on the edge of the lake and
50                  the water beyond.</p>
51                  <p>1 queen bed and 1 twin bed.</p>
52                  <h3 id="tree">Treehouse</h3>
53                  <p>A winding staircase takes you to your own private getaway at the top of
54                  the house, with view of the surrounding trees and meadows and the lake.</p>
55                  <p>1 queen bed.</p>
56                  <h3 id="garden">Garden Room</h3>
57                  <p>This room's French doors open onto our stone patio and flower garden.</p>
58                  <p>1 queen bed and 2 twin beds.</p>
59              </article>
```

New `nav` element created for navigating within the page

`id` values added to `h3` elements as targets for hash links

FIGURE F-18: Style rules for page nav bar

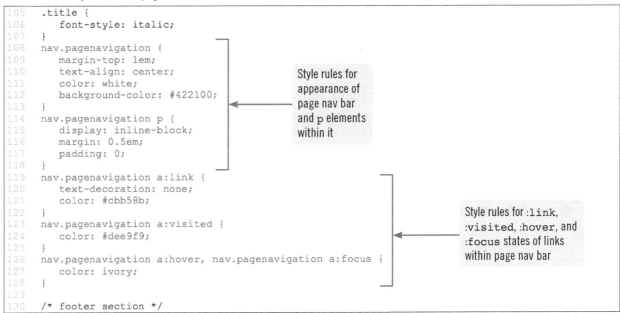

```
105     .title {
106         font-style: italic;
107     }
108     nav.pagenavigation {
109         margin-top: 1em;
110         text-align: center;
111         color: white;
112         background-color: #422100;
113     }
114     nav.pagenavigation p {
115         display: inline-block;
116         margin: 0.5em;
117         padding: 0;
118     }
119     nav.pagenavigation a:link {
120         text-decoration: none;
121         color: #cbb58b;
122     }
123     nav.pagenavigation a:visited {
124         color: #dee9f9;
125     }
126     nav.pagenavigation a:hover, nav.pagenavigation a:focus {
127         color: ivory;
128     }
129
130     /* footer section */
```

Style rules for appearance of page nav bar and `p` elements within it

Style rules for `:link`, `:visited`, `:hover`, and `:focus` states of links within page nav bar

Clearing browser history to retest link states

When changing properties for link pseudo-classes, you may find that all links in a page are formatted as `:visited` due to earlier testing. To reset the appearance of links to their default `:link` state, you need to clear your **browser history**, which is the log your browser maintains of URLs that you've visited. Browsers use browser history to enable features such as autocompleting addresses that you type in the Address bar. In addition, browsers render a link using declarations for the `:visited` pseudo-class if the link target appears in the browser history. Every browser enables you to clear the history list. Consult your browser documentation or search the web if you need help clearing your browser history.

Aid Navigational Accessibility

Learning
Outcomes
• Create a skip link
• Test accessibility
 with keyboard
 navigation

Users of screen readers and other users who navigate using a keyboard often experience a web page element-by-element in sequence from top to bottom. These users encounter the heading followed by each link in a nav bar before getting to the main content of the page. To allow users to skip straight to the main page content, it's good practice to include a **skip link**, which targets an `id` value at the start of the main page content and allows users to bypass navigation. **CASE** ▶ *You add a skip link to each web page in the Lakeland Reeds site, and you test the link using keyboard navigation.*

STEPS

1. **Return to** index.html **in your editor, place the insertion point just after the** p **in the opening <p> tag just below the opening <article> tag, press [Spacebar], then type** `id="contentstart"`
   This `id` value marks the start of the main page content.

2. **Add a blank line beneath the opening <div> tag for the** container **class, indent to align with the <header> tag that follows, then type** `<p class="skipnavigation"> <a href="#contentstart">Skip navigation</a></p>`
   FIGURE F-19 shows the code for the target `id` attribute and the skip link.

3. **Save your changes, open** index.html **in a browser, drag the bottom border of your browser up so only the skip link and the** h1 **heading are visible, then click** Skip navigation
   The skip link is displayed at the top of the browser window when the page opens, and when you click the link the browser displays the beginning of the main page content.

4. **Repeat Steps 1–3 for** aboutus.html, rooms.html, **and** reserve.html, **adding the** id **attribute in Step 1 to the** h2 **element in each document**

5. **Return to** styles.css **in your editor, above the** /* header section */ **comment, add the comment** /* skip navigation link */, **then create a style rule with the selector** p.skipnavigation a **containing the declarations** position: absolute; **and** left: -10000px;
   It's common to use absolute position to take a skip link out of the normal flow and then position it far outside the visible area of the page so users navigating by sight with a touch device don't see the link.

6. **Below the style rule you created in Step 5, create a new style rule with the selector** p.skipnavigation a:focus **containing the declarations** color: #34180f;, background-color: ivory;, top: 0.2em;, left: 0.4em;, **and** z-index: 2;
   This rule makes the link visible on the screen and highlights it when it has the focus so a user navigating with a keyboard can view and select the link when interacting with the page. **FIGURE F-20** shows the CSS code.

7. **Save your changes, refresh or reload** index.html **in your browser, then press [Tab] one or more times until the text Skip Navigation is displayed at the top of the page, as shown in FIGURE F-21**
   The skip link is not displayed when the page first opens, but becomes visible when it receives the focus while you navigate through the links on the page with the [Tab] key.

8. **Press the [Tab] key to select each of the remaining links on the page**
   When the skip link no longer has the focus, it is no longer displayed.

9. **Press [Enter]**
   Pressing [Enter] selects the element with focus. Selecting the skip link scrolls the page to the h2 heading.

10. **Validate the code for all your web pages and your style sheet**

FIGURE F-19: Skip link and target `id` value added to index.html

```
22          <div class="container">
23              <p class="skipnavigation"><a href="#contentstart">Skip navigation</a></p>
24              <header>
25                  <h1>Lakeland Reeds Bed &amp; Breakfast</h1>
26              </header>
27              <nav class="sitenavigation">
28                  <p><a href="index.html">Home</a></p>
29                  <p><a href="aboutus.html">About Us</a></p>
30                  <p><a href="rooms.html">Rooms</a></p>
                    <p><a href="reserve.html">Reservations</a></p>
                    <p><a href="http://wxug.us/lhn14" target="_blank">Local Weather</a></p>
                    <p><a href="https://goo.gl/maps/bwf5R" target="_blank">Directions</a></p>
                </nav>
                <article>
                    <p id="contentstart">Lakeland Reeds is a rustic bed and breakfast on Twin
37                      Lakes near rural Marble, Minnesota. Convenient to US 2 and 169, the fresh air
38                      and quiet make for an ideal weekend escape from the rush of city life.</p>
39              </article>
```

Target of skip link is the element with the id value `contentstart`

id value added to element at start of main page content

FIGURE F-20: CSS code to style skip link

```
47      /* skip navigation link */
48      p.skipnavigation a {
49          position: absolute;
50          left: -10000px;
51      }
52      p.skipnavigation a:focus {
53          color: #34180f;
54          background-color: ivory;
55          top: 0.2em;
56          left: 0.4em;
57          z-index: 2;
58      }
59
60      /* header section */
```

FIGURE F-21: Skip link displayed in response to keyboard navigation

Skip link displayed when element receives focus

Testing web pages with a screen reader

In addition to the keyboard, a screen reader is another common means of navigating a web page for people with certain disabilities. A screen reader is software that reads content on a computer, including web pages, out loud. Screen readers are commonly used by people with low vision and by blind people. As a developer, it can be useful to test your pages on screen readers to identify any issues with your documents that might prevent screen reader users from accessing all of your content.

Free, full-featured screen readers are available for both Windows and Mac computers. For Windows, you can download the free NVDA screen reader from nvaccess.org. For Mac, VoiceOver is a screen reader that's installed by default as part of the operating system; to enable and customize VoiceOver, open System Preferences, click Accessibility, then click VoiceOver. For more information on VoiceOver, see apple.com/accessibility/osx/voiceover/.

Practice

Concepts Review

Refer to FIGURE F-22 **to answer the questions that follow.**

FIGURE F-22

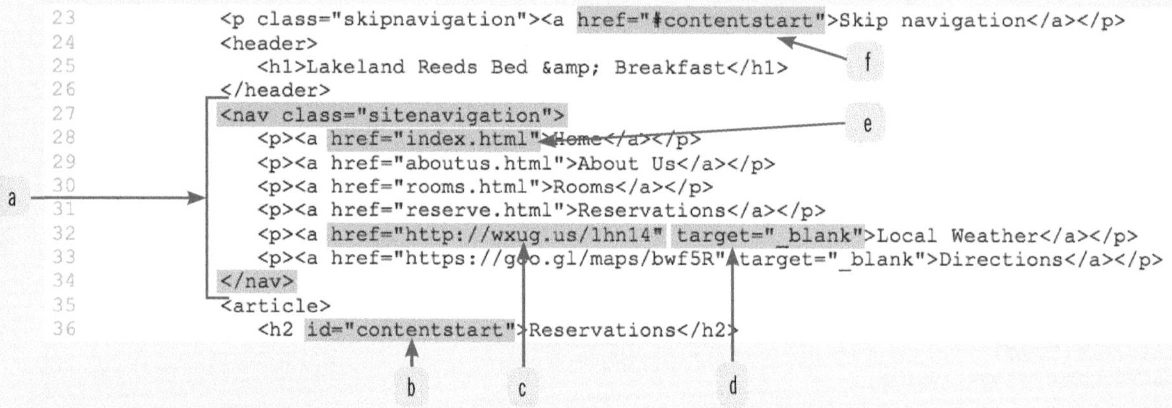

```
23          <p class="skipnavigation"><a href="#contentstart">Skip navigation</a></p>
24          <header>
25              <h1>Lakeland Reeds Bed &amp; Breakfast</h1>
26          </header>
27          <nav class="sitenavigation">
28              <p><a href="index.html">Home</a></p>
29              <p><a href="aboutus.html">About Us</a></p>
30              <p><a href="rooms.html">Rooms</a></p>
31              <p><a href="reserve.html">Reservations</a></p>
32              <p><a href="http://wxug.us/lhn14" target="_blank">Local Weather</a></p>
33              <p><a href="https://goo.gl/maps/bwf5R" target="_blank">Directions</a></p>
34          </nav>
35          <article>
36              <h2 id="contentstart">Reservations</h2>
```

a   b   c   d   e   f

1. **Which item marks a nav bar?**
2. **Which item is an absolute link?**
3. **Which item is a relative link?**
4. **Which item opens a link in a new tab?**
5. **Which item is a hash link?**
6. **Which item creates a target value for a link?**

Match each term with the statement that best describes it.

7. **Uniform resource locator (URL)**

8. **Relative link**

9. **Nav bar**

10. **Absolute link**

11. **Skip link**

12. **Pseudo-class**

   a. A link that gives only the path and filename information necessary to locate the target document based on the location of the current web page

   b. A type of link that specifies the full and complete address for the target document on the web

   c. A set of links for moving between web pages on a website

   d. A standard format for specifying how and where to access a resource on the Internet

   e. A categorization of a web page element based on a relationship or condition of the element at a given moment

   f. A link that targets an anchor at the start of the main page content and allows users to bypass navigation

Select the best answer from the list of choices.

13. **When creating a link, the web page or other document you link to is known as the _____ .**
   a. relative link   **c.** absolute link
   b. hash   **d.** target

14. **Which type of web reference contains a scheme, a server name, and a path?**
   a. hash   **c.** URL
   b. relative link   **d.** nav element

15. **Web servers make documents available using which protocol?**
    a. http
    b. ftp
    c. mailto
    d. telnet

16. **What does the value `#section3` for the `href` attribute target?**
    a. a URI
    b. a PDF file
    c. an `id` value
    d. a filename

17. **When you enter a URL, which of the following are you creating?**
    a. a hash link
    b. a skip link
    c. a relative link
    d. an absolute link

18. **Because web pages on a small website almost always share the same folder on a web server, it's most efficient to create which type of links when creating a nav bar?**
    a. relative
    b. absolute
    c. hash
    d. skip

19. **Which pseudo-class is applied when a user's mouse pointer is over the affected link?**
    a. a:link
    b. a:visited
    c. a:hover
    d. a:active

20. **You specify that a link should open in a new tab using which attribute?**
    a. `href`
    b. `target`
    c. `class`
    d. `id`

Skills Review

1. **Create relative links.**
   a. In your editor, open the file HTM_F-6.html from the SR folder where you store your Data Files for this unit, save it as **index.html**, then repeat to save the file HTM_F-7.html as **history.html**, HTM_F-8.html as **location.html**, and HTM_F-9.css as **styles.css**.
   b. Within the comment section at the top of each file, enter your first and last names and today's date, then save your changes.
   c. Return to index.html in your editor, then below the `header` element add a `nav` element with a `class` value of `sitenavigation`.
   d. Within the `nav` element, enter 4 p elements containing the text **Home**, **History**, **Menu**, and **Locations**.
   e. Create a relative link on the word **Home** that opens the page index.html, then repeat to add relative links to the text History to open the page history.html, Menu to open the file bigjmenu.pdf, and Locations to open location.html.
   f. Save your changes, return to styles.css in your editor, then above the main content section create a comment with the text **site navigation**.
   g. Below the comment you entered in the previous step, create a style rule for `nav` elements with the `class` value `sitenavigation` that sets the width to 19%, margins to 1em 0 0 2%, padding to 2%, float to `left`, and background color to `#ddd`.
   h. Save your changes, open index.html in your browser, then click the Locations link to test it.
   i. Return to index.html in your editor, copy the `nav` element including the opening and closing `<nav>` tags to the Clipboard, then paste the copied code after the `header` elements in history.html and in location.html.
   j. Save your changes to both documents, open index.html in your browser, then test the nav bar links on all 3 pages to ensure that all links work.

2. **Create absolute links.**
   a. Return to location.html in your editor, then copy the full address of the first location from the p element to the Clipboard. (*Hint*: Do not copy [Map].)
   b. Open a website that provides maps, such as maps.google.com or mapquest.com, paste the contents of the Clipboard into the location box on the web page, then press [Enter].

Skills Review (continued)

c. Copy the URL from the Address bar (or a short link if available).

d. Return to location.html in your editor, then add an absolute link on the word *Map* at the end of the first address, pasting the URL from the Clipboard as the `href` value. Be sure to add the closing tag for the a element just before the closing]. (*Hint*: If the URL you paste contains the ampersand (&) symbol, replace each occurrence with & to ensure your code validates.)

e. Repeat Steps a–d for the remaining two locations, save your work, then open location.html in your web browser and test each of the Map links.

3. **Change CSS display type.**

a. Return to styles.css in your editor, then in the `nav.sitenavigation` rule, comment out the declarations for the `width`, `padding`, and `float` properties.

b. Repeat Step a to comment out the `width` and `float` declarations in the `article` style rule and the `clear` declaration in the `footer` style rule.

c. Below the `nav.sitenavigation` rule, add a new style rule for p elements within the nav element with the `class` value `sitenavigation`, setting the display type to `inline-block` and the top and bottom padding to 0.3em.

d. Below the style rule you created in the previous step, add a new style rule for a elements within p elements within the nav element with the `class` value `sitenavigation`, setting the padding to 0.2em 0.6em and the display type to `inline-block`.

e. In the `nav.sitenavigation` rule, change the margins to 1em 1em 0 and the background color to `black`, then add a declaration to center-align text.

f. In the `article` rule in the main content section, change the margins to 0 1em 1em and the padding to 1em 1em 0.5em.

g. Save your changes, refresh or reload index.html in your browser, then use the nav bar links to view all the pages on the site and verify that the layout changes have been applied to all documents.

h. Return to styles.css in your editor, then in the media query at the end of the document, create a new style rule above the `@page` rule that sets the display type for nav elements to `none`.

i. Save your changes, refresh or reload index.html in your browser, open a print preview, then verify that the nav element is not part of the layout.

4. **Style links with a pseudo-class and style multiple link states.**

a. Return to styles.css in your editor, then in the body and container section below the rule for the p element, add a new style rule that formats the font color of a default link as `black`.

b. Below the rule you created in the previous step, add a rule to format the font colors of visited links with the color `#888`, then add another rule to relatively position active links 1px down from the top and 1px over from the left.

c. At the bottom of the site navigation section, add a rule that sets the font color of a default link to white and removes the link's underline, then add another rule that sets the font color for visited links to the value `#ccc`.

d. Below the rules you created in the previous step, add a rule that sets the font color of links that the mouse pointer is over and links that have the focus to `red` and sets the background color to `white`.

e. In the `nav.sitenavigation` rule, change the background color value to `black`.

f. Save your changes, return to your browser, then clear your browsing history.

g. Refresh or reload index.html in your browser, verify that the font and background colors change for links on the nav bar when the mouse pointer is over them and when the target pages have been viewed, verify that the position of links changes while they are being clicked, then repeat for history.html and location.html.

5. **Open links in new tabs.**

a. Return to location.html in your text editor, then in the opening <a> tag for the first Map link, add an attribute and value that opens the link in a new browser tab.

b. Repeat the previous step for the remaining two Map links.

c. Save your work, refresh or reload location.html in your browser, then test each Map link, verifying that it opens in a new tab.

Skills Review (continued)

6. **Link within a document.**

   a. Return to location.html in your editor.

   b. In the opening tag for the h3 element containing the text Queen’s Park, add an id attribute with the value queen.

   c. Repeat Step b to add an id attribute with the value stclair to the h3 element containing the text St. Clair, and an id attribute with the value dundas to the h3 element containing the text Dundas.

   d. Below the h2 element, enter a nav element with the class value pagenavigation.

   e. Within the new nav element, add 3 p elements containing the text **Queen’s Park/UT**, **St. Clair**, and **Dundas**.

   f. Link the text in the first p element to the element with the id value queen, the second to the element with the id value stclair, and the third to the element with the id value dundas.

   g. Save your changes, then return to styles.css in your editor.

   h. Above the main content section, add a comment with the text **page navigation**, then below the comment enter the following style rules:

   - For the nav element with the class value pagenavigation, set the margin to 0 1em and center-align text
   - For p elements within the nav element with the class value pagenavigation, set margins to 0 0.2em, display type to inline-block, and the background color to #ffcc66
   - For a elements within p elements within the nav element with the class value pagenavigation, set padding to 0.2em 0.6em and display type to inline-block
   - For default links within the nav element with the class value pagenavigation, create a 2px solid white border and remove the underline
   - For visited links within the nav element with the class value pagenavigation, create a 2px solid white border and set the text color to #999
   - For links that have the mouse pointer over them or that have the focus and that are within the nav element with the class value pagenavigation, create a 2px solid border with the color #ffcc66, set the text color to red, and set the background color to white

   i. Save your changes, open location.html in your browser, then test each of the links in the page navigation bar. (*Hint*: Reduce the height of your browser window if necessary to verify that all of the links work.) Your document should match **FIGURE F-23**.

7. **Aid navigational accessibility.**

   a. Return to index.html in your editor, then add an id attribute with a value of contentstart to the first p element within the article element.

   b. Above the header element, add a p element with the class value skipnavigation containing the text **Skip navigation**, then link the text Skip navigation to the id value contentstart.

   c. Save your changes, return to styles.css in your editor, then above the header section add a comment containing the text **skip navigation link**.

   d. Below the new comment, add a style rule for a elements within the p element with the class value skipnavigation that absolutely positions the elements -10000px from the left.

FIGURE F-23

Skills Review (continued)

e. Below the rule you added in the previous step, create a rule for a elements that have the focus and that are within the p element with the `class` value `skipnavigation` that sets the text color to `#34180f`, the background color to `white`, positions the elements 0.4em from the top and 0.4em from the right, sets the `left` value to `auto`, and assigns a z-index of 2.

f. Save your changes, refresh or reload index.html in your browser, then use the keyboard to verify that the Skip navigation link is displayed when it has the focus.

g. Repeat Steps a–b for history.html and location.html, adding the `id` attribute in Step a to the `h2` element in each file, then repeat Step f to test each file.

h. Validate the code for your web pages and style sheet.

Independent Challenge 1

As you continue your work on the website for the Spotted Wren Garden Center, you add a nav bar and links to gardening resources, along with navigational accessibility features.

a. In your editor, open the file HTM_F-10.html from the IC1 folder where you store your Data Files for this unit, save it as **index.html**, then repeat to save the file HTM_F-11.html as **hours.html**, and HTM_F-12.css as **styles.css**.

b. Within the comment section at the top of each file, enter your first and last names and today's date, then save your changes.

c. Return to index.html in your editor, then below the `header` element add a `nav` element with a `class` value of `sitenavigation`.

d. Within the `nav` element, create 4 p elements containing the text **Home, Hours, Location,** and **Tips**. Link the text Home to index.html, Hours to hours.html, and Tips to tipsheet.pdf.

e. In your browser, navigate to a map service, then using the address in the `footer` element of index.html, open a map showing that location. Copy the URL (or a short link) to the Clipboard, return to index.html in your editor, then, using the URL you copied, add a link to the word **Location** on the nav bar, specifying that the file should open in a new browser tab. Save your changes.

f. Copy the `nav` element from index.html, return to hours.html in your editor, then paste the `nav` element below the `header` element. Save your changes.

g. Return to styles.css in your editor, above the main content section add a comment containing the text **site navigation**, then below the comment, create the following style rules:

- For the `nav` element with the `class` value `sitenavigation`, set the background color to rgb(241,90,36) and center-align the text.
- For p elements within the `nav` element with the `class` value `sitenavigation`, set the display type to `inline-block`, the margins to 0.4em 0.6em, and the font size to 1.6em.
- For default links within the `nav` element with the `class` value `sitenavigation`, set text color to `yellow` and remove underlines.
- For visited links within the `nav` element with the `class` value `sitenavigation`, set text color to `white`.
- For links that the mouse pointer is over or that have the focus and that are within the `nav` element with the `class` value `sitenavigation`, set text color to `yellow` and create a text shadow with 1px horizontal offset, -1px vertical offset, 0 blur, and a color of `black`.
- For links that are being clicked and that are within the `nav` element with the `class` value `sitenavigation`, set a relative position 1px down from the top and 1px over from the left.

h. Save your changes to styles.css, return to index.html in your editor, then in the opening `<h2>` tag in the `article` element, add an `id` value of `contentstart`.

i. Below the opening `<div>` tag with the `class` value `container`, add a p element with the `class` value `skipnavigation`. Within the p element, add the text **Skip navigation** and link it to the element with the `id` value `contentstart`. Save your changes, then repeat Steps h and i for hours.html.

Independent Challenge 1 (continued)

j. Return to styles.css in your editor, then above the `header` section, add a comment containing the text **skip navigation link**. Below it, add the following style rules:
- For the `p` element with the `class` value `skipnavigation`, set margins to 0.
- For `a` elements within the `p` element with the `class` value `skipnavigation`, set an absolute position -10000px from the left.
- For `a` elements with the focus that are within the `p` element with the `class` value `skipnavigation`, set text color to `black`, background color to `white`, set a relative position 0.4em from the top and right, set the `left` value to `auto`, and set a z-index of 2.

k. In the print styles section, add a style rule before the `@page` rule that removes `nav` elements from the layout for printed output.

l. Save your changes, open index.html in a browser, then compare it to **FIGURE F-24**.

m. Test all the links on both index.html and hours.html, test the Skip navigation link using a keyboard, then create a print preview and verify that the nav bar is not displayed and the content is displayed as black text on a white background.

n. Validate the code for your web pages and style sheet.

FIGURE F-24

Independent Challenge 2

As you continue developing the website for the Murfreesboro Regional Soccer League, you create links between pages as well as links to anchors. You also incorporate features to make the site navigation more accessible.

a. In your editor, open the file HTM_F-13.html from the IC2 folder where you store your Data Files for this unit, save it as **index.html**, then repeat to save the file HTM_F-14.html as **started.html**, HTM_F-15.html as **schedule.html**, and HTM_F-16.css as **styles.css**.

b. Within the comment section at the top of each file, enter your first and last names and today's date, then save your changes.

c. Return to index.html in your editor, then below the `header` element add a `nav` element with a `class` value of `sitenavigation`.

d. Within the `nav` element, create 4 `p` elements containing the text **Home, Getting Started, Schedules**, and **Field Location**. Link the text Home to index.html, Getting Started to started.html, and Schedules to schedule.html.

e. In your browser, navigate to a map service, then open a map showing 515 Cherry Lane Drive, Murfreesboro, Tennessee. Copy the URL (or a short link) to the Clipboard, return to index.html in your editor, then add a link to the phrase Field Location on the nav bar using the URL you copied, specifying that the file should open in a new browser tab. Save your changes.

f. Copy the `nav` element from index.html, then paste it below the `header` element in started.html and schedule.html. Save your changes to both files.

g. Return to styles.css in your editor, above the main content section add a comment containing the text **site navigation**, then below the comment, create the following style rules:
- For the `nav` element with the `class` value `sitenavigation`, set padding to 2%, width to 25%, position to `absolute`, left to 0, and the background color to `#c8f098`.
- For `p` elements within the `nav` element with the `class` value `sitenavigation`, set the bottom margin to 0.6em, the padding to 0.2em, the background color to `black`, and the font weight to `bold`.

Independent Challenge 2 (continued)

- For default links within the nav element with the class value sitenavigation, set text color to white and remove underlines.
- For visited links within the nav element with the class value sitenavigation, set text color to #c8f098.
- For links that the mouse pointer is over or that have the focus and that are within the nav element with the class value sitenavigation, set text color to yellow.
- For links that are being clicked and that are within the nav element with the class value sitenavigation, set a relative position 1px down from the top and 1px over from the left.

h. Save your changes to styles.css, return to schedule.html, add the id value red to the first h3 element, then repeat for the remaining 3 h3 elements using the id values blue, green, and yellow.

i. Above the first h3 element, create a nav element with the class value pagenavigation.

j. Within the new nav element, add 4 p elements containing the text **Red**, **Blue**, **Green**, and **Yellow**. Link the text of each p element to the corresponding h3 element using its id value.

k. Save your changes, return to styles.css, then above the footer section create a comment containing the text page navigation. Below the comment, add the following style rules:

- For the nav element with the class value pagenavigation, set the left margin to 1em and the left padding to 7%.
- For p elements within the nav element with the class value pagenavigation, set display type to inline-block, margins to 0.4em 0.4em 1em, padding to 0.4em, the background color to #c8f098 and add a 1px solid black border.
- For default links within the nav element with the class value pagenavigation, remove the underline and set the text color to black.
- For links that have the mouse pointer over them or that have the focus and that are within the nav element with the class value pagenavigation, set the text color to red.

l. Return to index.html in your editor, then in the opening <h2> tag in the article element, add an id value of contentstart.

m. Below the opening <div> tag with the class value container, add a p element with the class value skipnavigation. Within the p element, add the text **Skip navigation** and link it to the element with the id value contentstart. Save your changes.

n. Repeat Steps l and m for started.html and for schedule.html.

o. Return to styles.css in your editor, then above the header section, add a comment containing the text **skip navigation link**. Below it, add the following style rules:

- For the a element within the p element with the class value skipnavigation, set an absolute position -10000px from the left.
- For the a element with the focus that is within the p element with the class value skipnavigation, set the left value to auto, position the element 0.2em from the top and right, set text color to black, background color to white, and set a z-index of 2.

p. In the print styles section, add a style rule before the first existing rule that positions the article element 0px from the left, then add a style rule before the @page rule that removes nav elements from the layout for printed output.

q. Save your changes, open schedule.html in a browser, then compare it to FIGURE F-25.

r. Test all the links on index.html, started.html, and schedule.html, test the Skip navigation link using a keyboard, then create a print preview and verify that the nav bar is not displayed, the article element is positioned at the left edge of the container, and all content is displayed as black text on a white background.

s. Validate the code for your web pages and style sheet.

FIGURE F-25

Independent Challenge 3

As you continue your work on the website for Hotel Natoma, you incorporate links between pages as well as to external websites, and incorporate navigational accessibility features.

a. In your editor, open the file HTM_F-17.html from the IC3 folder where you store your Data Files for this unit, save it as **index.html**, then repeat to save the file HTM_F-18.html as **nearby.html**, and HTM_F-19.css as **styles.css**.

b. Within the comment section at the top of each file, enter your first and last names and today's date, then save your changes.

c. Return to index.html in your editor, then below the `header` element add a nav element with a `class` value of `sitenavigation`.

d. Within the `nav` element, create 3 p elements containing the text **Home**, **What's Nearby**, and **Location**. Link the text Home to index.html and What's Nearby to nearby.html. (*Hint*: Replace the curly apostrophe in What's Nearby with the character reference `&rsquo;`.)

e. In your browser, navigate to a map service, then, using the address in the `footer` element of index.html, open a map showing that location. Copy the URL (or a short link) to the Clipboard, return to index.html in your editor, then, using the URL you copied, add a link to the word **Location** on the nav bar, specifying that the file should open in a new browser tab. Save your changes.

f. Copy the `nav` element from index.html, return to nearby.html in your editor, then paste the `nav` element below the `header` element. Save your changes.

g. Return to styles.css in your editor, above the main content section add a comment containing the text **site navigation**, then below the comment, create the following style rules:

   - For the nav element with the `class` value `sitenavigation`, set the width to 20%, padding to 2%, and float the element on the left.
   - For p elements within the nav element with the `class` value `sitenavigation`, set the bottom margin to 0.5em.
   - For default links within the nav element with the `class` value `sitenavigation`, set text color to `white`, the font weight to bold, and remove underlines.
   - For visited links within the nav element with the `class` value `sitenavigation`, set text color to `#ddd`.
   - For links that the mouse pointer is over or that have the focus and that are within the nav element with the `class` value `sitenavigation`, create a text shadow with 0 horizontal offset, 0 vertical offset, 5px blur, and a color of `#082008`.
   - For links that are being clicked and that are within the nav element with the `class` value `sitenavigation`, set a relative position 1px down from the top and 1px over from the left.

h. Save your changes to styles.css, return to index.html in your editor, then in the opening `<p>` tag in the `article` element, add an id value of `contentstart`.

i. Below the opening `<div>` tag with the `class` value `container`, add a p element with the `class` value `skipnavigation`. Within the p element, add the text **Skip navigation** and link it to the element with the id value `contentstart`. Save your changes.

j. Repeat Steps h and i for nearby.html, adding the id value to the h2 element.

k. Return to styles.css in your editor, then above the `header` section, add a comment containing the text **skip navigation** link. Below it, add the following style rules:

   - For a elements within the p element with the `class` value `skipnavigation`, set an absolute position -10000px from the left.
   - For a elements with the focus that are within the p element with the `class` value `skipnavigation`, set the position 0.2em from the left and 0.2em from the top, set the background color to `linen`, set the text color to `#082008`, and set a z-index of 2.

l. In the print styles section, add a style rule before the existing first style rule that sets `float` to `none` for the `article` element and sets its width to 100%, then add another style rule before the `@page` rule that removes `nav` elements from the layout for printed output.

Independent Challenge 3 (continued)

m. Save your changes, open nearby.html in a browser, then compare it to **FIGURE F-26**.

n. Test all the links on both index.html and nearby. html, test the Skip navigation link using a keyboard, then create a print preview and verify that the nav bar is not displayed, the article element is positioned at the left edge of the container, and all content is displayed as black text on a white background.

o. Validate the code for your web pages and style sheet.

FIGURE F-26

Independent Challenge 4—Explore

You continue your work building the website for Eating Well in Season by adding site navigation and accessibility features to existing pages.

a. In your editor, open the file HTM_F-20.html from the IC4 folder where you store your Data Files for this unit, save it as **index.html**, then repeat to save the file HTM_F-21.html as **sources.html**, HTM_F-22.html as **menus.html**, and HTM_F-23.css as **styles.css**.

b. Within the comment section at the top of each file, enter your first and last names and today's date, then save your changes.

c. Return to index.html in your editor, then below the `header` element create a `nav` element with links to the files index.html, sources.html, and menus.html. Copy the `nav` element to sources.html and menus.html, then save your changes to all 3 files.

d. Return to styles.css in your editor, above the main content section add a comment containing the text **site navigation**, then below the comment, create style rules to do the following:

- Set the background color of the `nav` element to black and center text within it.
- Use the inline-block display type for p elements within the nav element and add a 4px solid black border to each p element.
- Use the inline-block display type for each a element within the nav element and set the padding to 0.2em 0.8em.
- Set the default text color for links to `rgb(246,224,65)` and remove underlines from links.
- Set the text color for visited links to `#eee`.
- Set the text color for links with the mouse pointer over them or for links with the focus to black, with a background color of `rgb(246,224,65)`.
- Add the visual effect of a button being pushed to links that are being clicked.

e. Save your changes, then return to index.html in your editor. Below the opening `<div>` tag with the `class` value `container`, create a link with the text **Skip navigation** and link it to the first element nested within the article element. Save your changes, then repeat for sources.html and menus.html.

f. Return to styles.css in your editor, then above the `header` section, add a comment containing the text **skip navigation link**. Below it, add the following style rules for the skip navigation link you created:

- Position the link absolutely and out of the visible range of the page.
- When the link has the focus, give it a 2px solid black border, position it 0.2em from the left and 0.2em from the top of the containing element, set the background color to `white`, set the text color to `black`, and set a z-index of 2.

g. In the print styles section, add a style rule before the `@page` rule that removes `nav` elements from the layout for printed output.

Independent Challenge 4—Explore (continued)

h. Save your changes, open index.html in a browser, then compare it to FIGURE F-27.

i. Test all the links on index.html, sources.html, and menus.html, test the Skip navigation link using a keyboard, then create a print preview and verify that the nav bar is not displayed, the article element is positioned at the left edge of the container, and all content is displayed as black text on a white background.

j. Validate the code for your web pages and style sheet.

k. Install screen reader software and learn to use it.

- **Windows:** Download the free NVDA screen reader from nvaccess.org, then follow the instructions at http://community.nvda-project.org/documentation/userGuide.html to install and learn to use it. You do not have to make a donation to use the software for a trial run, although if you plan to use the software on a regular basis, you should consider donating. To turn off the program if it starts automatically, press [Insert] or [Caps Lock] + Q, then when you are prompted whether to end the program, select Yes, then Enter.

- **Mac:** Open System Preferences, click Accessibility, click VoiceOver, click the Enable VoiceOver box. In the dialog box that opens, click Learn More or Learn VoiceOver, then complete the tutorial to learn to use it.

l. Navigate index.html using your screen reader software, moving up and down within the page, and activating each link in the page. Open a new document in a word processor, then save it with the name **ScreenReaderSummary** to the IC4 folder where you save your files for this unit. Enter your name and today's date in the document, then write descriptions of 3 aspects of navigating the web with a screen reader that surprised you. For each aspect, describe what you were trying to do, how you would do that using a mouse, the steps required to complete it with a screen reader, and what part of the experience you found most surprising. Save your changes.

FIGURE F-27

Visual Workshop

In your text editor, open the file HTM_F-24.html from the VW directory where you store your Data Files for this unit and save it as **index.html**. Repeat to save HTM_F-25.html as **events.html**, HTM_F-26.html as **releases.html**, and HTM_F-27.css as **styles.css**. Add your first and last names and today's date to the comment section at the top of each file, then save your changes. Add a nav bar to all 3 web pages, formatting the default, visited, hover, and focus states as shown in FIGURE F-28, and adding a simulated push button effect for the active state. Link the first 3 nav bar links to the relevant pages in the website, and link the text *Location* to a map showing the business location listed at the bottom of the page that opens in a new tab. Create a skip navigation link for each document that is visible only when it has the focus and takes users to the first element in the main page content when selected. Edit the media query for printed output to exclude the navigation bars from printed output. Validate your HTML and CSS code. FIGURE F-28 shows the completed version of events.html.

FIGURE F-28

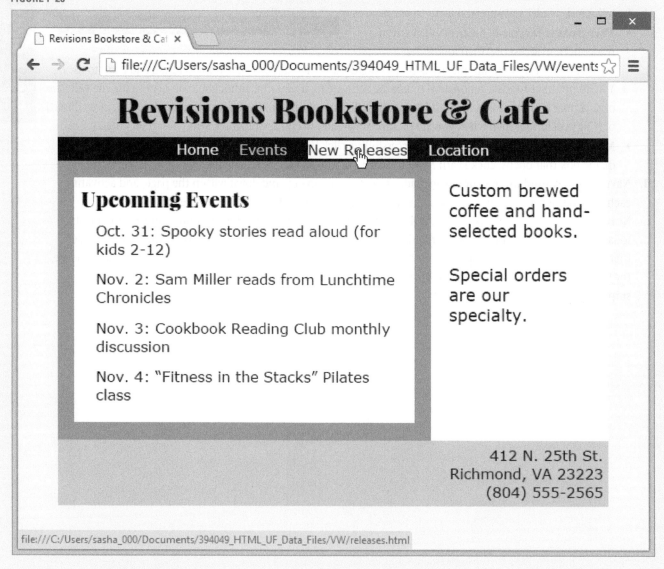

Inserting and Working with Images

CASE Your design colleagues at Lakeland Reed Bed & Breakfast have provided a logo image and several other graphics for the website you are creating. In this unit, you add the HTML and CSS code to incorporate these images into the site.

Unit Objectives

After completing this unit, you will be able to:

- Evaluate image file types
- Insert images
- Insert a background image
- Mark images as figures
- Create a figure caption

- Use images as links
- Create an image map
- Define additional hotspots
- Add a favicon and touch icons

Files You Will Need

 L   14 files   IC3   16 files

 SR   13 files   IC4   12 files

 IC1   11 files   VW   9 files

 IC2   11 files

For specific filenames, see Filenames_G.pdf in the Unit G Data Files folder.

Evaluate Image File Types

Learning
Outcomes
• Describe graphics
  file types
• Describe image
  sizing
  considerations

You can use HTML to incorporate images into your web pages and specify CSS properties to affect the way user agents display the images. Just as you can link to an external style sheet, you can add an image to a web page by linking to a separate image file, as illustrated in FIGURE G-1. **CASE** ▶ *As you prepare to incorporate graphics into the website for Lakeland Reeds Bed & Breakfast, you review the basics of images in HTML documents.*

DETAILS

To create optimal graphics for the web, it's important to understand a few concepts:

QUICK TIP
Both PNG and GIF
support transparent
pixels, allowing the
page background or
other elements to
show through parts
of an image. JPEG
does not support
transparency.

• **File types**

Images can be represented electronically in two ways: as bitmaps or as vectors. While a **bitmap image** represents an image as a grid of dots and specifies the color of each dot, a **vector graphic** encodes the appearance of a graphic as geometric shapes. Many file formats are available that render bitmap or vector representations in different ways. The three most widely used formats on the web are all different types of bitmap encoding. The **JPEG** or **JPG** format, named for the Joint Photographic Experts Group that created it, is optimized for images that contain many colors, such as photographs. **PNG**, short for portable network graphics, works best for art that contains a limited number of colors and areas with defined borders between areas. **GIF**, an abbreviation for graphics interchange format, is an older format with similar uses to PNG. An image in GIF format is generally larger than the same image in PNG format, and the GIF format supports fewer features than PNG, so PNG is generally preferred over GIF.

Browsers have long supported bitmap formats, but not vector graphics. However, all modern browsers support the **Scalable Vector Graphics (SVG)** format, which is optimal for encoding line art. Unlike bitmap formats like JPEG, which encode graphics at specific dimensions, an SVG file can be displayed at different dimensions with no decrease in quality. The only major browser that does not support SVG is IE8, so, if you need to maintain support for IE8 users, you should avoid use of SVG images.

• **Resolution and size**

When using any bitmap file formats, including JPEG, PNG, and GIF, it's important that an image is created and formatted with its use on the website in mind. All bitmap images are created to be displayed at a set resolution and size. **Resolution**, measured in **dots per inch (dpi)**, specifies how close the dots in the bitmap should appear on the output. While the standard for display on a monitor is 72 dpi, other media have different standards: for example, many home and office printers can print at 2400 dpi or greater. While a higher dpi image provides more detail, it also creates a file with a greater file size and takes up extra room on a web page. For this reason, it's important to save an image specifically for use on the web in a format and size that minimizes download time and ensures that the image fits in the page layout.

The size of a bitmap image is measured in **pixels**, which are the individual dots that make up the image. Every bitmap image is created with a specific length and width. While a vector graphic can be scaled larger or smaller with no change in quality, bitmap graphics display optimally only at their original, or **native**, length and width. As FIGURE G-2 illustrates, scaling a larger bitmap to a smaller size unnecessarily increases the amount of data users have to download. While scaling a smaller image to a larger size decreases the amount of data that users have to download, it also results in markedly poor image quality. For this reason, it's important that designers create graphics at the precise dimensions required for a layout, in addition to generating them with the correct resolution for the web.

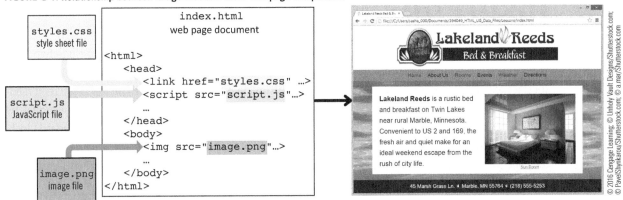

FIGURE G-2: Balancing bitmap file size and resolution

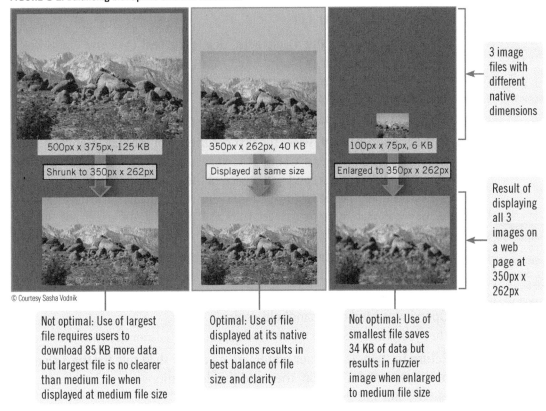

© Courtesy Sasha Vodnik

3 image files with different native dimensions

Result of displaying all 3 images on a web page at 350px x 262px

Not optimal: Use of largest file requires users to download 85 KB more data but largest file is no clearer than medium file when displayed at medium file size

Optimal: Use of file displayed at its native dimensions results in best balance of file size and clarity

Not optimal: Use of smallest file saves 34 KB of data but results in fuzzier image when enlarged to medium file size

Assessing the future of SVG

The most widely supported graphics formats—GIF, JPEG, and PNG—require external files created with image editors. SVG graphics, however, are written in a markup language similar to XML. As support for the format grows, you will be able to create simple graphics like you create style sheets—that is, by creating external documents in a text editor and linking them to your web pages. Browser makers are also beginning to incorporate support for SVG code within HTML documents, meaning that eventually you will have the option to embed graphics like you embed CSS. SVG is supported by all major browsers, but not IE8, so if it's important that your site be compatible with IE8, you should use other graphics formats instead.

Insert Images

Learning
Outcomes
• Add an image to a
web page
• Specify alt text for
an image

You add an image to an HTML document using the one-sided `img` element, which must include two attributes. The value of the `src` attribute is the path and filename of the image file to display. The `alt` attribute specifies text, known as **alt text**, to display in case the image is unavailable or is to be read by screen readers. TABLE G-1 details attributes for the `img` element. Like the `span` element, `img` is an inline element by default. You can nest an `img` element in a block-level element and align it horizontally using standard block-level alignment techniques. **CASE** ▶ *You add the Lakeland Reeds logo in place of the heading at the top of the page. You also replace the bullets separating the sections of the contact information with decorative graphics.*

STEPS

1. In your text editor, open HTM_G-1.html from the Lessons folder where you store your Data Files for this unit, save it as index.html, then repeat to save HTM_G-2.html as rooms.html, and HTM_G-3.css as styles.css

2. In the comment at the top of each file, enter your name and today's date where indicated, then save the files

QUICK TIP
Values for the width
and height
attributes are always
in pixels, so you do
not specify units.

3. In index.html, locate the `h1` element, delete the text Lakeland Reeds Bed & Breakfast, leaving the `<h1>` and `</h1>` tags, then between the `<h1>` tags, type
   `<img src="images/lakeland.gif" width="659" height="165" alt="Lakeland Reeds Bed and Breakfast">`
   Image files for a website are commonly stored in a separate folder to keep the files organized.

4. In the `footer` element, select the first occurrence of the character code `&bull;`, replace it with `<img src="images/flourish.gif" width="16" height="16" alt="">`, then repeat to replace the second occurrence of the character code with the same HTML code
   Because these images are merely decorative and do not add information to the page, you use an empty value for the `alt` attribute to let screen readers know that they can skip these elements. FIGURE G-3 shows the code containing the `img` elements you added.

QUICK TIP
When an `img`
element is the only
child of a parent
element, browsers
sometimes render
the image with extra
space below it. If
removing this space
is important, you can
use the declaration
`display: block;`
for the `img`.

5. Save your changes, then open index.html in a browser
   The logo image replaces the main heading text at the top of the page and the decorative graphic images replace the bullets in the footer, as shown in FIGURE G-4.

6. Open index.html on a handheld device
   The layout is narrowed to fit the device width, and then is narrowed further to fit the width of the logo.

7. Return to styles.css in your editor, create a new style rule for the `img` element at the end of the reset styles section, then add the declarations `max-width: 100%;`, `height: auto;`, and `width: auto;`
   The first declaration ensures that all images, including the logo image, are displayed no wider than the browser width, and the second declaration tells browsers to proportionally resize the height of an image if the width is resized. The third declaration is required for compatibility with IE8.

8. In the style rule that sets border, padding, and margin to 0 in the reset styles section, add the `img` selector to the list of selectors
   FIGURE G-5 shows the changes to the reset styles section of the style sheet.

QUICK TIP
Some layouts with
images don't work
well on both large
and small screens.
Developers some-
times create different
layouts for different
sizes, a practice
known as responsive
design.

9. Save your changes, then refresh or reload index.html on your handheld device
   The logo image is resized to fit the screen width, and the remaining page content fits the screen.

10. Repeat Steps 3-6 to add the logo and decorative graphic to the corresponding elements in rooms.html, then preview your changes on desktop and mobile browsers

```
23          <header>
24              <h1><img src="images/lakeland.gif" width="659" height="165" alt="Lakeland
25              Reeds Bed and Breakfast"></h1>
26          </header>
```

```
43          <footer>
44              <p>45 Marsh Grass Ln. <img src="images/flourish.gif" width="16" height="16"
45              alt=""> Marble, MN 55764 <img src="images/flourish.gif" width="16"
46              height="16" alt=""> (218) 555-5253</p>
47          </footer>
```

FIGURE G-4: Main web page with images inserted

Main heading text replaced by logo image

Bullet characters replaced by decorative graphics

© 2016 Cengage Learning; © Unholy Vault Designs/Shutterstock.com

FIGURE G-5: Reset styles for `img` element

```
10   /* reset styles */
11   html {
12       font-size: 16px;
13   }
14   a, article, body, div, footer, header, h1, h2, h3, img, nav, p {
15       border: 0;
16       padding: 0;
17       margin: 0;
18   }
19   img {
20       max-width: 100%;
21       height: auto;
22       width: auto;
23   }
```

TABLE G-1: Attributes for the `img` element

attribute	value
src	path and filename for image file to display
alt	text to display or read in place of image
height width	native height and width of image file in pixels

© 2016 Cengage Learning

Inserting and Working with Images

HTML5 & CSS3

Insert a Background Image

Learning
Outcomes
• Specify a back-
  ground image
• Specify a fallback
  background color

In addition to specifying a color as the background for a web page or web page element, you can provide a path and filename for a background image using the `background-image` property. As with background colors, it's important to choose a background image that provides contrast with other web page elements, especially text. If a background image does not fill the entire element, by default browsers **tile** it, meaning that, like tiles on a floor or wall, the image is displayed repeatedly both across and down the element to fill it up. **TABLE G-2** describes additional properties you can use to change the way a background image is displayed. **CASE** ▸ *The designers have provided a background image for the* `article` *element. Because the* `article` *element's content is within a separate* `div` *element with its own background color, the background image will be visible only at the edges of the page, maintaining readability.*

STEPS

1. **In your browser, open the file lake.jpg from the images folder**

   The image is small and square. This type of image, known as a **seamless image**, is designed to look like a single, uninterrupted image when tiled.

2. **Return to styles.css in your editor**

3. **In the `article` style rule, insert a blank line before the closing `}`, then indent and type**
   `background: url("images/lake.jpg");`

   When you specify a background image, the value for the `background` or `background-image` property always starts with the text `url`. The relative path, if necessary, and the filename for the background image are enclosed in parentheses and either single or double quotes.

4. **In the `background-color` declaration above the code you just entered, change the property name `background-color` to `background`**

   Even when you specify a background image, you should also continue to specify a background color as a fallback for user agents that don't display images, or for situations where the background image file is unavailable. When declarations conflict, the one that occurs later in the rule takes precedence. For example, when you specify both background color and background image using the shorthand `background` property, the final property that a browser can render is used, and the other is ignored. If a user agent is unable to load the image specified by the second `background` property, it falls back to the preceding `background` declaration and displays the background color instead. **FIGURE G-6** shows the code for the background color and image.

5. **Save your work, then reload index.html in your browser**

   As **FIGURE G-7** shows, the background image appears behind the `article` element. The image is repeated vertically and horizontally to fill the entire length and height of the element. The element contents are within a `div` element that has a background color of `ivory`; this prevents the background image from appearing behind the text and preserves readability.

6. **Return to styles.css in your editor, then in the print styles section at the end of the document and in the `body, h1, article, footer` style rule, replace the `background-color` property with `background`**

   FIGURE G-8 shows the edited code.

7. **Save your work, reload index.html in your browser, then open a print preview**

   The `article` element is displayed with a white background instead of a background image.

FIGURE G-6: Code for background color and background image

```
85   /* main content */
86   article {
87       margin: 0 auto;
88       padding: 1.4em;
89       background: #7eccec;
90       background: url("images/lake.jpg");
91   }
```

background-color property name changed to background
to serve as fallback for declaration that follows

background declaration added for
background image

FIGURE G-7: Main web page with tiled background image

Nested div
element has a
background
color of
ivory to
provide
contrast for
text

Background
image repeated
vertically and
horizontally to
cover entire
article
element

© 2016 Cengage Learning; © a.mar/Shutterstock.com

FIGURE G-8: background-color declaration changed to background in print styles section

```
147  /* print styles */
148  @media print {
149      body, h1, article, footer {
150          color: rgb(0,0,0);
151          background: rgb(255,255,255);
152      }
```

TABLE G-2: Properties that affect an element's background

property	specifies
background-attachment	whether a background image scrolls with document content (scroll, the default), scrolls only with element content (local), or does not scroll (fixed)
background-blend-mode	how overlapping background images blend with each other and with background color, using one or more keywords
background-clip	whether a background image extends only behind element content (content-box), up to the inner edge of the border (padding-box), or to the outer edge of the border (border-box, the default)
background-color	a background color using a color keyword or a hex, RGB, RGBa, HSL, or HSLa value
background-image	an image file to use as the background for an element with the syntax url("path/filename")
background-origin	whether a background image starts only behind element content (content-box), at the inner edge of the border (padding-box), or at the outer edge of the border (border-box, the default)
background-position	the position within an element of the edges of a background image using a combination of values and keywords
background-repeat	whether a background image is repeated horizontally, vertically, both, or neither, using one or more keywords
background-size	the size of a background image with keywords, lengths, or percentages
background	values for one or more properties related to background listed in a specific order

© 2016 Cengage Learning

Mark Images as Figures

HTML5 includes the semantic `figure` element to mark images that add information to a web page. To decide whether an image should be marked as a `figure`, think about whether the basic information conveyed by the page would still be complete if the image were not shown. If so, the image should be marked as a `figure`. For instance, a picture, chart, or map illustrating the topic of a paragraph would be marked as a figure because, while it illustrates the paragraph content, it isn't absolutely necessary for a user to understand the information. However, a logo image would not be marked as a `figure` because it's integral to conveying the overall subject of a page. **CASE** ▶ *You add a* `figure` *element for each room on the Rooms page.*

STEPS

1. Return to rooms.html in your editor, on a new line below the opening tag for the h3 element containing the text *Reed Room*, indent and type `<figure>`, press [Enter] twice, then indent and type `</figure>`

2. On the blank line between the opening and closing `<figure>` tags, indent and then type `<img src="images/reed.jpg" width="370" height="392" alt="a carpeted room with a high sloping ceiling, two small bright windows, and a two-person bed with a bedside table and lamp on each side">`

3. Repeat Steps 1 and 2 to add opening and closing `<figure>` tags below the h3 headings *Sun Room* and *Treehouse*, then on the blank line in each element, add the img elements shown in FIGURE G-9

   FIGURE G-9 shows the code for the figure and img elements added to rooms.html.

QUICK TIP

If the width of a
`figure` element is
not specified with a
percentage value,
you use the declara-
tion `max-width:`
`100%;` to ensure
that the element
automatically scales
to fit smaller screens.

4. Save your changes, return to styles.css in your editor, then, at the bottom of the main content section, add a style rule that uses the `article figure` selector with the declarations `max-width: 100%;`, `margin-left: 2em;`, and `float:right;`

5. Scroll to the reset styles section, then add the `figure` selector to the list of selectors in the style rule that sets border, padding, and margin to 0

6. Scroll to the main content section, add the declaration `overflow: auto;` to the `article div` style rule

   Because a floated element is not used in calculating the height of its parent element and the Treehouse image is taller than the text content it floats next to, the bottom of the parent element comes before the bottom of the image. Setting the `overflow` property to `auto` extends the height of the parent element to include the entire floated element, which will cause the ivory background of the `article` element to extend the entire length of the image. FIGURE G-10 shows the changes to the style sheet.

7. Save your changes, then refresh or reload rooms.html in your browser

   The three images you added within `figure` elements are floated to the right below the h3 elements. FIGURE G-11 shows one image as rendered by a browser.

Obtaining permission for image use

Although it's possible to find and copy images from the web for use on your own web pages, it's important to make sure you have permission to use a given image before incorporating it into your designs. In addition to avoiding potential legal action for unauthorized use of someone else's work, it's a show of respect to photographers and designers to ask for permission to use their work. For small projects, a photographer or designer may allow use in return for credit and a link to their site; for larger professional sites, a photographer or designer usually requires a use fee and agreed-on terms of use. If you're hiring a designer to create artwork for your website, make sure your agreement specifies how long and in what context you or your organization may use the work.

FIGURE G-9: `figure` and `img` elements added to rooms.html

```
38              <h3 id="reed">Reed Room</h3>
39              <figure>
40                  <img src="images/reed.jpg" width="370" height="392" alt="a carpeted room
41                  with a high sloping ceiling, two small bright windows, and a two-person
42                  bed with a bedside table and lamp on each side">
43              </figure>
44              <p>This first-floor room looks out over the reeds on the edge of the lake and
45              the water beyond.</p>
46              <p>1 queen bed and 1 twin bed.</p>
47              <h3 id="sun">Sun Room</h3>
48              <figure>
49                  <img src="images/sun.jpg" width="370" height="278" alt="room with a
50                  hardwood floor, bright windows on two sides, and a two-person bed with a
51                  bedside table and lamp on each side">
52              </figure>
53              <p>With windows on three sides, the sunlight in this second-floor room
54              supports a large selection of houseplants.</p>
55              <p>1 full bed.</p>
56              <h3 id="tree">Treehouse</h3>
57              <figure>
58                  <img src="images/tree.jpg" width="370" height="247" alt="a large room with
59                  a hardwood floor, a tall window overlooking trees, a two-person bed with a
60                  single bedside table, and a padded chair next to the window">
61              </figure>
62              <p>A winding staircase takes you to your own private getaway at the top of
```

FIGURE G-10: Style rules for `figure` elements

```
14    a, article, body, div, figure, footer, header, h1, h2, h3, img, nav, p {
15        border: 0;
16        padding: 0;
17        margin: 0;
18    }
```

```
92    article div {
93        max-width: 800px;
94        margin: 0 auto;
95        padding: 0 3% 1em;
96        background-color: ivory;
97        overflow: auto;
98    }
```

```
116   article p.pullquote {
117       font-size: 1.7em;
118   }
119   article figure {
120       max-width: 100%;
121       margin-left: 2em;
122       float: right;
123   }
```

FIGURE G-11: Style rules applied to `figure` elements

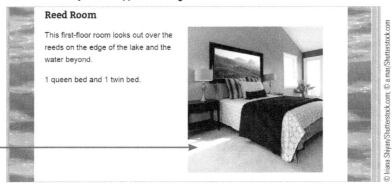

figure element
floated right

© Iriana Shiyan/Shutterstock.com; © a.mar/Shutterstock.com

Create a Figure Caption

In addition to providing alternative text for an image using the `alt` attribute, you can associate other types of text with an image. Many images benefit from a text caption that provides context, explanation, or credit. To associate caption text with an `img` element, you place the text in a `figcaption` element that is nested within the `figure` element for the image. **CASE** ▷ *Because the images on the Rooms web page are already explained by the surrounding content, you decide not to add captions to them. However, you add an image with a caption on the main page of the website.*

STEPS

1. Return to index.html in your editor, insert a new line below the opening tag for the `div` element with the `id` value `contentstart`, indent and type `<figure class="example">`, press [Enter] twice, then indent and type `</figure>`

2. On the blank line between the opening and closing `<figure>` tags, indent and then type `<img src="images/sun.jpg" width="370" height="278" alt="room with a hardwood floor, bright windows on two sides, and a two-person bed with a bedside table and lamp on each side">`

QUICK TIP
As a general rule, `alt` text should describe an image without adding additional information, but `figcaption` content can add information not provided by surrounding page content.

3. Insert a new line beneath the `<img>` tag you entered in the previous step, then indent and type `<figcaption><a href="rooms.html#sun">Sun Room</a></figcaption>`
   The `figcaption` element marks the text it contains as a caption for the associated image within the `figure` element. **FIGURE G-12** shows the code for the `figure`, `img`, and `figcaption` elements added to index.html.

4. Save your changes, then return to styles.css in your editor

5. At the bottom of the main content section, add a style rule that uses the `article figure.example` selector with the declaration `margin-top: 2em;`, then add another style rule with the `article figcaption` selector and the declaration `text-align: center;`

6. Scroll to the reset styles section, then add the `figcaption` selector to the list of selectors in the style rule that sets border, padding, and margin to 0
   FIGURE G-13 shows the changes to the style sheet.

7. Save your changes, then refresh or reload index.html in your browser
   The text *Sun Room* is centered beneath the image, as shown in **FIGURE G-14**.

Creating useful alt text

The text you provide using the `alt` attribute for an image is an important accessibility element for your website. It's also significant for users who are unable to download the image or who choose to browse without images. For graphics that include text, that text should be included in the value of the `alt` attribute, along with a description if it adds useful information. The `alt` value for photos and other graphics without text should include a description of the image. Because there are many ways to describe any given image, it's important to identify what aspect or aspects of a graphic are relevant to the web page, and then focus on those aspects. Finally, if a graphic is merely presentational and doesn't add information to the web page, include the `alt` attribute with nothing between the quotes. This lets screen readers know that the element isn't conveying information and that they can skip it, which saves blind and visually impaired users from wasting time listening to text such as "stylized bullet" repeatedly while learning nothing about the page contents.

```
34              <article>
                <div id="contentstart">
figcaption        <figure class="example">
element nested       <img src="images/sun.jpg" width="370" height="278" alt="room with a
within figure         hardwood floor, bright windows on two sides, and a two-person bed with a
element to provide    bedside table and lamp on each side">
caption for sibling   <figcaption><a href="rooms.html#sun">Sun Room</a></figcaption>
img element        </figure>
                <p class="pullquote"><span class="accent">Lakeland Reeds</span> is a rustic
```

FIGURE G-13: Style rules for `figure` element with `example` `class` value and for `figcaption` element

```
14    a, article, body, div, figcaption, figure, footer, header, h1, h2, h3, img, nav, p {
15       border: 0;
16       padding: 0;
17       margin: 0;
18    }
```

```
118   article figure {
119      max-width: 100%;
120      margin-left: 2em;
121      float: right;
122   }
123   article figure.example {
124      margin-top: 2em;
125   }
126   article figcaption {
127      text-align: center;
128   }
```

FIGURE G-14: Figure caption in main web page

© PavelShynkarou/Shutterstock.com; © a.mar/Shutterstock.com

Lakeland Reeds is a rustic bed and breakfast on Twin Lakes near rural Marble, Minnesota. Convenient to US 2 and 169, the fresh air and quiet make for an ideal weekend escape from the rush of city life.

Sun Room

Content of `figcaption` element displayed below `img` element

Understanding the `title` attribute

You can also specify additional information about an image using the `title` attribute, which is supported by the `img` and `figure` elements as well as most other HTML elements. Most visual user agents display the value of the `title` attribute as floating text when a user moves the mouse pointer over the associated element. However, modern desktop browsers do not provide access to the `title` value when navigating with a keyboard. In addition, mobile browsers do not support the display of the `title` attribute on touchscreen devices. For this reason, the W3C does not recommend that web developers use the `title` attribute until browser makers provide access for all users.

HTML5 & CSS3

Use Images as Links

You can add a link to an image in an HTML document by nesting the img element in an a element. Many websites add a link to the logo image on each page that returns the user to the main page of the site when the logo is clicked or touched. **CASE** ▶ *You link the logo image on the Rooms page back to index.html to provide a shortcut for visitors to the site. You also link the image of the Sun Room on the main web page to the information about that room on rooms.html.*

STEPS

1. **Return to rooms.html in your editor**

2. **Position the insertion point after the opening <h1> tag and before the <img> tag in the header element, then type <a href="index.html">**

3. **Position the insertion point between the closing > of the <img> tag and the closing </h1> tag, type </a>, then save your changes**

   FIGURE G-15 shows the added code.

4. **Return to index.html in your editor**

5. **Position the insertion point before the opening < of the <img> tag for the sun.jpg image in the article element, then type <a href="rooms.html#sun">**

6. **Position the insertion point after the closing > of the <img> tag, type </a>, then save your changes**

   FIGURE G-16 shows the added code.

TROUBLE

If the Rooms page opens but the Sun Room information is not at the top of the window, the window may be too tall for that section to scroll to the top. Reduce the height of your browser window, click your browser's Back button, then repeat Step 9.

7. **Refresh or reload rooms.html in your browser, then move the mouse pointer over the logo image**

   The pointer becomes a pointing hand when it moves over the image as shown in **FIGURE G-17**, indicating that the image is a link.

8. **Click the logo image at the top of the page**

   The main page opens.

9. **Click the Sun Room image**

   The Rooms page opens, with the Sun Room information at the top of the browser window.

Styling an image with opacity

Recent versions of all major browsers support the CSS opacity property for img elements. The opacity property sets how transparent an element is, from 0 (fully transparent) to 1 (fully opaque, which is the default). For instance, to set 50% opacity, you use the code

```
opacity: 0.5;
```

IE8 and older versions of Internet Explorer don't support this syntax, however, and require an additional declaration using a Microsoft-specific property:

```
filter: alpha(opacity=number);
```

where *number* is a percentage from 0 (fully transparent) to 100 (fully opaque). When you decrease the opacity of an image, you make it partially transparent. This can be useful if you want to increase the contrast between the image and other page elements or simply to alter the image to more closely match a site's design.

FIGURE G-15: a element enclosing `img` element for logo

```
22        <header>
23            <h1><a href="index.html"><img src="images/lakeland.gif" width="659" height="165"
24            alt="Lakeland Reeds Bed and Breakfast"></a></h1>
25        </header>
```

Opening and closing <a>
tags enclose <img> tag

FIGURE G-16: a element enclosing `img` element for Sun Room photo

```
36        <figure class="example">
              <a href="rooms.html#sun"><img src="images/sun.jpg" width="370"
              height="278" alt="room with a hardwood floor, bright windows on two sides,
              and a two-person bed with a bedside table and lamp on each side"></a>
              <figcaption><a href="rooms.html#sun">Sun Room</a></figcaption>
41        </figure>
```

Opening and
closing <a> tags
enclose <img> tag

FIGURE G-17: Link added to logo image

Pointer changes
to pointing hand
over logo image,
indicating that
the image is
a link

Using a background image and a background color together

When you specify a background color and a background image in separate declarations using the `background` property, only one of the declarations is rendered by browsers. However, in some cases you want to apply both a background color and a background image at the same time. This is most common when your background image has some transparent pixels and you want to control the color that's visible behind the image. To apply both a background color and a background image, you use a single shorthand `background` property and specify the background image name followed by the background color, separated by a space. For instance, to use the background image sky.jpg with a background color of `#001848`, you would use the declaration `background: url("sky.jpg") #001848;`. In this case, there's no need to create a second `background` declaration, as the specified color automatically serves as a fallback for the background image.

Create an Image Map

Learning
Outcomes
• Apply an image
map to an image
• Create a rectangu-
lar hotspot

Instead of linking an entire image to a single target document, it can be useful sometimes to link different areas of a single image to different targets. You can do so by creating an **image map**, which is HTML code associated with an image that specifies one or more shapes using sets of coordinates and provides a link target for each shape. Each shape is known as a **hotspot**. You create an image map with a single `map` element, in which you nest an `area` element for each hotspot. TABLE G-3 describes commonly used attributes of the `area` element. **CASE** *You add an image showing room sizes to the Rooms page, then create an image map containing a rectangular hotspot for the Reed room.*

STEPS

1. **In your browser, open the file** imagemap.png **from the images folder in the Lessons folder where you store your Data Files for this unit**

   The image includes shapes representing the 3 rooms at Lakeland Reeds. FIGURE G-18 shows the `shape` attribute value and the `coords` attribute for the rectangular Reed Room shape and illustrates the measurement of the coordinates from the top left corner of the image.

2. **Return to** rooms.html **in your editor, scroll as needed to the** `article` **element, add a blank line above the** `h3` **element with the text** *Reed Room*, **indent and type** `<p class="imagemap">`, **press [Enter] twice, then indent and type** `</p>`

3. **Click in the blank line within the** `p` **element you just created, then indent and type**
   `<img src="images/imagemap.png" width="500" height="250" alt="">`

4. **Add a blank line below the closing** `</p>` **tag for the image map, indent and type**
   `<map name="roomsmap">`, **press [Enter] twice, then indent and type** `</map>`

5. **Click in the blank line within the** `map` **element you just created, then indent and type**
   `<area shape="rect" coords="33,21,162,211" href="#reed" alt="Reed Room">`
   The `rect` value of the `shape` attribute indicates that the shape is a rectangle. For this shape, the value of the `coords` attribute starts with the *x* value of the top left corner of the rectangle, followed by the *y* value of the top left, then the *x* value of the bottom right, and finally the *y* value of the bottom right.

6. **In the** `<img>` **tag for the imagemap.png file, click just before the closing** `>`, **press [Spacebar], then type** `usemap="#roomsmap"`
   The `usemap` attribute specifies the `name` attribute value for a `map` element as a hash link. FIGURE G-19 shows the completed code for the image map.

7. **Save your changes, return to** styles.css **in your editor, in the main content section, below the** `article p` **style rule, add a style rule using the** `article p.imagemap` **selector with the declaration** `text-align: center;`, **then add a style rule using the** `article p.imagemap img` **selector with the declarations** `border: 1px solid black;` **and** `max-width: none;`
   Setting the `max-width` property to `none` prevents browsers from resizing the image, which would mean the coordinates no longer correspond to the intended parts of the image. FIGURE G-20 shows the rules added to the style sheet.

8. **Save your changes, refresh or reload rooms.html in your browser, move the mouse pointer over the rectangle labeled** Reed Room **in the map graphic**
   The mouse pointer changes to a pointing hand when it is over the rectangle, indicating that the rectangle is a link. Notice that when the mouse pointer moves off of the rectangle, it turns back to a pointing arrow.

9. **Click the** rectangle
   The browser scrolls the page down to the Reed Room section.

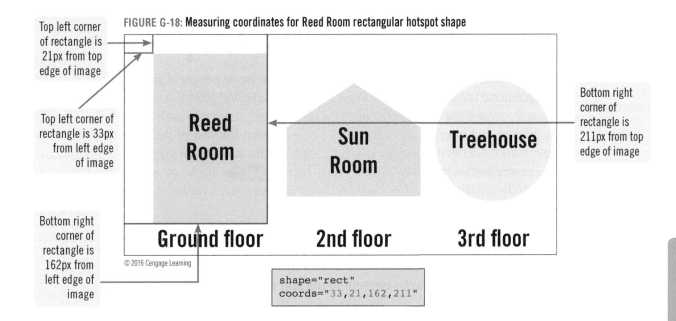

FIGURE G-18: Measuring coordinates for Reed Room rectangular hotspot shape

Top left corner of rectangle is 21px from top edge of image

Top left corner of rectangle is 33px from left edge of image

Bottom right corner of rectangle is 162px from left edge of image

Bottom right corner of rectangle is 211px from top edge of image

© 2016 Cengage Learning

```
shape="rect"
coords="33,21,162,211"
```

FIGURE G-19: `img`, `map`, and `area` elements for image map

```
38    each can accommodate an additional twin fold-out bed.</p>
39    <p class="imagemap">
40       <img src="images/imagemap.png" width="500" height="250" alt=""
41       usemap="#roomsmap">
42    </p>
43    <map name="roomsmap">
44       <area shape="rect" coords="33,21,162,211" href="#reed" alt="Reed Room">
45    </map>
46    <h3 id="reed">Reed Room</h3>
```

`usemap` attribute of `img` element specifies name value of `map` element to use as image map

`map` element contains one or more `area` elements for hotspots

`area` element with `shape` value of `rect` creates a rectangular hotspot

FIGURE G-20: Style rules for image map components

```
113   article p {
114      padding-top: 1em;
115   }
116   article p.imagemap {
117      text-align: center;
118   }
119   article p.imagemap img {
120      border: 1px solid black;
121      max-width: none;
122   }
```

Prevents image from resizing by causing browsers to use the `width` and `height` attribute values as fixed dimensions

TABLE G-3: Attributes of the `area` element

attribute	value
alt	Alternate text that describes the hotspot for users of screen readers or if the image doesn't load
coords	A comma-separated list of coordinates for the specified shape value measured from the top and left edges of the image
href	A URL, local filename, or hash link to the target document or location opened by the hotspot
shape	The value `circle` to create a circle, `poly` to create a polygon, or `rect` to create a rectangle

© 2016 Cengage Learning

Learning
Outcomes
• Create a polygonal
  hotspot
• Create a circular
  hotspot

Define Additional Hotspots

In addition to rectangular image map hotspots, you can also create polygonal and circular hotspots. To create a polygonal hotspot, you specify a shape value of poly and provide a list of coordinates for all vertices as the value of the coords attribute. To code a circular hotspot, you use the value circle for the shape attribute and specify the coordinates of the center point followed by the radius for the coords attribute. TABLE G-4 details the values for the coords attribute for each hotspot shape. FIGURE G-21 illustrates how the coordinates are measured for the circle shape. **CASE** ▶ *The image you're using for the image map depicts the Sun Room, which has 5 sides, and the Treehouse, which is circular. You add hotspots for these two rooms to the image map.*

STEPS

1. **Return to rooms.html in your editor**

2. **Insert a line below the area element in the map element, then indent and type**
   ```
   <area shape="poly" coords="258,54,335,101,335,180,184,180,184,101" href="#sun" alt="Sun Room">
   ```
   The poly value of the shape attribute indicates that the shape is a polygon, which allows you to create a triangle or a shape with more than 4 sides. For this shape, the value of the coords attribute starts with the *x* value of any vertex of the shape, followed by the *y* value of that vertex, then the *x* value of the next vertex in either direction, the *y* value of that vertex, and so on until all vertices have been specified in order.

3. **Insert a line below the area element you just created, then indent and type**
   ```
   <area shape="circle" coords="419,116,65" href="#tree" alt="Treehouse">
   ```
   The circle value of the shape attribute indicates that the shape is a circle. For this shape, the value of the coords attribute starts with the *x* value of the center of the circle, followed by the *y* value of the center, then the length of the circle's radius. FIGURE G-22 shows the final code for the image map.

4. **Save your changes, then refresh or reload rooms.html in your browser**

5. **Move the mouse pointer over the polygon labeled Sun Room in the map graphic, move the mouse pointer around the shape and on both sides of the shape border, then repeat for the circle labeled Treehouse**
   As with the Reed Room rectangle, the pointer is a pointing hand when it is over one of the shapes, as shown in FIGURE G-23, and returns to a default arrow pointer when it moves off of a shape.

6. **Click the Sun Room polygon**
   The browser scrolls the page down to the Sun Room section.

7. **Scroll back up to the image map graphic, then click the Treehouse circle**
   The browser scrolls the page down to the Treehouse section.

TABLE G-4: Values of the coords attribute for different hotspot shapes

shape value	coords value
circle	*x, y, r* where *x* and *y* are the *x* and *y* coordinates of the center point of the circle, and *r* is the radius
poly	*x1, y1, x2, y2, ...* where *x1, y1, x2, y2*, and so on are the *x* and *y* coordinates of the vertices of the polygon
rect	*x1, y1, x2, y2* where *x1* and *y1* are the *x* and *y* coordinates of the top left corner of the rectangle and *x2* and *y2* are the *x* and *y* coordinates of the bottom right corner of the rectangle

FIGURE G-21: Measuring coordinates for hotspot shapes

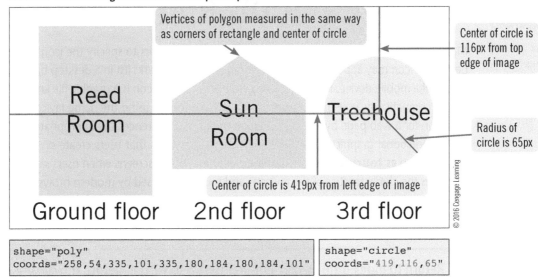

Vertices of polygon measured in the same way as corners of rectangle and center of circle

Center of circle is 116px from top edge of image

Radius of circle is 65px

Center of circle is 419px from left edge of image

Reed Room

Sun Room

Treehouse

Ground floor

2nd floor

3rd floor

© 2016 Cengage Learning

```
shape="poly"
coords="258,54,335,101,335,180,184,180,184,101"
```

```
shape="circle"
coords="419,116,65"
```

FIGURE G-22: `area` elements for polygonal and circular hotspots added

```
43        <map name="roomsmap">
44            <area shape="rect" c...
45            <area shape="poly" coords="258,54,335,101,335,180,184,180,184,101"
46            href="#sun" alt="Sun Room">
47            <area shape="circle" coords="419,116,65" href="#tree" alt="Treehouse">
48        </map>
```

`area` element with `shape` value of `poly` creates a polygonal hotspot

`area` element with `shape` value of `circle` creates a circular hotspot

FIGURE G-23: Testing link on Sun Room hotspot

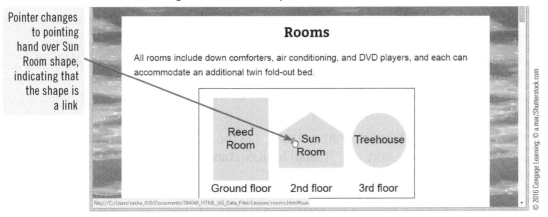

Pointer changes to pointing hand over Sun Room shape, indicating that the shape is a link

Rooms

All rooms include down comforters, air conditioning, and DVD players, and each can accommodate an additional twin fold-out bed.

Reed Room

Sun Room

Treehouse

Ground floor

2nd floor

3rd floor

file:///C:/Users/sasha_000/Documents/394049_HTML_UG_Data_Files/Lessons/rooms.html#sun

© 2016 Cengage Learning; © a.mar/Shutterstock.com

Generating hotspot coordinates

Identifying the precise coordinates for a hotspot shape can be the most challenging part of creating an image map. Using graphic design software such as Adobe Photoshop, you can identify the coordinates of any point in an image. By looking up the coordinates for each point in your image, you can create the area element for each hotspot manually. However, many tools are available that let you point and drag and identify shapes and then provide you with the shape's coordinates. GIMP, a free graphic design application, lets you generate an image map in this way. Adobe Fireworks, a paid application, supports this method as well. Additionally, some websites provide image map generation utilities for free. To locate them, use a search engine to search on the terms *free image map generator*.

Add a Favicon and Touch Icons

Learning
Outcomes
• Specify a favicon
• Specify touch
icons for iOS and
Android devices

Major browsers and operating systems allow web page authors to specify the icon associated with a web page. This icon may appear on the browser tab or the bookmarks list in a desktop browser or on the home screen of a mobile device. For desktop browsers, this custom icon is a graphic file known as a **favicon**. For widest compatibility, you create favicons with the .ico format using the name favicon.ico. You can specify a favicon for a web page by adding a link element that references the appropriate .ico file. You can also specify additional graphic files to serve as icons for shortcuts that users create on mobile devices. These icons, known as **touch icons**, are displayed on users' home screens when users save shortcuts. TABLE G-5 describes the characteristics of the favicons and touch icons used by modern browsers. **CASE** *The art department has created a favicon as well as touch icons for both iOS and Android systems. You add <link> tags to the main and Rooms pages for the Lakeland Reeds website for all three icons.*

STEPS

1. **Return to** index.html **in your editor, insert a blank line before the closing </head> tag, then indent**

QUICK TIP

The .ico format can contain multiple images, so you can create icons at all sizes listed in TABLE G-5 and include them all in the same .ico file.

2. **Type** `<link rel="shortcut icon" href="images/favicon.ico">`, **then press** [Enter]

   The rel value of shortcut icon is used to link to a favicon, which appears on the browser tab.

3. **Type** `<link rel="apple-touch-icon" href="images/apple-touch-icon.png">`, **then press** [Enter]

   The rel value of "apple-touch-icon" is used to link to a touch icon for iOS devices.

TROUBLE

Note that some browsers show favicons only for websites accessed over the Internet and don't look for the icons for local files. If you don't see the favicon, open the web page from a web server.

4. **Type** `<link rel="icon" sizes="192x192" href="images/android.png">`, **then save your changes**

   The rel value of "icon" is used to link to a touch icon for Android devices. Note that this link element should include the sizes attribute for maximum compatibility. FIGURE G-24 shows the code for the link elements inserted in the document.

5. **Reload index.html in your browser, then examine the browser tab for the Lakeland Reeds favicon, which resembles the stylized reeds in the logo image**

   FIGURE G-25 shows the favicon in a browser tab. Note that some browsers may display one of the touch icons instead, showing a dark brown background.

TROUBLE

If you're using a different smartphone or browser, follow your usual steps for adding an icon to your home screen.

6. **Open** index.html **on a smartphone or tablet, tap the** Menu button ⋮ **(Chrome for Android) or the** Share button ⬆ **(Safari for iOS), tap** Add to Home Screen, **tap** Add, **then examine the icon on your home screen**

   FIGURE G-26 shows the touch icon on the home screens of Android and iOS devices. Note that the two icons are almost identical, and simply have slightly different dimensions as described in TABLE G-5.

7. **Repeat Steps 2–6 for rooms.html**

8. **Validate the code for your web pages and your style sheet, then make changes as necessary to fix any errors**

FIGURE G-24: `link` elements for favicon and touch icons added

```
18          <link rel="stylesheet" href="styles.css">
19          <link rel="shortcut icon" href="images/favicon.ico">
20          <link rel="apple-touch-icon" href="images/apple-touch-icon.png">
21          <link rel="icon" sizes="192x192" href="images/android.png">
22      </head>
```

FIGURE G-25: Favicon displayed on desktop browser tab

Customized favicon from favicon.ico file

FIGURE G-26: Touch icons displayed on home screens of mobile devices

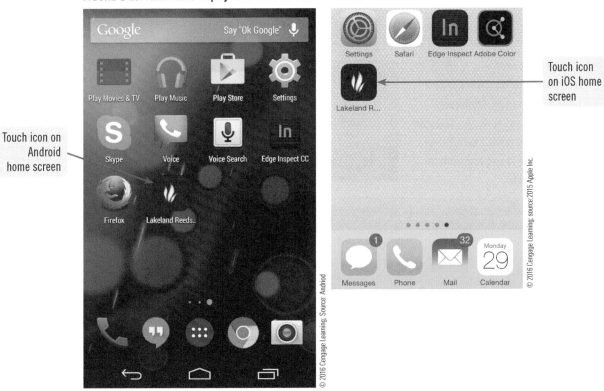

Touch icon on Android home screen

Touch icon on iOS home screen

TABLE G-5: Characteristics of favicons and touch icons

platform	format	dimensions	`link` tag
desktop (all)	.ico (all browsers) .png (all browsers except IE10 and earlier)	16px × 16px (standard resolution) 32px × 32px (high resolution) 48px × 48px (Taskbar)	`<link rel="shortcut icon" href="images/favicon.ico">`
Apple iOS	.png	180px × 180px	`<link rel="apple-touch-icon" href="images/apple-touch-icon.png">`
Google Android	.png	192px × 192px	`<link rel="icon" sizes="192x192" href="images/android.png">`

Practice

Concepts Review

Refer to FIGURE G-27 **to answer the following questions.**

FIGURE G-27

1. **Which item is an inline image?**
2. **Which item is styled by providing a url value for the** background **property?**
3. **Which item is created using the** link **element?**
4. **Which item is created using the** figcaption **element?**

Match each term with the statement that best describes it.

5. **pixel**
6. **image map**
7. **native**
8. **resolution**
9. **tile**
10. **hotspot**

    a. a term for the original dimensions of a bitmap image
    b. to display a background image repeatedly both across and down an element to fill it up
    c. a shape within an image that has its own link target
    d. specifies how close the dots in a bitmap should appear on the output
    e. one of the dots that make up a bitmap image
    f. HTML code associated with an image that specifies one or more shapes using sets of coordinates and provides a link target for each shape

Select the best answer from the list of choices.

11. Which type of image is represented as a grid of dots and their colors?

    a. vector

    b. native

    c. SVG

    d. bitmap

12. Which type of image encodes the appearance of a graphic as geometric shapes?

    a. bitmap

    b. vector

    c. GIF

    d. JPEG

13. Which image type is best for photographs?

    a. SVG

    b. JPEG

    c. PNG

    d. GIF

14. Which attribute do you use to specify text to display in case an image is unavailable or to be read in user agents by programs such as screen readers?

    a. title

    b. alt

    c. figcaption

    d. href

15. Which element specifies information about an image map and contains all of its hotspots?

    a. map

    b. area

    c. img

    d. link

16. The usemap attribute specifies the value of what attribute for the image map?

    a. id

    b. class

    c. name

    d. map

17. For widest compatibility, you create favicons using which format?

    a. .svg

    b. .jpg

    c. .png

    d. .ico

Skills Review

1. **Insert images.**

   a. In your editor, open HTM_G-4.html from the SR folder where you store your Data Files for this unit, save it as **index.html**, then repeat to save HTM_G-5.html as **events.html** and HTM_G-6.css as **styles.css**.

   b. In the comment at the top of each file, enter your name and today's date where indicated, then save the files.

   c. Return to events.html in your editor, add a p element below the h2 element in the article element with the class value decorative-image, then within the p element add an img element with a src value of images/bigjs.gif, a width of 280, a height of 280, and alt text of Big J's Deep Dish Pizza.

   d. Save your changes, then open events.html in a desktop browser and on a handheld device.

   e. Return to styles.css in your editor, create a new style rule for the img element at the end of the reset styles section, then add the declarations max-width: 100%;, height: auto;, and width: auto;.

   f. Scroll to the reset styles section, then add the img selector to the list of selectors in the style rule that sets border, padding, and margin to 0.

   g. In the main content section and below the h3 style rule, create a style rule with the selector p.decorative-image with the declarations max-width: 35%; and float: right;, then create another style rule with the selector p.introtext and the declaration width: 72%;.

   h. In the h3 style rule, add the declaration clear: both;.

   i. Save your changes, refresh or reload events.html on your handheld device, then verify that the logo image is scaled down.

2. **Insert a background image.**

   a. In your browser, open the file brick.jpg from the images folder.

   b. Return to styles.css in your editor.

   c. Scroll to the body style rule in the body and container section, insert a blank line before the closing }, then indent and type background: url("images/brick.jpg");.

Skills Review (continued)

d. In the `background-color` declaration above the code you just entered, change the property name `background-color` to `background`.

e. Scroll to the print styles section at the bottom of the style sheet, then, in the `body, h2, article` style rule, replace the `background-color` property with the `background` property.

f. Save your work, open index.html in your browser, then verify that the background of the `body` element is the tiled brick.jpg image.

3. Mark images as figures.

a. Return to events.html in your editor, then, on a new line below the opening tag for the h3 element with the `id` value `queen`, add a `figure` element.

b. Within the `figure` element, add an `img` element with a source of images/party.jpg, a width of 450, a height of 238, and alt text of **a long room with a high ceiling, hardwood floor, tables set for 2 and 4 people with tablecloths, and a small raised dais**.

c. Add a `figure` element below the opening tag for the h3 element with the `id` value `stclair`, then within the `figure` element add an `img` element with a source of images/gazebo.jpg, a width of 450, a height of 300, and alt text of **an outdoor brick patio containing several tables with chairs, interspersed with poles supporting a translucent covering, and surrounded by trees**.

d. Add a `figure` element below the opening tag for the h3 element with the `id` value `dundas`, then within the `figure` element add an `img` element with a source of images/special.jpg, a width of 450, a height of 300, and alt text of **a bright room with a high ceiling and tall windows, a hardwood floor, tables set with chairs, and lamps hanging from the ceiling**.

e. Save your changes, return to styles.css in your editor, scroll to the main content section, then below the h3 style rule, add a rule that uses the `figure` selector with the declarations `max-width: 50%;` and `float:right;`.

f. In the style rule that sets border, padding, and margin to 0 in the reset styles section, add the `figure` selector to the list of selectors.

g. In the main content section, add the declaration `overflow: auto;` to the `article` style rule.

h. Save your changes, then refresh or reload events.html in your browser.

4. Create a figure caption.

a. Return to events.html in your editor, then, within the `figure` element and below the h3 element with the `id` value `queen`, insert a `figcaption` element containing the text **The Party Room** below the `img` element.

b. Repeat Step a to add a `figcaption` element containing the text **The Gazebo** for the `figure` element below the h3 element with the `id` value `stclair`, and a `figcaption` element containing the text **The Special Events Room** for the `figure` element below the h3 element with the `id` value `dundas`.

c. Save your changes, then return to styles.css in your editor.

d. Within the main content section and below the `figure` style rule, add a style rule that uses the `figcaption` selector with the declarations `font-size: 1.6em;` and `text-align: center;`.

e. Scroll to the reset styles section, then add the `figcaption` selector to the list of selectors in the style rule that sets border, padding, and margin to 0.

f. Save your changes, then refresh or reload events.html in your browser.

5. Use images as links.

a. Return to events.html in your editor.

b. Scroll to the opening tag for the `article` element, then, within the p element with the `class` value `decorative-image`, add an a element enclosing the `img` element and set the `href` value for the a element to index.html. (*Hint*: Be sure to include the closing `</a>` tag after the `<img>` tag.)

c. Save your changes, then refresh or reload events.html in your browser.

d. Move the mouse pointer over the logo image, then verify the mouse pointer becomes a pointing hand.

e. Click the logo image, then verify that index.html opens.

Skills Review (continued)

6. Create an image map and define additional hotspots.

a. In your browser, open the file imagemap.png from the images folder in the SR folder where you store your Data Files for Unit G.

b. Return to events.html in your editor, in the `article` element add a blank line above the `h3` element with the `id` value `queen`, then add a p element with the `class` value `imagemap`.

c. Within the p element you just created, add an `img` element with a source of images/imagemap.png, width of 480, height of 240, and empty alt text.

d. Add a blank line below the closing `</p>` tag you created in Step b, then add a `map` element with a `name` value of `eventsmap`.

e. Within the `map` element, add an `area` element with a `shape` value of `rect`, `coords` of 22,15,137,204, an `href` value of `#queen`, and alt text of **Party Room**.

f. Below the `area` element you created in the previous step, add another `area` element with a `shape` value of `circle`, `coords` of 235,114,63, an `href` value of `#stclair`, and alt text of **Gazebo**.

FIGURE G-28

g. Below the `area` element you created in the previous step, add another `area` element with a shape value of `poly`, `coords` of 328,25,422,25, 422,75,470,75,470,202,328,202, an `href` value of `#dundas`, and alt text of **Special Events Room**.

h. In the `<img>` tag for the imagemap.png file, add a usemap attribute with a value of `#eventsmap`, then save your changes.

i. Return to styles.css in your editor, scroll to the main content section, then, in the style rule with the selector `p.introtext`, add the selector `p.imagemap`.

j. Below the style rule you just edited, create a new style rule using the selector `p.imagemap img` with the declaration `max-width:none;`, then save your changes.

k. Refresh or reload events.html in your browser. Your document should match **FIGURE G-28**.

l. Move the mouse pointer over each shape in the map graphic, then verify that the mouse pointer becomes a pointing hand only when it is over each shape.

m. Click each shape, then verify that the page scrolls to the correct section, decreasing the height of your browser window if necessary for testing.

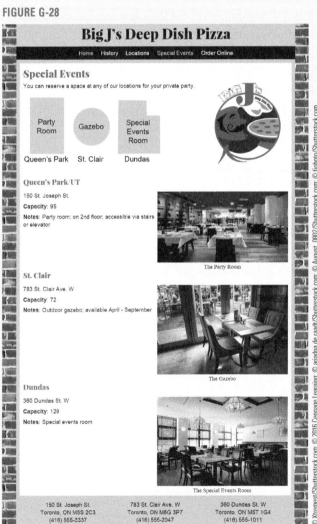

Skills Review (continued)

7. Add a favicon and touch icons.

a. Return to events.html in your editor, then before the closing `</head>` tag, enter a `link` element with a `rel` value of `shortcut icon` and an `href` value of `images/favicon.ico`.

b. Below the `link` element you created in the previous step, add another `link` element with a `rel` value of `apple-touch-icon` and an `href` value of `images/apple-touch-icon.png`.

c. Below the `link` element you created in the previous step, add another `link` element with a `rel` value of `icon`, a `sizes` value of `192x192`, and an `href` value of `images/android.png`.

d. Save events.html, then reload events.html in your browser and verify that the Big J's favicon is displayed in the browser tab.

e. Open index.html on a smartphone or tablet, tap the Menu button (Chrome for Android) or the Share button (Safari for iOS), tap Add to Home Screen, tap Add, then examine the icon on your home screen. (*Hint*: If you use a different browser or operating system, follow the steps you normally use.) **FIGURE G-29** shows the icon on the Android home screen.

f. Repeat Steps a-e for index.html

g. Validate the code for your web pages and your style sheet, then make changes as necessary to fix any errors

© 2016 Cengage Learning; Source: Android

FIGURE G-29

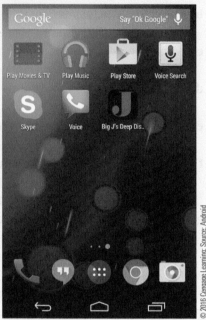

Independent Challenge 1

Sarah Nguyen, the owner of the Spotted Wren Garden Center, has provided you with a version of the company logo for the website, as well as related photos and a favicon. You add these images to the company's website.

a. In your editor, open HTM_G-7.html from the IC1 folder where you store your Data Files for this unit, save it as **index.html**, then repeat to save HTM_G-8.html as **hours.html** and HTM_G-9.css as **styles.css**. In the comment at the top of each file, enter your name and today's date where indicated, then save the files.

b. In index.html, replace the text of the h1 element with an `img` element referencing the file spotwren.gif in the images folder. Specify a width of 864 and a height of 184, and add **Spotted Wren Garden Center** as the alt text. Save your work, then repeat for hours.html.

c. In styles.css, create a new style rule for the `img` element at the end of the reset styles section, then add the declarations `max-width: 100%;`, `height: auto;`, `width: auto;`, and `display: block;`. In the style rule that sets border, padding, and margin to 0 in the reset styles section, add the `img` selector to the list of selectors. Save your changes, then preview index.html and hours.html in a browser.

d. Return to hours.html in your editor, then link the logo `img` element to index.html. Save your changes, refresh or reload hours.html in a browser, click the logo, then verify that index.html opens.

e. Return to index.html in your editor, then within the `article` element and before the `div` element, add a `figure` element. Within the `figure` element, add an `img` element that references the file cone.jpg in the images folder. Specify a width of 200 and a height of 301, and enter **a monarch butterfly on a purple coneflower** as alt text. Save your changes.

Independent Challenge 1 (continued)

f. Return to styles.css, then add the `figcaption` and `figure` selectors to the list of selectors in the style rule that sets border, padding, and margin to 0 in the reset styles section. At the bottom of the main content section, add a style rule based on the `figure` selector that specifies a width of 25% and floats the element to the right. Save your changes, then refresh or reload index.html in your browser.

g. Return to hours.html in your editor, then within the `article` element and before the `div` element, add a `figure` element. Within the `figure` element, add an `img` element that references the file quince.jpg in the images folder. Specify a width of 200 and a height of 301, and enter **the red blossom of a flowering quince** as alt text. Save your work, then refresh or reload hours.html in your browser.

h. Return to styles.css in your editor, then in the `.container` style rule in the body and page container section, change the existing `background-color` declaration to use the `background` shorthand property, then add a second `background` property that sets the grass.jpg file located in the images folder as the background. In the print styles section at the bottom of the style sheet, replace the `background-color` property with the `background` property in the `.container, h1, h2, p` style rule. Save your changes, then refresh or reload index.html and hours.html in your browser.

FIGURE G-30

i. Return to index.html in your editor, then in the head section add a `link` element that specifies the file favicon.ico in the images folder as the favicon. Add a second `link` element that specifies the file apple-touch-icon.png in the images folder as an Apple touch icon. Add a third `link` element that specifies the android.jpg file in the images folder as an icon and specifies its dimensions as 192x192. Save your changes, refresh or reload index.html in your browser, then verify that the favicon is displayed as shown in **FIGURE G-30**. Open index.html on a mobile device, save a link to the page on the home screen, then verify that the touch icon is displayed. **FIGURE G-31** shows the touch icon on an iOS device.

FIGURE G-31

j. Repeat Step i for hours.html.

k. Validate all your HTML and CSS documents.

Independent Challenge 2

You incorporate the logo for the Murfreesboro Regional Soccer League into the organizational website that you are creating. You also use an image map to link the parts of a soccer field to explanations of their functions.

a. In your editor, open HTM_G-10.html from the IC2 folder where you store your Data Files for this unit, save it as **index.html**, then repeat to save HTM_G-11.html as **field.html** and HTM_G-12.css as **styles.css**. In the comment at the top of each file, enter your name and today's date where indicated, then save the files.

b. In index.html, within the `header` element and beneath the `h1` element insert a `div` element, then within the `div` element add an `img` element that references the file mrsl.png in the images folder. Specify a width of 224, a height of 105, and a blank `alt` value. Save your changes, then repeat for field.html.

c. In styles.css, within the header section, add declarations to the `h1` style rule to set the width to 61% and float the element on the right. Create a rule based on the `header div` selector that sets the width to 33% and floats the element left. In the `header` style rule, add the declaration `overflow: auto;`.

d. Create a new style rule for the `img` element at the end of the reset styles section, then add the declarations `max-width: 100%;`, `height: auto;`, `width: auto;`, and `display: block;`. Add the `img` selector to the list of selectors in the style rule that sets border, padding, and margin to 0 in the reset styles section. Save your work, preview index.html and field.html in your browser, then verify that the logo graphic is displayed on the left side of the header and the h1 text is displayed on the right side of the header.

e. Return to field.html in your editor, then link the logo image to index.html. Save your changes, refresh or reload field.html in your browser, then verify that clicking the logo image opens index.html.

f. Return to styles.css in your editor, change the `background-color` declaration in the `.container` style rule in the body and page container section to use the `background` shorthand property, then add a second `background` property that specifies the file grass.jpg in the images folder as the background image. In the print styles section, replace the `background-color` property with the `background` property in the `aside, body, .container, footer, header` style rule. Save your changes, refresh or reload index.html in your browser, then verify that a background image of grass is displayed. (*Hint*: The `header` and `article` elements have their own background colors, so the background image should be visible only behind the nav bar.)

g. In your browser, open the file field.jpg from the images folder in the IC2 folder where you store your Data Files for this unit. Return to field.html in your editor, in the `article` element add a blank line above the h3 element containing the text Goal, then add a p element. Within the p element, add an `img` element that references field.jpg in the images folder, with a width of 450, a height of 293, alt text of **diagram of a soccer field**, and `class` value of `imagemap`.

h. Below the p element you just created, add a `map` element with a `name` value of `fieldmap`. In your editor, open the file areas.txt from the IC2 folder, then within the `map` element add `area` elements for the 9 shapes described in the file.

i. In the `<img>` tag for the field.jpg file, add a `usemap` attribute with a value of `#fieldmap`, then save your changes.

j. In styles.css, at the bottom of the main content section, add a style rule with the `.imagemap` selector and the declaration `max-width: none;`, then save your changes.

k. Refresh or reload events.html in your browser. Your document should match **FIGURE G-32**.

FIGURE G-32

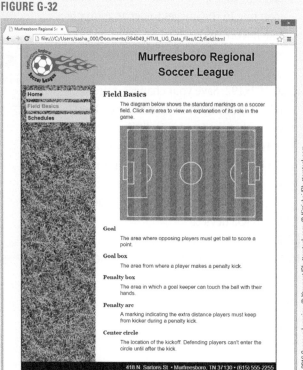

Independent Challenge 2 (continued)

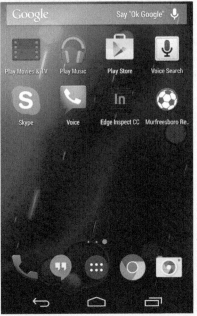

l. Test each shape in the image map, decreasing the height of your browser window if necessary for testing.

m. In index.html, add a `link` element that references favicon.ico in the images folder as a favicon. Add another link element that references apple-touch-icon.png in the images folder as an Apple touch icon. Add a third link element that references android.png in the images folder as a touch icon, specifying its dimensions as 192x192. Save your changes, then repeat for field.html.

n. Refresh or reload index.html in your browser, then verify that the favicon is displayed on the browser tab. Open index.html on a mobile device, save a link to the page on the home screen, then verify that the touch icon is displayed. FIGURE G-33 shows the touch icon on an Android device.

o. Validate all your HTML and CSS documents.

Independent Challenge 3

Diego Merckx, the manager of Hotel Natoma, has provided you with a web-ready version of the facility's logo as well as photos of a few local attractions. You incorporate these into the hotel's website.

a. In your editor, open HTM_G-13.html from the IC3 folder where you store your Data Files for this unit, save it as **index.html**, then repeat to save HTM_G-14.html as **nearby.html** and HTM_G-15.css as **styles.css**. In the comment at the top of each file, enter your name and today's date where indicated, then save the files.

b. In index.html, replace the text of the h1 element with an `img` element referencing the file logo.gif in the images folder. Specify a width of 368 and a height of 65, and add Hotel Natoma as the alt text. Save your work, then repeat for nearby.html.

c. In styles.css, create a new style rule for the `img` element at the end of the reset styles section, then add the declarations `max-width: 100%;`, `height: auto;`, `width: auto;`, and `display: block;`. Add the `img` selector to the list of selectors in the style rule that sets border, padding, and margin to 0 in the reset styles section. In the header section, create a new style rule using the h1 img selector with the declarations `margin: 0 auto;` and `display: block;`. Save your changes, then preview index.html and nearby.html in a browser.

d. Return to nearby.html in your editor, then link the logo `img` element to index.html. Save your changes, refresh or reload nearby.html in a browser, click the logo, then verify that index.html opens.

e. Return to index.html in your editor, then within the `article` element, before the p element, add a `figure` element. Within the `figure` element, add an `img` element that references the file bridge.jpg in the images folder. Specify a width of 350 and a height of 232, and enter **the Golden Gate Bridge, looking south from the Marin Headlands toward the Presidio, with downtown San Francisco on the left** as alt text. After the img element, add a `figcaption` element containing the text **Golden Gate Bridge**. Save your changes.

Independent Challenge 3 (continued)

f. Return to styles.css, then in the style rule that sets border, padding, and margin to 0 in the reset styles section, add the `figcaption` and `figure` selectors to the list of selectors. In the main content section and below the `article` h3 rule, add a style rule based on the `article figure` selector that specifies a maximum width of 100%, a left margin of 1em, and floats the element to the right. Below the rule you just added, add a style rule based on the `article figcaption` selector that center-aligns text and sets the font weight to bold. In the `article` style rule, add the declaration `overflow: auto;`. Save your changes, then refresh or reload index.html in your browser. Your document should match **FIGURE G-34**.

FIGURE G-34

g. Return to nearby.html in your editor, then within the `article` element and below the h3 element with the text Asian Art Museum, add a `figure` element. Within the `figure` element, add an img element that references the file aam.jpg in the images folder. Specify a width of 450 and a height of 337, and enter **the San Francisco Asian Art Museum, a beaux arts building composed of large granite bricks with columns above the entry doors** as alt text. Below the img element, add a `figcaption` element containing the same text as the preceding h3 element, **Asian Art Museum**. Repeat for the remaining four h3 elements using the details in **TABLE G-6**, then save your changes.

TABLE G-6

h3/figcaption Text	Filename	Width	Height	Alt Text
City Hall	cityhall.jpg	450	299	San Francisco City Hall, a beaux arts building with columns across the whole front and a gray dome over the center, illuminated from within at dusk
Civic Center Plaza	ccplaza.jpg	334	449	a bronze statue of Abraham Lincoln sitting in a chair, with the word Lincoln and an inscription on the stone base
United Nations Plaza	unplaza.jpg	300	450	a fountain shooting out from within granite slabs, with buildings rising up behind
Cable Car Turnaround	cablecar.jpg	450	300	a cable car on a circular platform made of wood planks, with people lined up in the background

Independent Challenge 3 (continued)

h. In styles.css, scroll to the main content section, then add the declaration `clear: right;` to the `article h3` style rule. Save your changes, then refresh or reload hours.html in your browser.

i. In your browser, open the file map.png from the images folder. Return to nearby.html in your editor, scroll as needed to the `article` element, add a p element above the h3 element containing the text Asian Art Museum. Within the p element, add an `img` element that references map.jpg in the images folder, with a width of 465, a height of 347, alt text of **map of the area around Hotel Natoma**, and `class` value of `imagemap`.

j. Below the p element you just created, add a `map` element with a `name` value of `nearby`. In your editor, open the file areas.txt from the IC3 folder, then within the `map` element add `area` elements for the 5 shapes described in the file.

k. In the `<img>` tag for the map.png file, add a `usemap` attribute to use the `map` element as an image map, then save your changes.

l. In styles.css, at the bottom of the main content section, add a style rule with the `.imagemap` selector and the declarations `border: 2px solid black;`, `margin: 0 auto;` and `max-width: none;`. Below this style rule, add a style rule with the `.imagemap img` selector that sets `max-width` to none. Save your changes.

m. Refresh or reload nearby.html in your browser. Your document should match **FIGURE G-35**.

n. Return to index.html in your editor, then add `link` elements for a favicon, an Apple touch icon, and an Android touch icon with a size of 192x192. Save your changes, refresh or reload index.html in your browser, then verify that the favicon is displayed on the browser tab. Open index.html on a mobile device, save a link to the page on the home screen, then verify that the touch icon is displayed. **FIGURE G-36** shows the touch icon on an iOS device.

o. Repeat Step n for nearby.html.

p. Validate all your HTML and CSS documents.

FIGURE G-35

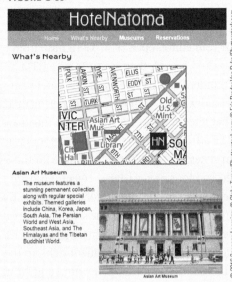

FIGURE G-36

Independent Challenge 4 – Explore

You continue your work building the website for Eating Well in Season by incorporating the company logo, a few marketing images, and an image map.

a. In your editor, open HTM_G-16.html from the IC4 folder where you store your Data Files for this unit, save it as **index.html**, then repeat to save HTM_G-17.html as **farms.html** and HTM_G-18.css as **styles.css**. In the comment at the top of each file, enter your name and today's date where indicated, then save the files.

b. In index.html, within the header element and below the h1 element, add a `div` element containing an `img` element that references the file logo.png in the images folder. Specify a width of 216 and a height of 146, and specify an `alt` attribute with no value. Repeat for farms.html, then save your changes to both files.

c. In styles.css, create a new style rule for the `img` element at the end of the reset styles section, then add the declarations `max-width: 100%;`, `height: auto;`, `width: auto;`, and `display: block;`. Add the `img` selector to the list of selectors in the style rule that sets border, padding, and margin to 0 in the reset styles section. In the header section of the style sheet, create a new style rule for the `div` element within the `header` element, setting the width to 26%, margins to 2% 4% 1%, and floating the element left. In the `header h1` style rule, add a declaration to float the element right. In the header style rule, add the declaration `overflow: auto;`. Save your changes, then preview index.html and farms.html in a browser.

d. Return to farms.html in your editor, then link the logo `img` element to index.html. Save your changes, refresh or reload farms.html in a browser, click the logo, then verify that index.html opens.

e. Return to index.html in your editor, then, within the `article` element, add a `figure` element. Within the `figure` element, add an `img` element that references the file meal.jpg in the images folder. Specify a width of 450 and a height of 299. View the image in your browser, then add alt text to index.html that describes the image. (*Hint*: Your alt text should describe the image in enough detail to convey its contents to someone accessing the page who cannot view the image.) After the `img` element, add a `figcaption` element containing the text **Healthy Meals.** Repeat to add `figure` elements using the details in TABLE G-7. Save your changes.

TABLE G-7

Filename	Width	Height	figcaption **Text**
veggies.jpg	450	298	Local sources.
delivery.jpg	450	299	Your schedule.

f. Return to styles.css, then, in the style rule that sets border, padding, and margin to 0 in the reset styles section, add the `figcaption` and `figure` selectors to the list of selectors. In the main content section and below the `article p` rule, add a style rule based on the `figure` selector that specifies a width of 75%, a margin of `1em auto`, and a 2px solid black border. Below the rule you just added, add a style rule based on the `figcaption` selector that sets padding to 0.25em, font size to 2em, font weight to `bold`, center-aligns text, and sets the background color to `white`. In the body and page container section, add the declaration `overflow: auto;` in the `.article-aside-inner-container` style rule. Save your changes, then refresh or reload index.html in your browser. Your document should match FIGURE G-37.

FIGURE G-37

Independent Challenge 4 – Explore (continued)

g. In your browser, open the file farm.jpg from the images folder. Return to farms.html in your editor, in the `article` element add a `p` element with a `class` value of `imagemap` above the h3 element containing the text Silo. Within the `p` element, add an `img` element that references farm.jpg in the images folder, with a width of 456, a height of 221, and empty alt text.

FIGURE G-38

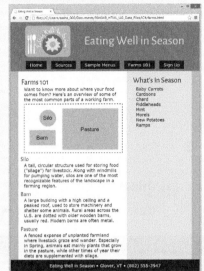

h. Below the p element you just created, add a `map` element. Decide on a name for the map and specify it with the `name` attribute. Using an application or a web service, create `area` elements for the 3 shapes on the map—one circle and two rectangles. (*Hint*: Use a search engine and the terms *image map coordinate generator* to locate free online services.)

i. Add the `area` elements you created within the `map` element, making sure to specify values for the `shape`, `alt`, `coords`, and `href` attributes. (*Hint*: The `href` values should be hash links to the corresponding h3 headings within the `article` element.)

j. In the `<img>` tag for the farm.png file, add an attribute to use the `map` element as an image map, then save your changes.

k. In styles.css, at the bottom of the main content section, add a style rule with the `.imagemap` selector with declarations that center-align text and create a 2px dashed black border. Below the style rule you just added, add a style rule with the `.imagemap img` selector that sets `max-width` to `none`. Save your changes.

FIGURE G-39

l. Refresh or reload farms.html in your browser. Your document should match **FIGURE G-38**. Test the image map and verify that all three hotspots work, decreasing the height of your browser window if necessary for testing.

m. Return to index.html in your editor, then add `link` elements for a favicon, an Apple touch icon, and an Android touch icon with a size of 192x192, using the relevant files in the images folder. Save your changes, refresh or reload index.html in your browser, then verify that the favicon is displayed on the browser tab. Open index.html on a mobile device, save a link to the page on the home screen, then verify that the touch icon is displayed. **FIGURE G-39** shows the touch icon on an Android device.

n. Repeat Step m for farms.html.

o. Validate all your HTML and CSS documents.

Visual Workshop

In your editor, open the file HTM_G-19.html from the VW folder where you store your Data Files for this unit and save it as **releases.html**. Repeat to save HTM_G-20.css as **styles.css**. Add your first and last names and today's date to the comment section at the top of each file, then save your changes. Use the files in the images folder to style the web page to match the one shown in FIGURE G-40, changing and adding to the style sheet as necessary. The logo graphic is logo.gif, the background image is books.png, and the photo of the girl reading a book is browsing.jpg. Specify favicon.ico as the favicon, android.png as the touch icon for Android devices (using dimensions of 192x192), and apple-touch-icon.png as the touch icon for iOS devices. Validate your HTML and CSS code.

FIGURE G-40

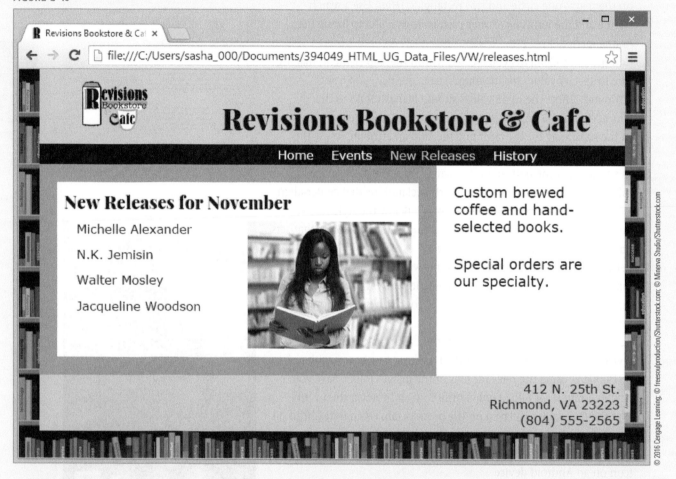

Organizing Content with Lists and Tables

CASE	As you continue your work on the website for the Lakeland Reeds Bed & Breakfast, you format content using lists and tables.

Unit Objectives

After completing this unit, you will be able to:

- Create an ordered list
- Create an unordered list
- Create a description list
- Create a nav bar using a list
- Insert a table

- Debug tables
- Span columns and rows
- Format a table with CSS
- Apply a table-like structure to other elements

Files You Will Need

 L 10 files   IC3 12 files

 SR 10 files   IC4 9 files

 IC1 10 files   VW 7 files

 IC2 9 files

For specific filenames, see Filenames_H.pdf in the Unit H Data Files folder.

©VikaSuh/Shutterstock.com

Create an Ordered List

You use the HTML ol element to create a list in which items are numbered or lettered sequentially. This type of list is known as an **ordered list** because the order in which the items are listed is important. You create each item in an ordered list with the li element. All the li elements for a list are nested within the opening and closing ol tags. The default marker for each list item is determined by the user agent rendering the web page but it is most often an Arabic numeral (1, 2, 3, . . .). You can use the values of the CSS list-style-type property shown in TABLE H-1 to change the markers to letters or to a different numbering style. **CASE** ▶ *Phillip Blaine, the owner of Lakeland Reeds Bed & Breakfast, has provided additional information that he'd like you to incorporate into the Reservations web page. You start by adding a list of the most popular weekends at Lakeland Reeds.*

STEPS

1. **In your editor, open HTM_H-1.html from the Lessons folder where you store your Data Files for this unit, save it as reserve.html, then repeat to save HTM_H-2.css as styles.css**

2. **In the comment at the top of each file, enter your name and today's date where indicated, then save the files**

3. **Return to reserve.html, insert a blank line beneath the paragraph *Our most sought-after weekends*, indent to the same level as the paragraph, type <ol>, press [Enter], indent to the same level, then type </ol>**
   All items in an ordered list are contained between the opening and closing tags for the ol element.

4. **Insert a blank line beneath <ol>, indent 3 additional spaces, then type** <li>Independence Day (Jul. 4)</li>
   The content of each list item is contained between the opening and closing tags for the li element.

5. **Press [Enter], indent as needed to the same level, then type** <li>Memorial Day (last Monday in May)</li>

6. **Press [Enter], indent as needed to the same level, type** <li>Labor Day (first Monday in Sep.)</li>, **then save your changes**
   FIGURE H-1 shows the completed HTML code for the ordered list.

7. **Return to styles.css in your editor, create a new style rule for the ol element at the end of the reset styles section, then add the declaration** list-style-type: none;
   This declaration removes the default numbering assigned by browsers from ol elements you create. Because you removed the default numbering, you are required to specify the list-style-type for each ordered list in your document.

8. **In the style rule that sets border, padding, and margin to 0 in the reset styles section, add the ol and li selectors to the list of selectors**

9. **Scroll down to the /* footer section */ comment and, above this comment, add the comment /* main content lists */, then, below this comment, create a style rule with the article ol selector and the declarations** margin: 1em 0 1em 2em;, font-size: 1.3em;, **and** list-style-type: decimal;
   FIGURE H-2 shows the changes to the style sheet.

10. **Save your changes, then open reserve.html in a browser**
    As FIGURE H-3 shows, the list is displayed with each list item numbered sequentially starting at the number 1. Note that the list markers for an ordered list are always displayed outside the content box and on the left. If the list has left padding or margin (as in this example), the markers are displayed within the padding or margin area. If not, the markers are displayed outside the element on the left side.

FIGURE H-1: HTML code for ordered list

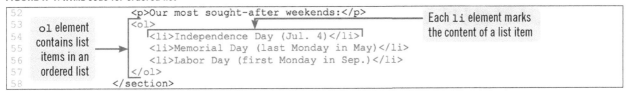

```
52              <p>Our most sought-after weekends:</p>
53    ol element <ol>
54    contains list   <li>Independence Day (Jul. 4)</li>
55    items in an     <li>Memorial Day (last Monday in May)</li>
56    ordered list    <li>Labor Day (first Monday in Sep.)</li>
57              </ol>
58          </section>
```

Each li element marks the content of a list item

FIGURE H-2: CSS code for ordered list

```
10    /* reset styles */
11    html {
12        font-size: 16px;
13    }
14    a, article, body, div, figcaption, figure, footer, header, h1,
15    h2, h3, img, li, nav, ol, p, section {
16        border: 0;
17        padding: 0;
18        margin: 0;
19    }
20    img {
21        max-width: 100%;
22        height: auto;
23        width: auto;
24    }
25    ol {
26        list-style-type: none;
27    }
```

li and ol selectors added to rule for border, padding, and margin in the reset styles section

list-style-type of none removes the default numbering assigned by browsers to ordered lists

```
137    /* main content lists */
138    article ol {
139        margin: 1em 0 1em 2em;
140        font-size: 1.3em;
141        list-style-type: decimal;
142    }
143
144    /* footer section */
```

list-style-type of decimal uses sequential numbers starting at 1

FIGURE H-3: Ordered list in Reservations web page

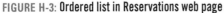
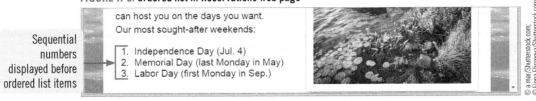

Sequential numbers displayed before ordered list items

can host you on the days you want.
Our most sought-after weekends:

1. Independence Day (Jul. 4)
2. Memorial Day (last Monday in May)
3. Labor Day (first Monday in Sep.)

TABLE H-1: Widely supported values for the CSS list-style-type property for the ol element

value	result	value	result
decimal	1. first item 2. second item	lower-latin lower-roman	i. first item ii. second item
decimal-leading-zero	01. first item 02. second item ... 10. tenth item 11. eleventh item	none	first item second item
		upper-alpha	A. first item B. second item
lower-alpha	a. first item b. second item	upper-latin upper-roman	I. first item II. second item

Create an Unordered List

HTML also enables you to create a list in which the order of list items doesn't matter. You create this type of list, known as an **unordered list**, using the ul element. You mark list item content with the same li element that you use for an ordered list. In an unordered list, list items are displayed with a bullet at the start of each line. The default bullet character is a solid circle, but you can use the CSS list-style-type property with one of the values shown in TABLE H-2 to specify a different bullet shape. **CASE** ▶ *Visitors sometimes reserve the entire facility for special events. You add Phillip's list of special events to the Reservations web page as an unordered list.*

STEPS

1. **Return to** reserve.html **in your editor, insert a blank line beneath the paragraph that begins** *Lakeland Reeds is also available,* **indent to the same level as the paragraph, type** <ul>**, press [Enter], indent to the same level, then type** </ul>

   All items in an unordered list are contained between the opening and closing tags for the ul element.

2. **Insert a blank line beneath** <ul>**, indent 3 additional spaces, then type**
   <li>Weddings</li>

   While the containing element is specific to the type of list you're creating, you use the li element for list items when creating either ordered or unordered lists.

3. **Press [Enter], indent as needed to the same level, type** <li>Birthdays</li>**, then repeat to enter the code** <li>Family Reunions</li>

   FIGURE H-4 shows the completed HTML code for the unordered list.

4. **Save your changes, then return to** styles.css **in your editor**

5. **In the style rule that sets border, padding, and margin to 0 in the reset styles section, add the** ul **selector to the list of selectors, then add the** ul **selector to the** ol **style rule in the reset styles section**

6. **Scroll down to the main content lists section, then, below the** article ol **rule, add a new style rule with the** article ul **selector and the declarations** margin: 1em 0 1em 2em;**,** font-size: 1.3em;**, and** list-style-type: disc;

   FIGURE H-5 shows the changes to the style sheet. Note that the value disc for list-style-type creates a filled circle, while the value circle creates an unfilled circle, as illustrated in TABLE H-2.

7. **Save your changes, then refresh or reload** reserve.html **in your browser**

   As FIGURE H-6 shows, the unordered list is displayed with a solid circular bullet next to each list item.

TABLE H-2: Values for the CSS list-style-type property for the ul element

value	description	example
circle	unfilled circle	○ list item
disc	filled circle (default)	● list item
square	filled square	■ list item
none	no character	list item

FIGURE H-4: HTML code for unordered list

```
60              <section>
61                  <h3>Special Events</h3>
62                  <figure class="alternate">
63                      <img src="images/frolic.jpg" width="350" height="209" alt="people
64                      swimming with a raft in the lake">
65                  </figure>
66                  <p>Lakeland Reeds is also available for booking group special events,
67                  including</p>
68                  <ul>
69                      <li>Weddings</li>
70                      <li>Birthdays</li>
71                      <li>Family Reunions</li>
72                  </ul>
73                  <p><a href="weddings.pdf">Guidelines and reservation form for a special
74                  event at Lakeland Reeds.</a> (PDF)</p>
75              </section>
```

ul element contains list items in an unordered list

Each li element marks the content of a list item

FIGURE H-5: CSS code for unordered list

```
10   /* reset styles */
11   html {
12       font-size: 16px;
13   }
14   a, article, body, div, figcaption, figure, footer, header, h1,
15   h2, h3, img, li, nav, ol, p, section, ul {
16       border: 0;
17       padding: 0;
18       margin: 0;
19   }
20   img {
21       max-width: 100%;
22       height: auto;
23       width: auto;
24   }
25   ol, ul {
26       list-style-type: none;
27   }
```

ul selector added to two rules in the reset styles section

```
137  /* main content lists */
138  article ol {
139      margin: 1em 0 1em 2em;
140      font-size: 1.3em;
141      list-style-type: decimal;
142  }
143  article ul {
144      margin: 1em 0 1em 2em;
145      font-size: 1.3em;
146      list-style-type: disc;
147  }
```

list-style-type of disc uses a filled circle

FIGURE H-6: Unordered list in Reservations web page

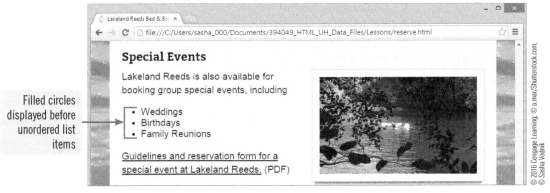

Filled circles displayed before unordered list items

© 2016 Cengage Learning; © a.mar/Shutterstock.com; © Sasha Vodnik

Create a Description List

The dl element creates a **description list**, which enables you to specify a set of items and descriptions. A description list was known in previous versions of HTML as a **definition list**. Unlike ol and ul, dl does not use the li element to specify list items. Instead, a list item uses two elements: dt marks the term or item being described, and dd marks the description. **CASE** ▶ *The contact information for Phillip Blaine on the Reservations page is a set of items and their descriptions. You change the markup for this section to a definition list.*

STEPS

1. **Return to** reserve.html **in your editor, locate the** div **element with the** class **value** contact, **then in the opening and closing tags, replace** div **with** dl
   This changes the div element to a description list element.

2. **In the next line, replace the code** <p><span> **with** <dt>, **replace the code** </span> **with** </dt>, **move the insertion point after the closing** </dt> **tag, then press [Enter]**

3. **Indent to match the previous line, type** <dd>, **then replace the closing** </p> **tag with** </dd>
   Your changes in Steps 2 and 3 have marked the Proprietor label as a dt element and the name Phillip Blaine as a dd element.

4. **Repeat Steps 2 and 3 to convert each of the remaining 3** p **elements to a** dt **and a** dd **element**
   FIGURE H-7 shows the completed HTML code for the description list.

5. **Save your changes, then return to** styles.css **in your editor**

6. **In the style rule that sets border, padding, and margin to 0 in the reset styles section, add the** dd, dl, **and** dt **selectors to the list of selectors**

7. **Scroll down to the main content lists section, then below the** article ul **rule, add a new style rule with the** article dl **selector and the declarations** margin: 1em 0; **and** font-size: 1.3em;

8. **Below the rule you created in the previous step, add a new style rule with the** article dt **selector and the declaration** font-weight: bold;, **then create a new style rule with the** article dd **selector and the declaration** margin-left: 2em;
   FIGURE H-8 shows the changes. The article dt style rule bolds the item in each set, and the article dd selector indents its description.

9. **Save your changes, then refresh or reload reserve.html in your browser**
   As **FIGURE H-9** shows, each dt element is displayed in bold and each dd element is indented.

Specifying custom bullets

In addition to choosing from the standard selection of bullet characters using the list-style-type property, you can instead choose to specify an image to display as the bullet character using the list-style-image property. The syntax is the same as that for specifying a background image: the text url followed by the path and filename of the image file,

enclosed in quotes and parentheses. For instance, the code

```
ul {
    list-style-image:url("images/browntri.gif");
}
```

specifies the file browntri.gif, located in the images folder, as the bullet character for unordered lists.

```
76              <section>
77                 <h3>Questions?</h3>
78                 <p>Feel free to contact us with any queries about Lakeland Reeds, or about
79                 planning your trip.</p>
80                 <dl class="contact">
81                    <dt>Proprietor</dt>
82                    <dd>Phillip Blaine</dd>
83                    <dt>Email</dt>
84                    <dd>lrbb@example.com</dd>
85                    <dt>Phone</dt>
86                    <dd>(218) 555-5253</dd>
87                    <dt>Fax</dt>
88                    <dd>(218) 555-0413</dd>
89                 </dl>
90              </section>
```

dt element marks the item in an item-description pair

dl element contains list items in a description list

dd element marks the description in an item-description pair

FIGURE H-8: CSS code for description list

```
10     /* reset styles */
11     html {
12         font-size: 16px;
13     }
14     a, article, body, dd, div, dl, dt, figcaption, figure, footer, header, h1,
15     h2, h3, img, li, nav, ol, p, section, ul {
16         border: 0;
17         padding: 0;
18         margin: 0;
19     }
```

dd, dl, and dt selectors added to rule for border, padding, and margin in the reset styles section

```
142    article ul {
143        margin: 1em 0 1em 2em;
144        font-size: 1.3em;
145        list-style-type: disc;
146    }
147    article dl {
148        margin: 1em 0;
149        font-size: 1.3em;
150    }
151    article dt {
152        font-weight: bold;
153    }
154    article dd {
155        margin-left: 2em;
156    }
```

Style rule bolds the item in each item-description pair

Style rule indents the description in each item-description pair

FIGURE H-9: Description list in Reservations web page

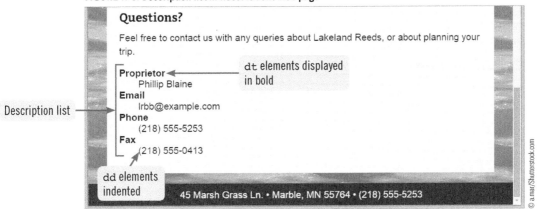

Description list

dt elements displayed in bold

dd elements indented

Organizing Content with Lists and Tables

HTML5 & CSS3

207

Create a Nav Bar Using a List

Learning
Outcomes
• Mark a nav bar as
  an unordered list

Some common web page content that at first glance may not appear to be a list may nevertheless benefit from being marked up using list elements. One example is a navigation bar, which is fundamentally a list of related links. By marking up a navigation bar using the ul and li elements, you add semantic information. In addition, list elements give you greater layout flexibility using fewer HTML tags, making your code easier to read. **CASE** ▶ *You convert the main navigation bar to an unordered list.*

STEPS

1. **Return to** reserve.html **in your editor, locate the opening <nav> tag with the** class **value** sitenavigation**, add a new line below it, indent an additional 3 spaces, then type** <ul>

2. **Add a new line above the closing </nav> tag for the main nav bar, indent an additional 3 spaces, then type** </ul>

> **TROUBLE**
> This is the <ul> tag you entered in step 1.

3. **In the line below the opening <ul> tag, indent an additional 3 spaces, replace the opening <p> tag with** <li>**, then replace the closing </p> tag with** </li>

4. **Repeat Step 3 to convert the remaining** p **elements in the nav bar to** li **elements**
   Your code should match **FIGURE H-11**.

5. **Save your changes, return to** styles.css **in your editor, then scroll up to the site navigation bar section**

6. **In the** nav.sitenavigation p **style rule, change the selector to** nav.sitenavigation li**, then add the declarations** font-size: 1.3em; **and** line-height: 1.4em;**, as shown in FIGURE H-12**

7. **Save your work, then reload reserve.html in your browser**
   As **FIGURE H-13** shows, there is no change in the appearance of the nav bar.

8. **Move the mouse pointer over the** Weather link **and verify that it still changes color, click the** Weather link **and verify that a weather page opens, then click your browser's** Back button **to return to reserve.html**

Creating nested lists

Sometimes nesting a list within another list is the clearest way to present information. It's easy to nest lists in HTML: you simply insert valid code for a list within the content of an li, dt, or dd element.

For instance, FIGURE H-10 shows the appearance in a browser of the nested lists created by the code shown to the right:

FIGURE H-10: **Nested list in browser**

```
1. Fruits
     ○ apples
     ○ pomegranates
2. Vegetables
     ○ carrots
     ○ beets
```

```
<ol>
   <li>
      Fruits
      <ul>
         <li>apples</li>
         <li>pomegranates</li>
      </ul>
   </li>
   <li>
      Vegetables
      <ul>
         <li>carrots</li>
         <li>beets</li>
      </ul>
   </li>
</ol>
```

FIGURE H-11: HTML code for nav bar using `ul` and `li` elements

```
29          <nav class="sitenavigation">
30            <ul>
              <li><a href="index.html">Home</a></li>
              <li><a href="aboutus.html">About Us</a></li>
              <li><a href="reserve.html">Reservations</a></li>
              <li><a href="events.html">Events</a></li>
              <li><a href="http://wxug.us/1hn14">Weather</a></li>
              <li><a href="https://goo.gl/maps/bwf5R">Directions</a></li>
37            </ul>
38          </nav>
```

Nav bar links nested within a `ul` element

Each `li` element marks a nav bar link

FIGURE H-12: Updated CSS code for nav bar

```
69     /* site navigation bar */
70     nav.sitenavigation {
71        color: #34180f;
72        text-align: center;
73        background-color: #B8944D;
74     }
75     nav.sitenavigation li {
76        margin: 0.3em 0.5em;
77        display: inline-block;
78        font-size: 1.3em;
79        line-height: 1.4em;
80     }
```

`nav.sitenavigation li` replaces `nav.sitenavigation p` selector

FIGURE H-13: Modified nav bar in browser

Nav bar appearance unchanged, but code now includes additional semantic meaning

© 2016 Cengage Learning; © Unholy Vault Designs/Shutterstock.com;
© a.mar/Shutterstock.com; © Elena Elisseeva/Shutterstock.com

Organizing Content with Lists and Tables

Insert a Table

In addition to a simple list of items or items and descriptions, HTML enables you to present a larger set of information as a table, which organizes data in horizontal **rows** and vertical **columns**. Each item in a table is displayed in a **cell**, which is the intersection of a row and a column. To create a table in HTML, you use the elements described in TABLE H-3. **CASE** ▸ *Phillip would like a table showing a breakdown of room rates. You add this table on the Reservations page.*

STEPS

QUICK TIP
Table content is placed between opening and closing table tags.

1. Return to reserve.html in your editor, insert a blank line below the h3 element containing the text *Rates*, indent to match the <h3> tag, type <table>, press [Enter], indent as needed, then type </table>

2. Insert a blank line beneath the opening <table> tag, indent 3 spaces more than the previous line, type <thead>, press [Enter], indent to match the previous line, then type </thead>

QUICK TIP
The thead and tbody elements group table rows into sections.

3. Press [Enter], indent to match the previous line, type <tbody>, press [Enter], indent as needed, then type </tbody>

4. Insert a blank line below the <thead> tag, indent 3 spaces more than the previous line, type <tr>, press [Enter], type </tr>, then repeat twice to add two more tr elements in the tbody section

QUICK TIP
The number of cells in each row is sufficient for a browser to calculate the number of columns; therefore, no element is required to specify the number or arrangement of columns.

5. Insert a blank line below the first <tr> tag in the thead section, indent 3 spaces more than the previous line, type <th>Period</th>, then enter the following additional th elements on separate lines: <th>Sun Room</th>, <th>Reed Room</th>, and <th>Treehouse</th>

6. Within the first tr element in the tbody section, enter the following td elements: <td>May 1 - Sep. 15</td>, <td>$110</td>, <td>$125</td>, and <td>$150</td>

7. Within the second tr element in the tbody section, enter the td elements <td>Sep. 16 - Apr. 30</td>, <td>$100</td>, <td>$110</td>, and <td>$150</td>, then save your changes
   Your HTML code should match FIGURE H-14.

8. Return to styles.css in your editor, in the reset styles section and in the rule that sets border, padding, and margin to 0, add table, tbody, td, tfoot, th, thead, and tr to the list of selectors

QUICK TIP
Specifying a border for the table element creates a border around the outside of a table, but not around individual cells within it.

9. Type /* main content tables */ above the /* footer section */ comment, then below the new comment create a new style rule with the selectors td, th and the declarations border: 1px solid black; and font-size: 1.3em;, as shown in FIGURE H-15
   Because browsers render tables without gridlines by default, you added a border declaration to create a line around each cell.

10. Save your changes, reload reserve.html in your browser, then scroll as necessary to the Rates section
    As FIGURE H-16 shows, the table content you entered is displayed in a grid, with a border around each cell.

FIGURE H-14: HTML code for table

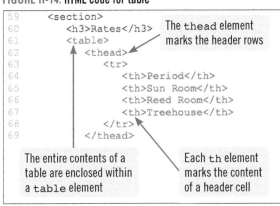

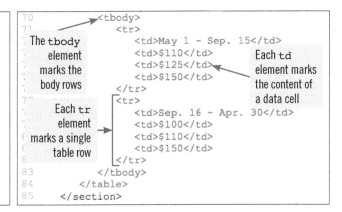

Code continued with line 70 in figure to the right   Code continued from figure on the left

FIGURE H-15: CSS code for table

```
14    a, article, body, div, dd, dl, dt, figcaption, figure, footer, header, h1,
15    h2, h3, img, nav, ol, p, section, table, tbody, td, tfoot, th, thead, tr, ul {
16        border: 0;
17        padding: 0;
18        margin: 0;
19    }
```

Selectors added to rule for border, padding, and margin in the reset styles section

```
160   /* main content tables */
161   td, th {
162       border: 1px solid black;
163       font-size: 1.3em;
164   }
165
166   /* footer section */
```

`border` property for `td` and `th` elements adds a line around each cell

FIGURE H-16: Table in Reservations web page

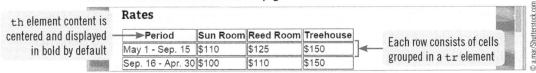

`th` element content is centered and displayed in bold by default

Each row consists of cells grouped in a `tr` element

TABLE H-3 HTML Table Structuring Elements

element	content	description
table	entire table	start and end of table content
thead		group of one or more rows that contain column headers; when printed, this content is displayed at the top of each page
tbody	group of rows	group of one or more rows that contain the main body of the table
tfoot		group of one or more rows that contain column footers; when printed, this content is displayed at the bottom of each page
tr	row	start and end of a row
th		content of a table header cell
td	cell	content of a standard table cell

Debug Tables

Learning
Outcomes
• Recognize and fix
  a table row with
  missing content
• Recognize and fix
  a table row with
  extra content

An error in the HTML code for a table can result in unique issues when rendered by a browser. If too many or too few cells are included in a row, then the result is a table that is not a rectangular grid, but one that has protruding cells or empty spaces instead. In addition, omitting or improperly placing a closing tag can result in an arrangement of data that's hard to understand. Some errors are easy to recognize, and therefore fix, as a result of their characteristic appearance in a browser. **CASE** ▶ *As you prepare to enhance the table of room rates, you introduce some errors into your code and examine the result in the browser to make sure you know how to spot these types of errors when you work with tables in the future.*

STEPS

1. **Return to reserve.html in your editor, locate the code `<td>$150</td>` within the second `tr` element, type `<!--` before the `<td>` tag, then type `-->` after the `</td>` tag**
   In order for a table to appear as a rectangular grid, each row must have the same amount of content. By commenting out this td element, you create a row that is missing a cell. **FIGURE H-17** shows the edited code.

QUICK TIP
You can visualize the role of each element in a table by opening your browser's developer tools, then mousing over each element to highlight it on the page.

2. **Save your changes, then refresh or reload reserve.html in your browser**
   As **FIGURE H-18** shows, the missing cell in the second row is reflected as an empty spot in the table.

3. **Return to reserve.html in your editor, then count the number of `th` or `td` elements that are not commented out within each `tr` element**
   The first and third rows each contain 4 th or td elements, while the second row contains only 3 td elements that are not commented out. This difference in the number of cells in each row results in the gap displayed in the browser.

4. **Remove the `<!--` and `-->` tags you added in Step 1**

5. **Below the final `td` element and within the second `tr` element, add a new line, indent to match the previous line, then type `<td>$150</td>`**
   When entering the code for a table manually, it's also possible to enter too much content in a single row. Adding an extra cell to this row creates such a row. **FIGURE H-19** shows the edited code.

QUICK TIP
The extra cell is narrower than the other cells because by default, browsers set width to fit the content in the widest cell of a column.

6. **Save your changes, then refresh or reload reserve.html in your browser**
   As **FIGURE H-20** shows, the extra cell in the second row protrudes from the rectangular shape of the table.

7. **Return to reserve.html in your editor, then count the number of `th` or `td` elements within each `tr` element**
   The first and third rows each contain 4 th or td elements, while the second row contains 5 td elements. This difference in the number of cells in each row results in the protruding cell displayed in the browser.

TROUBLE
If your table does not appear as expected, use **FIGURE H-14**, which shows the completed code for the table, to correct any errors.

8. **Remove the `td` element you added in Step 5, save your changes, then refresh or reload reserve.html in your browser**
   Your table once again appears as a rectangle with no protruding or missing cells.

FIGURE H-17: Table code to remove a cell

```
70              <tbody>
71                  <tr>
72                      <td>May 1 - Sep. 15</td>
73                      <td>$110</td>
74                      <td>$125</td>
75                      <!--<td>$150</td>-->
76                  </tr>
```

Commented out td element means this cell will not be displayed, so it creates a row with one fewer cells than other rows

FIGURE H-18: Table with a missing cell in a browser

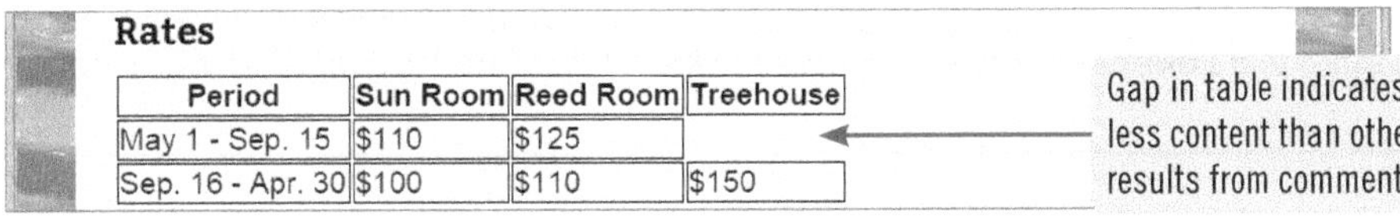

Rates

Period	Sun Room	Reed Room	Treehouse
May 1 - Sep. 15	$110	$125	
Sep. 16 - Apr. 30	$100	$110	$150

© a.mar/Shutterstock.com

Gap in table indicates that one row has less content than other rows; this results from commented out td element

FIGURE H-19: Table code to create a row with an extra cell

```
70              <tbody>
71                  <tr>
72                      <td>May 1 - Sep. 15</td>
73                      <td>$110</td>
74                      <td>$125</td>
75                      <td>$150</td>
76                      <td>$150</td>
77                  </tr>
```

Added td element results in a row with one more cell than other rows

FIGURE H-20: Table with an extra cell in a browser

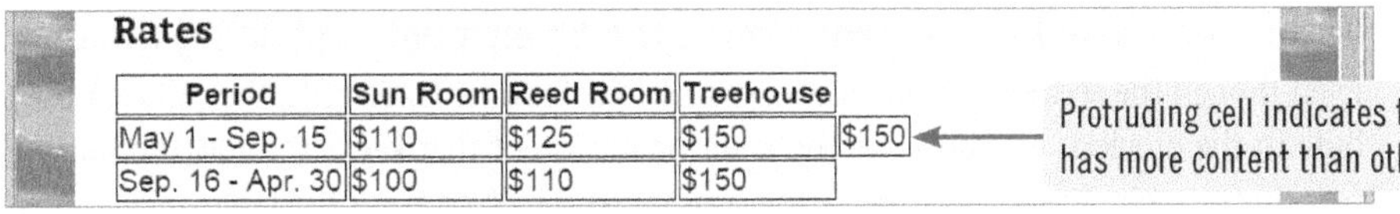

Rates

Period	Sun Room	Reed Room	Treehouse	
May 1 - Sep. 15	$110	$125	$150	$150
Sep. 16 - Apr. 30	$100	$110	$150	

© a.mar/Shutterstock.com

Protruding cell indicates that row has more content than other rows

Resisting the temptation to use tables for layout

You can style table borders with all the properties that are available for other web page elements, including removing borders completely. In the early days of the web, many developers combined spanned rows and columns with invisible borders to enable the positioning of text, images, and other elements side by side, and in specific areas of a web page. However, as CSS grew and user agent support for it matured, the CSS `position` and `float` properties became the preferred method for creating visual layouts. While you can place elements in arbitrary locations by manipulating the number and sizes of rows and columns in a table, doing so erroneously assigns semantic meaning to your web page content; this suggests that user agents should attempt to understand it as a table of related data. In addition, this use of a table creates particularly strong challenges for non-visual user agents such as screen readers in conveying the relationships between web page elements. For these reasons, you should restrict your use of tables only to data whose meaning can be best understood in a grid layout.

Span Columns and Rows

Learning
Outcomes
• Display cell
content in
multiple columns
• Display cell
content in
multiple rows

When a table contains cells that repeat the same content across a row or down a column, you can improve usability by removing all but one occurrence of the content and formatting the cell to be displayed across multiple columns or rows. To display the content of a cell across multiple columns in an HTML table, you use the colspan attribute in the opening th or td tag for the cell in order to specify the number of columns in which the content should be displayed. Likewise, you use the rowspan attribute to specify the number of rows for cell content to span. **CASE** *Your plans for the Rates table include an additional row at the top labeling the room listings, as shown in the sketch in* FIGURE H-21. *Once the new row is added, you plan to have Period span two rows in order to adjust for the space created by adding the new top row. You add* colspan *and* rowspan *attributes to make the Rates table easier to read while incorporating this new content.*

STEPS

1. **Return to** reserve.html **in your editor, insert a new line beneath the** <thead> **tag, indent 3 additional spaces, type** <tr>**, press [Enter], indent as needed, then type** </tr>

2. **Between the opening and closing** tr **tags you just entered, indent two additional spaces, type** <th>Period</th>**, press** [Enter]**, indent as needed, then type** <th colspan="3">Room</th>

    Although the new header row includes only two cells, the colspan attribute marks the second cell to be displayed in 3 columns, so the second cell will span the second, third, and fourth columns. As a result of the cell spanning multiple columns, the new row occupies the same number of columns as the other rows in the table, as shown in FIGURE H-21.

3. **Save your work, then reload reserve.html in your browser**

    As FIGURE H-22 shows, the text *Room* appears in a cell that spans three columns. However, the heading *Period* is now duplicated in the two heading rows.

4. **Return to** reserve.html **in your editor, within the first** tr **element, click before the closing > in the opening tag for the** th **element containing the text** *Period*, **press** [Spacebar]**, then type** rowspan="2"

5. **Within the second** tr **element, delete the** th **element containing the text** *Period*

    Even though the second heading row contains code for only three cells, the cell that use the rowspan attribute in the previous row provides the additional content that keeps the row the same length as the other rows in the table. FIGURE H-23 shows the completed HTML code for the table.

6. **Save your changes, then refresh reserve.html in your browser**

    As FIGURE H-24 shows, the cell containing the text *Period* spans two rows.

FIGURE H-21: Sketch of table with cells spanning rows and columns

Content of a single cell spans two rows →

Content of a single cell spans three columns ←

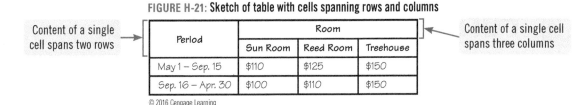

Period	Room		
	Sun Room	Reed Room	Treehouse
May 1 – Sep. 15	$110	$125	$150
Sep. 16 – Apr. 30	$100	$110	$150

© 2016 Cengage Learning

FIGURE H-22: Table cell spanning multiple columns

Redundant content in two rows →

colspan attribute causes cell content to be displayed across three columns

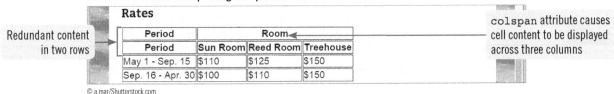

Rates

Period	Room		
Period	Sun Room	Reed Room	Treehouse
May 1 - Sep. 15	$110	$125	$150
Sep. 16 - Apr. 30	$100	$110	$150

© a.mar/Shutterstock.com

FIGURE H-23: Code containing `colspan` and `rowspan` attributes

New row added to thead section →

th element in second row containing the text *Period* removed →

rowspan attribute makes cell content part of multiple rows

colspan attribute makes cell content part of multiple columns

```
62      <thead>
63        <tr>
64          <th rowspan="2">Period</th>
65          <th colspan="3">Room</th>
66        </tr>
67        <tr>
68          <th>Sun Room</th>
69          <th>Reed Room</th>
70          <th>Treehouse</th>
71        </tr>
72      </thead>
```

FIGURE H-24: Table cell spanning multiple rows

`rowspan` attribute causes cell content to be displayed across two rows

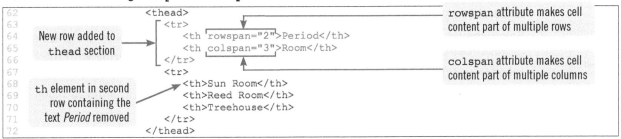

Rates

Period	Room		
	Sun Room	Reed Room	Treehouse
May 1 - Sep. 15	$110	$125	$150
Sep. 16 - Apr. 30	$100	$110	$150

© a.mar/Shutterstock.com

Calculating the number of columns in a row

When you use `colspan` and `rowspan` attributes, you still need to confirm that your content fits the table dimensions. To do so, start by adding the values for all `colspan` attributes used in the row. Next, add the number of `th` or `td` elements in the row without `colspan` attributes. Finally, add the number of `th` or `td` cells in earlier rows whose content is part of the current row due to `rowspan` values. In short:

    current row `colspan` total

+ cells in current row without `colspan`

+ cells spanning from previous rows with <u>rowspan</u>

= total columns

Running this calculation on any row of your table should produce the same value as for any other row.

If one or more rows appear to be shorter or longer than the surrounding rows, it can be helpful to preview your web page in a browser and inspect the table to identify the cell where the content of one row no longer corresponds to the content above or below it. You may simply need to adjust a `rowspan` or `colspan` value, or add or remove a cell.

In a table that doesn't use colspan or rowspan attributes, you can verify that each row includes content for every column simply by ensuring that each row contains the same number of th or td elements.

Format a Table with CSS

CSS enables you to style many aspects of a web page table. In addition to controlling fonts and backgrounds, you can use the `border-collapse` property to control the space between borders of adjacent cells and the `vertical-align` property to specify the vertical alignment of cell content. You can use these and other CSS properties to style an entire table, a table section (such as `thead` or `tbody`), or individual rows or cells. In addition, you can use the HTML `col` and `colgroup` elements to assign styles to a single column or to a group of columns. **CASE** ▶ *You style the borders and add background colors to different sections of your table to make it easier for users to read and understand.*

STEPS

QUICK TIP

The border-spacing property has no effect when border-collapse is set to collapse, but specifying a value of 0 ensures that browsers do not create extra space between the table's outermost cells and the border of the table element.

1. **Return to** styles.css **in your editor, then, in the reset styles section, add a style rule using the** `table` **selector with the declarations** `border-collapse: collapse;` **and** `border-spacing: 0;`

   Setting `border-collapse` to `collapse` eliminates the default space between the borders of adjacent cells.

2. **Scroll down to the main content tables section, then in the** `td, th` **style rule, add the declarations** `padding: 0.4em;` **and** `text-align: center;`

3. **Below the** `td, th` **rule, add a style rule with the** `table` **selector and the declarations** `width: 100%;` **and** `border: 2px solid black;`**, then add a style rule with the** `th` **selector and the declaration** `background-color: #aecdf4;`

   By default, a table occupies only the width necessary to display its content. At increased widths, each column is widened proportionally.

4. **Save your changes, then refresh or reload reservation.html in your browser**

   The content of all cells is centered and the cells have increased padding. The table occupies the entire width of the parent element and has a thicker outer border than the cell borders. In addition, the `th` cells have a light blue background.

QUICK TIP

Browsers render only the background (and related), border (and related), visibility, and width CSS properties applied to colgroup and col elements.

5. **Return to** reserve.html **in your editor, insert a blank line beneath the opening** `<table>` **tag, indent three additional spaces, type** `<colgroup>`**, press [Enter] twice, indent to match the previous code, then type** `</colgroup>`

QUICK TIP

Whenever you add col elements, they must cover all the columns in the table. Unless all columns are accounted for in col elements, your code won't validate.

6. **Within the opening and closing** `colgroup` **tags, indent and add the tags** `<col class="table-heading-column">` **and** `<col class="table-data-columns" span="3">` **on separate lines**

   FIGURE H-25 shows the HTML code. By default, each `col` element applies to a single column, starting from the left side of the table. However, you can group consecutive columns into a single `col` element by specifying the number of columns to include as the value of the `span` attribute. All `col` elements must be contained in a colgroup element.

7. **Save your work, return to** styles.css **in your editor, in the main content tables section, below the** `th` **rule, add a rule with the** `.table-heading-column` **selector and the declaration** `background-color: #f1eace;`**, then add a rule with the** `.table-data-columns` **selector and the declaration** `background-color: white;`

   Note that the second character in the color value is a number 1, not a letter l. **FIGURE H-26** shows the completed CSS code.

8. **Save your changes, then refresh or reload reserve.html in your browser**

   As **FIGURE H-27** shows, different background colors are applied to the columns based on the styling of the corresponding `col` elements. Styles specified for table cells, rows, or sections have a higher level of specificity than those applied to a `col` element; for this reason, the heading cells are rendered with the background color from the `th` rule rather than those specified for the `col` elements.

FIGURE H-25: `col` and `colgroup` elements added to HTML code for table

```
61              <table>
62   col elements   <colgroup>
63   nested within     <col class="table-heading-column">
64   colgroup          <col class="table-data-columns" span="3">
65   parent element  </colgroup>
66              <thead>
```

Styles for second `col` element apply to 3 columns

FIGURE H-26: Completed CSS code for table

```
28   table {
29       border-collapse: collapse;
30       border-spacing: 0;
31   }
32
33   /* document-wide styles */
```

```
164  /* main content tables */
165  td, th {
166      border: 1px solid black;
167      padding: 0.4em;
168      font-size: 1.3em;
169      text-align: center;
170  }
171  table {
172      width: 100%;
173      border: 2px solid black;
174  }
175  th {
176      background-color: #aecdf4;
177  }
178  .table-heading-column {
179      background-color: #f1eace;
180  }
181  .table-data-columns {
182      background-color: white;
183  }
```

Applies a background color to the first `col` element, which encompasses the leftmost column of the table

Applies a different background color to the second `col` element, which encompasses the remaining 3 columns

FIGURE H-27: Table with background color and other styles applied

Rates

Period	Room		
	Sun Room	Reed Room	Treehouse
May 1 - Sep. 15	$110	$125	$150
Sep. 16 - Apr. 30	$100	$110	$150

Special Events

Beige background applied to first column based on styling for first `col` element

Blue background applied to first two rows based on `th` style rule

White background applied to right three columns based on styling for second `col` element

© a.mar/Shutterstock.com

Organizing Content with Lists and Tables

Learning
Outcomes
• Arrange non-table
  elements in a grid
  using CSS

Apply a Table-Like Structure to Other Elements

Sometimes you may want to arrange web page elements so they appear visually in a grid, even if these elements would not normally belong in a table. To implement this layout, you first use block-level elements, such as `div` elements, to create a structure that parallels the nesting of `table`, `tr`, `th`, and `td` elements in an HTML table. You then set the CSS `display` property to `table-cell` for the elements containing the table content, `table-row` for the container elements for each row, and `table` for the main parent element. **CASE** *You duplicate the description list containing contact information for making reservations and convert the copy to a table-like layout using CSS.*

STEPS

1. Return to reserve.html in your editor, scroll down to the `h3` element that contains the text *Questions?*, select the entire `dl` element including the opening and closing `dl` tags, then copy it to the Clipboard

QUICK TIP
Commenting out code keeps the code available in case you later change your mind and want to use it.

2. Insert a new line before the opening `<dl>` tag, type `<!--`, insert a blank line after the closing `</dl>` tag, then type `-->`

3. Insert a new line before the opening `<!--` tag, paste the content of the Clipboard, then in the opening and closing tags for the pasted description list, replace `dl` with `div`, preserving the `class` value in the opening tag

4. Insert a new line above the first `dt` element, indent to the same level as the `dt` element, type `<div class="row">`, insert a new line below the first `dd` element, indent to the same level as the `dd` element, then type `</div>`

   The new div element serves the role of a `tr` element in a table.

5. Indent the `dt` and `dd` elements within the new `div` element an additional 3 spaces, replace the opening `<dt>` tag with `<div class="category">`, replace the closing `</dt>` tag with `</div>`, then, in the opening and closing dd tags, replace `dd` with `div`

6. Repeat Steps 4 and 5 for the remaining three sets of `dt` and `dd` elements, then compare your code to FIGURE H-28

7. Save your changes, return to styles.css in your editor, add a new line above the `/* footer section */` comment, then type `/* main content CSS tables */`

8. Below the new comment, add a style rule with the `.contact` selector and the declarations `margin: 1em 0;`, `display: table;`, and `font-size: 1.3em;`, add a style rule with the `.row` selector and the declaration `display: table-row;`, add a style rule with the `.row div` selector and the declarations `display: table-cell;` and `padding: 0.25em 0.5em;`, then add a style rule with the `.category` selector and the declaration `font-weight: bold;`, as shown in FIGURE H-29

9. Save your changes, refresh or reload reserve.html in your browser, then scroll down to the Questions? section

   As FIGURE H-30 shows, the contact information is now arranged in a grid without borders.

10. Validate the code for your web page and your style sheet, and make changes as necessary to fix any errors

FIGURE H-28: Completed HTML code for displaying contact information in a table-like layout

Outermost `div` element serves the role of a `table` element

`div` elements nested within outermost `div` element serve the role of `tr` elements

Most deeply nested `div` elements serve the role of `th` or `td` elements

```
110         <h3>Questions?</h3>
111         <p>Feel free to contact us with any queries about Lakeland Reeds, or about
112         planning your trip.</p>
113         <div class="contact">
114             <div class="row">
115                 <div class="category">Proprietor</div>
116                 <div>Phillip Blaine</div>
            </div>
            <div class="row">
                <div class="category">Email</div>
                <div>lrbb@example.com</div>
            </div>
            <div class="row">
                <div class="category">Phone</div>
124                 <div>(218) 555-5253</div>
125             </div>
126             <div class="row">
127                 <div class="category">Fax</div>
128                 <div>(218) 555-0413</div>
129             </div>
130         </div>
```

FIGURE H-29: Completed CSS code for displaying contact information in a table-like layout

Element with the `table` value for the `display` property serves the role of a `table` element

Element with the `table-row` value for the `display` property serves the role of a `tr` element

Element with the `table-cell` value for the `display` property serves the role of a `th` or `td` element

```
185   /* main content CSS tables */
186   .contact {
187     margin: 1em 0;
188     display: table;
189     font-size: 1.3em;
190   }
191   .row {
192     display: table-row;
193   }
194   .row div {
195     display: table-cell;
196     padding: 0.25em 0.5em;
197   }
198   .category {
199     font-weight: bold;
200   }
201
202   /* footer section */
```

FIGURE H-30: Contact information displayed in a table-like layout

Content displayed in a grid with two columns

Questions?

Feel free to contact us with any queries about Lakeland Reeds, or about planning your trip.

Proprietor	Phillip Blaine
Email	lrbb@example.com
Phone	(218) 555-5253
Fax	(218) 555-0413

Practice

Concepts Review

Refer to FIGURE H-31 **to answer the following questions.**

FIGURE H-31

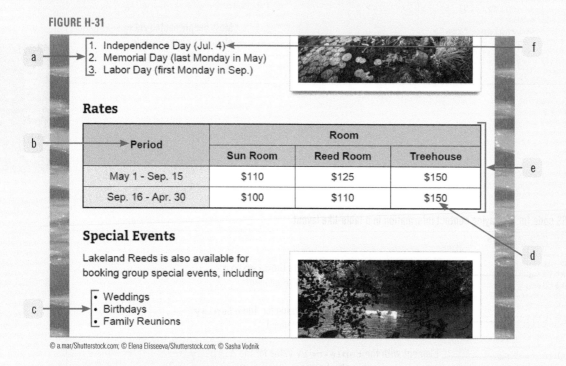

1. Independence Day (Jul. 4)
2. Memorial Day (last Monday in May)
3. Labor Day (first Monday in Sep.)

Rates

Period	Room		
	Sun Room	Reed Room	Treehouse
May 1 - Sep. 15	$110	$125	$150
Sep. 16 - Apr. 30	$100	$110	$150

Special Events

Lakeland Reeds is also available for booking group special events, including

- Weddings
- Birthdays
- Family Reunions

© a.mar/Shutterstock.com; © Elena Elisseeva/Shutterstock.com; © Sasha Vodnik

1. **Which item is created using the** td **element?**
2. **Which item is created using the** ul **element?**
3. **Which item is created using the** ol **element?**
4. **Which item is created using the** th **element?**
5. **Which item is created using the** table **element?**
6. **Which item is created using the** li **element?**

Match each term with the statement that best describes it.

7. **column**
8. **description list**
9. **ordered list**
10. **unordered list**
11. **row**
12. **cell**

a. a table component that displays a single item of data
b. a list in which items are numbered or lettered sequentially
c. a horizontal grouping of table content
d. a vertical grouping of table content
e. a list that enables you to specify an item and a description for each list item
f. a list in which the order of list items doesn't matter

Select the best answer from the list of choices.

13. **Which element do you use to create a list that is usually displayed with bullet characters?**
    - **a.** dd
    - **b.** ul
    - **c.** dl
    - **d.** ol

14. **What is a common cause of a protruding cell in a table?**
    - **a.** a missing thead element
    - **b.** a missing tbody element
    - **c.** a missing th or td element in one row
    - **d.** an extra th or td element in one row

15. **What is a common cause of an empty space in a table?**
    - **a.** a missing thead element
    - **b.** a missing tbody element
    - **c.** a missing th or td element in one row
    - **d.** an extra th or td element in one row

Skills Review

1. **Create an ordered list.**
   a. In your editor, open the file HTM_H-3.html from the SR folder where you store your Data Files for this unit, save it as **index.html**, then repeat to save the file HTM_H_4.html as **history.html**, HTM_H_5.html as **location.html**, and HTM_H_6.css as **styles.css**.
   b. Within the comment section at the top of each file, enter your first and last names and today's date, then save.
   c. Return to index.html in your editor, then below the p element containing the text *Eat in, carry out, or call for delivery*, insert a p element with the class value accent containing the text **Enjoy award winning pizza in your home in just three steps:**.
   d. Below the p element, insert starting and ending tags for an ordered list on separate lines at the same indent level.
   e. On a new line and between the tags you just entered, indent three additional spaces, add a list item element containing the text **Call the location nearest you.**, then repeat to insert two additional list items containing the text **Place your order and listen for your doorbell.** and **Open the box and dig in!**
   f. Save your changes, return to styles.css in your editor, then, in the reset styles section, add the ol and li selectors to the list of selectors in the style rule that sets border, padding, and margin to 0.
   g. At the end of the reset styles section, add a rule for the ol element that sets list-style-type to none.
   h. Scroll down as necessary to the /* footer section */ comment, then above it add the text **main content lists** as a new comment.
   i. Below the new comment you entered, create a style rule with the article ol selector that sets the width to 70%, the margin to 1em auto, the padding to 1em, left-aligns text, precedes each list item with a decimal number, and sets the background color to #ddd.
   j. Below the rule you created in the previous step, create a style rule with the article ol li selector that sets the left margin to 2em.
   k. Save your changes, open index.html in your browser, then verify that the three list items you entered are displayed in a list numbered 1, 2, and 3.

2. **Create an unordered list.**
   a. Return to history.html in your editor, locate the p element with the class value contrastbox, then edit the opening and closing tags for the element to make it an unordered list without a class value.
   b. Edit the opening and closing tags for each p element within the unordered list to make each a list item.
   c. Save your changes, return to styles.css in your editor, in the reset styles section add the ul selector to the list of selectors in the style rule that sets border, padding, and margin to 0, then add the ul selector to the style rule for ol elements that sets list-style-type to none.
   d. Scroll down to the /* main content lists */ comment, then in the two style rules above the comment, change the selector article div.contrastbox to article ul and change the selector article div.contrastbox p to article ul li.
   e. Cut and paste the /* main content lists */ comment so it is above the article ul style rule.

Skills Review (continued)

f. Save your changes, open history.html in your browser, then verify that the three words *flavor*, *aroma*, and *fresh* in the middle of the article are bold, centered, and displayed in a gray box and without bullet characters.

3. Create a description list.

a. Return to index.html in your editor, then within the `footer` element, add a blank line below the opening `<footer>` tag, indent an additional three spaces, enter the opening tag for a description list, add a blank line above the closing `</footer>` tag, indent an additional 3 spaces, then enter the closing tag for a description list.

b. For each p element within the `footer` element, increase the indent by three spaces, then remove the opening and closing p tags.

c. Mark the address *150 St. Joseph St.* as a description list term, move the `span` element and its content onto its own line at the same indent level, then mark the content of the new line as a description list description. (*Hint*: Include the `span` element within the code for the description item.) Repeat for the remaining two locations.

d. Save your changes, return to styles.css in your editor, then in the reset styles section add the `dl`, `dt`, and `dd` selectors to the list of selectors in the style rule that sets border, padding, and margin to 0.

e. Save your changes, reload index.html in your browser, then verify that each address and phone number is displayed on a separate line, and that each phone number is displayed in bold and indented in the contact information.

f. Return to index.html in your editor, copy the description list element to the Clipboard, including its opening and closing tags, return to history.html in your editor, replace the content of the `footer` element with the content of the Clipboard, save your changes, then repeat for location.html.

g. Reload history.html in your browser, verify that the footer content matches index.html, then repeat for location.html.

4. Create a navigation bar using a list.

a. Return to index.html in your editor, then within the nav element, add a blank line below the opening `<nav>` tag, indent an additional three spaces, enter the opening tag for an unordered list, add a blank line above the closing `</nav>` tag, indent an additional 3 spaces, then enter the closing tag for an unordered list.

b. For each `p` element within the nav element, increase the indent by three spaces, then replace the opening and closing p tags with tags that mark each element as a list item.

c. Save your changes, return to styles.css in your editor, scroll as necessary to the site navigation section, change the selector `nav.sitenavigation p` to `nav.sitenavigation li`, then change the selector `nav.sitenavigation p a` to `nav.sitenavigation li a`.

d. Save your changes, reload index.html in your browser, verify that the nav bar is displayed as shown in FIGURE H-32, click the History link, then verify that the History page is displayed. Note that the appearance of the nav bar on the History page will not match FIGURE H-32; you'll fix this in the following steps.

e. Return to index.html in your editor, then within the nav element, copy the unordered list tags and their content to the Clipboard.

f. Return to history.html in your editor, paste the content of the Clipboard to replace the content of the nav element, save your work, then repeat for location.html.

g. Refresh or reload history.html in your web browser, verify that the appearance of the nav bar matches that of index.html, click the Locations link, verify that the appearance of the nav bar matches the other pages, click the Home link, then verify that the index.html page is displayed.

FIGURE H-32

5. Insert a table.

a. Return to location.html in your editor, locate the h3 heading containing the text *Queen’s Park/UT*, insert a blank line beneath the p element containing the phone number, indent as needed to match the previous line, then insert opening and closing tags for a `table` element on separate lines at the same indent level.

b. Between the opening and closing tags you just entered, add opening and closing tags for table head and table body sections with each tag on its own line and indented three spaces more than the `table` tags.

c. Within the table head tags, add opening and closing tags for a table row, with each tag on its own line and indented three spaces more than the table head tags. Repeat to add opening and closing tags for three table rows in the table body section.

d. Within the table row element for the table head section, add table head cell elements containing the text **Day**, **Open**, and **Close** on separate lines, indented three spaces more than the opening table row tag. Repeat to add the following content to table data cell elements in the three table body rows:

Row 1: **Mon-Thu, 11am, 10pm**   Row 2: **Fri-Sat, 11am, 11pm**   Row 3: **Sun, Noon, 10pm**

e. Repeat Steps a–d to insert two more tables using the same content for the header row and the following content for the table body:

h3 heading *St. Clair*:

Row 1: **Mon-Thu, 11am, 9:30pm**   Row 2: **Fri-Sat, 11am, 11pm**   Row 3: **Sun, Noon, 9:30pm**

h3 heading *Dundas*:

Row 1: **Mon-Thu, 11am, 11pm**   Row 2: **Fri-Sat, 11am, Midnight**   Row 3: **Sun, Noon, 11pm**

f. Save your changes, return to styles.css in your editor, then in the reset styles section add the `table`, `thead`, `tbody`, `th`, and `td` selectors to the list of selectors in the style rule that sets border, padding, and margin to 0.

g. At the end of the reset styles section, create a style rule using the `table` selector that collapses borders and sets border spacing to 0.

h. Scroll down as necessary to the `/* footer section */` comment, then above it add the text **main content tables** as a new comment.

i. Below the new comment you entered, create a style rule with the `table` selector that sets the width to 50% and the margin to `0 auto`, create a rule with the `th` and `td` selectors that creates a 1px solid black border, create a rule with the `th` selector that sets padding to 0.1em 0.3em and background color to `#ffcc66`, then create a rule with the `td` selector that sets padding to 0.3em and left-aligns text.

j. Save your changes, reload location.html in your browser, then verify that each table makes sense and contains all the information specified in the previous steps.

6. Debug tables.

a. Return to location.html in your editor.

b. In the table below the h3 heading *Queen’s Park/UT*, add a table data cell containing the text **10pm** below the code for the final cell in the first row of the table body section.

c. Save your changes, refresh or reload location.html in your browser, then notice the effect of the extra cell.

d. Return to location.html in your editor, then comment out the line of code you added in Step b.

e. Comment out the code for the first table data cell in the second row of the table body section, save your changes, refresh or reload location.html in your browser, then notice the gap created by the missing cell.

f. Return to location.html in your editor, remove the comment tags from the first table data cell in the second row of the table body section, save your changes, refresh or reload location.html in your browser, then verify that all tables are displayed without extra or missing cells.

7. Span columns and rows.

a. Return to location.html in your editor, locate the table you inserted beneath the h3 heading *Queen’s Park/UT*, then insert opening and closing tags for a new row element just above the closing tag for the table head section.

b. In the first table row, select the code for the cells containing the text *Open* and *Close*, cut the text to the Clipboard, then paste it within the table row element for the second row in the table head section.

c. In the first table row, below the code for the table header cell containing the text *Day*, add code for a second table head element containing the text **Hours**.

d. In the table header cell containing the text *Day* in the first row of the table header section, add an attribute that indicates that the cell content should span 2 rows.

Skills Review (continued)

e. In the table header cell containing the text *Hours* in the first row of the table header section, add an attribute that indicates that the cell content should span 2 columns.

f. Copy the table head section including the opening and closing tags to the Clipboard, then paste it to replace the table head section in each of the remaining 2 tables in the document.

g. Save your changes, reload location.html in your browser, then verify that the table structure matches that shown in **FIGURE H-33**. Note that the table formatting will not match the figure; you'll fix this in Step 8.

FIGURE H-33

8. Format a table with CSS.

a. Return to location.html in your editor, insert a blank line beneath the opening `<table>` tag for the first table you created, indent three additional spaces, then add a container element for column groups.

b. Within the container element, add an element that applies the `class` value `table-heading-column` to the first column, add another element that applies the `class` value `table-data-columns` and spans the last two columns. Repeat Steps a and b for the other two tables.

c. Save your changes, return to styles.css in your editor, scroll as necessary to the main content tables section, then at the bottom of the section add a style rule for the `class` value `table-heading-column` that sets the background color to `#ccc`.

d. Save your changes, open location.html in your browser, then verify that the days of the week in each table have a gray background, as shown in **FIGURE H-33**.

9. Apply a table-like structure to other elements.

a. Return to index.html in your editor, scroll down to the `footer` element, select the entire description list including the opening and closing tags, then copy it to the Clipboard.

b. Comment out the description list element, then above the comment out code, paste the Clipboard content.

c. In the opening and closing tags for the pasted description list, replace `dl` with `div`, specifying the `class` value `contact` in the opening tag.

d. Insert a new line above the first `dt` element, indent to the same level as the `dt` element, enter an opening `<div>` tag with the `class` value `row`, insert a new line below the first `dd` element, indent to the same level as the `dd` element, then insert a closing `</div>` tag.

e. Indent the `dt` and `dd` elements within the new `div` element an additional three spaces, in the opening and closing `dt` tags replace `dt` with `div`, then in the opening and closing `dd` tags, replace `dd` with `div`, specifying the `class` value `phone` in the opening tag.

f. Repeat Steps d and e for the remaining two sets of `dt` and `dd` elements.

g. Save your changes, copy the CSS table you created to the Clipboard, including its opening and closing tags, return to history.html in your editor, replace the content of the `footer` element with the content of the Clipboard, save your changes, then repeat for location.html.

h. Return to styles.css in your editor, add a new line above the `/* print styles */` comment, then add a comment containing the text **footer CSS table**.

i. Below the new comment, add a style rule with the `.contact` selector and declarations that set margins to `0 auto` and `display` to `table`, add a style rule with the `.row` selector and a declaration that sets `display` to `table-row`, add a style rule with the `.row div` selector and declarations that set `display` to `table-cell` and padding to `0.25em 0.5em;`, then add a style rule with the `.phone` selector and a declaration that bolds text.

j. Save your changes, refresh or reload location.html in your browser, verify that the contact information in the page footer uses a table-like structure.

k. Validate the code for your web pages and your style sheet, and make changes as necessary to fix any errors.

Independent Challenge 1

Sarah Nguyen, the owner of the Spotted Wren Garden Center, has given you additional content to add to the website you've been creating for her. You add this information using lists and tables.

a. In your editor, open HTM_H-7.html from the IC1 folder where you store your Data Files for this unit, save it as **hours.html**, then repeat to save HTM_H-8.html as **resource.html** and HTM_H-9.css as **styles.css**. In the comment at the top of each file, enter your name and today's date where indicated, then save the files.

b. Return to resource.html in your editor. Beneath the h3 heading *Omaha area plant hardiness zone information*, insert the following table. (*Hint*: Use rowspan attributes for the cells containing the text *Zone, Last frost, First frost, May 1*, and *Oct 15*. Use a colspan attribute for the cell containing the text *Average annual minimum temp*. The HTML character code for the degree symbol is °).

TABLE H-4

| Zone | Average annual minimum temp | | Last frost | First frost |
	Fahrenheit	Celsius		
4b	–25°F to –20°F	–28.9°C to –31.6°C		
5a	–20°F to –15°F	–26.2°C to –28.8°C	May 1	Oct 15
5b	–15°F to –10°F	–23.4°C to –26.1°C		

c. Save your changes, return to styles.css in your editor, in the reset styles section add the table, thead, tbody, th, and td selectors to the list of selectors in the style rule that sets border, padding, and margin to 0. At the end of the reset styles section, create a style rule using the table selector that collapses borders and sets border spacing to 0.

FIGURE H-34

d. Above the /* footer section */ comment, add a comment containing the text **main content table**. Below the comment, add a style rule for th and td elements that creates a 1px solid black border and sets the padding to 0.5em, then add a rule for th elements that sets the background color to yellow. Save your changes.

e. Return to resource.html in your editor, then, in the code for the table, add a colgroup element that contains a child element with the class name zone for styling the first column, a child element with class name temps for styling the second and third columns, and a child element with the class name frost for styling the fourth and fifth columns. Save your changes, return to styles.css, in the main content table section add a style rule for the element with the class value temps that sets the background color to #87f547, then add a style rule for the element with the class value frost that sets the background color to #f5a88c. Save your changes, reload resource.html in your browser, then verify that the table appears as shown in **FIGURE H-34**.

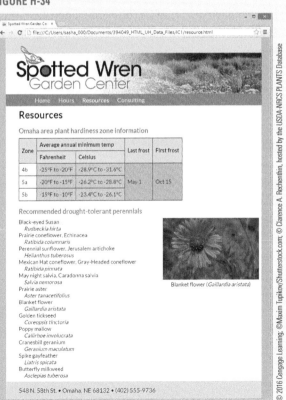

Independent Challenge 1 (continued)

f. Return to resource.html in your editor. Below the h3 element containing the text *Recommended drought-tolerant perennials* and the figure that follows it, mark up the list of plant names as a description list with the common names as terms and the Latin names that follow as descriptions. Save your changes, return to styles.css in your editor, then, above the /* footer section */ comment, add a comment containing the text **main content description list.** Below the comment, create a style rule to style the content of all description elements in a description list in italic and with a 1em left margin. Scroll up as necessary to the reset styles section, then add the dd, dl, and dt selectors to the list of selectors in the style rule that sets border, padding, and margin to 0. Save your changes, reload resource.html in your browser, then verify that the definition list matches the one shown in **FIGURE H-34**.

g. Return to resource.html in your editor. Convert the code for the nav bar to an unordered list by changing the p element that encloses each link to an li element, then enclosing the code for all the links within a ul element. Repeat for hours.html, then save your changes to both documents. Return to styles.css in your editor, scroll as necessary to the site navigation section, then change the selector for the nav.sitenavigation p rule to nav.sitenavigation li. Scroll up as necessary to the reset styles section, then add the ul and li selectors to the list of selectors in the style rule that sets border, padding, and margin to 0. At the end of the reset styles section, create a style rule using the ul selector that sets list-style-type to none. Save your changes, refresh or reload resource.html in your browser, then verify that the appearance of the navigation bar is unchanged. Click the Hours link, verify that the Hours page opens, then verify that the nav bar on that page is unchanged.

h. Return to hours.html in your editor. Beneath the h2 heading, insert a new line containing a div element with the class value table at the same indent level as the previous line. Add a closing tag for the div element below the last line of store hours information. Enclose each line of code containing store hours information in a div element with the class value row, then delete the opening and closing p tags from each line. For each line, enclose the abbreviation of the day of the week within a div element, delete the colon (:) that follows it, move the remainder of the line onto a new line, then enclose the content of the new line in a div element. Save your changes.

i. Return to styles.css in your editor. Above the /* footer section */ comment, add a comment containing the text **main content CSS table**. Below the comment, create a style rule for the table class that sets margins to 1em 0, font size to 1.3em, and makes the element display like a table, create a rule for the row class that makes the elements display like table rows, add a style rule for div elements within elements of the class row that sets padding to 0.25em 0.5em and makes the elements display like table cells, then add a style rule for the day class that makes text bold. Save your changes, reload hours.html in your browser, then verify that the list of hours matches the one shown in **FIGURE H-35**.

FIGURE H-35

j. Validate all your HTML and CSS documents.

Independent Challenge 2

You add new information about the Murfreesboro Regional Soccer League to the website that you are creating. You mark up the new information using an unordered list and several tables. You also change the markup for the nav bar to an unordered list.

a. In your editor, open HTM_H-10.html from the IC2 folder where you store your Data Files for this unit, save it as **started.html**, then repeat to save HTM_H-11.html as **schedule.html** and HTM_H-12.css as **styles.css**. In the comment at the top of each file, enter your name and today's date where indicated, then save the files.

b. In started.html, locate the paragraph that begins *If you're interested in joining up*, then insert a blank line below it. Add an unordered list containing the following four list items: **Child/Teen (6–18): $50, Student (19–24): $50, Adult (25–59): $65**, and **Senior (60+): $40**. Save your changes, then return to styles.css in your editor. In the reset styles section, add the ul and li selectors to the list of selectors in the style rule that sets border, padding, and margin to 0. At the end of the reset styles section, create a style rule using the ul selector that sets list-style-type to none. Above the /* footer section */ comment, add a comment containing the text **main content unordered list**. Below the comment, create a style rule for unordered lists within the article element that sets margins to 0 0 1em 3em, adds 7% padding on the left side, uses filled circles for list item markers, and sets the font size to 1.2em. Save your changes, open started.html in a browser, then verify that the bulleted list you created matches FIGURE H-36.

c. Return to started.html in your editor. Convert the code for the nav bar to an unordered list by enclosing the p elements that mark nav bar items within an element that marks an unordered list, then changing each p element that encloses a nav bar item to a list item element. Repeat for schedule.html, then save your changes to both documents. Return to styles.css in your editor. In the site navigation section, below the nav.sitenavigation rule, create a style rule that applies only to list item elements within the nav element with the class value sitenavigation that sets the font size to 1.2em. Save your work, reload started.html in your browser, then verify that the appearance of the nav bar matches FIGURE H-36. Click the Schedules link, ensure that the Schedules page opens, then verify the appearance of the nav bar also matches FIGURE H-36.

FIGURE H-36

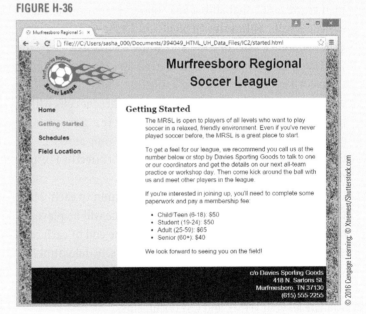

Independent Challenge 2 (continued)

d. Return to schedule.html in your editor, then convert the four lists of game dates and times into tables. Create a heading row for each table with heading cells containing the text **Date** and **Time**. Split the information for each game into two cells, the first containing the date and the second containing the start time. Set the `class` value for the first table to `red-team-schedule`, the second table to `blue-team-schedule`, the third table to `green-team-schedule`, and the fourth table to `yellow-team-schedule`. Save your changes, then return to styles.css in your editor. Above the comment `/* main content unordered list */`, add a comment containing the text **main content tables**, then below the new comment add a style rule for `table` elements that sets the width to 90% and sets margins to 0 auto. Add a style rule for table header cells and table data cells that creates 1px solid black borders and sets padding to 0.5em. Add a style rule for table header cell elements that sets the background color to #ddd. Create a rule for the element with the class value `red-team-schedule` that creates a 5px solid red border, then create a rule that adds a 5px solid red bottom border to header cells within this element Create a rule for the element with the class value `blue-team-schedule` that creates a 5px solid blue border, then create a rule that adds a 5px solid blue bottom border to header cells within this element and sets their text color to `blue`. Create a rule for the element with the class value `green-team-schedule` that creates a 5px solid green border, then create a rule that adds a 5px solid green bottom border to header cells within this element and sets their text color to `green`. Create a rule for the element with the class value `yellow-team-schedule` that creates a 5px solid border using the color #e6da57, then create a rule that adds a 5px solid bottom border using the color #e6da57 to header cells within this element and sets their text color to `yellow`. Save your changes, refresh or reload schedule.html in your browser, then verify that all four tables are displayed correctly. Fix any missing or extra cells.

e. Using **FIGURE H-37** as a guide, add a third column to each table that displays the field letter where each game will be played. (*Hint*: To add a column, add a new cell at the end of each row element.) Save your work, refresh or reload schedule.html in your browser, then verify that your tables match those shown in **FIGURE H-37**.

f. Validate all your HTML and CSS documents.

FIGURE H-37

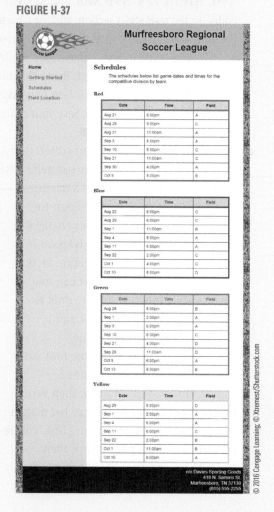

Independent Challenge 3

As you continue your work on the website for Hotel Natoma, you incorporate additional information about the hotel and local attractions using some of the techniques for organizing content that you learned in this unit.

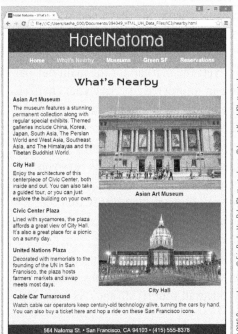

a. In your editor, open HTM_H-13.html from the IC3 folder where you store your Data Files for this unit, save it as **nearby.html**, then repeat to save HTM_H-14.html as **museums.html**, HTM_H-15.html as **greensf.html**, and HTM_H-16.css as **styles.css**. In the comment at the top of each file, enter your name and today's date where indicated, then save the files.

b. In nearby.html, mark the list of nearby locations and descriptions as a description list. Save your changes, then in styles.css, above the comment /* footer section */, create a comment containing the text **main content description list**. Add a style rule that bolds the text of description list term items, then add a rule that sets margins of 0.4em 0 1em for description list description items. In the reset styles section, add the dd, dl, and dt selectors to the list of selectors in the style rule that sets border, padding, and margin to 0. Save your changes, open nearby.html in a browser, then verify that it matches FIGURE H-38.

c. In museums.html, mark the list of museums as an unordered list. Save your changes, then in styles.css, above the comment /* main content description list */, create a comment containing the text **main content unordered lists**. Create a style rule for unordered lists that sets the left margin to 5%, displays a filled circle next to each list item, and sets the line height to 1.4em. In the reset styles section, add the ul and li selectors to the list of selectors in the style rule that sets border, padding, and margin to 0. At the end of the reset styles section, create a style rule using the ul selector that sets list-style-type to none. Save your changes, open museums.html in a browser, then verify that it matches FIGURE H-39.

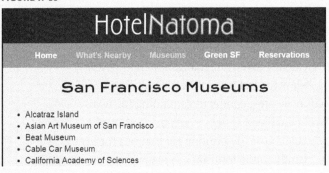

d. In greensf.html, mark the list of destinations as an ordered list. Save your changes, then in styles.css, above the comment /* footer section */, create a comment containing the text **main content ordered list**. Create a style rule for ordered lists that sets left and right margins to 5% and uses decimal numbering, then create a style rule for list items within an ordered list that creates 0.6em padding on the left. In the reset styles section, add the ol selector to the list of selectors in the style rule that sets border, padding, and margin to 0 and in the style rule that sets list-style-type to none.

Independent Challenge 3 (continued)

e. Save your changes, open greensf.html in a browser, then verify that it matches **FIGURE H-40**.

f. Return to greensf.html in your editor, then convert the markup for the main nav bar to use an unordered list. Save your changes, then in styles.css, in the site navigation section, change the selector for the `nav.sitenavigation p` rule to `nav.sitenavigation li`. Save your changes, refresh or reload greensf.html in your browser, then verify that the appearance of the nav bar remains unchanged.

g. Return to your editor, then repeat Step d for nearby.html and for museums.html.

h. Validate all your HTML and CSS documents.

FIGURE H-40

Independent Challenge 4 – Explore

As you continue your work on the website for *Eating Well In Season*, a provider of locally-sourced, healthy meals, you mark existing information using lists and you incorporate new information in a table.

a. In your editor, open HTM_H-17.html from the IC3 folder where you store your Data Files for this unit, save it as **menus.html**, then repeat to save HTM_H-18.html as **pricing.html**, and HTM_H-19.css as **styles.css**. In the comment at the top of each file, enter your name and today's date where indicated, then save the files.

b. In menus.html, mark the list of meals and menu items under the *Sample Menus* h2 heading as a description list. (*Hint*: More than one `dd` element can follow each `dt` element.) Save your changes, then in styles. css, below the last rule in the main content section, create a comment containing the text **main content description list**. Add a style rule for the description list that sets the font family to the font stack Verdana, Geneva, sans-serif and sets margins to 0 1em 1em, then create a rule for description list term items that formats text in bold and sets a top margin of 1em. In the reset styles section, add the `dd`, `dl`, and `dt` selectors to the list of selectors in the style rule that sets border, padding, and margin to 0. Save your changes, open menus.html in a browser, then verify that the display of the description list matches the one in **FIGURE H-41**.

FIGURE H-41

c. In menus.html, mark the content of the sidebar below the h2 element as an unordered list. Save your changes, then in styles.css, below the last rule in the sidebar section, create a comment containing the text **sidebar unordered lists**. Create a style rule for unordered lists within `aside` elements that sets the left margin to 2em and uses the image bullet.png from the images folder as the item marker (*Hint*: Use the `list-style-image` property with the syntax `url("path/filename")`). In the reset styles section, add the ul and li selectors to the list of selectors in the style rule that sets border, padding, and margin to 0. At the end of the reset styles section, create a style rule using the ul selector that sets `list-style-type` to none. Save your changes, refresh or reload menus.html in your browser, then verify that it matches FIGURE H-41.

d. Return to menus.html in your editor, then convert the markup for the main nav bar to use an unordered list. Save your changes, then in styles.css, in the site navigation section, change the selector for the `nav.sitenavigation` p rule to `nav.sitenavigation li`. Save your changes, refresh or reload menus.html in your browser, then verify that the appearance of the nav bar remains unchanged.

e. Return to menus.html in your editor, copy the unordered list from the sidebar, switch to pricing.html in your editor, then paste the unordered list in the code for the sidebar, replacing the existing content below the h2 element. Repeat to copy the ordered list in the nav bar for menus.html and paste it in pricing.html.

f. In the `article` element in pricing.html, create the table shown in TABLE H-5. Specify the `class` value `specific-headers` for the second row of the header section. Save your changes.

g. Return to styles.css in your editor, above the main content description list section, create a comment containing the text **main content table**. Create a style rule for the `table` element that sets a width of 90% and margins to `1em auto`. Create a rule for table header cells and table data cells that sets width to 33.3%, creates a 1px solid black border, sets padding to 0.3em 1em, and sets the font family to `Verdana, Geneva, sans-serif`. Create a rule for table header cells that sets the background color to `#98c13d`. Create a rule for table header cells nested in the element with the `class` value `.specific-headers` that sets the background color to `rgb(246,224,65)`. Save your changes, open pricing.html in a browser, then verify that it matches FIGURE H-42.

h. Validate all of your HTML and CSS documents and make any edits necessary to address any issues.

TABLE H-5

Meal	Monthly Cost	
	once a week	daily
Lunch	$60	$390
Dinner	$80	$520
Both	$125	$800

FIGURE H-42

Visual Workshop

In your editor, open the file HTM_H-20.html from the VW folder where you store your Data Files for this unit and save it as **events.html**. Repeat to save HTM_H-21.css as **styles.css**. Add your first and last names and today's date to the comment section at the top of each file, then save your changes. Add the table shown in FIGURE H-43, within the `div` element nested in the `article` element. (*Hint*: Use the `title` class to italicize the book title, and use the color `rgb(253,245,230)` for the table header background.) Convert the code for the nav bar to an unordered list, changing and adding to the style sheet as necessary. Validate your HTML and CSS code.

FIGURE H-43

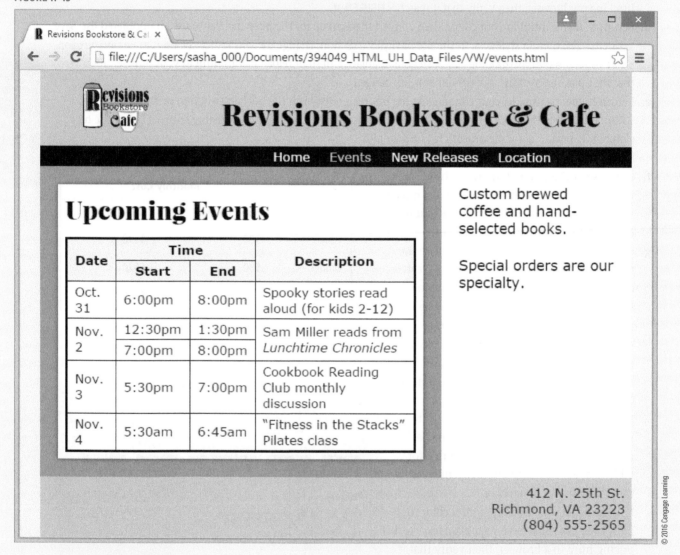

Organizing Content with Lists and Tables

Implementing Responsive Design

CASE In this unit, you'll implement responsive design practices to ensure that the Lakeland Reeds Bed & Breakfast website is displayed appropriately in any size browser window.

Unit Objectives

After completing this unit, you will be able to:

- Assess responsive design
- Construct a multipart media query
- Test layouts with an emulator
- Add a column with a media query

- Create a widescreen layout
- Create responsive navigation
- Implement adaptive content
- Use progressive enhancement

Files You Will Need

 L   15 files   IC3   13 files

 SR   12 files   IC4   13 files

 IC1   9 files   VW   11 files

 IC2   12 files

For specific filenames, see Filenames_I.pdf in the Unit I Data Files folder.

Assess Responsive Design

Learning
Outcomes
• Describe the
  techniques
  involved in
  responsive design

Web pages and applications can be viewed on a variety of devices, with screen sizes ranging from pocket-sized smartphones to large monitors. Although a browser on any device is capable of rendering any page written in HTML and CSS, a layout that's easy to use at one screen size can present challenges at a different screen size. A common solution to making a single web page or app usable at multiple sizes is **responsive design**, which allows a web developer to specify different CSS style rules for some or all of a page's elements depending on the width of the screen or browser window in which the document is displayed. **CASE** ▸ *As you prepare to update the layout for the Lakeland Reeds B & B website, you review the components of responsive design.*

DETAILS

Responsive design is based on a few techniques:

- **Sizing with percentages**

  Element widths in responsive designs are often specified in percentages, with the size of each element relative to the width of its parent. Using percentages, you could, for instance, place two images side by side, assigning each a width of 45% of the page width, and use the remaining 10% for the margin, padding, and border, which is a total of 100%. Because their box model properties are specified in percentages, these images would maintain their sizing relative to each other while preserving their layout on the page, regardless of the width of the browser window.

- **Identifying breakpoints**

  To create a web page using responsive design, you start by creating a layout that's optimized for the smallest or the largest screen size you want to support—but not both. You then use a desktop browser or other design tool to view the page at different widths. For instance, starting with a design optimized for smartphones, you view the page in a narrow window on a desktop browser, then widen the window gradually to see how the layout looks at larger widths. At a certain width—known as a **breakpoint**—the layout no longer looks good, or you may decide that you'd like to move elements or add or remove content to accommodate that window size.

- **Creating multipart media queries**

  Once you have identified your first breakpoint, you create a multipart @media rule known as a media query that specifies CSS style rules to apply. Like a print style rule, you use the @media keyword for responsive design but, instead of the print media type, you specify the screen media type. In addition, you follow the media type with one or more **media features**, which specify conditions that the media must satisfy for the rules in the media query to be applied. TABLE I-1 lists logical operators for multipart media queries and some media features. Responsive design relies mainly on the min-width and max-width media features. In general, you use min-width for all media queries when your starting layout is optimized for a small screen, and you use max-width for all media queries when your starting layout is optimized for a large screen. For instance, when your default layout is optimized for small screens, then the media query for your first breakpoint would use the min-width media feature, as follows:

  ```
  @media screen and (min-width: 880px) {
      style rules
  }
  ```

  This media query specifies that the style rules it contains should be applied when the associated HTML document is displayed on a screen and in a browser window that is at least 880px wide. This ensures that the rules for this media query are not applied to other media such as a printed page, and are not applied in browser windows narrower than 880px, such as when displayed on many smartphones. After creating your first media query, you reload the page in a browser, check if another breakpoint exists, create a media query for the next breakpoint if applicable, then repeat until your layout is displayed appropriately at the range of widths that you want to support. FIGURE I-1 shows a sample layout with media queries at different widths.

Nav bar hidden and represented by an icon

Default layout consists of a single column

Smartphone (default layout)

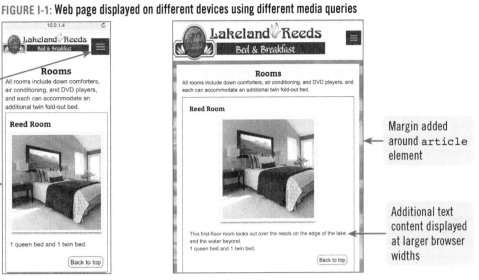

Margin added around article element

Additional text content displayed at larger browser widths

Tablet (min-width: 480px)

Nav bar displayed

Second column added to layout at larger browser widths

Figure moved to new column

Standard desktop (min-width: 880px)

Third column added to layout at largest browser widths

Button moved to new column

Large desktop (min-width: 1060px)

TABLE I-1: Selected logical operators and media features for media queries

type	keyword	description	example
logical operators	and	conditions before and after and keyword must be true	screen and (min-width: 880px)
	,	condition before or after comma must be true	screen, (min-width: 880px)
	not	condition following not keyword must be false	not screen
media features	min-width	minimum width to which media query applies	(min-width: 880px)
	max-width	maximum width to which media query applies	(max-width: 960px)

HTML5 & CSS3

Construct a Multipart Media Query

The first step in implementing responsive design is to create a default layout for the smallest or largest browser width you want to support. Next, you identify the first breakpoint, then you create a multipart media query that combines the `screen` media type with the appropriate media feature for your breakpoint—generally `min-width` or `max-width`. **CASE** ▶ *You examine the default layout for the Lakeland Reeds Rooms page, which is optimized for small screens. You then identify the next largest breakpoint and create a media query.*

STEPS

1. **In your editor, open HTM_I-1.html from the Lessons folder where you store your Data Files for this unit, save it as rooms.html, then repeat to save HTM_I-2.css as styles.css**

2. **In the comment at the top of each file, enter your name and today's date where indicated, then save the files**

3. **In your browser, open rooms.html, then adjust the width of the browser window to view the page as narrow as possible, as wide as possible, and then more narrow again until the boxes that enclose the room images are the same width as the images themselves, without causing the images to reduce in size**

   At a narrow width, all the content is displayed in a single, long column. As the browser window becomes wider, some of the content spreads across the page, and large areas of white space are introduced into the layout.

4. **Open the developer tools, hover over the `<article>` tag, then note the dimensions displayed in the browser window**

   The first dimension displayed is the width. Once you have identified a breakpoint, you can then use the developer tools to identify the width in pixels of the breakpoint. This breakpoint is at approximately 460px.

QUICK TIP
The comma before the word *print* in the media query means *or*, so the query applies to any printed output regardless of the browser width when the Print command is activated.

5. **Return to styles.css in your editor, scroll down to the end of the document, then above the `/* print styles */` comment, add the comment `/* small screen/tablet styles */`, press [Enter], type `@media screen and (min-width: 460px), print {`, press [Enter] twice, then type `}`**

   This code creates a breakpoint at a minimum browser width of 460px, or for any printed output. Smaller widths are displayed using default settings, while widths of 460px or greater use the style rules you specify in this media query.

6. **Within the braces for the new media query, enter the style rules shown in FIGURE I-2**

7. **Save your changes, reload rooms.html in your browser, drag the window to its narrowest width, then widen the window until the layout changes to match FIGURE I-3**

   At a width of at least 460px, padding is added around the `article` element, making the background image visible around the edges. In addition, a border, padding, and box shadow are added to `figure` elements and the display is set to `inline-block`, preventing the width of `figure` elements from expanding past the width of the images they contain.

QUICK TIP
The `@media print` style rule includes the declaration `page-break-before: always` for `section` elements, which causes each `section` element to start on a new page in printed output.

8. **Open a print preview of the page**

   Because your media query also applies to printed output, the layout of the print preview matches the layout of the page at widths larger than 460px.

FIGURE I-2: Media query for browser widths of 460px or greater

```
186    /* small screen/tablet styles */
187    @media screen and (min-width: 460px), print {
188        article {
189            padding: 2%;
190        }
191        figure {
192            border: 1px solid #ccc;
193            padding: 2%;
194            box-shadow: 0 10px 6px -6px #777;
195            display: inline-block;
196        }
197        section {
198            text-align: center;
199        }
200        section h3, section p {
201            text-align: left;
202        }
203    }
204
205    /* print styles */
```

Media feature enclosed in parentheses

Style rules applied in a browser window width of 460px or greater

FIGURE I-3: Rooms web page displayed narrower than 460px and wider than 460px

At width below 460px, the article element has no padding

At width of 460px or greater, the article element has 2% padding, making the background image visible

At width below 460px, figure elements have no border, padding, or box shadow

At width of 460px or greater, figure elements have gray border, 2% padding, and box shadow

© Unholy Vault Designs/Shutterstock.com; © 2016 Cengage Learning; © a.mar/Shutterstock.com; © Iriana Shiyan/Shutterstock.com

Implementing Responsive Images

The img element accepts a single filename as the value for the src attribute. When you create a responsive website that will be viewable in browser windows of different widths, you generally use a large image, which looks good on a large screen, and scale it down for smaller screens. However, large images can require a lot of bandwidth and time to download on a mobile device. For this reason, web developers have begun creating a standard for responsive images using the new srcset and sizes attributes

of the img element. Instead of specifying a single image filename, the srcset attribute enables you to specify the filenames of multiple sizes of the same image along with their widths, and the sizes attribute lets you indicate the browser widths at which each image should be used. You can read an overview of how these attributes are used at ericportis.com/posts/2014/srcset-sizes, and you can track their current level of browser support at caniuse.com.

Test Layouts with an Emulator

Before making a website publicly available, it's important to test it on as many devices that your audience may be using as possible. However, while developing the site, instead of using the actual devices, you can use an application known as an **emulator**, which runs on a computer and approximates the dimensions and behavior of a wide range of devices. While some device and mobile operating system makers release device-specific emulators, it can be simpler to use a single emulator that emulates a wide range of devices. One such emulator is built into the Chrome browser. **CASE** ▸ *You use Chrome Device Mode to emulate common Android and iOS smartphones and tablets to see how your layout is rendered on a range of devices.*

STEPS

Note: This lesson requires that you have a current version of Google Chrome installed. You can download the current version for free from google.com/chrome.

1. **Open** rooms.html **in Google Chrome**

2. **Click the** Customize and control Google Chrome button ☰**, point to** More tools, **then click** Developer tools

   The Developer tools pane is displayed.

TROUBLE
Click the Dock to main window button 🖵, if you don't see the device mode window or if the developer tools panel is floating.

3. **Click the** Toggle device mode button ▫**, click the** Device box, **click** Google Nexus 5, **then reload the page**

   The web page is displayed in Device Mode at the width and height of a Google Nexus 5 smartphone, as shown in FIGURE I-4. You might notice that as you move the mouse pointer over the document, it is displayed as a gray circle, indicating that the emulator is treating clicks as touches on a touchscreen.

TROUBLE
If the Media queries button turns white after you click it, click it a second time to turn it back to blue.

4. **Click the** Media queries button 📊 **so it turns blue**

   The Media queries button displays a representation of each media query that applies to the current document as a colored bar along the horizontal ruler. One colored bar is shown, representing the media query you created in the previous lesson for a minimum width of 460px.

5. **Click the** Swap dimensions button 🔄

   The Swap dimensions button simulates the device being used in landscape mode, or turned on its side. The default layout is applied to the document in a vertical, or portrait, orientation on the Google Nexus 5. However, when you swapped the dimensions, the width of the browser window became larger than 460px. As a result, the media query you created that applies to a minimum width of 460px is applied to the page when the device is in landscape mode, as shown in FIGURE I-5.

6. **Click the** Device box, **click** Apple iPhone 6, **then reload the page**

   The web page is displayed at the width and height of an Apple iPhone 6 smartphone.

7. **Click the** Swap dimensions button 🔄

   As with the Google Nexus 5, when you swap dimensions on the Apple iPhone 6, the media query you created is applied to the page.

TROUBLE
You can learn more about Chrome Device Mode at developer.chrome.com/devtools/docs/device-mode.

8. **Click the** Toggle device mode button ▫**, then close the Developer tools pane**

   Device Mode is turned off and the web page is displayed at the width of the browser window on your computer.

FIGURE I-4: Rooms page in Device Mode emulating Google Nexus 5

Google Nexus 5 selected in Device box

Media queries button

Swap dimensions button

Toggle device mode button

Web page displayed at width and height of Google Nexus 5 smartphone

Undock into separate window button

© Unholy Vault Designs/Shutterstock.com; © 2016 Cengage Learning; © a.mar/Shutterstock.com;
© Iriana Shiyan/Shutterstock.com

FIGURE I-5: Rooms page in Device Mode with media query shown and dimensions swapped

The Media queries button is blue, indicating that it is on

The width and height dimensions are swapped

The media query you created is represented as an orange bar that starts at 460px on the horizontal ruler

Because the browser window is now wider than 460px, the styles from your media query are applied, including the padding on the `article` element

© Unholy Vault Designs/Shutterstock.com; © 2016 Cengage Learning; © a.mar/Shutterstock.com;
© Iriana Shiyan/Shutterstock.com

Working With Device Pixel Ratios

The display for any electronic device, including a smartphone, a tablet, or a computer, is composed of a grid of dots known as **device pixels**. These pixels do not always correspond to the pixels used in either CSS media queries or property values, which are known as **logical pixels**. Traditionally, a device's display showed each pixel of an image using a single pixel of the display. Over time, displays became denser, packing more pixels into the same amount of space, which makes the content appear sharper. However, displaying content on a high-density screen at a 1:1 ratio of logical pixels to device pixels means that the content would be smaller than if it were viewed on a low-density screen, potentially making the content hard to read. To address this issue, some devices with especially dense displays use multiple device pixels to show a single logical pixel. The number of device pixels

used to display each logical pixel is a value known as the device **pixel ratio**. For instance, suppose the width of a smartphone display is 640 pixels. If the device pixel ratio for the device is 2, then the browser would behave as if the display was only 320 pixels wide (640 ÷ 2 = 320). When researching the dimensions of devices that you want to support, it is important to learn not only the screen dimensions (in device pixels) but also the device pixel ratio. Using these 2 values, you can calculate the width that the browser behaves as. The options in Google Chrome Device Mode include a Device pixel ratio button, which lets you specify the device pixel ratio in your testing. When you select a device from the Device menu, its device pixel ratio is automatically set to the value for that device—for instance, the device pixel ratio for the Galaxy Nexus 5 is 3, while that of the iPhone 6 is 2.

Learning
Outcomes
• Use a media query
to add a column

Add a Column with a Media Query

When adapting a layout for multiple screen widths, it can be helpful to vary the number of columns in which content is displayed. On small screens, it generally makes the most sense to display content in a single column. However, at larger sizes, you can move some content into a sidebar, or even show some elements next to others. You can use a media query to create columns by setting properties such as `float`, `width`, and `position`. **CASE** *On wider displays, you want the images of the rooms to be displayed to the right of their descriptions, rather than below their descriptions. You create a media query to do this at a breakpoint of 880px.*

STEPS

1. **Return to rooms.html in your browser, then widen the browser window and observe how the layout responds**

   As the browser window widens, the image of each room remains centered, with increasing white space on both sides, while the description of each room is displayed across the page below the image.

2. **Return to styles.css in your editor, scroll down to the end of the document and above the `/* print styles */` comment, add the comment `/* standard screen styles */`, then press [Enter]**

3. **Type `@media screen and (min-width: 880px) {`, press [Enter] twice, then type `}`**

   This code creates a breakpoint at a minimum browser width of 880px.

4. **Within the braces for the new media query, enter the style rules shown in** FIGURE I-6

5. **Save your changes, reload rooms.html in your browser, drag the window to its narrowest width, then widen the window until the layout changes to match** FIGURE I-7

   At its narrowest, the browser displays the web page using the default settings. As the page becomes wider than 460px, the default layout changes to show the style rules identified in your first media query, the one set for screens with a `min-width` of 460px. This layout continues to be displayed, even as the browser window widens, until you reach 880px, at which point the style rules from the new media query are applied. Note that declarations from your first media query are still applied at a width greater than 880px because the media query condition of `min-width` 460px is still met. However, if a declaration in a later media query targets a property used in an earlier media query with the same selector, the later declaration is applied instead of the earlier one.

FIGURE I-6: Media query for browser widths of 880px or greater

```
205    /* standard screen styles */
206    @media screen and (min-width: 880px) {
207        h3 {
208            float: left;
209        }
210        figure {
211            float: right;
212            max-width: 50%;
213            margin: 2% 0 2% 2%;
214        }
215        section {
216            padding-bottom: 2%;
217        }
218        .top-link {
219            right: auto;
220            left: 0;
221        }
222    }
223
224    /* print styles */
```

h3 elements floated left so `figure` elements can appear to the right

`figure` elements floated right with a `max-width` of 50% to create second column

Padding reduced at bottom of `section` elements because of new position of `top-link` buttons

`top-link` button repositioned on left side of parent element

FIGURE I-7: Rooms web page displayed wider than 880px

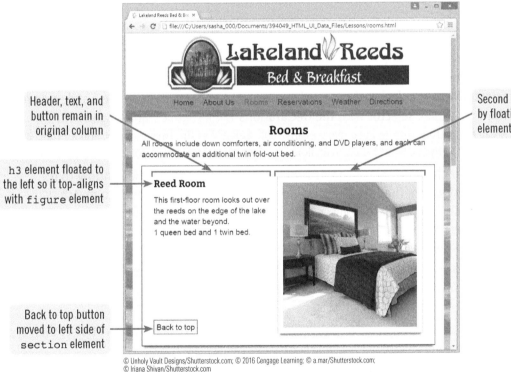

Header, text, and button remain in original column

h3 element floated to the left so it top-aligns with `figure` element

Back to top button moved to left side of `section` element

Second column created by floating `figure` element on the right

© Unholy Vault Designs/Shutterstock.com; © 2016 Cengage Learning; © a.mar/Shutterstock.com; © Iriana Shiyan/Shutterstock.com

Understanding mobile-specific websites

Although the practice of responsive design has become common, some developers choose to create and maintain multiple versions of the same website instead. In this situation, users of desktop computers see the default website, while mobile users see a version of the website with a layout optimized for small screens. Maintaining separate websites comes with its own challenges. For instance, it can be easy to mistakenly include different information in each site, or to update the content of one site without updating the other. In addition, while some content might be excluded from the mobile site for ease of use on a small screen, in some cases mobile users are unable to access that information. Finally, using multiple sites involves the use of different URLs – for instance, www.example.com vs m.example.com – meaning that shared links do not always work predictably across devices. No matter which approach you or an organization you work with chooses, it is important to understand and implement the best practices around your chosen approach.

Create a Widescreen Layout

Learning
Outcomes
• Use a media query
  to create a
  widescreen layout

Media queries can be used to take advantage of the extra width that larger screens provide. For instance, a site with a lot of information to deliver to users, such as a media organization, may add an additional column that highlights new or popular content. Whether you add an additional column or not, in many cases, you want to set a maximum width for your layout by specifying a breakpoint at which the content width stops increasing. **CASE** ▶ *You create another media query to move the Back to top button into its own column when the browser window is larger than 1060px, and you set a maximum width for the layout when the browser window reaches a width of 1400px.*

STEPS

1. **Return to rooms.html in your browser, then widen the browser window and observe how the layout responds**

   As the two-column layout widens, the left column widens, spreading out the descriptive text. This creates a large white space on the left and creates distance between the header and the photo.

2. **Return to styles.css in your editor, scroll down to the end of the document, above the /* print styles */ comment, add the comment** /* large screen styles */, **then press [Enter]**

3. **Type** @media screen and (min-width: 1060px) {, **press [Enter] twice, then type** }

   This code creates a breakpoint at a minimum browser width of 1060px.

4. **Within the braces for the new media query, create a style rule for the** figure **selector with the declaration** margin: 2% 25% 2% 2%;, **then create a style rule for the** .top-link **selector with the declarations** left: auto; **and** right: 0;

   Recall that setting left to auto removes any value assigned to the left property, and a right value of 0 positions the right edge of the element along the right edge of the closest positioned ancestor element.

5. **Save your changes, reload rooms.html in your browser, drag the window to its narrowest width, then widen the window until the layout changes to match FIGURE I-8**

   At the smaller widths, the page still uses the default layout and your earlier media queries. But, when the browser window reaches 1060px in width, the Back to top button for each article element moves to a new third column on the right side of the image, as shown in FIGURE I-8.

6. **Return to styles.css in your editor, scroll down to the end of the document and above the /* print styles */ comment, add the comment** /* maximum width screen styles */, **then press [Enter]**

7. **Type** @media screen and (min-width: 1400px) {, **press [Enter] twice, then type** }

   This code creates a breakpoint at a minimum browser width of 1440px.

8. **Within the braces for the new media query, enter the** article div **style rule shown in FIGURE I-9 on lines 237–239**

   The min-width media feature is used to apply this media query to any browser window width 1400px or larger. The article element has 2% padding on the left and right, and the article div element has 3% padding on the left and right, occupying a total of 10% of the width of the browser window. You set the width of the article div element to 1260px, which is 90% of the screen width at the breakpoint. The comment shows the math used to arrive at the width value. FIGURE I-9 shows the code for the 2 media queries.

9. **Save your changes, reload rooms.html in your browser, then if you have a widescreen display, drag the window as wide as possible**

   As shown in FIGURE I-10, the Back to top button moves to a third column to the right of each image, balancing out the page. At widths larger than 1260px, the container div no longer increases in width.

FIGURE I-8: Rooms web page displayed wider than 1060px

Third column created by positioning Back to top button to the right of each photo

© Unholy Vault Designs/Shutterstock.com; © 2016 Cengage Learning;
© a.mar/Shutterstock.com; © Iriana Shiyan/Shutterstock.com

FIGURE I-9: Media queries for browser widths of 1060px or greater and 1400px or greater

```
224   /* large screen styles */
225   @media screen and (min-width: 1060px) {
226       figure {
227           margin: 2% 25% 2% 2%;
228       }
229       .top-link {
230           left: auto;
231           right: 0;
232       }
233   }
234
235   /* maximum width screen styles */
236   @media screen and (min-width: 1400px) {
237       article div {
238           width: 1260px; /* 1400 * 90% */
239       }
240   }
241
242   /* print styles */
```

25% right margin added to `figure` elements to create third column

Back to top buttons positioned against the right edge of parent element

Comment details the math used to calculate container width

Fixed width applied to container `div` when browser window is 1400px or wider

FIGURE I-10: Rooms web page displayed wider than 1400px

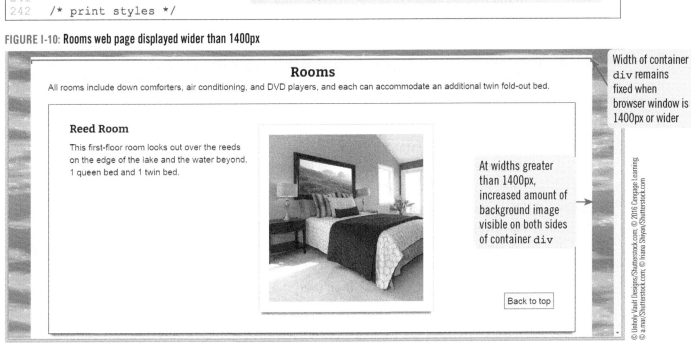

Width of container `div` remains fixed when browser window is 1400px or wider

At widths greater than 1400px, increased amount of background image visible on both sides of container `div`

© Unholy Vault Designs/Shutterstock.com; © 2016 Cengage Learning;
© a.mar/Shutterstock.com; © Iriana Shiyan/Shutterstock.com

Create Responsive Navigation

Learning
Outcomes
• Replace a nav bar
  with a button

It's sometimes useful to hide elements, rather than showing them by default, in layouts for smaller screens and then give users the means to show them as needed. One of the most commonly hidden web page elements is the nav bar. On smaller screens, it's standard to replace the nav bar with a button showing 3 horizontal lines, which is often referred to as a **hamburger menu**. Users click (or touch) the button to view the nav bar, then either click a nav bar option or click the button again to hide the menu. To create a hamburger menu, a button image is added to the page and positioned, the nav bar is hidden, and then a `script` element that toggles the `display` setting of the nav bar when the button is clicked or touched is added to the HTML document. **CASE** ▸ *Because the nav bar takes up significant vertical space on the default layout and the small screen/tablet layout, you implement a hamburger menu for these screen widths.*

STEPS

1. **Return to rooms.html in your editor, below the opening <nav> tag with the class value sitenavigation, create a div element with the class value navigation-menu-button, then, within the div element, type** `<img src="images/menu.png" width="63" height="57" alt="Show navigation">`
   The `img` element for the menu button is inserted within the `nav` element.

QUICK TIP
The script.js file contains JavaScript code that toggles the menu button between `display` values of `block` and `none` when it is clicked or touched.

2. **Scroll down to the bottom of the document, then, above the closing </body> tag, add the code** `<script src="script.js"></script>`
   FIGURE I-11 shows the code for the `img` and `script` elements.

3. **Save your changes, return to styles.css in your editor, scroll up to the site navigation bar section, then, above the nav.sitenavigation ul selector, add a style rule with the div.navigation-menu-button selector and the declaration** `float: right;`

4. **In the nav.sitenavigation style rule, add the declarations** `width: 18%;`, `padding: 5% 1%;`, `float: right;`, **and** `position: relative;`, **then delete the declaration** `text-align: center;`

QUICK TIP
Removing the `display` value `inline-block` from the nav bar list items causes browsers to display them as a vertical list.

5. **In the nav.sitenavigation ul style rule, add the declarations** `border: 3px solid #34180f;`, `display: none;`, `position: absolute;`, `right: 5%;`, `top: 70%;`, **and** `z-index: 2;`

6. **In the nav.sitenavigation li style rule, delete the declaration** `display: inline-block;`

7. **Scroll up to the header section, then, in the header style rule, add the declarations** `width: 80%;` **and** `float: left;`

8. **Scroll down to the standard screen styles section, then, above the h3 style rule, add the style rules shown in the right image in FIGURE I-12**
   FIGURE I-12 shows the new declarations you added to the style sheet in this lesson.

TROUBLE
Be sure to click the brown menu button to the right of the header and not the menu button in your browser's toolbar.

9. **Save your changes, reload rooms.html in your browser, drag the window to its narrowest width, then click the menu button** ▪
   The menu button is displayed to the right of the header. Clicking the button displays the nav bar options below it in a vertical list, as shown in **FIGURE I-13**.

10. **Click the menu button again, then drag the window wider until a second column is added to the section elements**
    When you click the menu button again, the menu is hidden. At greater browser widths, the menu returns to its horizontal appearance and the menu button is hidden.

FIGURE I-11: HTML code for menu button and script

```
31        <nav class="sitenavigation">
32            <div class="navigation-menu-button">
33                <img src="images/menu.png" width="63" height="57" alt="Show navigation">
34            </div>
35            <ul>
```

```
101          </footer>
102          <script src="script.js"></script>
103      </body>
```

FIGURE I-12: CSS code for responsive navigation

```
62   header {
63       width: 80%;
64       background-color: white;
65       float: left;
```

```
78   /* site navigation bar */
79   nav.sitenavigation {
80       width: 18%;
81       padding: 5% 1%;
82       color: #34180f;
83       float: right;
84       position: relative;
85   }
86   div.navigation-menu-button {
87       float: right;
88   }
89   nav.sitenavigation ul {
90       border: 3px solid #34180f;
91       display: none;
92       background-color: #B8944D;
93       position: absolute;
94       right: 5%;
95       top: 70%;
96       z-index: 2;
97   }
```

```
218  /* standard screen styles */
219  @media screen and (min-width: 880px) {
220      header {
221          float: none;
222          width: auto;
223      }
224      div.navigation-menu-button {
225          display: none;
226      }
227      nav.sitenavigation {
228          width: 100%;
229          padding: 0;
230      }
231      nav.sitenavigation ul {
232          border: none;
233          width: 100%;
234          display: block;
235          position: static;
236          text-align: center;
237      }
238      nav.sitenavigation li {
239          display: inline-block;
240      }
241      h3 {
```

Code continued in figure on right   Code continued from figure on left

FIGURE I-13: Modified nav bar in browser

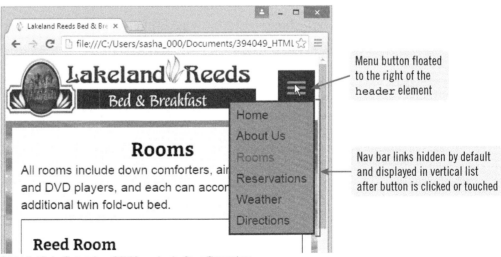

Menu button floated to the right of the header element

Nav bar links hidden by default and displayed in vertical list after button is clicked or touched

© Unholy Vault Designs/Shutterstock.com; © 2016 Cengage Learning; © a.mar/Shutterstock.com

Implement Adaptive Content

Learning
Outcomes
• Hide and display
  content using
  media queries

In general, all content that is available on your website for users of a large screen should also be available for users of smaller devices, such as smartphones. In some cases, however, it is useful to limit the amount of content shown by default and make related information available only if a user requests it. This aspect of responsive design is sometimes called **adaptive content**. One method of implementing adaptive content is to change the display of elements in media queries using class names. Another common method is to use one or more of the structural pseudo-classes described in TABLE I-2. **CASE** ▶ *To consolidate the information shown on small screens, you hide the first paragraph of text within each section by default and use the standard screen width media query to make it visible on larger screens.*

STEPS

1. **Return to** styles.css **in your editor, then scroll up to the main content section**

2. **Below the closing } for the** section p **style rule, insert a blank line, then add a new style rule with the selector** section p:first-of-type **and the declaration** display: none;

   The section p:first-of-type selector selects the first p element within each section element. This style rule hides these elements in the default small screen layout.

3. **Scroll down to the small screen/tablet styles section**

4. **Before the closing } for the media query with a** min-width **of 460px, add a blank line, then add a new style rule with the selector** section p:first-of-type **and the declaration** display: block;

   This style rule displays the first p element within each section element when the screen width is 460px or greater. FIGURE I-14 shows the new style rules in the style sheet.

5. **Save your changes, reload rooms.html in your browser, then drag the window to its narrowest width**

   The first paragraph of text under each room image is not displayed, leaving only the description of beds, as shown in FIGURE I-15.

6. **Drag the window to widen it until the background image is visible at the left and right edges**

   The first paragraph of text under each room image is now visible, as shown in FIGURE I-16.

TABLE I-2: Structural pseudo-classes

pseudo-class	description*	example	selects
:first-child :last-child	the first or last child element if it is of the specified type	p:first-child	first p child element if it is also the first child
:first-of-type :last-of-type	the first or last child element of the specified type	p:last-of-type	last p child element
:nth-child(n)	the nth child element of the specified type	li:nth-child(3)	the third li child element
:nth-last-child(n)	the nth from last child element of the specified type	li:nth-last-child(3)	the third from last li child element
:nth-of-type(n)	the nth occurrence of the specified child element	p:nth-of-type(5)	the fifth p child element
:nth-last-of-type(n)	the nth from last occurrence of the specified child element	p:nth-last-of-type(5)	the fifth from last p child element

* where *n* is a number or a calculation in the form *an+b*; note that IE8 does not support the structural pseudo-classes listed in this table

© 2016 Cengage Learning

FIGURE I-14: Styles for adaptive content added to style sheet

```
136    section p {
137        clear: left;
138    }
139    section p:first-of-type {
140        display: none;
141    }
```

Selector uses `:first-of-type` pseudo-class to select the first p element within each `section` element

The first p element in each `section` element is not displayed in the default handheld layout

```
216        section h3, section p {
217            text-align: left;
218        }
219        section p:first-of-type {
220            display: block;
221        }
222    }
```

The first p element in each `section` element is displayed when the browser window is at least 460px wide

FIGURE I-15: Text hidden at smaller browser width

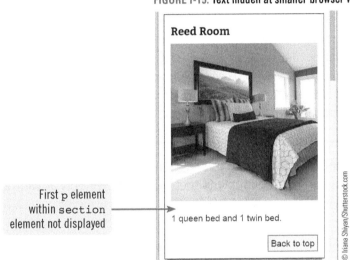

First p element within `section` element not displayed

FIGURE I-16: Adaptive content displayed in wider browser window

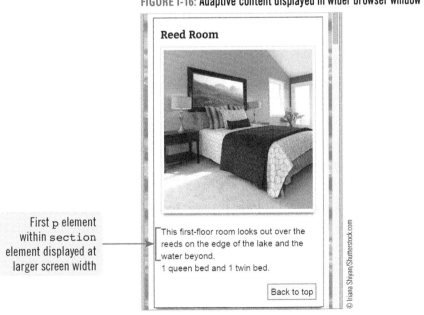

First p element within `section` element displayed at larger screen width

Implementing Responsive Design

Use Progressive Enhancement

Learning
Outcomes
• Add a feature
  using progressive
  enhancement
• Use a shim

While modern browsers support many recently added CSS properties, an older browser, such as IE8, generally doesn't support features developed after the browser was released. Because the main content and capabilities of a website should be available for users of the oldest browsers employed by a significant share of your users, it may seem at first glance that you need to exclude newer features from your websites for compatibility reasons. However, multiple methods are available for incorporating newer features. JavaScript files known as shims have been developed for many recent HTML and CSS features. A **shim** recreates a feature for older browsers using JavaScript code. Another option is to accept that a newer feature will be unavailable for users of older browsers and to use it in a way that doesn't affect the meaning or functionality of the page content. This practice is known as **progressive enhancement** because the newer features enhance the basic content for users of some browsers. You've already implemented progressive enhancement in your web development work for more widely supported features; for instance, when specifying an image as a web page background, you also specified a color as a fallback. However, progressive enhancement is especially important when working with new features that aren't universally supported, such as the `border-radius` property, which rounds the corners of elements. TABLE I-3 describes the basic syntax of the `border-radius` property. **CASE** ▶ *Media queries using the `@media` rule are not recognized by IE8, so you add a shim to the Rooms web page in order to insure that your media queries are applied in IE8. You also use the `border-radius` property to add rounded corners to the* Back to top *buttons in modern browsers, while still displaying functional buttons with square corners in older browsers.*

STEPS

1. **If you have access to Internet Explorer 8, use it to open rooms.html from a web server, drag the window to its narrowest width, and then widen the window as wide as possible**
   IE8 does not support media queries, so only the default styles are applied to the page no matter the width of the browser window.

2. **Return to** rooms.html **in your editor, scroll to the** head **element near the top of the file, insert a new line below the** link **element that references styles.css, then insert the following element:**
   `<script src="respond.min.js"></script>`
   This `script` element references the file respond.min.js, which is a shim for media queries in IE8. FIGURE I-17 shows the updated code.

3. **Save your changes, return to** styles.css **in your editor, then scroll as necessary to the main content section**

4. **Within the** .top-link a **style rule, add a line before the closing** }, **then add the declaration** border-radius: 0.6em;
   The `border-radius` property rounds the corners of an element. FIGURE I-18 shows the updated style rule.

5. **Save your changes, reload rooms.html in your browser, then scroll as necessary to view one of the** Back to top **buttons**
   In modern browsers, the buttons now have rounded corners, as shown in FIGURE I-19.

6. **If you have access to Internet Explorer 8, use it to open rooms.html from a web server**
   IE8 does not support the `border-radius` property, so the buttons still have square corners as shown in FIGURE I-20.

7. **Validate your HTML and CSS files**

FIGURE I-17: `script` element for shim added to rooms.html

```
18              <link rel="stylesheet" href="styles.css">
19              <script src="respond.min.js"></script>
20              <link rel="shortcut icon" href="images/favicon.ico">
```

FIGURE I-18: `border-radius` declaration added to style sheet

```
162    .top-link a {
163        padding: 3px 6px;
164        border: 2px solid #777;
165        display: inline-block;
166        background-color: #ebf8fa;
167        border-radius: 0.6em;
168    }
```

FIGURE I-19: Rounded corners applied to button in modern browser

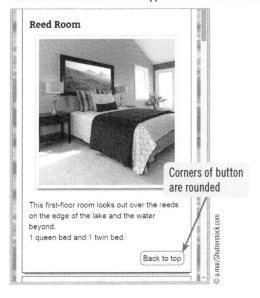

Corners of button are rounded

This first-floor room looks out over the reeds on the edge of the lake and the water beyond.
1 queen bed and 1 twin bed.

Back to top

© a.mar/Shutterstock.com

FIGURE I-20: Button without rounded corners in IE8

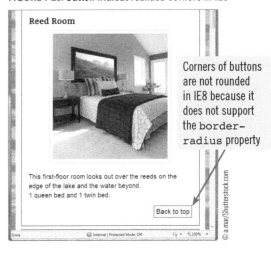

Corners of buttons are not rounded in IE8 because it does not support the `border-radius` property

This first-floor room looks out over the reeds on the edge of the lake and the water beyond.
1 queen bed and 1 twin bed.

Back to top

© a.mar/Shutterstock.com

TABLE I-3: The `border-radius` property

property	description	example

`border-top-left-radius`
`border-top-right-radius`
`border-bottom-right-radius`
`border-bottom-left-radius`
	specific properties that set the border radius of a single corner	`border-top-right-radius: 10px;`

`border-radius`	shorthand property that sets all corners	`border-radius: 2em;`

© 2016 Cengage Learning

Practice

Concepts Review

Refer to the code shown in FIGURE I-21 **to answer the following questions.**

FIGURE I-21

```
162   .top-link a {
163       padding: 3px 6px;
164       border: 2px solid #777;
165       display: inline-block;
166       background-color: #ebf8fa;
167       border-radius: 0.6em;◄———— d
168   }

202   /* small screen/tablet styles */
203   @media screen and (min-width: 460px), print {
204       article {
205           padding: 2%;
206       }
207       figure {
208           border: 1px solid #ccc;
209           padding: 2%;
210           box-shadow: 0 10px 6px -6px #777;
211           display: inline-block;
212       }
213       section {
214           text-align: center;
215       }
216       section h3, section p {
217           text-align: left;
218       }
219       section p:first-of-type {
220           display: block;
221       }
222   }
```

1. Which item is a media feature?
2. Which item is an example of progressive enhancement?
3. Which item is a media query?
4. Which item is a breakpoint?

Match each term with the statement that best describes it.

5. responsive design
6. emulator
7. hamburger menu
8. shim

a. a button showing 3 horizontal lines that is often used to replace the nav bar on smaller screens

b. allows a web page designer to specify different CSS style rules for some or all of a page's elements, depending on the width of the screen or browser window in which the document is displayed

c. a JavaScript file that uses code to create a newer CSS feature for users of older browsers

d. an application that runs on a computer and approximates the dimensions and behavior of a wide range of devices

Select the best answer from the list of choices.

9. **Which of the following is a valid media feature for a media query?**
   a. and
   b. max-width
   c. or
   d. not

10. **Which of the following explains why you might create a widescreen layout?**
   a. To save space on devices with smaller screens.
   b. To take advantage of extra space available on larger displays.
   c. To ensure that all your content is visible at all display sizes.
   d. Because responsive design only works on smaller screens.

11. **Which of the following explains why you might implement responsive navigation?**
   a. To save space on devices with smaller screens.
   b. To take advantage of extra space available on larger displays.
   c. To ensure that all your content is visible at all display sizes.
   d. Because responsive design only works on smaller screens.

12. **Which of the following explains why you might use progressive enhancement?**
   a. To save space on devices with smaller screens.
   b. To take advantage of extra space available on larger displays.
   c. To implement newer features for browsers that support them.
   d. To replicate newer features in older browsers.

13. **Which of the following explains why you might use a shim?**
   a. To save space on devices with smaller screens.
   b. To take advantage of extra space available on larger displays.
   c. To implement newer features for browsers that support them.
   d. To replicate newer features in older browsers.

Skills Review

1. **Construct a multipart media query.**
   a. In your editor, open the file HTM_I-3.html from the SR folder where you store your Data Files for this unit, save it as **index.html**, then repeat to save the file HTM_I-4.css as **styles.css**.
   b. Within the comment section at the top of each file, enter your first and last names and today's date, then save your changes.
   c. Open index.html in a desktop browser, resize the browser window to its smallest width, then resize it to its largest width.
   d. Return to styles.css in your editor, then in the header section and within in the h1 style rule, change the text-align property to left-align text.
   e. Above the /* print styles */ comment near the end of the file, add the comment /* small screen/ tablet styles */.
   f. Below the new comment, create a media query for devices with a screen and at a minimum width of 720px, or for printed output. Within the media query, add style rules that do the following:
      * For the body element, set padding to 1em
      * For the h1 element, set font size to 2.5em, line height to 1.4em, and center-align text
      * For the p element with the class value decorative-image, set the width to 30%, set top padding to 1em, float the element to the left, and set the display to inline
      * For the footer element, set the left margin to 30%

Skills Review (continued)

g. Save your changes, refresh or reload index.html in your browser, resize the browser window to its smallest width, widen the window, then verify that the media query you created in Steps e-f is applied at approximately 720px, as shown in **FIGURE I-22**.

FIGURE I-22

2. **Test layouts with an emulator.**

   a. Open index.html in Google Chrome, open the Developer Tools, then turn on Device Mode.

   b. Select the Google Nexus 5 as the device, then reload the page.

   c. Swap the device dimensions. (*Note*: The layout may not change.)

   d. Select the Apple iPhone 6 as the device, then reload the page

   e. Swap the device dimensions. (*Note*: The layout may not change.)

   f. Turn off Device Mode.

3. **Add a column with a media query.**

   a. Return to styles.css in your editor, then, above the `/* print styles */` comment near the end of the file, add the comment `/* standard screen styles */`.

   b. Below the new comment, create a media query for devices with a screen and at a minimum width of 1000px. Within the media query, add style rules that do the following:

   FIGURE I-23

   - For the element with the `class` value `info`, set the width to 65%, set the top margin to 1em, and float the element on the left.
   - For the element with the `class` value `locations`, set the width to 35%, float the element on the right, and right-align text.

   c. Save your changes, refresh or reload index.html in your browser, resize the browser window to its smallest width, widen the window, then verify that the media query you created in Steps a-b is applied at approximately 1000px, as shown in **FIGURE I-23**.

4. **Create a widescreen layout.**

   a. Return to styles.css in your editor, then, above the `/* print styles */` comment near the end of the file, add the comment `/* large screen styles */`.

   b. Below the new comment, create a media query for devices with a screen and at a minimum width of 1238px. Within the media query, add a style rule for the `body` element that sets the width to 1200px.

   c. Save your changes, refresh or reload index.html in your browser, resize the browser window to its smallest width, widen the window, then verify that the width of the body element becomes fixed at a browser window width of approximately 1238px.

5. Create responsive navigation.

a. Return to index.html in your editor, below the opening `<nav>` tag with the `class` value `sitenavigation`, create a `div` element with the `class` value `navigation-menu-button`, then, within the `div` element, add an `img` element with a source of images/menu.png, width of 60, height of 60, and alt text of **Show navigation**.

b. Scroll down to the bottom of the document, then above the closing `</body>` tag, add the code `<script src="script.js"></script>`.

c. Save your changes, return to styles.css in your editor, scroll up to the site navigation bar section, then above the `nav.sitenavigation ul` style rule, add a style rule for `img` elements within the nav element with the `class` value `sitenavigation` that sets the display to inline-block.

d. In the `nav.sitenavigation` style rule, change the `text-alignment` declaration to right-align text, then add declarations to absolutely position the element 5px from the right and 76px from the top with a z-index of 2.

e. In the `nav.sitenavigation ul` style rule, add declarations to turn off the display of the element and relatively position it -6px from the top.

f. In the `nav.sitenavigation li` style rule, delete the declaration `display: inline-block;`.

g. Scroll down to the standard screen styles section, then add the following style rules:

- For the nav element with the `class` value `sitenavigation`, set the position to static and center-align text.
- For `img` elements within the nav element with the `class` value sitenavigation, turn off display of the element.
- For `ul` elements within the nav element with the `class` value sitenavigation, set the display to `block` and the position to `static`.
- For `li` elements within the nav element with the `class` value sitenavigation, set the display to `inline-block`.

h. Save your changes, reload index.html in your browser, drag the window to its narrowest width, then click the menu button and verify that the menu options are displayed as shown in FIGURE I-24.

i. Click the menu button again to hide the menu, drag the window wider until the locations and hours are displayed in a separate column, then verify that the menu button is no longer displayed and the menu options are displayed below the header as seen previously in FIGURE I-23.

FIGURE I-24

© 2016 Cengage Learning

6. Implement adaptive content.

a. Return to styles.css in your editor, then scroll up to the main content section.

b. Below the closing } for the `.accent` style rule, add a new style rule for elements with the `class` value subsection that turns the display off.

c. Below the style rule you added in the previous step, add a new style rule for the `img` element that is the last child of the element with the `class` value info that turns the display off. (*Hint*: Use the selector `.info img:last-child`.)

d. In the small screen/tablet styles section and above the `footer` style rule in that same section, add a new style rule for elements with the `class` value subsection that sets display to `block`.

e. In the standard screen styles section and above the `.locations` style rule, add a rule for the `img` element that is the last child of the element with the `class` value info that sets display to `inline`. (*Hint*: Use the selector `.info img:last-child`.)

f. Save your changes, refresh or reload index.html in your browser, then drag the window to its narrowest width and verify that the hours for each location and the photo in the middle of the page are hidden.

Skills Review (continued)

g. Drag the window to widen it until the yellow column is visible on the left and verify that the hours are displayed.

h. Drag the window to widen it until the locations and hours are displayed in their own column on the right and verify that the photo is displayed in the center column.

7. Use progressive enhancement.

a. Return to index.html in your editor, scroll to the `head` element, insert a blank line below the `link` element that references styles.css, insert the following element in that blank line: `<script src="respond.min.js"></script>`, then save your work.

b. Return to styles.css in your editor, then scroll as necessary to the small screen/tablet styles section.

c. Above the `h1` style rule in the small screen/tablet styles section, add a new style rule for the element with the `class` value `container` that sets the border radius to 2em.

d. Within the same section, in the `footer` style rule, add a declaration that sets the border radius for the bottom right corner to 2em. (*Hint*: Use the `border-bottom-right-radius` property.)

e. Save your changes, refresh or reload index.html in your browser, drag the window to its narrowest width, then verify that the corners of the container element are not rounded.

f. Drag the window to widen it until the yellow column is visible on the left, then verify that all four corners of the container element are rounded and the bottom right corner of the `footer` element, which coincides with the bottom right corner of the container element, is rounded.

g. If you have access to Internet Explorer 8, use it to open index.html from a web server and verify that the corners remain square but the content is unaffected. Drag the window to its narrowest width, then widen the window and verify that all media queries are applied at the appropriate size.

h. Validate the code for your web pages and your style sheet, and make changes as necessary to fix any errors.

Independent Challenge 1

The layout of the Spotted Wren Garden Center website has been updated to work on smaller screen sizes. The manager, Sarah Nguyen, has asked you to make the layout responsive to take better advantage of larger displays.

a. In your editor, open HTM_I-5.html from the IC1 folder where you store your Data Files for this unit, save it as **index.html**, then repeat to save HTM_I-6.css as **styles.css**. In the comment at the top of each file, enter your name and today's date where indicated, then save the files. Open index.html in a browser, resize the browser window to its narrowest width, then resize it to its widest width while observing the layout.

b. Return to styles.css in your editor, then above the print styles section, add the text **small screen/tablet styles** as a comment. Below the new comment, create a media query that applies to devices with screens when the browser window has a minimum width of 500px, or to printed output. Within that media query, add a style rule for the `figure` element that sets display to block. Save your changes, refresh or reload index.html in your browser, resize the browser window to its narrowest width, then resize it to at least 500px wide and verify that the purple coneflower image and caption shown in FIGURE I-25 are displayed. (*Note*: The layout will not match that shown in FIGURE I-25.)

FIGURE I-25

Independent Challenge 1 (continued)

c. Return to styles.css in your editor, then above the print styles section, add the text **standard/large screen styles** as a comment. Below the new comment, create a media query that applies to devices with screens when the browser window has a minimum width of 864px. Within the media query, add a style rule for the `header` element that sets background color to white, for the `span` element within the `h1` element that sets display to `none`, for the `img` element within the `h1` element that sets its display to `block`, for the `article` element that floats it on the left and sets its width to 64%, and for the `aside` element that sets its display to `block`. Save your changes, refresh or reload index.html in your browser, resize the browser window to its narrowest width, then resize it to at least 864px wide and verify that its layout matches FIGURE I-25.

d. Return to styles.css in your editor, then in the sidebar section, add a style rule for each `td` element that is the first child of its parent element, setting the font weight to `bold`. (*Hint*: Use the selector `td:first-child`.) Save your changes, refresh or reload index.html in your browser, then verify that the abbreviations for the days of the week are displayed in bold as shown in FIGURE I-25.

e. Open index.html in Google Chrome, open the Developer Tools, then turn on Device Mode. Select the Google Nexus 5 as the device, then view the page using both orientations. Repeat for the Apple iPhone 6, and for a third device of your choosing, then turn off Device Mode.

f. In your browser, open a print preview, then verify that the small screen/tablet layout is used. (*Note*: You should see the purple coneflower image.)

g. Return to index.html in your editor, then in the `head` element and below the `link` element for styles.css, add the code `<script src="respond.min.js"></script>`. Save your changes. If you have access to IE8, open index.html in IE8, resize the browser window to its narrowest width, then resize it as wide as possible and verify that both media queries are applied at the appropriate widths.

h. Validate your HTML and CSS documents.

Independent Challenge 2

As you continue your work on the website for the Murfreesboro Regional Soccer League, you want to ensure that the layout adapts to different screen sizes. You use media queries and other techniques to make the design of the site responsive.

a. In your editor, open HTM_I-7.html from the IC2 folder where you store your Data Files for this unit, save it as **index.html**, then repeat to save HTM_I-8.css as **styles.css**. In the comment at the top of each file, enter your name and today's date where indicated, then save the files. Open index.html in a browser, resize the browser window to its narrowest width, then resize it to its widest width while observing the layout.

b. Return to index.html in your editor, then within the `nav` element, add a `div` element with the `class` value `navigation-menu-button` before the `ul` element. Within the `div` element, add an img element for the file menu.png within the images folder with a width of 60, a height of 60, and alt text of **Show navigation**. Scroll down to the bottom of the file, then above the closing `</body>` tag enter the code `<script src="script.js"></script>`. Save your changes.

c. Return to styles.css in your editor, then scroll as necessary to the site navigation section. In the `nav.sitenavigation` rule, change the padding to 2% on all sides, the width to 16%, and float the element on the right. In the `nav.sitenavigation ul` style rule, turn off the display of the element, then absolutely position the element 2% from the right side of the parent. In the `nav.sitenavigation a` style rule, remove the declaration that sets the bottom margin.

d. Scroll to the header section, change the width of the `header` element to 76%, and turn off the display of the `header div` element.

e. Scroll to the main content section, change the width of the `article` element to 100%. Save your changes, refresh or reload index.html in your browser, then view the page at its narrowest and widest widths and verify that the navigation sidebar is not displayed and the menu button is displayed to the right of header. Click the menu button and verify that the navigation menu is displayed below it, then click the button again and verify that the navigation menu is hidden.

Independent Challenge 2 (continued)

f. Return to styles.css in your editor, then above the print styles section, add the text **small screen/tablet styles** as a comment. Below the new comment, create a media query that applies to devices with screens when the browser window has a minimum width of 500px, or to printed output. Within the media query, add a style rule for the `aside` element that sets display to block, then add a style rule for the `article` element that sets the width to 70% and the font size to 2em and floats the element on the left without requiring either side to be clear of other elements. Save your changes, refresh or reload index.html in your browser, resize the browser window to its narrowest width, then resize it to at least 500px wide and verify that the sidebar is displayed on the right side of the layout as shown in **FIGURE I-26**.

g. Return to styles.css in your editor, then above the print styles section, add the text **standard screen styles** as a comment. Below the new comment, create a media query that applies to devices with screens when the browser window has a minimum width of 760px, or to printed output. Within the media query, add style rules for the following:

- For the `body` element, set the padding to 1em on all sides.
- For the element with the `class` value `container`, set the border radius to 2em and the background color to #c8f098.
- For the `header` element, set the width to `auto`, set the element so it no longer floats, and set the border radius for the top left and top right corners to 2em.
- For the `div` element within the `header` element, set the display to `block`.
- For the `nav` element with the `class` value `sitenavigation`, set padding to 2% on all sides, set the width to 21%, and float the element on the left.
- For the `img` element within the `nav` element with the `class` value `sitenavigation`, turn off the display of the element.
- For the `ul` element within the `nav` element with the `class` value `sitenavigation`, set the display to block and return positioning to the default setting (*Hint*: Use the declaration `position: static;`).
- For `a` elements within the `nav` element with the `class` value `sitenavigation`, set the bottom margin to 0.6em.
- For the `article` element, set the width to 50%.
- For the `aside` element, set the width to 19%.
- For the `footer` element, set the border radius of the bottom left and bottom right corners to 2em.

h. Save your changes, refresh or reload index.html in your browser, resize the browser window to its narrowest width, then resize it to at least 760px wide and verify that its layout matches **FIGURE I-27**.

FIGURE I-26

FIGURE I-27

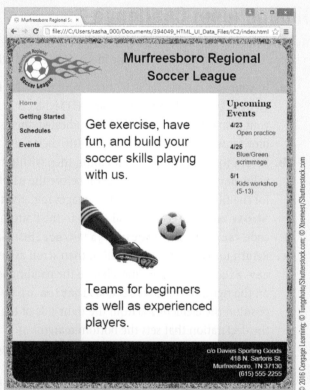

Independent Challenge 2 (continued)

i. Return to styles.css in your editor, then above the print styles section, add the text **large screen styles** as a comment. Below the new comment, create a media query that applies to devices with screens when the browser window has a minimum width of 1080px. Within the media query, add a style rule for the element with the `class` value `container` that sets the width to 1040px. Save your changes, refresh or reload index.html in your browser, resize the browser window to greater than 1080px wide and verify that the width of the page content remains constant as the browser window widens.

j. Return to styles.css in your editor, then in the main content section, add a style rule for each p element within the `article` element that is the first child of its parent element, setting the top margin to 0. (*Hint*: Use the selector `article p:first-child`.) Save your changes, refresh or reload index.html in your browser, then verify that the height of the empty space above the first paragraph of text in the center column is reduced.

k. Open index.html in Google Chrome, open the Developer Tools, and then turn on Device Mode. Test your layout in both orientations using the Google Nexus 5, the Apple iPhone 6, and a third device of your choosing.

l. In your browser, open a print preview, then verify that the layout matches the browser rendering for the standard screen styles media query.

m. Return to index.html in your editor, then in the `head` element and below the `link` element for styles.css, add the code `<script src="respond.min.js"></script>`. Save your changes. If you have access to IE8, open index.html in IE8, resize the browser window to its narrowest width, then resize it as wide as possible and verify that both media queries are applied at the appropriate widths.

n. Validate your HTML and CSS documents.

Independent Challenge 3

Many of the clients of the Hotel Natoma navigate the area during their stays using smartphones, so the hotel has created a layout for handheld devices for the site. You use media queries to add responsive layouts for standard and large desktop screens, starting with the What's Nearby page.

a. In your editor, open HTM_I-9.html from the IC3 folder where you store your Data Files for this unit, save it as **nearby.html**, then repeat to save HTM_I-10.css as **styles.css**. In the comment at the top of each file, enter your name and today's date where indicated, then save the files. Open nearby.html in a browser, resize the browser window to its narrowest width, then resize it to its widest width while observing the layout.

b. Return to nearby.html in your editor, then in the `section` element with the `class` name `aam`, insert a `figure` element before the `div` element. Within the `figure` element, add an img element for the file images/aam.jpg with a width of 450, a height of 337, and alt text of **the San Francisco Asian Art Museum, a beaux arts building composed of large granite bricks with columns above the entry doors**. After the img element and still within the `figure` element, add a `figcaption` element containing the text **Asian Art Museum**. Repeat to add a `figure` element to the `section` element with the `class` name `cityhall`, adding an img element for images/cityhall.jpg with a width of 450, a height of 299, and alt text of **San Francisco City Hall, a beaux arts building with columns across the whole front and a gray dome over the center, illuminated from within at dusk**, and a `figcaption` element containing the text **City Hall**. Save your changes.

c. Return to styles.css in your editor, then in the main content section, add a style rule for `figure` elements within the `article` element below the `article h3` rule that turns off the display of the elements.

d. Above the print styles section, add a comment containing the text **small screen/tablet styles**. Below the new comment, create a media query for devices with screens where the browser window is at least 550px wide, or for printed output. Within the media query, create a style rule for `figure` elements within the `article` element that sets the maximum width to 50%, the margins to 0 0 1em 1em, floats the elements on the right, and sets the display to `block`, then create a style rule for `figcaption` elements within the `article` element that center-aligns text and bolds it.

Independent Challenge 3 (continued)

e. Save your changes, then refresh or reload nearby.html in your browser. View the page at its narrowest width, then resize the browser window to at least 550px wide and verify that the images of the Asian Art Museum and city hall are displayed as shown in **FIGURE I-28**.

f. Return to styles.css in your editor, then above the print styles section, add the text **standard/wide screen styles** as a comment. Below the new comment, create a media query that applies to devices with screens when the browser window has a minimum width of 800px. Within the media query, add style rules for the following:

- For the `article` element, set the padding to 0.6em 0 0.
- For the `figure` elements within the `article` element, turn off the display.
- For the `section` elements within the `article` element, set the width to 100%, the height to 1000px, set the element so it does not float, set the `background-size` property to `cover`, then set the `background-position` property to `center`.
- For the `section` elements with the `class` value `aam` within the `article` element, set images/aam.jpg as the background image, then repeat for the remaining four `section` elements using the `class` values and filenames shown in **TABLE I-4**.

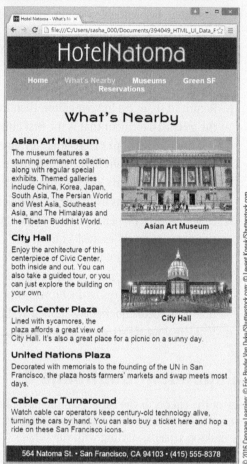

FIGURE I-28

TABLE I-4

class name	image filename
cityhall	images/cityhall.jpg
ccplaza	images/ccplaza.jpg
unplaza	images/unplaza.jpg
cablecar	images/cablecar.jpg

- For `div` elements within `section` elements within the `article` element, set the width to 100%, absolutely position the elements at the top left corner of the positioned ancestor element, set the z-index to 2, set the background color to rgba(255,255,255,0.6), then set a fallback background color of `white` for older browsers. (*Hint:* Specify the fallback background color before the declaration that uses the RGBa value.)
- For the `h3` elements within the `article` element and the `p` elements within the `article` element, set the margins to 0.6em.

Independent Challenge 3 (continued)

g. Save your changes, refresh or reload nearby. html in your browser, resize the browser window to at least 800px wide and verify that its layout matches **FIGURE I-29**.

h. Test your layout in Google Chrome Developer Tools in both orientations using the Google Nexus 5, the Apple iPhone 6, and a third device of your choosing.

i. In your browser, open a print preview, then verify that the small screen/tablet layout is used.

j. Return to nearby.html in your editor, then in the `head` element and below the `link` element for styles.css, add the code `<script src="respond.min.js"> </script>`. Save your changes. If you have access to IE8, open nearby.html in IE8, resize the browser window to its narrowest width, then resize it as wide as possible and verify that both media queries are applied at the appropriate widths.

k. Validate your HTML and CSS documents.

FIGURE I-29

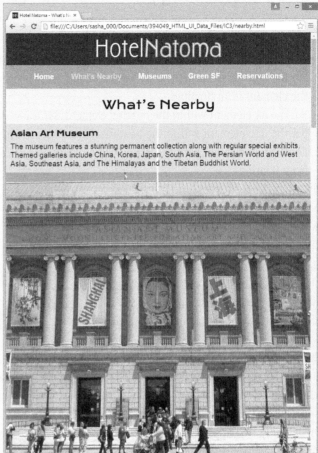

Independent Challenge 4 – Explore

Your clients at Eating Well in Season have commissioned a layout that takes advantage of the space on large screens. They've asked you to make the layout responsive so it also works on smaller screens.

a. In your editor, open HTM_I-11.html from the IC4 folder where you store your Data Files for this unit, save it as **index.html**, then repeat to save HTM_I-12.css as **styles.css**. In the comment at the top of each file, enter your name and today's date where indicated, then save the files.

b. Return to styles.css in your editor, then in the site navigation section, within the `nav.sitenavigation li` style rule, add a declaration to set the border radius to 0.8em. Within the `nav.sitenavigation a` style rule, set the border radius to 0.6em.

c. Scroll down to the main content section, then below the style rule for the `figure` element, add a style rule for the first `figure` element that sets its background image to images/meal.jpg, then repeat to set the background image for the second `figure` element to images/veggies.jpg and for the third `figure` element to images/delivery.jpg. Save your work. (*Hint*: You can select the first and last `figure` elements with the `:first-of-type` and `:last-of-type` pseudo-classes, respectively. You can select the second `figure` element using the `:nth-of-type()` pseudo-class with a value of 2. *Note*: These structural pseudo-classes are not recognized by IE8.)

d. Open index.html in a browser, resize the browser window to its widest width, then resize it to its narrowest width while observing the layout.

Independent Challenge 4 – Explore (continued)

e. Return to styles.css in your editor, then above the print styles section, add a comment containing the text **standard screen styles**. Below the new comment, create a media query for devices with screens where the browser window has a maximum width of 1500px, or for printed output. Within the media query, create the following style rules:

- For the `header` element, set the width to `auto`, the maximum width to 800px, the margins to `0 auto`, and stop the element from floating.
- For the `h1` element within the `header` element, set the width to 60% and the margins to 8% 3% 0 3%.
- For the `div` element within the `header` element, set the margins to 2% 4% 1% and float the element on the left.
- For the `nav` element with the `class` value `sitenavigation`, set the margins to `0 auto` and stop the element from floating.

f. Save your changes, then refresh or reload index.html in your browser. View the page at its widest width, then resize the browser window to less than 1500px wide and verify that the nav bar is displayed below the header and both elements are centered, as shown in FIGURE I-30. (*Note*: Depending on the size of your monitor, the text *Eating Well in Season* may be displayed on a single line.)

FIGURE I-30

g. Return to styles.css in your editor, then above the print styles section, add the text **small screen/tablet styles** as a comment. Below the new comment, create a media query that applies to devices with screens when the browser window has a maximum width of 1100px, or for printed output. Within the media query, add style rules for the following:

- For the `article` element, set the width to 62.5%.
- For `figure` elements, set the width to 100%, the height to `auto`, the bottom margin to 1em, remove the background images, and stop the elements from floating.
- For the `img` elements within the `figure` elements, set the display to `block`.
- For the `aside` element, set the width to 33.5%.

h. Save your changes, refresh or reload index.html in your browser, resize the browser window to less than 1100px wide and verify that its layout matches FIGURE I-30. (*Note*: Depending on the size of your monitor, the text *Eating Well in Season* may be displayed on a single line.)

i. Return to index.html in your editor, then within the `nav` element, add a `div` element before the `ul` element. Within the `div` element, add an img element for the file menu.png within the images folder with a width of 63, a height of 57, and alt text of **Show navigation**. Above the closing `</body>` tag, enter the code `<script src="script.js"></script>`. Save your changes.

j. Return to styles.css in your editor, then above the print styles section, add the text **handheld styles** as a comment. Below the new comment, create a media query that applies to devices with screens when the browser window has a maximum width of 800px. Within the media query, add style rules for the following:

- For the `header` element, set the margins to 0 95px 0 0 and float the element on the left.
- For the `h1` element within the `header` element, set the width to `auto`, set the margins to 0.4em 2%, and float the element on the left.
- For the `div` element within the `header` element, set the display to `none`.
- For the `nav` element with the `class` value `sitenavigation`, set the margins to 16px and absolutely position the element 0px from both the top and right edges of the nearest positioned ancestor element.
- For the element with the `class` value `navigation-menu-button`, set the display to `block` and float the element on the right.

Independent Challenge 4 – Explore (continued)

- For the `ul` element within the `nav` element with the `class` value `sitenavigation`, set the display to `none`, give the element a fixed position 73px from the top and 6px from the right, and set the z-index to 2.
- For `li` elements within the `nav` element with the `class` value `sitenavigation`, set the margins to 0, remove the border, set the display to `block`, left-align the text, and set the border radius to 0.
- For `a` elements within the `nav` element with the `class` value `sitenavigation`, set the width to 83% and set the border radius to 0.
- For the `aside` element, set the display to `none`.

k. Save your changes, refresh or reload index.html in your browser, resize the browser window to less than 800px wide, click the menu button, and verify that the layout matches **FIGURE I-31**.

l. Test your layout in Google Chrome Developer Tools in both orientations using the Google Nexus 5, the Apple iPhone 6, and a third device of your choosing.

m. Return to styles.css in your editor, then in the print styles section, within the media query, add the following style rules:
- For the `header` element, set the margins to 0 0 1em.
- For the `div` element within the `header` element, set the top margin to 0.
- For the h1 element within the `header` element, set the margins to 0 auto.
- For the `nav` element, set display to `none`.
- For the `figure` elements, add a 3px solid black border.

n. Save your changes, refresh or reload index.html in your browser, open a print preview, then verify that the header, main content, and sidebar are displayed and that the nav bar is not displayed.

o. Return to index.html in your editor, then in the `head` element and below the `link` element for styles.css, add the code `<script src="respond.min.js"></script>`. Save your changes. If you have access to IE8, open index.html in IE8, resize the browser window to its narrowest width, then resize it as wide as possible and verify that all media queries are applied at the appropriate widths.

p. Validate your HTML and CSS documents.

FIGURE I-31

Visual Workshop

In your editor, open the file HTM_H-13.html from the VW folder where you store your Data Files for this unit and save it as **index.html**. Repeat to save HTM_H-14.css as **styles.css**. Add your first and last names and today's date to the comment section at the top of each file, then save your changes. Incorporate the file menu.png in the images folder as a menu button, and add a script element referencing the file script.js so that clicking the button toggles the display of the menu items. Use a media query to create the layout shown in **FIGURE I-32** – but without the photo in the center of the page – for browser windows at least 800px wide and for printed output. Use another media query and the image browsing.jpg in the images folder to create the full layout shown in **FIGURE I-32** for browser windows at least 1100px wide. Add an additional media query for browser windows 1400px wide or wider that fixes the width of the body at 1400px and centers the content within the browser window. Test your layouts using Chrome Device Mode in both orientations on at least 3 devices, including 1 iOS device and 1 Android device. Validate your HTML and CSS code.

FIGURE I-32

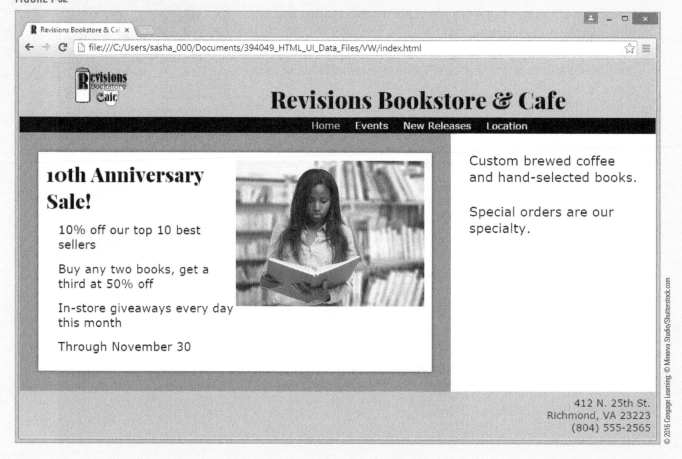

Implementing Responsive Design

Creating and Processing Web Forms

CASE Lakeland Reeds Bed & Breakfast would like visitors to be able to make reservations and ask questions on the site directly. To meet this need, you design and create a contact form.

Unit Objectives

After completing this unit, you will be able to:

- Design a form
- Create a form
- Create text fields
- Customize text fields
- Create check boxes
- Create option buttons
- Add drop-down menus
- Enable form submission

Files You Will Need

L	9 files	IC3	8 files
SR	8 files	IC4	8 files
IC1	8 files	VW	8 files
IC2	9 files		

For specific filenames, see Filenames_J.pdf in the Unit J Data Files folder.

Learning
Outcomes
• Identify the
 components of a
 web form

Design a Form

HTML enables you to receive user input by creating a **form**, which is a group of elements that let users type text, select from lists, check boxes, and/or click option buttons to provide information, and then submit that information. Understanding what information you need to collect, identifying the type of data required for each item, and ensuring that your form is logically organized and includes adequate explanations can increase usability as well as improve the accuracy and relevance of information that users provide. **CASE** ▸ *FIGURE J-1 shows a sketch of the form you will create for the Lakeland Reeds website. Before you finalize the form, you review some important steps in designing a form.*

DETAILS

A few tasks are particularly important in designing a usable form:

- **Identify the types of information you need to collect**

  Users provide most information in a form through input elements, which support different types of user interaction depending on the value of the type attribute. **TABLE J-1** lists and describes the most commonly used input type values. Form elements in which users enter or select data are known as **fields** or **controls**.

  To make the data a user submits as useful as possible, it is important to ask for information in distinct pieces. For instance, if your web form includes a single field into which users enter their first and last names, you would not be able to sort the resulting information by last name easily. Providing separate input elements—one for first name and one for last name—instead would make it possible to sort resulting records by last name. **TABLE J-2** details some of the most commonly used HTML elements used to create forms.

- **Create a logical flow**

  A form should display related fields near each other; for example, if you are collecting name and mailing address information, you will want to display the fields in the order that users are accustomed to specifying an address: first name, last name, street, city, etc. In addition, when you want users to complete the fields in a specific order, place the first field at the top of the form and subsequent fields below it. Many forms end with a field where users can enter a question, a comment, or additional information. Placing such a field at the end of a form ensures that users first have the opportunity to enter information in specific fields.

- **Integrate labels and legends**

  Fields are displayed on web pages as boxes to check, boxes in which to enter text, or menu options to select. To make the significance of each field clear to users, it's important to associate each field with a **label**, which is an element containing descriptive text that is associated with a field.

  In most forms, groups of fields form logical units. In a web page form, these groups are known as **fieldsets**. By default, most browsers surround the fields in a fieldset with a box, creating a visual cue that the fields share a common subject. You can further increase the usability of your form by adding a descriptive title to each fieldset. Such a title is known as a **legend** and is created using the legend element.

TABLE J-1: Commonly used input type values

value	creates	example
checkbox	a check box, which allows users to select a single item	☑ Sun Room
radio	an option button, which lets users select one option from a set of choices	⦿ Vacation ○ Celebration
submit	a submit button, which users can click to send the data they have provided to the server	Submit
text	a text box into which users can type a single line of text	Phone

Creating and Processing Web Forms

FIGURE J-1: Sketch of Lakeland Reeds contact form

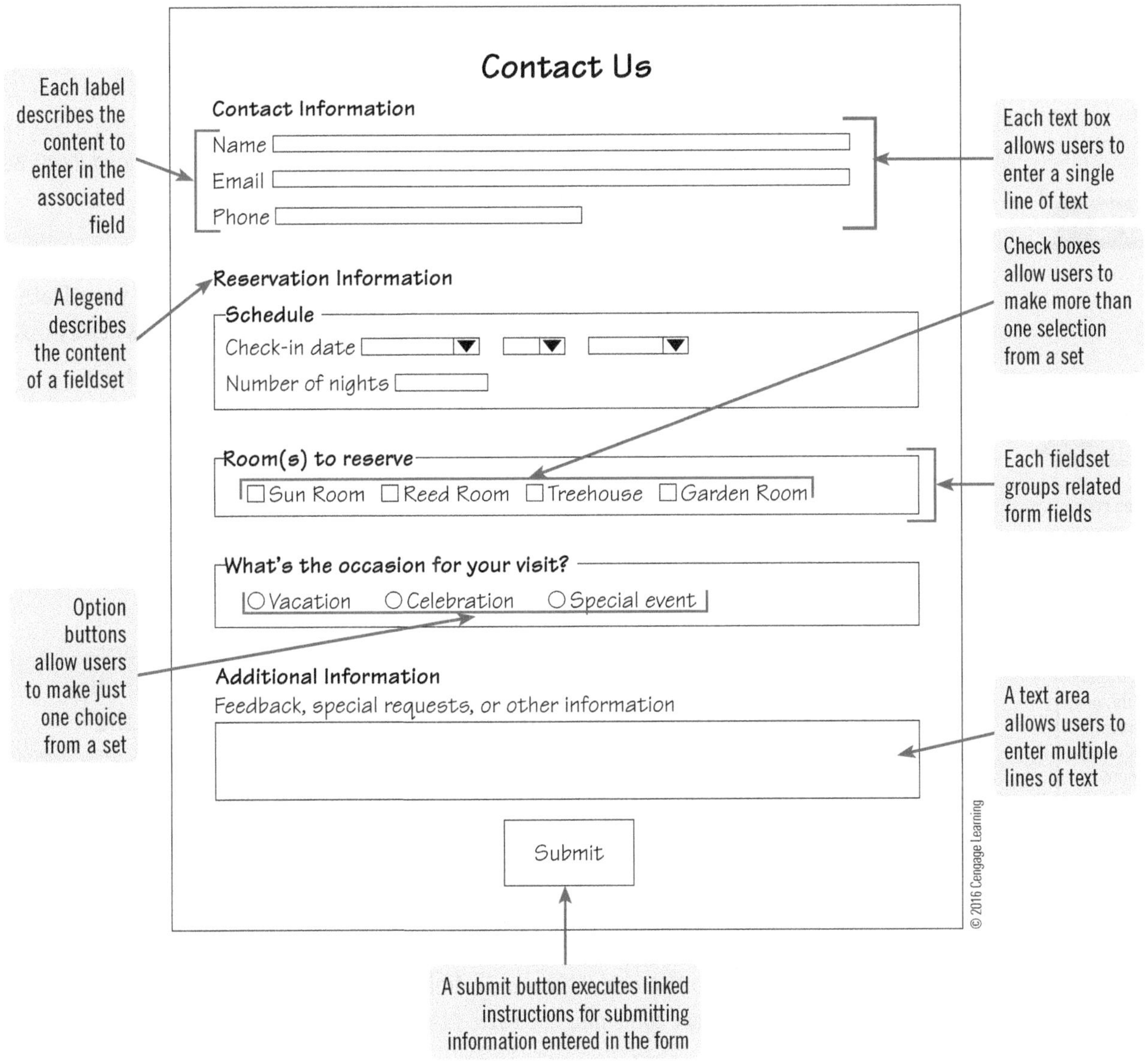

Each label describes the content to enter in the associated field

A legend describes the content of a fieldset

Option buttons allow users to make just one choice from a set

Each text box allows users to enter a single line of text

Check boxes allow users to make more than one selection from a set

Each fieldset groups related form fields

A text area allows users to enter multiple lines of text

A submit button executes linked instructions for submitting information entered in the form

Contact Us

Contact Information
Name
Email
Phone

Reservation Information
Schedule
Check-in date
Number of nights

Room(s) to reserve
☐ Sun Room ☐ Reed Room ☐ Treehouse ☐ Garden Room

What's the occasion for your visit?
○ Vacation   ○ Celebration   ○ Special event

Additional Information
Feedback, special requests, or other information

Submit

© 2016 Cengage Learning

HTML5 & CSS3

TABLE J-2: HTML form elements

element	marks	element	marks
fieldset	a group of related form fields and associated labels	legend	a heading describing the topic of the fieldset
form	all the elements that are part of a form	optgroup	a group of option elements in a drop-down list
input	an individual item of data that users can enter, or a button for form interaction	option	a single entry in a drop-down list
		select	a set of entries to display as a drop-down list
label	a heading describing the associated field	textarea	a multiline area where users can enter text

© 2016 Cengage Learning

Create a Form

Like a table, a web page form contains a series of nested elements. You mark form contents with the `form` element. A `fieldset` element contains the elements in each section of the form, including a `legend` element describing the contents of the fieldset. **CASE** ➤ *As you begin to create the Lakeland Reeds B&B contact form, you enter the basic structuring elements.*

STEPS

1. In your editor, open HTM_J-1.html from the Lessons folder where you store your Data Files for this unit, save it as contact.html, then repeat to save HTM_J-2.css as styles.css

2. In the comment at the top of each file, enter your name and today's date where indicated, then save the files

TROUBLE
FIGURE J-2 shows the completed code. Refer to it as needed as you complete these steps.

3. In contact.html, add a new line below the `h2` element, indent to match the opening `<h2>` tag, then insert opening and closing `form` tags on separate lines

4. Between the opening and closing `form` tags, add 4 sets of opening and closing `fieldset` tags on separate lines with the `class` values `contactinfo`, `reserveinfo`, `additionalinfo`, and `submitbutton`

QUICK TIP
As you work through the steps in this unit, be sure to indent your code as needed to make it more readable.

5. Within the `contactinfo fieldset` element, add the code `<legend>Contact Information</legend>`, then repeat to add the legend Reservation Information within the `reserveinfo` fieldset and the legend Additional Information to the `additionalinfo` fieldset

6. Below the `legend` element in the `reserveinfo` fieldset, add 3 sets of opening and closing `<fieldset>` tags on separate lines with the `class` values `schedule`, `roominfo`, and `occasioninfo`

7. Within the `schedule` fieldset, add the code `<legend>Schedule</legend>`, then repeat to add the legends Room(s) to reserve to the `roominfo` fieldset, and What's the occasion for your visit? to the `occasioninfo` fieldset

   FIGURE J-2 shows the HTML code containing the `form`, `fieldset`, and `legend` elements.

8. Save your changes, return to styles.css in your editor, then above the `/* footer section */` comment, add the comments and rules shown in FIGURE J-3

QUICK TIP
Most browsers display a border around each fieldset by default.

9. Save your changes, open contact.html in a browser, then compare your form to FIGURE J-4

10. Return to styles.css in your editor, go to the reset styles section, add the `fieldset`, `form`, and `legend` selectors to the rule that sets `border`, `padding`, and `margin`, save your changes, then refresh or reload contact.html in your browser

    The default borders are removed from the fieldsets, and only the nested fieldsets show borders, based on the `fieldset fieldset` style rule you created.

FIGURE J-2: Structuring code for the contact form

```
40                    <h2>Contact Us</h2>
41                    <form>
42                        <fieldset class="contactinfo">
43                            <legend>Contact Information</legend>
44                        </fieldset>
45                        <fieldset class="reserveinfo">
46                            <legend>Reservation Information</legend>
47                            <fieldset class="schedule">
48                                <legend>Schedule</legend>
49                            </fieldset>
50                            <fieldset class="roominfo">
51                                <legend>Room(s) to reserve</legend>
52                            </fieldset>
53                            <fieldset class="occasioninfo">
54                                <legend>What's the occasion for your visit?</legend>
55                            </fieldset>
56                        </fieldset>
57                        <fieldset class="additionalinfo">
58                            <legend>Additional Information</legend>
59                        </fieldset>
60                        <fieldset class="submitbutton">
61                        </fieldset>
62                    </form>
```

fieldset elements nested within reserveinfo fieldset (lines 47–55)

FIGURE J-3: Style rules for form structuring elements

```
126    /* form styles */
127    form {
128        padding: 10px;
129    }
130
131    /* fieldset styles */
132    fieldset {
133        margin-bottom: 0.8em;
134    }
135    fieldset fieldset {
136        margin-top: 1em;
137        padding: 0.8em;
138        border: 1px solid #777;
139    }
```

Placing multiple selectors on separate lines does not affect their meaning

This style rule applies only to `fieldset` *elements nested within other* `fieldset` *elements*

```
140    legend {
141        font-size: 1.25em;
142    }
143    .contactinfo legend,
144    .reserveinfo > legend,
145    .additionalinfo legend {
146        margin-left: -0.1em;
147        font-weight: bold;
148    }
149
150    /* footer section */
```

Selectors are separated by commas

> selects direct child, so this selector applies to the child `legend` *element, but not grandchild* `legend` *elements*

Code continued with line 140 in figure to the right

Code continued from figure on the left

FIGURE J-4: Styled form outline in browser

legend elements in nested fieldset elements have different styles than other legend elements

Final `fieldset` *element has no legend*

© a.mar/Shutterstock.com

Create Text Fields

Learning
Outcomes
• Create text boxes
• Create a text area

You use the `input` element to create many different types of fields that accept user input in your forms. Setting the `type` attribute to `text` creates a single-line text field known as a **text box**, in which users can type a small amount of text. Modern browsers support a number of additional `type` values that create text boxes with specific semantic meanings; TABLE J-3 details the most common of these. The `textarea` element is used to create a **text area**, which is a field that allows users to enter multiple lines of text. **CASE** ▶ *You add text boxes for name, email, phone number, and length of stay, along with a text area and labels.*

STEPS

1. **Return to** contact.html **in your editor**

2. **Within the** `contactinfo` **fieldset and below the** `legend` **element, enter opening and closing** `<label>` **tags on separate lines, then on a new line between the tag, type** Name
   Text within the `label` element serves as the label for the associated field.

3. **Repeat Step 2 to create two more** `label` **elements below the one you just created, containing the text** Email **and** Phone **respectively, add a** `label` **element containing the text** Number of nights **below the legend in the** `schedule` **fieldset, then add a** `label` **element containing the text** Feedback, special requests, or other information **below the legend in the** `additionalinfo` **fieldset**

4. **Below the text** *Name* **in the first** `label` **element, enter the code**
   `<input type="text" name="name" id="nameinput">`
   Specifying the value `text` for the `type` attribute creates a generic text box. The `input` element can be nested in the `label` element to make it easier to work with the two elements as a unit.

5. **Repeat Step 4 to enter the** `input` **elements highlighted in green in** FIGURE J-5 **below the text** *Email* **in the second** `label` **element, below the text** *Phone* **in the third** `label` **element, and below the text** *Number of nights* **in the fourth** `label` **element**
   The values `email`, `tel`, and `number` for the `type` attribute create text boxes and enable any special features a user agent might apply to those field types.

6. **Below the label text in the** `additionalinfo` **fieldset, enter the code**
   `<textarea name="feedback" id="feedback" rows="4" cols="55"></textarea>`
   The `rows` attribute specifies how many lines of input the box accommodates—that is, how tall the box will be—while the `cols` attribute approximates how many characters should fit across the box.

7. **In the opening tag for the first** `label` **element, add a space before the closing >, then type** `for="nameinput"`
   For accessibility purposes, it's important to associate each label with its corresponding field. To do so, you give the `label` element a `for` attribute and assign it the field's `id` value.

8. **Repeat Step 7 to assign the second** `label` **element a** `for` **value of** `emailinput`, **the third** `phoneinput`, **the fourth** `stay-nights`, **and the fifth** `feedback`, **as shown in the code highlighted in yellow in** FIGURE J-5

9. **Save your changes, then refresh or reload contact.html in your browser**
   As FIGURE J-6 shows, the text of each label is displayed along with a text box corresponding to each `input` element.

10. **Click the first text box, type any first and last name, press [Tab], then repeat to enter information in each box, typing the text of this step in the text area**
    As you reach the end of a line in the text area, the text wraps, beginning a new line.

FIGURE J-5: Code for text boxes and text areas

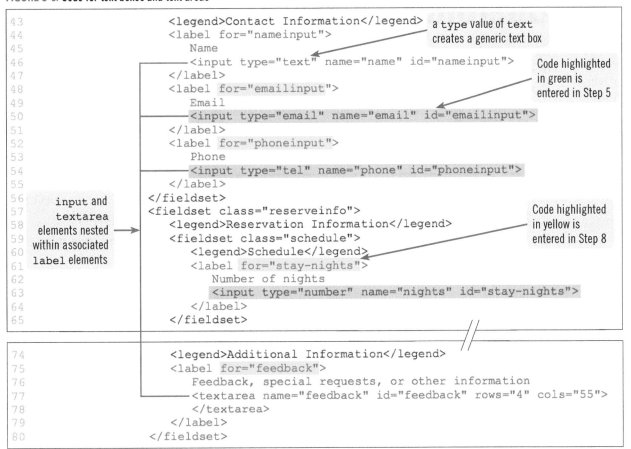

```
43                        <legend>Contact Information</legend>      a type value of text
44                        <label for="nameinput">                   creates a generic text box
45                            Name
46                          ──<input type="text" name="name" id="nameinput">
47                        </label>                                  Code highlighted
48                        <label for="emailinput">                  in green is
49                            Email                                 entered in Step 5
50                          ──<input type="email" name="email" id="emailinput">
51                        </label>
52                        <label for="phoneinput">
53                            Phone
54                          ──<input type="tel" name="phone" id="phoneinput">
55                        </label>
56    input and        </fieldset>
57    textarea         <fieldset class="reserveinfo">               Code highlighted
58    elements nested      <legend>Reservation Information</legend>  in yellow is
59    within associated    <fieldset class="schedule">              entered in Step 8
60    label elements           <legend>Schedule</legend>
61                            <label for="stay-nights">
62                                Number of nights
63                              ──<input type="number" name="nights" id="stay-nights">
64                            </label>
65                        </fieldset>

74                        <legend>Additional Information</legend>
75                        <label for="feedback">
76                            Feedback, special requests, or other information
77                          ──<textarea name="feedback" id="feedback" rows="4" cols="55">
78                            </textarea>
79                        </label>
80                    </fieldset>
```

FIGURE J-6: Text fields and associated labels displayed in form

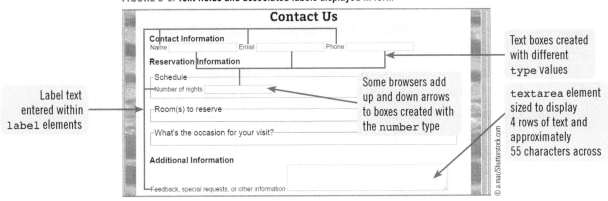

TABLE J-3: type values for special data types and effects in browsers

value	result
email	modern browsers may validate to ensure that entries are valid email addresses; touchscreen devices with on-screen keyboards may display customized buttons for email input, such as an @ key and a . or .com key
number	modern browsers may validate to ensure that entries are numbers; touchscreen devices with on-screen keyboards may display numeric keyboards
password	most browsers display text entered by users as bullets or asterisks rather than showing the actual characters
search	modern browsers may style input to match styling of search boxes in other parts of the user interface
tel	touchscreen devices with on-screen keyboards may display numeric keyboards with -, *, and # keys
url	modern browsers may validate entries to ensure that they are valid web addresses; touchscreen devices with on-screen keyboards may display customized buttons for input, such as /, ., and .com keys

Customize Text Fields

Learning
Outcomes
• Apply style rules to
form components
• Add placeholder
text to text boxes

Labels and fields usually require styling to optimize usability. Good layout can transform a disorganized list of words and boxes into sets of labels and fields with clear relationships. It's common to use positioning to align multiple sets of `label` and `input` elements in a grid, but some developers prefer CSS table styling instead. You can also use the `placeholder` attribute to populate text boxes with instructions in modern browsers. **CASE** ▸ *You add styles to the style sheet to display the labels and text boxes in parallel columns. You also add placeholder text to two of the fields in your form.*

STEPS

1. **Return to** styles.css **in your editor, then add the** `input`, `label`, **and** `textarea` **selectors to the rule that sets** `border`, `padding`, **and** `margin` **in the reset styles section**

2. **Above the** `/* footer section */` **comment, enter the comments and style rules shown in FIGURE J-7**

   The `.contactinfo input` rule positions the `input` elements in the Contact Information section 5em from the left so they do not overlap their labels and remain left aligned relative to each other. The `.schedule input` rule does the same for the Schedule section using a value of 10em.

3. **Save your changes, then return to** contact.html **in your editor**

QUICK TIP

Placeholder text
can be useful in
providing examples
of formats for input
or for describing
what users should
enter in a given
text box.

4. **In the** `<input>` **tag with the** `id` **value** `nameinput`, **add a space before the closing** `>`, **then type** `placeholder="First and last name"`

   Modern browsers display the value of the `placeholder` attribute as light-colored text in the associated text box and remove it when a user selects the box in preparation for text entry.

5. **Repeat Step 4 for the** `<input>` **tag with the** `id` **value** `emailinput` **to add the code** `placeholder="address@example.com"`

   FIGURE J-8 shows the updated code.

QUICK TIP

The placeholder
attribute is ignored
by older browsers, so
it should not be used
to display crucial
information.

6. **Save your changes, then refresh or reload** contact.html **in your browser**

   As FIGURE J-9 shows, placeholder text appears in gray in the first two text boxes.

7. **Click the** Name **text box, type a name, then click in the** Email **text box**

   When you begin typing in a text box, the placeholder text is hidden.

8. **Click the** Number of nights **text box**

   Some browsers display up and down arrows that allow you to select a number by clicking rather than by typing.

Changing styles on focus

You can use the `:focus` pseudo-class to change the style of an `input` or `textarea` element when a user is working with it. This technique is commonly used to change the background color of a field to help users visually identify their position in a form.

Unlike links, which use different pseudo-classes for mouse and keyboard interaction, the `:focus` pseudo class responds to both mouse and keyboard interaction in a form. A field has focus when a user clicks it, touches it, or navigates to it with a keyboard.

FIGURE J-7: Field and label styles

```
143   .schedule {
144      position: relative;
145   }
146
147   /* field styles */
148   .contactinfo input, #stay-nights, textarea {
149      border: 1px solid #ccc;
150      padding: 0.2em;
151      font-size: 1em;
152   }
153   select {
154      margin-bottom: 0.6em;
155   }
156   .contactinfo input {
157      position: absolute;
158      left: 5em;
159   }
160   .schedule input {
161      position: absolute;
162      left: 10em;
163   }
```

```
164   #nameinput, #emailinput {
165      width: 25em;
166   }
167   #phoneinput {
168      width: 12em;
169   }
170   #stay-nights {
171      width: 3em;
172   }
173
174   /* label styles */
175   label {
176      font-size: 1em;
177      line-height: 1.6em;
178   }
179   .contactinfo label {
180      display: block;
181      position: relative;
182      margin: 0.8em 0;
183   }
184
185   /* footer section */
```

Code continued with line 164 in figure to the right   Code continued from figure on the left

FIGURE J-8: placeholder attributes added to input elements

```
44                    <label for="nameinput">
45                       Name
46                       <input type="text" name="name" id="nameinput" placeholder="First and
47                       last name">
48                    </label>
49                    <label for="emailinput">
50                       Email
51                       <input type="email" name="email" id="emailinput"
52                       placeholder="address@example.com">
53                    </label>
```

FIGURE J-9: Text boxes with positioning, size, and placeholder text applied

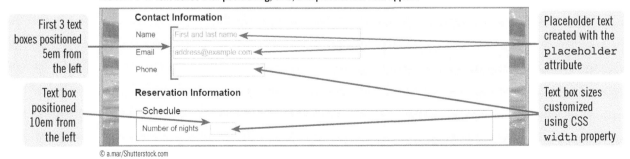

First 3 text boxes positioned 5em from the left

Text box positioned 10em from the left

Placeholder text created with the `placeholder` attribute

Text box sizes customized using CSS `width` property

© a.mar/Shutterstock.com

Creating and Processing Web Forms   271

Create Check Boxes

Sometimes rather than allowing users to enter text, you want to present them with a predetermined set of choices. When you want users to be able to select one or more predefined choices independent of each other, a check box usually makes the most sense. A **check box** is a box that users can click or touch to add or remove a check mark, enabling users to select or deselect it. A check box is ideal for allowing users to indicate whether a particular statement applies to them. A check box is created using the `input` element with a `type` value of `checkbox`. **CASE** *Because a user may wish to reserve more than one room at Lakeland Reeds, you use check boxes for choices in the "Room(s) to reserve" fieldset.*

STEPS

1. **Return to contact.html in your editor, then in the fieldset with the `class` value `roominfo` and below the *Room(s) to reserve* `legend` element, enter 4 pairs of `<label>` tags on separate lines**

2. **In the opening tag for the first `label` element, add the code `for="sun"`, then repeat for the remaining 3 `label` elements using the `for` values `reed`, `tree`, and `garden`**

QUICK TIP
A check box should
always precede its
label text for optimal
usability.

3. **Within the first `label` element, enter the tag `<input type="checkbox" id="sun" value="Sun Room">`, then on a new line type Sun Room**
   Because users do not enter text in a check box, you use the `value` attribute to specify text to be submitted with the form if the check box is selected.

4. **Repeat Step 3 for the remaining `label` elements, creating `input` elements with the following attributes and label text:**

   ```
   id="reed" value="Reed Room"          Reed Room
   id="tree" value="Treehouse"          Treehouse
   id="garden" value="Garden Room"      Garden Room
   ```

5. **Add the code `name="room"` to each of the four `input` tags**
   FIGURE J-10 shows the completed code for the check boxes and labels.

6. **Save your changes, then return to styles.css in your editor**

7. **Above the `/* footer section */` comment, add a style rule for `label` elements within the element with the `class` value `roominfo` that sets the right margin to 1.6em**
   FIGURE J-11 shows the new style rule, which adds space between each label and the check box that follows it.

QUICK TIP
Different browsers
format check boxes
differently by
default, so the check
boxes in your
browser may not
match those in the
figure.

8. **Save your changes, then refresh or reload contact.html in your browser**
   A check box is displayed to the right of each label below the Room(s) to reserve legend, as shown in **FIGURE J-12**.

9. **Click each check box to select it, then click each check box again to deselect it**
   You can select as many or as few check boxes at once as you want.

FIGURE J-10: HTML code for check boxes

```
66                          <fieldset class="roominfo">
67                              <legend>Room(s) to reserve</legend>
68                              <label for="sun">
69                                  <input type="checkbox" id="sun" value="Sun Room" name="room">
70                                  Sun Room
71                              </label>
72                              <label for="reed">
73                                  <input type="checkbox" id="reed" value="Reed Room" name="room">
74                                  Reed Room
75                              </label>
76                              <label for="tree">
77                                  <input type="checkbox" id="tree" value="Treehouse" name="room">
78                                  Treehouse
79                              </label>
80                              <label for="garden">
81                                  <input type="checkbox" id="garden" value="Garden Room"
82                                  name="room">
83                                  Garden Room
84                              </label>
85                          </fieldset>
```

FIGURE J-11: CSS code to add space to the right of check box labels

```
183     .roominfo label {
184         margin-right: 1.6em;        ← Creates a space of 1.6em
185     }                                 to the right of each label
186
187     /* footer section */
```

FIGURE J-12: Check boxes displayed in form

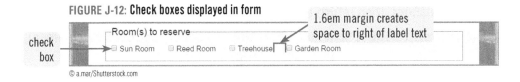

check box → ☐ Sun Room   ☐ Reed Room   ☐ Treehouse ☐ Garden Room

Room(s) to reserve

1.6em margin creates space to right of label text

© a.mar/Shutterstock.com

Marking fields as required

Often one or more fields on a web form are marked as required—that is, fields the user must complete. Many websites implement scripts to check if required fields are completed; if not, these scripts can prevent the submission of the form and display an error message. Modern browsers also support the HTML5 required attribute, which can replace script-based verification. You simply add the attribute required (or required="required" in XHTML documents) to any required field element. For instance,

to create a text box that users must complete, you use the code `<input type="text" required>`. You should also include a visual cue on your web page for each required field, along with an explanation of what the cue means. A red asterisk is commonly used to denote required fields on web forms. The required attribute can't replace script-based validation for websites that must support older browsers, but it can supplement script-based validation for many websites.

Learning Outcomes
• Create option buttons

Create Option Buttons

Another type of form field, the **option button**, presents users with a circular box for selecting one option from a set of choices. An option button is also known as a **radio button** and is best suited for prompting users to select only one item from a group, such as the age range that applies to a user. Option buttons and check boxes ensure that user input for particular questions matches a standard list of options, which prevents typographical errors. Each `input` element in a set of option buttons must include the `name` attribute with a value identical to all other members of the set. You can also include the `checked` attribute for one option button in a set, causing browsers to display the button as selected by default. **CASE** *Phillip Blaine would like users to select only one answer when indicating the occasion for their visit, so you use option buttons for the* input *elements. Because most visitors are on* vacation, *he'd like the* Vacation *option to be selected by default when users open the web page.*

STEPS

1. **Return to** contact.html **in your editor, then in the** `occasioninfo` **fieldset and below the** *What's the occasion for your visit?* legend **element, enter three pairs of** `<label>` **tags on separate lines**

2. **In the opening tag for the first** `label` **element, add the code** `for="vacation"`, **then repeat for the remaining two** `label` **elements using the** `for` **values** `celebration` **and** `event`

3. **Within the first** `label` **element, enter the tag** `<input type="radio" name="occasion" id="vacation" value="Vacation">`, **then on a new line type** Vacation

4. **Repeat Step 3 for the remaining** `label` **elements, creating** `input` **elements with the following attributes and label text:**

`id="celebration"`	`value="Celebration"`	`Celebration`
`id="event"`	`value="Special Event"`	`Special Event`

   Be sure to include the code `type="radio"` and `name="occasion"` for all three `input` elements.

5. **Within the** `input` **element with the** `id` **value** `vacation`, **add the attribute** `checked`
   FIGURE J-13 shows the completed code for the option buttons and their labels.

6. **Save your changes, then return to** styles.css

7. **In the** `.roominfo label` **style rule above the** `/* footer section */` **comment, add the** `.occasioninfo label` **selector as shown in** FIGURE J-14
   This style adds space between each label and the option button that follows it.

8. **Save your changes, then refresh or reload contact.html in your browser**
   The *Vacation* option button is automatically selected as shown in FIGURE J-15.

9. **Click the** Celebration **and** Special Event **option buttons to select them**
   As you click each button in the set, the previously selected button is deselected.

> **QUICK TIP**
> HTML5 allows the checked attribute with no value; for XHTML code, you must supply the full attribute-value pair: `checked= "checked"`.

> **QUICK TIP**
> Be sure to use a comma to separate the selectors.

> **QUICK TIP**
> Check boxes also support the checked attribute.

Implementing selection interfaces

HTML5 implemented several new `type` values that provide users with specific types of predefined options. TABLE J-4 details several of these values. All of these values create web page features known as **selection interfaces**, which present users with allowable options visually or enable them to manipulate values without entering text. However, older browsers, such as IE8, do not recognize or support these `input` values. This means that if your web page design relies on any of these `type` values, you'll likely need to include scripts or other field types that mimic their functions as backups in order for your pages to degrade gracefully.

FIGURE J-13: HTML code for option buttons

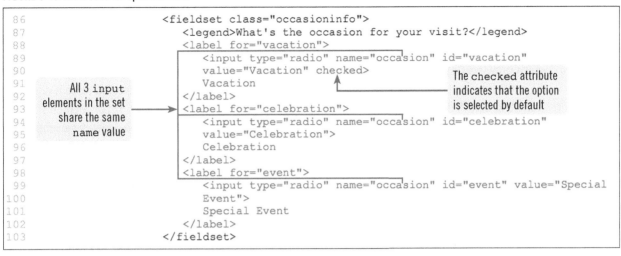

```
86                        <fieldset class="occasioninfo">
87                            <legend>What's the occasion for your visit?</legend>
88                            <label for="vacation">
89                                <input type="radio" name="occasion" id="vacation"
90                                value="Vacation" checked>
91                                Vacation
92                            </label>
93                            <label for="celebration">
94                                <input type="radio" name="occasion" id="celebration"
95                                value="Celebration">
96                                Celebration
97                            </label>
98                            <label for="event">
99                                <input type="radio" name="occasion" id="event" value="Special
100                               Event">
101                               Special Event
102                           </label>
103                       </fieldset>
```

All 3 input elements in the set share the same name value

The checked attribute indicates that the option is selected by default

FIGURE J-14: CSS code to add space to the right of option button labels

```
184    .roominfo label, .occasioninfo label {
185        margin-right: 1.6em;
186    }
187
188    /* footer section */
```

Creates a space of 1.6em to the right of each label

The Vacation option is selected by default because its `<input>` tag includes the `checked` attribute

FIGURE J-15: Option buttons displayed in form

1.6em margin creates space to right of label text

© a.mar/Shutterstock.com

TABLE J-4: `type` values that may invoke selection interfaces

value(s)	description	browser implementations
color	supports hexadecimal color values	a color picker that visually represents colors and lets users click colors to select them
date, month, week, time, datetime, datetime-local	accepts dates, times, and related values using a standard format	a calendar that users can scroll through and click to select date-related values
file	accepts the path and filename for a file to upload from a user's device	file navigation features that let users select a file from local storage
number	enables developer to specify a range of valid numbers that users can input	arrows that users can click to increase or decrease the value; numeric keyboards (touchscreen devices)
range	enables developer to specify a range of valid numbers that users can input	a slider bar that enables users to increase or decrease the value by dragging a pointer along a line

Add Drop-Down Menus

Learning
Outcomes
• Create drop-down
  menus
• Add options to
  drop-down menus

Another option for creating a list of options from which users can select is to create a **drop-down menu**, which browsers display as a text box with an arrowhead next to it. Users can click the arrowhead to view the entire list of options; once a user selects an option, the list is hidden and the selected value is displayed in the text box. A drop-down menu is created using the `select` element, with `option` elements nested within the `select` element to specify the list items. **CASE** *You create drop-down menus for arrival date, month, and year.*

STEPS

QUICK TIP

An element that creates a field does not need to be nested within the associated `label` element; this is only done when convenient for positioning fields and label text.

QUICK TIP

The `select` and `option` elements are not included in your reset style rules because browsers have custom layouts for these elements that use the `padding`, `border`, and/or `margin` properties.

QUICK TIP

You can use the `font-size` property to set the size of text in a drop-down menu; however, not all browsers recognize this property for `select` elements.

QUICK TIP

In order to make a different option the default, you add the `selected` attribute to that `option` element.

1. **Return to** contact.html **in your editor, go to the** schedule **fieldset. create a blank line below the** *Schedule* legend **element, enter a** p **element containing the text** Check-in date, **then below the** p **element create a** div **element with a** class **value of** date-picker

    You will create 3 `select` elements to collect the month, day, and year, so you group them within a `div` element. Each form field must have its own label, so you use a p element to add additional text that indicates the overall function of the group.

2. **Within the** div **element, create a** label **element with the** for **value** checkin-month **and the text** Check-in Month, **below it create a second** label **with the** for **value** checkin-day **and the text** Check-in Day, **then below it create a third** label **with the** for **value** checkin-year **and the text** Check-in Year

3. **Below the** label **with the text** *Check-in Month,* **enter opening and closing** <select> **tags on separate lines with the** id **value** checkin-month **and the** name **value** checkin-month, **then repeat to create a** select **element with the** id **and** name **values** checkin-day **below the** label **with the text** *Check-in Day* **and a** select **element with the** id **and** name **values** checkin-year **below the** label **with the text** *Check-in Year*

4. **Within the first** select **element, enter opening and closing** <option> **tags containing the text** January, **then add the code** value="01" **within the opening** <option> **tag**

5. **Repeat Step 4 to add an** option **element containing the text** February **with the value** 02, **an** option **element containing the text** March **with the value** 03, **and so on for the remaining months of the year, ending with the text** December **and a** value **of** 12

6. **Within the second** select **element, enter opening and closing** <option> **tags containing the text** 1, **add the code** value="01" **within the opening** <option> **tag, then repeat to create** option **elements for the remaining days in the longest month, ending with the text** 31 **and a** value **of** 31

7. **Within the third** select **element, enter opening and closing** <option> **tags containing the text** 2019, **add the code** value="2019" **within the opening** <option> **tag, repeat to create an** option **element containing the text** 2020 **and a** value **of** 2020, **then repeat to create an** option **element containing the text** 2021 **and a value of** 2021

    FIGURE J-16 shows the completed code for the drop-down menus.

8. **Save your changes, return to** styles.css **in your editor, then, above the** /* footer section */ **comment, add the style rules shown in** FIGURE J-17

9. **Save your changes, refresh or reload contact.html in your browser, then click the arrowhead next to the year 2019**

    As **FIGURE J-18** shows, the first `option` element within each `select` element is displayed as the default choice.

10. **Use the drop-down menus to select a check-in date of August 3, 2020**

```
61 <fieldset class="schedule">
62    <legend>Schedule</legend>
63    <p>Check-in date</p>
64    <div class="date-picker">
65       <label for="checkin-month">Check-in Month
66       </label>
67       <select id="checkin-month"
68       name="checkin-month">
69          <option value="01">January</option>
70          <option value="02">February</option>
71          <option value="03">March</option>
72          <option value="04">April</option>
73          <option value="05">May</option>
74          <option value="06">June</option>
75          <option value="07">July</option>
76          <option value="08">August</option>
77          <option value="09">September</option>
78          <option value="10">October</option>
79          <option value="11">November</option>
80          <option value="12">December</option>
81       </select>
82       <label for="checkin-day">Check-in Day
83       </label>
84       <select id="checkin-day"
85       name="checkin-day">
86          <option value="01">1</option>
87          <option value="02">2</option>
88          <option value="03">3</option>
89          <option value="04">4</option>
90          <option value="05">5</option>
91          <option value="06">6</option>
92          <option value="07">7</option>
93          <option value="08">8</option>
```

```
94          <option value="09">9</option>
95          <option value="10">10</option>
96          <option value="11">11</option>
97          <option value="12">12</option>
98          <option value="13">13</option>
99          <option value="14">14</option>
100         <option value="15">15</option>
101         <option value="16">16</option>
102         <option value="17">17</option>
103         <option value="18">18</option>
104         <option value="19">19</option>
105         <option value="20">20</option>
106         <option value="21">21</option>
107         <option value="22">22</option>
108         <option value="23">23</option>
109         <option value="24">24</option>
110         <option value="25">25</option>
111         <option value="26">26</option>
112         <option value="27">27</option>
113         <option value="28">28</option>
114         <option value="29">29</option>
115         <option value="30">30</option>
116         <option value="31">31</option>
117      </select>
118      <label for="checkin-year">Check-in Year
119      </label>
120      <select id="checkin-year"
121      name="checkin-year">
122         <option value="2019">2019</option>
123         <option value="2020">2020</option>
124         <option value="2021">2021</option>
125      </select>
126   </div>
```

Each **option** element defines a single menu option

Code continued with line 94 in figure to the right

Each **select** element creates a drop-down menu

Code continued from figure on the left

HTML5 & CSS3

```
190   .schedule p {
191      width: 9.2em;
192      float: left;
193   }
```

p element floated to left of drop-down lists to indicate the type of information requested

```
194   .date-picker label {
195      position: absolute;
196      left: -10000px;
197   }
198
199   /* footer section */
```

label elements positioned offscreen for use with screen readers

Code continued with line 194 in figure to the right

Code continued from figure on the left

FIGURE J-18: Drop-down menus for check-in date in browser

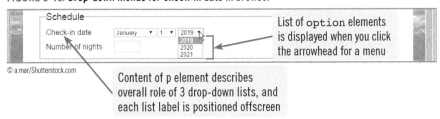

List of **option** elements is displayed when you click the arrowhead for a menu

Content of p element describes overall role of 3 drop-down lists, and each list label is positioned offscreen

© a.mar/Shutterstock.com

Enable Form Submission

Learning
Outcomes
• Create a submit
  button
• Test form
  submission

A form needs to include a **submit button**, which is a button that users can click to submit the data they've entered. An `input` element with a `type` value of `submit` is used to create a submit button. TABLE J-5 details 3 other input values that also create buttons. The `action` attribute is added to the opening `form` tag to specify the name and location of a script that will accept the form data. In addition, every field with information to be submitted must have a value for the `name` attribute. Then, when submitting a form, user agents group the `name` attribute of each field with the value entered or selected by a user. **CASE** *You create a submit button, add an attribute that sends form input to a script, and test your work.*

STEPS

1. **Return to** contact.html **in your editor, then within the fieldset with the** `class` **value** `submitbutton`, **add an** `input` **element with a** `type` **value of** `submit`, **an** `id` **value of** `submit`, **and a value for the** `value` **attribute of** Submit
   The `value` attribute specifies the text displayed on the button.

2. **In the opening** <form> **tag, add the code** `action="results.html"`
   FIGURE J-19 shows the updated document. The value of the `action` attribute specifies the file or application that receives the form data.

3. **Save your changes, return to** styles.css **in your editor, then above the** `/* label styles */` **comment, enter the style rule shown in** FIGURE J-20

4. **Save your changes, then open contact.html in your browser**
   The submit button is displayed at the bottom of the form. By default, most browsers display form buttons with black text on a gray background with a subtle box shadow.

5. **Click the** Number of nights **box, type** car, **then press [Tab]**
   Because this field has the `type` value `number`, some modern browsers flag or reject non-numerical input. Firefox outlines the field in red to indicate invalid input, as shown in FIGURE J-21.

6. **Complete the form with fictitious information, making sure to enter a number in the** *Number of nights* **field and checking at least 2 boxes in the Rooms(s) to reserve section, then click** Submit
   The results.html page opens showing the data submitted by the form, as shown in FIGURE J-22. For each form field, the `name` attribute is submitted followed by an equal sign and the entered or selected value. A page like results.html can be useful for testing a form during development. When a form is finalized and incorporated into a public website, the data is transmitted to an application running on a web server.

7. **Validate contact.html and your style sheet, then make changes as necessary to fix any errors**

TABLE J-5: `type` **values for form buttons**

value	description	attributes
button	creates a generic button that can be programmed using a script	value specifies text displayed on the button
image	creates a submit button using an image	src specifies the image file name and location alt provides alternative text for users of non-visual user agents
reset	clears all user input and resets fields to defaults; not used by some designers because users can confuse it with a submit button and inadvertently lose all input	value specifies text displayed on button
submit	creates a default submit button that submits user input based on form or button attributes	value specifies text displayed on button

FIGURE J-19: HTML code for form action and submit button

```
40              <h2>Contact Us</h2>
41              <form action="results.html">
42                  <fieldset class="contactinfo">

171                 <fieldset class="submitbutton">
172                     <input type="submit" id="submit" value="Submit">
173                 </fieldset>
```

FIGURE J-20: CSS code for submit button

```
173    #submit {
174        border: none;
175        padding: 0.4em 0.6em;
176        background-color: #e3d5ba;
177        font-size: 1.25em;
178        border-radius: 10px;
179    }
180
181    /* label styles */
```

FIGURE J-21: Invalid input in Firefox

© a.mar/Shutterstock.com

FIGURE J-22: results.html page showing submitted form data

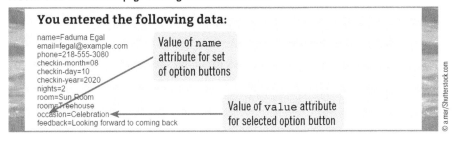

© a.mar/Shutterstock.com

Practice

Concepts Review

Refer to FIGURE J-23 **to answer the questions.**

FIGURE J-23

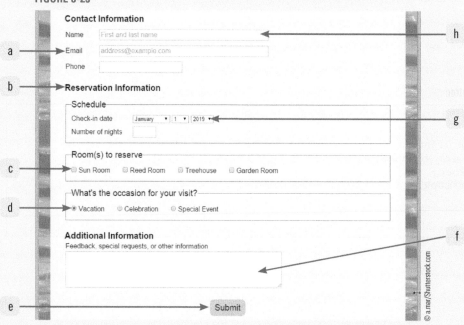

1. **Which element is created using an** input **element with a** type **value of** submit?
2. **Which element is created using an** input **element with a** type **value of** checkbox?
3. **Which element is created using an** input **element with a** type **value of** text?
4. **Which element is created using an** input **element with a** type **value of** radio?
5. **Which item is created with a** textarea **element?**
6. **Which item is created with a** legend **element?**
7. **Which item is created with a** select **element?**
8. **Which item is created with a** label **element?**

Match each term with the statement that best describes it.

9. **check box**	**a.** a box that users can click to add or remove a check mark
10. **fieldset**	**b.** a group of fields that form a logical unit
11. **text box**	**c.** descriptive text associated with a form element
12. **option button**	**d.** a box for selecting one option from a set of choices
13. **submit button**	**e.** a field that allows users to enter multiple lines of text
14. **field**	**f.** a single-line text field
15. **text area**	**g.** a button that users can click to submit the data they've entered
16. **label**	**h.** a descriptive title for a fieldset
17. **legend**	**i.** a form element in which users enter or select data

Select the best answer from the list of choices.

18. Modern browsers display the value of the _____ attribute as light-colored text in the associated text box and remove it when a user enters text in the box.
    - **a.** placeholder
    - **b.** type
    - **c.** legend
    - **d.** label

19. Each input element in a set of option buttons must include the _____ attribute with a value identical to all other members of the set.
    - **a.** selected
    - **b.** id
    - **c.** name
    - **d.** value

20. Which element do you use to create a drop-down menu?
    - **a.** fieldset
    - **b.** textarea
    - **c.** input
    - **d.** select

21. Which element do you use to add an item to a drop-down menu?
    - **a.** input
    - **b.** option
    - **c.** label
    - **d.** legend

22. When submitting a form, user agents group the _____ attribute of each field with the value entered or selected by a user.
    - **a.** name
    - **b.** id
    - **c.** placeholder
    - **d.** value

Skills Review

1. **Create a form.**
    a. In your editor, open HTM_J-3.html from the SR folder where you store your Data Files for this unit, save it as **order.html**, then repeat to save the file HTM_J-4.css as **styles.css**.

    b. Within the comment section at the top of each file, enter your first and last names and today's date, then save your changes.

    c. In order.html, insert a form element below the h2 element, then within the form element add four fieldset elements with the class values deliveryinfo, orderinfo, additionalinfo, and submitbutton.

    d. Within the first fieldset element, add a legend element containing the text **Delivery Information**, then repeat to add the legend **Order** within the second fieldset element and the legend **Special Instructions** within the third fieldset element.

    e. Below the legend element in the orderinfo fieldset, add three fieldset elements with the class values **crustinfo**, **sizeinfo**, and **toppinginfo**.

    f. Within the crustinfo fieldset, add a legend element containing the text **Crust**, then repeat to add the legends **Size** to the sizeinfo fieldset and **Topping(s)** to the toppinginfo fieldset. Save your changes.

    g. Return to styles.css in your editor, then in the reset styles section, add the fieldset, form, and legend selectors to the style rule that sets border, padding, and margin to 0.

    h. Above the /* footer section */ comment, create a comment containing the text **form styles**, then below the comment, add a style rule for the form element that sets the padding to 10px and the background color to #e3d5ba.

    i. Below the style rule you created in the previous step, create a comment containing the text **fieldset styles**, then below the comment, add the following style rules:
    - For fieldset elements, set the bottom margin to 1em.
    - For fieldset elements nested within other fieldset elements, set the top margin to 1em, padding on all sides to 0.8em, and create a 1px solid border with the color #777.
    - For legend elements, set the font size to 1.25em.

Skills Review (continued)

- For the `legend` element within the element with the `class` value `deliveryinfo`, for the `legend` element that is a direct child of the element with the `class` value `orderinfo`, and for the `legend` element within the element with the `class` value `additionalinfo`, set the left margin to -0.1em and bold text.

j. Save your changes, open order.html in your browser, then verify that all of the `legend` elements are displayed.

2. **Create text fields.**

a. Return to order.html in your editor, then within the fieldset with the `class` value `deliveryinfo`, below the `legend` element, add a `label` element containing the text **Name** on a line between the `<label>` tags. Repeat to create four more `label` elements below the one you just created, containing the text **Street Address**, **City**, **Email**, and **Phone**, respectively, then add an additional `label` element below the Special Instructions legend in the fieldset with the class value `additionalinfo` containing the text **Special requests, delivery details**.

b. Below the text *Name* in the first `label` element, create an `input` element for a text field with the `name` value `name` and the `id` value `nameinput`, then add a for attribute to the opening `<label>` tag that associates it with the `input` element you created. Repeat to create a text field below the text *Street Address* with the `name` value `address` and the `id` value `addressinput`, a text field below the text *City* with the `name` value `city` and the `id` value `cityinput`, an email field below the text *Email* with the `name` value `email` and the `id` value `emailinput`, and a telephone field below the text *Phone* with the `name` value `phone` and the `id` value `phoneinput`.

c. Below the label text in the fieldset with the `class` value `additionalinfo`, insert an element to create a text area with the `name` value `instructions` and the `id` value `instructions` that displays 3 rows and 50 columns of input. Add an attribute to the opening `<label>` tag that associates it with the text area you created.

d. Save your changes, return to styles.css in your editor, then in the reset styles section, add the `input`, `label`, and `textarea` selectors to the style rule that sets border, padding, and margin to 0.

e. Save your changes, then refresh or reload order.html in your browser. Verify that all the labels and text entry fields are displayed, then enter text in each of the fields you just created.

3. **Customize text fields.**

a. Return to styles.css in your editor, then above the `/* footer section */` comment, add a comment containing the text **field styles**. Below the new comment, add the following style rules:

- For `input` elements within the element with the `class` value `deliveryinfo` and for the `textarea` element, create a 1px solid border using the color #ccc, 0.2em of padding on all sides, and set the font size to 1em.
- For `input` elements within the element with the `class` value `deliveryinfo`, absolutely position the elements 8em from the left.
- For the elements with the `id` values `nameinput`, `addressinput`, and `emailinput`, set the width to 20em.
- For the elements with the `id` values `cityinput` and `phoneinput`, set the width to 12em.

b. Below the styles you created in the previous step, add a comment containing the text **label styles**. Below the new comment, add the following style rules:

- For `label` elements, set the font size to 1em.
- For `label` elements within the element with the `class` value `deliveryinfo`, set `display` to `block`, relatively position the elements, and set margins to 0.8em 0.

c. Save your changes, return to order.html in your editor, then add the placeholder text **First and last name** to the input element with the `id` value `nameinput`. Repeat to add **Building number and street** for the input tag with the `id` value `addressinput` and **address@example.com** for the input element with the id value `emailinput`.

d. Save your changes, then refresh or reload order.html in your browser. Verify that the placeholder text is displayed in the fields where you added it.

4. **Create check boxes.**
   a. Return to order.html in your editor, then below the `legend` element in the fieldset with the `class` value `toppinginfo`, create four `label` elements.
   b. In the opening tag for the first `label` element, add an attribute to associate it with the element with the `id` value `pepperoni`. Within the `label` element, enter code to create an `input` element for a check box with the `id` value `pepperoni` and the value `Pepperoni` for the `value` attribute. Add a new line below the `input` element and enter the text **Pepperoni**.
   c. Repeat Step b to complete the remaining `label` elements with `input` elements with the attributes and label text shown in **TABLE J-6**:

   TABLE J-6

id	value	label text
sausage	Sausage	Sausage
greenpepper	Green Peppers	Green Peppers
onion	Onions	Onions

   © 2016 Cengage Learning

   d. Add the `name` attribute with the value `toppings` to each of the four `input` elements.
   e. Save your changes, then return to styles.css. Above the `/* footer section */` comment, create a style rule for `label` elements within the element with the `class` value `toppinginfo` that sets the right margin to 1.6em.
   f. Save your changes, then refresh or reload order.html in your browser. Click each check box to select it, then click each check box again to deselect it.

5. **Create option buttons.**
   a. Return to order.html in your editor, then below the `legend` element in the `crustinfo` fieldset, create two `label` elements.
   b. In the opening tag for the first `label` element, add an attribute to associate it with the element with the `id` value `thin`. Within the `label` element, enter code to create an `input` element for an option button with the `id` value `thin` and the value `Thin` for the `value` attribute. Add a new line below the `input` element and enter the text **Thin Crust**.
   c. Repeat Step b to associate the second `label` element with the element with the `id` `thick` and to create an `input` element for an option button with the `id` value `thick`, the value `Deep Dish` for the `value` attribute, and label text **Deep Dish**. Add an attribute to make this option selected by default.
   d. Add the `name` attribute with the value `crust` to each of the two `input` elements
   e. Save your changes, return to styles.css in your editor, then in the label styles section in the style rule for `label` elements within the element with the `class` value `toppinginfo`, add a selector for `label` elements within the element with the `class` value `crustinfo`.
   f. Save your changes, then refresh or reload order.html in your browser. Click the *Thin Crust* and *Deep Dish* option buttons to select them.

6. **Add drop-down menus.**
   a. Return to order.html in your editor, add a new line below the `legend` element in the fieldset with the `class` value `sizeinfo`, then add a `select` element with the value `size` for the `id` and `name` attributes.
   b. Within the `select` element, add an `option` element with a value of `small` for the `value` attribute, and the text **Small**. Repeat to create `option` elements with a `value` value of `medium` and text **Medium**, a `value` value of `large` and text **Large**, and a `value` value of `XL` and text **Extra Large**.
   c. Save your changes, return to styles.css in your editor, then in the reset styles section, add the `option` and `select` selectors to the style rule that sets border, padding, and margin to 0.

Skills Review (continued)

d. Above the /* label styles */ comment, add a style rule for the `select` element that creates a bottom margin of 0.6em and sets the font size to 1em. Above the /* footer section */ comment, add a style rule for the `label` element within the element with the `class` value `sizeinfo` that absolutely positions the element -10000px from the left.

e. Save your changes, then refresh or reload order.html in your browser. Use the drop-down menu to select each of the size options.

7. Enable form submission.

a. Return to order.html in your editor.

b. Within the `submitbutton` fieldset, enter code for an `input` element that creates a submit button with an `id` value of `submit` and value for the `value` attribute of `Add to Cart`.

c. In the opening <form> tag, add an attribute that sends the collected form data to the file results.html when the form is submitted.

d. Save your changes, then return to styles.css in your editor. Above the comment /* label styles */, add a style rule for the element with the `id` value `submit` that removes the border, sets the padding to `0.4em 0.6em`, sets the background color to `#ffcc66`, sets the font size to 1.25em, and creates a border radius of 10px. Above the /* field styles */ comment, add a style rule for the element with the `class` value `submitbutton` that adds 0.5em of padding on top and center-aligns text.

FIGURE J-24

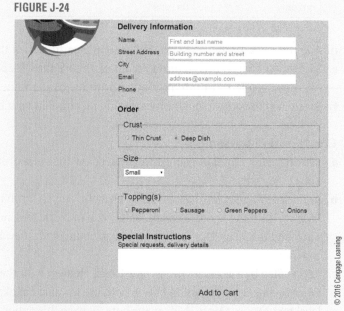

e. Save your changes, then refresh or reload order.html in your browser. Compare your screen to **FIGURE J-24**.

f. Complete all the sections of the form, click the Add to Cart button, then verify that the results.html page opens and displays the information you entered or selected.

g. Validate the code for order.html and styles.css, then make changes as necessary to fix any errors.

Independent Challenge 1

The Spotted Wren Garden Center has begun offering free landscaping consultations. Sarah Nguyen, the owner, would like to add a form to the website to enable users to request an appointment. You create and style the form.

a. In your editor, open HTM_J-5.html from the IC1 folder where you store your Data Files for this unit, save it as **quote.html**, then repeat to save HTM_J-6.css as **styles.css**. In the comment at the top of each file, enter your name and today's date where indicated, then save the files.

b. In quote.html, insert tags for a `form` element before the closing </article> tag. Within the `form` element, add tags for 5 `fieldset` elements with the `class` values `contactinfo`, `timinginfo`, `jobtype`, `additionalinfo`, and `submitbutton`.

c. Save your changes, then in styles.css, add the selectors `fieldset`, `form`, `input`, `label`, `legend`, and `textarea` to the style rule in the reset styles section that sets border, padding, and margin to 0.

Independent Challenge 1 (continued)

d. Above the `/* footer section */` comment, add a comment containing the text **form styles**. Below the comment, add a style rule for the `form` element that sets the margin to 2%, the padding to 2%, creates a 2px solid black border, and sets the background color to `#ff9c78`.

e. Below the `form` style rule, add a comment containing the text **fieldset styles**. Below the comment, add a style rule for `fieldset` elements that sets the margins to `0 0 1em 1em`, then add a style rule for `legend` elements that sets margins to `0 0 0.4em -1em`, font size to `1.2em`, and font weight to `bold`.

f. In quote.html, in the fieldset with the `class` value `contactinfo`, add the legend text **Contact Info** followed by five `label` elements. Within the first `label` element, add the label text **Name**, then add code to create a text box with the `id` value `nameinput` and the `name` value `name`. Add a `for` attribute to the opening `<label>` tag to associate it with the `input` element you created. Repeat for the remaining `label` elements, using the values shown in **TABLE J-7**:

TABLE J-7

id	name	label text
addressinput	address	Street Address
zipinput	zip	Zip Code
emailinput	email	Email
phoneinput	phone	Phone

© 2016 Cengage Learning

g. Edit the `emailinput` element to specify the `type` for an email address, then edit the `phoneinput` element to specify the `type` for a phone number. Add the placeholder text **First and last name** to the `nameinput` element and **address@example.com** to the `emailinput` element.

h. Save your changes, then in styles.css and above the `/* footer section */` comment, add a new comment with the text **field styles**. Below the new comment, add the following style rules:

- For the `input` element, create a 1px solid border with the color `#777`, set the padding to 0.2em on all sides, and set the font size to 1em.
- For `input` elements within the element with the `class` value `contactinfo`, absolutely position the elements 8em from the left.
- For the elements with the `id` values `nameinput`, `emailinput`, and `addressinput`, set the width to 30em.
- For the elements with the `id` values `zipinput` and `phoneinput`, set the width to 12em.

i. Below the style rules you created in the previous set, add a new comment with the text **label styles**. Below the new comment, create a style rule for `label` elements that sets the font size to 1em, then create a style rule for `label` elements within the element with `class` value `contactinfo` that sets margins to `0.7em 0`; sets `display` to `block`; and relatively positions the elements. Save your changes, then preview quote.html in a browser.

j. Return to quote.html in your editor, then in the fieldset with the `id` value `timinginfo`, add the legend **Best day(s) to schedule a visit** followed by 7 `label` elements. Within the first `label` element, add code to create a check box with the `id` value `monday`, the `name` value `days`, and the value `Monday` for the `value` attribute, then add the label text **Monday**. Add a `for` attribute to the opening `<label>` tag to associate it with the `input` element you created. Repeat for the remaining `label` elements to create check boxes for the other 6 days of the week in chronological order.

k. Save your changes, then in styles.css and above the `/* footer section */` comment, add a style rule for `label` elements in the element with the `class` value `timinginfo` that sets the right margin to 0.5em. Save your changes to styles.css, then refresh or reload quote.html in your browser.

Independent Challenge 1 (continued)

l. Return to quote.html in your editor, then in the fieldset with the `id` value `jobtype`, add the legend **Project Area** followed by 4 `label` elements. Within the first `label` element, add code to create an option button with the `id` value `front`, the `name` value `area`, and the value `House front` for the `value` attribute, then add the label text **Front of House**. Add a `for` attribute to the opening `<label>` tag to associate it with the `input` element you created. Repeat for the remaining `label` elements, using the same `name` value and the additional values shown in TABLE J-8:

TABLE J-8

id	value	label text
border	Border	Border of Property
multiple	Multiple	Multiple Areas (please specify in Notes box below)
other	Other	Other (please specify in Notes box below)

© 2016 Cengage Learning

m. Save your changes, then in styles.css and above the `/* footer section */` comment, add a style rule for `label` elements in the element with the `class` value `jobtype` that sets `display` to `block` and a bottom margin of 0.2em. Save your changes to styles.css, then refresh or reload quote.html in your browser.

n. Return to quote.html in your editor, then in the fieldset with the `class` value `additionalinfo`, add the legend **Additional Information** followed by a `label` element. Within the label element, add the label text **Notes**, then add code to create a text area with `notes` for the `id` and `name` values, displaying 4 rows and 60 columns of input. Add a `for` attribute to the opening `<label>` tag to associate it with the text area you created. Save your changes. In styles.css and above the `/* label styles */` comment, create a style rule that applies to the element with the `id` value `notes` that sets its `display` to `block`. Save your changes, then refresh or reload quote.html in your browser.

o. Return to quote.html in your editor, then in the fieldset with the `class` value `submitbutton`, add code to create a submit button with the `id` value `submit` and the value `Submit Request` for the `value` attribute. In the opening `<form>` tag, add an attribute that passes submitted data to the file results.html. Save your changes. In styles.css and above the `/* field styles */` comment, create a style rule that applies to the element with the `class` value `submitbutton` that removes the bottom margin. Save your changes to styles.css. Refresh or reload quote.html in your browser, then compare your document with FIGURE J-25.

FIGURE J-25

p. Complete all sections of the form, click Submit Request, then verify that the results.html page opens and displays the data you entered or selected.

q. Validate your HTML and CSS documents.

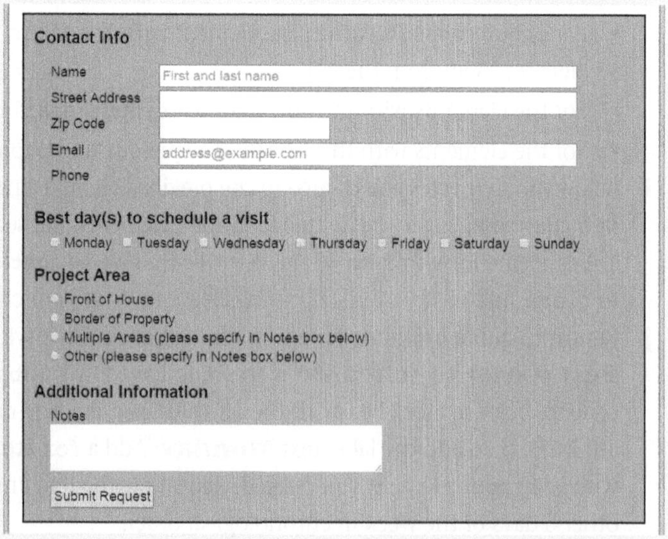

Independent Challenge 2

The coordinators of the Murfreesboro Regional Soccer League would like to allow prospective new members to sign up on the website. You create a form to allow users to enter basic information.

a. In your editor, open HTM_J-7.html from the IC2 folder where you store your Data Files for this unit, save it as **signup.html**, then repeat to save HTM_J-8.css as **styles.css**. In the comment at the top of each file, enter your name and today's date where indicated, then save the files..

b. In signup.html, below the h2 element, add a `form` element containing 5 fieldsets. Add the following class values to the fieldsets: `contactinfo`, `ageinfo`, `membershipinfo`, `additionalinfo`, `submitbutton`. Add legends to the first four fieldsets containing the text **Contact Information**, **Age Range**, **Special Memberships**, and **Additional Information**.

c. Save your changes, then in styles.css, add the selectors `fieldset`, `form`, `input`, `label`, `legend`, and `textarea` to the style rule in the reset styles section that sets border, padding, and margin to 0.

d. Above the `/* footer section */` comment, add a comment containing the text fieldset styles, then below the comment create the following style rules:
- For `fieldset` elements, create a 2px solid black border, set padding to 2% on all sides, and add a bottom margin of 0.8em.
- For `legend` elements, set the font size to 1.4em, the font weight to `bold`, and the font family to a font stack including Georgia, Times New Roman, Times, and serif.

Save your changes to styles.css, open signup.html in a browser, then verify that the fieldsets and legends are displayed.

e. Return to signup.html in your editor, then in the first fieldset, add four `label` elements. Add the label text **First Name**, **Last Name**, **Email**, and **Phone**. Add a text input field below the label text in the first label element, using the id value fnameinput and the name value fname. Add a for attribute to the opening `<label>` tag to associate it with this element. Repeat to add a text input field to the second `label` element with the id value lnameinput and the name value lname, an email input field to the third `label` element with the id value emailinput and the name value email, and a phone input field to the fourth `label` element with the id value phoneinput and the name value phone. Specify First name as placeholder text for the first text field, Last name for the second, and address@example.com for the third. Save your changes.

f. In styles.css and above the `/* footer section */` comment, add a comment with the text **field styles**, then below the comment create the following style rules:
- For `input` elements, add a 1px solid border using the color #777, set padding to 0.2em on all sides, and set the font size to 1em.
- For `input` elements within the element with the `class` value `contactinfo`, absolutely position the elements 6em from the left.
- For the elements with the id values fnameinput, lnameinput, and emailinput, set the width to 20em.
- For the element with the id value phoneinput, set the width to 12em.

g. Below the styles you created in the previous step, add a comment with the text **label styles**, then below the comment create the following style rules:
- For `label` elements, set the font size to 1.2em.
- For `label` elements within the element with the `class` value `contactinfo`, set `display` to `block`, position to `relative`, and margins to 1em 0.

Save your changes to styles.css, refresh or reload signup.html in a browser, then verify that the Contact Information `input` elements and labels are displayed.

Independent Challenge 2 (continued)

h. Return to signup.html in your editor, then in the fieldset with the `class` value `ageinfo` and below the Age Range legend, add a `select` element with `agerange` for both the `id` and `name` values. Create 8 options for the drop-down list, displaying the text **4–6**, **7–9**, **10–12**, **13–15**, **16–17**, **18–35**, **36–54**, and **55+**. Set the value for the `value` attribute for the first option to **D1**, the second to **D2**, and so on through the final element, which will have the value **D8**.

i. In the fieldset with the `class` value `membershipinfo` and below the Special Memberships legend, add two `label` elements. Within the first `label` element, add code to create a check box with the `id` value `student`, the `name` value `memberships`, and the value `Student` for the `value` attribute, then add the label text **Student**. Add a `for` attribute to the opening `<label>` tag to associate it with the `input` element you created. Repeat for the second `label` element to create a check box with the `id` value `senior`, the `name` value `memberships`, and the value `Senior` for the `value` attribute, then add the label text **Senior**. Add a `for` attribute to the opening `<label>` tag to associate it with the `input` element you created. Save your changes, return to styles.css in your editor, then above the /* footer section */ comment, add a style rule for the `label` elements within the element with the `class` value `membershipinfo` that sets the right margin to 1em. Save your changes.

j. Return to signup.html, then in the fieldset with the `class` value `additionalinfo` and below the Additional Information legend, add a `label` element. Within the `label` element, add the label text **Questions or special requests**, then add code to create a text area with `feedback` for the `id` and `name` values, displaying 7 rows of input. Add a `for` attribute to the opening `<label>` tag to associate it with the text area you created. Save your changes. Go to styles.css in your editor, then in the field styles section, add the `textarea` selector to the `input` style rule. Move to the end of the field styles section, then create a new style rule for the element with the `id` value `feedback` that sets the width to 98% and sets `display` to `block`. Save your changes to styles.css, then refresh or reload signup.html in your browser and verify that the Age Range, Special Memberships, and Additional Information sections all include the appropriate content.

k. Return to signup.html in your editor, then in the fieldset with the `class` value `submitbutton`, add code to create a submit button with the `id` value `submit` and the value `Submit` for the `value` attribute. In the opening `<form>` tag, add an attribute that passes submitted data to the file results.html. Save your changes. In styles.css and above the /* field styles */ comment, create a style rule that applies to the element with the `class` value `submitbutton`, removing the border and center-aligning text. Above the /* label styles */ comment, create a style rule for the element with the `id` value `submit`, creating a 1px solid border using the color `#999`, setting the font size to 1.5em, the font weight to `bold`, the background color to `#c8f098`, and the border radius to 0.5em. Save your changes to styles.css, then refresh or reload signup.html in your browser and compare your document to **FIGURE J-26**.

l. Complete all sections of the form, click Submit, then verify that the results.html page opens and displays the data you entered or selected.

m. Validate your HTML and CSS documents.

FIGURE J-26

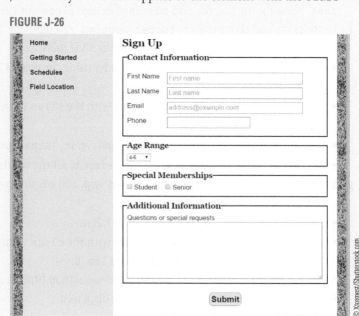

Independent Challenge 3

Diego Merckx, the manager of the Hotel Natoma, wants to allow guests to initiate reservations using the website. You create a web page form based on the information he wants to collect from potential visitors.

a. In your editor, open HTM_J-9.html from the IC3 folder where you store your Data Files for this unit, save it as **reserve.html**, then repeat to save HTM_J-10.css as **styles.css**. In the comment at the top of each file, enter your name and today's date where indicated, then save the files.

b. In reserve.html, add a `form` element below the h2 element, then add four fieldsets. Add the legend text **Contact Information**, **Reservation Information**, and **Additional Information** to the first three fieldsets. Add an appropriate `class` name to each fieldset (the fourth fieldset will contain the Submit button). Within the fieldset with the legend Reservation Information, nest five additional fieldsets, add the legends **Party size**, **Bed preference**, **Check-in date**, **Check-out date**, and **Parking**, then add an appropriate `class` name to each fieldset.

c. Save your changes, then in styles.css, add the selectors `fieldset`, `form`, `input`, `label`, `legend`, and `textarea` to the style rule in the reset styles section that sets border, padding, and margin to 0.

d. Above the `/* footer section */` comment, add a comment containing the text **form styles**, then below the comment, create a style rule for the `form` element that sets padding to 0.5em and the background color to #082008. Below this style rule, add a comment containing the text **fieldset styles**, then below the comment create the following style rules:

   • For `fieldset` elements, set the bottom margin to 0.5em, set the padding to `2.5em 2% 0.5em`, relatively position the elements, and set the background color to #93AD78.

   • For `fieldset` elements nested within other `fieldset` elements, set the top padding to 0.4em and create a 2px solid border using the color #082008.

   • For `legend` elements that are direct children of fieldset elements that are themselves direct children of the form element, set the font size to 1.25em; the font family to a font stack including PTSansCaption, Georgia, Times New Roman, Times, and serif; and absolutely position the elements 0.6em from the top. (*Hint*: Use the selector `form > fieldset > legend`.)

   • For the fieldset containing the legend text *Check-in date*, set the width to 40% and float the element on the left.

   • For the fieldset containing the legend text *Check-out date*, set the width to 40% and float the element on the right.

   • For the fieldset containing the legend text *Parking*, clear floated elements on both the left and right sides.

   • For the last fieldset (the one for the submit button), set the padding to `0.5em 0`, the bottom margin to 0, and center-align text.

   Save your changes to styles.css, open reserve.html in a browser, then verify that the fieldsets and legends are displayed.

e. In reserve.html, add three `label` elements to the first fieldset (the one that contains the legend Contact Information), containing the label text **Name**, **Email**, and **Phone**. Add code for a text box within each `label` element, using the relevant input types and appropriate `name` and `id` values. Add placeholder text if appropriate. Associate each `label` element with the enclosed text box. Save your changes, then in styles.css, above the `/* footer section */` comment, add a comment containing the text **field styles**, then below the comment create create the following style rules:

   • For `input` elements, set padding to 0.2em on all sides and font size to 1em.

   • For `input` elements within the first fieldset, absolutely position the elements 5em from the left.

   • For the `input` elements associated with the label text *Name* and *Email*, set the width to 30em.

   • For the `input` element associated with the label text *Phone*, set the width to 12em.

Independent Challenge 3 (continued)

Below the style rules you just created, add a comment containing the text **label styles**, then below the comment create the following style rules:

- For `label` elements, set the bottom margin to 0.2em and the line height to 1.6em.
- For `label` elements within the first fieldset, set margins to `0.6em 0`, `display` to `block`, and `position` to `relative`.

Save your changes to styles.css, refresh or reload reserve.html in your browser, then verify that the text boxes and labels are displayed in the first fieldset.

f. Return to reserve.html and in the fieldset with the legend *Party size*, add two `label` elements containing the label text **Number in your party** and **Number of rooms required**. Add code for a text box within each `label` element using appropriate `type`, `name`, and `id` values. Associate each `label` element with the enclosed text box. Save your changes, then in styles.css and above the `/* label styles */` comment, create a style rule for input elements within the fieldset with the legend *Party size*, set the right margin to 2em and the width to 3em. Save your changes, refresh or reload the web page in your browser, then verify that the text boxes and labels are displayed.

g. Return to reserve.html and in the fieldset with the legend *Bed preference*, add three `label` elements containing the label text **King/Queen**, **Twin**, and **Other/Mix (specify in Additional Information)**. Add code for a check box before the label text within each `label` element, using appropriate values for the `name`, `id`, and `value` attributes. Associate each `label` element with the enclosed check box. Save your changes, then in styles.css and above the `/* footer styles */` comment, add a style rule for `label` elements within the fieldset with the legend *Bed preference* that sets the right margin to 1.6em. Save your changes, refresh or reload the web page in your browser, then verify that the check boxes and labels are displayed.

h. In the fieldset with the legend *Check-in date*, create 3 `label` elements, containing the text **Check-in month**, **Check-in day**, and **Check-in year**. Below each `label` element, create a drop-down list containing the appropriate content – the months of the year, the days of the month, and the years 2019-2021, respectively. Add appropriate `id` and `name` values to the lists, and associate each label with its list. Copy the code for the three drop-down lists and paste it into the fieldset with the legend *Check-out date*, then change the label text to **Check-out month**, **Check-out day**, and **Check-out year**, and change the `id` and `name` values for the pasted items to unique values. Save your changes, then in styles.css and above the `/* footer section */` comment, create a style rule for the `label` elements within the fieldsets with the legends *Check-in date* and *Check-out date* that absolutely positions the elements -10000px from the left. Save your changes, refresh or reload the web page in your browser, then verify that all the drop-down lists are displayed.

i. Return to reserve.html and in the fieldset with the legend *Parking*, add a `label` element containing the label text **I need parking for**. Add code for a text box within the `label` element using appropriate `type`, `name`, and `id` values. Associate the `label` element with the enclosed text box. After the code for the text box, add the text **vehicle(s)** followed by a period (.). Save your changes, then in styles.css and above the `/* label styles */` comment, add a style rule for the text box you just created that sets its width to **3em**. Save your changes, refresh or reload the web page in your browser, then verify that the text box and the label text are displayed.

Independent Challenge 3 (continued)

j. Return to reserve.html and in the fieldset containing the legend text *Additional Information*, add a `label` element. Within the `label` element, add the label text **Feedback, special requests, or other information**, then add code to create a text area with appropriate `id` and `name` values, displaying four rows of input. Associate the `label` element with the text area element. Save your changes, then in styles.css and in the field styles section, add the `textarea` selector to the `input` style rule, then below the `input` style rule create a new style rule for the `textarea` element that sets its width to 99% and `display` to `block`. Save your changes, refresh or reload the web page in your browser, then verify that the text area and the label text are displayed.

k. In the final fieldset, add code to create a submit button with an appropriate `id` value and the value **Submit** for the `value` attribute. In the opening `<form>` tag, add an attribute that passes submitted data to the file results.html. Save your changes. In styles.css and above the `/* label styles */` comment, create a style rule for the submit button, setting the font family to a font stack that includes PTSansCaption, Georgia, Times New Roman, Times, and serif; a background color of `#e3d5ba`; font size to 1.25em; and a 10px border radius on the top-left and bottom-right corners. Save your changes, then refresh or reload the web page in your browser and compare your screen to **FIGURE J-27**.

l. Complete all sections of the form, click Submit, then verify that the results.html page opens and displays the data you entered or selected.

m. Validate your HTML and CSS documents.

FIGURE J-27

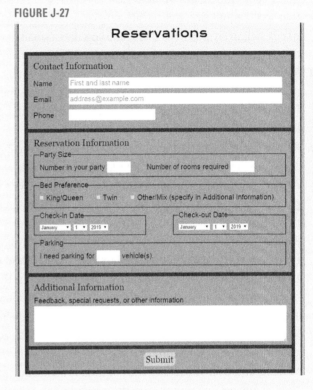

Independent Challenge 4 – Explore

As you continue your work on the website for Eating Well in Season, a provider of locally-sourced, healthy meals, you create a form that will allow new customers to sign up for the service online.

a. In your editor, open HTM_J-11.html from the IC4 folder where you store your Data Files for this unit, save it as **signup.html**, then repeat to save HTM_J-12.css as **styles.css**. In the comment at the top of each file, enter your name and today's date where indicated, then save the files.

b. In signup.html below the first `h2` element, containing the text Sign Up, add a `form` element. Within the `form` element, add 7 `fieldset` elements. In the first six fieldsets, specify the legend text **Contact information**, **Meal(s)**, **Delivery frequency**, **Start date**, **How did you hear about us?**, and **Food allergies**. In styles.css, add the selectors `fieldset`, `form`, `input`, `label`, `legend`, and `textarea` to the style rule in the reset styles section that sets border, padding, and margin to 0. Create new style rules to specify padding for the fieldsets and to specify an appropriate font size, weight, and family for the legends. Preview the document in a browser.

Independent Challenge 4 – Explore (continued)

c. Return to signup.html and in the first fieldset, create 7 text boxes with the labels **Name**, **Email**, **Phone**, **Address**, **City**, **State**, and **Zip**. Specify an appropriate data type for each text box and include placeholder text for at least one text box. Associate all the text boxes with their labels, and provide appropriate values for the `id` and `name` properties. In styles.css, create a style rule for `input` elements that creates a border, sets a small bottom margin, and specifies a font size. Create another style rule for text boxes in the first fieldset that absolutely positions them far enough from the left to avoid overlapping the labels and sets a maximum width. Create style rules that specify appropriate maximum widths for individual text boxes as necessary. Create a style rule for `label` elements that sets the font size, then create a style rule for `label` elements in the first fieldset that sets their `display` to `block`, relatively positions them, and specifies a small bottom margin. Preview the document in a browser, enter data in each of the new fields, and verify all fields work as expected.

d. Return to signup.html and in the second fieldset, create 2 checkboxes with the labels **Lunch** and **Dinner**. Associate the text boxes with their labels, and provide appropriate values for the `id`, `name`, and `value` properties. In styles.css, create a style rule that adds a small margin on the right side of each label in this fieldset. Preview the document in a browser and test the new fields.

e. Return to signup.html and in the third fieldset, create 2 option buttons with the labels **Daily** and **Weekly**. Associate the text boxes with their labels, and provide appropriate values for the `id`, `name`, and `value` properties. Add an attribute that selects Weekly by default. In styles.css, edit the selector for the style rule you created in the previous step so it applies to the content of this fieldset as well. Preview the document in a browser and test the new fields.

f. Return to signup.html and in the fourth fieldset, create a text box with the label Start date. Use the `type` value `date` for the text box. Associate the text box with its label, and provide appropriate values for the `id` and `name` properties. In styles.css, create a style rule that absolutely positions the label in the fourth fieldset out of the visible area of the browser window. Preview the document in multiple browsers and explore what, if any, selection interface is available when you move the mouse pointer over the field or click the field.

g. Return to signup.html and in the fifth fieldset, create a drop-down menu with the label **How did you hear about us?** containing the options --, **web search, friend/word of mouth, saw a delivery truck**, and **other**. (Note: The -- option is the default and allows users to skip the question without the form logging any default answer.) Specify an appropriate value for the `value` attribute for each option and associate the label text with the drop down menu. In styles.css, add the selector for this fieldset to the style rule that absolutely positions other labels out of the visible area of the browser window, then specify a larger font size for the drop-down menu. Preview the document in a browser and test the new field.

h. Return to signup.html and in the sixth fieldset, create a text area with the label **Food allergies** that displays three lines of text. In styles.css, add the selector for this fieldset to the style rule that absolutely positions other labels out of the visible area of the browser window, specify a font size for the contents of the text area, then specify a width of 99% for the text area. Preview the document in a browser and test the new field.

Independent Challenge 4 – Explore (continued)

i. Return to signup.html and in the seventh fieldset, create a submit button that displays the text **Sign Up**. Add an attribute to the form element that submits the data entered by users to the file results.html. In styles.css, create a style rule that specifies a padding, border, font size, and border radius for the button, and sets the background color to `rgb(246,224,65)`. Preview the document in a browser, then verify that the button looks as you expect. Complete each field in the form, click Sign Up, then verify that the results.html page opens and displays the data you entered.

j. Return to signup.html and in the first fieldset, add the `required` attribute to the element that creates each text box. Just after the opening `<legend>` tag, enter the code `<span>*</span>` to insert an asterisk. Repeat for each label in the first fieldset, and for the legends in the second and third fieldsets. In styles.css, add a style rule for span elements within fieldset elements that sets the color to red. Preview the document in a browser. Your document should match **FIGURE J-28**.

k. Click the Sign Up button without completing any of the form fields and notice what, if any, validation feedback the browser provides for the required fields. Repeat for at least one other browser and notice any differences between browsers.

l. Validate your HTML and CSS documents.

FIGURE J-28

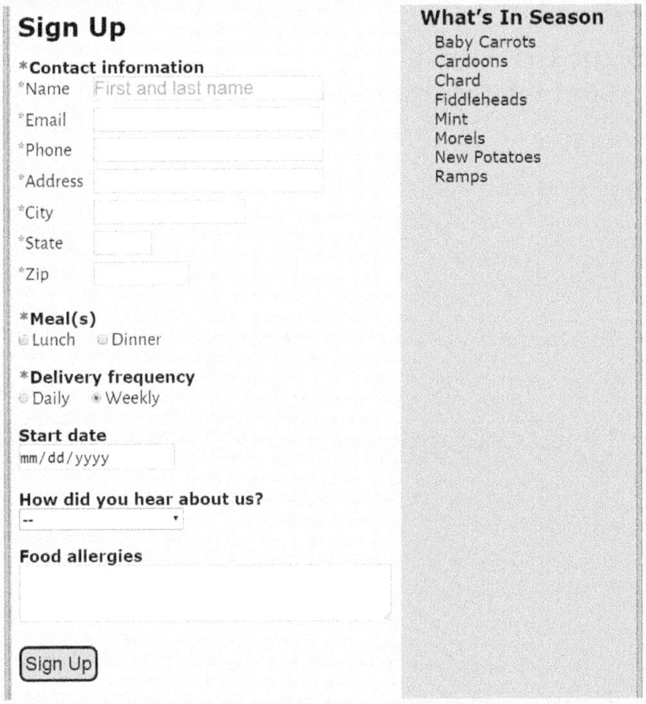

Visual Workshop

In your editor, open the file HTM_J-13.html from the VW folder where you store your Data Files for this unit and save it as **signup.html**. Repeat to save HTM_J-14.css as **styles.css**. Add your first and last names and today's date to the comment section at the top of each file, then save your changes. Add and style a form to match the page shown in FIGURE J-29. Configure your form to submit data to the file results.html. Test your form, then validate your HTML and CSS code.

FIGURE J-29

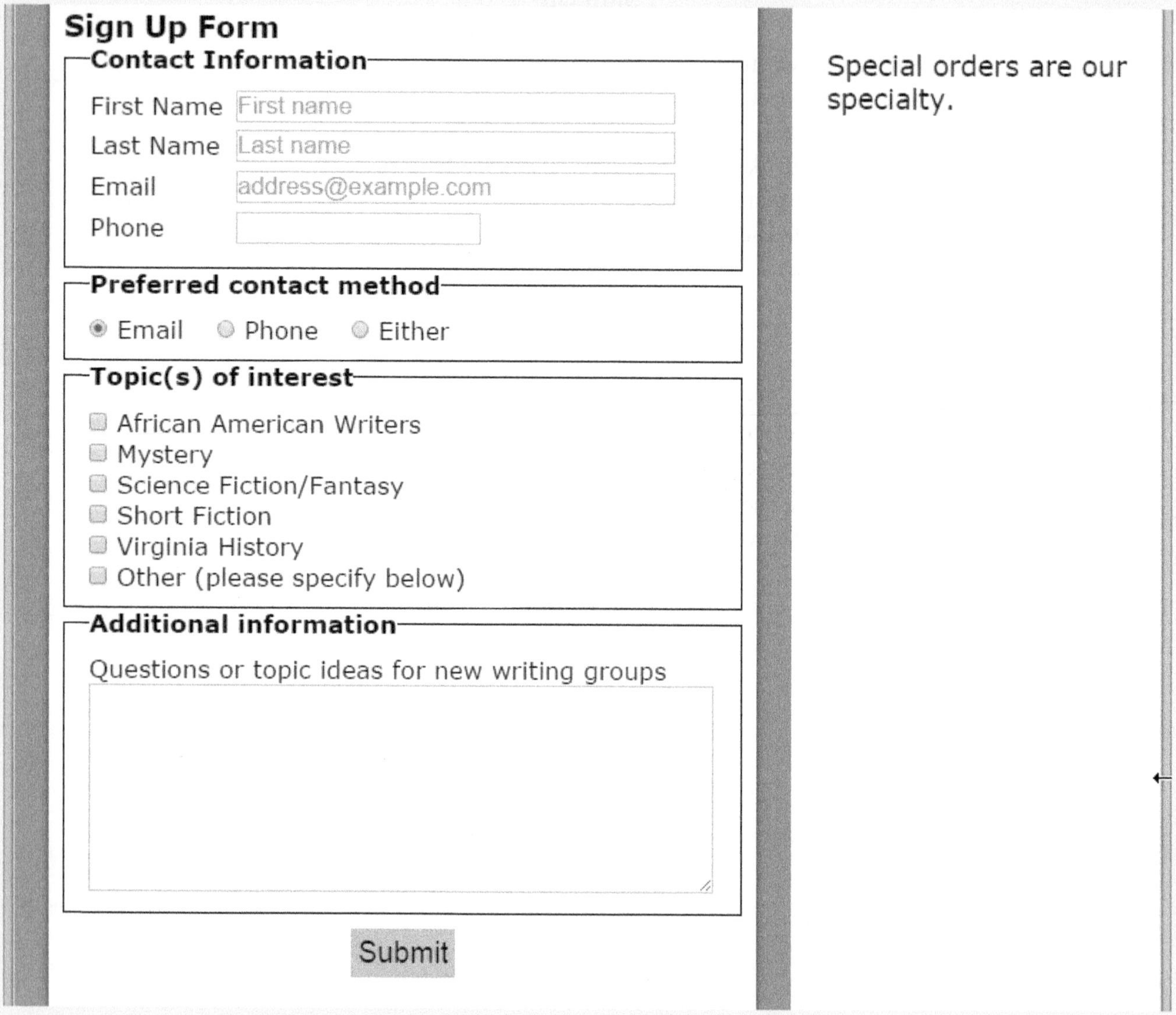

Creating Visual Effects and Animation

> **CASE** ▶ In this unit, you'll add visual effects and animation to enhance the appearance of the Lakeland Reeds Bed & Breakfast website.

Unit Objectives

After completing this unit, you will be able to:

- Add generated content
- Add visual form feedback
- Create a gradient
- Create a CSS shape

- Apply styles based on feature detection
- Apply a transform
- Create a transition
- Animate content

Files You Will Need

L	10 files	IC3	12 files
SR	10 files	IC4	8 files
IC1	8 files	VW	8 files
IC2	9 files		

For specific filenames, see Filenames_K.pdf in the Unit K Data Files folder.

Add Generated Content

Learning
Outcomes
• Add generated
  content to a web
  page

Unlike the other pseudo-elements, which simply select parts of existing web page elements, the :before and :after pseudo-elements enable you to insert content into web pages using style rules. The content added using these pseudo-elements is known as **generated content**. You can use these selectors to add text, images, or other content before or after the content specified for an element in its HTML code. For instance, you might use the :after pseudo-element to insert an icon after the text of headings. Style rules based on either of these pseudo-elements generally use the content property to specify either text or the path and name for an image file to be displayed. TABLE K-1 shows the syntax for the most common values of the content property. **CASE** *You have built a new form for the Lakeland Reeds website that contains several required fields. You use the :before pseudo-element to add a red asterisk before the label for each required field as a visual indication that the field is required.*

STEPS

1. **In your editor, open HTM_K-1.html from the Lessons folder where you store your Data Files for this unit, save it as quote.html, then repeat to save HTM_K-2.css as styles.css**

2. **In the comment at the top of each file, enter your name and today's date where indicated, then save the files**

3. **Open quote.html in your browser, then examine the form**
   Below the form heading is a note explaining the meaning of the asterisks. Currently, the asterisks are not displayed next to the form labels.

4. **Return to styles.css in your editor, scroll down to the label styles section, then below the label, .reserveinfo p style rule, add a new style rule with the selector**
   label:before, .reserveinfo p:before
   This selector selects the pseudo-element before each label element as well as before the p element within the fieldset with the class value reserveinfo.

QUICK TIP
Be sure to type a space after the * and before the closing ".

5. **Within the new style rule, add the declarations** content: "* "; **and** color: red;
   The content property specifies what content should be displayed before each selected element.

6. **Below the new style rule, create another style rule with the selector**
   .additionalinfo label:before **and the declaration** content: "";
   Because the textarea element in the fieldset with the class value additionalinfo is not required, you set the content shown before its label to an empty string ("") so no asterisk is displayed. FIGURE K-1 shows the completed code.

QUICK TIP
In the box model, generated content is considered part of an element's content.

7. **Save your changes, then refresh or reload quote.html in your browser**
   A red asterisk is displayed to the left of each label element except the last one, as well as before the p element containing the text Start date, as shown in FIGURE K-2.

FIGURE K-1: Style rules using the `:before` pseudo-element

```
195    /* label styles */
196    label, .reserveinfo p {
197        font-size: 1em;
198        line-height: 1.6em;
199        font-weight: bold;
200    }
201    label:before, .reserveinfo p:before {
202        content: "* ";
203        color: red;
204    }
205    .additionalinfo label:before {
206        content: "";
207    }
```

The `:before` pseudo-element specifies content displayed before the content specified for an element in its HTML code

Include a space after the asterisk to create white space between the asterisk and the element content

A pair of quotes with no content creates an empty string, which you use to remove any content created in other style rules

FIGURE K-2: * character and space added before labels and p element

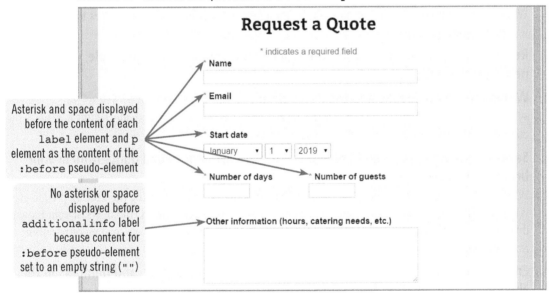

Asterisk and space displayed before the content of each `label` element and `p` element as the content of the `:before` pseudo-element

No asterisk or space displayed before `additionalinfo` label because content for `:before` pseudo-element set to an empty string (`""`)

TABLE K-1: Common values for the `content` property

content type	syntax	example
text	`"text"`	`content: "Chapter: ";`
image	`url("path/image")`	`content: url("images/bed.png");`

Add Visual Form Feedback

Learning Outcomes
• Change form properties in response to user actions and input

While you can use generated content to enhance many types of elements, including those in forms, CSS supports several pseudo-classes specifically for use with forms. You can use the pseudo-classes detailed in **TABLE K-2** to change the properties of `input` elements and other elements in forms in response to user actions. **CASE** ▶ *You use the :valid pseudo-class to set a green background color on text boxes in which the user input conforms to the data type. In addition, you use the :focus pseudo-class to set a blue background color on the selected text box to help draw a user's eye to the current location in the browser window.*

STEPS

QUICK TIP
The :valid and :invalid pseudo-classes are supported by all modern browsers but are not part of the official CSS specification, so they generate errors when validating CSS code. You can safely ignore these errors.

1. **Return to** styles.css **in your editor, scroll up to the field styles section, then, below the** `input, textarea` **style rule, create a style rule with the selector** `input:valid` **and the declaration** `background-color: #d1f4bd;`

   This style rule changes the background color to light green in fields where the user entry meets all the rules. In the Request a Quote form, a text box with the `required` attribute would have to contain a user entry to be valid. In addition, text boxes with the `email` or `number` type values would have to contain data that fits these data types.

2. **Save your changes, refresh or reload** quote.html **in your browser, enter** Faduma Egal **in the Name box,** fegal@example.com **in the Email box,** 5 **in the Number of days box, and** 15 **in the Number of guests box, then click the** Other information box

   When the content you enter meets all the rules for a field, its background color changes to light green as shown in **FIGURE K-3**.

3. **Return to** styles.css **in your editor, then, below the** `input:valid` **style rule, create a new style rule with the selectors** `input:focus` **and** `textarea:focus`

4. **Within the new style rule, add the declaration** `background-color: #cce5ef;`

   When a field is selected, this style rule sets the background color to a light blue shade. **FIGURE K-4** shows the completed style rules for the :valid and :focus pseudo-classes.

QUICK TIP
Some browsers treat form fields as valid before users enter data in them, so form fields may have green backgrounds while the form is still empty.

5. **Save your changes, press and hold** [Shift] **as you refresh or reload** quote.html **in your browser, then click the** Name box

   When you click a field, it has the focus and the declaration in the style rule using the :focus pseudo-class is applied. The background of the Name field changes to light blue as shown in **FIGURE K-5**. If your browser does not clear form data when you refresh or reload the page, hold [Shift] while reloading or refreshing to reset the form.

6. **Enter a name in the Name box, an email address in the Email box, and numbers in the Number of days and Number of guests boxes, then click the** Other information box

   Each time you click or tab to a box, it receives the focus and the blue background color is applied. When you switch to a different field, the background of a completed field with valid input changes to the green color you specified in Step 1.

FIGURE K-3: Fields with acceptable input formatted with :valid pseudo-class

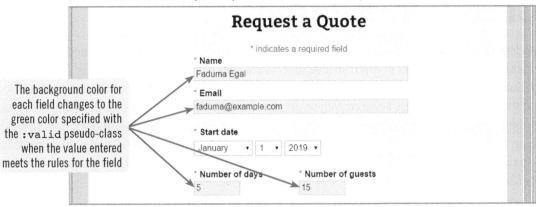

The background color for each field changes to the green color specified with the :valid pseudo-class when the value entered meets the rules for the field

FIGURE K-4: Completed CSS for visual form feedback

```
158    /* field styles */
159    input, textarea {
160        border: 1px solid #ccc;
161        padding: 0.2em;
162        font-size: 1em;
163        display: block;
164    }
165    input:valid {
166        background-color: #d1f4bd;
167    }
168    input:focus, textarea:focus {
169        background-color: #cce5ef;
170    }
```

The :valid pseudo-class applies to form elements with user input that meets the rules for the field

The :focus pseudo-class applies to the element that currently has the focus

FIGURE K-5: Field that has the focus formatted with :focus pseudo-class

The background color for a text box or text area changes to the blue color specified with the :focus pseudo-class when the field has the focus

TABLE K-2: Commonly used pseudo-classes for forms

pseudo-class	applies to	description
:active	buttons (button elements or input elements with type value of button, reset, or submit)	the element is in the process of being clicked or otherwise activated
:checked	check boxes, option buttons, or options in a drop-down list	the element is checked or otherwise selected
:focus	input, select, and textarea elements	the element has the focus
:invalid	input or textarea elements with type or other attributes that limit valid values	the content entered by a user does not meet the rules for the field
:optional	input, select, and textarea elements	the element does not have the required attribute, meaning that user entry in the field is optional
:required	input, select, and textarea elements	the element has the required attribute, meaning that user entry in the field is required
:valid	input or textarea elements with type or other attributes that limit valid values	the content entered by a user meets the rules for the field

Create a Gradient

Learning Outcomes
• Add a background gradient to an element

Modern browsers support images and solid colors as backgrounds. In addition, they support gradients. A **gradient** is a visual effect in which an area starts as a single color on one edge or corner and transitions gradually to one or more other colors, as shown in FIGURE K-6. To create a basic background gradient, you use the `linear-gradient` keyword with values describing the gradient. TABLE K-3 describes the syntax of the `linear-gradient` keyword. A gradient is considered a generated image, and you specify it as a value of the `background-image` property. You can also specify a gradient using the shorthand `background` property. **CASE** *You change the page background to a gradient that gradually shifts from sky blue to white and back to sky blue.*

STEPS

QUICK TIP
You can use the `radial-gradient` keyword to create gradients that start at a single point and transition outward in a circle. You can read more at developer.mozilla.org/en-US/docs/Web/CSS/radial-gradient.

1. **Return to** styles.css **in your editor, then scroll up as necessary to the document-wide styles section**

2. **Within the** body **style rule and below the existing** background **declaration, add the declaration** `background: linear-gradient(#7eccec, white);`
   This declaration creates a linear gradient that starts as sky blue and gradually transitions to white. Using the `background` property allows older browsers that don't support gradients to fall back to the background color specified in the previous declaration. Unless you specify otherwise, a linear gradient starts at the top of an element and transitions down in a vertical line.

3. **Save your changes, then refresh or reload quote.html in your browser**
   The page background is now a gradient that starts at the top as sky blue and transitions to white at the bottom of the body element. In a browser window that's longer than the page content, the gradient starts again below the page content as shown in FIGURE K-7.

4. **Return to** styles.css **in your editor, then, within the declaration you created in Step 2, click between the closing**) **and the** ;, **insert a** space, **then type** no-repeat
   The `no-repeat` keyword prevents the gradient from repeating. FIGURE K-8 shows the completed code for your gradient.

5. **Save your changes, refresh or reload quote.html in your browser, then if possible resize the browser window so it's longer than the page content**
   The gradient no longer repeats, and the area below the page content remains white.

TABLE K-3: Syntax for the `linear-gradient` keyword

component	description	example
starting point/direction	An angle in degrees from 0 to 360 followed by the text `deg` that indicates the direction of the gradient and determines the starting point; or the keyword `to` followed by the keyword `top` or `bottom` and/or the keyword `left` or `right`. The default angle, `0deg`, is from top to bottom; `90deg` is from left to right, `180deg` is from bottom to top, and `270deg` is from right to left.	`90deg` orients the gradient from left to right
color stops	A color name or value followed by a measurement (usually in percent) indicating where the color is fully displayed (and the previous color is no longer displayed); color stops are separated by commas (a gradient requires at least 2 color stops); if no value is stated, 0% is assumed as a default for the first color stop and 100% for the last one; as the gradient moves from the current color to the color stop for the next color, the two colors blend creating the gradient effect	`#7eccec, white 50%, #aabd7e` creates a gradient that starts with the color `#7eccec`, changes to `white` when the gradient is 50% across the element, then changes to `#aabd7e` at the end of the element; the colors blend as the gradient moves from one color to another color

FIGURE K-6: Examples of linear gradients

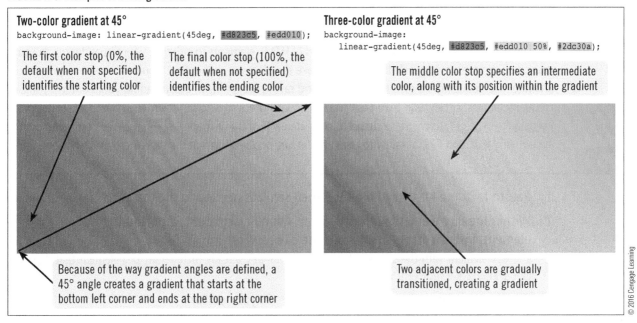

Two-color gradient at 45°

`background-image: linear-gradient(45deg, #d823c5, #edd010);`

The first color stop (0%, the default when not specified) identifies the starting color

The final color stop (100%, the default when not specified) identifies the ending color

Because of the way gradient angles are defined, a 45° angle creates a gradient that starts at the bottom left corner and ends at the top right corner

Three-color gradient at 45°

`background-image:`
`    linear-gradient(45deg, #d823c5, #edd010 50%, #2dc30a);`

The middle color stop specifies an intermediate color, along with its position within the gradient

Two adjacent colors are gradually transitioned, creating a gradient

FIGURE K-7: Linear gradient applied to page background

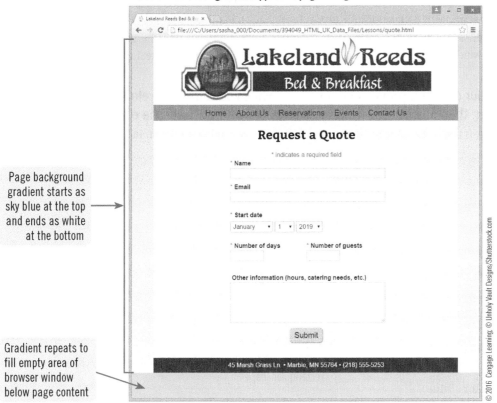

Page background gradient starts as sky blue at the top and ends as white at the bottom

Gradient repeats to fill empty area of browser window below page content

FIGURE K-8: CSS code for gradient

```
29    /* document-wide styles */
30    body {
31       margin: 0 auto;
32       font-family: Arial, Helvetica, sans-serif;
33       background: #7eccec;
34       background: linear-gradient(#7eccec, white) no-repeat;
35    }
```

Create a CSS Shape

You can use CSS properties to change the shapes of HTML elements to enhance your visual design. In some cases, you can even modify HTML elements to take the places of shapes that would otherwise require use of an image file, reducing the sizes of your pages and saving users time in downloading your content. You can create rectangles, circles, and triangles by applying CSS properties to `div` elements, which are rectangular by default. **TABLE K-4** shows the code used to create each of these shapes. **CASE** *You create an orange circle using HTML and CSS, format it to resemble the sun, and position it in the top left corner of your page.*

STEPS

1. **Return to** quote.html **in your editor, then scroll as needed to the top of the** body **element**

2. **Within the** `div` **element with the** `class` **value** `background-art` **and before the** `img` **element, insert a** `div` **element with the** `class` **value** `sun-shape`

   The `div` element with the `class` value `background-art` already includes an `img` element that depicts a cloud. **FIGURE K-9** shows the inserted `div` element.

3. **Save your changes, then return to** styles.css **in your editor**

4. **In the document-wide styles section and below the** `.background-art` **style rule, add a rule with the selector** `.sun-shape`, **then add the declarations shown in FIGURE K-10**

   The rule starts with declarations for width, height, background color, and border radius, which create a circle with a yellow-orange color. The remaining declarations position the circle partly outside of the browser window in the top left corner, place it behind other elements, and create both outside and inset box shadows.

5. **Save your changes, press and hold [Shift] while you refresh or reload quote.html in your browser, then if necessary widen your browser window until the circle is visible**

   The circle is displayed at the top left corner of the browser window, as shown in **FIGURE K-11**.

TABLE K-4: Syntax for creating common CSS shapes

shape	code	explanation

rectangle	`width: 100px;`
	`height: 100px;`
	`background-color: blue;`
		define dimensions and add a background color to create a rectangular shape

circle	`width: 100px;`
	`height: 100px;`
	`background-color: red;`
	`border-radius: 50%;`
		specify a border radius of 50% for a square to create a perfect circle

triangle	`width: 0;`
	`height: 0;`
	`border-left: 50px solid transparent;`
	`border-right: 50px solid transparent;`
	`border-bottom: 87px solid green;`
		add a large bottom border using the desired color and add transparent borders on the left and right sides to reduce the amount of the bottom border that is visible to create a triangle; for an equilateral triangle (in which all 3 sides are the same length), the width of the left border plus the width of the right border × 0.87 = the width of the bottom border

FIGURE K-9: `div` element inserted

```
25          <div class="background-art">
26              <div class="sun-shape"></div>
27              <img src="images/cloud.png" class="cloud-image" width="234" height="150" alt="">
28          </div>
```

FIGURE K-10: CSS code for circle shape

```
42      .background-art {
43          position: absolute;
44      }
45      .sun-shape {
46          width: 200px;
47          height: 200px;
48          background-color: rgb(253,148,42);
49          border-radius: 50%;
50          position: absolute;
51          left: -80px;
52          top: -80px;
53          z-index: -2;
54          box-shadow: 0 0 25px rgb(254,230,55),
55                      0 0 50px rgb(254,230,55) inset;
56      }
```

Minimal properties needed to create a circle using CSS

Additional declarations to change the appearance of the circle

FIGURE K-11: CSS circle displayed in browser

Cloud image inserted using an img element

Circle created using a div element and the border-radius property, and positioned partly off of the web page

Creating Visual Effects and Animation

Learning
Outcomes
• Specify an
alternate style rule
for browsers that
do not support a
CSS property

Apply Styles Based on Feature Detection

Recall that some newer styles, such as the `border-radius` property, are not recognized by older browsers, such as IE8. When using newer styles, it's important to ensure that your design still works in older browsers. A design exhibits **graceful degradation** when it uses newer styles in modern browsers while displaying a usable layout and all page content in older browsers. One popular tool for implementing graceful degradation is Modernizr, a free script library. When a browser opens and loads a web page that incorporates Modernizr, Modernizr tests the browser to detect which properties are supported, a process known as **feature detection**. Based on the results, Modernizr applies a set of CSS classes to the `html` element. **CASE** ▸ *You use a Modernizr class to specify a background image of a sun for the `div` element in browsers that don't support the `border-radius` property.*

STEPS

QUICK TIP
The class values that Modernizr adds are only available when the page is open and do not become part of the HTML code for your web page. The Modernizr library tests for supported features each time the HTML file is opened.

1. **If you have access to IE8, use it to open quote.html, then if necessary widen the browser window until an orange rectangle is visible in the top left corner**

   Because IE8 does not support the `border-radius` property, the div is displayed as a rectangle as shown in **FIGURE K-12**.

2. **Return to quote.html in your editor, scroll up to the head section, then locate the `script` element that references the file `modernizr.custom.28018.js`**

   When the modernizr.custom.28018.js file is executed, it adds a predetermined class name if the feature is supported, or a different class name if the feature is not supported. To ensure that only the code that can be interpreted by a user's browser is rendered, you can write style rules that apply only to children of elements with specific class values.

QUICK TIP
The `class` values that Modernizr creates for supported features are listed at modernizr.com/docs. For unsupported features, Modernizr adds no- to the start of the supported `class` value.

3. **Return to styles.css in your editor, then in the document-wide styles section and above the `.cloud-image` rule, add a new style rule with the selector**

   `.no-borderradius .sun-shape`

   Recall that for each feature that Modernizr tests, it adds a class value to the `html` element. For the `border-radius` property, Modernizr adds the class value `borderradius` if the property is supported by the browser or the class name `no-borderradius` if the property is not supported by the browser. The selector you created in this step applies to the element with the `class` value `sun-shape` only if it is a descendant of an element with the `class` value `no-borderradius`. If this class value exists, it means that Modernizr has found that the browser does not support the `border-radius` property, and this rule is implemented; if Modernizr has found that the browser supports the `border-radius` property, the `no-borderradius` class value isn't added, and the browser ignores this style rule.

4. **Within the style rule you created in Step 3, add the declaration**

   `background: url("images/sun.png");`

   This declaration uses the `background` property to override the `background-color` declaration applied in the `.sun-shape` style rule. **FIGURE K-13** shows the completed code.

5. **Save your changes, then refresh or reload quote.html in a modern browser**

   Because modern browsers support the `border-radius` property, the CSS circle you created is still displayed, and the rule specifying the sun.png background image is ignored.

6. **If you have access to IE8, refresh quote.html in IE8**

   Because IE8 does not support the `border-radius` property, the sun.png background image is displayed instead of the CSS circle, as shown in **FIGURE K-14**.

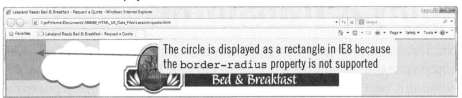

FIGURE K-13: CSS code for Modernizr fallback

```
57    .no-borderradius .sun-shape {
58        background: url("images/sun.png");
59    }
60    .cloud-image {
```

Modernizr adds the no-borderradius class value to the html element in browsers that do not support the border-radius property

FIGURE K-14: Background image displayed in IE8

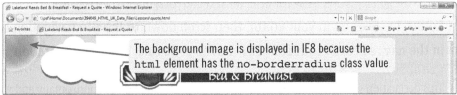

The background image is displayed in IE8 because the html element has the no-borderradius class value

Understanding the difference between browser sniffing and feature detection

Ensuring cross-browser compatibility has been an important task in web development since early in the web's existence. For much of that time, web developers tried to identify the brand and version of each user's browser by using a script to ask the browser to identify itself, a technique known as **browser sniffing**. While you may encounter browser sniffing scripts in your work on existing web sites, the technique has an important drawback—browsers may not always identify themselves accurately. Instead of trying to identify the browser, Modernizr runs a series of tests and uses the results to decide which features a user's browser supports, a process known as feature detection. Feature detection is more reliable than browser sniffing and also provides a more detailed picture of the capabilities of a user's browser.

Customizing and downloading the Modernizr library

The Modernizr library is available for free download from modernizr.com. The site offers two options for downloading the library—development and production. If you choose the Development link, you download the full version of the library containing all default features. This is appropriate for use when you are building and testing a website. However, when you are ready to make your website available to users, the full Modernizr library may contain many features that you aren't using, meaning that each user is required to download a much larger file than necessary. At this point, you can return to modernizr.com and choose the Production link, which presents a list of all supported features and allows you to choose only those features that your site relies on. Based on your choices, the site then generates an optimized version of Modernizr for your needs. This results in a smaller file than the full library and helps make your site more responsive for users.

Apply a Transform

Modern browsers support using the CSS `transform` property to apply a **transform**, which is a change in the appearance of an element in one or more specific ways, including rotating, scaling, skewing, or moving (translating) it. **TABLE K-5** details some of the keywords used with the `transform` property and the syntax for each. **FIGURE K-15** shows an example of the effect of each of those keywords. Because the `transform` property is a relatively new CSS feature, it was implemented in some browsers with **browser prefixes**, which are words or abbreviations that are added to the start of a property name and that are specific to one or more browsers or rendering engines. When some browser makers implement a property with a browser prefix, you can provide support for that property in as many browsers as possible by creating a declaration using the property's unprefixed form, and preceding that declaration with a duplicate declaration for each browser prefix. This ensures that all browsers that support the property, whether using prefixes or not, can process your code. **CASE** *When a user moves the mouse pointer over a list item in the nav bar, you want to increase the size of the item to draw the user's eye to it. You use the* `transform` *property and the* `scale` *keyword to add this style to the page, and you add browser-prefixed versions of the property for wide browser support.*

STEPS

QUICK TIP
You can apply
multiple transforms
using a single
property by including
a space between
the transform
descriptions; for
instance,
`transform:`
`scale(1.2)`
`rotate(30deg);`.

1. **Return to quote.html in a modern browser, then move the mouse pointer over a nav bar link**
   When the pointer is over a nav bar item, the text and background colors change.

2. **Return to styles.css in your editor, then scroll down to the site navigation bar section**

3. **In the `nav.sitenavigation li: hover` style rule, add the declaration**
   `transform: scale(1.2);`
   This declaration scales the `li` element to 1.2 times its default size both horizontally and vertically.

4. **Above the declaration you added in Step 3, add the declarations**
   `-ms-transform: scale(1.2);` **and** `-webkit-transform: scale(1.2);`
   At the time this book was written, some older Microsoft browsers (using the `-ms-` prefix) and browsers using the WebKit rendering engine (`-webkit-` prefix) required prefixed versions of the `transform` property. So, in this example, the first declaration specifies the `transform` value with the `-ms-` prefix for older Microsoft browsers, and the second does the same with the `-webkit-` prefix for some browsers that use the WebKit rendering engine. **FIGURE K-16** shows the completed style rules.

5. **Save your changes, then refresh or reload quote.html in your browser**

QUICK TIP
When you apply a
transform to an
element, the
element continues to
occupy the same
amount of space in
the normal flow, so
scaling an element
up does not affect
the size of its parent
element.

6. **Move the mouse pointer over the links in the nav bar**
   When the mouse pointer is over a link, the corresponding `li` element is scaled up in size, as shown in **FIGURE K-17**.

7. **If you have access to IE9, Safari on a Mac, Safari on iOS, or UC browser for Android, repeat Steps 5 and 6 with each of those browsers to verify that the vendor-prefixed declarations work correctly**

Working with browser-prefixed properties

Browser-prefixed properties are sometimes used by browser makers for CSS properties whose functions and syntax haven't yet reached consensus in the W3C development process. Commonly used prefixes include `-webkit-` (Chrome, Safari, Android browser, Opera), `-moz-` (Firefox), and `-ms-` (IE, Edge).

The support tables for CSS properties on caniuse.com indicate which versions of different browsers require prefixes for specific properties.

FIGURE K-15: Examples of 4 types of transforms

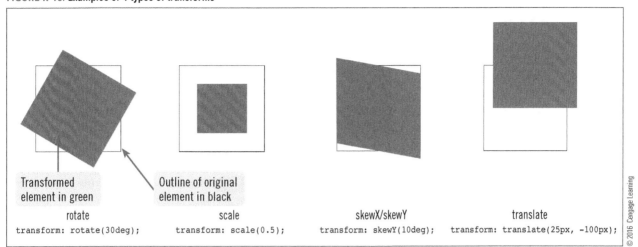

Transformed element in green

Outline of original element in black

rotate	scale	skewX/skewY	translate
transform: rotate(30deg);	transform: scale(0.5);	transform: skewY(10deg);	transform: translate(25px, -100px);

FIGURE K-16: `transform` declarations added to style rule

```
112    nav.sitenavigation li:hover {
113        background-color: #34180f;
114        -ms-transform: scale(1.2);
115        -webkit-transform: scale(1.2);
116        transform: scale(1.2);
117    }
```

Prefixed properties included before declaration using unprefixed property name

FIGURE K-17: Result of `transform` property in browser

`li` element scales up to 1.2 times its original size when it has the focus as a result of the `transform: scale(1.2);` declaration

TABLE K-5: `transform` property keywords and syntax

keyword	effect	syntax
rotate	rotates the element the specified number of degrees clockwise for positive values or counter-clockwise for negative values	/* rotate 30 degrees clockwise */ transform: rotate(30deg);
scale scaleX scaleY	resizes the element, with values less than 1 reducing the size and with values greater than 1 increasing the size	/* scale down to 50% of default horizontal and vertical size */ transform: scale(0.5);
skewX skewY	moves the top and bottom sides (skewX) or the left and right sides (skewY) in opposite directions (but remaining parallel) until the remaining 2 sides are angled the specified number of degrees	/* angle the top and bottom sides 10 degrees */ transform: skewY(10deg);
translate translateX translateY	repositions the element the specified amount from its default position horizontally and/or vertically, with positive values moving down or to the right, and negative values moving up or to the left	/* move 25px to the right and 100px up */ transform: translate(25px, -100px);

Create a Transition

Modern browsers support **transitions**, which are CSS features that gradually apply changes to properties in response to user actions over a number of seconds. In essence, transitions can be used to add simple animations to web pages. For instance, when you apply rotation to an element using the `transform` property with the `rotate` keyword, you can add a transition to configure the element to spin into its final position over several seconds rather than simply appearing in the transformed position. To create a transition the shorthand `transition` property or one or more of the specific properties for transitions is added to the style rule for the default state of the affected element. In addition to the length of time a transition takes, additional effects can be implemented using the properties detailed in TABLE K-6. **CASE** ➤ *You add a transition to the* `li` *elements in the nav bar so the change in size and background color on hover is animated over 2 seconds.*

STEPS

1. **Return to** styles.css **in your editor, then scroll as needed to the site navigation bar section**

2. **Within the** `nav.sitenavigation li` **style rule and before the final }, insert the declarations**
   `-webkit-transition-duration: 2s;` **and** `transition-duration: 2s;`
   These declarations specify that any property changes applied to these elements take 2 seconds from start to finish. You added the declaration with the `-webkit-` prefix because, at the time this book was written, some browsers using the WebKit rendering engine required prefixed versions of the transition properties.

3. **Below the declarations you created in Step 2, insert the declarations**
   `-webkit-transition-timing-function: ease-in;` **and**
   `transition-timing-function: ease-in;`
   The `ease-in` keyword creates a transition that starts slowly and picks up speed.

4. **Save your changes, refresh or reload quote.html in your browser, then move the mouse pointer over a nav bar item**
   The scaling up created by the transform property and the change in background color take place slowly over 2 seconds. FIGURE K-18 shows a nav bar item in the midst of the transition.

5. **Return to** styles.css **in your editor, then in the** `-webkit-transition-duration` **and** `transition-duration` **declarations, change the value to** `0.2s`
   This change makes the transition happen more quickly, to avoid making interactions with the page feel slow. FIGURE K-19 shows the revised code.

6. **Save your changes, refresh or reload quote.html in your browser, then move the mouse pointer over a nav bar item**
   The transition now happens much more quickly.

7. **If you have access to UC browser for Android, repeat Step 6 with that browser to verify that the vendor-prefixed declarations work correctly**

Using Transitions and Animations Effectively

Transitions and animations can be useful in drawing your users' attention to different parts of your web pages. However, if you use transitions and animations too much, your pages can seem cluttered, busy, or overwhelming to some users, so it's important not to overuse these features. In general, you should not include a transition on a web page that takes more than a few seconds. Some of the most effective uses of transitions are quite subtle, such as transitioning the :focus pseudo-class on a form field over a fraction of a second. Transitions used in this way can give users the impression that your site is polished and high-quality—sometimes without the users even being able to explain why. It can be useful to examine a number of high traffic websites and identify where they use transitions and animation and what the purpose of each is. You may then want to try to replicate some of these features on your own site and see how these features change the overall feel of your site.

FIGURE K-19: CSS code for transition

```
104   nav.sitenavigation li {
105       margin: 0.3em 0.5em;
106       padding: 0.2em 0.4em;
107       display: inline-block;
108       font-size: 1.3em;
109       line-height: 1.4em;
110       border-radius: 10px;
111       -webkit-transition-duration: 0.2s;
112       transition-duration: 0.2s;
113       -webkit-transition-timing-function: ease-in;
114       transition-timing-function: ease-in;
115   }
116   nav.sitenavigation li:hover {
117       background-color: #34180f;
118       -ms-transform: scale(1.2);
119       -webkit-transform: scale(1.2);
120       transform: scale(1.2);
121   }
```

The -webkit-transition-duration and transition-duration properties set how long the transition takes

The -webkit-transition-timing-function and transition-timing-function properties determine how the transition is applied

The transition applies to all properties with values that change in response to user interaction

TABLE K-6: Transition-related CSS properties

property	description	example
transition-delay	time in seconds after a transition is triggered and before the transition begins	transition-delay: 5s;
transition-duration	time in seconds from the start of transition to the end of transition	transition-duration: 3s;
transition-property	the name(s) of one or more properties to be transitioned	transition-property: transform;
transition-timing-function	a function expression or keyword that determines the rhythm of the animation; commonly used keywords include ease, ease-in, ease-in-out, ease-out, linear, step-end, and step-start	transition-timing-function: ease-in;
transition	shorthand property that takes space-separated values in the order *property duration timing-function delay*; values for multiple properties can be specified, separated by spaces	transition: transform 3s ease-in 5s;

© 2016 Cengage Learning

HTML5 & CSS3

Animate Content

In addition to transitions, modern browsers support another approach to animating elements using animation properties and the `@keyframes` rule. An animation created this way is referred to as a **keyframe animation**. Keyframe animations enable you to control more aspects of an animation, including what the animation looks like at various points between the start and end of the animation, as well as the number of times the animation plays. TABLE K-7 describes some commonly used animation properties. To create an `@keyframes` rule, you specify a name for the rule after the keyword `@keyframes`. Within the braces for the rule, you specify nested rules using percentages as selectors. For instance, a selector of 0% contains declarations for the state of the animation at the start (0% of the way through the animation), and a selector of 75% indicates what the property values should be when the animation is 75% or three-quarters of the way finished. **CASE** ▸ *You animate the cloud image in the top left corner of your web page so it covers the sun when the page loads, then moves right to reveal the sun.*

STEPS

1. **If necessary, widen your browser window so that the cloud image is visible to the right of the sun**

2. **Return to** styles.css **in your editor, then scroll up to the document-wide styles section**

3. **Below the** `.cloud-image` **style rule, add the** `@-webkit-keyframes` **and** `@keyframes` **rules shown in** FIGURE K-20

   At the time this book was written, the `@-webkit-keyframes` syntax was used only in some versions of Chrome, Opera, and Safari. Other browsers that don't recognize this syntax ignore it and implement the `@keyframes` rule instead.

4. **Within the** `.cloud-image` **style rule and before the closing** `}`, **add the six animation properties shown in** FIGURE K-21

   The `animation-duration` property and its `-webkit-` variant specify that the animation will take 3 seconds. The `animation-timing-function` property and its variant use the keyword `linear`, meaning that the speed of the animation is constant from start to finish. The `animation-name` property and its variant specify the name assigned to the animation in the `@-webkit-keyframes` and `@keyframes` rules.

5. **Save your changes, then refresh or reload quote.html in your browser**

   When the page reloads, the cloud is positioned partly off-screen, and mostly obscures the sun. The cloud moves right 100px in 1.5 seconds, which is 50% of the length of the animation, then moves the remaining 150px in the last 1.5 seconds. FIGURE K-22 shows the page halfway through the animation.

6. **If you have access to Safari for OS X or for iOS, Chrome for desktop or for Android, or Android browser, repeat Step 5 with each of those browsers to verify that the vendor-prefixed declarations work correctly**

7. **Validate your HTML and CSS documents**

   Because the `@-webkit-keyframes` rule and the `:valid` pseudo-class are not part of the CSS specification, they cause validation errors. As long as your CSS code generates no additional errors, you can treat your code as valid.

FIGURE K-20: `@-webkit-keyframes` and `@keyframes` rules added

```
67    @-webkit-keyframes reveal-sun {
68       0% {
69          left: -150px;
70       }
71       50% {
72          left: -50px;
73       }
74       100% {
75          left: 100px;
76       }
77    }
```

The `@-webkit-keyframes` rule is required by Chrome, Safari, Opera, and Android Browser

The content of the `@-webkit-keyframes` rule is identical to that of the `@keyframes` rule

@-webkit-keyframes rule

```
78    @keyframes reveal-sun {
79       0% {
80          left: -150px;
81       }
82       50% {
83          left: -50px;
84       }
85       100% {
86          left: 100px;
87       }
88    }
```

The name is any string you choose to identify the animation

The declarations in each percentage rule specify the state of the element at that point in the animation

@keyframes rule

FIGURE K-21: Animation rules added to `.cloud-image` style rule

```
60    .cloud-image {
61       max-width:
62       display: bl
63       position: a
64       left: 100px;
65       z-index: -1;
66       -webkit-animation-duration: 3s;
67       animation-duration: 3s;
68       -webkit-animation-timing-function: linear;
69       animation-timing-function: linear;
70       -webkit-animation-name: reveal-sun;
71       animation-name: reveal-sun;
72    }
```

The content of each `-webkit-`prefixed declaration is the same as its corresponding unprefixed property

The `animation-duration` property specifies the time the animation takes from start to finish

The `animation-timing-function` value is a keyword for the rhythm of the animation

The `animation-name` declaration references the name specified in the corresponding `@keyframes` rule

FIGURE K-22: Animation of cloud image in progress

Cloud image moving to the right based on animation properties and `@keyframes` rules

© 2016 Cengage Learning; © Unholy Vault Designs/Shutterstock.com; © Pixel Embargo/Shutterstock.com; © Epsicons/Shutterstock.com

TABLE K-7: Animation-related CSS properties

property	description
animation-delay	time in seconds after an animation is triggered and before the animation begins
animation-direction	whether the animation should play forward (normal) or in reverse (reverse)
animation-duration	time in seconds from the start of animation to the end of animation
animation-iteration-count	number of times the animation is played
animation-name	the name of the @keyframe rule to use
animation-timing-function	a function expression or keyword that determines the rhythm of the animation; commonly used keywords include ease, ease-in, ease-in-out, ease-out, linear, step-end, and step-start
animation	shorthand property that takes space-separated values in the order *name duration timing-function delay iteration-count direction*

© 2016 Cengage Learning

Practice

Concepts Review

Refer to FIGURE K-23 **to answer the following questions.**

FIGURE K-23

```
1   body {
2       margin: 0 auto;
3       font-family: Arial, Helvetica, sans-serif;
4       background: #7eccec;
5       background: linear-gradient(#7eccec, white) no-repeat;
6   }
7   .sun-shape {
8       width: 200px;
9       height: 200px;
10      background-color: rgb(253,148,42);
11      border-radius: 50%;
12  }
13  .no-borderradius .sun-shape {
14      background: url("images/sun.png");
15  }
16  nav.sitenavigation li {
17      transition-duration: 0.2s;
18      transition-timing-function: ease-in;
19  }
20  nav.sitenavigation li:hover {
21      background-color: #34180f;
22      transform: scale(1.2);
23  }
24  label:before, .reserveinfo p:before {
25      content: "* ";
26      color: red;
27  }
```

(a → lines 3–5)
(b → lines 9–10)
(c → lines 14–15)
(d → lines 17–18)
(e → lines 21–22)
(f → lines 25–26)

1. Which style rule applies a transform?
2. Which style rule adds generated content?
3. Which style rule applies styles based on feature detection?
4. Which style rule creates a transition?
5. Which style rule creates a gradient?
6. Which style rule creates a CSS shape?

Match each term with the statement that best describes it.

7. gradient
8. feature detection
9. transform
10. transition
11. keyframe animation
12. browser prefix

a. a change in the appearance of an element in one or more specific ways, including moving, scaling, skewing, or rotating it

b. the process of testing a user's browser to detect which CSS properties are supported

c. a word or abbreviation added to the start of a property name that is specific to one or more browsers or rendering engines

d. a visual effect in which an area starts as a single color on one edge or corner and changes to one or more other colors

e. an animation created using animation properties and the @keyframes rule

f. a CSS feature that gradually applies changes to one or more properties in response to user actions over a number of seconds

Select the best answer from the list of choices.

13. You use the `:before` and `:after` pseudo-classes to add _____ to a web page.

   a. a gradient   **c.** a CSS shape

   b. generated content   **d.** a transition

14. Which pseudo-class can you use to provide visual form feedback?

   a. `:valid`   **c.** `:first-of-type`

   b. `:visited`   **d.** `:first-letter`

15. In addition to the `background` shorthand property, which other property can you use to add a gradient to an element?

   a. `color`   **c.** `background-color`

   b. `opacity`   **d.** `background-image`

16. Which geometric shape can you create by specifying a border-radius value of 50% for a block-level element with matching height and width?

   a. circle   **c.** triangle

   b. square   **d.** pentagon

17. Which transform property or properties resize an element?

   a. `rotate`   **c.** `skewX/skewY`

   b. `scale`   **d.** `translate`

Skills Review

1. **Add generated content.**

   a. In your editor, open HTM_K-3.html from the SR folder where you store your Data Files for this unit, save it as **catering.html**, then repeat to save the file HTM_K-4.css as **styles.css**.

   b. Within the comment section at the top of each file, enter your first and last names and today's date, then save your changes.

   c. Return to styles.css in your editor, then in the label styles section and below the `label, .reserveinfo p` style rule, add a new style rule with selectors for the `:before` pseudo-element for the `label` element and the `:before` pseudo-element for p elements within the element with the `class` value `reserveinfo`. Within the style rule, add declarations that specify a color of `red`, and an asterisk (*) followed by a space for the content.

   d. Below the new style rule, create another style rule for the `:before` pseudo-element for `label` elements within the element with the `class` value `additionalinfo`. Within the style rule, add a declaration that specifies an empty string for the content. (*Hint*: Use `""` to specify an empty string.)

   e. Save your changes, then open catering.html in your browser and verify that a red asterisk is displayed to the left of each text label except the label for the text area at the bottom of the form.

2. **Add visual form feedback.**

   a. Return to styles.css in your editor, then in the field styles section below the `input, textarea` style rule, create a style rule that selects the `:valid` pseudo-class for `input` elements and specifies a background color of `#d1f4bd`.

   b. Below the new style rule, create a new style rule that selects the `:focus` pseudo-class for `input` elements and the `:focus` pseudo-class for `textarea` elements and specifies a background color of `#ffcc66`.

   c. Save your changes, refresh or reload catering.html in your browser, click in the Name field, then verify that the background color of the field changes to gold.

   d. Enter valid data in the Name, Email, and Number of guests field and verify that the background of each field changes to green.

3. **Create a gradient.**

   a. Return to styles.css in your editor, then scroll up as needed to the body and container section.

   b. Within the `body` style rule and below the existing `background` declaration, add a declaration using the `background` property that creates a linear gradient starting with the color `rgb(153,102,51)` and ending with the color `orange`.

c. Save your changes, refresh or reload catering.html in your browser, if necessary resize your browser window wider than the content, then verify that a gradient from brown to orange is displayed behind the content.

d. Return to styles.css in your editor, then within the declaration you created in Step b, add a keyword that prevents the gradient from repeating.

e. Save your changes, refresh or reload catering.html in your browser, if possible resize the browser window so it's longer than the page content, then verify that the gradient does not repeat below the end of the content.

4. Create a CSS shape.

a. Return to styles.html in your editor, then scroll down as necessary to the sidebar section.

b. In the .decorative-image style rule, add declarations that create a 3px solid black border, a 50% border radius in all corners, and a background color of white.

c. Save your changes, refresh or reload catering.html in your browser, then verify that the logo image is displayed on a white circular background with a black border.

5. Apply styles based on feature detection.

a. If you have access to IE8, use it to open catering.html, then examine the shape behind the logo image, which should be a square instead of a circle.

b. Return to catering.html in your editor, scroll up to the head section, then locate the script element that references the file modernizr.custom.10704.js.

c. Scroll down as necessary to the aside element, then before the p element, insert a div element with the class value fallback-background. Within the new div element, add an img element that uses the circle.png file within the images folder as its source and set the alt text to an empty string.

d. Save your changes, return to styles.css in your editor, then in the sidebar section and below the aside rule, add a new style rule with the selector .fallback-background that sets the width and height to 100%, absolutely positions the element at the top of the parent element, and turns off display of the element. Below the new rule, add a style rule with the selector .fallback-background img that sets the width and height to 100% and relatively positions the element. Below the .fallback-background rule, add a rule with the selector .no-borderradius .fallback-background that sets display to block. Below the .decorative-image rule, add a new rule with the selector .no-borderradius .decorative-image that removes the element's border and background.

e. Save your changes, refresh or reload catering.html in a modern browser, then if you have access to IE8, refresh catering.html in IE8 and verify that the logo image is displayed in front of an image of a white circle with a black border.

6. Apply a transform.

a. Return to catering.html in a modern browser, then move the mouse pointer over a nav bar link and notice the changes that take place.

b. Return to styles.css in your editor, scroll down to the site navigation section, then below the nav.sitenavigation li style rule, add a style rule with a selector for the :hover pseudo-class of li elements within the nav element with the class value sitenavigation. Add a declaration that creates a transform by scaling the element to 1.2 times its default size. Above this declaration, add browser-specific declarations for Microsoft and Webkit browsers.

Skills Review (continued)

c. Save your changes, refresh or reload quote. html in your browser, move the mouse pointer over the links in the nav bar, then verify that the size of each nav bar item increases when the mouse pointer is over it, as shown in **FIGURE K-24**.

7. Create a transition.

a. Return to styles.css in your editor, then scroll as needed to the site navigation section.

b. Within the `nav.sitenavigation li` style rule and before the final `}`, add declarations that set transition duration to 2 seconds and specify a transition timing function of `ease-in`. Above each declaration, add a browser-specific declaration for Microsoft browsers and another for Webkit browsers.

c. Save your changes, refresh or reload catering.html in your browser, move the mouse pointer over a nav bar item, then notice how long the transition takes.

d. Return to styles.css in your editor, then change the transition duration to 0.2 seconds.

e. Save your changes, refresh or reload catering.html in your browser, move the mouse pointer over a nav bar item, then verify that the transition happens quickly.

8. Animate content.

a. Return to catering.html in your editor, then in the `aside` element and before the closing `</aside>` tag, add a `div` element with the `class` value `cover`.

b. Save your changes, return to styles.css, then above the `/* site navigation */` comment, add a style rule for the element with the `class` value `cover` with declarations that set the width and height to 100%, absolutely position the element at the top of the parent element, set the background color to `#ffcc66`, and set opacity to 0. (*Hint*: Use the declaration `opacity: 0;`.)

c. Save your changes, refresh or reload catering.html in your browser, then verify that the logo image is still visible. (*Note*: You added a div element in front of the image but set the opacity to 0, making the element transparent, so the logo is still visible.)

d. Return to styles.css in your editor, then below the `.cover` style rule, add an `@-webkit-keyframes` rule with the animation name `show-logo`. Within the `@-webkit-keyframes` rule, add a rule with the `0%` selector and the declaration `opacity: 1;`, add another rule with the `75%` selector and the declaration `opacity: 0.8;`, and a third rule with the `100%` selector and the declaration `opacity: 0;`.

e. Below the `@-webkit-keyframes` rule, add a generic `@keyframes` rule with the same name and content.

f. In the `.cover` style rule, add a declaration that sets the length of the animation to 2 seconds, sets the timing function to `ease-in`, and specifies the name of the animation that you set in the first line of the `@keyframes` rule. Before each of the 3 declarations you added, add the `-webkit-` prefixed version using the same value.

g. Save your changes, refresh or reload catering.html in your browser, then verify that the logo image is hidden at first and is slowly revealed.

h. Validate your HTML and CSS documents. Verify that your CSS contains no validation errors apart from the presence of the `@-webkit-keyframes` rule and the `:valid` pseudo-class.

Independent Challenge 1

As you continue your work on the web site of the Spotted Wren Garden Center, you enhance the layout with visual effects and animation.

a. In your editor, open HTM_K-5.html from the IC1 folder where you store your Data Files for this unit, save it as **contact.html**, then repeat to save HTM_K-6.css as **styles.css**. In the comment at the top of each file, enter your name and today's date where indicated, then save the files.

b. In styles.css, in the label styles section, add a style rule for `label` elements within the element with the `class` value `contactinfo` that inserts an asterisk (*) followed by a space before each element and formats the inserted character in green. Save your changes, open contact.html in a browser, then verify that a green asterisk followed by a space is displayed to the left of the labels Name, Email, and Phone.

c. Return to styles.css in your editor, then in the field styles section, add a style rule for valid `input` elements within the element with the `class` value `contact` info that sets the background color to `#d1f4bd`. (*Hint*: Use the `:valid` pseudo-class.) Add another style rule for `input` elements with the focus and `textarea` elements with the focus that sets the background color to `yellow`. Save your changes, then refresh or reload contact.html in your browser. Click the Name field and verify that the background color of the field changes to yellow. Type your name, click the Email field, then verify that the background color of the Name field changes to light green.

d. Return to styles.css in your editor, scroll to the body and page container section, then in the `body` style rule, add a declaration before the final } that specifies a background gradient starting with the color `#eeccdd` and finishing with the color `#6ac238`. Add code to specify that the gradient does not repeat. Save your changes, refresh or reload contact.html in your browser, then verify that the solid background color to the left and right of the main content is a gradient that starts as light purple at the top of the page and changes to green by the bottom. Also verify that the gradient does not extend below the `footer` element.

e. Return to styles.css in your editor, then in the site navigation section and below the `nav.sitenavigation li` style rule, add a new rule for `li` elements that are being hovered over and that are within the `nav` element with the `class` value `sitenavigation`. Within the new style rule, create a transform that makes the element 1.3 times its default size. (*Hint*: Be sure to include browser-specific properties for Microsoft and WebKit browsers, as well as the generic property.) Save your changes, refresh or reload contact.html in your browser, then move the mouse pointer over one of the items in the nav bar. Your page should match the one shown in **FIGURE K-25**.

FIGURE K-25

Independent Challenge 1 (continued)

f. Return to styles.css in your editor, then in the site navigation section, within the `nav.sitenavigation li` style rule, add declarations that create a transition with a duration of 0.1 second using the `ease-out` timing function. (*Hint*: Be sure to include browser-specific properties for WebKit browsers, as well as the generic properties.) Save your changes, refresh or reload contact.html in your browser, move the mouse pointer over one of the items in the nav bar, then verify that the transform takes a short amount of time to happen, rather than happening immediately.

g. Validate your HTML and CSS documents. Verify that your CSS contains no validation errors apart from the presence of the `:valid` pseudo-class.

Independent Challenge 2

As you continue your work on the Murfreesboro Regional Soccer League web site, you enhance the layout with visual effects and animation.

a. In your editor, open HTM_K-7.html from the IC2 folder where you store your Data Files for this unit, save it as **report.html**, then repeat to save HTM_K-8.css as **styles.css**. In the comment at the top of each file, enter your name and today's date where indicated, then save the files.

b. Return to styles.css in your editor, then in the label styles section, add a style rule that adds a red asterisk followed by a space before each `label` element within the element with the `class` value `contactinfo`. Save your changes, then open report.html in a browser and verify that the generated content is displayed.

c. Return to styles.css in your editor, then in the field styles section, create a style rule that sets the background color to `#eee` for `input` elements that have the focus. Create another style rule that sets the background color to `#d1f4bd` for `input` elements that are valid and that are within the element with the `class` value `contactinfo`. Save your changes, refresh or reload report.html in your browser, click the **Home Team box**, type **Red**, click the **Home Score box**, type **5**, click the **Away Team box**, then verify that the background color of the completed fields is light green, and the background color for the selected field is light gray.

d. Return to styles.css in your editor, then in the header section and in the `header` style rule, add a declaration below the existing `background` declaration that specifies a gradient for the background. The gradient should have an angle of 90 degrees, start with the color `rgb(140,198,63)`, and end with the color `white`. (*Hint*: Within the parentheses for your property value, type `90deg` to specify the angle, type a comma, then specify the colors.) Save your changes, refresh or reload report.html in your browser, then verify that the background of the header section is a gradient that changes from light green on the left to white on the right.

e. Return to report.html in your editor, then within the `fieldset` element with the `class` value `contactinfo` and just below the opening `<fieldset>` tag, create a `div` element with the `class` value `circle`. Save your changes, then return to styles.css in your editor. In the fieldset styles section, create a style rule for the `div` element with the `class` value `circle`. Set the width to 16em, the height to 84%, the border to 10px solid white, the border radius to 50%, absolutely position the element –10em from the left, and set the z-index to –1. Save your changes, refresh or reload report.html in your browser, then verify that half of a white circle is visible on the left side of the form behind the labels and `input` elements.

f. If you have access to IE8, use it to open report.html, then verify that a white rectangle is visible on the left side of the form behind the labels and `input` elements. Return to styles.css in your editor, then in the fieldset styles section, add a style rule for the `div` element with the `class` value `circle` when it is nested within an element with the `class` value `no-borderradius`. Add a declaration that turns off the display of the element. Save your changes, refresh report.html in IE8, then verify that the rectangle is no longer displayed behind the form elements. Refresh or reload report.html in a modern browser and verify that the half circle is still displayed behind the form elements.

Independent Challenge 2 (continued)

g. Return to styles.css in your editor, then in the site navigation section, create a style rule for `li` elements that are being hovered over and that are nested with the `nav` element with the `class` value `sitenavigation`. Apply a transform that moves the elements to the left 25px. (*Hint*: Use the `translateX` keyword with a value of `25px`.) Add browser-specific declarations for Microsoft and WebKit browsers. Save your changes., refresh or reload report.html in your browser, move the mouse pointer over a nav bar item, then verify that the item moves slightly to the right, as shown in **FIGURE K-26**.

FIGURE K-26

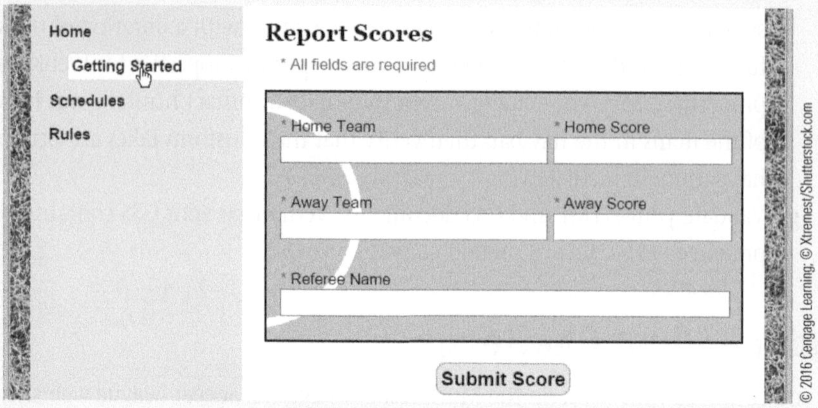

h. Return to styles.css in your editor, then in the site navigation section, add declarations to the `nav.sitenavigation li` style rule that create a transition with a duration of 0.5 seconds that uses the timing function `ease-in-out`. Add browser-specific declarations for WebKit browsers. Save your changes, refresh or reload report.html in your browser, move the mouse pointer over a nav bar item, then verify that the transform is applied gradually over half a second.

i. Return to styles.css in your editor, then in the header section and in the `header div` style rule, add declarations to create a keyframe animation, setting the duration to 2 seconds, the timing function to `ease-out`, and an animation name of `logozoom`. Add browser-specific declarations for WebKit browsers. Below the `header div` style rule, add an `@keyframes` rule that specifies the name `logozoom`, specifies a `left` value of `800px` at 0%, and specifies a `left` value of `0` at 100%. Add a browser-specific version of the `@keyframe` rule for WebKit browsers. Save your changes, refresh or reload report.html in your browser, then verify that the logo is initially not displayed, then moves in from the right side of the page, and after 2 seconds is displayed in its default location.

j. Validate your HTML and CSS documents. Verify that your CSS contains no validation errors apart from the presence of the `@-webkit-keyframes` rule and the `:valid` pseudo-class.

Independent Challenge 3

As you continue to work with Diego Merckx to refine the design of the Hotel Natoma web site, you enhance the layout with visual effects and animation.

a. In your editor, open HTM_K-9.html from the IC3 folder where you store your Data Files for this unit, save it as **museums.html**, then repeat to save HTM_K-10.css as **styles.css**. In the comment at the top of each file, enter your name and today's date where indicated, then save the files.

b. Return to styles.css in your editor, in the main content section and below the `article p` style rule, add a new rule for content before `p` elements within the `article` element. Add declarations to set the width and height to 90px and to create 5px of padding on the right. Below the style rule you just added, add a new rule for content before elements with the `class` value `art`. Add a declaration that specifies the image art.png in the images folder as the content. (*Hint*: Use the property value `url("images/art.png")`.) Repeat to add a rule for content before elements with the `class` value `culture` that specifies the image culture.png in the images folder, and a rule for content before elements with the `class` value `kids` that specifies the image kids.png in the images folder. Save your changes, open museums.html in a browser, then verify that an icon is displayed to the left of the name of each museum, with a different icon for art museums, culture museums, and kids' museums.

Independent Challenge 3 (continued)

c. Return to styles.css in your editor, then in the main content section and within the `article figure` style rule, add a declaration that creates a background gradient at a 45 degree angle that starts with the color `#93AD78` and ends with the color `yellow`. Save your changes, refresh or reload museums.html in your browser, then verify that a gradient is displayed behind the Haight-Ashbury Museum of Psychedelic Art and History caption. The gradient should start in the bottom left corner as light green and become more yellow moving up and toward the right.

d. If you have access to IE8, open museums.html in IE8 and verify that no gradient is displayed behind the Haight-Ashbury Museum of Psychedelic Art and History caption. Return to styles.css in your editor, then in the main content section and below the `article figure` style rule, add a new rule for the `figure` element within the `article` element and descended from an element with the `class` value `.no-cssgradients`. Add a declaration that specifies the file gradient.png within the images folder as the value for the `background` property, then below it, add the declaration `background-size: cover;` to ensure that the background image does not repeat. Save your changes, refresh museums.html in IE8, then verify that the gradient image is displayed behind the Haight-Ashbury Museum of Psychedelic Art and History caption.

e. Return to styles.css in your editor, then in the site navigation section and within the `nav.sitenavigation li:hover` style rule, add a declaration to apply a transform that displays the element at 1.3 times its default size. Add browser-specific declarations for Microsoft and WebKit browsers. Save your changes, refresh or reload museums.html in your browser, move your mouse pointer over one of the items in the nav bar, then verify that the item increases in size as shown in **FIGURE K-27**.

FIGURE K-27

f. Return to styles.css in your editor, then in the site navigation section and within the `nav.sitenavigation li` style rule, add declarations that create a 0.1 second transition that uses the `ease-out` timing function. Include browser-specific properties for WebKit browsers. Save your changes, refresh or reload museums.html in your browser, move your mouse pointer over one of the items in the nav bar, then verify that the item takes a moment to grow to its final size.

g. Return to styles.css in your editor, then in the main content section and above the `article figcaption` style rule, add a style rule for the `img` element within the `figure` element within the `article` element. Add declarations that create a 3 second animation with the name `spin` that uses the `ease-out` timing function. Add declarations using browser-specific properties for WebKit browsers. Below the new style rule, add an `@keyframes` rule with the name `spin` that applies a transform at 0% that rotates the element 360 degrees, and specifies 0 degrees of rotation at 100%. Duplicate the `@keyframes` rule using the browser-specific properties for WebKit browsers. (*Hint*: Specify WebKit properties for both the `@keyframes` rule itself and for the transform states.) Save your changes, refresh or reload museums.html in your browser, then verify that the image below the San Francisco Museums heading makes a full rotation when the page opens.

h. Validate all your HTML and CSS documents. Verify that your CSS contains no validation errors apart from the presence of the `@-webkit-keyframes` rule.

Independent Challenge 4 – Explore

You enhance the layout of the Eating Well in Season website with visual effects and animation.

a. In your editor, open HTM_K-11.html from the IC4 folder where you store your Data Files for this unit, save it as **farms.html**, then repeat to save HTM_K-12.css as **styles.css**. In the comment at the top of each file, enter your name and today's date where indicated, then save the files. Examine the contents and structure of each file, then open farms.html in a browser and review the contents of the page.

b. Return to styles.css in your browser, then in the main content section, add declarations to the `.silo` style rule to make the element a circle 4.5em in diameter. Add declarations to the `.barn` style rule to make the element a rectangle 7em wide and 4em high. Add declarations to the `.pasture` style rule to make the element a right triangle 10em high and 14em wide. (*Hint*: Set the height and width to 0. Create a 14em solid transparent right border and a 10em solid bottom border using the color `rgb(170,189,126)`.) Save your changes, refresh or reload farms.html in your browser, then verify that all three shapes are displayed as expected.

c. If you have access to IE8, open farms.html using IE8 and verify that the silo is displayed as a square rather than as a circle. Return to styles.css in your editor, then below the `.pasture p` style rule, add a style rule that sets the background image of the element with the `class` value `map-container` to the farm.png file in the images folder when the `border-radius` property is not supported. (*Hint*: Use the relevant class name generated by Modernizr.) Add another style rule below the one you just created that turns off the display of the `div` elements nested within the element with the `class` value `map-container` when the `border-radius` property is not supported. Save your changes, then refresh farms.html in IE8 and verify that a similar image of the farm map is displayed showing the silo as a circle.

d. Return to styles.css in your editor, then below the `.silo` style rule, add a rule for content displayed after the element with the `class` value `silo` when the mouse pointer is over it. (*Hint*: Use the selector `.silo:hover:after`.) Return to farms.html in your editor, copy the text of the paragraph below the h3 heading Silo to the Clipboard, return to styles. css, then in the new style rule, add a declaration to specify the content and paste the contents of the Clipboard as the value. Repeat to create new style rules for content displayed after the elements with the `class` values `barn` and `pasture`, using the contents of the paragraphs below the h3 headings Barn and Pasture, respectively. Scroll up and below the `.map-container p` style rule, add a style rule for the `div` element that the mouse pointer is over and that is within the element with the `class` value `map-container`, setting its z-index to 2. Below this style rule, add a new style rule for content after the same element. (*Hint*: Use the selector `.map-container div:hover:after`.) Add declarations that set the width to 12em, specify a top margin of 1.6em, a 1px solid black border, and padding of `0.2em 0.4em`, make the element a block-level element, set the background color to `rgb(246,224,65)`, and left-align text. Save your changes, refresh or reload farms.html in a modern browser, then move the mouse pointer over the map shapes and verify that a box displaying descriptive text about the current shape is displayed when the mouse pointer is over that shape.

e. Return to styles.css in your editor, then scroll up to the body and page container section. In the `.article-outside-outer-container` style rule, change the `background-color` declaration to use the `background` shorthand property with the same value. Below the existing `background` declaration, add a second `background` declaration that specifies a linear gradient oriented at 90 degrees, starting with the color `#aabd7e`, changing to white at 50%, then changing back to `#aabd7e`. Save your changes, refresh or reload farms.html in your browser, then verify that the green background behind the main body section fades from green to white on the left and white to green on the right.

Independent Challenge 4 – Explore (continued)

f. Return to styles.css in your editor, then in the site navigation section, below the nav.sitenavigation li style rule, add a rule for the li elements within the nav element with the class value sitenavigation when the mouse pointer is over them. Add a declaration that applies transforms that increase their size to 1.2 times the default and move them 4px up. (*Hint*: To move the elements up, use the keyword translateY with the value -4px. You can apply multiple transforms using a single property by separating them with a space.) Add

FIGURE K-28

any necessary browser-specific declarations for compatibility with major modern browsers. Save your changes, refresh or reload farms.html in your browser, move your mouse pointer over an item in the nav bar, then verify that the specified transforms are applied, as shown in **FIGURE K-28.**

g. Return to styles.css in your editor, then in the site navigation section, in the nav.sitenavigation li style rule, add declarations to create a 0.2 second transition using the ease-in timing function. Add any necessary browser-specific declarations for compatibility with major modern browsers. Save your changes, refresh or reload farms.html in your browser, move your mouse pointer over an item in the nav bar, then verify that the transforms now take a moment to be applied.

h. Return to styles.css in your editor, then in the header section, add code to animate the header div element using the ease-in-out timing function over 3 seconds. The animation should start with a scale of 0, making it invisible, and end with a scale of 1. Add any necessary browser-specific declarations and rules for compatibility with major modern browsers. Save your changes, refresh or reload farms.html in your browser, then verify that the logo image is initially not visible, then slowly grows to full size over 3 seconds.

i. Validate your HTML and CSS documents. Verify that your CSS contains no validation errors apart from the presence of any browser-prefixed style rules.

Visual Workshop

In your editor, open the file HTM_K-13.html from the VW folder where you store your Data Files for this unit and save it as **order.html**. Repeat to save HTM_K-14.css as **styles.css**. Add your first and last names and today's date to the comment section at the top of each file, then save your changes. Add background gradients to the `header` and `footer` elements as shown in **FIGURE K-29**, using the existing background color as the ending color and `white` as the starting color, and setting an angle of 90 degrees. Add and style the red asterisk before each label as generated content. Create the visual form feedback shown for valid fields and for the currently selected field. Apply the transform shown to the navigation bar item that the mouse pointer is over, and add a transition using settings of your choice. Validate your HTML and CSS code.

FIGURE K-29

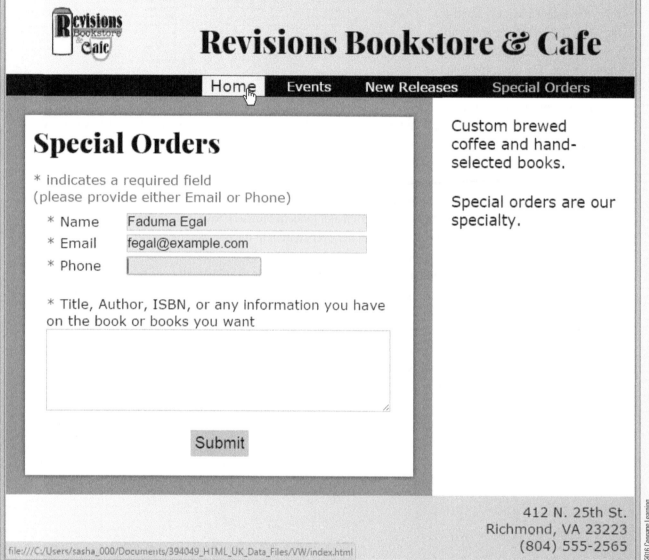

Incorporating Video and Audio

CASE ▶ Phillip Blaine wants to add video and audio to the website for his business to give users a flavor of local happenings near Lakeland Reeds Bed & Breakfast. In this unit, you will add video and audio to the website.

Unit Objectives

After completing this unit, you will be able to:

- Assess web video and audio
- Use the `video` element
- Control playback
- Incorporate the `source` element
- Add video support for older browsers
- Provide poster and fallback images
- Make videos accessible
- Implement the `audio` element

Files You Will Need

L	22 files	IC3	15 files
SR	22 files	IC4	12 files
IC1	16 files	VW	12 files
IC2	16 files		

For specific filenames, see Filenames_L.pdf in the Unit L Data Files folder.

©VikaSuh/Shutterstock.com

Assess Web Video and Audio

Learning
Outcomes
• Describe encoding
and container
formats for web
video and audio

In addition to the text and graphics you've worked with so far, HTML also supports incorporating video and animated elements into web pages. Used appropriately, these elements can contribute significant content and can complement the design of a website. Video and audio are widespread on the web today, with tools available that let users manipulate and publish videos straight from cameras or phones, and upload podcasts and self-produced music. As a web developer, you must make choices about how you incorporate video and audio into your web pages so as to accommodate the technologies that your intended audience uses. As a result, understanding the details of how video and audio are encoded, published, and viewed for the web is crucial. **CASE** ▶ *As you prepare to add the new content to the Lakeland Reeds B & B website, you review the nuts and bolts of online video and audio encoding and publishing.*

DETAILS

Publishing video and audio on the web relies on a few main concepts:

- **Encoding and containers**

  The process of transforming a moving image and/or sound into a digital file is known as **encoding**. Video and audio can be encoded in many different ways, and researchers are continually trying to find new ways to encode video and audio that result in smaller file sizes while still preserving image and sound quality. Each encoding method is known as a **codec**—short for coder/decoder. Four main video codecs are in wide use on the web today: **H.264**, **Theora**, **VP8**, and **VP9**. Likewise, most audio on the web is encoded as **AAC**, **MP3**, **Opus**, or **Vorbis**. TABLE L-1 describes these codecs.

  For video, codecs are not the end of the story, however. Because video is most often accompanied by audio, an encoded set of video data, known as a **stream**, is packaged for distribution within a file known as a **container**. A container file may contain an accompanying audio stream as well. Several container formats are popular on the web today, including **MPEG-4**, **Ogg**, **WebM**, and **Flash Video**. While most container formats can accommodate a variety of codecs, each container is commonly used with one or two specific audio codecs and video codecs. TABLE L-2 describes the common container formats.

- **Helper programs**

  Playing a video or audio file on a computer has traditionally required a program, known as a **helper program** or a **plugin**, that can both unpack the relevant container and decode the video and audio streams. Because not all helper programs have been able to deal with all containers or codecs, users have long needed to download and install multiple plugins to play web video and audio from different sources. The most commonly used helper programs include Adobe Flash Player and Microsoft Silverlight.

QUICK TIP
For the current state of browser video support, see en.wikipedia.org/wiki/HTML5_video.

- **Browser support**

  Recent versions of major browsers have simplified web video and audio somewhat by incorporating the ability to process media files and play web video and audio within browser software itself. Combined with the `video` and `audio` elements introduced in HTML5, these new browser abilities provide web developers with more control over how media is presented on a web page as well as the options available to users for interacting with it. FIGURE L-1 illustrates the relationship between video files, audio files, and other web page components, and it shows a web page containing a video with relevant controls along with the controls for an audio file.

  At the time this book was written, only one video codec is natively supported by all major browsers: H.264. However, different combinations of containers and codecs still have advantages in certain situations. In addition, older browsers, such as IE8, cannot decode video or audio, meaning that web developers have to take extra steps when publishing media—especially video—to ensure the files are available to a wide spectrum of users. You'll explore some of these methods in this unit.

FIGURE L-1: Relationship between video files, audio files, and other web page components

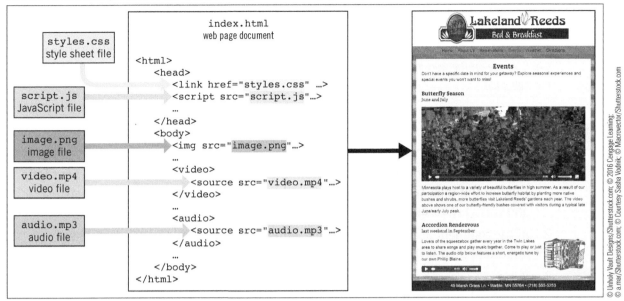

© Unholy Vault Designs/Shutterstock.com; © 2016 Cengage Learning;
© a.mar/Shutterstock.com; © Courtesy Sasha Vodnik; © Macrovector/Shutterstock.com

TABLE L-1: Main web video and audio codecs

codec type	name	developed by
video	H.264; also known as MPEG-4 part 10, Advanced Video Coding (MPEG-4 AVC)	the Video Coding Experts Group (VCEG) and the Moving Pictures Experts Group (MPEG)
	Theora	the Xiph.org Foundation
	VP8	On2; owned by Google
	VP9	Google
audio	AAC	a consortium of companies; declared a standard by MPEG
	MP3; also known as MPEG-1 or MPEG-2 Audio Layer 3 (or III)	MPEG
	Opus	the Internet Engineering Task Force (IETF)
	Vorbis	the Xiph.org Foundation

© 2016 Cengage Learning

TABLE L-2: Most popular container formats

name	extension	common video encoding	common audio encoding
MPEG-4	.mp4, .m4v	H.264 video	AAC or MP3 audio
Ogg	.ogv	Theora video	Vorbis or Opus audio
WebM	.webm	VP8 or VP9 video	Vorbis or Opus audio
Flash Video	.flv	various proprietary and public formats	various proprietary and public formats

© 2016 Cengage Learning

Use the `video` Element

Learning
Outcomes
• Add video to a
web page with the
video element

To add video to a web page, you use the `video` element. **CASE** ▶ *Phillip has provided you the video he wants to use on the website in an MPEG-4 container. You use the* `video` *element to incorporate the file into the web page.*

STEPS

QUICK TIP
You will learn about the use and syntax of .vtt files later in this unit.

1. In your editor, open HTM_L-1.html from the Lessons folder where you store your Data Files for this unit, save it as events.html, then repeat to save HTM_L-2.css as styles.css and HTM_L-3.vtt as descriptions.vtt

2. In the comment at the top of each file, enter your name and today's date where indicated, then save the files

QUICK TIP
Refer to the figures as you work through the steps to confirm code placement.

3. Return to events.html in your editor, then beneath the p element containing the text June and July, insert opening and closing video tags on separate lines

4. Within the opening <video> tag, place the insertion point before the closing >, insert a space, then type `src="media/bfly.m4v"`
   The src attribute specifies the name and location of the video file to display.

5. After the code you entered in the previous step, insert a space, then type
   `type="video/mp4"`
   The `type` attribute of the `video` element specifies the container format used to encode the file referenced by the `src` attribute. The container format is specified using the relevant **MIME type**, which is a standardized value used to reference a data type. **TABLE L-3** lists `type` values for the container formats described in **TABLE L-2**. **FIGURE L-2** shows the completed HTML code for the `video` element.

TROUBLE
If your browser displays a message saying that some web page items are blocked, follow the steps provided to allow the blocked content.

6. Save your changes, return to styles.css in your editor, then in the reset styles section, add the video selector to the reset rule that sets border, padding, and margin to 0

7. In the img style rule, add the video selector
   FIGURE L-3 shows the completed CSS code.

8. Save your changes, then open events.html in a modern browser
   The opening frame of the video is displayed as shown in **FIGURE L-4**.

TROUBLE
If Play is not a menu option in Safari, click Show Controls, then click the Play button ▶.

9. Right-click the video, then on the menu that opens, click Play
   The video, which is just over 30 seconds long, plays through once.

TABLE L-3: `video` element `type` values

container format	MIME type
MPEG-4	video/mp4
Ogg	video/ogg
WebM	video/webm
Flash Video	video/x-flv

FIGURE L-2: video element added to HTML code

```
45          Opening and       <h3>Butterfly Season</h3>
46          closing tags      <p class="eventdate">June and July</p>
47          for the video    <video src="media/bfly.m4v" type="video/mp4">
48          element           </video>
49                            <p>Minnesota plays host to a variety of beautiful butterflies in high
```

The value of the src attribute specifies the filename and location of the video file

The value of the type attribute indicates the container format of the video file using its MIME type

FIGURE L-3: CSS code for video element

```
10    /* reset styles */
11    html {
12        font-size: 16px;
13    }
14    a, article, body, div, figcaption, figure, footer, header, h1,
15    h2, h3, img, li, nav, p, section, ul, video {
16        border: 0;
17        padding: 0;
18        margin: 0;
19    }
20    img, video {
21        max-width: 100%;
22        height: auto;
23        width: auto;
24    }
```

FIGURE L-4: Video displayed on web page

Butterfly Season
June and July

Minnesota plays host to a variety of beautiful butterflies in high summer. As a result of our participation a region-wide effort to increase butterfly habitat by planting more native bushes

The first frame of the video is displayed by default when the page opens

© a.mar/Shutterstock.com; © Courtesy Sasha Vodnik

Control Playback

Learning
Outcomes
• Add browser-
generated controls
to a video
element

The `video` element supports a number of attributes, which are detailed in TABLE L-4. Several of these attributes give you control over how the element is displayed and what types of interactions are available to users. The presence of the `controls` attribute instructs browsers to add their default controls to the `video` element; this enables user control over actions like playing and pausing content and adjusting audio volume. Likewise, the `preload` attribute indicates whether a browser should download the relevant video file before a user plays it, the `loop` attribute indicates that the browser should restart playback each time it reaches the end of the video, and the `autoplay` attribute tells browsers to start playback of the video immediately when the page is loaded. **CASE** ▶ *Rather than require users to right-click the video, you add the `controls` attribute to display video controls by default.*

STEPS

1. **Return to events.html in your editor**

2. **In the opening <video> tag, add the attribute** `controls`

   FIGURE L-5 shows the completed code.

3. **Save your changes, then refresh or reload events.html in your browser**

   As **FIGURE L-6** shows, browsers display controls in conjunction with the `video` element. These controls typically include a play button, a position bar for visualizing the progress of the video during playback with a slider for moving forward or backward in the video, one or more options for adjusting the audio level, and a full-screen button.

4. **Click the Play button in the bottom left corner of the video, which should resemble** ▶

   The video begins to play. In some browsers, the Play button is replaced by a Pause button.

5. **Click the Pause button, which should resemble** ▮▮

   If your browser does not display a Pause button, but continues to show a Play button, click the Play button instead. The video pauses, and the frame where you paused it continues to be displayed.

6. **Click the Play button, drag the position slider back to the beginning, click the Full-screen button, then press the [Esc] key on your keyboard to exit full-screen mode**

   When you click the Full-screen button, the browser enlarges the video to occupy your entire screen.

Including video from an external site

Uploading video to a video hosting site such as YouTube can be a shortcut to including it in your web pages. Such sites generally display buttons that you can click to automatically generate HTML code for any video they host and then embed that video in your web pages. This process can remove a lot of specialized technical work from the task of adding a video to a website, while preserving your control over the appearance of your web pages. However, many free video hosting services display advertisements before or during videos, which is not the case with videos that you host yourself.

FIGURE L-5: controls attribute added to video element

```
45                        <h3>Butterfly Season</h3>
46                        <p class="eventdate">June and July</p>
47                        <video src="media/bfly.m4v" type="video/mp4" controls>
48                        </video>
```

FIGURE L-6: Default video controls in some modern browsers

© a.mar/Shutterstock.com; © Courtesy Sasha Vodnik

TABLE L-4: video element attributes

attribute	usage	value(s)
audio	enables control over the audio channel	muted
autoplay	specifies that the video should begin playing immediately when the page is loaded	(no value)
controls	requests that the browser display its default playback controls	(no value)
height	specifies the height of the element in pixels; omit for responsive sizing	the height in pixels
loop	indicates that the browser should restart playback each time it reaches the end of the video	(no value)
poster	specifies a path and filename for an image to display before video playback starts	path/filename
preload	indicates whether the browser should download the video file when opening the web page (auto), download only metadata related to the video file (metadata), or wait to download until the video is played (none)	auto metadata none
src	specifies the path and filename of the video file; not needed if using source elements	path/filename
width	specifies the width of the element in pixels; omit for responsive sizing	the width in pixels

© 2016 Cengage Learning

Incorporate the source Element

Although all modern browsers can play MPEG-4 videos encoded with the H.264 codec, some browsers are optimized to play other formats more efficiently. In addition, a small percentage of users still access the web with older browsers that support the video element but not the H.264 codec. For this reason, it's generally best to reference multiple video files, each specifying the same video but in different encoding and container formats, to accommodate the potential range of your users' browser capabilities. You can nest multiple instances of the source element within a video element to specify the location and encoding of multiple versions of the same video encoded in different formats. **CASE** *In addition to the MP4 video file, Phillip also provided you with a WebM version of the same file encoded with the VP8 video codec and the Vorbis audio codec. You add* source *elements to reference both of the video files.*

STEPS

1. **Open File Explorer (or the file manager for your operating system), navigate to the Lessons folder where you store your Data Files for this unit, then open the media folder**

   This folder contains the video and audio files that Phillip has provided you for this web page. Notice that in addition to the bfly.m4v file that you referenced in your video element, the folder contains the file bfly.webm, which is the WebM version of the same video.

2. **Return to events.html in your editor**

3. **Between the opening and closing `<video>` tags, add two one-sided `<source>` tags on separate lines**

4. **Delete the `src` and `type` attributes and their values from the opening `<video>` tag**

   Even though you're specifying two alternative source files, you continue to specify `controls` in the opening `<video>` tag.

5. **Within the first `<source>` tag, add the code `src="media/bfly.m4v" type="video/mp4"`**

6. **In the second `<source>` tag, add the code `src="media/bfly.webm" type="video/webm"`**

   This `source` element references a file containing the same video in a WebM container. **FIGURE L-7** shows the completed code.

7. **Save your changes, then reload events.html in your browser**

   The opening frame of the video is displayed as shown in **FIGURE L-8**. The video loaded based on the values in one of the `source` elements, rather than in the opening `<video>` tag as it did previously.

8. **Click the Play button**

   The video plays through once, just as it did previously when it loaded from the `video` element.

FIGURE L-7: Multiple `source` elements added within `video` element

```
45                          <h3>Butterfly Season</h3>
46    Second source         <p class="eventdate">June and July</p>
47    element references     <video controls>
48    the WebM version           <source src="media/bfly.m4v" type="video/mp4">
49    of the same video          <source src="media/bfly.webm" type="video/webm">
50                          </video>
```

Second source element references the WebM version of the same video

`src` and `type` properties from `video` element moved into first `source` element

FIGURE L-8: Video displayed on web page from `source` element

Butterfly Season
June and July

Minnesota plays host to a variety of beautiful butterflies in high summer. As a result of our participation a region-wide effort to increase butterfly habitat by planting more native bushes

Encoding video in web-ready formats

If you're developing web pages on your own, you will probably need to convert a single video file into multiple formats. Many tools are available to handle this conversion. While some software that simplifies and automates the process is available for purchase, some powerful tools are available free or on a donation basis as well. These free and low-cost alternatives are often just as powerful as their more expensive counterparts, but they may require more configuration and may not be as well documented. If you're working on a well-funded project with a tight deadline, purchasing software may make the most sense; however, if you're working within a low budget, it can be well worth your time to familiarize yourself with the free or low-cost tools. Try searching on *HTML5 video encoder* or *video encoder* plus the name of the container type to which you want to convert.

Whichever type of software you choose, be sure to download or purchase it from a company or organization that you're familiar with or that is recommended to you by someone you trust. Obtaining software from an untrusted source can expose your computer system to malware.

Add Video Support for Older Browsers

Learning
Outcomes
• Use the object
element to add a
Flash fallback for a
video

In spite of the promise of HTML5 video, some web users are running older browsers, such as IE8, that don't recognize HTML5 elements like video and source. Fortunately, HTML5 enables you to incorporate support for video that works for users of older browsers, while maintaining the benefits of HTML5 video for browsers that support it. Older browsers rely on additional software to play videos, and many such programs are available. Adobe Flash Player is the most widely installed program, and for this reason it is a common choice for supporting a wide array of older browsers. To make a Flash video available to older browsers, you use the object and param elements, which are detailed in TABLE L-5. These elements specify the file type and location, along with other settings. **CASE** *A colleague has encoded the movie for you in the appropriate format for the Flash player. You add this version as a fallback option to maximize the number of users that will be able to view the video.*

STEPS

1. **Return to events.html in your editor, then above the closing </video> tag, enter opening and closing tags for the object element on separate lines**

2. **In the opening <object> tag, add the code** type="application/x-shockwave-flash" width="854" height="508"

    The value for the type attribute is a MIME type, but instead of describing the video encoding, it specifies the software that should be used to play the content of the object element. Although you can control the size of the video element, which is the parent element, with CSS style rules, you still need to specify the width and height of the object element using attributes.

QUICK TIP
Check the documentation for a helper program to identify which param names and values it requires.

3. **Between the opening and closing <object> tags, enter the following** param **elements on separate lines:**

    ```
    <param name="movie" value="media/bfly.swf">
    <param name="base" value="media">
    ```

    You specify the name and path to the video file in the first param element. Different types of content for the object element make use of their own customized parameter names and values, such as the base parameter. FIGURE L-9 shows the completed code.

TROUBLE
If no video is displayed, check that your browser has Flash Player installed by visiting adobe.com/software/ flash/about/; if Flash Player is not installed, follow the instructions to install it, then refresh events.html.

4. **Save your changes, then if you have access to IE8, open events.html in IE8**

    IE8 does not support the HTML5 video element, so it ignores the video and source tags and renders the object element instead. In this case, the Flash player is displayed, as shown in FIGURE L-10.

5. **Use the controls to start and stop the video, move forward and backward within it, and adjust the audio level**

    Note that the provided Flash Player file incorporates its own video captions. You will learn how to add captions to the video element later in this unit.

FIGURE L-9: Code to incorporate the Flash version of the video

```
45                      <h3>Butterfly Season</h3>
46                      <p class="eventdate">June and July</p>
47                      <video controls>
48                          <source src="media/bfly.m4v" type="video/mp4">
49                          <source src="media/bfly.webm" type="video/webm">
    object and          <object type="application/x-shockwave-flash" width="854" height="508">
50  param elements          <param name="movie" value="media/bfly.swf">
51  specify attributes       <param name="base" value="media">
52  and settings for      </object>
53  Flash Player        </video>
54
```

FIGURE L-10: Video displayed in Flash Player

Butterfly Season
June and July

Controls are embedded within Flash Player video and are displayed the same way across browsers

Minnesota plays host to a variety of beautiful butterflies in high summer. As a result of our participation a region-wide effort to increase butterfly habitat by planting more native

© Courtesy Sasha Vodnik

TABLE L-5: The object and param elements

element	description	attributes
object	includes the content of an external resource, such as a Flash video, in the current web page	type="*MIME type*" width="*width*" height="*height*"
param	defines one or more parameters related to the external resource in the containing object element	name="*parameter name*" value="*parameter value*"

© 2016 Cengage Learning

Provide Poster and Fallback Images

Learning Outcomes
- Specify a poster image for a video
- Specify a fallback image for a video

Before a user chooses to play a video, the first frame of the video is displayed by default. However, you can customize what users see by specifying a **poster image**, which is an image displayed before the video is played. In addition, some potential users of any given web page will be unable to view video content. To preserve the layout of your web pages for such users and to give them a taste of the content in the video, you can provide a **fallback image** by nesting an img element within the object element; this image is displayed in browsers that do not recognize the video element and cannot render the video specified by the object element. **CASE** ▸ *Phillip Blaine has provided an image file that consists of a single frame of the butterfly video along with some text. You add this image as both a poster and a fallback image.*

1. **In your file manager, navigate to the images folder in the Lessons folder where you store your Data Files for this unit, then double-click bfly.png to open it in your default application for viewing images**

   The image shows a frame from the butterfly video with the Lakeland Reeds logo and the text Butterfly Season.

2. **Return to events.html in your editor, then in the opening <video> tag, add the code** `poster="images/bfly.png"`

   The poster attribute specifies a poster image for the video element.

3. **Above the closing </object> tag, insert a new line, create an <img> tag, then add attributes to specify the source as** images/bfly.png, **alternative text of** a bush with purple flowers covered in dark butterflies, **width of** 854, **and height of** 480

   This code specifies bfly.png as the fallback image, which will be shown if the browser does not support any of the specified video formats. **FIGURE L-11** shows the completed code for the poster and fallback images.

4. **Save your changes, then reload events.html in a modern browser**

   The poster image is shown instead of the first frame of the video, along with the video controls. **FIGURE L-12** shows the poster image in Chrome.

5. **If you have access to an older browser without Flash installed, open events.html in that browser**

   In browsers that don't support the video element or Flash video, the fallback image is displayed without any video controls.

```
45          <h3>Butterfly Season</h3>
46          <p class="eventdate">June and July</p>
47          <video controls poster="images/bfly.png">
48             <source src="media/bfly.m4v" type="video/mp4">
49             <source src="media/bfly.webm" type="video/webm">
50             <object type="application/x-shockwave-flash" width="854" height="508">
51                <param name="movie" value="media/bfly.swf">
52                <param name="base" value="media">
53                <img src="images/bfly.png" alt="a bush with purple flowers covered
54                in dark butterflies" width="854" height="480">
55             </object>
56          </video>
```

The poster image is specified with the poster attribute

The fallback image is specified with an img element nested within the object element

FIGURE L-12: Poster image displayed

When the video first opens, the poster image is displayed instead of the first frame of the video

© Unholy Vault Designs/Shutterstock.com; © 2016 Cengage Learning; © a.mar/Shutterstock.com; © Courtesy Sasha Vodnik

Make Videos Accessible

To make a video accessible to a wide range of users, you accompany the video with text content. To ensure that users who are deaf or hard of hearing can access the information in the audio track, you add **captions**, which consist of text that is overlaid on the video image and describes the audio portion. In addition to narration or dialog, captions also include a description of other sounds that are part of the video, such as the sound of a door closing. To provide access to the visual portion of a video for users who are blind or have low sight, you create **descriptions**, which explain in words what is happening in the video and can be read by a screen reader. Both captions and descriptions are external text files written in **WebVTT**, which is a markup language for creating text tracks to accompany video. Caption and descriptions files are linked to a web page using the `track` element. **CASE** *You add captions and descriptions to the video on the Events page.*

STEPS

1. **Return to descriptions.vtt in your editor, then examine the contents of the file**

   A WebVTT file must start with the text `WEBVTT FILE` on the first line. The line containing `NOTE` identifies the text that follows as a comment. The comment ends at the first blank line after `NOTE`.

QUICK TIP
In a WebVTT file, all times must include 2 digits for minutes followed by a colon, 2 digits for seconds followed by a period, and 3 digits for fractions of a second. They can also start with 2 digits for hour followed by a colon.

2. **Create 2 blank lines at the end of the file, then position the insertion point on the last line**

3. **Type** `1`, **press [Enter], then type** `00:00.000 --> 00:31.000`, **then press [Enter]**

   A WebVTT file consists of one or more **cues**, which are sections consisting of a unique name, a time range, and associated text. The code you typed uses 1 as the cue name and specifies a time range starting at 0 minutes and 0.0 seconds (the start of the video) and ending at 0 minutes and 31.0 seconds (the end of the video).

4. **Type A bush with purple flowers is covered with many dark butterflies, some of which slowly beat their wings.**

   FIGURE L-13 shows the completed code for the descriptions file. Because the butterfly video consists of a single, continuous shot of one object, it requires only one cue.

QUICK TIP
You can use screen reader software to test text descriptions.

5. **Save your changes, return to events.html in your editor, then below the second `source` element, add the following element on a new line:**

   ```
   <track  src="descriptions.vtt"  kind="descriptions"  srclang="en"  label="English
   descriptions">
   ```

   This `track` element specifies that the descriptions.vtt file contains descriptions for the video. **TABLE L-6** describes commonly used attributes for the `track` element.

6. **In your editor, open captions.vtt from the Lessons folder where you store your Data Files for this unit**

   This file contains captions that describe the sounds in the video and provide a transcript of the video narration. The text for each cue is displayed on the screen only between the start and end times indicated for that cue.

7. **Return to events.html in your editor, then below the existing `track` element, add the following element on a new line:**

   ```
   <track src="captions.vtt" kind="captions" srclang="en" label="English captions">
   ```

   This `track` element uses the value `captions` for the `kind` attribute to indicate that the associated file contains captions. **FIGURE L-14** shows the updated HTML code.

TROUBLE
At the time this book was written, Firefox did not support captions, no browsers supported captions when files were opened from the local file system, and IE required additional server configuration to display them. If necessary, open events.html from a web server in Chrome or Safari, then repeat Step 8.

8. **Save your changes, reload events.html in your browser, then examine the video controls**

   Some browsers display a button that lets you turn captions on or off, including Chrome **cc**, IE **cc**, and Safari **.** If the captions button is not displayed, review your captions.vtt file and fix any errors.

9. **Click the Play button, if necessary click the Captions button to turn on captions and click English captions to select the captions you created, then verify that the cues in the captions.vtt file are displayed at the appropriate times, as shown in FIGURE L-15**

FIGURE L-13: Completed descriptions.vtt file

```
1    WEBVTT FILE ◄──── First line must consist of WEBVTT FILE
2
3    NOTE
4    Lakeland Reeds Butterfly Season video descriptions
5    Filename: descriptions.vtt
6    Author:                                              A comment starts with a line consisting
7    Date:                                                of NOTE and ends with a blank line
8    HTML5 and CSS3 Illustrated Unit L, Lessons
9                                                                                    Cue text
10   1 ◄──── Cue name
11   00:00.000 --> 00:31.000 ◄──── Cue time range
12   A bush with purple flowers is covered with many dark butterflies, some of which slowly
13   beat their wings.
```

FIGURE L-14: track elements added to HTML file

```
47            <video controls pos  kind value of descriptions specifies text descriptions of visual content
48              <source src="media/bfly.mp4" type="video/mp4">
49              <source src="media/bfly.webm" type="video/webm">
50              <track src="descriptions.vtt" kind="descriptions" srclang="en"
51              label="English descriptions">
52              <track src="captions.vtt" kind="captions" srclang="en"
53              label="English captions">
54              <object type="applicat  kind value of captions specifies text transcript of audio content
```

FIGURE L-15: Video captions displayed during playback

© a.mar/Shutterstock.com; © Courtesy Sasha Vodnik

Captions displayed at the bottom of the video

Button for controlling display of captions in Chrome

TABLE L-6: Commonly used attributes of the track element

attribute	description
kind	the type of information contained in the source file using one of the following keywords: captions (transcript of all audio content); chapters (video navigation tool); descriptions (transcript of visual content); metadata (content used by track-related scripts); or subtitles (transcript of spoken content, the default)
label	a unique, user-readable description of track content for inclusion in a list of available tracks
src	the path and name of the file containing the track data
srclang	an abbreviation from the list at iana.org/assignments/language-subtag-registry indicating the language of the track data

© 2016 Cengage Learning

Implement the `audio` Element

Learning
Outcomes
• Add audio to a
  web page with the
  audio element

In addition to the `video` element, HTML also includes an `audio` element for linking audio files to a web page and enabling users to control playback. The `audio` element makes use of the same attributes as the `video` element and accepts nested `source` elements for source files in multiple formats. TABLE L-7 details the MIME types for 4 of the most common audio file formats for the web. **CASE** ▶ *Phillip would like you to add the option for users to play a recording of a short song in the Accordion Festival section of the Events page. You'll add the file in two formats, mp3 and Ogg, with a fallback to Flash Player for older browsers.*

STEPS

1. **Return to events.html in your editor**

2. **Just above the closing `</section>` tag for the Accordion Rendezvous section, insert opening and closing `<audio>` tags on separate lines**

3. **In the opening `<audio>` tag, add the attribute `controls`**

   An audio element includes no visual content unless it specifies a poster image. This means that an audio element is invisible on a web page unless controls are displayed.

4. **Within the `audio` element, add a `source` element containing the attributes `src="media/bonfire.mp3"` and `type="audio/mpeg"`**

5. **Below the code you just entered, add a second `source` element containing the attributes `src="media/bonfire.ogg"` and `type="audio/ogg"`**

6. **Below the second `source` element, enter opening and closing `<object>` tags on separate lines, then in the opening `<object>` tag, add the attributes `type="application/x-shockwave-flash"`, `width="320"`, and `height="30"`**

7. **Within the `object` element, enter the following `param` elements on separate lines:**
   ```
   <param name="movie" value="media/bonfire.swf">
   <param name="base" value="media">
   ```
   Even though the file contains no video, you still indicate its location with the `movie` parameter. FIGURE L-16 shows the completed code.

QUICK TIP
Because the controls
that each browser
displays can vary in
dimensions, you
should not specify
height or width
for the audio
element.

8. **Save your changes, return to styles.css in your editor, then in the reset styles section, add the `audio` selector to the reset rule that sets border, padding, and margin to 0**
   FIGURE L-17 shows the completed CSS code.

9. **Save your changes, then reload events.html in your browser**
   Audio controls are displayed below the text describing the accordion festival, as shown in FIGURE L-18.

10. **Use the audio controls to start and stop the song, move forward and backward within it, and adjust the volume**

11. **Validate your HTML and CSS files**

FIGURE L-16: `audio` element added to HTML document

```
67                    <section>
68                        <h3>Accordion Rendezvous</h3>
69                        <p class="eventdate">last weekend in September</p>
70                        <figure>
71                            <img src="images/accordion.png" width="208" height="160">
72                        </figure>
73                        <p>Lovers of the squeezebox gather every year in the Twin Lakes area to
74                        share songs and play music together. Come to play or just to listen. The
75                        audio clip below features a short, energetic tune by our own Phillip
76                        Blaine.</p>
77                        <audio controls>
78                            <source src="media/bonfire.mp3" type="audio/mpeg">
79                            <source src="media/bonfire.ogg" type="audio/ogg">
80                            <object type="application/x-shockwave-flash" width="320" height="30">
81                                <param name="movie" value="media/bonfire.swf">
82                                <param name="base" value="media">
83                            </object>
84                        </audio>
85                    </section>
```

The audio element adds audio content to a web page

source elements specify audio source files

The object element specifies Flash content for older browsers

HTML5 & CSS3

FIGURE L-17: CSS code for `audio` element

```
10    /* reset styles */
11    html {
12        font-size: 16px;
13    }
14    a, article, audio, body, div, figcaption, figure, footer, header, h1,
15    h2, h3, img, li, nav, p, section, ul, video {
16        border: 0;
17        padding: 0;
18        margin: 0;
19    }
```

FIGURE L-18: Audio player displayed in Chrome

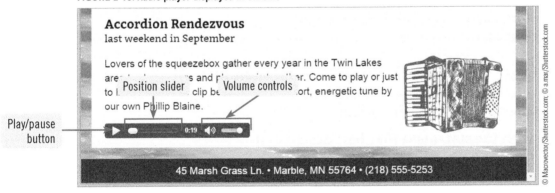

Play/pause button

Position slider

Volume controls

TABLE L-7: MIME types for common audio formats

name	MIME type	name	MIME type
AAC	audio/aac	Opus	audio/ogg
mp3	audio/mpeg	Vorbis	audio/ogg

Practice

Concepts Review

Refer to FIGURE L-19 **to answer the following questions.**

FIGURE L-19

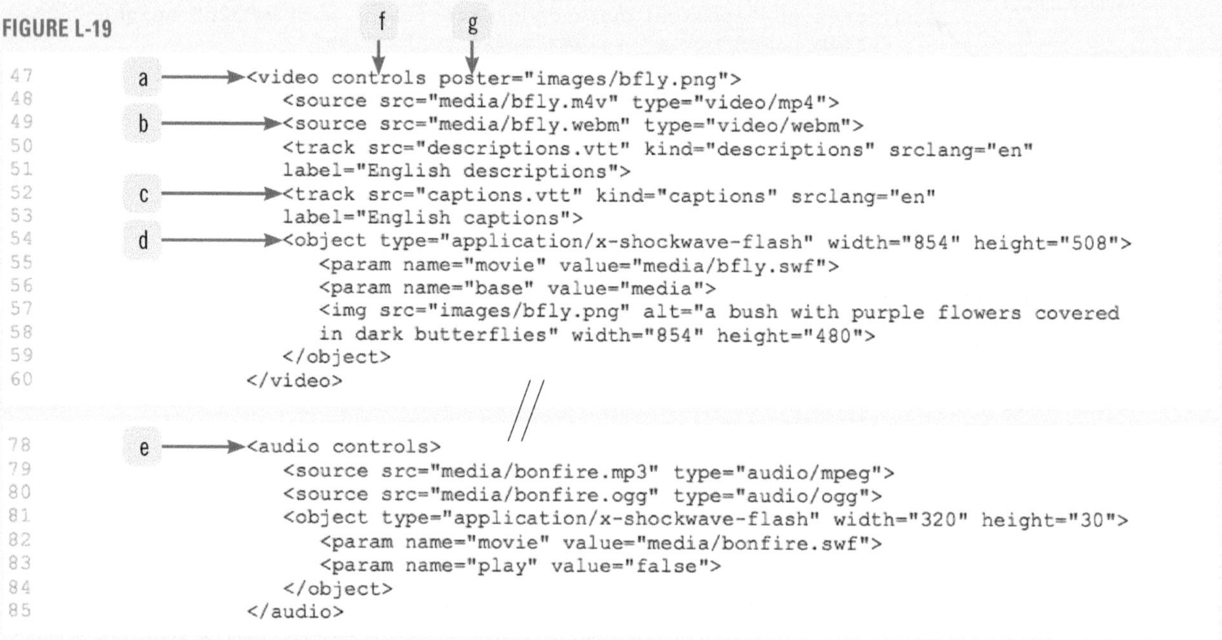

```
                              f        g
                              ↓        ↓
47   a  ──────→  <video controls poster="images/bfly.png">
48                   <source src="media/bfly.m4v" type="video/mp4">
49   b  ──────→      <source src="media/bfly.webm" type="video/webm">
50                   <track src="descriptions.vtt" kind="descriptions" srclang="en"
51                   label="English descriptions">
52   c  ──────→      <track src="captions.vtt" kind="captions" srclang="en"
53                   label="English captions">
54   d  ──────→      <object type="application/x-shockwave-flash" width="854" height="508">
55                       <param name="movie" value="media/bfly.swf">
56                       <param name="base" value="media">
57                       <img src="images/bfly.png" alt="a bush with purple flowers covered
58                       in dark butterflies" width="854" height="480">
59                   </object>
60               </video>
                              //
78   e  ──────→  <audio controls>
79                   <source src="media/bonfire.mp3" type="audio/mpeg">
80                   <source src="media/bonfire.ogg" type="audio/ogg">
81                   <object type="application/x-shockwave-flash" width="320" height="30">
82                       <param name="movie" value="media/bonfire.swf">
83                       <param name="play" value="false">
84                   </object>
85               </audio>
```

1. Which item makes video available for modern browsers?
2. Which item makes audio available for modern browsers?
3. Which item specifies a poster image for modern browsers?
4. Which item specifies that browsers should display controls for interacting with the related video content?
5. Which item specifies a file that contains text related to the media file?
6. Which item specifies the type and name of a media file?
7. Which item specifies a fallback Flash file for older browsers?

Match each term with the statement that best describes it.

8. stream
9. codec
10. container
11. encoding
12. MIME type
13. plugin

    a. a specific encoding method; short for coder/decoder
    b. an encoded set of video or audio data
    c. a program that can both unpack a video or audio container and decode the video and audio streams
    d. a file in which video and/or audio is packaged for distribution
    e. a standardized data type that describes a container format
    f. the process of transforming a moving image and/or sound into a digital file

Select the best answer from the list of choices.

14. H.264, Theora, and VP8 are examples of popular _____ on the web today.
    a. plugins   **c.** MIME types
    b. container formats   **d.** codecs

15. Which of the following is a codec used to encode audio?
    a. H.264   **c.** m4v
    b. AAC   **d.** VP8

16. Which of the following is a codec used to encode video?
    a. Ogg   **c.** m4v
    b. AAC   **d.** VP9

17. Which of the following is a container format?
    a. Vorbis   **c.** WebM
    b. H.264   **d.** MP3

18. Flash Player is an example of which of the following?
    a. a plugin   **c.** an HTML element
    b. a container format   **d.** a codec

19. Which element do you use to provide video for older browsers?
    a. source   **c.** audio
    b. video   **d.** object

Skills Review

1. Use the `video` element.
    a. In your editor, open HTM_L-4.html from the SR folder where you store your Data Files for this unit, save it as **news.html**, then repeat to save the file HTM_L-5.css as **styles.css**. and the file HTM_L-6.vtt as **descriptions.vtt**.
    b. Within the comment section at the top of each file, enter your first and last names and today's date, then save your changes.
    c. Return to news.html in your editor, then insert a `video` element just before the closing `</section>` tag for the first section, which has the `h2` heading *News*.
    d. Within the opening `<video>` tag, add attributes to specify the file market.m4v in the media folder as the source, and MP4 as the container type.
    e. Save your changes, then return to styles.css in your editor. Add the `video` selector to the style rule in the reset styles section that sets border, padding, and margin to 0, then in the `img` style rule in the reset styles section, add the `video` selector.
    f. Save your changes, then open news.html in your browser. Right-click the opening frame of the video, then click Play.

2. Control playback.
    a. Return to news.html in your editor, then in the `video` element, add an attribute to indicate that browsers should display controls for the video.
    b. Save your changes, then refresh or reload news.html in your browser. Use the controls to navigate through the video and adjust the volume.

3. Incorporate the `source` element.
    a. Return to news.html in your editor, then between the opening and closing `<video>` tags, add two `source` elements on separate lines.
    b. Within the first `<source>` tag, cut and paste the attributes and values from the opening `<video>` tag that specify the source file and container type.

c. Within the second `<source>` tag, add attributes to specify the file market.webm in the media folder as the source and WebM as the container type.

d. Save your changes, then refresh or reload news.html in your browser. Use the controls to navigate through the video and adjust the volume.

4. Add video support for older browsers.

a. Return to news.html in your editor, then above the closing `</video>` tag, add an `object` element.

b. In the opening `<object>` tag, add attributes to specify Flash as the object type, a width of 854, and a height of 508.

c. Between the opening and closing `<object>` tags, add a `param` element that specifies a name of `movie` and value of `media/market.swf`, then add another `param` element that specifies a name of `base` and a value of `media`.

d. Save your changes, then if you have access to IE8, open news.html in that browser.

e. Use the Flash Player controls to play and pause the video, navigate through it, and adjust the volume.

5. Provide poster and fallback images.

a. Return to news.html in your editor, then in the opening `<video>` tag, add an attribute to specify a poster image of images/market.png.

b. Above the closing `</object>` tag, add an element to specify a backup image for browsers that can't play any of the provided formats, specifying market.png in the images folder as the source, alternative text of Big J's Pizza, a width of 854, and a height of 480.

c. Save your changes. If you have access to a browser that doesn't support HTML5 elements or Flash, open news.html in that browser, then verify that the static image showing the Big J's logo on a black background is displayed.

6. Make videos accessible.

a. Return to descriptions.vtt in your editor, then create 2 blank lines at the end of the file.

b. On the last line of the file, create a cue with a name of 1, a start time of 00:00.000, an end time of 00:09.000, and content of **An outdoor farmers' market with vendors selling their wares under white pop-up canopies.** Repeat to add the cues described in TABLE L-8.

TABLE L-8

name	start time	end time	content
2	00:10.000	00:17.000	Different types of mushrooms for sale in small baskets, including portabella, button, brown, lion's mane, maitake, tree oyster, and shiitake.
3	00:18.000	00:22.000	Big J's logo, showing a chef with a mustache and a chef's hat holding out a pepperoni pizza, with the words "Big J's Deep Dish Pizza."

© 2016 Cengage Learning

c. Save your changes, return to news.html in your editor, then below the second `source` element, add a `track` element for the descriptions.vtt file with attributes specifying `descriptions` as the kind of content, a source language of English, and a label of **English descriptions**.

d. In your editor, open captions.vtt from the SR folder where you store your Data Files for this unit, then review the contents of the file.

e. Return to news.html in your editor, then below the existing `track` element, add a new `track` element for the captions.vtt file with attributes specifying `captions` as the kind of content, a source language of English, and a label of **English captions**.

f. Save your changes, refresh or reload news.html in your browser, then verify that a captions button is displayed as part of the video controls.

g. Click the **Play button**, if necessary click the **Captions button** to turn on captions, then verify that the cues in the captions.vtt file are displayed at the appropriate times. [*Hint*: You may need to open news.html from a web server and in Chrome for captions to be displayed.]

7. Implement the `audio` element.

a. Return to news.html in your editor, then just above the closing `</section>` tag for the second section, which has the h3 heading *Music to Eat Pizza By*, insert an `audio` element.

b. In the opening `<audio>` tag, add an attribute to indicate that browsers should display controls for the element.

c. Within the `audio` element, add a `source` element specifying dance.mp3 in the media folder as the source and MP3 as the container type. Add a second `source` element specifying dance.ogg in the media folder as the source and Ogg as the container type.

d. Save your changes, then return to styles.css in your editor. Add the `audio` selector to the style rule in the reset styles section that sets border, padding, and margin to 0.

e. Save your changes, then reload news.html in your browser. Use the audio controls to start and stop the song, move forward and backward within it, and adjust the volume. **FIGURE L-20** shows the display of the `video` and `audio` elements in Chrome.

FIGURE L-20

f. Return to news.html in your editor, then below the second `source` element, add an `object` element.

g. In the opening `<object>` tag, add attributes to specify Flash as the object type, a width of 320, and a height of 30.

h. Between the opening and closing `<object>` tags, add a `param` element that specifies a name of `movie` and value of `media/dance.swf`, then add another `param` element that specifies a name of `base` and a value of `media`.

i. Save your changes, then if you have access to IE8, open news.html in that browser. Use the Flash Player controls to play and pause the audio, navigate through it, and adjust the volume.

j. Validate the code for your HTML and CSS files, then make changes as necessary to fix any errors.

Independent Challenge 1

The Spotted Wren Garden Center is adding videos of gardens and landscaping projects to their website to give current and potential customers ideas that they might want to implement for their own homes and businesses. Sarah Nguyen, the manager, has provided you with a set of files containing the first project to be spotlighted. You'll add it to a new page on the website.

a. In your editor, open HTM_L-7.html from the IC1 folder where you store your Data Files for this unit, save it as **great.html**, then repeat to save HTM_L-8.css as **styles.css** and HTM_L-9.vtt as **captions.vtt**. In the comment section at the top of each file, enter your name and today's date where indicated, then save the files.

b. Return to great.html in your editor, then below the h3 heading, add code to incorporate a video for modern browsers. Specify hodgkins.png in the images folder as the poster image and indicate that browsers should display video controls. Add a reference to the file hodgkins.m4v in the media folder as a source file and specify that the file is in MP4 format. Add a reference to the file hodgkins.webm in the media folder as a second source file and specify that the file is in WebM format.

c. Save your changes, then return to styles.css in your editor. Add the `video` selector to the style rule in the reset styles section that sets border, padding, and margin to 0, then in the `img` style rule in the reset styles section, add the `video` selector. In the main content section, create a style rule for the `video` element that specifies margins of `0  0.5em`, sets the maximum width to 50%, creates a 1px solid black border, and floats the element on the right.

Independent Challenge 1 (continued)

d. Save your changes. Open great.html in a modern browser that supports the video element and verify that the video plays. **FIGURE L-21** shows the web page displaying the video.

© Courtesy Sasha Vodnik

FIGURE L-21

Great Gardens

Looking for inspiration for your outdoor areas? We're collecting photos and videos of some of our garden projects, as well as other settings that inspire us.

The Hodgkins family, Papillion, NE

"We wanted to make our land into a place that drew us in, a place we wanted to go back to again and again," says Lila Hodgkins. She and her husband Dave settled on a brook as the centerpoint of their project after a visit to some friends. "We sat in wooden chairs sipping lemonade on a warm summer day next to this babbling creek -- but we were in the middle of a big city! Papillion isn't as dense or as loud, but we still wanted that kind of escape."

e. Return to great.html in your editor, then add code for a Flash version of the video to the web page. Specify a media type of Flash, a width of 854, and a height of 508. Add a `param` element that specifies a name of `movie` and value of `media/hodgkins.swf`, then add another `param` element that specifies a name of `base` and a value of `media`.

f. Save your changes. If you have access to a browser such as IE8 that does not recognize the `video` element and that has the Flash Player plugin installed, open great.html and verify that the video plays.

g. Return to great.html, then add the file hodgkins.png in the images folder as a fallback image for the Flash code. Specify a width of 854 and a height of 480, and provide appropriate alt text.

h. Save your changes. If you have access to a browser that does not recognize the `video` element and does not have the Flash Player plugin installed, open great.html and verify that the fallback image is displayed.

i. Return to captions.vtt in your editor, then add the cues shown in **TABLE L-9**.

TABLE L-9

name	start time	end time	content
1	00:01.000	00:01.800	[Water running, wind blowing]
2	00:02.000	00:03.900	We just love the water features.
3	00:04.200	00:06.000	I bring my morning coffee out here,
4	00:06.200	00:07.300	close my eyes,
5	00:07.500	00:11.500	and just enjoy the sound of the water as I prepare for my day.
6	00:12.000	00:42.000	[Water running, wind blowing]

© 2016 Cengage Learning

j. Save your changes, return to great.html in your browser, then add a reference to the captions.vtt file within the `video` element, specifying `captions` as the kind of content, en as the source language, and label of **English captions**. Add a reference to the descriptions.vtt file within the `video` element as well, specifying a `descriptions` as the kind of content, en as the source language, and label of **English descriptions**.

Independent Challenge 1 (continued)

k. Save your changes, refresh or reload great.html in a modern browser that supports captions, then play the video and verify that the captions you created are displayed.

l. Validate your HTML and CSS files.

Independent Challenge 2

The coordinators of the Murfreesboro Regional Soccer League would like to add a public service announcement advocating outdoor activities to the website. They've provided you the video in multiple formats.

a. In your editor, open HTM_L-10.html from the IC2 folder where you store your Data Files for this unit, save it as **started.html**, then repeat to save HTM_L-11.css as **styles.css** and HTM_L-12.vtt as **captions.vtt**. In the comment section at the top of each file, enter your name and today's date where indicated, then save the files.

b. Return to started.html in your editor, then in the `article` element and below the `h2` heading, add code to incorporate a video for modern browsers. Specify outdoors.png in the images folder as the poster image and indicate that browsers should display video controls. Add a reference to the file outdoors.m4v in the media folder as a source file and specify that the file is in MP4 format. Add a reference to the file outdoors.webm in the media folder as a second source file and specify that the file is in WebM format.

c. Save your changes, then return to styles.css in your editor. Add the `video` selector to the style rule in the reset styles section that sets border, padding, and margin to 0, then in the `img` style rule in the reset styles section, add the `video` selector. In the main content section, create a style rule for the `video` element that sets the maximum width to 50%, specifies margins of `0 0.4em 0.4em`, and floats the element on the right.

d. Save your changes. Open started.html in a modern browser that supports the video element and verify that the video plays. **FIGURE L-22** shows the web page displaying the video.

FIGURE L-22

e. Return to started.html in your editor, then add code for a Flash version of the video to the web page. Specify a media type of Flash, a width of 854, and a height of 508. Add a `param` element that specifies a name of `movie` and value of `media/outdoors.swf`, then add another `param` element that specifies a name of `base` and a value of `media`.

f. Save your changes. If you have access to a browser, such as IE8, that does not recognize the `video` element and that has the Flash Player plugin installed, open started.html and verify that the video plays.

g. Return to started.html, then add the file outdoors.png in the images folder as a fallback image for the Flash code. Specify a width of 854 and a height of 480, and provide appropriate alt text.

h. Save your changes. If you have access to a browser that does not recognize the `video` element and does not have the Flash Player plugin installed, open started.html and verify that the fallback image is displayed.

Independent Challenge 2 (continued)

i. Return to captions.vtt in your editor, then add the cues shown in TABLE L-10.

TABLE L-10

name	start time	end time	content
1	00:01.000	00:02.900	Experts tell us that kids need 60 minutes
2	00:03.000	00:05.900	of activity a day to grow up healthy,
3	00:06.000	00:08.900	and we know that regular physical activity boosts kids'
4	00:09.000	00:12.900	concentration and creativity, and is even linked to improved
5	00:13.000	00:14.900	academic performance.
6	00:15.000	00:18.900	Best of all, moving around is just plain fun.
7	00:19.000	00:22.900	And one of the most fun ways to get moving is by exploring
8	00:23.000	00:24.900	America's great outdoors.
9	00:25.000	00:27.900	No matter where you live, there are places near you to get out
10	00:28.000	00:31.900	and get active, from biking around your neighborhood to playing
11	00:32.000	00:34.900	tag or capture the flag in an urban park,
12	00:35.000	00:37.900	from hiking on a mountain trail to paddling around a lake or
13	00:38.000	00:39.900	catching an early morning wave.
14	00:40.000	00:44.900	The great outdoors is America's first and best playground.
15	00:45.000	00:46.900	So what are you waiting for?
16	00:47.000	00:50.900	Grab a backpack and get moving outside with your family today.
17	00:51.000	00:54.900	For more information on where to go and what to do outside,
18	00:55.000	00:59.000	visit LetsMove.gov.

j. Save your changes, return to started.html in your browser, then add a reference to the captions.vtt file within the `video` element, specifying a `captions` as the kind of content, `en` as the source language, and label of **English captions**. Add a reference to the descriptions.vtt file within the `video` element as well, specifying a `descriptions` as the kind of content, `en` as the source language, and label of **English descriptions**.

k. Save your changes, refresh or reload started.html in a modern browser that supports captions, then play the video and verify that the captions you created are displayed.

l. Validate your HTML and CSS files.

Independent Challenge 3

Diego Merckx, the manager of the Hotel Natoma, would like to add videos of local attractions within walking distance of the hotel to help potential guests visualize its great location. To start, he's given you multiple versions of a video of a cable car being turned around at the terminus on Powell Street. You'll add this video to the website.

a. In your editor, open HTM_L-13.html from the IC3 folder where you store your Data Files for this unit, save it as **nearby.html**, then repeat to save HTM_L-14.css as **styles.css**, HTM_L-15.vtt as **captions.vtt**, and HTM_L-16.vtt as **descriptions.vtt**. In the comment section at the top of each file, enter your name and today's date where indicated, then save the files.

Independent Challenge 3 (continued)

b. Within the `section` element with the `class` value `cablecar` and above the `h3` heading Cable Car Turnaround, add code to incorporate a video for modern browsers. Specify cablecar.png in the images folder as the poster image and indicate that browsers should display video controls. Add a reference to the file cablecar.m4v in the media folder as a source file and specify that the file is in MP4 format. Add a reference to the file cablecar.webm in the media folder as a second source file and specify that the file is in WebM format.

c. Save your changes, then return to styles.css in your editor. Add the `video` selector to the style rule in the reset styles section that sets border, padding, and margin to 0, then in the `img` style rule in the reset styles section, add the `video` selector. In the main content section, create a style rule for the `video` element that sets the maximum width to 50%, specifies margins of `0.2em 0 0.2em 0.5em`, and floats the element on the right.

d. Save your changes, open nearby.html in a modern browser that supports the `video` element, and verify that the video plays. **FIGURE L-23** shows the web page displaying an HTML5 video.

FIGURE L-23

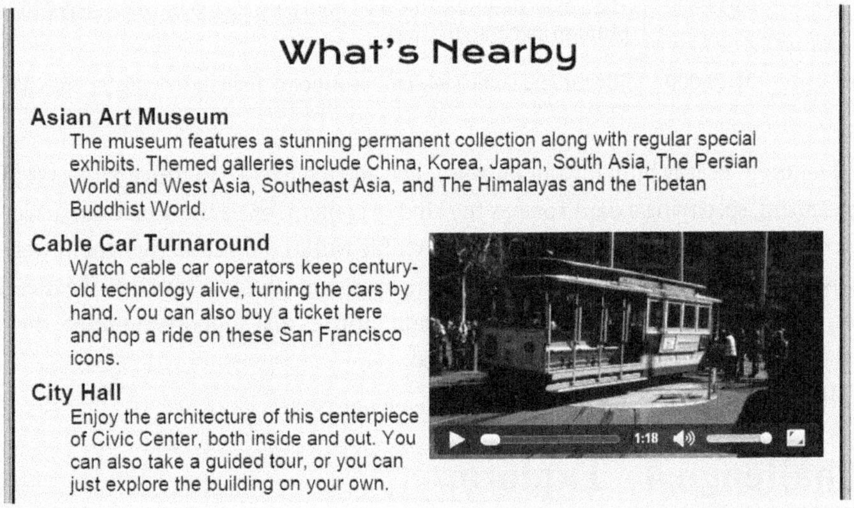

© Courtesy Sasha Vodnik

e. Return to nearby.html in your editor, then add code for a Flash version of the video to the web page. Specify a media type of Flash, a width of 854, and a height of 508. Add a `param` element that specifies a name of `movie` and value of `media/cablecar.swf`, then add another `param` element that specifies a name of `base` and a value of `media`.

f. Save your changes. If you have access to a browser, such as IE8, that does not recognize the `video` element and that has the Flash Player plugin installed, open nearby.html and verify that the video plays.

g. Return to nearby.html, then add the file cablecar.png in the images folder as a fallback image for the Flash code. Specify a width of 854 and a height of 480, and provide appropriate alt text.

h. Save your changes. If you have access to a browser that does not recognize the `video` element and does not have the Flash Player plugin installed, open nearby.html and verify that the fallback image is displayed.

i. Return to captions.vtt in your editor, then add the cues shown in **TABLE L-11**.

TABLE L-11

name	start time	end time	content
1	00:01.000	00:08.000	[Train running on rails]
2	00:10.000	00:49.000	[People talking indistinctly]
3	00:50.000	01:18.000	[Train running on rails]

© 2016 Cengage Learning

Independent Challenge 3 (continued)

j. Save your changes, return to descriptions.vtt in your editor, then add the cues shown in **TABLE L-12**.

TABLE L-12

name	start time	end time	content
1	00:00.000	00:06.000	A cable car runs down a track toward a circular wooden platform.
2	00:08.000	00:10.000	The train stops on the platform and the conductor hops off the side of the car.
3	00:15.000	00:18.000	The conductor uses a metal rod to start the wooden platform rotating.
4	00:25.000	00:43.000	The conductor pushes against the side of the car as it continues to rotate with the platform.
5	00:44.000	00:46.000	The platform stops rotating with the car aligned with a different track.
6	00:47.000	00:55.000	The conductor pushes the train from behind, and the train begins to roll off the platform and onto the track.
7	00:56.000	01:18.000	The car rolls completely off the platform, then the conductor hops back on the car.

© 2016 Cengage Learning

k. Save your changes, return to nearby.html in your browser, then add a reference to the captions.vtt file within the `video` element, specifying a `captions` as the kind of content, `en` as the source language, and label of **English captions**. Add a reference to the descriptions.vtt file within the `video` element as well, specifying a `descriptions` as the kind of content, `en` as the source language, and label of **English descriptions**.

l. Save your changes, refresh or reload nearby.html in a modern browser that supports captions, then play the video and verify that the captions you created are displayed.

m. Validate your HTML and CSS files.

Independent Challenge 4 – Explore

The owners of Eating Well in Season would like to incorporate a video of food being prepared on the page that lists sample menus.

a. In your editor, open HTM_L-17.html from the IC4 folder where you store your Data Files for this unit, save it as **menus.html**, then repeat to save HTM_L-18.css as **styles.css**, and HTM_L-19.vtt as **descriptions.vtt**. In the comment section at the top of each file, enter your name and today's date where indicated, then save the files.

b. Return to menus.html in your editor, then in the `article` element and above the `div` element with the `class` value `article-content-container`, add code to incorporate a video for modern browsers. Specify chef.png in the images folder as the poster image. Add attributes to indicate that browsers should play the video automatically when the page loads and that they should automatically start the video again from the beginning when it finishes. (*Hint*: Use the `autoplay` attribute to start the video automatically and the `loop` attribute to automatically restart the video. Do not include the `controls` attribute.) Add a reference to the file chef.m4v in the media folder as a source file and specify that the file is in MP4 format. Add a reference to the file chef.webm in the media folder as a second source file and specify that the file is in WebM format.

c. Save your changes, then return to styles.css in your editor. Add the `video` selector to the style rule in the reset styles section that sets border, padding, and margin to 0, then in the `img` style rule in the reset styles section, add the `video` selector. In the main content section, create a style rule for the `video` element that absolutely positions the element at the top of the containing element. In the `.article-content-container` style rule, add declarations that relatively position the element, set the z-index to 2, and set the opacity to 0.7. (*Hint*: Use the `opacity` property to set the opacity.) In the `article` style rule, add the declaration `overflow: hidden;`, then add a declaration that relatively positions the element.

Independent Challenge 4 – Explore (continued)

d. Save your changes. Open menus.html in a modern browser that supports the video element and verify that the video plays. The video should be displayed behind the menu text, and the white background of the menu content should be mostly opaque, as shown in **FIGURE L-24**. In addition, the video should play automatically when the page loads, and the video should automatically restart from the beginning when it reaches the end. (*Note*: The video may take several seconds to load and play after the page opens.)

FIGURE L-24

e. Return to menus.html in your editor, then add code for a Flash version of the video to the web page. Specify a media type of Flash, a width of 854, and a height of 480. Add a `param` element that specifies a name of `movie` and value of `media/chef.swf`, add another `param` element that specifies a name of `base` and a value of `media`, then add a third `param` element that specifies a name of `loop` and a value of `true`. (*Note*: The `param` element with the `loop` name performs the same function for a Flash video as the `loop` attribute for the `video` element.)

f. Save your changes. If you have access to a browser, such as IE8, that does not recognize the `video` element and that has the Flash Player plugin installed, open started.html and verify that the video plays. (*Note*: Older browsers including IE8 do not support the `opacity` property, so the video may not be visible in these browsers.)

g. Return to menus.html, then add the file chef.png in the images folder as a fallback image for the Flash code. Specify a width of 854 and a height of 480, and provide appropriate alt text.

h. Save your changes. If you have access to a browser that does not recognize the `video` element and does not have the Flash Player plugin installed, open menus.html and verify that the fallback image is displayed.

i. Return to descriptions.vtt in your editor, then create a cue that describes the visual content of the video. Be sure that the cue has a unique name, correctly formatted starting and ending times, and text content.

j. Save your changes, return to menus.html in your browser, then add a reference to the descriptions.vtt file within the `video` element as well, specifying a `descriptions` as the kind of content, `en` as the source language, and label of **English descriptions**. (*Note*: Because the video does not contain an audio track, there is no need for captions.)

k. Save your changes, then validate your HTML and CSS files.

Visual Workshop

In your editor, open the file HTM_L-20.html from the VW folder where you store your Data Files for this unit and save it as **readers.html**. Repeat to save HTM_L-21.css as **styles.css**. Add your first and last names and today's date to the comment section at the top of each file, then save your changes. Use your editor to add the audio clips rumi.mp3, rumi.ogg, and rumi.swf from the media folder. When you're finished, your web page should match FIGURE L-25. Verify that your file works in modern browsers as well as in older browsers. Validate your HTML and CSS code.

FIGURE L-25

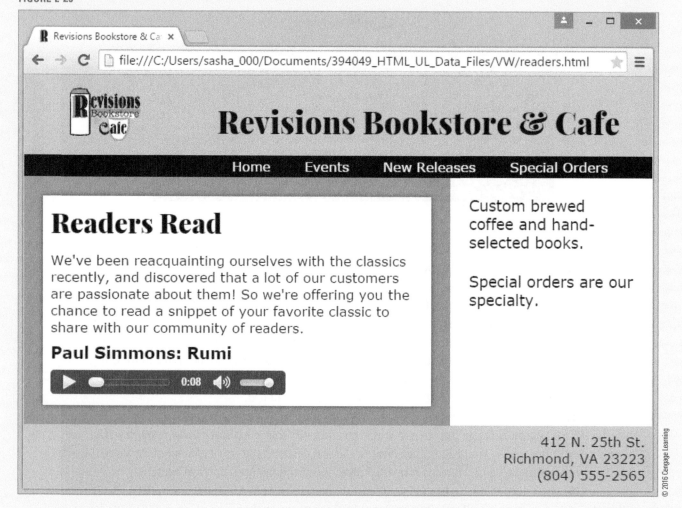

Incorporating Video and Audio

Programming Web Pages with JavaScript

| **CASE** | Phillip Blaine, the owner of Lakeland Reeds Bed & Breakfast, would like the feedback form on his website to show a preview of the message that will be sent. You will create the code for this feature using JavaScript. |

Unit Objectives

After completing this unit, you will be able to:

- Explore the Document Object Model
- Access elements and properties using JavaScript
- Create statements
- Store and access data in variables

- Create a function
- Add an event listener
- Change CSS with JavaScript
- Create an `if` statement

Files You Will Need

 L   9 files   IC3   13 files

 SR   10 files   IC4   8 files

 IC1   11 files   VW   8 files

 IC2   9 files

For specific filenames, see Filenames_M.pdf in the Unit M Data Files folder.

Explore the Document Object Model

Learning
Outcomes
• Describe the
  components of
  the Document
  Object Model

HTML and CSS enable you to create and manipulate a limited set of web page elements and properties. You can increase the range of actions you can perform on web page elements by writing and including programs with your web pages. The most widely used programming language for modern web browsers is **JavaScript**, which you can use to reference and change data associated with parts of HTML documents. Writing code to accomplish this requires a standardized way of referring to the parts of a web page; this system is known as the **Document Object Model (DOM)**. You can think of the DOM as a hierarchical arrangement of the content of an HTML document into a tree-like structure, which is known as the **DOM tree**. **FIGURE M-1** shows the code for a simple web page along with its corresponding DOM tree. Each item in the DOM tree—including elements, attributes, and text content—is known as a **node.** **CASE** ▶ *You review the underlying concepts of the DOM in preparation for working with JavaScript.*

DETAILS

You create code by combining several types of information associated with a node:

*   **Objects**

    In the DOM, each HTML element is considered an **object**. To retrieve data from or make changes to a web page element, you must first write code that identifies the specific object you want to work with. One of the most straightforward ways to reference an object is by using a CSS selector that identifies it. You can also reference an object using its id or class attribute value.

*   **Properties**

    Each DOM node is associated with a standard set of information; each piece of information is known as a **property**. Standard properties for objects include the text content associated with an object, the name of the object, and the name of an associated attribute. Each attribute represents its own node and is associated with its own properties, including its value. **TABLE M-1** lists a few commonly referenced properties.

*   **Methods**

    The DOM also defines **methods**, which are actions that are associated with an object. For instance, you can access any HTML element by specifying a CSS selector using the querySelector() method. Method names are always followed by parentheses. When using a method, you specify information that the method uses between the parentheses. For the querySelector() method, you specify within the parentheses a CSS selector that identifies the desired element. For instance, to access an element with the id value nameinput, you would use the CSS selector #nameinput, so the code to access this element would be querySelector("#nameinput"). **TABLE M-2** lists a few commonly used methods.

TABLE M-1: Commonly used properties

property	refers to	example
classValue	the value of an element's class attribute	one or more class names, separated by spaces
innerHTML	the content of an object, including any nested HTML tags; compatible with IE8	the text in a p element
src	the path and source filename for an element with an src attribute	the path and filename for an image
textContent	the text content of an object, excluding any nested HTML tags; not compatible with IE8	the text in a p element
value	the current value of a form field or an object property	the value of the href property for an a element

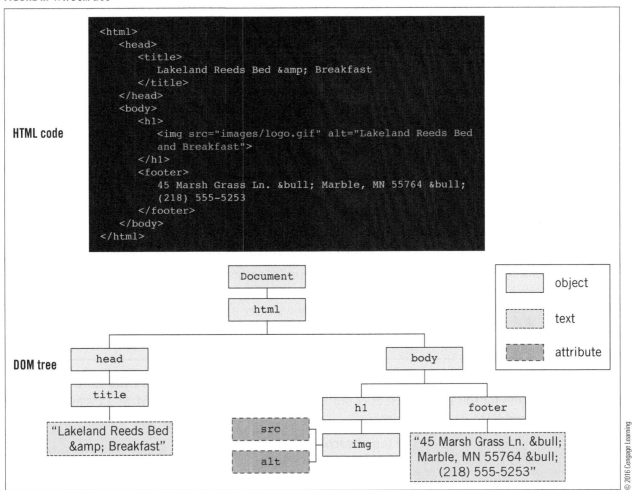

HTML code

DOM tree

TABLE M-2: **Commonly used methods**

method	associated action
addEventListener("*event*", *code*, *useCapture*)	monitors the specified object for the occurrence of *event*, and runs *code* in response
querySelector("*selector*")	accesses the element specified by *selector*, which is a CSS selector

Changing pointer appearance with CSS

The mouse pointer can take several different shapes in a browser, depending on the content it is over. The most common shapes are a pointing hand 👆 when over a link, an I-beam ⌶ when over text, and an arrow ⬉ when over an image. However, you can use JavaScript to make elements clickable even when they aren't links. As a result, the pointer may, for example, be displayed as an I-beam ⌶ even when the text it's over is clickable. This can be confusing for users, who may, without even realizing it consciously, expect that if the pointer is not a pointing hand 👆, then an item is not clickable. Fortunately, you can specify which pointer a browser should display over a given element using the CSS cursor property. To specify a pointing hand 👆, you use the pointer value; an I-beam ⌶, the text value; and an arrow ⬉, the default value.

HTML5 & CSS3

Learning
Outcomes
• Reference an
  element with
  JavaScript
• Reference a
  property with
  JavaScript

Access Elements and Properties Using JavaScript

One of the basic building blocks of JavaScript code is references to objects and properties on a web page using methods such as querySelector(). Every method is the child of an object, and querySelector() is a child of the **Document object**, which is the parent element of the DOM tree. Whenever you use a method, you specify its parent object first, followed by a period and then the method name, so any time you use the querySelector() method, you specify it in your code as document.querySelector(). You specify a CSS selector in quotes within the parentheses of the querySelector() method to reference an object. You can also add another dot and the name of a property associated with the selected element to reference that property. For example, you could use the code document.querySelector("aside") to reference the aside element, and then add a dot and the textContent property name to access the text content of this element, resulting in the code document.querySelector("aside").textContent. The **console**, which is part of the developer tools in a modern web browser, can be used to enter test code and view error messages related to JavaScript. **CASE** ▸ *Before you create a JavaScript document, you practice referencing objects and their properties using a browser console.*

STEPS

QUICK TIP
You will learn about
the use and syntax
of .js files later in
this unit.

1. **In your editor, open HTM_M-1.html from the Lessons folder where you store your Data Files for this unit, save it as contact.html, then repeat to save HTM_M-2.css as styles.css and HTM_M-3.js as script.js**

2. **In the comment at the top of each file, enter your name and today's date where indicated, then save the files**

   The script.js file will contain JavaScript code. Multi-line comments in JavaScript use the same format as CSS comments.

3. **Open contact.html in a modern browser**

   The document contains a contact form for submitting questions to Lakeland Reeds. It also includes a section at the bottom of the page that shows a preview of the message that will be sent based on the form contents.

TROUBLE
If your browser
indicates that it is
blocking some
content, click the
Allow blocked
content button or
similar button to
allow the content to
be processed.

4. **Open the console using the appropriate command from** TABLE M-3

   The console may be displayed as a pane at the bottom of the browser window or as a separate window. If your console displays error messages, you can ignore them for now.

5. **Click on the command line, type** document.querySelector("h2").textContent, **then press [Enter]**

   Below the code you typed, the console displays "Contact Us", which is the content of the h2 heading. FIGURE M-2 shows the code and the result in the consoles of the 3 major browsers.

6. **On the command line, type** document.querySelector("#nameinput").value, **then press [Enter]**

   The element with the id value nameinput is the first text box in the form. You use the value property to reference the value entered in a form field. In this case, the form field is blank, so the value returned in the console is an empty string ("").

7. **Click in the Name box on the form, type Faduma Egal, then press [Tab]**

8. **Click on the command line, type** document.querySelector("#nameinput").value, **then press [Enter]**

   Because you entered a name in the first form field, the console reports that value, as shown in FIGURE M-3.

FIGURE M-2: The browser console in modern browsers

Chrome

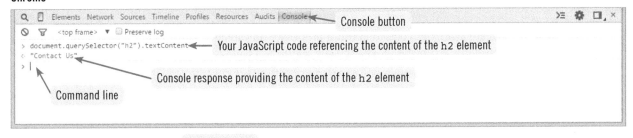

Firefox

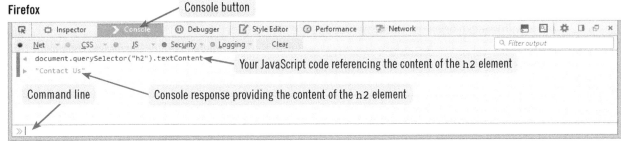

Internet Explorer

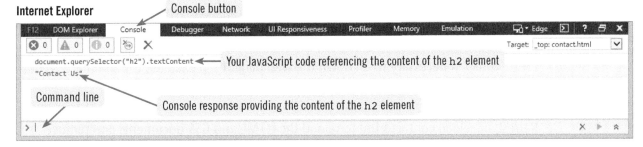

FIGURE M-3: Value of first form field in Chrome console

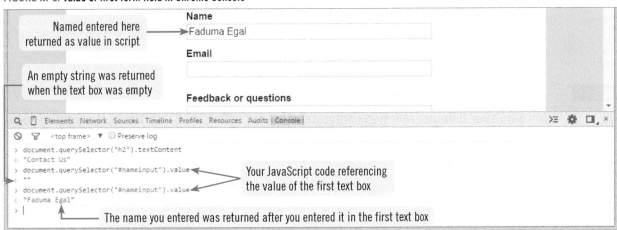

TABLE M-3: Steps to open the console in major browsers

browser	keyboard shortcut	menu steps
Chrome	Ctrl + Shift + J (Win) option + command + J (Mac)	Click the Customize and control Google Chrome button ≡, point to More tools, then click JavaScript console.
Firefox	Ctrl + Shift + K (Win) option + command + K (Mac)	Click the Open menu button ≡, click Developer, then click Web Console.
Internet Explorer	F12, then Ctrl + 2	Click the Tools button ⚙, click F12 Developer Tools on the menu, then in the window that opens, click the Console button.

Create Statements

Learning
Outcomes
• Write a JavaScript
statement

Once you create JavaScript code to access a property, you can add to the code to make changes to that property. You do so by creating a **statement**, which is a JavaScript instruction that performs an action. One of the most common actions you can perform with a Javascript statement is to assign a new property value. To do so, you use the **assignment operator**, which is simply an equal sign (=). The code on the left side of the equal sign accesses the property. The code to the right of the equal sign specifies the new value for the property, and is often enclosed in quotes. Every JavaScript statement ends with a semicolon (;). Statements are created in an external JavaScript file, which is a text file with a name that ends with the extension .js. Then, the `script` element is added to an HTML document to reference the external JavaScript file. **CASE** ▶ *You experiment with the assignment operator by creating statements that assign sample values to the two empty paragraphs in the summary section below the form.*

STEPS

TROUBLE
Be sure to enter
the selector as
`.feedback-from`
rather than
`.feedback-form`.

1. **On the command line, type**
   ```
   document.querySelector(".feedback-from").textContent = "Faduma Egal"
   ```
   The code to the left of the equal sign references the text content of the element with the `class` value `feedback-from`, which is the p element that follows the text "From:" in the summary section below the form. The name to the right of the equal sign is the value you want to assign.

2. **Press [Enter], if necessary scroll down the web page, then examine the summary section below the form**
   The name Faduma Egal is now displayed to the right of the text From:, as shown in **FIGURE M-4**.

TROUBLE
If reloading does not
remove the changes,
open contact.html in
a new tab.

3. **Refresh or reload contact.html to reload the HTML and CSS documents and remove your command line changes**

4. **Return to script.js in your editor, type the following code below the comment section, then press [Enter]:**
   ```
   document.querySelector(".feedback-from").textContent = "Faduma Egal";
   ```

5. **Type** `document.querySelector(".feedback-content").textContent = "Do you allow pets?";`
   Your script.js file contains two statements, as shown in **FIGURE M-5**.

TROUBLE
If the text shown in
FIGURE M-7 is not
displayed in your
browser, return to
script.js in your editor,
compare your
statements with the
code shown in
Steps 4 and 5, and
ensure that both lines
end with a semicolon.

6. **Save your changes, return to contact.html in your editor, then near the bottom of the document, just before the closing </body> tag, type** `<script src="script.js"></script>`
   The `script` element associates the specified JavaScript file with the current HTML document. **FIGURE M-6** shows the updated HTML code.

7. **Save your changes, refresh or reload contact.html in your browser, then scroll down to the bottom of the page**
   The two statements in the script.js file are executed when the page loads, and the text content is added as shown in **FIGURE M-7**.

Debugging JavaScript code

As with HTML and CSS code, sometimes the JavaScript code that you write doesn't produce the results you expect. In such cases, your first step should be to open the browser console, check for any error messages, and then examine the referenced location in your code for possible errors. In cases when errors are difficult to locate, a few simple troubleshooting steps can help you identify and fix most errors. First, check capitalization. Because JavaScript is case-sensitive, references to properties, methods, objects, or variables with inconsistent capitalization can produce unpredictable results. Next, check punctuation. Each statement should end with a semicolon, and, single and double quotes, parentheses, and braces ({ }) must occur in matched sets.

FIGURE M-4: Text content assigned to an element with JavaScript

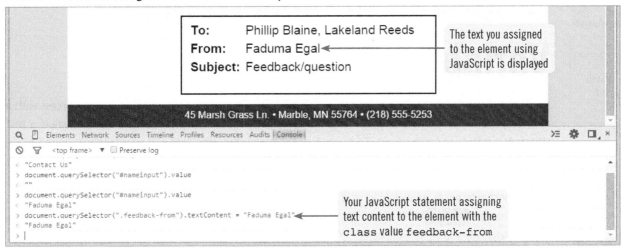

The text you assigned to the element using JavaScript is displayed

Your JavaScript statement assigning text content to the element with the `class` value `feedback-from`

FIGURE M-5: Statements added to script.js file

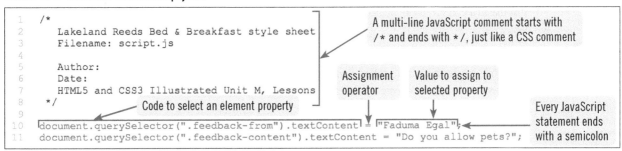

A multi-line JavaScript comment starts with `/*` and ends with `*/`, just like a CSS comment

Assignment operator

Value to assign to selected property

Code to select an element property

Every JavaScript statement ends with a semicolon

FIGURE M-6: `script` element added to HTML document

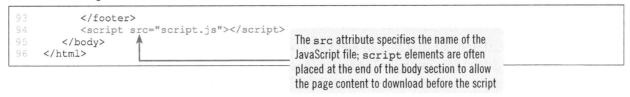

The `src` attribute specifies the name of the JavaScript file; `script` elements are often placed at the end of the body section to allow the page content to download before the script

FIGURE M-7: Content added to web page elements by JavaScript statements in external file

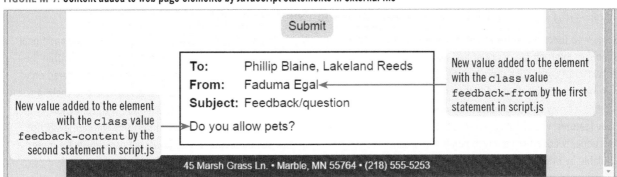

New value added to the element with the `class` value `feedback-from` by the first statement in script.js

New value added to the element with the `class` value `feedback-content` by the second statement in script.js

Learning
Outcomes
• Create a variable
  and assign it a
  value

Store and Access Data in Variables

JavaScript allows you to create **variables**, which are values that are stored and that you can access with a name that you specify. A variable can store many types of information, including a numeric value, a text string, or a reference to an object. To create a variable, you type the keyword `var` followed by the name to assign to the variable, an equal sign, and the variable value, as shown in **FIGURE M-8**. Because shorter JavaScript statements are generally easier for developers to understand and troubleshoot, it's common to store object references as variables, and then reference the objects in subsequent statements using the variable names. **CASE** ▶ *To shorten the statements in your JavaScript code, you create variables to store the object references, and replace the object references in your statements with the variable names.*

STEPS

1. **Return to** script.js **in your editor, then below the opening comment, insert two new lines**

2. **Type** `/* create variables */`**, then press [Enter]**
   Just like in a CSS file, it can be helpful to add a comment at the start of each section of a longer JavaScript file.

QUICK TIP
Some editors display keywords like `var` in italics. Like other formatting applied in a text editor, this is ignored when the code is rendered in a browser.

3. **Type** `var fromValue = document.querySelector(".feedback-from");`**, then press [Enter]**
   This code creates a variable called `fromValue`. As its value, it stores a reference to the element with the `class` value `feedback-from`, which is an element that one of your existing statements modifies.

4. **Type** `var feedbackValue = document.querySelector(".feedback-content");`
   This code creates a variable named `feedbackValue` and stores a reference to the element with the `class` value `feedback-content` as its value. JavaScript variable names cannot include spaces, so when creating a name that contains multiple words, it's common to use **camel case**, in which the first letter of the first word is lowercase and the first letter of each new word is capitalized.

QUICK TIP
Be sure not to delete `.textContent` at the end of the element reference in the statement.

5. **In the statement that sets an element's text value to "Faduma Egal", replace the code** `document.querySelector(".feedback-from")` **with** `fromValue`
   This change shortens your existing statement by replacing the element reference with a variable name.

6. **In the statement that sets an element's text value to "Do you allow pets?", replace the code** `document.querySelector(".feedback-content")` **with** `feedbackValue`
   The completed code to create and reference variables is shown in **FIGURE M-9**.

QUICK TIP
Although the page is unchanged, your statements are now shorter and more legible.

7. **Save your changes, then refresh or reload** contact.html **in your browser**
   Because the variables reference the same elements that your code previously referenced, the page is unchanged, as shown in **FIGURE M-10**.

Preserving accessibility for user agents that don't support scripting

Some web users access pages with browsers or devices that are unable to interpret JavaScript or that can't access the full range of JavaScript code. Such users may be using older browsers, may have JavaScript disabled in their browsers for security reasons, or may be using assistive devices. As with other web page features, you should ensure that any content or functionality added to your web pages with a script is also available by other means. While it's generally straightforward to create pages that degrade gracefully without any additional code, it's sometimes useful to add fallback content within the HTML `noscript` element, whose contents are rendered only when JavaScript isn't available. If it isn't possible to make a scripted page accessible, another option is to create an alternative page that is displayed for users without JavaScript access. Search on the phrase *JavaScript accessibility* for more details on creating accessible scripts.

FIGURE M-8: Syntax for creating a variable

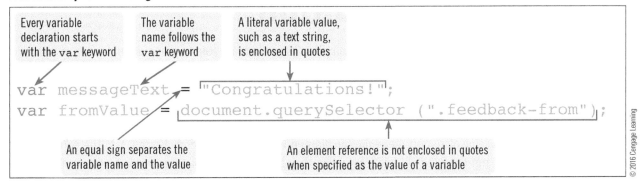

Every variable declaration starts with the `var` keyword

The variable name follows the `var` keyword

A literal variable value, such as a text string, is enclosed in quotes

```
var messageText = "Congratulations!";
var fromValue = document.querySelector (".feedback-from");
```

An equal sign separates the variable name and the value

An element reference is not enclosed in quotes when specified as the value of a variable

© 2016 Cengage Learning

FIGURE M-9: Statements creating and referencing variable values

```
1    /*
2        Lakeland Reeds Bed & Breakfast style sheet
3        Filename: script.js
4
5
6
7                          lustrated Unit M, Lessons
8
9
10   /* create variables */
11   var fromValue = document.querySelector(".feedback-from");
12   var feedbackValue = document.querySelector(".feedback-content");
13
14   fromValue.textContent = "Faduma Egal";
15   feedbackValue.textContent = "Do you allow pets?";
```

You use the variable name to reference the variable's value in other statements

The variable value is a reference to an object in the HTML document

The variable names take the place of the object references

FIGURE M-10: Web page unchanged after element references stored in variables

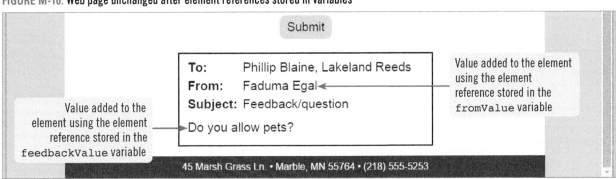

Submit

To: Phillip Blaine, Lakeland Reeds
From: Faduma Egal
Subject: Feedback/question

Do you allow pets?

45 Marsh Grass Ln. • Marble, MN 55764 • (218) 555-5253

Value added to the element using the element reference stored in the `feedbackValue` variable

Value added to the element using the element reference stored in the `fromValue` variable

Create a Function

As your JavaScript code becomes more complex, it's useful to be able to group multiple lines of code and reference them as a single unit. JavaScript enables you to do this by creating a **function**, which is a group of one or more statements with an assigned name. A function starts with the keyword `function` followed by a name for the function and a pair of parentheses. The punctuation for a function is similar to that of a CSS style rule: an opening curly brace ({) goes at the beginning; each line of code within the function ends with a semicolon; and the entire function ends with a closing curly brace (}). The contents of a function are not executed automatically when they are parsed by a browser. Instead, you must include a reference to the function name, known as a **function call**, elsewhere in your JavaScript code to indicate when the statements in the function should be executed. FIGURE M-11 illustrates function syntax and execution. **CASE** *You group the two statements that add text content to the preview section within a function and you add a function call to execute them.*

STEPS

1. **Return to** script.js **in your editor**

2. **Indent the statement** `fromValue.textContent = "Faduma Egal";`, **insert a new line above the statement, then type** `/* add text to preview section */`
   A function should always be preceded by a comment that describes what the function does.

3. **Press [Enter], then type** `function completePreview() {`

4. **Indent the statement** `feedbackValue.textContent = "Do you allow pets?";`, **then below it, type** `}`
   FIGURE M-12 shows the completed code for the function.

5. **Save your changes, refresh or reload contact.html in your browser, then scroll down to the preview section**
   The name "Faduma Egal" and the feedback "Do you allow pets?" are not displayed because your JavaScript code does not include a function call for the `completePreview()` function. This means that the statements in the function are parsed by the browser but never executed.

6. **Return to** script.js **in your editor**

7. **Below the closing** } **for the function, add 2 blank lines, then type** `completePreview();`
   This statement is a function call for the `completePreview()` function. FIGURE M-13 shows the completed code.

8. **Save your changes, refresh or reload contact.html in your browser, then scroll down to the preview section**
   The name and question are once again added to the preview section as a result of the function call you added in Step 7, which instructed the browser to execute the statements contained in the function.

FIGURE M-11: Syntax for creating and calling a function

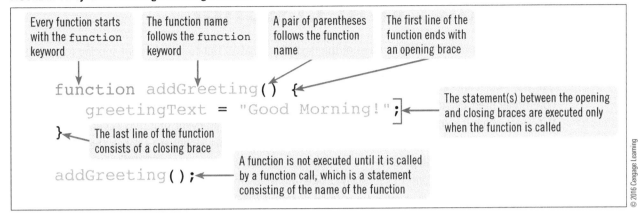

Every function starts with the `function` keyword

The function name follows the `function` keyword

A pair of parentheses follows the function name

The first line of the function ends with an opening brace

```
function addGreeting() {
    greetingText = "Good Morning!";
}
addGreeting();
```

The statement(s) between the opening and closing braces are executed only when the function is called

The last line of the function consists of a closing brace

A function is not executed until it is called by a function call, which is a statement consisting of the name of the function

FIGURE M-12: `completePreview()` function created

```
12    var feedbackValue = document.querySelector(".feedback-content");
13
14    /* add text to preview section */
15    function completePreview() {
16        fromValue.textContent = "Faduma Egal";
17        feedbackValue.textContent = "Do you allow pets?";
18    }
```

New function created with the name `completePreview()`

Statements within function indented for readability

FIGURE M-13: Function call added to script.js file

```
14    function completePreview() {
15        fromValue.textContent = "Faduma Egal";
16        feedbackValue.textContent = "Do you allow pets?";
17    }
18
19    completePreview();
```

Function call for the `completePreview()` function

Implementing jQuery and other libraries

Web developers using JavaScript for more complex applications often find that they need to use the same sets of code repeatedly in different contexts to create the same effects. In response to this common situation, developers group reusable code in collections known as **libraries**. By attaching a single script file containing a library to a web page document, developers instantly have access to all the functions stored in the file. Many freely distributable libraries are available online; currently, jQuery is one of the most popular libraries in use. Developers who use jQuery or other libraries still create programs with JavaScript, but they use libraries to simplify the process of writing complex code.

© 2016 Cengage Learning

HTML5 & CSS3

Programming Web Pages with JavaScript

361

Add an Event Listener

Developers commonly take advantage of the flexibility of JavaScript to add content specific to each user and in response to a user's actions. Developers can write JavaScript that responds to actions, known as **events**, which include many actions commonly performed on a web page. TABLE M-4 lists several commonly used events. To call a function in response to a user action, a developer creates an **event listener**, which is a statement that specifies a web page object, an event that may occur on that object, and the name of a function that is called when that event happens. FIGURE M-14 details the code for event listeners and the relationship between event listeners, events, and functions. **CASE** *You want the value of the Name field in the form to be displayed after the word From: in the preview section, and you want the contents of the Feedback or questions box to be displayed below the Subject line in the preview section. You update the function and create an event listener to transfer this information after users type it.*

STEPS

1. **Return to script.js in your editor, then below the statement that creates the** `feedbackValue` **variable, add a new line, then enter the statements in Lines 13–15 of** FIGURE M-15
   These new variables store references to the Name box, the Feedback or questions box, and the form itself.

2. **Within the** `completePreview()` **function and in the first statement, delete the value** `"Faduma Egal"` **(including the quotes), then replace it with** `nameField.value`
   The edited statement adds the text in the Name box to the preview section.

3. **Within the** `completePreview()` **function and in the second statement, delete the value** `"Do you allow pets?"` **(including the quotes), then replace it with** `feedbackField.value`
   The edited statement adds the text in the Feedback or questions box to the preview section.

4. **Above the statement** `completePreview();`**, insert a line, type** `/*`**, then below the statement, insert a line and type** `*/`
   You will not need the function call after you create an event listener, so it is now commented out.

5. **Add two new lines to the end of the file, then add the comment and the event listener shown in Lines 27 and 28 of** FIGURE M-15
   The event listener references the form and when the `change` event occurs for that element, calls the `completePreview()` function. Note that when you reference a function in an event listener, you do not include the parentheses after the function name. The completed code is shown in FIGURE M-15.

TROUBLE
If reloading does not
clear the information
you entered earlier,
open the page in a
new tab.

6. **Save your changes, refresh or reload contact.html in your browser, then scroll down to the preview section**
   No text is displayed after the word From: or below the Subject line. With the changes you just made to your code, this is the expected behavior.

7. **Click the Name box in the form, type your first and last name, press [Tab], then scroll down to the preview section**
   When you pressed Tab and moved to a different form field, the `change` event was initiated on the Name box. The event listener then called the `completePreview()` function, which copied your entry from the Name box to the preview section after the word From:.

8. **Click the Feedback or questions box on the form, type What time is checkout?, press [Tab], then scroll down to the preview section**
   Again, when you pressed Tab, the `change` event was initiated on the Feedback or questions box. The event listener then called the `completePreview()` function, which copied your entry from the Feedback or questions box to the preview section below the Subject line.

FIGURE M-14: Syntax for creating an event listener and relationship with events and functions

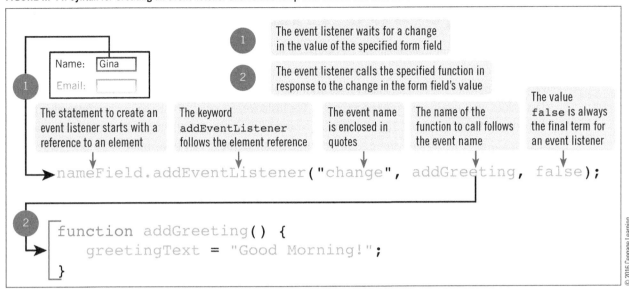

① The event listener waits for a change in the value of the specified form field

② The event listener calls the specified function in response to the change in the form field's value

The statement to create an event listener starts with a reference to an element

The keyword `addEventListener` follows the element reference

The event name is enclosed in quotes

The name of the function to call follows the event name

The value `false` is always the final term for an event listener

```
nameField.addEventListener("change", addGreeting, false);

function addGreeting() {
    greetingText = "Good Morning!";
}
```

FIGURE M-15: Updated code with event listener

```
10   /* create variables */
11   var fromValue = document.querySelector(".feedback-from");
12   var feedbackValue = document.querySelector(".feedback-content");
13   var nameField = document.querySelector("#nameinput");
14   var feedbackField = document.querySelector("#other-info");
15   var form = document.querySelector(".contact-form");
16
17   /* add form text to preview section */
18   function completePreview() {
19       fromValue.textContent = nameField.value;
20       feedbackValue.textContent = feedbackField.value;
21   }
22
23   /*
24   completePreview();
25   */
26
27   /* create event listener for changes to form */
28   form.addEventListener("change", completePreview, false);
```

New variables reference values in form fields

The updated statement copies the value from the Name field to the summary section

The updated statement copies the value from the Feedback or questions field to the summary section

Function call commented out

The event listener is set on the object referenced by the `form` variable

The event listener responds to the `change` event

The event listener calls the `completePreview` function

TABLE M-4: Commonly used events

event	description	event	description
change	the value of an element changes	mouseover	a user moves the mouse pointer over an element or touches an element
click	a user clicks or touches an element	submit	a user submits a form
load	a document or image loads	touchend	a user removes a finger or stylus from the screen
mouseout	a user moves the mouse pointer off an element or stops touching an element	touchstart	a user touches a finger or stylus to the screen

Change CSS with JavaScript

Learning
Outcomes
• Add a class
  value to an object
  with JavaScript

You can use JavaScript to change the CSS styles of an element in response to a user's actions. A common method is to create a style rule for the new appearance of an element using a `class` selector, and then use JavaScript to add or remove class values from the element in response to events. To access an element's class values, you use its `className` property. For instance, to assign the `highlight` class value to the element identified by the `pullQuote` variable, you would use the statement `pullQuote.className = "highlight";`. Recall that the `class` attribute of an element can have more than one value, with multiple values separated by spaces. If the element already had a `class` value of `main-article`, you could add the `class` value `highlight` with the statement `pullQuote.className = "main-article highlight";`, which preserves the existing `class` value and adds the new one as well. **FIGURE M-16** illustrates this process. **CASE** *The preview section isn't particularly helpful until a user enters text in the form. You change the CSS for the page to hide the preview section by default; you create a style rule based on a CSS class selector to change the `display` property to `block`; and then you add a JavaScript statement to add the new `class` value to the preview section when a user makes a change to the form.*

STEPS

1. **Return to** styles.css **in your editor, scroll down to the feedback preview section, then in the** `.feedback-preview` **style rule, add the declaration** `display: none;`

QUICK TIP
A style rule like the
`.show` rule that
should overrule
another rule with the
same specificity must
appear below the
other style rule in the
style sheet.

2. **Below the closing } for the** `.feedback-preview` **style rule, add a new style rule using the** `.show` **selector and the declaration** `display: block;`
   FIGURE M-17 shows the updates to the CSS code.

3. **Save your changes, then return to** script.js **in your editor**

4. **In the create variables section, below the statement that begins with** `var form`**, add a new line, then type the following statement:**
   `var feedbackPreview = document.querySelector(".feedback-preview");`
   This statement creates a new variable named `feedbackPreview` that references the element with the `class` value `feedback-preview`. This is the `div` element that contains the preview section below the form on the web page.

5. **In the code for the** `completePreview()` **function, above the final }, insert a new line and type** `feedbackPreview.className = "feedback-preview show";`
   The code to the left of the equal sign specifies the `className` property for the element selected by the `feedbackPreview` variable, and the code to the right of the equal sign specifies a new value that includes the `class` values `feedback-preview` and `show`. Because the HTML code for the element already specifies the `class` value `feedback-preview`, the statement you entered has the effect of adding the `class` value `show` to the element. **FIGURE M-18** shows the updated JavaScript code.

6. **Save your changes, refresh or reload** contact.html **in your browser, then scroll to the bottom of the page**
   The preview section is hidden as a result of the change you made to the `.feedback-preview` style rule in Step 1. **FIGURE M-19** shows the bottom of the web page when it is opened.

7. **Click the** Name box**, type your first and last name, then press** [Tab]
   The preview section is now displayed and includes your name after the text From:, as in previous lessons. This is because the new JavaScript statement you added is part of the function that is called every time a change is made to the form.

FIGURE M-16: Adding a `class` value with JavaScript

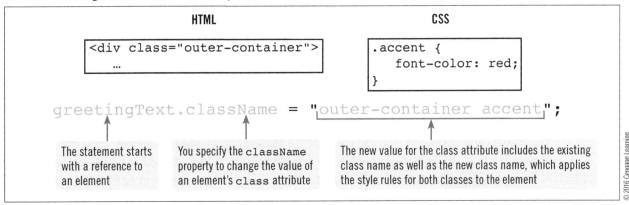

HTML	CSS

`<div class="outer-container">`
    `...`
	`.accent {`
	    `font-color: red;`
	`}`

`greetingText.className = "outer-container accent";`

The statement starts with a reference to an element

You specify the `className` property to change the value of an element's `class` attribute

The new value for the class attribute includes the existing class name as well as the new class name, which applies the style rules for both classes to the element

© 2016 Cengage Learning

FIGURE M-17: Changes to style rules

```
177    /* feedback preview section */
178    .feedback-preview {
179        max-width: 400px;
180        padding: 10px;
181        margin: 0 auto;
182        border: 2px solid black;
183        font-size: 1.3em;
184        background-color: white;
185        display: none;
186    }
187    .show {
188        display: block;
189    }
```

The preview section is no longer displayed by default when the page opens

You can add the `class` value `show` to an element to make it visible on the page

FIGURE M-18: Statements added to create new variable and change `class` value

```
10    /* create variables */
11    var fromValue = document.querySelector(".feedback-from");
12    var feedbackValue = document.querySelector(".feedback-content");
13    var nameField = document.querySelector("#nameinput");
14    var feedbackField = document.querySelector("#other-info");
15    var form = document.querySelector(".contact-form");
16    var feedbackPreview = document.querySelector(".feedback-preview");
17
18    /* add form text to preview
19    function completePreview() {
20        fromValue.textContent = nameField.value;
21        feedbackValue.textContent = feedbackField.value;
22        feedbackPreview.className = "feedback-preview show";
23    }
```

Specifies the `className` property for the element selected by the `feedbackPreview` variable

Specifies a new value that includes the `class` values `feedback-preview` and `show`

FIGURE M-19: Preview section hidden when web page opens

The preview section is between the Submit button and the footer, but it is no longer displayed by default

Submit

45 Marsh Grass Ln. • Marble, MN 55764 • (218) 555-5253

Create an `if` Statement

JavaScript supports the use of symbols known as **operators** to compare or change the values of multiple objects or properties. You've already used the assignment operator (=), which enables you to assign a value to an object. In addition, JavaScript lets you analyze and manipulate values in more complex ways. You can compare values of different elements using **comparison operators**, which let you determine whether two values are the same or different. TABLE M-5 describes 3 of the most commonly used operators. Using comparison operators, you can create an **if statement**, in which two values are compared and if the result is true, one or more statements are executed. FIGURE M-20 illustrates the syntax and usage of `if` statements. **CASE** ▶ *Because all fields in the form are required, you decide to turn off the display of the Submit button until all fields are completed. You use an `if` statement to show the Submit button again when the form is ready to submit.*

STEPS

1. **Return to** script.js **in your editor**

2. **In the create variables section, below the final variable declaration, add a new line, then type** `var submitButton = document.querySelector(".submitbutton");`
   This statement creates a new variable named `submitButton` that references the element with the `class` value `submitbutton` (the `fieldset` element containing the Submit button).

3. **In the code for the** `completePreview()` **function, add a new line above the closing },** **indent 3 spaces, then type** `if (form.checkValidity() === true) {`
   The keyword `if` starts the `if` statement. The code in parentheses is the condition that must be true for the remaining code to be executed. This condition uses the equal operator (===) to check if the value provided by the `checkValidity()` method for the element referenced by the `form` variable is `true`.

4. **Press [Enter], indent 6 spaces, then type**
   `submitButton.className = "submitbutton show";`
   If the condition in the previous line is true, this statement is executed; if not, this statement is not executed.

5. **Press [Enter], indent 3 spaces, then type** }
   The braces ({ }) enclose the code to be executed if the condition is true. FIGURE M-21 shows the updated code for the `completePreview()` function.

6. **Save your changes, return to styles.css in your editor, scroll down to the fieldset styles section, then below the** `.reserveinfo` **style rule, add the style rule shown in** FIGURE M-22

7. **Save your changes, refresh or reload contact.html in your browser, then scroll to the bottom of the page**
   The Submit button is now hidden by default along with the preview section.

8. **Click the** Name box, **type your first and last name, press [Tab], type your email address, press [Tab], type** What time is checkout?, **then press [Tab]**
   After you complete all 3 fields and move the focus out of the final field, the form is valid and the condition in the `if` statement becomes true. As a result, the `class` value `show` is added to the fieldset with the `class` value `submitbutton` and the Submit button is displayed once again.

9. **Validate your HTML and CSS code**

FIGURE M-20: Syntax for creating an `if` statement

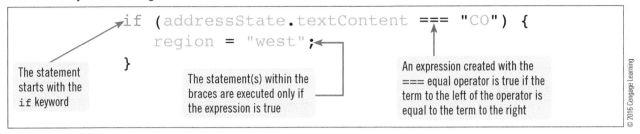

The statement starts with the `if` keyword

The statement(s) within the braces are executed only if the expression is true

An expression created with the `===` equal operator is true if the term to the left of the operator is equal to the term to the right

© 2016 Cengage Learning

FIGURE M-21: New variable created and conditional statement added

```
16    var feedbackPreview = document.querySelector(".feedback-preview");
17    var submitButton = document.querySelector(".submitbutton");
18
19    /* add form text to preview section */
20    function completePreview() {
21        fromValue.textContent = nameField.value;
22        feedbackValue.textContent = feedbackField.value;
23        feedbackPreview.className = "feedback-preview show";
24        if (form.checkValidity() === true) {
25            submitButton.className = "submitbutton show";
26        }
27    }
```

The condition must be true for the code in braces to be executed

Conditional statement

FIGURE M-22: `.submitbutton` style rule added

```
144    .submitbutton {
145        display: none;
146    }
147
148    /* field styles */
```

TABLE M-5: Operators

operator name	operator	description	example
assignment	=	assigns the value on the right to the object on the left	`var name = "Faduma"`
equal	===	true if the value on the left is equal to the value on the right	`if (a === b)`
not equal	!==	true if the value on the left is not equal to the value on the right	`if (a !== b)`

© 2016 Cengage Learning

Scripting fallback options with Modernizr

You've already seen how to use the `class` values that the Modernizr library generates to provide fallback code for some features within a stylesheet. However, some modern HTML and CSS capabilities cannot be duplicated in older browsers using CSS alone. You can create fallback code for additional features using JavaScript. To do so, you create a conditional statement that checks for objects that Modernizr generates when it checks for browser features. For instance, if the `placeholder` attribute of the `input` element is supported, Modernizr generates an object named `Modernizr.input.placeholder`. You can add code to a JavaScript document that replicates some or all of the behavior of the `placeholder` attribute, then place the code within a conditional statement that checks whether the relevant Modernizr object exists. The additional code is executed only if the object does not exist. This ensures that your code does not interfere with browser functionality in modern browsers but still replicates desired features in older browsers.

Practice

Concepts Review

Refer to FIGURE M-23 **to answer the following.**

FIGURE M-23

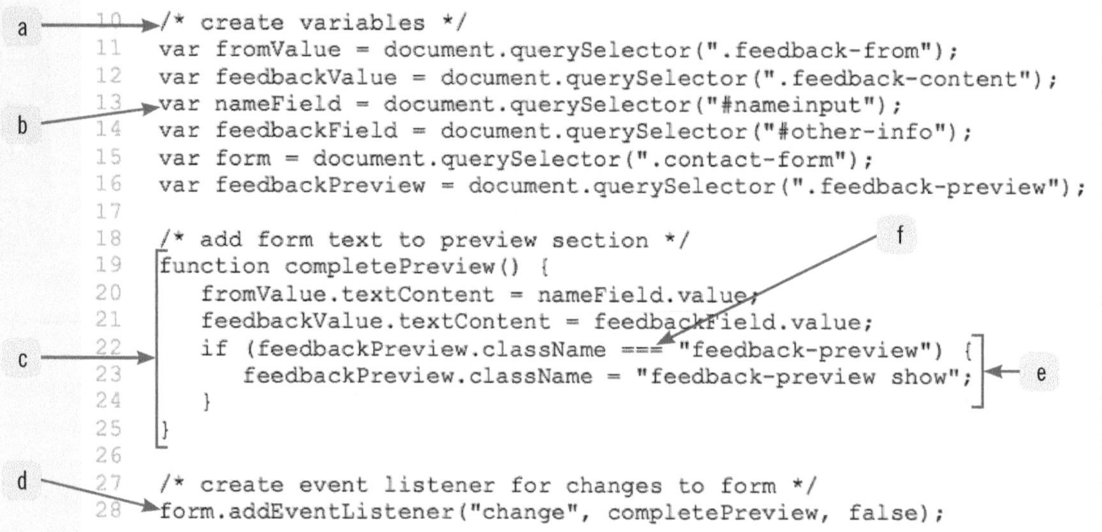

```
10   /* create variables */
11   var fromValue = document.querySelector(".feedback-from");
12   var feedbackValue = document.querySelector(".feedback-content");
13   var nameField = document.querySelector("#nameinput");
14   var feedbackField = document.querySelector("#other-info");
15   var form = document.querySelector(".contact-form");
16   var feedbackPreview = document.querySelector(".feedback-preview");
17
18   /* add form text to preview section */
19   function completePreview() {
20       fromValue.textContent = nameField.value;
21       feedbackValue.textContent = feedbackField.value;
22       if (feedbackPreview.className === "feedback-preview") {
23           feedbackPreview.className = "feedback-preview show";
24       }
25   }
26
27   /* create event listener for changes to form */
28   form.addEventListener("change", completePreview, false);
```

a — 10
b — 13
c — 22
d — 27
f
e — 23

1. **Which item is a conditional operator?**
2. **Which item creates a variable?**
3. **Which creates an if statement?**
4. **Which item creates a function?**
5. **Which item creates a comment?**
6. **Which item creates an event listener?**

Match each term with the statement that best describes it.

7. **DOM**
8. **object**
9. **property**
10. **statement**
11. **variable**
12. **function**

a. a JavaScript instruction that performs an action
b. a group of one or more statements with an assigned name
c. a piece of information associated with a DOM node
d. a value that is stored and that you can access with a name that you specify
e. a standardized way of referring to the parts of a web page
f. an HTML element in the DOM

Select the best answer from the list of choices.

13. The equal sign (=) is known in JavaScript as the _____.

  a. assignment operator   **c.** inequality operator

  b. equality operator   **d.** comparison operator

14. To execute the statements in a function, you use a(n) _____.

  a. property   **c.** function call

  b. object   **d.** `if` statement

15. An action on a web page that JavaScript code can respond to is known as a(n) _____.

  a. property   **c.** event listener

  b. event   **d.** function

16. You can use a(n) _____ to call a function in response to an event.

  a. event listener   **c.** property

  b. function call   **d.** variable

17. Code that compares two values and executes one or more statements if the result is true is a(n) _____?

  a. variable   **c.** function

  b. node   **d.** `if` statement

Skills Review

1. Access elements and properties using JavaScript.

  a. In your editor, open HTM_M-4.html from the SR folder where you store your Data Files for this unit, save it as **catering.html**, then repeat to save the file HTM_M-5.css as **styles.css**. and the file HTM_M-6.js as **script.js**.

  b. Within the comment section at the top of each file, enter your first and last names and today's date, then save your changes.

  c. Open catering.html in a modern browser, then open the browser console.

  d. On the command line, type `document.querySelector("h1").textContent`, press **[Enter]**, then verify that the response in the console matches the h1 element. (*Note*: If your browser indicates that it is blocking some content, click the Allow blocked content button or similar button to allow the content to be processed.)

  e. On the command line, type `document.querySelector("#emailinput").value`, press **[Enter]**, then verify that the response in the console is an empty string ("").

  f. In the Email box on the form, type your email address, then press **[Tab]**.

  g. On the command line, type `document.querySelector("#emailinput").value`, press **[Enter]**, then verify that the console responds with the email address you entered.

2. Create statements.

  a. On the command line, type `document.querySelector(".request-from").textContent = "Jan Mercutio"`.

  b. Press **[Enter]**, if necessary scroll down the web page, verify that Jan Mercutio is displayed after the word From: in the summary section below the form, then refresh or reload catering.html. (*Note*: If reloading does not remove the changes, open contact.html in a new tab.)

  c. Return to script.js in your editor, type `document.querySelector(".request-from").textContent = "Jan Mercutio";` below the comment section, then press **[Enter]**.

  d. Type `document.querySelector(".request-content").textContent = "How far in advance do I need to reserve?";`.

  e. Save your changes, return to catering.html in your editor, then near the bottom of the document, just before the closing `</body>` tag, enter a `script` element with script.js as its source.

Skills Review (continued)

f. Save your changes, refresh or reload contact.html in your browser, scroll down to the bottom of the page, then verify that *Jan Mercutio* is displayed after the word From: and *How far in advance to I need to reserve?* is displayed below the Subject line.

3. Store and access data in variables.

a. Return to script.js in your editor, below the opening comment insert two new lines, then enter a comment containing the text **create variables**.

b. Type `var nameContent = document.querySelector(".request-from");`, then press **[Enter]**.

c. Type `var feedbackContent = document.querySelector(".request-content");`.

d. In the statement that sets an element's text value to "Jan Mercutio", replace the code `document.querySelector(".request-from")` with **nameContent**.

e. In the statement that sets an element's text value to "How far in advance do I need to reserve?", replace the code `document.querySelector(".request-content")` with **feedbackContent**.

f. Save your changes, refresh or reload contact.html in your browser, then verify that the same text is displayed in the preview section as described in Step 2f.

4. Create a function.

a. Return to script.js in your editor.

b. Indent the statement `nameContent.textContent = "Jan Mercutio";`, insert a new line above the statement, then add a comment containing the text **add form text to preview section**.

c. Press **[Enter]**, then type `function updatePreview() {`.

d. Indent the statement `feedbackContent.textContent = "How far in advance do I need to reserve?";`, insert a new line below it, then on the new line type `}`.

e. Save your changes, refresh or reload contact.html in your browser, scroll down to the preview section, then verify that no text appears after the word From: or below the Subject line.

f. Return to script.js in your editor, below the closing `}` for the function, add 2 blank lines, then type `updatePreview();`.

g. Save your changes, refresh or reload contact.html in your browser, scroll down to the preview section, then verify that the same text is displayed in the preview section as described in Step 2f.

5. Add an event listener.

a. Return to script.js in your editor, then below the statement that creates the `feedbackContent` variable, add a new line, then enter the following three statements:

```
var nameInput = document.querySelector("#nameinput");
var feedbackInput = document.querySelector("#other-info");
var form = document.querySelector(".catering-form");
```

b. Within the `updatePreview()` function and in the first statement, delete the value `"Jan Mercutio"` (including the quotes), then replace it with **nameInput.value**.

c. Within the `updatePreview()` function and in the second statement, delete the value `"How far in advance do I need to reserve?"` (including the quotes), then replace it with **feedbackInput.value**.

d. Add opening and closing comment characters around the statement `updatePreview();` at the bottom of the document to transform it into a comment.

e. Add two new lines to the end of the file, add a comment containing the text **create event listener for changes to form**, then on a new line add the statement `form.addEventListener("change", updatePreview, false);`.

f. Save your changes, refresh or reload contact.html in your browser, scroll down to the preview section, then verify that no text appears after the word From: or below the Subject line.

Skills Review (continued)

g. Click the Name box in the form, type your first and last name, click the Event information box on the form, type **What is the minimum event size that you cater?**, press **[Tab]**, scroll down to the preview section, then verify that the text you entered is displayed in the expected locations in the preview section, as shown in FIGURE M-24.

FIGURE M-24

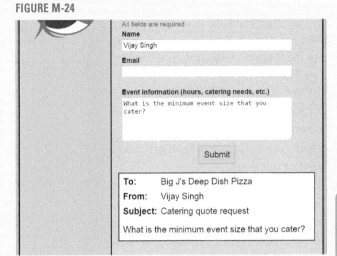

6. **Change CSS with JavaScript.**

a. Return to styles.css in your editor, scroll down to the catering preview section, then in the `.catering-preview` style rule, add the declaration `display: none;`.

b. Below the closing } for the `.catering-preview` style rule, add a new style rule using the `.show` selector and the declaration `display: block;`.

c. Save your changes, then return to script.js in your editor

d. In the create variables section, below the statement that begins with `var  form`, add a new line, then type the following statement:

`var cateringPreview = document.querySelector(".catering-preview");`

e. In the code for the `updatePreview()` function and above the final }, insert a new line, indent as needed, then type `cateringPreview.className = "catering-preview show";`.

f. Save your changes, refresh or reload contact.html in your browser, scroll to the bottom of the page, then verify that the preview section is not displayed.

g. Click the Name box, type your first and last name, press **[Tab]**, then verify that the preview section is displayed at the bottom of the page and your name is displayed after the From: text.

7. **Create an `if` statement.**

a. Return to script.js in your editor.

b. In the create variables section, below the final variable declaration, add a new line, then type

`var submitButton = document.querySelector(".submitbutton");`

c. In the code for the `updatePreview()` function, add a new line above the closing }, indent as needed, then type

`if (form.checkValidity() === true) {`.

d. Press **[Enter]**, indent as needed, then type `submitButton.className = "submitbutton show";`.

e. Press **[Enter]**, indent 3 spaces, then type }.

f. Save your changes, return to styles.css in your editor, scroll down to the fieldset styles section, then in the `.submitbutton` style rule, add the declaration `display: none;`.

g. Save your changes, refresh or reload contact.html in your browser, scroll to the bottom of the page, then verify that neither the Submit button nor the preview section is displayed.

h. Click the Name box, type your first and last name, press **[Tab]**, then verify that the preview section is displayed while the Submit button is still not displayed.

i. Type your email address, press **[Tab]**, type **What is the minimum event size that you cater?**, press **[Tab]**, then verify that the Submit button is displayed.

j. Validate your HTML and CSS code.

Independent Challenge 1

Sarah Nguyen, the manager of the Spotted Wren Garden Center, would like you to add a couple features to the form on the company's website. She'd like the specified placeholder text to be displayed no matter what browser a user opens the site on. In addition, she'd like boilerplate text automatically inserted in the Additional Information section if users select certain options in the Project Area section. You'll incorporate scripts into the website to add the requested features.

a. In your editor, open HTM_M-7.html from the IC1 folder where you store your Data Files for this unit, save it as **resource.html**, then repeat to save HTM_M-8.css as **styles.css** and HTM_M-9.js as **script.js**. In the comment section at the top of each file, enter your name and today's date where indicated, then save the files.

b. Open resource.html in a browser, click the text Blanket flower, Hedge rose, and Little bluestem, and verify that nothing happens.

c. Return to script.js in your editor, below the comment section add a comment for a section in which you will create variables, then below the new comment add statements to create the following variables:
- A variable named `list` that references an element using the selector `.choices-list`
- A variable named `blanket` that references an element using the selector `.choices-list li:first-of-type`
- A variable named `hedge` that references an element using the selector `.choices-list li:nth-of-type(2)`
- A variable named `bluestem` that references an element using the selector `.choices-list li:last-of-type`
- A variable named `figureImage` that references an element using the selector `article figure img`
- A variable named `figureCaption` that references an element using the selector `article figure figcaption`

d. Below the statement for the final variable, insert 2 blank lines, then add a comment for a function that will change the image to show the blanket flower. Create a function with the name `showBlanket()` that includes 3 statements:
- A statement that selects the `src` property of the element selected by the `figureImage` variable and sets its value to `"images/blanket.jpg"` (including the quotes)
- A statement that selects the `alt` property of the element selected by the `figureImage` variable and sets its value to `"a single blossom of a blanket flower"` (including the quotes)
- A statement that selects the `textContent` property of the element selected by the `figureCaption` variable and sets its value to `"Blanket flower"` (including the quotes)

e. Repeat Step d to create a second function named `showHedge()` that selects the same properties and sets the value of the first to `"images/rugosa.jpg"`, the second to `"a sprawling, low hedge rose plant with several flowers"`, and the third to `"Hedge rose"`.

f. Repeat Step d to create a third function named `showBluestem()` that selects the same properties and sets the value of the first to `"images/bluestem.jpg"`, the second to `"a cluster of little bluestem in a field"`, and the third to `"Little bluestem"`.

g. Below the third function, insert 2 blank lines, then add a comment for the event listeners section. Below the comment, create an event listener for the element selected by the `blanket` variable that responds to the `click` event and calls the `showBlanket()` function. (*Hint:* Do not include the parentheses after `showBlanket` when naming the function in the event listener statement.) Repeat to create an event listener for the element selected by the `hedge` variable that calls the `showHedge()` function, then repeat again to create an event listener for the element selected by the `bluestem` variable that calls the `showBluestem()` function.

h. Save your changes, return to resource.html, then at the bottom of the document, just above the closing `</body>` tag, add a `script` element and specify script.js as its source.

Independent Challenge 1 (continued)

i. Save your changes, then refresh or reload resource.html in your browser. Click **Hedge rose**, then verify that the image on the right changes as shown in **FIGURE M-25**. Click **Little bluestem** and verify that the image changes to a different image. Click **Blanket flower** and verify that the image changes back to the original image that was displayed when you opened the page.

j. Validate your HTML and CSS files.

FIGURE M-25

Independent Challenge 2

As you continue to develop the website for the Murfreesboro Regional Soccer League, you decide to compact the contents of the Schedules page and make the content interactive using scripts. You'll add JavaScript code that displays the schedule for a single team at a time based on which button a user clicks.

a. In your editor, open HTM_M-10.html from the IC2 folder where you store your Data Files for this unit, save it as **schedule.html**, then repeat to save HTM_M-11.css as **styles.css** and HTM_M-12.js as **script.js**. In the comment section at the top of each file, enter your name and today's date where indicated, then save the files.

b. Open schedule.html in a browser, click the Red, Green, Blue, and Yellow buttons, and verify that nothing happens.

c. Return to script.js in your editor, below the comment section add a comment for a section in which you will create variables, then below the new comment add statements to create the following variables:
  - A variable named `redButton` that references the element with the class value `.red-team-button`
  - A variable named `blueButton` that references the element with the class value `.blue-team-button`
  - A variable named `greenButton` that references the element with the class value `.green-team-button`
  - A variable named `yellowButton` that references the element with the class value `.yellow-team-button`
  - A variable named `redSchedule` that references the element with the class value `.red-team-schedule`
  - A variable named `blueSchedule` that references the element with the class value `.blue-team-schedule`
  - A variable named `greenSchedule` that references the element with the class value `.green-team-schedule`
  - A variable named `yellowSchedule` that references the element with the class value `.yellow-team-schedule`

d. Save your changes, return to styles.css in your editor, then in the main content tables section, below the `th` style rule, add a style rule for the elements with the `class` values `red-team-schedule`, `blue-team-schedule`, `green-team-schedule`, and `yellow-team-schedule` that turns off the display of these elements. Below the new style rule, add a rule for elements with the `class` value `show` that sets `display` to `block`. Save your changes, refresh or reload schedule.html in your browser, then verify that no schedules are displayed.

e. Return to script.js in your editor, below the statement for the final variable, insert 2 blank lines, then add a comment for a function that will show the red team schedule and hide the other schedules. Create a function with the name `showRed()` that includes 4 statements:
  - A statement that selects the `className` property of the element selected by the `redSchedule` variable and sets its value to `"red-team-schedule show"` (including the quotes)
  - A statement that selects the `className` property of the element selected by the `blueSchedule` variable and sets its value to `"blue-team-schedule"` (including the quotes)
  - A statement that selects the `className` property of the element selected by the `greenSchedule` variable and sets its value to `"green-team-schedule"` (including the quotes)
  - A statement that selects the `className` property of the element selected by the `yellowSchedule` variable and sets its value to `"yellow-team-schedule"` (including the quotes)

Independent Challenge 2 (continued)

f. Repeat Step e three times to create three additional functions:
- a function named `showBlue()` that selects the same properties and sets the value of the first property to `"red-team-schedule"`, the second property to `"blue-team-schedule show"`, the third property to `"green-team-schedule"`, and the fourth property to `"yellow-team-schedule"`.
- a function named `showGreen()` that selects the same properties and sets the value of the first property to `"red-team-schedule"`, the second property to `"blue-team-schedule"`, the third property to `"green-team-schedule show"`, and the fourth property to `"yellow-team-schedule"`.
- a function named `showYellow()` that selects the same properties and sets the value of the first property to `"red-team-schedule"`, the second property to `"blue-team-schedule"`, the third property to `"green-team-schedule"`, and the fourth property to `"yellow-team-schedule show"`.

g. Below the fourth function, insert 2 blank lines, then add a comment for the event listeners section. Below the comment, create an event listener for the element selected by the `redButton` variable that responds to the `click` event and calls the `showRed()` function. (*Hint*: Do not include the parentheses after `showRed` when naming the function in the event listener statement.) Repeat to create an event listener for the element selected by the `blueButton` variable that calls the `showBlue()` function, an event listener for the element selected by the `greenButton` variable that calls the `showGreen()` function, and an event listener for the element selected by the `yellowButton` variable that calls the `showYellow()` function.

h. Save your changes, return to schedule.html, then at the bottom of the document, just above the closing `</body>` tag, add a `script` element and specify script.js as its source.

i. Save your changes, refresh or reload schedule.html in your browser, then verify that none of the schedules are displayed. Click the **Red button**, then verify that the Red schedule is displayed as shown in FIGURE M-26. Click the **Blue button**, the **Green button**, and the **Yellow button** and verify that the appropriate schedule is displayed after you click each one.

j. Validate your HTML and CSS files.

FIGURE M-26

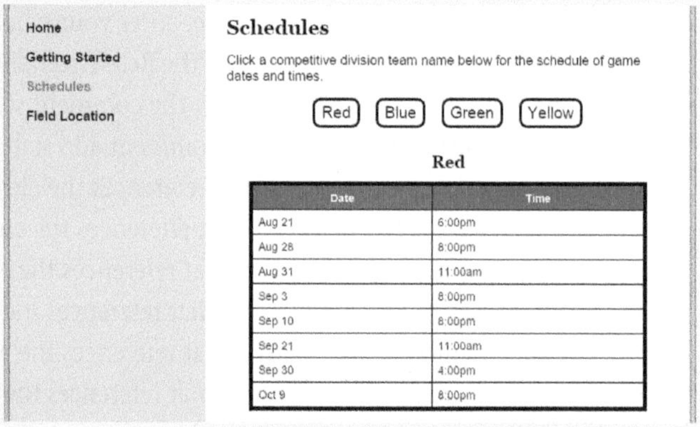

Independent Challenge 3

Diego Merckx, the manager of the Hotel Natoma, would like to make the list of local attractions on the hotel's website interactive. When a user clicks the name of an attraction, he'd like the web page to display an image of the attraction as well as a description. You create JavaScript code to add this functionality.

a. In your editor, open HTM_M-13.html from the IC3 folder where you store your Data Files for this unit, save it as **nearby.html**, then repeat to save HTM_M-14.css as **styles.css** and HTM_M-15.js as **script.js**. In the comment section at the top of each file, enter your name and today's date where indicated, then save the files.

b. Open nearby.html in a browser, click each of the 5 headings on the right side of the page, and verify that nothing happens.

Independent Challenge 3 (continued)

c. Return to script.js in your editor, below the comment section add a comment for a section in which you will create variables, then below the new comment add statements to create the 12 variables described in TABLE M-6.

TABLE M-6

variable name	CSS selector	variable name	CSS selector
aamHead	.aam h3	ccplazaHead	.ccplaza h3
aamParagraph	.aam p	ccplazaParagraph	.ccplaza p
cablecarHead	.cablecar h3	unplazaHead	.unplaza h3
cablecarParagraph	.cablecar p	unplazaParagraph	.unplaza p
cityhallHead	.cityhall h3	figureImage	figure img
cityhallParagraph	.cityhall p	figureCaption	figcaption

© 2016 Cengage Learning

d. Save your changes, return to styles.css in your editor, then in the main content section, add a declaration to the `article p` style rule that turns off the display of these elements. Below the `figcaption` style rule, add a rule for elements with the `class` value `show` that sets `display` to `block`. Save your changes, refresh or reload schedule.html in your browser, then verify that the description paragraphs are no longer displayed.

e. Return to script.js in your editor, below the statement for the final variable, insert 2 blank lines, then add a comment for a function that will show the Asian Art Museum paragraph and image and hide the other paragraphs. Create a function with the name `showAam()` that includes 8 statements that do the following:

- select the `className` property of the element selected by the `aamParagraph` variable and sets its value to `"show"` (including the quotes)
- select the `className` property of the element selected by the `cablecarParagraph` variable and sets its value to `""` (an empty string)
- select the `className` property of the element selected by the `cityhallParagraph` variable and sets its value to `""` (an empty string)
- select the `className` property of the element selected by the `ccplazaParagraph` variable and sets its value to `""` (an empty string)
- select the `className` property of the element selected by the `unplazaParagraph` variable and sets its value to `""` (an empty string)
- select the `src` property of the element selected by the `figureImage` variable and sets its value to `"images/aam.jpg"` (including the quotes)
- select the `alt` property of the element selected by the `figureImage` variable and sets its value to appropriate alt text for the image (enclosed in quotes)
- select the `textContent` property of the element selected by the `figureCaption` variable and sets its value to `"Asian Art Museum"` (including the quotes)

Independent Challenge 3 (continued)

f. Repeat Step e four times to create four additional functions. Select the same properties and variable references, and set them to the values described in **TABLE M-7**.

TABLE M-7

function name	value 1	value 2	value 3	value 4	value 5	value 6	value 8*
showCablecar()	""	"show"	""	""	""	"images/cablecar.jpg"	Cable Car Turnaround
showCityhall()	""	""	"show"	""	""	"images/cityhall.jpg"	City Hall
showCcplaza()	""	""	""	"show"	""	"images/ccplaza.jpg"	Civic Center Plaza
showUnplaza()	""	""	""	""	"show"	"images/unplaza.jpg"	United Nations Plaza

© 2016 Cengage Learning

* Value 7 should be appropriate alt text for the image specified by value 6.

g. Below the fifth function, insert 2 blank lines, then add a comment for the event listeners section. Below the comment, create an event listener for the element selected by the `aamHead` variable that responds to the `click` event and calls the `showAam()` function. (*Hint*: Do not include the parentheses after `showAam` when naming the function in the event listener statement.) Repeat to create an event listener for the element selected by the `cablecarHead` variable that calls the `showCablecar()` function, an event listener for the element selected by the `cityhallHead` variable that calls the `showCityhall()` function, an event listener for the element selected by the `ccplazaHead` variable that calls the `showCcplaza()` function, and an event listener for the element selected by the `unplazaHead` variable that calls the `showUnplaza()` function.

h. Save your changes, return to nearby.html, then at the bottom of the document, just above the closing `</body>` tag, add a `script` element and specify script.js as its source.

FIGURE M-27

i. Save your changes, then refresh or reload nearby.html in your browser. Click the heading **Asian Art Museum**, then verify that the descriptive paragraph is displayed below the heading and the image of the Asian Art Museum is displayed to the right with the appropriate caption as shown in **FIGURE M-27**. Click each of the remaining 4 headings and verify that the appropriate descriptive text, image, and caption are displayed after you click each one.

j. Validate your HTML and CSS files.

What's Nearby

Asian Art Museum
The museum features a stunning permanent collection along with regular special exhibits. Themed galleries include China, Korea, Japan, South Asia, The Persian World and West Asia, Southeast Asia, and The Himalayas and the Tibetan Buddhist World.

Cable Car Turnaround

City Hall

Civic Center Plaza

United Nations Plaza

Asian Art Museum

568 Natoma St. • San Francisco, CA 94103 • (415) 555-8378

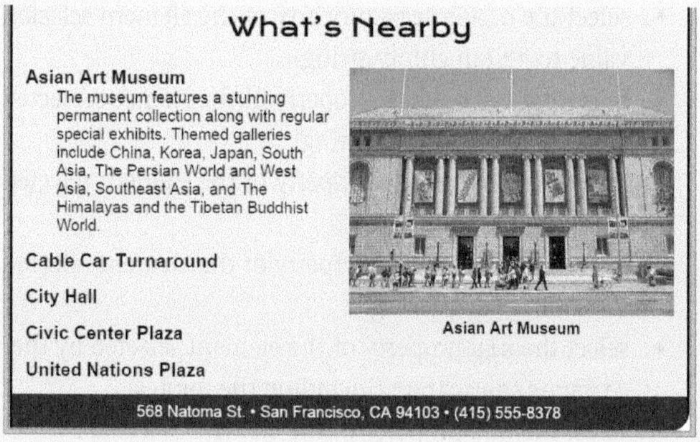

© Eric Broder Van Dyke/Shutterstock.com

Independent Challenge 4 – Explore

The staff at Eating Well in Season is adding functionality to their website that will allow customers to pay for an order online. For users whose information is already on file, they'd like the billing page to let them choose from a list of saved addresses and have the address information automatically filled in in the form fields. You'll write JavaScript to accomplish this.

a. In your editor, open HTM_M-16.html from the IC4 folder where you store your Data Files for this unit, save it as **order.html**, then repeat to save HTM_M-17.css as **styles.css** and HTM_M-18.js as **script.js**. In the comment section at the top of each file, enter your name and today's date where indicated, then save the files.

b. Open order.html in a browser, click Home and Work options buttons, and verify that the form fields remain empty.

Independent Challenge 4 – Explore (continued)

c. Return to script.js in your editor, below the comment section add a comment for a section in which you will create variables, then below the new comment add statements to create the following variables. (*Hint*: Refer to the HTML code for the elements described below to identify the best selector to use for each.)

- A variable named `homeOption` that references the option button with the label Home
- A variable named `workOption` that references the option button with the label Work
- A variable named `streetInput` that references the text box with the label Street Address
- A variable named `cityInput` that references the text box with the label City
- A variable named `stateInput` that references the text box with the label State
- A variable named `zipInput` that references the text box with the label Zip

d. Below the statement for the final variable, insert 2 blank lines, then add a comment for a function that will populate the form fields with home address information. Create a function with a name that you choose and that includes 5 statements:

- A statement that assigns "1 Main St." (including quotes) as the value of the element selected by the `streetInput` variable
- A statement that assigns "Sicilia" (including quotes) as the value of the element selected by the `cityInput` variable
- A statement that assigns "ME" (including quotes) as the value of the element selected by the `stateInput` variable
- A statement that assigns "03900" (including quotes) as the value of the element selected by the `zipInput` variable
- An `if` statement that assigns the `class` names `submitbutton` and `show` to the element selected by the `submitButton` variable if the data entered in the form is valid

e. Below the function you created in the previous step, insert 2 blank lines, then add a comment for a function that will populate the form fields with work address information. Create a function with a name that you choose and that includes 5 statements:

- A statement that assigns "15 Columbine Ln." (including quotes) as the value of the element selected by the `streetInput` variable
- A statement that assigns "Crab City" (including quotes) as the value of the element selected by the `cityInput` variable
- A statement that assigns "ME" (including quotes) as the value of the element selected by the `stateInput` variable
- A statement that assigns "04993" (including quotes) as the value of the element selected by the `zipInput` variable
- An `if` statement that assigns the `class` names `submitbutton` and `show` to the element selected by the `submitButton` variable if the data entered in the form is valid

f. Below the second function, insert 2 blank lines, then add a comment for the event listeners section. Below the comment, create an event listener for the element selected by the `homeOption` variable that responds to the `click` event and calls the function that you created in Step d. Repeat to create an event listener for the element selected by the `workOption` variable that calls the function that you created in Step e.

g. Save your changes, return to order.html, then at the bottom of the document, just above the closing `</body>` tag, add a `script` element and specify script.js as its source.

h. Save your changes, refresh or reload order.html in your browser, click the **Home option button**, then verify that the address information displayed below the Home option button is added to the appropriate form fields as shown in FIGURE M-28. Click the **Work option button**, then verify that the address information displayed below the Work option button is added to the appropriate form fields.

i. Validate your HTML and CSS files.

FIGURE M-28

Visual Workshop

In your editor, open the file HTM_M-19.html from the VW folder where you store your Data Files for this unit and save it as **readers.html**. Repeat to save HTM_M-20.css as **styles.css** and HTM_M-21.js as **script.js**. Add your first and last names and today's date to the comment section at the top of each file, then save your changes. To the left of the nav bar, the web page includes small, medium, and large sizes of the letter A. Create a script that reduces the font size for the entire web page when a user clicks the small A, increases the font size for the entire web page when a user clicks the large A, and returns the font size to its default when a user clicks the middle A. (*Hint*: The style sheet includes a rule for the class value `smaller-size` that sets the font size to a value smaller than the default and a rule for the class value `larger-size` that sets the font size to a value larger than the default. To change the font size for the entire page, you need to change its value for the `html` element.) Also include code that changes the background color to white and the font color to black for the A that corresponds to the style currently assigned to the page, and changes the background color to black and the font color to white for the other buttons. (*Hint*: The style sheet includes a rule for the class value `selected-button` that is assigned by default to the middle A. Create JavaScript code to change which element is assigned this class value.) FIGURE M-29 shows the web page after a user clicks the small A. Validate your HTML and CSS code.

FIGURE M-29

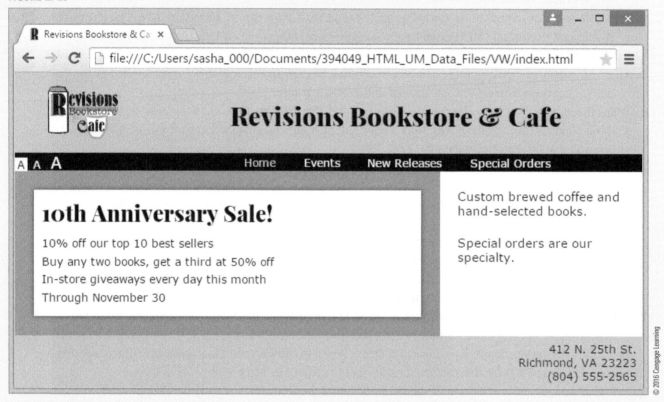

Integrating Social Media

CASE Phillip Blaine would like your help understanding social media and integrating social media tools into the Lakeland Reeds Bed & Breakfast website. In this unit, you'll incorporate some of these tools into the company's website.

Unit Objectives

After completing this unit, you will be able to:

- Evaluate social media
- Add a Facebook Like button
- Add a Twitter Tweet button
- Embed a tweet

- Embed a YouTube video
- Embed an Instagram image
- Integrate a Twitter account feed
- Add a Twitter hash tag feed

Files You Will Need

L	11 files	IC3	9 files
SR	12 files	IC4	10 files
IC1	7 files	VW	7 files
IC2	8 files		

For specific filenames, see Filenames_N.pdf in the Unit N Data Files folder.

Evaluate Social Media

Learning
Outcomes
• Describe the
main ways to
incorporate social
media into a
website

Providing users, customers, and community members with methods for sharing online content and integrating their own comments is at the heart of **social media**. Used correctly, social media can enhance your web presence by enabling people to share information about your business or cause, as well as news that you post on your site, with their friends and colleagues. **CASE** *As you prepare to show Phillip different options for social media tools on the Lakeland Reeds website, you review some of the main ways to incorporate social media into a website.*

DETAILS

There are a few main ways to incorporate social media content into your website:

• **Buttons and other widgets**

Many social media sites offer **widgets**, which consist of prewritten HTML and/or JavaScript code that enables users to provide easy access to their social content from a web page. Different sites provide a variety of tools that developers can use to create widgets. The most commonly used widgets are simple buttons that include the logo of the social network and text describing their function. For instance, Facebook users can include a Like button on a web page, which visitors can click to automatically mark the content on Facebook as something they like. This new like is reflected both on the visitor's Facebook timeline, and on the Facebook page of the person or organization on whose site the button was clicked. Twitter offers buttons that enable visitors to follow a user on Twitter, or to easily tweet a link to the content. **FIGURE N-1** shows a web page with Facebook and Twitter buttons.

• **Embedded content**

Sometimes, you may want to incorporate content posted on social media into your website. All major social media platforms provide tools for the content they host to be embedded on other websites. When content is **embedded** on another site, it is displayed with formatting that matches the host site and it includes links back to the context in which it was originally posted. A single post on Twitter (known as a **tweet**) is one type of social content that is commonly embedded in other sites. In addition, videos from sites such as YouTube and pictures from Instagram and other image hosting sites are often embedded as well. **FIGURE N-2** shows a web page with an embedded video and an embedded tweet.

• **Feeds**

In addition to buttons and embeds, social media sites include other types of widgets. A **feed** is a widget that shows a fixed number of recent posts to a given social media account or shows posts that meet certain criteria. The content of a feed is constantly updated so that it always shows the most recent content matching its criteria. Larger websites tend not to include feeds to avoid cluttering their layouts. However, on a smaller website—especially on one whose content does not often change—incorporating a feed can be a useful way to keep the site's content fresh and to incorporate new information without needing to edit the pages. **FIGURE N-1** shows a web page with a feed.

FIGURE N-2: Web page containing an embedded video and tweet

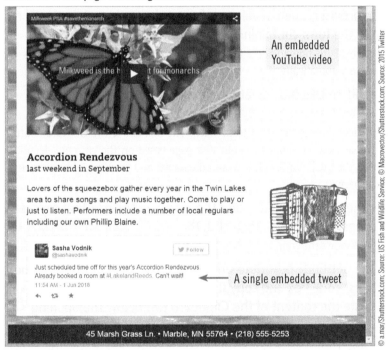

Choosing an appropriate social networking site for your audience

A **social networking site** is a website such as Facebook or LinkedIn that enables people to share information about common interests, news, and events with friends, colleagues, and any other people they choose. While a few social networking sites are widely known across much of the world, many such sites exist. Because different sites are prevalent in different countries or regions or with different groups of people, it's important to consider which site best suits your needs when planning to integrate social media into your website. If the geographic focus of your business or organization is limited, you should familiarize yourself with the most popular sites for the relevant area. For instance, while Facebook is a popular social networking site in North America,

you may find a significant number of European users on VK, and Chinese users on Sina Weibo. It's also crucial to consider which sites the people you want to connect with are likely to be using; for instance, in North America, Facebook is a popular general-purpose site, while LinkedIn is popular for business and professional networking. Keep in mind as well that while you may already use one or more social networking sites personally, it may make sense to choose an entirely different site for networking for your business or organization. Finally, although membership in a social networking site is generally open to most anyone, users may choose to restrict access to their information and news only to other users whom they know or with whom they share a common interest.

Add a Facebook Like Button

When potential customers view your website, it's a great opportunity to invite them to connect with you on one or more social networks. One of the most commonly used button widgets is the Facebook Like button. The fact that a visitor has liked you is visible to the people in that visitor's network. **CASE** ➤ *You add a Facebook Like button to the Lakeland Reeds home page.*

STEPS

1. **In your editor, open HTM_N-1.html from the Lessons folder where you store your Data Files for this unit, save it as index.html, then repeat to save HTM_N-2.html as events.html and HTM_N-3.js as styles.css**

2. **In the comment at the top of each file, enter your name and today's date where indicated, then save the files**

3. **In your browser, open developers.facebook.com/docs/plugins/like-button, then scroll down to the form containing the Get Code button**
   This page explains how to add a Like button. Completing the form fields lets you generate the code for a Like button automatically.

4. **In the URL to Like box, delete the existing content, then type https://facebook.com/cengagebrain**
   This URL identifies the content to be liked. The box above the Get Code button shows a preview of the content that would be added to your web page based on the current selections, including buttons to be generated, the total number of likes, and the names and thumbnail images of any of your friends who have liked the page.

5. **Under the Layout heading, click the arrow on the box that says standard; from the list that opens, click button, then click the Include Share Button box to uncheck it**
   FIGURE N-3 shows the completed form along with a preview of the button it will generate.

6. **Click the Get Code button to open the Your Plugin Code dialog box, select the content of the first code box and copy it to the Clipboard, return to index.html in your editor, then paste the content of the Clipboard just below the opening <body> tag**

7. **Return to your browser, select the content of the second code box and copy it to the Clipboard, return to index.html in your editor, then paste the contents of the Clipboard just before the closing </nav> tag**
   FIGURE N-4 shows the inserted code.

8. **Save your changes, close the Your Plugin Code window in your browser, then open index.html in your browser**
   As FIGURE N-5 shows, the Like button is displayed to the right of the nav bar.

9. **Click the Like button**
   If you are not logged into Facebook, clicking the Like button opens a window prompting you to log in. Otherwise, a checkmark is added to the Like button and the You like cengagebrain.com. window opens.

10. **Click the Close button, right-click the Like button, click Inspect Element, then examine the code for the Like button in the developer tools**
    The JavaScript code you pasted at the start of the body section added a number of nested elements within the div element for the Like button. The style sheet includes a style for the nav element that sets the display of nested ul, div, and other elements to inline-block, which makes them appear side by side.

FIGURE N-3: Completed form to generate Like button code

The URL of the page to like

The Layout option is changed to button

Click to generate the button code

The Include Share Button box is unchecked

A preview of the button that will be displayed based on your settings

Source: Facebook © 2015

FIGURE N-4: HTML code for Like button inserted in document

```
23      <body>
24          <div id="fb-root"></div>
25          <script>(function(d, s, id) {
26            var js, fjs = d.getElementsByTagName(s)[0];
27            if (d.getElementById(id)) return;
28            js = d.createElement(s); js.id = id;
29            js.src = "//connect.facebook.net/en_US/sdk.js#xfbml=1&version=v2.3";
30            fjs.parentNode.insertBefore(js, fjs);
31          }(document, 'script', 'facebook-jssdk'));</script>
32          <p class="skipnavigation"><a href="#contentstart">Skip navigation</a></p>
33          <header>
34              <h1><img src="images/lakeland.gif" width="659" height="165"
35              alt="Lakeland Reeds Bed and Breakfast"></h1>
36          </header>
37          <nav class="sitenavigation">
38              <ul>
39                  <li><a href="index.html">Home</a></li>
40                  <li><a href="aboutus.html">About Us</a></li>
41                  <li><a href="reserve.html">Reservations</a></li>
42                  <li><a href="events.html">Events</a></li>
43                  <li><a href="https://goo.gl/maps/bwf5R">Directions</a></li>
44              </ul>
45              <div class="fb-like" data-href="https://facebook.com/cengagebrain"
46              data-layout="button" data-action="like" data-show-faces="true"
47              data-share="false"></div>
48          </nav>
```

This code, which was copied from the first box, makes facebook.com scripts available on your site but does not create an element that is visible on the page

This code, which was copied from the second box, contains the code for the Like button

FIGURE N-5: Facebook Like button displayed on web page

The location of the Like button is based on the second set of code you inserted

© Unholy Vault Designs/Shutterstock.com; © 2016 Cengage Learning; Source: Facebook © 2015

Integrating Social Media   383

Add a Twitter Tweet Button

In addition to the Facebook Like button, other common social networking widgets include the Follow and Tweet buttons from Twitter. Visitors click the Follow button to follow the linked account on their Twitter stream. After clicking the Follow button, future updates for the linked account are displayed in the visitor's Twitter feed. The Tweet button provides a shortcut for a visitor to share a link to the current page with their followers on Twitter. **CASE** *You add a Twitter Tweet button to the main Lakeland Reeds web page.*

STEPS

TROUBLE
If entering this URL
doesn't open the
page for generating
code for buttons, use
a search engine to
search on the phrase
twitter buttons.

1. **In your browser, open about.twitter.com/resources/buttons**
   The page provides options for creating several different buttons.

2. **Click the Share a link option button**
   Button options and a preview section are displayed for the selected option.

3. **Below the Tweet text label, click the Check out this site box, then type Sweet BnB in Northern MN!**

4. **Click the Show count box to uncheck it**
   FIGURE N-6 shows the completed form along with a preview of the button it will generate.

5. **Click the box containing code below the Preview and code heading, then copy it to the Clipboard**

6. **Return to index.html in your editor, then paste the contents of the Clipboard just before the closing </nav> tag**
   FIGURE N-7 shows the inserted code. The code includes an a element, which will display the button, and a script element, which incorporates code from Twitter.

7. **Save your changes, refresh or reload index.html in your browser, then click the Tweet button**
   As **FIGURE N-8** shows, the Tweet button is displayed to the right of the Like button on the nav bar. Clicking the Tweet button opens a window that shows a preview of the tweet and a button you can click to post the tweet.

8. **Close the Share a link on Twitter window**

9. **Right-click the Tweet button, click Inspect Element, then examine the code for the Tweet button in the developer tools**
   As with the Like button, the JavaScript code for the Tweet button added a number of nested elements to the code, including an iframe element.

FIGURE N-6: Completed form to generate Tweet button code

Share a link option button selected

Custom text added in Tweet text section

Show count check box unchecked

Preview of the button that will be added to your web page

Automatically generated code to create the button (your code might wrap differently)

Source: 2015 Twitter

FIGURE N-7: HTML code for Tweet button inserted in document

```
37        <nav class="sitenavigation">
38           <ul>
39              <li><a href="index.html">Home</a></li>
40              <li><a href="aboutus.html">About Us</a></li>
41              <li><a href="reserve.html">Reservations</a></li>
42              <li><a href="events.html">Events</a></li>
43              <li><a href="https://goo.gl/maps/bwf5R">Directions</a></li>
44           </ul>
45           <div class="fb-like" data-href="https://facebook.com/cengagebrain"
46           data-layout="button" data-action="like" data-show-faces="true"
47           data-share="false"></div>
48           <a href="https://twitter.com/share" class="twitter-share-button"
49           data-text="Sweet BnB in Northern MN!" data-count="none">Tweet</a>
50           <script>!function(d,s,id){var js,fjs=d.getElementsByTagName(s)[0],p=/^http:/.
51           test(d.location)?'http':'https';if(!d.getElementById(id)){js=d.createElement(s);
52           js.id=id;js.src=p+'://platform.twitter.com/widgets.js';fjs.parentNode.
53           insertBefore(js,fjs);}} (document, 'script', 'twitter-wjs');</script>
54        </nav>
```

FIGURE N-8: Results of clicking the Tweet button

The custom tweet text you entered in the form

The URL of the current page (yours will differ)

Tweet button added to the end of the nav bar

If you are logged into Twitter on your computer, these options may be different

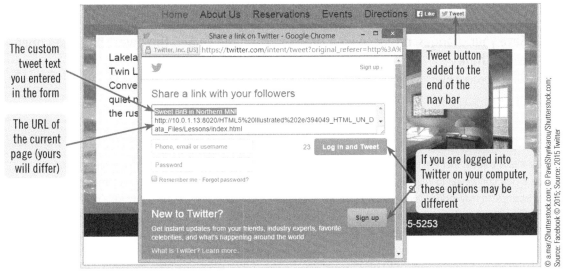

Integrating Social Media

Embed a Tweet

**Learning
Outcomes**
• Embed a tweet in
a web page

In addition to making it easier for users to link to your website on social media, you can embed social
media content into your website. Twitter provides tools that enable you to copy and paste code to embed
any tweet into your own web pages. **CASE** ▶ *Phillip would like to see how the Events web page might be
enhanced with embedded social media. You start by copying the code for the Like and Follow buttons from the
index.html file and pasting that code to the events.html file, then you embed a sample tweet.*

STEPS

1. **Return to index.html in your editor, copy the code after the opening <body> tag and
   before the p element with the class value skipnavigation to the Clipboard, return
   to events.html in your editor, then paste the code after the opening <body> tag**

2. **Return to index.html in your editor, copy the code after the closing </ul> tag and
   before the </nav> tag to the Clipboard, return to events.html in your editor, paste the
   code before the </nav> tag, then save your changes**
   Including the Like and Tweet buttons on every page of your website keeps the layout consistent.

3. **In your browser, open twitter.com**
   If you are logged in, your Twitter feed is displayed, showing tweets from people you follow. Otherwise, a
   generic site overview loads.

   QUICK TIP
   If your search results
   do not show tweets,
   click **Live** above the
   search results.

4. **Type accordion in the Search Twitter or Search for stuff box, then press [Enter]**
   A list of tweets that include the word *accordion* is displayed.

5. **Scroll down if necessary, choose a tweet from the search results, then click the
   More button ⋯ for that tweet**
   A menu opens as shown in FIGURE N-9.

6. **Click Embed Tweet on the menu**
   The Embed this Tweet window opens, containing code to copy and paste into your web page, as shown in
   FIGURE N-10.

7. **Copy the selected code to the Clipboard, return to events.html in your editor, paste the
   code above the closing </section> tag for the section element containing the h3
   heading Accordion Rendezvous, then delete the script element from the code that
   you just inserted**
   You only need the Twitter script element once per page. Because it is already included with the code for
   the Tweet button, you delete it from the code for this widget. The updated code is shown in FIGURE N-11.

8. **Save your changes, return to your browser, close the Embed this Tweet box, then open
   events.html**
   The embedded tweet is displayed in a box on your web page, as shown in FIGURE N-12.

Selecting social media content to embed

In general, the social media content that you embed on your
website should have a clear connection to your business
or organization. For example, it may include content that your
organization itself has generated, such as a tweet from your
organization's Twitter account. Another source is other users
who mention your organization or something related to it.

For instance, a nonprofit organization that sponsors a major
annual event might embed a glowing tweet from an event
participant. Likewise, a business located near a landmark might
embed tweets that mention visits to that location. Remember
that the social media content that you choose to embed reflects
on your organization, so it's important to be selective.

FIGURE N-9: More menu displayed for tweet in search results

Source: 2015 Twitter

FIGURE N-10: Code to embed the previewed Tweet

Source: 2015 Twitter

FIGURE N-11: HTML code for embedded tweet

```
68          <section>
69              <h3>Accordion Rendezvous</h3>
70              <p class="eventdate">last weekend in September</p>
71              <figure>
72                  <img src="images/accordion.png" width="208" height="160"
73                  alt="line drawing of an accordion">
74              </figure>
75              <p>Lovers of the squeezebox gather every year in the Twin Lakes area to
76              share songs and play music together. Come to play or just to listen.
77              Performers include a number of local regulars including our own Phillip
78              Blaine.</p>
79              <blockquote class="twitter-tweet" lang="en"><p lang="en" dir="ltr">Just
80              scheduled time off for this year&#39;s Accordion Rendezvous. Already
81              booked a room at <a href="https://twitter.com/hashtag/LakelandReeds?
82              src=hash">#LakelandReeds</a>. Can&#39;t wait!</p>&mdash; Sasha Vodnik
83              (@sashavodnik) <a href="https://twitter.com/sashavodnik/status/
84              605447223917187072">June 1, 2015</a></blockquote>
85          </section>
```

FIGURE N-12: Embedded tweet displayed on events.html

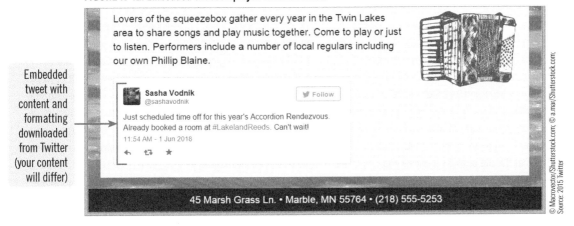

Source: 2015 Twitter

Embed a YouTube Video

Facebook, Twitter, and other social networks give users the ability to upload videos that are hosted by those sites. In addition, dedicated video hosting sites such as YouTube allow anyone to upload and share video content, whether on a social network or elsewhere. **CASE** *As you continue to enhance the Events page, you embed a video hosted by YouTube.*

STEPS

1. **In your browser, go to youtube.com/user/usfws/videos**

   The YouTube channel for the United States Fish and Wildlife Service opens.

2. **Scroll through the video thumbnails and descriptions shown to identify one that is about butterflies**

3. **Click the preview image for the video you've selected, view the video that opens, then if a message indicates that another video is about to play, click Cancel**

4. **Below the video, click the Share button ☒, then in the pane that opens below the Share button, click Embed**

   HTML code for embedding the video is displayed, and the code is automatically selected, as shown in **FIGURE N-13**. Note that the code uses the HTML `iframe` element, which enables developers to embed content from another website while preserving formatting and presentation that may look quite different from the surrounding web page. The `src` attribute for the `iframe` element specifies the URL of the content to be displayed.

5. **Copy the code to the Clipboard, return to events.html in your editor, then paste the code from the Clipboard above the closing </section> tag for the `section` element containing the h3 header Butterfly Season**

   The updated code is shown in **FIGURE N-14**.

6. **Save your changes, refresh or reload events.html in your browser, then scroll down if necessary to view the video**

   The embedded video is displayed below the text in the first section of the web page, as shown in **FIGURE N-15**.

7. **Move the mouse pointer over the video, click the play button to start the video, then click the pause button to pause it**

   The embedded video plays on your website just as it did on youtube.com.

Understanding video hosting

As a web developer, you can use the `video`, `source`, and `track` elements to add videos to your website and upload the video files to your own web server. However, there are several reasons why you might choose to upload a video to a video hosting site like YouTube and embed the video using that site's widget instead. One of the main advantages of using a video hosting site is that you can upload the video in whatever format you have and the site takes care of converting it to any other formats needed. In addition, the widget that the site provides is backward-compatible for older browsers, letting you maximize the reach of your videos to any user of your site whose browser can render video. Because the more technical aspects of integrating video into your website are automated by a video hosting site, using one can allow members of your organization with less technical expertise to work on the website, potentially decreasing the amount of work that web developers need to do. Finally, major video hosting sites use web servers that are optimized to deliver video to users more quickly than many web hosting providers can. One drawback of hosting with a free video hosting site is that sometimes users are shown ads before viewing your video. If it's important to you that users not be shown ads, you may find it worthwhile to subscribe to a paid video hosting service.

FIGURE N-13: HTML code for embedding video

Thumbnail previews of related videos are displayed after the current video plays

Share button

Embed option

The code for embedding the video is automatically selected

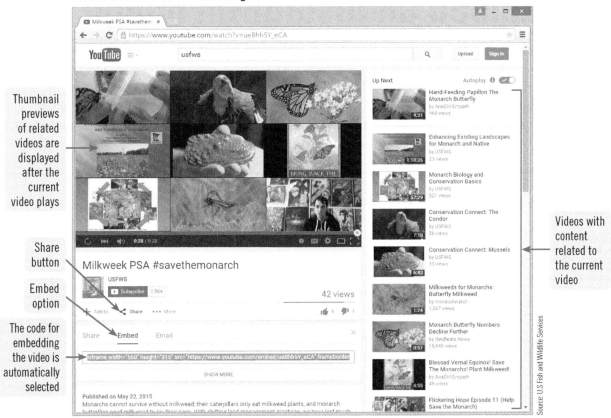

Videos with content related to the current video

Source: U.S Fish and Wildlife Services

FIGURE N-14: HTML code for embedded video

```
43              <section>
44                  <h3>Butterfly Season</h3>
45                  <p class="eventdate">June and July</p>
46                  <p>Minnesota plays host to a variety of beautiful butterflies in high
47      summer. As a result of our participation a region-wide effort to increase butterfly
48      habitat by planting more native bushes and shrubs, more butterflies visit Lakeland Reeds'
49                  year. You can count on our butterfly-friendly bushes being covered with
50                  ing late June and early July.</p>
51                  <iframe width="560" height="315"
52                  src="https://www.youtube.com/embed/ueBhh5Y_eCA" frameborder="0"
53                  allowfullscreen></iframe>
54              </section>
```

The code for embedded video uses the `iframe` element

FIGURE N-15: Embedded video displayed on events.html

The embedded video

Play button

Source: U.S Fish and Wildlife Services; © 2016 Cengage Learning;
© a.mar/Shutterstock.com

Integrating Social Media

Embed an Instagram Image

In addition to supporting video uploads, many social networking sites also enable users to upload images that they want to share. While social networks like Facebook and Twitter enable users to share photos, other sites serve as dedicated hubs for photo hosting and sharing. Perhaps the best known of these photo-centered sites is Instagram. Although Instagram is owned by Facebook, Instagram content can be shared on other social networks including Twitter. **CASE** *You finish enhancing the Events page with social media from one additional source: a photo from Instagram.*

STEPS

1. **In your browser, open instagram.com/usfws**

   The Instagram feed for the United States Fish and Wildlife Service opens. The most common way to find images on Instagram is to log into the Instagram app on a mobile device, search, and mark a photo as a favorite.

2. **Scroll through the images to locate an image of a butterfly, then click that image**

   A window showing the image and comments about it is displayed, as shown in **FIGURE N-16**.

3. **Click the More button ⋯, then click Embed**

   The Embed window opens, displaying the code for embedding the file.

4. **Click the Copy Embed Code button**

   The HTML code for embedding the image is copied to the Clipboard.

5. **Return to events.html in your editor, then paste the embed code above the closing </section> tag for the section element containing the h3 header Butterfly Season**

   A large block of code for embedding the image is added to your code just before the closing </section> tag.

6. **Save your changes, refresh or reload events.html in your browser, then scroll down if necessary to view the image**

   The embedded image is displayed below the YouTube video, as shown in **FIGURE N-17**.

Integrating widgets into responsive design

Most social media widgets automatically adjust in size to fit the layout in which they are embedded. As a result, widgets generally adapt well to responsive layouts as long as your stylesheet sets the width as a percentage for the widget or its container. As with any layout, it's important to test a web page that incorporates social media widgets on different devices and at different browser window widths.

The selected image

The account name of the user who uploaded the image

A description of the image

usfws
3 months ago
A western tiger swallowtail #butterfly feeds on a lily. Spring is coming soon! Have you thought about planting a #pollinator garden? http://1.usa.gov/1IMPfdh (Photo:#NRCS) #USFWS #nature #conservation

Follow

Click to follow the user who posted this image on Instagram

Comments about this image by Instagram users

Leave a comment...

More button

Source: U.S. Fish and Wildlife Service; Source: 2015 Instagram

Lakeland Reeds Bed & Br

10.0.1.13:8020/HTML5%20Illustrated%202e/394049_HTML_UN_Data_Files/Lessons/events.html

YouTube video

usfws · 3 months ago

+ Follow

Instagram image and caption added to web page and formatted

A western tiger swallowtail #butterfly feeds on a lily. Spring is coming soon! Have you thought about planting a #pollinator garden? http://1.usa.gov/1IMPfdh (Photo:#NRCS) #USFWS #nature #conservation

2,696 likes   54 comments

Instagram

Accordion Rendezvous

Source: U.S. Fish and Wildlife Service; Source: 2015 Instagram

Integrate a Twitter Account Feed

In addition to widgets that create buttons or embed tweets, Twitter also supports widgets that display a regularly updated series of tweets, known as a feed, on a web page. One of the most commonly displayed feeds is an account feed, which shows tweets from a specific Twitter account. For example, a business or organization with an active Twitter presence might add a Twitter account feed to its website to keep the site fresh even when the page content itself does not change regularly. **CASE** *Lakeland Reeds does not currently have a Twitter presence, so you add a feed for your personal Twitter account to the main web page to show Phillip how it works.*

STEPS

Note: If you do not have a Twitter account and want to complete the steps in this lesson, first visit twitter.com, sign up for an account, then add at least one tweet to your timeline.

1. **In your browser, open twitter.com and then sign into your account as needed**
   Your main page displays the tweets from other Twitter accounts that you follow.

2. **Click the Profile and settings button, then click Settings**
   The Settings page for your account is displayed.

3. **Click Widgets in the list of options on the left side of the page, then on the Widgets page that opens, click the Create new button**
   The Create a user widget page opens, displaying settings for generating code for a widget based on your timeline.

4. **Click the Height box, then type 300**
   The value in the Height box is your widget's height in pixels. FIGURE N-18 shows the completed settings.

5. **Review the remaining settings, click Create widget, then click the close button on the Your widget has been created message**
   HTML code for the widget is displayed, as shown in FIGURE N-19.

6. **Click in the box displaying the widget code, press [Ctrl][A] (Win) or [command][A] (Mac) to select all of the code, copy the code to the Clipboard, then return to index.html in your editor**

7. **Within the article element and just above the opening <figure> tag, insert a new figure element, paste the code for your Twitter widget within the new figure element, then delete the script element you just inserted as part of the pasted code**
   Because the page already contains a Twitter widget with the necessary script element, you delete it from the code for this widget. The updated HTML for index.html is shown in FIGURE N-20.

8. **Save your changes, then refresh or reload index.html in your browser**
   The Twitter widget you created for your timeline is displayed on the right side of the page as shown in FIGURE N-21.

Obtaining code for widgets

Many large social networking sites make widget code available on their websites. While sites may label this code differently, you can usually find what you need by searching on the term *widget* along with the name of the website in a search engine.

The sites generally provide interfaces that let you configure the options you'd like to show and hide for a given widget, and then the sites generate the code for you based on your selections.

FIGURE N-18: Create a user widget page

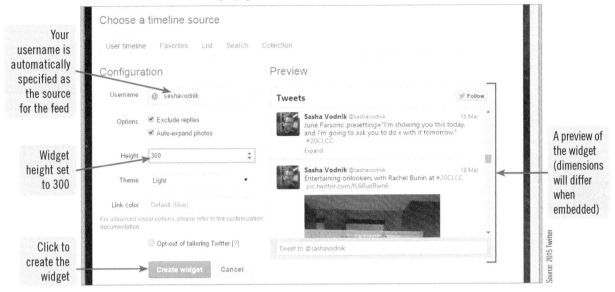

Your username is automatically specified as the source for the feed

Widget height set to 300

Click to create the widget

A preview of the widget (dimensions will differ when embedded)

FIGURE N-19: HTML code for feed widget generated

Code to embed the feed in a web page

FIGURE N-20: HTML code for Twitter account feed

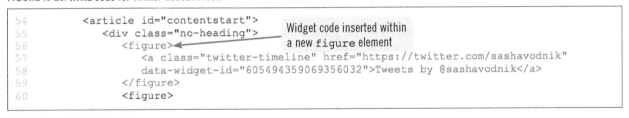

```
54          <article id="contentstart">
55              <div class="no-heading">
56                  <figure>
57                      <a class="twitter-timeline" href="https://twitter.com/sashavodnik"
58                      data-widget-id="605494359069356032">Tweets by @sashavodnik</a>
59                  </figure>
60                  <figure>
```

Widget code inserted within a new figure element

FIGURE N-21: Twitter account feed widget in index.html

Lakeland Reeds is a rustic bed and breakfast on Twin Lakes near rural Marble, Minnesota. Convenient to US 2 and 169, the fresh air and quiet make for an ideal weekend escape from the rush of city life.

The feed shows your most recent tweets (including retweets)

The Twitter account feed widget is 300px in height, based on your settings

45 Marsh Grass Ln. • Marble, MN 55764 • (218) 555-5253

Integrating Social Media

Add a Twitter Hash Tag Feed

Learning
Outcomes
• Add a Twitter hash
  tag feed to a web
  page

Instead of incorporating a widget displaying your account feed into your website, Twitter offers code for other widgets, including a feed based on a search for a word or hash tag. Twitter was among the first of the social networks to popularize the inclusion of searchable codes known as **hash tags** that allow users to find posts on a given topic. A hash tag begins with the hash or pound symbol (#), giving the tag its name. A hash tag feed is especially useful for organizations that are promoting the use of a certain hash tag related to their work. As part of such a campaign, the business can easily display the most recent tweets containing that hash tag right on its website. **CASE** ▶ *You replace the account feed on the main page of the Lakeland Reeds website with a hash tag feed to show Phillip the difference.*

STEPS

TROUBLE
If you have navigated
away from the Create
a user widget page,
open twitter.com,
click the Profile and
settings button, click
Settings, then click
Widgets.

1. **Return to the Create a user widget page in your browser, then click the** Back to widget settings button

   Your main page displays the tweets from other Twitter accounts that you follow.

2. **On the Widgets page, click the** Create new button

   The Create a user widget page opens.

3. **Below the Choose a timeline source heading, click** Search

   The configuration settings are displayed for creating a widget based on one or more search terms you specify.

4. **Delete the value in the Search Query box, type** #minnesotasummer, **click the Height box, then type** 300

   The preview is updated to show tweets that contain the hash tag #minnesotasummer. **FIGURE N-22** shows the final settings.

5. **Click** Create widget, **copy the widget code to the Clipboard, then return to index.html in your editor**

6. **Within the first** `figure` **element, comment out the existing** `a` **element, paste the code for your Twitter widget before the closing** `</figure>` **tag, then delete the** `script` **element you just inserted in the pasted code**

   The updated HTML code for index.html is shown in **FIGURE N-23**.

TROUBLE
You may receive
validation errors
stemming from
widgets you inserted;
it's safe to ignore
warnings about
deprecated attributes
because the layout of
your page does not
rely on them.

7. **Save your changes, then refresh or reload index.html in your browser**

   The Twitter search widget you just created replaces the timeline widget on the right side of the page, as shown in **FIGURE N-24**.

8. **If you are using a shared computer, log out of Twitter**

9. **Validate your HTML and CSS code**

Assessing the drawbacks of a hash tag feed

Although a hash tag feed can be useful for incorporating certain types of content into a website, it's important to recognize its potential pitfalls. Because the feed is generated based on a hash tag that anyone could include in any tweet, you may find that the feed includes some tweets that you consider inappropriate for your website. When you create the widget, Twitter turns on the Safe search mode feature by default, which filters out some content based on profanity and other criteria. However, this does not guarantee that all the content in the feed will be

content that you would choose to show on your website. If keeping tight control on the feed is important, a few alternatives are available. Twitter allows you to create a collection of tweets, which are tweets that you add individually to a named group. Once you have created a collection, you can create a feed widget based on that collection. Another option is to retweet any tweets that you approve of, and then embed your account feed, which will show your retweets along with tweets you generate yourself.

FIGURE N-22: Create a search widget page

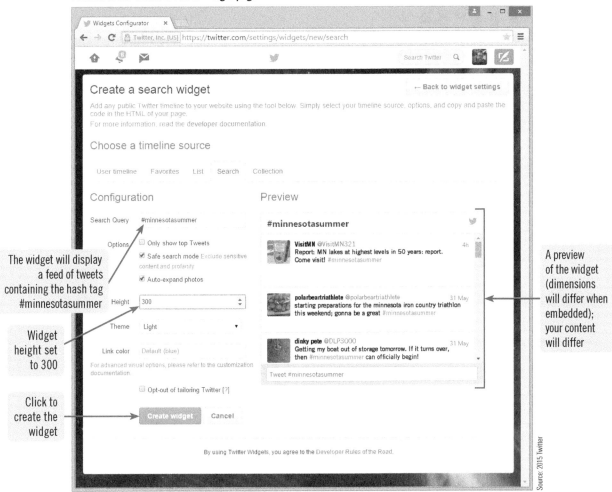

The widget will display a feed of tweets containing the hash tag #minnesotasummer

Widget height set to 300

Click to create the widget

A preview of the widget (dimensions will differ when embedded); your content will differ

FIGURE N-23: HTML code for Twitter hash tag feed

```
56              <figure>
57    <!--         <a class="twitter-timeline" href="https://twitter.com/sashavodnik"
58              data-widget-id="605494359069356032">Tweets by @sashavodnik</a>-->
59              <a class="twitter-timeline"
60              href="https://twitter.com/hashtag/minnesotasummer"
61              data-widget-id="605510013868572674">#minnesotasummer Tweets</a>
62    </figure>
```

Code for account feed commented out

FIGURE N-24: Twitter hash tag feed widget in index.html

Lakeland Reeds is a rustic bed and breakfast on Twin Lakes near rural Marble, Minnesota. Convenient to US 2 and 169, the fresh air and quiet make for an ideal weekend escape from the rush of city life.

Sun Room

The feed shows the most recent tweets containing the #minnesotasummer hash tag

The Twitter hash tag feed widget is 300px in height, based on your settings

45 Marsh Grass Ln. • Marble, MN 55764 • (218) 555-5253

Integrating Social Media

Practice

Concepts Review

Refer to FIGURE N-25 **to answer the following questions.**

FIGURE N-25

1. **Which item is a Twitter button?**
2. **Which item is a Facebook button?**
3. **Which item is a hash tag?**
4. **Which item is a feed?**

Match each term with the statement that best describes it.

5. **social media**
6. **widget**
7. **feed**
8. **social networking site**
9. **hash tag**

a. a searchable term beginning with #

b. prewritten HTML and/or JavaScript code that enables users to provide easy access to their social content from a web page

c. a method for sharing online content and integrating comments

d. a widget that shows a fixed number of recent posts to a given social media account or shows posts that meet certain criteria

e. a website such as Facebook or LinkedIn that enables people to share information about common interests, news, and events with friends, colleagues, and any other people they choose

Select the best answer from the list of choices.

10. When content is _____ on another site, it is displayed with formatting that matches the host site and includes links back to the context in which it was originally posted.

    a. linked

    b. copied

    c. embedded

    d. hosted

11. The _____ element enables developers to embed a self-contained web page within another HTML document.

    a. figure

    b. iframe

    c. aside

    d. html

12. An organization may add a _____ to its website to keep the site fresh even when the page content itself does not change regularly.

    a. button

    b. hash tag

    c. tweet

    d. feed

Skills Review

1. **Add a Facebook Like button.**

    a. In your editor, open HTM_N-4.html from the SR folder where you store your Data Files for this unit, save it as **index.html**, then repeat to save the file HTM_N-5.html as **news.html**, and the file HTM_N-6.css as **styles.css**.

    b. Within the comment section at the top of each file, enter your first and last names and today's date, then save your changes.

    c. In your browser, open developers.facebook.com/docs/plugins/like-button, delete the existing content in the URL to Like box, then type **https://facebook.com/cengagebrain**.

    d. Under the Layout heading, click the arrow in the box that says standard, click button on the list that opens, then click the Include Share Button box to uncheck it.

    e. Click the Get Code button, copy the content of the first code box in the window that opens, return to index.html in your editor, then paste the content of the Clipboard just below the opening `<body>` tag.

    f. Return to your browser, copy the content of the second code box to the Clipboard, return to index.html in your editor, then paste the content of the Clipboard just before the closing `</nav>` tag.

    g. Save your changes, close the Your Plugin Code window in your browser, open index.html in your browser, then click the Like button. (*Note*: To see the Like button, you must open the web page from a web server.)

    h. Click the Close button, right-click the Like button, click Inspect Element, then examine the code for the Like button in the developer tools.

2. **Add a Twitter Tweet button.**

    a. Open about.twitter.com/resources/buttons in your browser, then click the Share a link option button.

    b. Below the Tweet text label, click the Check out this site box, then type **The best deep dish #pizza in Toronto!**

    c. Click the Show count box to uncheck it, click the box containing code below the Preview and code heading, then copy it to the Clipboard.

    d. Return to index.html in your editor, then paste the content of the Clipboard just before the closing `</nav>` tag.

    e. Save your changes, refresh or reload index.html in your browser, then click the Tweet button.

    f. Close the Share a link window.

Skills Review (continued)

3. Embed a tweet.

   a. Return to index.html in your editor, copy the code after the opening `<body>` tag and before the `div` element with the `class` value `outer-container` to the Clipboard, return to news.html in your editor, then paste the code after the opening `<body>` tag.

   b. Return to index.html in your editor, copy the code after the closing `</ul>` tag and before the `</nav>` tag to the Clipboard, return to news.html in your editor, paste the code before the `</nav>` tag, then save your changes.

   c. In your browser, open twitter.com, type **pizza** in the Search Twitter or Search for stuff box, then press [Enter].

   d. Scroll down if necessary, choose a tweet from the search results, then click the More button [···] for that tweet.

   e. Click Embed Tweet on the menu, copy the selected code to the Clipboard, return to news.html in your browser, paste the code above the closing `</section>` tag for the section element containing the h3 heading Music to Eat Pizza By, then delete the `script` element you just inserted.

   f. Save your changes, return to your browser, close the Embed this Tweet box, open news.html, then verify that the embedded tweet is displayed.

4. Embed a YouTube video.

   a. In your browser, go to youtube.com, click the Search box, type **pizza recipe**, press [Enter], then click the preview image for a video about making pizza.

   b. Below the video, click the Share button [<], then in the pane that opens below the Share button, click Embed.

   c. Copy the code to the Clipboard, return to news.html in your editor, then paste the code from the Clipboard above the closing `</section>` tag for the `section` element containing the h3 header Big J's Behind the Scenes – Part 1.

   d. Save your changes, refresh or reload events.html in your browser, then scroll down if necessary to view the video.

   e. Click the play button to start the video, then click the pause button to pause it.

5. Embed an Instagram image.

   a. In your browser, open instagram.com/usdagov, scroll through the images to locate an image of food or food production, then click that image.

   b. Click the More button [···], click Embed, then click the Copy Embed Code button.

   c. Return to news.html in your editor, then paste the embed code above the closing `</section>` tag for the `section` element containing the h3 header Big J's Behind the Scenes – Part 1.

   d. Save your changes, refresh or reload events.html in your browser, then scroll down if necessary to view the image. Your page should resemble **FIGURE N-26**.
(*Note*: The specific tweet, video, and image on your page may differ from those shown in the figure.)

FIGURE N-26

Skills Review (continued)

6. **Integrate a Twitter account feed.**

   a. Open twitter.com in your browser and sign into your account if you are not already signed in, click the Profile and settings button, then click Settings.

   b. Click Widgets in the list of options on the left side of the page, then on the Widgets page that opens, click the Create new button.

   c. Click the Height box, type **250**, then click Create widget.

   d. Click in the box displaying the widget code, press [Ctrl][A] (Win) or [command][A] (Mac) to select all of the code, copy the code to the Clipboard, then return to index.html in your editor.

   e. Within the `article` element and just above the opening tag for the `div` element with the `class` value `info`, insert a new `figure` element, paste the code for your Twitter widget within the new `figure` element, then delete the `script` element you just inserted.

   f. Save your changes, refresh or reload index.html in your browser, then verify that the feed is displayed on the right side of the page as shown in FIGURE N-27. (*Note*: The content of the feed on your page will differ from that shown in the figure.)

   FIGURE N-27

7. **Add a Twitter hash tag feed.**

   a. Return to the Create a user widget page in your browser, click the Close button on the window containing the message Your widget has been created, then click the Back to widget settings button.

   b. On the Widgets page, click the Create new button.

   c. Below the Choose a timeline Source heading, click Search, delete the value in the Search Query box, then type **#pizza**.

   d. Click the Height box, type **250**, click Create widget, copy the widget code to the Clipboard, then return to index.html in your editor.

   e. Within the `figure` element, comment out the existing a element, paste the code for your Twitter widget before the closing `</figure>` tag, then delete the `script` element you just inserted.

   f. Save your changes, refresh or reload index.html in your browser, then verify that the widget content shows tweets that include the hash tag #pizza.

   g. Validate your HTML and CSS code. (*Note*: You can ignore any validation errors stemming from widgets you inserted, including warnings about deprecated attributes.)

Independent Challenge 1

Sarah Nguyen, the manager of the Spotted Wren Garden Center, would like to incorporate social media into the company's website. You add buttons and a feed to the site's main page.

a. In your editor, open HTM_N-7.html from the IC1 folder where you store your Data Files for this unit, save it as **index.html**, then repeat to save HTM_N-8.css as **styles.css**. In the comment section at the top of each file, enter your name and today's date where indicated, then save the files.

b. In index.html, add an empty `div` element with the `class` value `social-media-buttons` within the `nav` element and after the `ul` element. Within the new `div` element, add code for a Facebook Like button for a URL of your choice and a Twitter Tweet button with the default text **Spotted Wren is the place for plants and garden supplies**. (*Hint*: Be sure to add the `div` and `script` elements for the Facebook Like button just after the opening `<body>` tag.) Save your changes.

c. In styles.css and within the site navigation section, add a style rule for the element with the `class` value `social-media-buttons` that sets margins to `0.4em 0.6em`. Add a rule for the `ul` element within the `nav` element, for `div` elements within the `nav` element, and for `iframe` elements within the `nav` element that sets the `display` property to `inline-block` and sets the `vertical-align` property to `middle`. Save your changes, open index.html in a browser, then verify that the buttons are displayed on the far right side of the nav bar. (*Note*: To view the Like button, the web page must be opened from a web server.)

d. Return to index.html in your editor, then just after the opening `<article>` tag, add an empty `figure` element. Within the new `figure` element, add code to create a Twitter account feed for your Twitter account with a height of 400. (*Hint*: Set the height of the widget when you generate the code at twitter.com, not in the CSS for your website.) Save your changes, return to styles.css in your editor, then in the main content section, add a style rule for the `figure` element that sets its width to 50%, creates a left margin of 1em, and floats it on the right. Save your changes, refresh or reload index.html in your browser, then verify that the feed is displayed to the right of the main content as shown in **FIGURE N-28**.

e. Validate your HTML and CSS code. (*Note*: You can ignore any validation errors stemming from widgets you inserted, including warnings about deprecated attributes.)

FIGURE N-28

Independent Challenge 2

As you continue to develop the website for the Murfreesboro Regional Soccer League, you add social media features to help participants stay informed about the league and to assist new member recruitment efforts. You embed a YouTube video and a tweet, and you add Facebook Like and Twitter Tweet buttons.

a. In your editor, open HTM_N-9.html from the IC2 folder where you store your Data Files for this unit, save it as **news.html**, then repeat to save HTM_N-10.css as **styles.css**. In the comment section at the top of each file, enter your name and today's date where indicated, then save the files.

b. In news.html, add an empty `div` element with the `class` value `social-media-buttons` within the `nav` element and after the `ul` element. Within the new `div` element, add code for a Facebook Like button for a URL of your choice and a Twitter Tweet button with the default text **Get moving – play soccer!** (*Hint*: Be sure to add the `div` and `script` elements for the Facebook Like button just after the opening `<body>` tag.) Save your changes.

c. In styles.css and within the site navigation section, add a style rule for the element with the `class` value `social-media-buttons` that floats the element to the left and clears other floats on both sides. Add a rule for the `ul` element within the `nav` element, for `div` elements within the `nav` element, and for `iframe` elements within the `nav` element that sets the `display` property to `inline-block` and sets the `vertical-align` property to `middle`. Save your changes, open news.html in a browser, then verify that the buttons are displayed at the bottom of the nav bar. (*Note*: To view the Like button, the web page must be opened from a web server.)

d. Return to news.html in your editor, then below the p element that follows the h3 heading *Epic Game*, add code to embed a YouTube video with content related to soccer. Save your changes, refresh or reload news.html in your browser, then verify that the video is displayed and that you can play it.

e. Return to news.html in your editor, then below the p element that follows the h3 heading *Shout-out from a Pro*, add code to embed a tweet related to soccer. (*Hint*: Delete the `script` element that is part of the code generated by Twitter for a tweet to avoid duplication.) Save your changes, refresh or reload news.html in your browser, then verify that the tweet is displayed. Your page should resemble the one shown in **FIGURE N-29**.

f. Validate your HTML and CSS code. (*Note*: You can ignore any validation errors stemming from widgets you inserted, including warnings about deprecated attributes.)

FIGURE N-29

Independent Challenge 3

Diego Merckx, the manager of the Hotel Natoma, would like you to incorporate social media tools into the Hotel Natoma website. You'll add Like and Tweet buttons, embedded content, and a Twitter feed.

a. In your editor, open HTM_N-11.html from the IC3 folder where you store your Data Files for this unit, save it as **index.html**, then repeat to save HTM_N-12.html as **guest.html** and HTM_N-13.css as **styles.css**. In the comment section at the top of each file, enter your name and today's date where indicated, then save the files.

b. In index.html, add an empty `div` element with the `class` value `social-media-buttons` after the `nav` element and before the `article` element. Within the new `div` element, add code for a Facebook Like button for a URL of your choice and a Twitter Tweet button with the default text **Check out this great Earth-friendly hotel in the heart of San Francisco!** (*Hint*: Be sure to add the `div` and `script` elements for the Facebook Like button just after the opening `<body>` tag.) Save your changes, then repeat for guest.html.

c. In styles.css and below the site navigation section, create a new section with the comment text **social media buttons**, then below the comment add a style rule for the element with the `class` value `social-media-buttons` that creates margins of `0.4em 0.6em` and absolutely positions the element 1em from the top and 1em from the right of the positioned parent element. Add a rule for `div` elements within the element with the `class` value `social-media-buttons` and for `iframe` elements within the element with the `class` value `social-media-buttons` that sets the `display` property to `inline-block` and sets the `vertical-align` property to `middle`. Save your changes, open index.html in a browser, verify that the buttons are displayed at the bottom of the nav bar, then repeat for guest.html. (*Note*: To view the Like button, the web page must be opened from a web server.)

d. Return to guest.html in your editor, then below the h2 heading *Guestbook*, add code to embed a tweet that contains the text San Francisco (or #sanfrancisco). Below the code for the tweet, add code to embed an Instagram image related to San Francisco. (*Hint*: If you don't have access to an Instagram account and a mobile device, you can choose a photo from one of the URLs used in this unit, such as instagram.com/usfws.) Save your changes, refresh or reload guest.html in your browser, then verify that the tweet and the image are displayed. Your page should resemble the one shown in **FIGURE N-30**.

e. Return to index.html in your editor, then replace the content of the `figure` element with code to display your Twitter account feed with a height of 250px. (*Hint*: Set the height when generating the widget at twitter.com, not in your CSS code.) Save your changes, refresh or reload index.html in your browser, then verify that the feed is displayed. Your page should resemble the one shown in **FIGURE N-31**.

f. Validate your HTML and CSS code. (*Note*: You can ignore any validation errors stemming from widgets you inserted, including warnings about deprecated attributes.)

FIGURE N-30

FIGURE N-31

Independent Challenge 4 – Explore

The owners of Eating Well in Season would like to incorporate social media into their website. You add customized Facebook Like and Twitter Tweet buttons, as well as a customized Twitter account feed.

a. In your editor, open HTM_N-14.html from the IC4 folder where you store your Data Files for this unit, save it as **index.html**, then repeat to save HTM_N-15.css as **styles.css**. In the comment section at the top of each file, enter your name and today's date where indicated, then save the files.

b. In index.html, replace the contents of the `aside` element with an empty `div` element with the `class` value `social-media-widgets`. Within the new `div` element, add code for Facebook Like and Share buttons for a URL of your choice. (*Hint*: To include a Share button, be sure the Include Share Button box is checked when generating the code.) Use the `button_count` layout for the widget, and be sure the Show Friends' Faces box is unchecked. Save your changes to index.html, then in styles.css and within the sidebar section, add a style rule for the element with the class value social-media-widgets that center-aligns text. Save your changes, open index.html in a browser, and verify that Facebook Like and Share buttons are displayed to the right of the main content, with a bubble next to the Share button showing the total number of shares.

c. Return to index.html in your editor, then within the `div` element with the `class` value `social-media-widgets` and below the code for the Facebook buttons, create an empty `div` element. Within the new `div` element, add code for a Twitter Hashtag button for the hashtag #eatlocal. (*Hint*: Go to about.twitter.com/resources/buttons, click the Hashtag option button, then in the Hashtag box type **eatlocal**.) Save your changes, return to styles.css in your editor, then in the sidebar section, add a style rule for the `div` elements within the element with the `class` value `social-media-widgets` that sets the bottom margin to 1em. Save your changes, refresh or reload index.html in your browser, then verify that a Twitter Hashtag button is displayed below the Facebook buttons.

FIGURE N-32

d. Return to index.html in your editor, then within the `div` element with the `class` value `social-media-widgets` and below the code for the Facebook buttons, create an empty `div` element. Within the new `div` element, add code for a Twitter account feed with a height of 600px. (*Hint*: Set the height when generating the widget at twitter.com, not in your CSS code.) Before you generate the widget, click the Theme box, then click Dark, click the Link color box, then click the light green square. Save your changes, refresh or reload index.html in your browser, then verify that the feed is displayed. Your page should resemble the one shown in **FIGURE N-32**.

e. Validate your HTML and CSS code. (*Note*: You can ignore any validation errors stemming from widgets you inserted, including warnings about deprecated attributes.)

Visual Workshop

In your editor, open the file HTM_N-16.html from the VW folder where you store your Data Files for this unit and save it as **index.html**. Repeat to save HTM_N-17.css as **styles.css**. Add your first and last names and today's date to the comment section at the top of each file, then save your changes. Add a Facebook Like button, a Twitter Tweet button, and a Twitter account feed to the web page so your page matches the one shown in **FIGURE N-33**. Validate your HTML and CSS code. (*Note*: You can ignore any validation errors stemming from widgets you inserted, including warnings about deprecated attributes.)

FIGURE N-33

Integrating Social Media

Optimizing Your Website for Search Engines

> **CASE** The owner of Lakeland Reeds Bed and Breakfast, Phillip Blaine, wants you to do everything you can to ensure that his website is easy for potential customers to find when they search with Google or another search engine. In this unit, you'll learn and apply several techniques that can increase the likelihood that the Lakeland Reeds B&B website is suggested to users who search by the name of the business or on search terms relevant to it.

Unit Objectives

After completing this unit, you will be able to:

- Understand search engine optimization (SEO)
- Write indexable content
- Add a description with the `meta` element
- Incorporate microdata
- Create a sitemap file
- Create a robots.txt file
- Preview and finalize your site
- Submit your site

Files You Will Need

L	12 files	IC3	8 files
SR	8 files	IC4	7 files
IC1	9 files	VW	8 files
IC2	9 files		

For specific filenames, see Filenames_O.pdf in the Unit O Data Files folder.

Learning
Outcomes
• Describe the
  benefits of
  search engine
  optimization

Understand Search Engine Optimization (SEO)

In addition to people looking for information on websites, search engines are also looking for information. Just as you've practiced a number of techniques for making websites accessible and usable for people, you can implement techniques that make the content of your pages more understandable to the programs that index and add information to search engine databases. The process of tailoring the structure and content of a web page with search engines in mind is known as **search engine optimization (SEO)**. Implementing SEO techniques increases the likelihood that people searching on a query relevant to your website will be presented with a link to your website. In addition to their potential effects on search results, SEO techniques enable you to make more of the existing information in your web pages available for inclusion in search results and for use with other applications that might interpret the data on your website. **FIGURE O-1** illustrates some of these SEO practices. **CASE** *Before you begin implementing SEO practices on the Lakeland Reeds B&B website, you review the benefits of using SEO.*

DETAILS

SEO brings two main benefits to your web pages:

• **Increasing your site's priority in search results**

Search engines balance many factors to decide the priority of search results; these factors are combined into a set of instructions known as an **algorithm**. One of the goals of SEO is to address factors that are part of search engine algorithms in order to move a site up in the list of search results returned for relevant queries. A site's position in this list is known as its **search rank**. To improve a site's search rank, SEO techniques focus on clarifying the overall topic of a web page, as well as the subject of each section. By using SEO techniques to make the most accurate and specific information about a web page available to search engines in a format that they can easily use, you increase the likelihood of potential users reaching your site through a search engine query. For example, including high-quality content can improve your website's search rank. In addition, the number and text of links to your site from other websites can be an important factor in determining your search rank.

• **Giving web applications useful semantic information about your site**

In addition to increasing your web site's priority in search results, you also want to include semantic elements in your web site that can be used by other web applications. For example, when you design a web page, you use HTML semantic elements to describe the types of content represented in your web page. In addition, you use the text specified by the `title` and `meta` elements in the head section to describe the content of a page more generally. You can further mark up web page elements using **microdata**, which is a standard for using attributes to add more types of semantic data to web page content. Search engines can use microdata to present and format relevant web page content in search results. In addition, other web applications, such as search engines and online directories, can use microdata to group and present marked data in ways that make it easier to understand or to connect with data from other places. **FIGURE O-2** compares the link to a web page in sample search results before and after improving `title` text, adding a description with the `meta` element, and incorporating microdata.

FIGURE O-1: Factors in search engine indexing and search rank

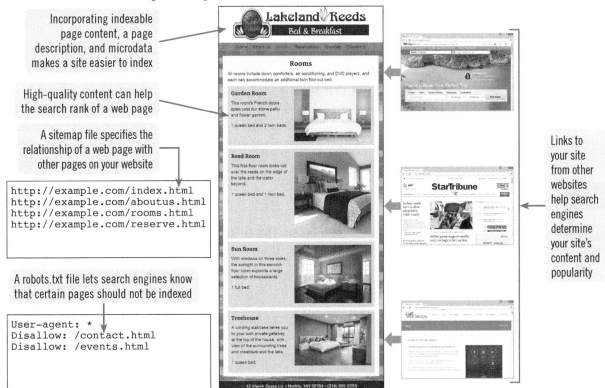

Incorporating indexable page content, a page description, and microdata makes a site easier to index

High-quality content can help the search rank of a web page

A sitemap file specifies the relationship of a web page with other pages on your website

```
http://example.com/index.html
http://example.com/aboutus.html
http://example.com/rooms.html
http://example.com/reserve.html
```

A robots.txt file lets search engines know that certain pages should not be indexed

```
User-agent: *
Disallow: /contact.html
Disallow: /events.html
```

Links to your site from other websites help search engines determine your site's content and popularity

FIGURE O-2: Sample search results showing the effects of SEO techniques

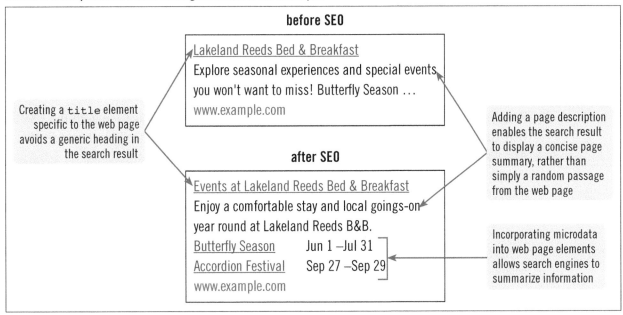

before SEO

Lakeland Reeds Bed & Breakfast
Explore seasonal experiences and special events you won't want to miss! Butterfly Season ...
www.example.com

after SEO

Events at Lakeland Reeds Bed & Breakfast
Enjoy a comfortable stay and local goings-on year round at Lakeland Reeds B&B.
Butterfly Season   Jun 1 –Jul 31
Accordion Festival   Sep 27 –Sep 29
www.example.com

Creating a `title` element specific to the web page avoids a generic heading in the search result

Adding a page description enables the search result to display a concise page summary, rather than simply a random passage from the web page

Incorporating microdata into web page elements allows search engines to summarize information

Write Indexable Content

**Learning
Outcomes**
• Edit web page
content to make it
easily indexable

Making a website search engine friendly starts with one of the most basic components: your content. Making even small adjustments to the content you're presenting to users can improve the accuracy of search engines when they index your pages. The `title` element, heading elements, `img` elements, and linked text play important roles in indexing, so you should pay special attention to them in your web documents. In addition, elements such as the `title` element play unique roles in results for some search engines, as **FIGURE O-3** illustrates. **TABLE O-1** outlines guidelines for increasing the effectiveness of these elements for SEO. **CASE** *You begin optimizing the Lakeland Reeds B&B website by maximizing the effectiveness of the* `title`, `link`, *and* `img` *elements.*

STEPS

QUICK TIP
You will not make
changes to the CSS
file for your website
in this unit, so there's
no need to create a
copy of it.

1. In your editor, open HTM_O-1.html from the Lessons folder where you store your Data Files for this unit, then save it as rooms.html

2. In the comment at the top of the file, enter your name and today's date where indicated, then save the file

3. In the head section, edit the text of the `title` element to read Room selection at Lakeland Reeds Bed & Breakfast

   A clear title helps search engine users recognize when your web page contains the information they're seeking. **FIGURE O-4** shows the edited `title` element.

4. Near the bottom of the `section` element with the `id` value `garden`, change the link text Contact to Ask a question, then change the link text Book to Make a reservation

   Search engines can use link text to help them understand the content of the target page. Replacing these single words with phrases makes them more descriptive without making them cumbersome.

5. Repeat Step 4 for the `section` elements with the `id` values `reed`, `sun`, and `tree`

6. In the file manager for your operating system, navigate to the images folder within the Lessons folder where you store your Data Files for this unit, then rename garden.jpg to garden-room.jpg, reed.jpg to reed-room.jpg, sun.jpg to sun-room.jpg, and tree.jpg to treehouse.jpg

   Giving your images short, descriptive names adds to the information that search engines can collect about your web pages.

7. Return to rooms.html in your editor, edit the `img` element in the section with the `h3` text Garden Room to change the `src` value to images/garden-room.jpg, then edit the `src` values for the remaining three room images to images/reed-room.jpg, images/sun-room.jpg, and images/treehouse.jpg, respectively

   FIGURE O-5 shows the changed code for the first `section` element.

8. Save your changes, then open rooms.html in your browser

   In your browser, the changed button text may be the only visible sign of your content optimization. However, all the changes you made will be available to search engines when indexing the page once it's published.

FIGURE O-3: Text of the `title` element in sample search result

Search engines often use the content of the `title` element as the heading of the search result

Events at Lakeland Reeds Bed & Breakfast
Explore seasonal experiences and special events you won't want to miss! Butterfly Season …
www.example.com

FIGURE O-4: Edited `title` element in rooms.html document

```
1    <!DOCTYPE html>
2    <html lang="en">
3       <head>
4          <title>Room selection at Lakeland Reeds Bed &amp; Breakfast</title>
5          <!--
```

Title content edited to clearly indicate the page topic

FIGURE O-5: Changed code for first `section` element

```
46              <section>
47                  <h3 id="garden">Garden Room</h3>
48                  <figure>
49                      <img src="images/garden-room.jpg" width="370" height="248" alt="a room
50                      with a low, two-person bed, with shelves built into the walls holding a
51                      lamp on each side of the bed">
52                  </figure>
53                  <p>This room's French doors open onto our stone patio and flower
54                  garden.</p>
55                  <p>1 queen bed and 2 twin beds.</p>
56                  <p class="contact-button"><a href="contact.html">Ask a question</a></p>
57                  <p class="book-button"><a href="reserve.html">Make a reservation</a></p>
58              </section>
```

Link text changed from words to phrases for clarity

Image name edited to short, multi-word phrase

TABLE O-1: Guidelines for creating indexable content

element(s)	do	don't
title	create short, descriptive titles customize the title text to accurately describe the current page	use generic or long titles copy the same title text for every page in a website
h1–h6	add headings to major subdivisions of the page	mark text with a heading element merely for visual formatting
img	give image files short, descriptive names supply alternative text using the `alt` attribute	give image files long or nondescriptive names include text in images that's not available elsewhere on the page
a	make links concise use text that describes the link target	add links to long sections of text link generic text such as *click here*

Add a Description with the meta Element

Learning
Outcomes
• Use the meta
element to add a
description to a
web page

Along with fine-tuning the content of your site to increase comprehension by search engines, you can add several types of code to your web pages to provide information specifically for search engines. Among the easiest types to implement is a page summary using an attribute of the meta element. You've already used the meta element to indicate the character encoding of your web documents with the charset attribute and to specify settings for mobile devices using the viewport attribute. To add a summary of your page content, you create a new meta element with the description attribute. While search engines aren't likely to use your description text to decide which user queries match a page, this text is commonly used as a summary in search results, similar to the example in FIGURE O-6. **CASE** ▶ *Phillip has provided you with a one-sentence summary of each page in the Lakeland Reeds B&B website. You add the description for the Rooms page using a* meta *element.*

STEPS

1. **Return to rooms.html in your editor**

2. **In the head section, insert a blank line beneath the meta tag with the viewport attribute, indent if necessary, then type <meta>**

3. **In the tag you just entered, add a space before the closing >, then type**
   name="description"
   Like the meta element for setting the viewport of a web page, you specify a description using two attributes. The value of the name attribute indicates the type of data provided in the element.

4. **Add a space, then type** content="Lakeland Reeds Bed & Breakfast offers 4 comfortable rooms that accommodate from 2 to 5 people. All have private baths and views of Twin Lakes."
   Whenever you use the name attribute for a meta element, it must be paired with a content attribute, which contains the actual value. FIGURE O-7 shows the completed meta tag for the page description.

5. **Save your changes**
   Because browsers don't display the content of meta elements, there's no need to view the changes in your browser.

Recognizing the limits of SEO techniques

Fundamentally, SEO is about providing search engines with as much information as possible regarding the focus of your web pages and relying on the search engines themselves to decide how relevant each page is to a given query. Each search engine continuously adjusts its algorithm to keep it up to date and fine-tune its accuracy. Some people who work with web technologies approach SEO as a way to provide search engines with a website description that's calculated to score a higher position in search results but which doesn't necessarily accurately represent the site presented to human users. While this approach may work for limited periods of time, search engine algorithms grow over time to accommodate this approach and lessen its impact. In addition, some of the coding required for this approach can negatively impact the experience of human users on your web pages. Instead of trying to push the limits of SEO in pursuit of higher search rankings, your time will likely be better spent on creating great web pages and complementing search engine results with other ways of spreading the word about them, such as through social media.

Events at Lakeland Reeds Bed & Breakfast
Enjoy a comfortable stay and local goings-on
year round at Lakeland Reeds B&B.
www.example.com

If a web page includes a meta element with the value description for the name attribute, search engines often use the value of its content attribute as a summary for the search result

FIGURE O-7: Code for description meta element

```
1   <!DOCTYPE html>
2   <html lang="en">
3      <head>
4         <title>Room selection at Lakeland Reeds Bed &amp; Breakfast</title>
5         <!--
6            Lakeland Reeds Bed & Breakfast Rooms page
7            Filename: rooms.html
8
9            Author:
10           Date:
11           HTML5 and CSS3 Illustrated Unit O, Lessons
12        -->
13        <meta charset="utf-8">
14        <meta name="viewport" content="width=device-width">
15        <meta name="description" content="Lakeland Reeds Bed &amp; Breakfast offers 4
16        comfortable rooms that accommodate from 2 to 5 people. All have private baths and
17        views of Twin Lakes.">
18        <script src="modernizr.custom.40753.js"></script>
```

Understanding the keywords meta element

In addition to description, another value for the name attribute of the meta element is keywords. In a keywords meta element, the value of the content attribute is a list of words or terms that describe the page content, separated by commas. Originally, the idea was that such an element would be used to list keywords that a developer would expect to be search terms entered in a search query in order to help match the page with the search terms. For instance, a keywords meta element for a bed and breakfast in Minnesota with lake access might look like

```
<meta name="keywords" content="bed and
breakfast, lake, boating, fishing, minnesota">
```

Because the algorithms used by many major search engines have become quite sophisticated, keywords meta elements have greatly decreased in importance in recent years. Both Google and Bing disregard the content of a keywords meta element when indexing a page. In addition, Bing has indicated that the presence of a keywords meta element may cause it to flag a web page as potential spam, which negatively impacts its search rank, and the same is likely true for Google. For this reason, you should avoid using keywords meta elements in web pages you develop. In addition, if you take over maintenance of an older website, you should check for and remove any keywords meta elements that might be present in the code.

Incorporate Microdata

HTML also supports a syntax known as microdata that enables you to add semantic information to specific web page elements. Microdata is based on **vocabularies**, which are sets of terms and definitions that can be used to indicate the semantic value of specific types of information. Although anyone can define and use a custom vocabulary, implementing an established and widely used one increases the usability of the data in your web pages. Several vocabularies exist for marking microdata, but the most widely supported is schema.org. This vocabulary is composed of a number of **schemas**, which are groups of terms and definitions related to different types of information. You reference a schema in your code using the unique string that identifies it. **CASE** ▸ *Phillip would like you to mark up the address of Lakeland Reeds in the page footer using microdata to make it easier for search engines and other web applications to index.*

STEPS

QUICK TIP

The string that
identifies a schema is
a URI, which is
similar to a URL but
does not necessarily
reference an actual
web document.

1. **In the opening `<footer>` tag near the bottom of the document, add the attributes**
   `itemtype="http://schema.org/LocalBusiness" itemscope`
   The `itemtype` attribute specifies the unique string that identifies the schema you're using—in this case, the LocalBusiness schema. The `itemscope` attribute signifies that the schema specified using the `itemtype` attribute applies to all descendent elements of the element in which it is declared, unless a descendent element declares a different schema.

2. **Add line breaks and indents to your code as needed to place the name, street address, city, state, zip and phone number on separate lines**

QUICK TIP

You can view a list
of property names
and descriptions for
this schema at
schema.org/
LocalBusiness.

3. **Enclose the text Lakeland Reeds Bed & Breakfast but not the code for the bullet symbol in a `span` element with the attribute** `itemprop="name"`
   This code signifies that the content of the `span` element corresponds to the `name` property in the schema you declared in Step 1. For most web page elements, the microdata value is the text an element contains.

4. **Enclose the street address, city, state, and zip code but not the code for the bullet symbol in a single `span` element with the following attributes:**
   `itemprop="address" itemtype="http://schema.org/PostalAddress" itemscope`
   The LocalBusiness schema specified in Step 1 applies to the complete address. You will use the PostalAddress schema for postal address data to mark each part of the address.

5. **Repeat Step 3 to add `span` elements with `itemprop` values of `streetAddress` for 45 Marsh Grass Ln., `addressLocality` for Marble, `addressRegion` for MN, `postalCode` for 55764, and `telephone` for (218) 555-5253**
   FIGURE O-8 shows the completed code. **TABLE O-2** shows the microdata properties and values based on the code you added, along with their corresponding schemas.

QUICK TIP

Google also offers a
tool that automates
generating markup
for structured data
at google.com/
webmasters/
markup-helper.

6. **Save your changes, copy the code for the `footer` element to the Clipboard, go to your browser, then open developers.google.com/structured-data/testing-tool**
   This tool enables you to validate microdata markup.

7. **Click the text Input your source code, paste the contents of the Clipboard, then click Validate**
   The right side of the page displays a labeled list of the items you marked, along with an indicator of whether the code contains errors, as shown in **FIGURE O-9**.

8. **Refresh or reload rooms.html in your browser, then scroll to view the footer text**
   The microdata markup you added has no effect on the appearance of the footer text. **FIGURE O-10** shows an example of how a search engine might take advantage of the microdata in a business listing.

FIGURE O-8: Code for microdata in footer section

```
103        <footer itemtype="http://schema.org/LocalBusiness" itemscope>
104        ➤<span itemprop="name">Lakeland Reeds Bed &amp; Breakfast</span> &bull;
105        ➤<span itemprop="address" itemtype="http://schema.org/PostalAddress" itemscope>
106            <span itemprop="streetAddress">45 Marsh Grass Ln.</span> &bull;
107            <span itemprop="addressLocality">Marble</span>,
108            <span itemprop="addressRegion">MN</span>
109            <span itemprop="postalCode">55764</span>
110        </span>&bull;
111        ➤<span itemprop="telephone">(218) 555-5253</span>
112        </footer>
```

The business name, address, and phone number are marked with properties from the LocalBusiness schema

The parts of the address are marked with properties from the PostalAddress schema

FIGURE O-9: Results of using Google's Structured Data Testing Tool

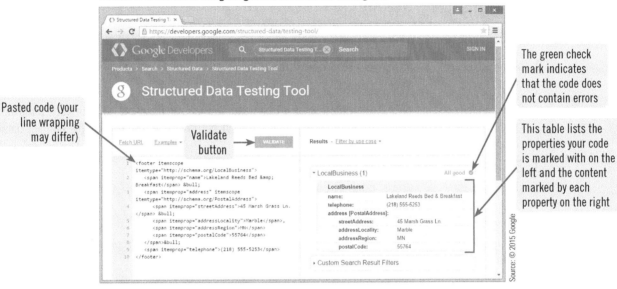

Pasted code (your line wrapping may differ)

Validate button

The green check mark indicates that the code does not contain errors

This table lists the properties your code is marked with on the left and the content marked by each property on the right

Source: © 2015 Google

FIGURE O-10: Microdata in sample search result

Room selection at Lakeland Reeds Bed & Breakfast
Marble, MN - (218) 555-5253
Lakeland Reeds Bed & Breakfast offers 4 comfortable rooms that accommodate from 2 to 5 people. All have private baths and views of Twin Lakes.
www.example.com

Search engine results could supplement a summary of web page content with items marked using microdata, such as the city, state, and phone number

TABLE O-2: Microdata marked in Rooms web page

schema	property	value
http://schema.org/LocalBusiness	name	Lakeland Reeds Bed & Breakfast
	address	45 Marsh Grass Ln., Marble, MN 55764, (218) 555-5253
	telephone	(218) 555-5253
http://schema.org/PostalAddress	streetAddress	45 Marsh Grass Ln.
	addressLocality	Marble
	addressRegion	MN
	postalCode	55764

© 2016 Cengage Learning

Create a Sitemap File

Ensuring that the relationships between pages on your website are easy to understand is an important part of making your site usable for visitors. Users should be able to get to any page on the site using links from other pages, and links should be organized in such a way that it's clear to users how to navigate to desired content. In a large website, it can be especially beneficial to ensure that search engines see and index all the web pages on the site. You can accomplish this by creating and publishing a **sitemap** file, which is a file in a specific format that lists all the pages available to users in a website, and may include information about web page content such as images or video. Although sitemap files for large or complex websites are generally written in XML, for a small website you can create a basic sitemap as a plain text file, without using a markup language. **CASE** ▶ *Phillip is planning to make just 3 of the Lakeland Reeds web pages available to users. Even though the Lakeland Reeds B&B website is currently small, Phillip would like you create a sitemap file for the site.*

STEPS

1. **In your editor, create a new text document**

2. **Type** `http://www.example.com/index.html`**, then press** [Enter]
   The simplest version of a sitemap file contains only text. You list the complete URL for each published page in your website on a separate line. For demonstration purposes, you use the sample domain name example.com.

3. **Add the following URLs on separate lines:**
   ```
   http://www.example.com/aboutus.html
   http://www.example.com/rooms.html
   http://www.example.com/reserve.html
   ```
   FIGURE O-11 shows the completed code for the sitemap file. Note that this file lists only the 3 web pages that Phillip is making available to users.

4. **Save the file with the filename** sitemap.txt **to the Lessons folder where you store your Data Files for this unit**
   When search engines index a site, they identify a sitemap file based on its location on the web server where web documents are stored. A sitemap file does not need to be linked within a site's HTML code.

```
1    http://www.example.com/index.html
2    http://www.example.com/aboutus.html
3    http://www.example.com/rooms.html
4    http://www.example.com/reserve.html
```

Creating an XML sitemap file

While a plain-text sitemap file can meet the needs of a small, simple website, larger sites and sites with a lot of content can benefit from sitemap files that provide more information. You can add more data about your web pages and their contents by creating a file using XML with the Sitemap protocol, which is detailed at sitemaps.org. XML is a markup language like HTML and uses similar rules for tags and attributes; however, XML files require some elements that HTML files don't, and XML files have their own specific rules. To facilitate the creation of XML sitemap files like the one shown in FIGURE O-12, many free utilities are available. In addition, many blogging platforms generate sitemap files automatically for blog content.

FIGURE O-12: The start of an XML sitemap file

```
1    <?xml version="1.0" encoding="UTF-8"?>
2    <urlset
3            xmlns="http://www.sitemaps.org/schemas/sitemap/0.9"
4            xmlns:xsi="http://www.w3.org/2001/XMLSchema-instance"
5            xsi:schemaLocation="http://www.sitemaps.org/schemas/sitemap/0.9
6                    http://www.sitemaps.org/schemas/sitemap/0.9/sitemap.xsd">
7
8    <url>
9       <loc>http://example.com/</loc>
10      <lastmod>2018-10-06T01:39:16+00:00</lastmod>
11   </url>
12   <url>
13      <loc>http://example.com/compatibility.html</loc>
14      <lastmod>2019-03-18T10:53:03+00:00</lastmod>
15   </url>
16   <url>
17      <loc>http://example.com/blog/</loc>
18      <lastmod>2019-04-06T16:35:05+00:00</lastmod>
19   </url>
20   <url>
21      <loc>http://example.com/mobile/</loc>
22      <lastmod>2019-02-17T19:09:25+00:00</lastmod>
23   </url>
24   <url>
25      <loc>http://example.com/about/</loc>
26      <lastmod>2019-01-13T22:33:35+00:00</lastmod>
27   </url>
28   <url>
29      <loc>http://example.com/blog/index.html</loc>
30      <lastmod>2019-04-06T16:35:05+00:00</lastmod>
31   </url>
32   <url>
33      <loc>http://example.com/sitemap.html</loc>
```

HTML5 & CSS3

Create a robots.txt File

Learning Outcomes
• Create a robots.txt file

Sometimes your website may contain pages or folders that you don't want indexed by search engines. Search engines index web pages using programs known as **bots** or **crawlers**. By convention, bots look for a file named robots.txt in the root directory of a website for instructions on any files or folders to exclude from indexing. Because any publicly available document on the web can be viewed by anyone with Internet access, you can't rely on a robots.txt file to keep a document on your web server hidden; if restricting access is your goal, you'll likely want to implement a password-based system to restrict access. However, for influencing which pages are indexed by major search engines, a robots.txt file is an invaluable tool. The role of a robots.txt file in website indexing by search engines is illustrated in FIGURE O-13. **CASE** *Phillip wants to publish only a subset of the web pages you've created on the Lakeland Reeds B&B website to start. However, he'd like to put all the pages up on the web server so he can continue to test the pages that aren't yet part of the main site structure. You create a robots.txt file to prevent these extra web pages from being indexed by search engines.*

STEPS

QUICK TIP

The website at robotstxt.org includes a database that lists the names of robots for different search engines, which you can use to apply rules selectively.

1. **In your editor, create a new text document**

2. **Type** `User-agent: *`**, then press [Enter]**
   Before listing specific pages to include or exclude from indexing, you use a `User-agent` entry to specify which bots the rules apply to. The * wildcard indicates that all bots should respect the rule or rules that follow.

3. **Type** `Disallow: /contact.html`**, then press [Enter]**
   Every value should begin with a slash (/).

QUICK TIP

After specifying a group of files to exclude from indexing, you can create one or more `Allow` entries to specify files that should be indexed.

4. **Type** `Disallow: /events.html`
   FIGURE O-14 shows the completed code for the robots.txt file. In addition to listing a specific file, you can specify filename patterns to exclude all files with given characteristics in their names. TABLE O-3 lists some common patterns.

5. **Save the file with the filename** robots.txt **to the Lessons folder where you store your Data Files for this unit**

Excluding pages from indexing with the noindex meta element

Even if you exclude a web page from indexing in your robots.txt file and other pages in your site don't link to the excluded page, search engines may index the page anyway if another website links to it. To avoid this, you can add the following meta element to the excluded page:

`<meta name="robots" content="noindex">`
   You can select a specific bot to which the element should apply by using a name from the robots database at robotstxt.org in place of the value `robots` for the `name` attribute.

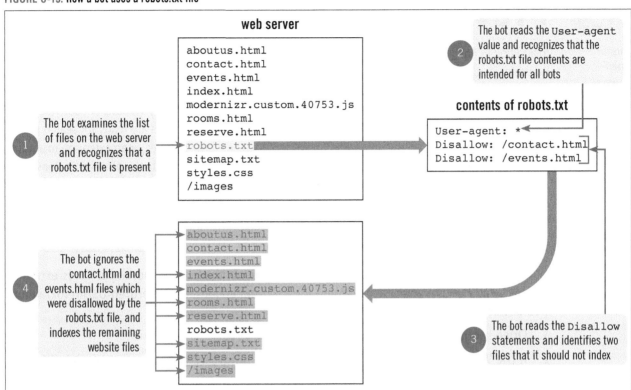

© 2016 Cengage Learning

FIGURE O-14: Code for robots.txt file

```
1    User-agent: *
2    Disallow: /contact.html
3    Disallow: /events.html
```

TABLE O-3: Common patterns used in a robots.txt file

pattern	matches	example
/	entire website	Disallow: /
/filename	the file with the name filename	Disallow: /contact.html
/directory	all the contents of the directory with the name directory	Disallow: /test
/*.extension$	all files in the site with a file extension that matches extension	Disallow: /*.pdf$

© 2016 Cengage Learning

Preview and Finalize Your Site

In addition to previewing and validating your web pages from usability and accessibility standpoints, it can be useful to give your documents a final check from the point of view of a bot. Search engines index mainly text, as well as selected attribute values such as `alt` values for `img` elements. In addition, style sheets don't influence what bots encounter. For this reason, viewing text-only versions of your web pages can help you identify missing or hidden content and ensure that your pages are ready for search engine indexing. You can install a program such as the free, open-source Lynx browser, or an extension to another browser to let you view only the text of a web page. You can also approximate this view without installing any additional software by changing some settings in any modern web browser. **CASE** ▶ *As you prepare to finalize the optimized version of the Lakeland Reeds B&B website, you use a browser extension to review it in text-only mode in your browser to double-check the content that bots will encounter.*

STEPS

Note: The following steps require that you use Firefox with the Web Developer Tools extension installed. You can download the extension for free from addons.mozilla.org/en-US/firefox/addon/web-developer.

1. **Open rooms.html in your browser from a web server**

2. **If the Web Developer Toolbar is not displayed, right-click (Win) or control-click (Mac) the Open Menu button ▤, then click Web Developer Toolbar**
   The Web Developer Toolbar is displayed, as shown in **FIGURE 0-15**.

TROUBLE
At the time this book
was written,
disabling images did
not work for local
files. If images are
still displayed, open
rooms.html from a
web server, then
repeat Step 3.

3. **On the Web Developer Toolbar, click Images, point to Disable Images, click Disable All Images, then reload the web page**
   The images are no longer displayed.

4. **On the Web Developer Toolbar, click CSS, point to Disable Styles, then click Disable All Styles**
   The web page is displayed without images and with only browser default styling, as shown in **FIGURE 0-16**.

5. **Scroll through the web page to view the content as a bot is likely to encounter it**
   Text-only view is especially useful for noticing when site content is available only through technologies such as JavaScript or Flash, which are not accessible by most bots. Because the content of the rooms.html page is made up only of text and graphics, all of the content remains visible in the current view, with alt text taking the place of images.

6. **On the Web Developer Toolbar, click CSS, point to Disable Styles, then click Disable All Styles**
   Styles are re-enabled and CSS is once again applied to the web page.

QUICK TIP
The Disable All
Styles option is
automatically turned
off when a page is
reloaded or when a
new page is opened.
The Disable All
Images option
remains selected
until you turn it off.

7. **On the Web Developer Toolbar, click Images, point to Disable Images, click Disable All Images, then reload the web page**
   The display of images is re-enabled.

8. **Validate rooms.html**

Web Developer Toolbar

Click to set CSS options

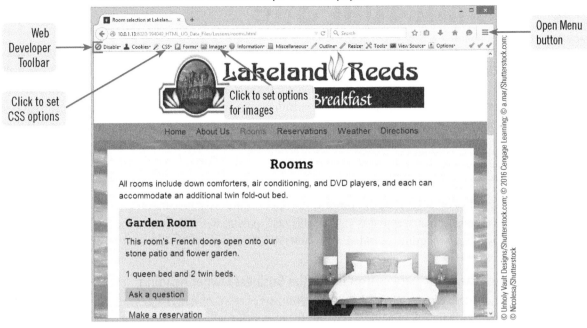

Open Menu button

Elements displayed without the style sheet, using only the default styling applied by the browser

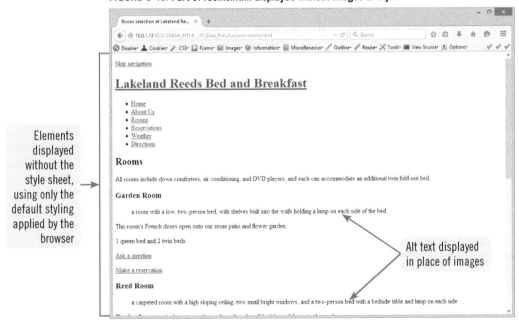

Alt text displayed in place of images

Submit Your Site

Learning
Outcomes
• Describe the
process of
submitting site
information to
search engines

When you are finished optimizing your website, you can simply publish it to the web to make it available to potential users as well as to search engine bots. However, you can take other measures as well to increase the chances that search engines that are popular among your target audience index your pages accurately. **CASE** ▶ *As Phillip prepares to publish his site, you review with him some additional steps he can take to submit information about the site to search engines and to maximize his site's exposure.*

STEPS

QUICK TIP
Because web page designs and content change regularly, your screen may not match exactly the pages shown in these steps.

1. **In your browser, open the page** google.com/submityourcontent

   Major search engines, as well as some smaller ones, provide web forms where you can submit the address of a website for indexing. As **FIGURE O-17** shows, this web page enables different types of users to submit a website to Google.

2. **Click the** Participate button **under the Business Owner heading**

   Major search engines offer tools to help **webmasters**, the people in charge of websites, administer sites. In addition to a link for submitting your site, the page includes links to help with incorporating microdata and submitting a sitemap.

TROUBLE
If you do not have a Google account, you can create one at accounts.google. com/SignUp.

3. **Click** Add your URL, **then if necessary sign into your Google account**

   The page that opens includes a field where you can enter the URL of your website. Note that when submitting a website, you need to submit only the link to the main page. Because Phillip's site is not yet published, you won't submit a URL right now.

QUICK TIP
You do not need to sign in to continue with the steps.

4. **Open the web page** bing.com/toolbox/webmaster

   Like the page you visited at Google, this page at Bing, shown in **FIGURE O-18**, includes links to help you accomplish tasks such as uploading sitemaps.

5. **Click** Submit your Site to Bing **under the KEY RESOURCES heading**

   As with the Google page you viewed earlier, the page that opens includes a field where you can enter the URL of your website.

6. **In your browser, open the URL** webmaster.yandex.com **and examine the resources available, then repeat for** zhanzhang.baidu.com **(Chinese)**

   Yandex is a popular search engine in Russia and Eastern Europe, while Baidu is the dominant search engine in China. If the target audience for your website is in a specific geographic location, you should submit your website to the most popular search engine(s) in that region.

7. **Use a search engine to search on the phrase** Minnesota bed and breakfast

   The first page of results likely includes links to one or two major sites that list and rate bed and breakfasts. Because search engines use links to your site both for indexing and to set the priority of your site in search results, it's important to let owners of relevant websites know when your site is up. In addition to using your professional and/or personal contacts to identify other sites where links to your pages make sense, conducting your own searches using the keywords you'd expect people seeking your site to use, as you did in this step, is an invaluable research tool.

FIGURE O-17: Submit your content page at google.com

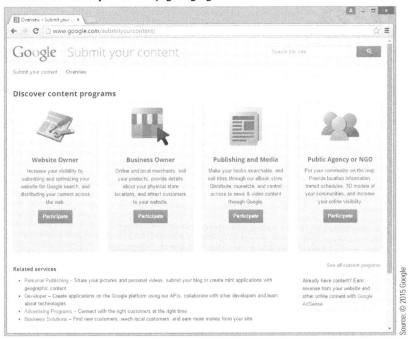

Source: © 2015 Google

FIGURE O-18: Bing Webmaster Tools page at bing.com

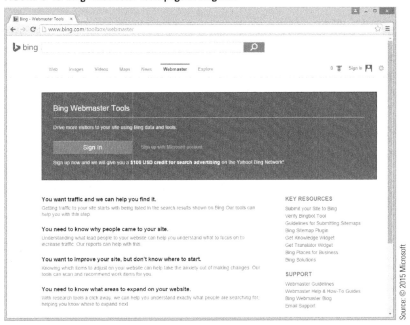

Source: © 2015 Microsoft

Using search engine webmaster tools

In addition to enabling you to submit your site for indexing, the webmaster tools provided by search engines can help you accomplish many other tasks as well. One of the main benefits to using these tools includes the ability to submit additional information to complement microdata from your website that appears in search results. For instance, you can submit a photo of your business to be displayed, along with other specific information, such as your business hours. Major search engines also allow you to purchase targeted advertising for your business, which is displayed on the websites of other businesses that are paid by the search engine to run ads on their sites. For a bed and breakfast, for example, this might result in an ad linking to your business being shown to users of a travel website when they search for travel information about your geographical region, or to users of a website whose audience matches your target demographic. Finally, webmaster tools also include easy-to-follow guidelines for further optimizing your website for indexability and guides for accomplishing basic tasks in administering a website.

Practice

Concepts Review

Refer to the sample search result in FIGURE O-19 **to answer the following questions.**

FIGURE O-19

1. Which content is based on a description `meta` element?
2. Which content is based on microdata?
3. Which content is based on the `title` element?

Match each term with the statement that best describes it.

4. **search engine optimization (SEO)**
5. **algorithm**
6. **search rank**
7. **microdata**
8. **vocabulary**
9. **bot**

    a. a website's position in the list of search results returned for a query

    b. a program used by a search engine to index web pages

    c. a standard for using attributes to add semantic data to web page content

    d. a set of terms and definitions that can be used to indicate the semantic value of a specific type of information

    e. a set of instructions used by search engines to decide the priority of search results

    f. the process of tailoring the structure and content of a web page with search engines in mind

Select the best answer from the list of choices.

10. **Which of the following is a strategy for making the content of a title element more indexable?**
    a. make it long
    b. make it generic
    c. copy the same title text from another page on the site
    d. customize it to accurately describe the current page

11. **Which of the following is a strategy for making an image element more indexable?**
    a. give the image file a long name
    b. give the image file a generic name
    c. give the image file a descriptive name
    d. remove the alt attribute and its value

12. **To create a `meta` element that provides site summary text, what value do you specify for the `name` attribute?**
    a. `robots`
    b. `description`
    c. `charset`
    d. `keywords`

13. **Which attribute signifies that a specified microdata vocabulary applies to all descendent elements of the element in which it is declared?**
    a. `itemtype`
    b. `itemdata`
    c. `itemscope`
    d. `itemprop`

14. **By convention, what is the name of the file that bots look for in the root directory of a website for instructions on any files or folders to exclude from indexing?**
    a. robots.txt
    b. sitemap.txt
    c. sitemap.xml
    d. index.html

Skills Review

1. **Write indexable content.**
   a. In your editor, open HTM_O-2.html from the SR folder where you store your Data Files for this unit, then save it as **location.html**.
   b. Within the comment section at the top of the file, enter your first and last names and today's date, then save your changes.
   c. In the head section, edit the text of the `title` element to read **Big J’s Deep Dish Pizza Toronto Locations**.
   d. Within the first `section` element and in the second p element beneath the h3 heading Queen’s Park/UT, change the link text Map to **Map of Big J’s Queen’s Park/UT**. Repeat for the second and third `section` elements, changing the link text to **Map of Big J’s St. Clair** and **Map of Big J’s Dundas**, respectively.
   e. In the file manager for your operating system, navigate to the images folder within the SR folder where you store your Data Files for this unit, then rename bigjs.gif to **big-js-pizza.gif**.
   f. Return to location.html in your editor, then edit the img element in the `header` element to change the src value to **images/big-js-pizza.gif**.
   g. Save your changes, then open location.html in your browser. Your updated page should match the one shown in **FIGURE O-20**.

FIGURE O-20

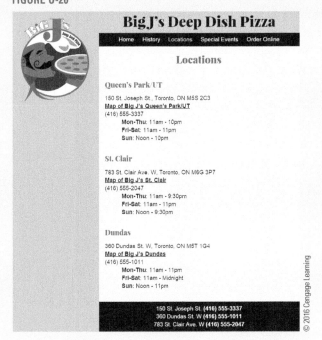

Skills Review (continued)

2. Add a description with the `meta` element.

   a. Return to location.html in your editor

   b. In the head section, insert a `meta` element with a `name` value of **description** and a `content` value of **Get Big J’s Pizza at Queen’s Park/UT, St. Clair, or Dundas**.

   c. Save your changes.

3. Incorporate microdata.

   a. In the `footer` element near the bottom of the document, add an attribute referencing the microdata schema identified by the string **http://schema.org/LocalBusiness**. Add another attribute setting the specified schema as the scope.

   b. Add an attribute that marks the text *Big J’s Queen’s Park/UT* as corresponding to the `name` property in the current schema.

   c. Add an attribute that marks the street address *150 St. Joseph St.* as corresponding to the `address` property in the current schema. Add a second attribute referencing the microdata schema identified by the string **http://schema.org/PostalAddress**. Add a third attribute setting the specified schema as the scope. Enclose the text 150 St. Joseph St. within a `span` element, then add an attribute that marks the contents as corresponding to the `streetAddress` property in the current schema.

   d. Add an attribute that marks the text *(416) 555-3337* as corresponding to the **telephone** property in the current schema.

   e. Repeat Steps b–d to mark the contents of the remaining two `div` elements.

   f. Save your changes, reload location.html in your browser, then scroll down to verify that the display of the footer text is unchanged.

4. Create a sitemap file.

   a. In your editor, create a new text document.

   b. On separate lines, enter the following URLs:

     http://www.example.com/index.html

     http://www.example.com/location.html

   c. Save the file with the filename **sitemap.txt** to the SR folder where you store your Data Files for this unit.

5. Create a robots.txt file.

   a. In your editor, create a new document.

   b. Add code specifying that the file applies to all bots.

   c. Add code specifying that order.html should not be indexed.

   d. Save the file with the filename robots.txt to the SR folder where you store your Data Files for this unit.

6. Preview, finalize, and submit your site.

   a. Return to location.html in your browser, then display the Web Developer Toolbar.

   b. Disable images and CSS within the current web page.

   c. Scroll through the web page to view the content as a bot is likely to encounter it.

   d. Re-enable the display of images and the use of CSS code within the page.

   e. Use a search engine to search on the phrase **Toronto pizza**, then examine the results to identify websites on which this business should create a listing.

   f. Validate location.html.

Independent Challenge 1

Sarah Nguyen, the manager of the Spotted Wren Garden Center, is preparing to publish the website you have been working on. She would like you to implement some search engine optimization measures before the site goes live.

a. In your editor, open HTM_O-3.html from the IC1 folder where you store your Data Files for this unit, then save it as **resource.html**. In the comment section at the top of the file, enter your name and today's date where indicated, then save the file.

b. Change the text of the `title` element to **Gardening Resources from Spotted Wren Garden Center**.

c. In the file manager for your operating system, navigate to the images folder within the IC1 folder where you store your Data Files for this unit. Rename spotwren.gif to **spotted-wren.gif**, rename blanket.jpg to **blanket-flower.jpg**, then rename rugosa.jpg to **hedge-rose.jpg**. Return to your editor, then change the `img` element referencing each file to match the new name. Save your changes, open resource.html in your browser, then verify that it matches **FIGURE O-21**.

FIGURE O-21

Blanket flower (*Gaillardia aristata*)

Hedge rose (*Rosa rugosa*)

d. Mark the contents of the `footer` element using microdata. Use the schema with the identifier http://schema.org/LocalBusiness, marking the text Spotted Wren Garden Center as corresponding to the `name` property, the complete address as corresponding to the `streetAddress` property, and the phone number as corresponding to the `telephone` property. Use the schema with the identifier http://schema.org/PostalAddress to mark the street, city, and state—marking 548 N. 58th St. as corresponding to the `streetAddress` property, Omaha as corresponding to the `addressLocality` property, NE as corresponding to the `addressRegion` property, and 68132 as corresponding to the `postalCode` property. (*Hint*: Be sure to add the attribute that sets each specified schema as the scope.) Save your changes, refresh or reload resource. html in your browser, then verify that the appearance of the page has not changed.

e. Create a sitemap file listing the files index.html, resource.html, and hours.html at the sample domain http://www.example.com. Save the file with the name **sitemap.txt**.

f. Create a **robots.txt** file that applies to all user agents and excludes the file quote.html from indexing.

g. Return to resource.html in your browser, display the Web Developer Toolbar, disable images and CSS within the current web page, then scroll through the web page to view the content as a bot is likely to encounter it. (*Note*: Remember to re-enable the display of images and CSS within the page when you are done.)

h. Use a search engine to search on the phrase **Omaha gardening**, then examine the results to identify websites on which this business should create a listing.

i. Validate resource.html.

Independent Challenge 2

As you prepare to publish the website for the Murfreesboro Regional Soccer League, you add some search engine optimizations.

a. In your editor, open HTM_O-4.html from the IC2 folder where you store your Data Files for this unit, then save it as **started.html**. In the comment section at the top of the file, enter your name and today's date where indicated, then save the file.

b. Change the text of the title element to include the name of the organization as well as the phrase **Getting Started**.

c. In the file manager for your operating system, navigate to the images folder within the IC2 folder where you store your Data Files for this unit. Rename mrsl.gif to **murfreesboro-regional-soccer-league.png**, then rename outdoors.jpg to **children-playing.png**. Return to your editor, then change the img element referencing each file to match the new name. Save your changes, open resource. html in your browser, then verify that it matches **FIGURE O-22**.

FIGURE O-22

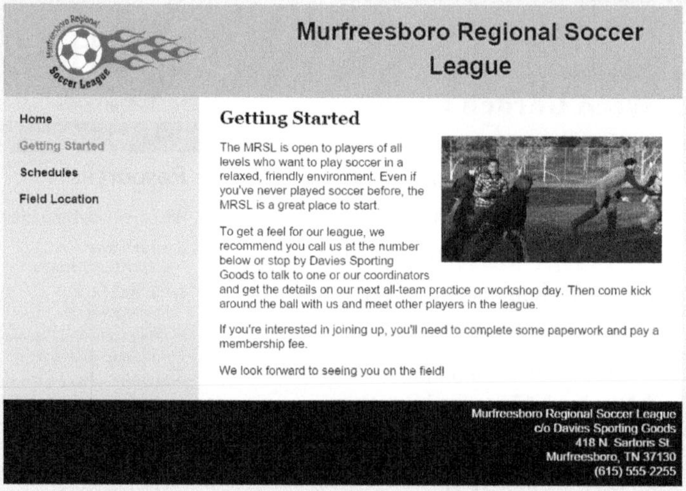

Murfreesboro Regional Soccer League

Getting Started

The MRSL is open to players of all levels who want to play soccer in a relaxed, friendly environment. Even if you've never played soccer before, the MRSL is a great place to start.

To get a feel for our league, we recommend you call us at the number below or stop by Davies Sporting Goods to talk to one of our coordinators and get the details on our next all-team practice or workshop day. Then come kick around the ball with us and meet other players in the league.

If you're interested in joining up, you'll need to complete some paperwork and pay a membership fee.

We look forward to seeing you on the field!

Murfreesboro Regional Soccer League
c/o Davies Sporting Goods
418 N. Sartoris St.
Murfreesboro, TN 37130
(615) 555-2255

© 2016 Cengage Learning; Source: letsmove.gov

d. Mark the contents of the footer element using microdata. Use the schema with the identifier http://schema.org/LocalBusiness, marking the text Murfreesboro Regional Soccer League as corresponding to the name property, the lines containing the c/o, street address, city, state, and zip as corresponding to the streetAddress property, and the phone number as corresponding to the telephone property. Use the schema with the identifier http://schema.org/PostalAddress to mark the address information, marking c/o Davies Sporting Goods
 415 N. Sartoris St. as corresponding to the streetAddress property, Murfreesboro as corresponding to the addressLocality property, TN as corresponding to the addressRegion property, and 37130 as corresponding to the postalCode property. (*Hint:* Be sure to add the attribute that sets each specified schema as the scope.) Save your changes, refresh or reload resource. html in your browser, then verify that the appearance of the page has not changed.

e. Create a sitemap file listing the files index.html, started.html, and schedule.html at the sample domain http://www.example.com. Save the file with the name **sitemap.txt**.

f. Create a **robots.txt** file that applies to all user agents and excludes the file signup.html from indexing.

g. Write a concise description of the page contents, then add it to your HTML file using a description meta element. Save your changes.

h. Return to started.html in your browser, display the Web Developer Toolbar, disable images and CSS within the current web page, then scroll through the web page to view the content as a bot is likely to encounter it. (*Note:* Remember to re-enable the display of images and CSS within the page when you are done.)

i. Use a search engine to search on the phrase **Tennessee soccer**, then examine the results to identify websites on which this business should create a listing.

j. Validate started.html.

Independent Challenge 3

As you continue your work on the website for the Hotel Natoma, you add search engine optimizations to the site, starting with the Local Events page.

a. In your editor, open HTM_O-5.html from the IC3 folder where you store your Data Files for this unit, then save it as **nearby.html**. In the comment section at the top of the file, enter your name and today's date where indicated, then save the file.

b. Edit the text of the `title` element so it appropriately reflects the page content.

c. Rename the logo image file using descriptive words separated by hyphens, then edit the `img` element in the document to match. Repeat for the cablecar image. Save your changes, open nearby.html in a browser, then verify that both images are still displayed as shown in **FIGURE O-23**.

d. Mark the contents of the `footer` element using microdata. Use the

FIGURE O-23

schema with the identifier http://schema.org/LocalBusiness, marking the hotel name as corresponding to the `name` property, the complete address as corresponding to the `address` property, and the phone number as corresponding to the `telephone` property. Use the schema with the identifier http://schema.org/PostalAddress to mark the street, city, and state—marking the street address as corresponding to the `streetAddress` property, the city as corresponding to the `addressLocality` property, the state abbreviation as corresponding to the `addressRegion` property, and the postal (zip) code as corresponding to the `postalCode` property. (*Hint*: Be sure to add the attribute that sets each specified schema as the scope.) Save your changes, refresh or reload nearby.html in your browser, then verify that the appearance of the page has not changed.

e. Create a sitemap file listing the files index.html, nearby.html, and museums.html at the sample domain http://www.example.com. Save the file with the name **sitemap.txt**.

f. Create a **robots.txt** file that applies to all user agents and excludes the file reserve.html from indexing.

g. Write a concise description of the page contents, then add it to your HTML file using a description `meta` element. Save your changes.

h. Return to nearby.html in your browser, display the Web Developer Toolbar, disable images and CSS within the current web page, then scroll through the web page to view the content as a bot is likely to encounter it. (*Note*: Remember to re-enable the display of images and CSS within the page when you are done.)

i. Use a search engine to search on the phrase **San Francisco hotel**, then examine the results to identify websites on which this business should create a listing.

j. Validate nearby.html.

Independent Challenge 4 – Explore

As you near the end of your work on the website for Eating Well in Season, you optimize the website for search engines.

a. In your editor, open HTM_O-6.html from the IC4 folder where you store your Data Files for this unit, then save it as **menus.html**. In the comment section at the top of the file, enter your name and today's date where indicated, then save the file.

b. Edit the text of the `title` element so it appropriately reflects the page content.

c. Rename the logo image file using descriptive words separated by hyphens, then edit the `img` element in the document to match. Save your changes, open menus.html in a browser, then verify that the image is still displayed as shown in **FIGURE O-24**.

FIGURE O-24

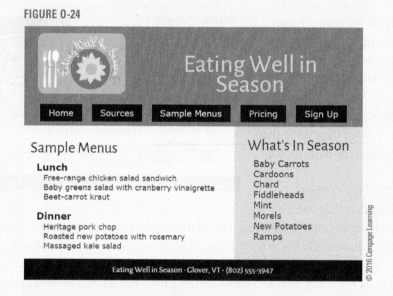

d. Return to menus.html in your editor, copy the `footer` element to the Clipboard, then in your browser open google.com/webmasters/markup-helper. Click the Local Businesses option button, below the buttons click the HTML tab, click the text area, paste the contents of the Clipboard, then click Start Tagging. On the screen that is displayed, select the text Eating Well in Season at the top of the page, then click Name on the menu that opens. Click the word Glover, point to Address on the menu that opens, then click Locality/City. Click VT, point to Address on the menu that opens, then click Region/State. Select the phone number, then point to Telephone on the menu that opens. Review the properties and data on the right side of the page, then click Create HTML. In the HTML Source with Microdata Markup panel, select the `footer` element and copy it to the Clipboard. (*Hint*: <html>, <head>, <body>, and other tags may be generated as part of the code. You should copy only the starting and ending <footer> tags and the text between them.) Return to menus.html in your editor, delete the existing `footer` element, then paste the contents of the Clipboard in its place. Add line breaks and indents as necessary to make the generated code readable, and replace any bullet characters with the character code `&bull;`. Save your changes, refresh or reload menus.html in your browser, then verify that the appearance of the page has not changed.

Independent Challenge 4 – Explore (continued)

e. Create a sitemap file listing the files index.html, sources.html, and signup.html at the sample domain http://www.example.com. Save the file with the name **sitemap.txt**.

f. Create a **robots.txt** file that applies to all user agents and excludes the file menus.html from indexing.

g. Return to menus.html in your editor, then add a `meta` element with the `name` value `robots` and the `content` value `noindex`. Save your changes.

h. Write a concise description of the page contents, then add it to your HTML file using a description `meta` element. Save your changes.

i. Refresh or reload menus.html in your browser, display the Web Developer Toolbar, disable images and CSS within the current web page, then scroll through the web page to view the content as a bot is likely to encounter it. (*Note*: Remember to re-enable the display of images and CSS within the page when you are done.)

j. Use a search engine to search on the phrase **Vermont local food**, then examine the results to identify websites on which this business should create a listing.

k. Validate menus.html.

Visual Workshop

In your editor, open the file HTM_O-7.html from the VW folder where you store your Data Files for this unit and save it as **releases.html**. Add your first and last names and today's date to the comment section at the top of each file, then save your changes. Edit the file so that when a search engine indexes the file, the search result might appear as shown in FIGURE O-25. Save your changes, then validate releases.html.

FIGURE O-25

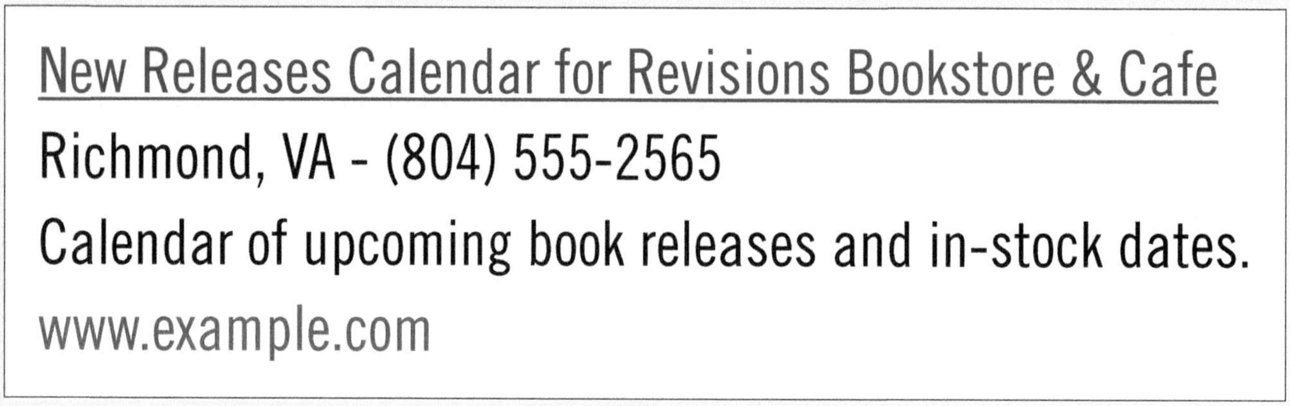

New Releases Calendar for Revisions Bookstore & Cafe

Richmond, VA - (804) 555-2565

Calendar of upcoming book releases and in-stock dates.

www.example.com

Testing and Improving Performance

CASE As you prepare to finalize the website you've developed for Lakeland Reeds Bed & Breakfast, you test it and make changes to improve its usability and performance.

Unit Objectives

After completing this unit, you will be able to:

- Assess performance
- Plan usability tests
- Perform browser tests
- Test page loading speed

- Incorporate a spritesheet
- Optimize images
- Reduce the size of CSS files
- Customize modernizr.js

Files You Will Need

L	20 files	IC3	18 files
SR	17 files	IC4	13 files
IC1	14 files	VW	10 files
IC2	17 files		

For specific filenames, see Filenames_P.pdf in the
Unit P Data Files folder.

Assess Performance

Testing a website's layout and functionality using your own computer and a browser does not account for how quickly a published site loads and responds to user interaction over the Internet – a measure known as the site's **performance**. When a user's browser requests files over the Internet, several factors influence how quickly the files are delivered. Some of these factors, such as the user's Internet connection speed, are out of your control as a developer. However, you can perform tests that simulate the experience of accessing your site in different browsers and over different types of connections to identify any bottlenecks in your site. You can also optimize several aspects of your code to ensure that your content is available as quickly as possible to users who want to access it. **TABLE P-1** describes some of the best practices for decreasing page load time. **CASE** ▶ *Phillip Blaine has given his final approval to the layout and content of the website you have created for Lakeland Reeds Bed & Breakfast. As you prepare to publish the site, you review the adjustments you can make to optimize the site's performance.*

DETAILS

Two factors significantly impact the time it takes for a web page to load or respond:

• **The size of embedded or linked files**

When a user requests a web page, different types of content contribute to the total download size, which affects download time. In addition to the HTML file, the CSS files, any referenced media files, and JavaScript files must also be downloaded. For each of these file types, a developer can take steps to reduce the file size, which in turn decreases the amount of time that the download takes and potentially enables users to view the site more quickly. HTML, CSS, and JavaScript files can all be **minified**, which involves an automated process that removes any characters that are not needed by a browser to parse the files. **FIGURE P-1** shows CSS code before and after minifying. Image files can likewise be **optimized**—a similar process that ensures that the files are as compressed as possible without losing significant visual information. Another option is to remove **orphaned styles**, which are style rules based on selectors that no longer apply to any elements on your web pages. Finally, you should also consider using a custom build of any JavaScript library incorporated into your website, such as Modernizr. A **custom build** is a version of the library that includes only the features that your site uses. Although minifying code, optimizing images, removing orphaned styles, and using custom builds of JavaScript libraries may result in only a small reduction in overall file size, every byte matters, especially for those users who will access your website over expensive mobile connections.

• **The number of HTTP requests**

When a browser requests files from a web server, it uses Hypertext Transfer Protocol (HTTP), which is a set of rules for exchanging information about requests for web documents. Browsers generally limit the number of files that can be requested from a single server simultaneously. This means that for sites that include many external CSS, JavaScript, image, and other files, the browser must wait to request some files until after other files have been downloaded because it does not request all the files all at once. The practice of waiting to request additional files results in a longer download time. Developers reduce the amount of time required to wait for requests by combining files of the same type into a single file, where possible. For instance, on a website that uses multiple CSS files, you could combine them into a single document. Similarly, developers generally combine all decorative images and other images that do not relate directly to the content of a web page into a single image called a **spritesheet**. This enables all these images to be retrieved with a single HTTP request. The spritesheet is then specified in the style sheet as the background image for each element that incorporates one of the included images, with properties specifying the area of the spritesheet image to be displayed. Similar to the way coordinates are generated for an image map, third-party software is usually used to generate the properties for the images in a spritesheet. Reducing the number of HTTP requests is another way to make a small but meaningful improvement in how quickly your page is available for users who request it, as illustrated in **FIGURE P-2**.

```
/*
    Lakeland Reeds Bed and Breakfast style sheet
    Filename: styles.css

    Author:
    Date:
    HTML5 and CSS3 Illustrated Unit P, Lessons
*/

/* reset styles */
html {
    font-size: 16px;
}
```

Original CSS code, which includes comments, spaces, and line breaks

Minified version of the CSS code on the left, with comments, spaces, and line breaks removed

```
html{font-size:16px}a,article,body,div,fieldset,figcaption,figure,footer,form,header,h1,h2,h3,img,input,label,legend,li,nav,p,section,textarea,ul{border:0;padding:0;margin:0}img{max-width:100%;height:auto;width:auto}ul{list-style-type:none}body{margin:0 auto;font-family:Arial,Helvetica,sans-serif}p{line-height:1.4em;font-size:1.3em}a:link{color:#000}a:visited{color:#888}p.skipnavigation a{position:absolute;left:-10000px}p.skipnavigation a:focus{color:ivory;background-
```

FIGURE P-2: Reducing HTTP requests by combining files

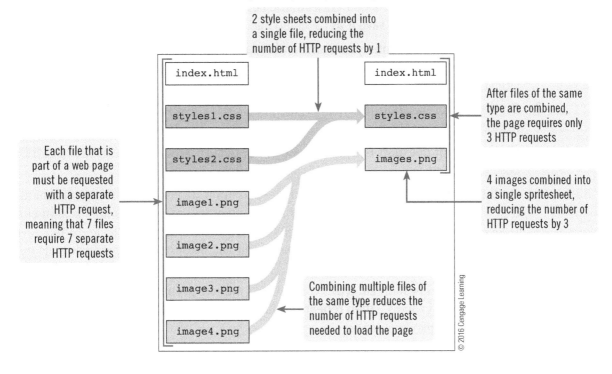

2 style sheets combined into a single file, reducing the number of HTTP requests by 1

Each file that is part of a web page must be requested with a separate HTTP request, meaning that 7 files require 7 separate HTTP requests

After files of the same type are combined, the page requires only 3 HTTP requests

4 images combined into a single spritesheet, reducing the number of HTTP requests by 3

Combining multiple files of the same type reduces the number of HTTP requests needed to load the page

© 2016 Cengage Learning

TABLE P-1: Selected best practices for decreasing page load time

best practice	effect
implement spritesheets	downloads all decorative images in a single HTTP request
optimize images	reduces amount of data user must download over a potentially slow or expensive connection
remove orphaned styles	
minify CSS files	
customize JavaScript libraries	limits download to only code used for your website

© 2016 Cengage Learning

HTML5 & CSS3

Plan Usability Tests

Planning and structuring your website logically is an important aspect of making the site usable. The best way to test the usability of your site is by collecting feedback from the site's users. While the process of collecting feedback from likely users can require significant planning and energy, the information these users provide can be invaluable in making your site one that people want to use and in ensuring that the information you're publishing is as widely available as possible. FIGURE P-3 illustrates a common setup for conducting a usability test. To collect the best information possible from usability tests, it's important to identify questions you want all test participants to answer. To ensure that your questions don't vary between testers, it's considered a good practice to create a script and to use it consistently throughout the process. **CASE** ▶ *Before you publish the site, Phillip wants you to check that the website conveys the impression that he is responsible and treats guests with respect, and that the business is a midrange B & B. He also wants to ensure that users can easily locate contact information, room descriptions, and room rates. You create a usability testing plan and script to address these questions.*

STEPS

1. **In your editor, open HTM_P-1.txt from the Lessons folder where you store your Data Files for this unit, then save it as** Lakeland Reeds Test Plan.txt

2. **At the top of the file, enter your name and today's date where indicated, then save the file**
   The document includes *Feedback* and *Tasks* sections, along with two additional questions. The *Feedback* section already includes two questions asking users for general impressions.

3. **On the line for question 1b, type** "Would you expect the owner of this business to be responsible?"

4. **On the line for question 1c, type** "Would you expect to be treated respectfully at this bed & breakfast?"

5. **On the line for question 1d, type** "Compared to other bed & breakfast establishments that you're familiar with, would you rank this one as low-end, mid-range, or high-end?"
   These questions cover Phillip's queries about the impression conveyed by the site. In the Tasks section, you'll ask users to locate certain information on the site and watch whether they're able to do so, and how easily.

6. **On the line for question 2a, type** "contact information", **repeat for question 2b to enter** "descriptions of rooms", **then repeat for question 2c to enter** "rates"
   FIGURE P-4 shows the completed test plan.

7. **Save your changes**

Performing usability tests

You can choose from several methods of performing usability tests based on your testing budget and the equipment available to you. On the high end, some larger organizations have dedicated testing facilities that may include rooms with two-way mirrors for observing testers unobtrusively, as well as computer systems configured to record and play back the keystrokes and mouse movements of testers. In a more modest testing setup, you may simply sit next to a user and write down as accurately as possible what the user does; positioning a video camera with a clear view of the screen and recording the tester's activities for later scrutiny can be a useful addition to this setup. When testing a user's ability to navigate a website, some developers find it easiest to print out all the pages involved in the tasks at hand, ask testers to point to the location on the page where they'd click to find certain information, then show the testers a printout of the page that would open based on their response and ask questions about it.

A professional testing facility may allow observers to watch the test from behind mirrored glass

The person conducting the test is generally in the room with the user and positioned to be able to see what the user does

The user sits at a computer and attempts to complete the tasks requested by the person conducting the test

© 2016 Cengage Learning

FIGURE P-4: Completed usability testing plan

```
 1   Author:
 2   Date:
 3   HTML5 and CSS3 Illustrated Unit P, Lessons
 4
 5   Lakeland Reeds Bed & Breakfast
 6   Website Usability Testing Plan
 7
 8   1. Feedback
 9      With user viewing index.html, ask
10      a. "Based only on this web page, please give me three words that describe this
11   business."
12      b. "Would you expect the owner of this business to be responsible?"
13      c. "Would you expect to be treated respectfully at this bed & breakfast?"
14      d. "Compared to other bed & breakfast establishments that you're familiar with, would
15   you rank this one as low-end, mid-range, or high-end?"
16      e. "Do you have any other impressions of this bed & breakfast based on this web page?"
17   [If yes: "Please describe them."]
18
19   2. Tasks
20      "Now, using the website, please locate the following:"
21      a. "contact information"
22      b. "descriptions of rooms"
23      c. "rates"
24
25   3. "Based on this website, if you were looking to make a reservation at a bed &
26   breakfast, how likely would you be to consider Lakeland Reeds? Definitely not, unlikely,
27   likely, or definitely?"
28
29   4. "Do you have any other feedback about this website?"
30
31   "Thank you for your time and your help."
```

Learning
Outcomes
• Test web pages in
  target browsers

Perform Browser Tests

When you're preparing to publish a website, scrutinizing your pages on different browsers one more time is especially important. While you may not always find errors, testing your pages exhaustively on the most common user agents among your target audience helps ensure that you don't publish web pages that display obvious errors or that don't work as expected for some of your audience members. No matter what your audience, the majority of users are likely to be using Windows. If you are developing on a Mac, it's important to ensure that you have access to a Windows system for testing. In addition, both Android and iOS phones are used by significant numbers of people, so testing on the most widely used versions of these mobile operating systems is also important. **CASE** *You test the links and functionality on each web page using the major Windows and Mac browsers, as well as the default browsers on Android and iOS phones.*

STEPS

TROUBLE
Microsoft Edge is the default Windows browser starting with Windows 10. If you are using an earlier version of Windows, open index.html in Internet Explorer instead.

1. In your editor, open HTM_P-2.html from the Lessons folder where you store your Data Files for this unit, save it as index.html, then repeat to save HTM_P-3.html as aboutus.html, HTM_P-4.html as rooms.html, HTM_P-5.html as contact.html, and HTM_P-6.css as styles.css

2. At the top of each file, enter your name and today's date where indicated, then save the files

3. Open index.html in Edge (Win) or Safari (Mac)

4. Click the About Us link, verify that it opens the About Us page, then click your browser's Back button

5. Repeat Step 4 to test all the links on the web page, then repeat this process for each of the remaining web pages, verifying that the content of each page is displayed as expected
   Clicking each link lets you verify that all the links work and point to the appropriate pages.

6. Compare the appearance of the nav bar on aboutus.html with other pages
   As FIGURE P-5 shows, the icon displayed to the left of the current page is missing on aboutus.html.

QUICK TIP
In Edge or IE, you can press F12 to display the developer tools, click the Emulation button, then select an older version of IE to see how the page would be rendered by that browser.

7. Return to aboutus.html in your editor, within the nav element and in the second li element, add the attribute class="current_page", then save your changes
   The icon is missing because the class value wasn't added to the nav bar link on this page. FIGURE P-6 shows the edited code.

8. Reload aboutus.html in your browser and verify that the nav bar icon is displayed to the left of About Us on the nav bar as on the other web pages

9. View each page of the website in Firefox and in Chrome on your system, then repeat on the other major desktop operating system (Mac or Windows) and test in Firefox, Chrome, and Edge (Win) or Safari (Mac)

QUICK TIP
If necessary, explore trading computer time with a friend or colleague who has a different operating system than yours.

10. View each page of the website on an Android device in Firefox and Chrome or Android Browser, then repeat on an iOS device using Safari

The layout for each page includes an icon before the nav bar link for the current page

On aboutus.html, the icon is missing before the nav bar link

FIGURE P-6: Updated code for About Us page

```
31        <nav class="sitenavigation">
32          <ul>
33            <li><a href="index.html">Home</a></li>
34            <li class="current_page"><a href="aboutus.html">About Us</a></li>
35            <li><a href="rooms.html">Rooms</a></li>
36            <li><a href="contact.html">Contact Us</a></li>
37          </ul>
38        </nav>
```

The `current_page` class is added to the `li` element containing a link to the current page, which is styled with an icon using the `:before` pseudo-element

Using automated test suites

The manual testing method used in this lesson is most realistic for smaller websites with few web pages. As a site grows in size and complexity, however, you can save time and catch more errors through **automated testing**, which is a set of testing measures performed by specialized software. Some free testing services are available online, such as the W3's link checker at validator.w3.org/checklink. In addition, professional web development software

such as Adobe Dreamweaver includes link checking options. These options check for **dead links**, which are links whose targets don't exist. For more advanced testing, you can use a configurable testing suite like Selenium (docs.seleniumhq.org). Testing suites enable you to set up a series of actions that a user might take and have them executed automatically by the software, which then provides the results.

HTML5 & CSS3

Learning
Outcomes
• Simulate web
  page downloads
  at different
  connection speeds

Test Page Loading Speed

Fast downloads are especially important for mobile users. However, optimizing page load time improves the experience of desktop users as well. Any improvements that cause your pages to load more quickly can help avoid users becoming impatient with your site as it loads, which might result in those users abandoning your site and going to a different site instead. It can be useful to test your website at different connection speeds to see how quickly it might load for different users. Chrome Device Mode includes a utility that lets you view a simulation of a web page loading at different connection speeds. **CASE** ▸ *You use Chrome Device Mode to see how fast or slow your pages might load at different connection speeds.*

STEPS

Note: This lesson requires that you have a current version of Google Chrome installed. You can download the current version for free from google.com/chrome.

QUICK TIP

Modeling connection speeds in Chrome does not work when you open files from your local hard drive, so you must open them from a web server instead.

1. **Open index.html from a web server in Google Chrome**

2. **Click the Customize and control Google Chrome button 🞀, point to More tools, then click Developer tools to display the Developer tools pane**

3. **Click the Toggle device mode button 🞀, then click the Emulate screen resolution box to uncheck it if necessary**

4. **Click the Network box, click WiFi (30 Mbps 2ms RTT), then reload the page**

   The first number, measured in megabits per second (Mbps) specifies the maximum amount of data that the connection can carry per second. The second number, measured in milliseconds, represents the maximum time from a request being sent to data being returned from the server. The WiFi option simulates a very fast connection to a web server, so the page reloads almost instantly. FIGURE P-7 shows the selected option in Chrome Device Mode. TABLE P-2 explains the other options in the Network box list.

5. **Click the Network box, click Regular 2G (250 Kbps 300ms RTT), then reload the page**

   The page may take a moment to reload, after which one or more of the images should load slowly. FIGURE P-8 shows the page in the process of loading at Regular 2G speed.

QUICK TIP

You can get an estimate of the cost for a user to view your published web pages in different parts of the world at whatdoesmysite cost.com.

6. **Repeat Step 4 to test at least two other connection speeds**

   Notice that although download time may not be noticeable on a fast connection, it can take a while for your page to be rendered totally on a slower connection. By reducing the number of files downloaded and their size, you can improve your site's performance for all users.

7. **Click the Toggle device mode button 🞀, then close the Developer tools pane**

TABLE P-2: Connection speed options in Chrome Device Mode

option	values	description
GPRS	50 Kbps 500ms RTT	Earliest widespread protocol for cellular data
Regular 2G	250 Kbps 300ms RTT	Lowest connection speed supported by many wireless carriers
Good 2G	450 Kbps 150ms RTT	
Regular 3G	750 Kbps 100ms RTT	Connection speed supported by most wireless carriers starting in the mid 2000's
Good 3G	1 Mps 40ms RTT	
Regular 4G	4 Mbps 20ms RTT	LTE and other modern wireless technologies
DSL	2 Mbps 5ms RTT	Home Internet connection provided over telephone lines
WiFi	30 Mbps 2ms RTT	Communication between a client and server over a local WiFi connection
No Throttling	(varies)	Your actual connection speed, with no simulated slowing

© 2016 Cengage Learning

FIGURE P-7: Web page loading at simulated WiFi speed

Web page opened from a web server

Emulate screen resolution box unchecked

The background and Sun Room images load almost instantly after the page is reloaded at simulated WiFi speed

Toggle Device Mode button

Customize and control Google Chrome button

WiFi selected in Network box

FIGURE P-8: Web page loading at simulated Regular 2G speed

Regular 2G selected in Network box

One or more of the images may take several seconds to load at simulated Regular 2G speed

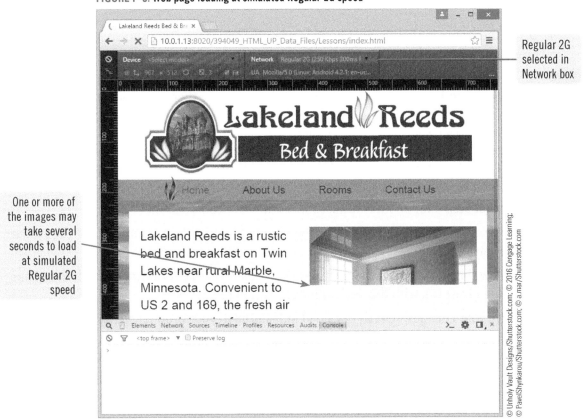

© Unholy Vault Designs/Shutterstock.com; © 2016 Cengage Learning;
© PavelShynkarou/Shutterstock.com; © a.mar/Shutterstock.com

Incorporate a Spritesheet

One of the most commonly used methods for reducing the time it takes for your pages to load over mobile connections is to incorporate spritesheets. To create a spritesheet, you use image editing software to add multiple images to a single, larger image. The resulting image, known as a spritesheet, includes all of the smaller images arranged side-by-side or in a grid. Because the spritesheet is a single image file, you can download it with a single HTTP request. To use a spritesheet on a web page, you specify it as the background image for multiple elements and use CSS properties to control which part of the spritesheet is displayed for each element. **CASE** ▸ *In the nav bar for the Lakeland Reeds B&B, an image is displayed to the left of the link for the current page, and a different decorative image is displayed as a separator in the contact information in the footer. You've been provided a spritesheet that combines these two images, and you replace the current code for the images on the nav bar and in the footer with CSS to show the appropriate part of the spritesheet.*

STEPS

QUICK TIP
You can view the spritesheet images used on any web page by using browser developer tools to view a site's image files.

1. **In your file manager, navigate to the images folder within the Lessons folder where you store your data files for this unit, then double-click** sprites.png **to open it in your default image viewer**

   The sprites.png file contains two images and is your spritesheet for this website. **FIGURE P-9** illustrates how spritesheets work.

2. **Return to** styles.css **in your editor, then in the site navigation bar section and in the** .current_page:before **style rule, change the value for the** content **property to** "" **(empty quotes)**

   The existing page layout specifies an image before the element with the class value current_page. Because a spritesheet is specified as an element's background image, you remove the value for the content property.

3. **In the** .current_page:before **style rule, add the declarations shown in red in** FIGURE P-10, **then save your changes**

QUICK TIP
Because an image from a spritesheet must be specified as a background image, you can't specify alt text for it. For this reason, you should use spritesheets only for decorative images and not for images that relate directly to the content of a web page.

4. **Return to** index.html **in your editor and in the** footer **element, replace each** <img> **tag with the code** <span class="flourish"></span>, **then save your changes**

   FIGURE P-11 shows the updated HTML code for index.html. You must specify a spritesheet as a background image, so you cannot use an img element with a spritesheet. Instead, it's common practice to use span elements, as you've done here. Shortly, you will add a style rule to specify the spritesheet as the background image for elements with the class value flourish, but first you will replace the img elements in the footer on the other web pages with span elements.

5. **Repeat Step 4 for aboutus.html, rooms.html, and contact.html**

6. **Return to** styles.css **in your editor, then in the footer section, comment out the** footer img **style rule**

7. **Below the** footer img **style rule, create a new style rule for elements with the** class **value** flourish **with the declarations shown in red in** FIGURE P-12

QUICK TIP
By using a spritesheet, you've reduced the number of items a browser must request from the server by one without changing your layout.

8. **Save your changes, refresh or reload index.html in your browser, verify that the decorative images in the nav bar and in the footer are still displayed as they were previously, then repeat for aboutus.html, rooms.html, and contact.html**

FIGURE P-9: Using a spritesheet in a web page layout

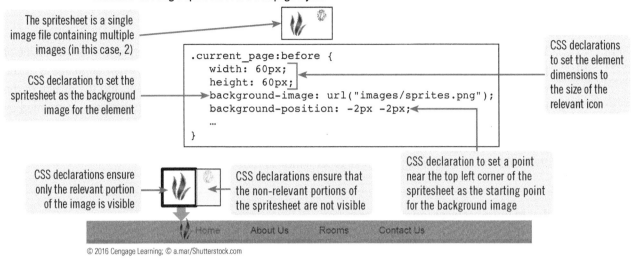

The spritesheet is a single image file containing multiple images (in this case, 2)

CSS declaration to set the spritesheet as the background image for the element

CSS declarations to set the element dimensions to the size of the relevant icon

```
.current_page:before {
    width: 60px;
    height: 60px;
    background-image: url("images/sprites.png");
    background-position: -2px -2px;
    ...
}
```

CSS declarations ensure only the relevant portion of the image is visible

CSS declarations ensure that the non-relevant portions of the spritesheet are not visible

CSS declaration to set a point near the top left corner of the spritesheet as the starting point for the background image

Home   About Us   Rooms   Contact Us

© 2016 Cengage Learning; © a.mar/Shutterstock.com

FIGURE P-10: Updated style rule incorporating spritesheet into nav bar

```
99      display: inline-block;
100     position: absolute;
101     top: -16px;
102     left: -50px;
103     content: "";
104     overflow: hidden;
105     background-repeat: no-repeat;
106     background-image: url("images/sprites.png");
107     background-position: -2px -2px;
108 }
```

The value of the content property is changed to an empty string

The overflow property prevents other parts of the spritesheet from being displayed

The sprites.png image file is specified as the background image

The background is displayed starting near the top left corner of the spritesheet; these values are usually generated automatically by a program that creates spritesheets

FIGURE P-11: img elements replaced by span elements in HTML code

```
52      <footer>
53          <p>45 Marsh Grass Ln. <span class="flourish"></span> Marble, MN 55764
54          <span class="flourish"></span> (218) 555-5253</p>
55      </footer>
```

FIGURE P-12: Updated style rule incorporating spritesheet into footer

```
222 /* footer img {
223     vertical-align: baseline;
224 } */
225 .flourish {
226     width: 36px;
227     height: 23px;
228     background-position: -64px -2px;
229     vertical-align: baseline;
230     display: inline-block;
231     overflow: hidden;
232     background-repeat: no-repeat;
233     background-image: url("images/sprites.png");
234 }
```

The footer img style rule is commented out because the footer element no longer contains img elements

The dimensions of the flourish icon

The background position; these values are usually generated automatically by a program that creates spritesheets

Optimize Images

You can reduce the size of some files that are part of your website without affecting their content. One of the most important targets of this type of size reduction is image files. Even when an image is at the correct size for your web page, it's often possible to reduce the file size by reducing the quality of the image in a way that humans can't perceive. This process, known as image optimization, is performed by specialized software. In some cases, an optimized image can be one-half or one-quarter the size of the original file. **CASE** *You upload the largest images—the background image of the water and the images of the rooms—to an online image optimizer to see if their sizes can be reduced.*

STEPS

1. **In your browser, open** tinypng.com
   This is a website that offers online image optimization for .png and .jpg images.

2. **In your file manager, navigate to the images folder within the Lessons folder where you store your data files for this unit, resize and/or rearrange your windows if necessary so both your file manager and browser are visible, then drag the file** garden.jpg **over the Drop your .jpg or .png files here! box as shown in** FIGURE P-13
   The website processes the file and then displays the results of its optimization.

3. **Repeat Step 2 to optimize the files reed.jpg, sun.jpg, tree.jpg, and water.jpg**
   When all 5 files are processed, the website lists the results as shown in FIGURE P-14.

4. **Click the** download link **for garden.jpg, then save the file with the filename** garden-sm.jpg **in the images folder within the Lessons folder where you store your data files for this unit**

5. **Repeat Step 4 to save reed.jpg as** reed-sm.jpg, **sun.jpg as** sun-sm.jpg, **tree.jpg as** tree-sm.jpg, **and water.jpg as** water-sm.jpg

6. **Return to** rooms.html **in your editor, in the** img **elements for the first 4 image files you optimized, change the filenames to the new versions, then save your changes**
   The updated img elements are shown in FIGURE P-15.

7. **Return to** styles.css **in your editor, in the main content section and in the** article **style rule, change the filename for the second** background **property value to** water-sm.jpg, **then save your changes**
   The updated style rule is shown in FIGURE P-16.

8. **Refresh or reload rooms.html in your browser**
   The appearance of the page is unchanged because the optimized images are not perceptibly different from the earlier versions.

Including appropriately sized images

While sprites work only for background images, you can implement other techniques to optimize the balance between image size and download speed for other images in your web pages. It can be tempting to use the largest available size for an image and scale it down to fit the browser window using media queries; however, this technique requires all browsers, even those using mobile connections, to download huge files. A more efficient solution is to create multiple versions of an image at the sizes and resolutions that your web page targets and load only the appropriate image for each device. Implementing this strategy requires the use of JavaScript. Another option is to use an online service that resizes images for you on the fly as users load your pages.

FIGURE P-13: Dragging garden.jpg to the tinypng image optimizer

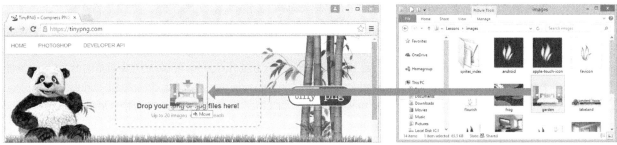

© Nicolesa/Shutterstock; © Unholy Vault Designs/Shutterstock.com; © 2016 Cengage Learning; Courtesy Jason Bucy; © PavelShynkarou/Shutterstock.com; Source: tinypng.com

FIGURE P-14: Results of image optimization on tinypng.com

The five files you uploaded to the tinypng website

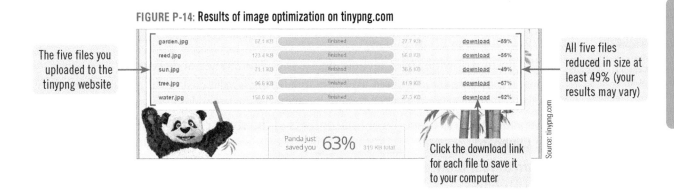

All five files reduced in size at least 49% (your results may vary)

Click the download link for each file to save it to your computer

Source: tinypng.com

FIGURE P-15: `img` elements updated to reference optimized image files

```
47          <img src="images/garden-sm.jpg" width="370" height="248" alt="a room
48          with a low, two-person bed, with shelves built into the walls holding a
49          lamp on each side of the bed">
```

```
58          <img src="images/reed-sm.jpg" width="370" height="392" alt="a carpeted
59          room with a high sloping ceiling, two small bright windows, and a two-
60          person bed with a bedside table and lamp on each side">
```

```
69          <img src="images/sun-sm.jpg" width="370" height="278" alt="room with a
70          hardwood floor, bright windows on two sides, and a two-person bed with
71          a bedside table and lamp on each side">
```

```
80          <img src="images/tree-sm.jpg" width="370" height="247" alt="a large
81          room with a hardwood floor, a tall window overlooking trees, a two-
82          person bed with a single bedside table, and a padded chair next to the
83          window">
```

FIGURE P-16: `article` style rule updated to reference optimized image file

```
110    /* main content */
111    article {
112        margin: 0 auto;
113        padding: 1.4em;
114        background: #7eccec;
115        background: url("images/water-sm.jpg");
116    }
```

Reduce the Size of CSS Files

Learning Outcomes
• Remove Orphaned Styles
• Minify a style sheet

As you add, change, and remove features and formatting while developing a website, you can end up with orphaned styles, which are style rules based on selectors that no longer apply to any elements on your web pages. Removing orphaned styles reduces the amount of code users have to download, shrinking download time. In addition, streamlined code makes it easier for other developers to work with. Once you are satisfied that your style sheet includes only necessary code, it's a common practice to minify it before uploading it. Minifying removes all unnecessary characters, which reduces file size. While minifying results in a file that's hard for a human to read, it makes no difference to a user agent's ability to parse it. **CASE** ▶ *You've identified an orphaned style in styles.css left over from an older version of the layout. You remove this style rule and minify the style sheet to reduce the amount of time it takes for users to download the CSS file.*

STEPS

QUICK TIP
You can use a browser extension such as Dust-Me Selectors (brothercake.com/ dustmeselectors) to automatically identify style rules that are not in use.

1. **In your editor, return to** styles.css

2. **In the document-wide styles section, delete the** .container **style rule**
   Earlier versions of the layout included an element with the class value container, but this class value is not part of the current layout. **FIGURE P-17** shows the updated document-wide styles section of the style sheet.

3. **Save your changes, select the entire contents of the styles.css file, then copy the code to the Clipboard**

4. **Return to your browser, open cssshrink.com, then scroll down as necessary to the IN and OUT boxes**

QUICK TIP
You can perform basic CSS minification manually by deleting all line breaks from the code and deleting all spaces between curly braces.

5. **Click the code box below the word IN, press [Ctrl]+A (Win) or [command]+A (Mac), press [Delete] to delete the code, then paste the contents of the Clipboard**
   The pasted code is displayed on the left side of the page and a minified version is shown on the right side, as shown in **FIGURE P-18**.

6. **Click the code box below the word OUT, press [Ctrl]+A (Win) or [command]+A (Mac), then copy the selected code to the Clipboard**

7. **Return to your editor, create a new CSS file, paste the contents of the Clipboard, then save the file as** styles.min.css **to the Lessons folder where you save your files for this unit**
   Notice that the code is all on one long line. Including .min in the filename before the file extension is a standard way to indicate that a file contains minified code.

QUICK TIP
The difference in page loading time as a result of your changes may not be noticeable, but it can make a big difference in a larger website and in conjunction with other optimizations.

8. **Return to** index.html, **update the** link **element to reference** styles.min.css, **save your changes, then repeat to update the** link **elements in aboutus.html, rooms.html, and contact.html**
   FIGURE P-19 shows an updated link element.

9. **Refresh or reload index.html in your browser, verify that the changes you made to the style sheet don't impact the appearance of the page, then repeat for aboutus.html, rooms.html, and contact.html**

Working with minified files

When you maintain a website, it can be tedious to go through the process of minifying a file every time you make a change to your site's CSS. Fortunately, many tools are available for developers that can automate tasks such as minifying. When it's time to publish their files, many developers execute a customized script that performs the set of tasks required to upload the new version of the site. Among these tasks is automatic minification of CSS files. This enables developers to work only with human-readable versions of their files, while ensuring that minified versions are published to their web servers when it's time to publish changes to the code.

```
29    /* document-wide styles */
30    body {
31       margin: 0 auto;
32       font-family: Arial, Helvetica, sans-serif;
33    }
34    p {
35       line-height: 1.4em;
36       font-size: 1.3em;
37    }
38    a:link {
39       color: black;
40    }
41    a:visited {
42       color: #888;
43    }
44                                              .container
45    /* skip navigation link */               style rule deleted
```

FIGURE P-18: CSS minification tool at cssshrink.com

Pasted code

Formatted version of code for comparison

Minified code; notice the comments are not included in the minified code

Formatted version of minified code for comparison with original version

Source: cssshrink.com

FIGURE P-19: `link` element updated to reference minified style sheet

```
13        <meta charset="utf-8">
14        <meta name="viewport" content="width=device-width">
15        <script src="modernizr-latest.js"></script>
16        <link href='http://fonts.googleapis.com/css?family=Bitter:400,700' rel='stylesheet'
17        type='text/css'>
18        <link rel="stylesheet" href="styles.min.css">
19        <link rel="shortcut icon" href="images/favicon.ico">
20        <link rel="apple-touch-icon" href="images/apple-touch-icon.png">
21        <link rel="icon" sizes="192x192" href="images/android.png">
22    </head>
```

Customize modernizr.js

Including the Modernizr JavaScript library in your web pages is an easy way to ensure that code that uses HTML and CSS features can still be rendered by older browsers. Because the features you incorporate into your website can change as you develop it, it's common to download and include the entire Modernizr library during the process of building a site. However, when you are ready to publish a site, it's a good idea to create a custom build of Modernizr, which is a version of the library that includes only the features that your site uses. By excluding code that your site doesn't need, you reduce the size of the Modernizr file that users have to download, further increasing the speed at which your site downloads. The modernizr.com website includes a configuration tool you can use to select the Modernizr features you need and download a custom build based on the selected features. **CASE** ➤ *You create a custom Modernizr build to support the modern features incorporated in index.html, aboutus.html, rooms.html, and contact.html.*

STEPS

1. **In your browser, open Modernizr.com**

   The main page for the Modernizr website opens as shown in **FIGURE P-20**.

2. **Click the** Production button

   The Download Modernizr page opens, which displays check boxes for all of the features that it can support.

TROUBLE
The version number on your screen may not match the version number shown in this step (v3.7.1).

3. **In the CSS3 column, click the check boxes for** @font-face **and** CSS Generated Content

4. **In the HTML5 column, click the check boxes for** Input Attributes **and** Input Types

5. **In the Extra section, click the check box for** html5shiv v3.7.1 w/ printshiv

   The completed form is shown in **FIGURE P-21**.

6. **Click the** Generate! button

   A minified version of your custom build is generated and displayed in the text box below the Generate! button.

TROUBLE
Because you are downloading a JavaScript file, your browser may warn you that the file is potentially harmful; click the option that ignores the warning and downloads the file.

7. **Click the** Download Custom Build button, **then save the custom build file to the Lessons folder where you store your data files for this unit**

   You may need to use your file manager to navigate to your downloads folder and then move or copy the custom build file from the downloads folder to your Lessons folder.

8. **Return to** index.html **in your editor, in the** script **element in the head section, replace the filename** modernizr-latest.js **with the filename of your custom build, save your changes, then repeat for aboutus.html, rooms.html, and contact.html**

   Sample updated code for index.html is shown in **FIGURE P-22**.

9. **Refresh or reload index.html in your browser, verify that the layout is unchanged, repeat for the other three pages, then if you have access to IE8, use it to test all 4 pages and verify that the layouts are displayed as expected**

10. **Validate your HTML and CSS code**

FIGURE P-20: Modernizr.com main web page

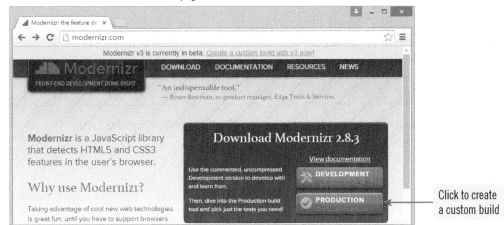

Click to create
a custom build

Source: modernizr.com

FIGURE P-21: Download Modernizr page with options selected

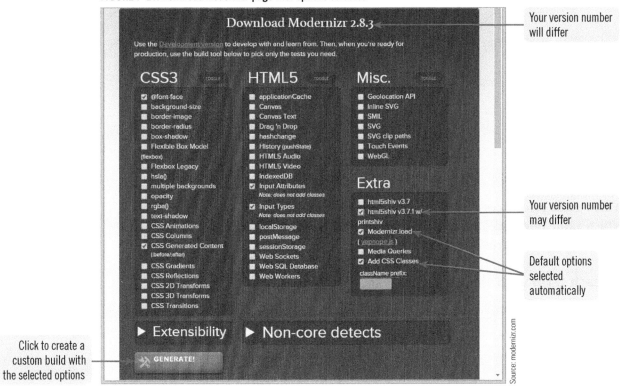

Your version number
will differ

Your version number
may differ

Default options
selected
automatically

Click to create a
custom build with
the selected options

Source: modernizr.com

FIGURE P-22: Link to Modernizr library updated for custom build

```
14        <meta name="viewport" content="width=device-width">    Your filename may differ
15        <script src="modernizr.custom.97014.js"></script>
16        <link href='http://fonts.googleapis.com/css?family=Bitter:400,700' rel='stylesheet'
```

Practice

Concepts Review

Refer to the code shown in FIGURE P-23 **to answer the following questions.**

FIGURE P-23

```
14        <meta name="viewport" content="width=device-width">
15        <script src="modernizr.custom.97014.js"></script>
16        <link href='http://fonts.googleapis.com/css?family=Bitter:400,700' rel='stylesheet'
17        type='text/css'>
18        <link rel="stylesheet" href="styles.min.css">
19        <link rel="shortcut icon" href="images/favicon.ico">
20        <link rel="apple-touch-icon" href="images/apple-touch-icon.png">
21        <link rel="icon" sizes="192x192" href="images/android.png">
22    </head>

46            <figure>
47                <img src="images/garden-sm.jpg" width="370" height="248" alt="a room
48                with a low, two-person bed, with shelves built into the walls holding a
49                lamp on each side of the bed">
50            </figure>
```

1. **Which value references a minified style sheet?**
2. **Which value references a custom build of the Modernizr library?**
3. **Which value references an optimized image?**

Match each term with the statement that best describes it.

4. **performance**
5. **minified**
6. **optimized**
7. **automated testing**
8. **dead links**
9. **orphaned styles**

a. describes HTML, CSS, or JavaScript code that has had all characters removed that are not needed by a browser to parse the files

b. links whose targets don't exist

c. a measure of how quickly a published site loads and responds to user interaction over the Internet

d. describes an image file that has been compressed as much as possible without losing significant visual information

e. style rules based on selectors that no longer apply to any elements in your web pages

f. a set of browser testing measures performed by specialized software

Select the best answer from the list of choices.

10. **What can you do to reduce the size of a CSS file?**
    - **a.** minify it
    - **b.** optimize it
    - **c.** create a spritesheet
    - **d.** create a custom build

11. **What can you do to reduce the size of an image file?**
    - **a.** minify it.
    - **b.** optimize it
    - **c.** remove dead links
    - **d.** create a custom build

12. **To collect the best information possible from usability tests, it's important to**
    - **a.** purchase specialized testing software
    - **b.** have access to a testing facility
    - **c.** skip such testing if you don't really have time for it
    - **d.** identify questions you want all test participants to answer

13. **Which of the following is a reasonable alternative to performing manual browser testing on your entire website?**
    - **a.** testing on only one operating system
    - **b.** automated browser testing
    - **c.** skipping browser testing altogether
    - **d.** testing on only a single browser

14. **Which of the following is an advantage of removing unused styles?**
    - **a.** It makes your code more likely to work on different browsers
    - **b.** It makes your code easier for other developers to work with
    - **c.** It ensures that your code is valid
    - **d.** It eliminates large images from your site

Skills Review

1. **Plan usability tests**
    - **a.** In your editor, open HTM_P-7.txt from the SR folder where you store your Data Files for this unit, then save it as **Big J Test Plan.txt**.
    - **b.** At the top of the file, enter your first and last names and today's date where indicated, then save your changes.
    - **c.** In section 1, add questions asking if test participants would expect to have fun at the restaurant, if they would expect the restaurant to be kid friendly, and if it's a restaurant where they would take a date.
    - **d.** In section 2, add instructions for test participants to locate a menu and the phone number for the Dundas location.
    - **e.** Save your changes.

2. **Perform browser tests**
    - **a.** In your editor, open HTM_P-8.html from the SR folder where you store your Data Files for this unit, save it as **index.html**, then repeat to save HTM_P-9.html as **history.html**, HTM_P-10.html as **location.html**, HTM_P-11.html as **catering.html**, and HTM_P-12.css as **styles.css**.
    - **b.** In the comment section at the top of each file, enter your first and last names and today's date, then save your changes.
    - **c.** Open index.html in Edge (Win) or Safari (Mac). (*Hint*: If you are using Windows 8 or earlier, open index.html in Internet Explorer instead.)
    - **d.** Click the History link, verify that it opens the History page, then click your browser's Back button. Repeat to test all the links on the web page, then repeat this process for each of the remaining web pages, verifying that the content of each page is displayed as expected.
    - **e.** Compare the appearance of the main heading on catering.html with the main headings on other pages
    - **f.** Return to catering.html in your editor, within the `article` element, change the h3 element containing the text *Catering* to an h2 element, then save your changes.

g. Reload catering.html in your browser and verify that the format and size of the main heading text Catering matches the main headings on other pages, as shown in **FIGURE P-24**.

h. View each page of the website in Firefox and in Chrome on your system, then repeat on the other major desktop operating system (Mac or Windows) using Firefox, Chrome, and Edge (Win) or Safari (Mac).

i. View each page of the website on an Android device in Firefox and Chrome or Android Browser, then repeat on an iOS device using Safari.

FIGURE P-24

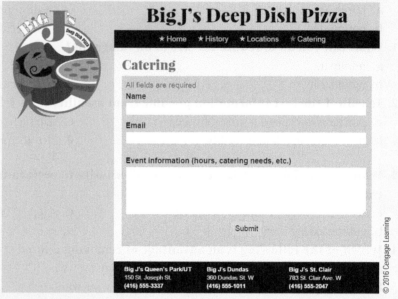

3. Test page loading speed

a. Open index.html from a web server in Google Chrome.

b. Open the developer tools, then enable Device Mode.

c. Choose WiFi (30 Mbps 2ms RTT) as the network speed, then reload the page.

d. Choose Good 2G (450 Kbps 150ms RTT) as the network speed, then reload the page.

e. Repeat Step d to test at least two other connection speeds.

f. Disable device mode, then close the developer tools.

4. Incorporate a spritesheet

a. In your file manager, navigate to the images folder within the SR folder where you store your data files for this unit, then double-click the sprites.png file to open it in your default image viewer.

b. Return to styles.css in your editor, then in the site navigation section and in the `nav.sitenavigation li:before` style rule, change the value for the `content` property to `""` (empty quotes). Above the `content` declaration, add the declarations `width: 15px;` and `height: 15px;`. Below the `content` declaration, add the declarations `display: inline-block;`, `overflow: hidden;`, `background-repeat: no-repeat;`, `background-image: url("images/sprites.png");`, and `background-position: -2px -2px`.

c. In the `nav.sitenavigation li.current_page:before` style rule, comment out the `content` declaration, then add the declaration `background-position: -19px -2px;`.

d. Save your changes, refresh or reload index.html in your browser, verify that the decorative images in the nav bar are still displayed as they were previously, then repeat for history.html, location.html, and catering.html.

5. Optimize images

a. In your browser, open tinypng.com. (*Hint*: If you are unable to open tinypng.com, use a search engine to search on the terms online image optimization, open a service from the results, follow the directions on the site to optimize the 2 images listed in Step b, download the results using the filenames in Step c, then skip to Step d.)

b. In your file manager, navigate to the images folder within the SR folder where you store your data files for this unit, then drag the file slices.jpg over the Drop your .jpg or .png files here! box. Repeat to optimize the file brick.jpg.

c. Click the download link for slices.jpg, then save the file with the filename slices-sm.jpg in the images folder within the SR folder where you store your data files for this unit. Repeat to download brick.jpg and save it as brick-sm.jpg. (*Hint*: If the files are automatically saved to your Downloads folder, navigate to the Downloads folder in your file manager, rename the files if necessary, then move the files to the images folder within the SR folder where you store your data files for this unit.)

Skills Review (continued)

d. Return to history.html in your editor, in the img element for slices.jpg, change the filename to slices-sm.jpg, then save your changes.

e. Return to styles.css in your editor, in the body and container section and in the `body` style rule, change the filename for the second `background` property value to brick-sm.jpg, then save your changes.

f. Refresh or reload history.html in your browser, then verify that the appearances of the image of the neon sign and of the background brick pattern is unchanged.

6. **Reduce the size of CSS files**

a. In your editor, return to styles.css. In the main content section, delete the `div.subsection p` style rule. In the fieldset styles section, delete the `.reserveinfo` style rule. Save your changes.

b. Select the entire contents of the styles.css file, then copy the code to the Clipboard.

c. Return to your browser, open cssshrink.com, then scroll down as necessary to the IN and OUT boxes.

d. Click the code box below the word IN, select and delete the code, then paste the contents of the Clipboard.

e. Click the code box below the word OUT, select all the code, then copy the selected code to the Clipboard.

f. Return to your editor, create a new CSS file, paste the contents of the Clipboard, then save the file as styles.min.css to the SR folder where you save your files for this unit.

g. Return to index.html, update the `link` element to reference styles.min.css, save your changes, then repeat to update the `link` elements in history.html, location.html, and catering.html.

h. Refresh or reload index.html in your browser, verify that the changes you made to the style sheet don't impact the appearance of the page, then repeat for history.html, location.html, and catering.html.

7. **Customize modernizr.js**

a. In your browser, open Modernizr.com, then click the Production button.

b. In the CSS3 column, click the check boxes for @font-face and CSS Generated Content.

c. In the HTML5 column, click the check boxes for Input Attributes and Input Types.

d. In the Extra section, click the check box for html5shiv v3.7.1 w/ printshiv. (*Note*: The version number on your screen may not match the version number shown in this step (v3.7.1).)

e. Click the Generate! button, click the Download Custom Build button, then save the custom build file to the SR folder where you store your data files for this unit.

f. Return to index.html in your editor, in the `script` element in the head section, replace the filename modernizr-latest.js with the filename of your custom build, save your changes, then repeat for history.html, location.html, and catering.html.

g. Refresh or reload index.html in your browser, verify that the layout is unchanged, repeat for the other three pages, then if you have access to IE8, use it to test all 4 pages and verify that the layouts are displayed as expected.

h. Validate your HTML and CSS code.

Independent Challenge 1

As you prepare to publish the website for the Spotted Wren Garden Center, you test and enhance the performance of the website.

a. In your editor, open HTM_P-13.html from the IC1 folder where you store your Data Files for this unit, save it as **index.html**, then repeat to save HTM_P-14.html as **hours.html**, HTM_P-15.html as **resource.html**, HTM_P-16.html as **contact.html**, and HTM_P-17.css as **styles.css**. In the comment section at the top of each file, enter your name and today's date where indicated, then save the files.

Independent Challenge 1 (continued)

b. Examine all four web pages in the browser of your choice. The code for the footer in resource.html page uses a different structure of elements than the other pages; use browser developer tools to examine the footer code for resource.html and one other page in the same site to identify the difference. Return to resource.html in your editor, correct the code for the footer, save your changes, then reload the page in your browser and verify that you have fixed the error. The web page should match **FIGURE P-25**.

c. Test all links in all four pages. Preview all pages in Edge (or IE on an older version of Windows, or Safari on a Mac), Firefox, and Chrome, then repeat on the other major platform (Windows or Mac). Use a web server to test all pages on a mobile device running Android and on an iOS device.

d. Use Chrome Device Mode to simulate the loading speed of resource.html at 3 different connection speeds.

e. Optimize the blanket.jpg and rugosa.jpg images on resource.html, the cone.jpg image on index.html, and the planting.jpg image on hours.html. (Note: All images are in the images folder for IC1.) Link the relevant HTML files to the optimized images, then run the loading speed simulation again and notice any differences.

FIGURE P-25

f. Return to styles.css in your editor, remove the orphaned h4 style rule, then save your changes. Create a minified version of styles.css with the filename styles.min.css, link to the minified style sheet in all 4 HTML files, then save your changes.

g. Create a custom build of Modernizr that includes only the features used on the Spotted Wren website, save the file to the IC1 folder where you store your data files for this unit, then change the Modernizr `script` element in each HTML file to reference the custom build file. (*Hint*: In the CSS3 column, select @font-face and CSS Generated Content, in the HTML5 column, select Input Attributes and Input Types, then in the Extra section, select html5shiv v3.7.1 w/ printshiv (the version number shown may differ).) If you have access to IE8, use it to test all 4 HTML documents and verify that the pages appear and function as expected.

h. Validate your HTML and CSS files. (*Note*: You can ignore any CSS errors generated due to the use of the `:valid` pseudo-class.)

Independent Challenge 2

As you prepare to publish the website for the Murfreesboro Regional Soccer League, you test and enhance the performance of the website.

a. In your editor, open HTM_P-18.txt from the IC2 folder where you store your Data Files for this unit, save it as **MRSL Test Plan.txt**, then repeat to save HTM_P-19.html as **index.html**, HTM_P-20.html as **started.html**, HTM_P-21.html as **schedule.html**, HTM_P-22.html as **report.html**, and HTM_P-23.css as **styles.css**. In the comment section at the top of each file, enter your name and today's date where indicated, then save the files.

Independent Challenge 2 (continued)

b. Examine all four web pages in the browser of your choice. Identify the two inconsistencies in layout between the pages, use browser tools and/or your editor to identify the code responsible, then fix and save the files. (*Hint:* One inconsistency involves the nav bar and the other involves the footer.) All of your web pages should match the layout shown in **FIGURE P-26**.

FIGURE P-26

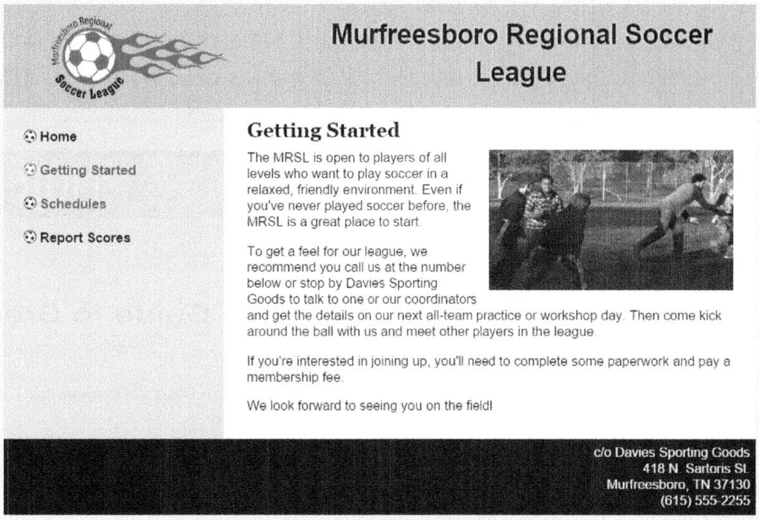

©2016 Cengage Learning; Source: letsmove.gov

c. Return to MRSL Test Plan.txt in your editor, then add questions to complete the test plan. (*Hint:* Think about what goals an organization like MRSL might have—for instance, creating a welcoming environment for people of different ages, genders, races, and abilities—then write questions that would help the organization understand whether the site was meeting those goals.) Save your changes.

d. Test all links in all four pages. Preview all pages in Edge (or IE on an older version of Windows, or Safari on a Mac), Firefox, and Chrome, then repeat on the other major platform (Windows or Mac). Use a web server to test all pages on a mobile device running Android and on an iOS device.

e. Use Chrome Device Mode to simulate the loading speed of started.html at 3 different connection speeds.

f. Optimize the outdoors.png image on started.html, the kick.jpg image on index.html, and the grass.jpg image used on all pages, link to the optimized images in the associated HTML files, then run the loading speed simulation again and notice any differences.

g. Return to styles.css in your editor, then in the site navigation section and within the `nav.sitenavigation li a:before` style rule, change the value for the `content` property to `""` (an empty string). Add the declarations `width: 20px;` and `height: 20px;` before the `padding-right` declaration. Below the `top` declaration, add the declarations `display: inline-block;`, `overflow: hidden;`, `background-repeat: no-repeat;`, `background-image: url("images/sprites.png");`, and `background-position: -2px -2px;`.

h. In the `nav.sitenavigation li.current_page a:before` style rule, comment out the `content` declaration, then add the declaration `background-position: -24px -2px;`. Save your changes, refresh or reload index.html in your browser, verify that a red soccer ball icon is still displayed next to the current link (Home) in the nav bar and that black soccer ball icons are displayed next to all the other links in the nav bar, then check that the icons are displayed correctly on the remaining pages as well.

i. Return to styles.css in your editor, remove the orphaned `aside` style rule and the sidebar comment above it. Also remove the `aside` selector in the print styles section, then save your changes.

j. Create a minified version of styles.css with the filename styles.min.css, link to the minified style sheet in all 4 HTML files, then save your changes.

k. Create a custom build of Modernizr that includes only the features used on the MRSL website, save the file to the IC2 folder where you store your data files for this unit, then change the Modernizr `script` element in each HTML file to reference the custom build file. (*Hint:* In the CSS3 column, select @font-face and CSS Generated Content, in the HTML5 column, select Input Attributes and Input Types, then in the Extra section, select html5shiv v3.7.1 w/ printshiv (the version number shown may differ).) If you have access to IE8, use it to test all 4 HTML documents and verify that the pages appear and function as expected.

l. Validate your HTML and CSS files. (*Note:* You can ignore any CSS errors generated due to the use of the `:valid` pseudo-class.)

Independent Challenge 3

As you prepare to publish the website for Hotel Natoma, you test and enhance the performance of the website.

a. In your editor, open HTM_P-24.html from the IC3 folder where you store your Data Files for this unit, save it as **index.html**, then repeat to save HTM_P-25.html as **nearby.html**, HTM_P-26.html as **museums.html**, HTM_P-27.html as **greensf.html**, and HTM_P-28.css as **styles.css**. In the comment section at the top of each file, enter your name and today's date where indicated, then save the files.

FIGURE P-27

HotelNatoma

Home   What's Nearby   Museums   Green SF

Guide to Green San Francisco
Top-ranked must-see green destinations in San Francisco

Cable Cars + Cable Car museum
Crissy Field
Quesada Gardens
Angel Island
Bike network
Transit Museum
Conservatory of Flowers
Golden Gate Park

Cable Car

564 Natoma St. • San Francisco, CA 94103 • (415) 555-8378

b. Examine all four web pages in the browser of your choice. Identify the layout issue on one of the pages, use browser tools and/or your editor to identify the code responsible, then fix and save the file. (*Hint*: All figures should float on the right.) The Green San Francisco web page should match the layout shown in **FIGURE P-27**.

c. Test all links in all four pages. Fix any broken links. Preview all pages in Edge (or IE on an older version of Windows, or Safari on a Mac), Firefox, and Chrome, then repeat on the other major platform (Windows or Mac). Use a web server to test all pages on a mobile device running Android and on an iOS device.

d. Use Chrome Device Mode to simulate the loading speed of index.html at 3 different connection speeds.

e. Optimize the bridge.jpg image on index.html, the cablecar.png image on nearby.html, the tiedye.jpg image on museums.html, and the cablecar.jpg image on greensf.html, link to the optimized images in the corresponding HTML files, then run the loading speed simulation again and notice any differences.

f. Return to museums.html in your editor, convert the list of museums from list items to paragraphs, preserving the `class` attributes and values, then remove the ul element. Save your changes, then return to styles.css in your editor. In the main content section, before the `li.art` rule, add a style rule for content before p elements with the `class` values `art`, `culture`, or `kids`. Add the declarations `width: 30px;`, `height: 30px;`, `content: "";`, `display: inline-block;`, `overflow: hidden;`, `background-repeat: no-repeat;`, and `background-image: url("images/sprites.png");`. In the `li.art` rule, change the selector to `p.art:before`, then replace the `list-style-image` declaration with `background-position: -2px -2px;`. Repeat to change `li.culture` to `p.culture:before` with a background position of `-34px -2px`, and to change `li.kids` to `p.kids:before` with a background position of `-66px -2px`. Save your changes, refresh or reload museums.html in your browser, then verify that the 3 different museum icons are still displayed next to the museum names.

g. Return to styles.css in your editor, in the main content section, delete the orphaned `article ul` style rule, delete the form styles, fieldset styles, field styles, and label styles sections and all the style rules within them, then save your changes. Create a minified version of styles.css with the filename styles.min.css, link to the minified style sheet in all 4 HTML files, then save your changes.

h. Create a custom build of Modernizr that includes only the features used on the Hotel Natoma website, save the file to the IC3 folder where you store your data files for this unit, then change the Modernizr `script` element in each HTML file to reference the custom build file. (*Hint*: In the CSS3 column, select @font-face and CSS Generated Content, then in the Extra section, select html5shiv v3.7.1 w/ printshiv (the version number shown may differ).) If you have access to IE8, use it to test all 4 HTML documents and verify that the pages appear as expected.

i. Validate your HTML and CSS files.

Independent Challenge 4 – Explore

As you prepare to publish the website for Eating Well in Season, you test and enhance the performance of the website.

a. In your editor, open HTM_P-29.txt from the IC4 folder where you store your Data Files for this unit, save it as **EWIS Test Plan.txt**, then repeat to save HTM_P-30.html as **index.html**, HTM_P-31.html as **sources.html**, HTM_P-32.html as **menus.html**, and HTM_P-33.css as **styles.css**. In the comment section at the top of each file, enter your name and today's date where indicated, then save the files.

b. Examine all three web pages in the browser of your choice. Identify the two inconsistencies in content or layout between the pages, use browser tools and/or your editor to identify the code responsible, then fix and save the files. All of your web pages should match the layout shown in **FIGURE P-28**.

c. Return to EWIS Test Plan.txt in your editor, then complete the document by writing questions you would ask usability test participants about the website. Save your changes.

d. Test all links in all three pages, fix any issues, then save your changes. Preview all pages in Edge (or IE on an older version of Windows, or Safari on a Mac), Firefox, and Chrome, then repeat on the other major platform (Windows or Mac). Use a web server to test all pages on a mobile device running Android and on an iOS device.

e. Use Chrome Device Mode to simulate the loading speed of started.html at 3 different connection speeds. Optimize the delivery.jpg, meal.jpg, and veggies.jpg images on index.html, link to the optimized images, then run the loading speed simulation again and notice any differences.

f. Open Firefox, download the Dust-Me Selectors extension from brothercake.com/dustmeselectors, then install it. Open index.html in Firefox, then click the Scan this page button ☑ added by Dust-Me Selectors to check for unused styles. Repeat for sources.html and menus.html. The resulting list shows the selectors for style rules that are not used by your site. (*Hint*: If you are using a computer on which Dust-Me Selectors was already installed when you started this step, after you scan the first page, click the Trash this site's data button in the Dust-Me Data window, then rescan all three pages.) Return to styles.css in your editor, remove the orphaned style rules, then save your changes. Create a minified version of styles.css with the filename styles.min.css, link to the minified style sheet in all 3 HTML files, then save your changes.

g. Create a custom build of Modernizr that includes only the features used on the EWIS website, save the file to the IC4 folder where you store your data files for this unit, then change the Modernizr `script` element in each HTML file to reference the custom build file. If you have access to IE8, use it to test all 3 HTML documents and verify that the pages appear and function as expected.

h. Validate your HTML and CSS files.

Visual Workshop

In your editor, open the file HTM_P-34.html from the VW folder where you store your Data Files for this unit, save it as **index.html**, then repeat to save HTM_P-35.html as **releases.html**, HTM_P-36.html as **order.html**, and HTM_P-37.css as **styles.css**. Add your first and last names and today's date to the comment section at the top of each file, then save your changes. Open all 3 pages in a browser and compare them to each other and to the page shown in **FIGURE P-29**. Make any changes necessary so the layout and common content is consistent and matches the figure. Optimize the image on releases.html, minify styles.css, and download and link to a custom build of Modernizr for all 3 pages. Save your changes, then validate your HTML and CSS code.

FIGURE P-29

Revisions Bookstore & Cafe

Home   New Releases   Special Orders

New Releases for November

Michelle Alexander

N.K. Jemisin

Walter Mosley

Jacqueline Woodson

Custom brewed coffee and hand-selected books.

Special orders are our specialty.

412 N. 25th St.
Richmond, VA 23223
(804) 555-2565

HTML

HTML Elements

This table includes all HTML elements covered in this text, along with selected attributes.

element	content/function
global attributes that apply to all HTML elements	
id="*id*"	a unique identifier for the current element
lang="*keyword*"	the primary language of the element contents, from a standard list of abbreviations
class="*class*"	one or more classes that the element is part of, separated by spaces
style="*style*"	one or more CSS declarations that apply only to the current element
!	contains comment text within the <!-- --> tag pair
a	links enclosed text or elements to another web page or other resource
href="*filename* | *url*"	address of web page or other resource that opens when the link is clicked or activated
target="_blank | _self"	a keyword for the window or tab in which the linked resource opens
area	creates a shape within an image map
alt="*text*"	text to display or be read aloud in place of the shape
coords="*x1,y1,…*"	a comma-separated list of coordinates for the specified shape value measured from the top and left edges of the image
href="*filename* | *url*"	a URL, local filename, or hash link to the target document or location opened by the hotspot
shape="circle | poly | rect"	the type of shape to create
article	contains a stand-alone piece of work, such as a single entry in a blog
aside	contains a part of a page that's tangential to the main page content
audio	inserts an audio clip
audio="muted"	mutes audio
autoplay	specifies that audio should begin playing immediately when page is loaded
controls	requests that the browser display its default playback controls
height="*height*"	specifies the height of the element in pixels
loop	indicates that the browser should restart playback each time it reaches the end of the clip
preload="auto | metadata | none"	indicates whether the browser should download the audio file when opening the web page (auto), download only the metadata related to the audio file (metadata), or wait to download until the audio clip is played (none)
src="*path/filename*"	specifies the path and filename of the audio file
type="*type*"	specifies the container format used to encode the file referenced by the src attribute, where type is the MIME type of the container format
width="*width*"	specifies the width of the element in pixels
body	contains the contents visible in the main window of a web browser
br	inserts a line break
col	encloses one or more table columns to treat as a unit
span="*value*"	specifies the number of columns to include in the element
colgroup	encloses the col elements for a table
span="*value*"	specifies the number of columns to include in the element when no col elements are specified

element	content/function
dd	marks a description associated with a dt element in a description list
div	marks block-level content with no specific semantic meaning
dl	marks a description list, in which each item is comprised of a term and its description
dt	marks a term or an item being described in a description list
fieldset	marks a group of related form fields and associated labels
figcaption	marks caption text associated with an img element; always enclosed within a figure element
figure	contains an image that adds information to a web page; a user agent should be able to link the content of a figure element and move it to another location without affecting the information conveyed by the web page
footer	contains information about a section or document that usually appears at the end of a web page, such as attributions and/or footnotes
form action="action"	marks all the elements that are part of a form specifies the file or application that receives form data
h1, h2, h3, h4, h5, h6	mark heading text; h1 is the highest level heading on a web page and h6 is the lowest
head	contains information about a web page, including elements that are not visible within the browser window
header	contains information about a section or document that usually appears at the beginning, such as a heading, logo, and/or table of contents
html	encloses all the code for a web page
iframe	embeds content from another website while preserving formatting and presentation

img
    alt="text"
    src="url | filename"
    width="value"
    height="value"
    usemap="name"
	inserts an image
	text to display or be read aloud in place of the image
	path and filename for the image file to display
	native width of the image in pixels
	native height of the image in pixels
	name attribute value of map element to use as image map

input
    alt="text"
    checked
    maxlength="value"
    name="name"
    placeholder="text"
    required
    src="path/filename"
    type="button"
    type="checkbox"
    type="color"
    type="date | month |
      week | time | datetime |
      datetime-local"
    type="email"
 	
    type="file"
    type="image"
    type="number"
 	
    type="password"
 	
    type="radio"
    type="range"
    type="reset"
	marks an individual item of data that users can enter, or a button for form interaction
	provides alternative text for users of non-visual user agents (used with type="image")
	marks an option button or a check box as selected by default
	specifies the maximum number of characters a user can enter
	specifies the group name that all option buttons in a group must share
	text that appears in an input box until the user is ready to type
	indicates that users must complete the field, and that browsers should enforce this requirement
	specifies the image file name and location (used with type="image")
	creates a generic button that can be programmed using a script
	creates a check box, which allows users to select a single item
	supports input of hexadecimal color values
	accepts dates, times, and related values using a standard format
	
	modern browsers may validate to ensure that entries are valid email addresses; touchscreen devices with on-screen keyboards may display customized buttons for email input, such as an @ key or a . or .com key
	accepts the path and filename for a file to upload from a user's device
	creates a submit button using an image
	modern browsers may validate to ensure that entries are numbers; touchscreen devices with on-screen keyboards may display numeric keyboards
	most browsers display text entered by users as bullets or asterisks rather than showing the actual characters
	creates an option button, which lets users select one option from a set of choices
	enables you to specify a range of valid numbers that users can input
	creates a button that clears all user input and resets all form fields to defaults

element	content/function
type="search"	modern browsers may style input to match styling of search boxes in other parts of the user interface
type="submit"	creates a submit button that submits user input based on form or button attributes
type="tel"	touchscreen devices with on-screen keyboards may display numeric keyboards with -, *, and # keys
type="text"	creates a text box into which users can type a single line of text
type="url"	modern browsers may validate entries to ensure they are valid web addresses; touchscreen devices with on-screen keyboards may display customized buttons for input, such as /, ., and .com keys
value="*value*"	specifies the text to be submitted if an element is selected, or the text to appear on a button
label	marks a heading describing the associated field
for="*id*"	specifies the id value of the element being labeled
legend	marks a heading describing the topic of the fieldset
li	marks list item content in an ordered list or an unordered list
link	makes the content of an external file available in an HTML document
href="*filename* | *url*"	specifies the destination
rel="keyword"	keyword specifying the type of link
media="*media*"	media for which the linked resource is intended (default: all)
type="*type*"	MIME type of the linked resource
map	parent element for area elements that make up an image map
name="*name*"	name value referenced by usemap attribute in img element
meta	enables you to pass information about a web page to user agents that open it
name="*name*"	the type of metadata being provided, from list of standard metadata names
http-equiv="*keyword*"	directions to the user agent on handling the web page
content="*content*"	the content of the metadata described by the name value
charset="*charset*"	the character encoding that the document uses
nav	contains site or page navigation elements
object	includes the content of an external resource in the current web page
type="*type*"	specifies the MIME type of the external resource
height="*height*"	specifies the height of the element in pixels
width="*width*"	specifies the width of the element in pixels
ol	marks an ordered list, in which items are numbered or lettered sequentially
optgroup	marks a group of option elements in a drop-down list
option	marks a single entry in a drop-down list
selected	marks an entry as selected by default
value="*value*"	specifies the text to be submitted if an element is selected
p	marks a paragraph of text
param	defines one or more parameters related to the external resource in the containing object element
name="*name*"	parameter name
value="*value*"	parameter value
script	contains script code or a link to an external file containing script code
src="*filename*"	path and filename for the external script file
type="*type*"	the script language or data format
section	encloses a section of content focused on a common theme, such as a chapter of a larger work
select	encloses a set of entries to display as a drop-down list
source	specifies the location and encoding of an audio or video file
src="*path/filename*"	specifies the path and filename of the audio or video file
type="*type*"	specifies the container format used to encode the file referenced by the src attribute, where *type* is the MIME type of the container format
span	contains inline text or elements; enables you to style inline elements

element	content/function
style type="*type*"	encloses style sheet code a MIME value indicating the language of the style sheet code
table	marks content to present as a table
tbody	encloses table body rows

td
    colspan="*value*"
    rowspan="*value*"
	marks the content of a table data cell
	the number of columns that the cell spans
	the number of rows that the cell spans

textarea
    cols="*value*"
    rows="*value*"
	marks a multiline area where users can enter text
	approximates how many characters in a monospace font should fit across the box
	specifies how many rows of input are visible

tfoot	encloses table footer rows

th
    colspan="*value*"
    rowspan="*value*"
	marks the content of a table header cell
	the number of columns that the cell spans
	the number of rows that the cell spans

thead	encloses table header rows
title	specifies text that appears on the title bar or tab of a web browser opening the page
tr	encloses table cell elements that make up a single table row

track
    kind="captions |
        chapters |
        descriptions |
        metadata |
        subtitles"
    label="*label*"
 	
    src="*path/filename*"
    srclang="*language*"
	links a VTT caption or description file to the current web page
	specifies the type of information contained in the source file using one of the following keywords: captions (transcript of all audio content); chapters (video navigation tool); descriptions (transcript of visual content); metadata (content used by track-related scripts); or subtitles (transcript of spoken content, the default)
	specifies a unique, user-readable description of track content for inclusion in a list of available tracks
	specifies the path and name of the file containing the track data
	specifies the language of the track data using an abbreviation from the list at iana.org/assignments/language-subtag/registry

ul	marks an unordered list, in which the order of items doesn't matter

video
    audio="muted"
    autoplay
    controls
    height="*height*"
    loop
    poster="*path/filename*"
    preload="auto | metadata |
        none"
 	
    src="*path/filename*"
    type="*type*"
 	
    width="*width*"
	inserts a video
	mutes audio
	specifies that video should begin playing immediately when page is loaded
	requests that the browser display its default playback controls
	specifies the height of the element in pixels
	indicates that the browser should restart playback each time it reaches the end of the video
	specifies a path and filename for an image to display before video playback starts
	indicates whether the browser should download the video file when opening the web page (auto), download only the metadata related to the video file (metadata), or wait to download until the video is played (none)
	specifies the path and filename of the video file
	specifies the container format used to encode the file referenced by the src attribute, where type is the MIME type of the container format
	specifies the width of the element in pixels

CSS

CSS Properties

This table includes all CSS properties covered in this text, along with selected values.

property	values	specifies
@keyframes	*name*	a keyframe animation that indicates values of properties that change at two or more points during the animation, where *name* is the name of the animation to be referenced by the animation-name or animation property
@media	all; max-width: *value*; min-width: *value*; print; screen; or speech	style rules that apply only to indicated media or media features
@page	(none)	style rules for a limited set of properties that apply only to paged output (such as printed output)
animation	*name duration timing-function delay iteration-count direction*	values for animation-name, animation-duration, animation-timing-function, animation-delay, animation-iteration-count, and animation-direction using a shorthand syntax
animation-delay	*n*s, where *n* is a value in seconds	time in seconds after an animation is triggered and before the animation begins
animation-direction	*normal* or *reverse*	whether the animation should play forward (normal) or in reverse (reverse)
animation-duration	*n*s, where *n* is a value in seconds	time in seconds from the start of the animation to the end of the animation
animation-iteration-count	a whole number, *n*	number of times the animation is played
animation-name	*name*	the name of the @keyframe rule to use
animation-timing-function	ease, ease-in, ease-in-out, ease-out, linear, step-end, or step-start	a function expression or keyword that determines the rhythm of the animation
background	*background-image background-position [/background-size] background-repeat background-attachment background-clip background-color*	one or more properties related to background listed in a specific order (shorthand property)
background-attachment	scroll; local; or fixed	whether a background image scrolls with document content (scroll, the default), scrolls only with element content (local), or does not scroll (fixed)
background-blend-mode	normal; multiply; screen; overlay; darken; lighten; color-dodge; color-burn; hard-light; soft-light; difference; exclusion; hue; saturation; color; or luminosity	how overlapping background images blend with each other and with background color

property	values	specifies
background-clip	content-box; padding-box; or border-box (default)	whether a background image extends only behind element content (content-box), up to the inner edge of the border (padding-box), or to the outer edge of the border (border-box, the default)
background-color	color name from list of supported colors; rgb triplet in the format rgb(rrr,ggg,bbb); rgba value in the format rgba(rrr,ggg,bbb,a); hsl value in the format hsl(hhh,sss,lll); hsla value in the format hsla(hhh,sss,lll,a); or hexadecimal triplet in the format #rrggbb	an element's fill color, behind any content such as text
background-image	url("path/filename") or linear-gradient(color_stops)	an image file to use as the background for an element
background-origin	content-box; padding-box; or border-box (default)	whether a background image starts only behind element content (content-box), at the inner edge of the border (padding-box), or at the outer edge of the border (border-box, the default)
background-position	one to four values from the keywords static; relative; absolute; sticky; or fixed, or values in CSS units	the position within an element of the edges of a background image
background-repeat	one or two values from the keywords repeat; repeat-x; repeat-y; space, round; or no-repeat	whether a background image is repeated horizontally, vertically, both, or neither, using one or two keywords
background-size	one or two values from the keywords auto; cover; or contain; or values in CSS units	the size of a background image with keywords, lengths, or percentages
border	a space-separated list of a thickness value in a CSS unit, a style keyword, and a CSS color name or value (% values are not supported for thickness), in the format thickness style color	the visible border around an element
border-collapse	collapse or separate (the default)	whether space is displayed between the borders of adjacent table cells (separate) or not (collapse)
border-color border-top-color border-right-color border-bottom-color border-left-color	color name from list of supported colors; rgb triplet in the format rgb(rrr,ggg,bbb); rgba value in the format rgba(rrr,ggg,bbb,a); hsl value in the format hsl(hhh,sss,lll); hsla value in the format hsla(hhh,sss,lll,a); or hexadecimal triplet in the format #rrggbb	the color of an element border on one or more sides

border-radius
border-top-left-radius
border-top-right-
   radius
border-bottom-right-
   radius
border-bottom-left-
   radius
	value in em, pixels, or another supported unit; percent of the height of the parent element	the roundness of specified corner(s) of an element

border-spacing	1 or 2 values in CSS units	the distance between the borders of adjacent table cells if the value of border-collapse is separate
border-style border-top-style border-right-style border-bottom-style border-left-style	dashed; dotted; double; groove; hidden; inset; none; ridge; outset; or solid	the style of an element border on one or more sides

property	values	specifies
border-width border-top-width border-right-width border-bottom-width border-left-width	thin; medium; thick; or a value in a CSS unit (% values not supported)	the thickness of an element border on one or more sides
bottom	value in ems, pixels, or another supported unit; or percent of the height of the browser window	the distance the element is moved up from the bottom edge of the browser window (fixed positioning) or positioned ancestor element (relative or absolute positioning); the default value, 0, leaves the element in its original vertical position
box-shadow	a horizontal offset in pixels; a vertical offset in pixels; a blur radius in pixels (optional); a shadow color (optional); a spread distance in pixels (optional); and the inset keyword (optional)	the shadow to create behind a block-level element
clear	left; right; both; or none	floated elements are not displayed to the left, right, or on either side of another element
color	color name from list of supported colors; rgb triplet in the format rgb(rrr,ggg,bbb); rgba value in the format rgba(rrr,ggg,bbb,a); hsl value in the format hsl(hhh,sss,lll); hsla value in the format hsla(hhh,sss,lll,a); or hexadecimal triplet in the format #rrggbb	an element's foreground color; for elements containing text, this is the text color
content	"text" or url("path/image")	text or external content used with the :before or :after pseudo-element
display	block; inline; inline-block; none; table; table-cell; table-row	how an element is rendered
float	left; right; or none	horizontal alignment of an element with the left or right edge of the parent element, and allows elements that follow to fill in the remaining horizontal space
font	[font-style] [font-variant] [font-weight] font-size [/line-height] font-family; at minimum, both font-size and font-family values must be specified, and all values within square brackets are optional	multiple font-related properties listed in a specific order (shorthand property)
font-family	font family name or font stack	the font family in which the text of an element is displayed
font-size	a value in a CSS unit	the relative or absolute size of text
font-style	italic; oblique; or normal	whether characters are displayed slanted or in standard orientation
font-variant	small-caps; other language-specific and font-specific keywords	a variant of the default font to use, including a font family's small caps style or other language-specific and font-specific styles
font-weight	normal; bold; 100; 200; 300; 400; 500; 600; 700; 800; or 900	the weight of text
height	a value in a CSS unit; % value based on width of parent element	the vertical size of an element's content, excluding border, padding, and margin
left	value in ems, pixels, or another supported unit; or percent of the width of the browser window	the distance the element is moved from the left toward the right edge of the browser window (fixed positioning) or positioned ancestor element (relative or absolute positioning); the default value, 0, leaves the element in its original horizontal position

property	values	specifies
line-height	a value in a CSS unit; or a value without units to specify a multiple of the default line height	the amount of blank space above and below each line of text
list-style-image	url("path/filename")	the image used as a list item marker
list-style-type	ordered list: decimal; decimal-leading-zero; lower-alpha; lower-latin; lower-roman; none; upper-alpha; upper-latin; upper-roman; or language-specific values unordered list: circle; disc; square; or none	the list item marker for an ordered or an unordered list
margin margin-top margin-right margin-bottom margin-left	a value in a CSS unit; % value based on width of parent element	the space outside a border between the border and adjacent or parent elements
max-height	a value in a CSS unit; % value based on width of parent element	the maximum vertical size of an element's content, excluding border, padding, and margin
max-width	a value in a CSS unit; % value based on width of parent element	the maximum horizontal size of an element's content, excluding border, padding, and margin
min-height	a value in a CSS unit; % value based on width of parent element	the minimum vertical size of an element's content, excluding border, padding, and margin
min-width	a value in a CSS unit; % value based on width of parent element	the minimum horizontal size of an element's content, excluding border, padding, and margin
opacity	a decimal value from 0 (fully transparent) to 1 (fully opaque)	how transparent an element is
padding padding-top padding-right padding-bottom padding-left	a value in a CSS unit; % value based on width of parent element	the space inside a border between the border and the element content
position	absolute; fixed; relative; static (default)	precisely where an element should be positioned on the web page
right	value in ems, pixels, or another supported unit; or percent of the width of the browser window	the distance the element is moved from the right toward the left edge of the browser window (fixed positioning) or positioned ancestor element (relative or absolute positioning); the default value, 0, leaves the element in its original horizontal position
text-align	left; right; center; justify; inherit (same value as enclosing element)	the horizontal alignment of text and other inline or inline-block elements within a parent element
text-shadow	a horizontal offset in pixels; a vertical offset in pixels; a blur radius in pixels (optional); and a shadow color (optional)	the shadow created behind text
top	value in ems, pixels, or another supported unit; or percent of the height of the browser window	the distance the element is moved down from the top edge of the browser window (fixed positioning) or positioned ancestor element (relative or absolute positioning); the default value, 0, leaves the element in its original vertical position
transform	rotate(ndeg), where n is a value in degrees; scale(n), scaleX(n), scaleY(n), where n is a decimal value between 0 and 1; skewX(ndeg), skewY(ndeg), where n is a value in degrees; or translate(n, m), translateX(n), translateY(n), where n and m are values in CSS units	changes to appearance of element by rotating, scaling, skewing, and/or moving (translating)

property	values	specifies
transition-delay	*n*s, where *n* is a value in seconds	time in seconds after a transition is triggered and before the transition begins
transition-duration	*n*s, where *n* is a value in seconds	time in seconds from the start of transition to the end of transition
transition-property	*property*	the name(s) of one or more properties to be transitioned
transition-timing-function	ease, ease-in, ease-in-out, ease-out, linear, step-end, or step-start	a function expression or keyword that determines the rhythm of the animation
transition	*property duration timing-function delay*	values for transition-property, transition-duration, transition-timing-function, and transition-delay using a shorthand syntax
vertical-align	top; middle (the default); or bottom	the vertical alignment of table cell contents
width	a value in a CSS unit; % value based on width of parent element	the horizontal size of an element's content, excluding border, padding, and margin
z-index	positive or negative integer, or 0	the position of an element in the stacking order; an element with a larger value is displayed on top of an element with a smaller value

CSS Pseudo-elements

pseudo-element	selects
:after	content that appears in the document before the element content
:before	content that appears in the document after the element content
:first-letter	the first letter of text in the current element
:first-line	the first line of text in the current element
:selection	web page content selected by the users

CSS Pseudo-classes

pseudo-class	selects an element when
:active	the element is in the process of being clicked or otherwise activated
:checked	the element is checked or otherwise selected
:first-child	the first child element if it is of the specified type
:first-of-type	the first child element of the specified type
:focus	the element is currently selected or active
:hover	the mouse pointer is over the element
:invalid	the content entered by a user does not meet the rules for the field
:last-child	the last child element if it is of the specified type
:last-of-type	the last child element of the specified type
:link	the link has not been visited, does not currently have the focus or the mouse pointer over it, and is not being clicked
:nth-child(*n*)	the *n*th child element of the specified type

pseudo-class	selects an element when
:nth-last-child(*n*)	the *n*th from last child element of the specified type
:nth-last-of-type(*n*)	the *n*th from last occurrence of the specified child element
:nth-of-type(*n*)	the *n*th occurrence of the specified child element
:optional	the element does not have the required attribute, meaning that user entry in the field is optional
:required	the element has the required attribute, meaning that user entry in the field is required
:valid	the content entered by a user meets the rules for the field
:visited	the element links to a document that has already been viewed

Note: *n* is a number or a calculation in the form *an+b*;
Note: IE8 supports only :active, :focus, :hover, :link, and :visited

Glossary

@font-face rule A variation of a style rule that indicates the name of a downloadable font and the location of the necessary files.

AAC One of four main audio codecs in wide use on the web today; developed by a consortium of companies and declared a standard by the Moving Pictures Experts Group (MPEG).

absolute link A link that specifies the full and complete address for a target document on the web.

absolute positioning A positioning technique that takes an element out of the normal flow and positions it in a location you specify.

absolute units Units such as pixels that represent a specific length or height that doesn't change.

adaptive content Content in a responsive design whose display is changed based on media queries.

algorithm The set of instructions combining the factors that search engines use to decide the priority of search results.

alt text Text to display in case an image is unavailable or needs to be read in user agents by software such as screen readers; created with the alt attribute of the img element.

assignment operator The = operator, which assigns a value in a JavaScript expression.

attribute Additional code within an opening element tag that specifies information about that element.

automated testing A set of browser testing measures performed by specialized software.

Bitmap image An electronic representation of an image as a grid of dots, with a color specified for each dot.

block-level element An element rendered as a box occupying the full length of its parent element, with a line break before and after.

body section A web page section whose contents include elements that are visible in the main window of a web browser, such as paragraphs and headings.

border In the box model, a line around an element formatted with a width, style, and color.

bot A program used by a search engine to index web pages. *Also called* crawler.

box model The model CSS uses to represent the characteristics of every web page element as a rectangular box with several global properties.

breakpoint In responsive design, a browser width where a change in layout should occur.

browser history The log your browser maintains of URLs that you've visited.

browser prefix A word or an abbreviation added to the start of a property name that is specific to a browser or rendering engine.

browser sniffing A technique that attempts to identify the brand and version of each user's browser by using a script to ask the browser to identify itself.

bug A problem that results from incorrectly written code.

Camel case A method of capitalization that uses a lowercase letter for the first letter of the first word in a JavaScript variable name and capitalizes the first letter of each new word in the name.

captions Text that is overlaid on a video image and that describes the audio portion.

Cascading Style Sheets (CSS) A companion language to HTML designed for describing the appearance of web page elements.

cell The intersection of a row and a column in a table, in which each item of data is displayed.

character encoding The system user agents should employ to translate the electronic information representing a web page into human-recognizable symbols, such as letters and numbers.

character reference A specially formatted code that represents characters in the HTML document character set.

check box A box that users can click to add or remove a check mark, enabling users to select or deselect it.

child element An element nested within another element.

class selector A selector that creates a style rule based on values assigned to elements using the HTML class attribute.

clients Computers that access web documents over a network from a web server.

code editor A text editor that is optimized for writing code in a programming language.

codec An encoding method for audio or video; short for coder/decoder.

collapse The term for what happens in the box model when adjacent top and bottom margins combine into a single margin equal to the greater of the two values.

column A vertical set of data in a table.

comment A text element in your web page code that is not rendered by user agents and is viewable only by people who examine the HTML code of your web pages.

commenting out Enclosing a declaration within comment characters so user agents won't apply it to your documents while preserving it in your style sheet.

comparison operator An operator that lets you determine whether two values are the same or different.

container A file within which a video stream and any accompanying audio are packaged for distribution.

control *See* field.

crawler *See* bot.

CSS *See* Cascading Style Sheets (CSS).

CSS3 The most recent version of CSS.

custom build A version of a JavaScript library such as Modernizr that includes only the features that your site uses.

custom font A font that is not installed on a user's computer but that a user agent can download and apply.

Dead links Links whose targets don't exist.

debugging The process of finding and removing bugs from code.

declaration The basic building block of CSS code, which is a combination of a property name and a value.

definition list The name for a description list in previous versions of HTML.

description list A list that enables you to specify a set of items and descriptions.

descriptions Text that explains in words what is happening in a video and that can be read by a screen reader.

design document *See* project plan.

developer tools Utilities that are built into all modern browsers that you can use to debug your code.

device pixel ratio The number of device pixels used to display each logical pixel on a given device.

device pixels Dots in the grid that makes up the display for any electronic device.

DNS *See* domain name service (DNS).

DNS server A specialized web server that looks up the IP address that corresponds to a given domain name and passes that information to a web client, which then uses it to access a website.

Document object The parent element of the DOM tree.

Document Object Model (DOM) A standardized way of referring to the parts of a web page.

DOM *See* Document Object Model (DOM).

DOM tree The hierarchical arrangement of the content of an HTML document.

domain name registrar A person or organization authorized by ICANN to reserve domain names.

domain name service (DNS) The central directory for the web, similar to a phone book, which connects the IP address of a web resource with its domain name.

dots per inch (DPI) The unit of measurement for image resolution, which specifies how close the dots in the bitmap image should appear on the output.

downloadable font *See* custom font.

DPI *See* dots per inch (DPI).

drop-down menu A list of options from which users can select, and which browsers display as a small text box with an arrowhead next to it.

Em A CSS unit that represents a multiple of the computed font size for the current element, where 1em represents 100% of this size.

email harvester A program that continually explores web pages looking for email addresses that in turn receive spam emails.

embedded Content from another site that is displayed with formatting that matches the host site and includes links back to the context in which it was originally posted.

embedded style sheet CSS style rules entered in the head element of an HTML document.

emulator An application that runs on a computer and approximates the dimensions and behavior of a wide range of devices.

encoding The process of transforming a moving image and/or sound into a digital file.

event An action on a web page that JavaScript code can respond to.

event listener A statement that specifies a web page object, an event that may occur on that object, and the name of a function that is called when that event happens.

Extensible Hypertext Markup Language (XHTML) A version of HTML that conforms to the rules of Extensible Markup Language (XML).

Extensible Markup Language (XML) A markup language whose rules are combined with those of HTML to create XHTML.

extension A small application that changes the way web pages are rendered in a browser or integrates features with the content of a web page.

external style sheet A separate file containing style information that multiple web pages can link to.

Fallback image An image displayed in place of a video when a user's browser is unable to render the video content.

favicon A custom graphic file for a website, displayed on the browser tab or bookmarks list in a desktop browser.

feature detection The process of testing a user's browser to detect which CSS properties are supported.

feed A widget that shows a fixed number of recent posts to a given social media account or shows posts that meet certain criteria.

field A form element in which users enter or select data. Also called control.

fieldset A group of fields that forms a logical unit.

fixed positioning A visual effect that involves an element remaining in the same position in the browser window while a user scrolls the remaining page content.

Flash Video A container format commonly used to encode various proprietary and public audio and video formats.

fluid layout A layout in which content size is constrained with the min-width and max-width properties and the columns are sized using percentages.

font family A collection of a single typeface and its variants.

font stack A list of font families in order of preference, separated by commas.

form A group of elements that lets users type text, select from lists, check boxes, and/or click buttons to provide information, and then submit that information.

function A group of one or more statements with an assigned name.

function call A reference to a function name that causes its statements to be executed.

Generated content Content added using style rules with the `:before` and `:after` pseudo-elements.

generic font family A grouping of font families according to shared characteristics.

GIF An older graphics format that works best for art that contains limited numbers of colors and areas with defined borders between areas; short for Graphics Interchange Format.

graceful degradation When a design uses newer styles in modern browsers, the process of displaying a usable layout and all page content in older browsers.

gradient A visual effect in which an area starts as a single color on one edge or corner and transitions gradually to one or more other colors.

grandchild element The child element of an element's child element.

grandparent element The parent element of an element's parent element.

H.264 One of four main video codecs in wide use on the web today; developed by the Video Coding Experts Group (VCEG) and the Moving Pictures Experts Group (MPEG).

hamburger menu A button showing three horizontal lines that is often used to replace the nav bar on smaller screens.

hand-coding The process of creating a web page by entering HTML directly.

hash link A link to an `id` property value.

hash tag A searchable code that begins with the hash or pound symbol (#) and that allows users to find posts on a given topic.

head section The section of an HTML document containing elements that are not part of the main web page, such as the `title` element.

helper program A program traditionally required for playing a video or audio file on a computer; the program can both unpack the relevant container and decode the video and audio streams.

hex system *See* hexadecimal system.

hexadecimal system A system for specifying colors that uses a pound sign (#) followed by six digits, which may include the numbers 0–9 and the letters a–f; the first two digits specify the red value, the middle two digits indicate the green value, and the final pair of digits represents the blue value.

hotspot A linked shape in an image map.

HTML *See* Hypertext Markup Language (HTML).

HTML5 The most recent version of HTML.

http *See* Hypertext Transfer Protocol (http).

https *See* Hypertext Transfer Protocol Secure (https).

hyperlink *See* link.

Hypertext Markup Language (HTML) The language in which web pages are written, which provides a standardized format for specifying the structure of a web page.

Hypertext Transfer Protocol (http) One of the schemes that web servers use to make documents available.

Hypertext Transfer Protocol Secure (https) One of the schemes that web servers use to make documents available.

ID selector A CSS selector that applies code in its associated style rule to the element with the specified `id` attribute value.

if statement Code that compares two values and executes one or more statements if the result is true.

image map HTML code associated with an image that specifies one or more shapes using sets of coordinates and provides a link target for each shape.

image optimization The process of reducing the file size of an image by reducing its quality in a way that humans can't perceive.

inheritance The process of applying an element's declarations to all of its descendant elements.

inline element An element that does not expand to fill the space of its parent and that is not rendered with line breaks before or after.

inline style A style rule inserted into the opening tag of an element using the `style` attribute.

IP address The four-part address used to access web resources; the address is made up of four numbers, each of which can have a value from zero to 255, separated by periods.

JavaScript The most widely used programming language for modern web browsers.

JPEG An image format optimized for images that contain many colors, such as photographs; *also called* JPG; short for Joint Photographic Experts Group, the organization that created it.

JPG *See* JPEG.

Keyframe animation A CSS animation created using animation properties and the `@keyframes` rule.

Label An element containing descriptive text that is associated with a form element.

layer A new level displayed on top of the normal flow, into which a positioned element is placed.

legend A descriptive title for a fieldset.

library A group of reusable JavaScript code.

link Text or another web page element that users can select to move to related content in the same page or in another document.

liquid layout *See* fluid layout.

logical pixels The pixels used in CSS media queries or property values.

lorem ipsum Text from an essay by the Roman philosopher Cicero that has been standard filler for print layouts since the 1500s.

Mailto link A link that creates a new email to a specified recipient.

margin In the box model, the space outside the border between the border and adjacent or parent elements.

media features Keywords such as min-width or max-width that specify conditions that the media must satisfy for the rules in a media query to be applied.

media query A variation of a style rule that you use to create a group of rules for a specific device.

method An action that is associated with an object.

microdata A standard for using attributes to add semantic data to web page content.

microformats A predecessor to microdata as a specification for adding semantic data to web page elements.

MIME type A standardized value used to reference a data type, such as the container format for a file in an audio, video, or source element.

minified HTML, CSS, or JavaScript code that has had all characters removed that are not needed for a browser to parse it.

MP3 One of four main audio codecs in wide use on the web today; developed by the Moving Pictures Experts Group (MPEG).

MPEG-4 A container format commonly used to encode H.264 video and AAC audio.

multi-line comment A comment that occupies multiple lines, with the opening and closing tags often on their own lines.

Named character reference A character reference that uses an abbreviation-based code.

native For a bitmap image, the native dimensions are the original width and height at which the image was saved.

nav bar *See* navigation bar.

navigation bar A set of links for moving between web pages in a website.

nested The state of being located within; when a tag pair occurs within another tag pair, the inner pair is said to be nested within the outer pair.

node An item in the DOM tree, including elements, attributes, and text content.

normal flow The default arrangement of elements in a web document, in which elements are displayed in the order they appear, with most elements displayed below the element that precedes them.

numeric character reference A character reference that uses a number code.

Object An HTML element in the DOM.

Ogg A container format commonly used to encode Theora video and Vorbis audio.

one-sided tag An HTML tag that is used by itself, rather than in a pair.

operator A symbol that a developer can use to compare or change the value of an object or a property.

optimized Describes an image file that has been compressed as much as possible without losing significant visual information.

option button A type of form field that presents users with a circular box for selecting one option from a set of choices.

Opus One of four main audio codecs in wide use on the web today; developed by the Internet Engineering Task Force (IETF).

ordered list A list in which items are numbered or lettered sequentially.

orphaned styles Style rules based on selectors that no longer apply to any elements on your web pages.

Padding In the box model, the space inside a border between the border and the element content.

parent element An element with another element nested within it.

path The part of a URL composed of the sequence of folders in which the target document is stored on the server.

percent A CSS unit that represents a percentage of another value for the current element or an ancestor element; each CSS property that takes a value in % specifies what value the % calculation is based on.

performance A measure of how quickly a published site loads and responds to user interaction over the Internet.

pixel A CSS unit that represents a unit equal to approximately 1/96 inch or 0.26 millimeter.

pixels The individual dots that make up an image, used to measure the size of a bitmap image.

plugin *See* helper program.

PNG A graphics format that works best for art that contains limited numbers of colors and areas with defined borders between areas; short for Portable Network Graphics.

poster image An image displayed before a video is played.

preview To open a web page in one or more browsers and examine the result.

progressive enhancement A practice that accepts that newer CSS features are unavailable for users of older browsers and uses these newer features in a way that doesn't affect the meaning or functionality of the page content.

project plan A summary of a client's parameters for a web site, including audience, budget, and timeline. *Also called* design document.

property (DOM) A piece of information associated with a DOM node.

property (CSS) An aspect of the appearance of a web page element that can be modified.

pseudo-class A categorization of a web page element based on a relationship or condition of the element at a given moment, rather than on a static attribute value.

pseudo-element A selector that identifies a specific part of an element and lets you style the selection as if it were its own element.

R

Radio button *See* option button.

RDFa A specialized version of the Resource Description Framework (RDF) language; RDFa is another specification for adding semantic data to web page elements.

relative link A link that gives only the path and filename information necessary to locate the target document based on the location of the current web page.

relative positioning A positioning technique that lets you make adjustments to the default position of an element while preserving the space allotted to the element in the normal flow.

relative units Units such as ems, percent, and rems that are calculated based on the sizes of other elements on a web page.

rem A CSS unit that represents a multiple of the computed font size for the html element, where 1rem represents 100% of this size; term is short for *root em*.

rendering engine Software that translates web page elements into visual, auditory, or tactile representations based on web standards.

reset rule A style rule that resets one or more common properties of multiple elements to a common baseline, ensuring that default values that may be different between browsers do not cause a web page to be displayed inconsistently.

resolution Specifies how close the dots in a bitmap image should appear on the output; measured in dots per inch (DPI).

responsive design A common solution to making a single web page or app usable at multiple screen or browser sizes; responsive design allows a web page designer to specify different CSS style rules for some or all of a page's elements, depending on the width of the screen or browser window in which the document is displayed.

rgb system A system that uses rgb triplets to specify colors.

rgb triplet A set of comma-separated values, each ranging from 0–255 or 0–100%, which represent the amounts of red, green, and blue in a color.

row A horizontal set of data in a table.

S

Sans-serif font A font that does not incorporate serifs.

Scalable Vector Graphics (SVG) A graphics format that's optimal for encoding line art and that can be displayed at different dimensions with no decrease in quality.

schema In microdata, a single group of terms and definitions related to a specific type of information.

scheme The way that computers ask for and communicate about a requested document.

screen reader Devices that many people with visual impairments use to access the web, which read aloud web page text and descriptions that a user selects.

search engine optimization (SEO) The process of tailoring the structure and content of a web page with search engines in mind.

search rank A website's position in the list of search results returned for a query.

selection interface A web page feature that presents users with allowable form field options visually or enables them to manipulate values without entering text.

selector The part of a style rule that identifies the HTML element or elements to which the declarations apply.

semantic Describes languages such as HTML5, which are intended to indicate the meanings of elements such as headings and paragraphs, but not to tell web browsers how the elements should appear.

semantic element An HTML5 element that indicates the role of its content.

SEO *See* search engine optimization.

serif A small finishing stroke at the end of a line making up a character in some fonts.

serif font A font that uses serifs.

server farm A specifically designed facility for web servers that provides a constant flow of electricity and uninterrupted Internet access.

server name The part of a URL that identifies the general location of a target document on the web.

shim A JavaScript file that uses code to create a newer CSS feature for users of older browsers.

short link A generated URL that uses an especially short domain name and a specially crafted path to represent a large, unwieldy link as a short, manageable URL.

shortcut property A property that assigns values to multiple other CSS properties with a single declaration.

sibling element When two elements are both children of the same element, they are sibling elements.

single-line comment A comment that includes the opening tag, comment text, and closing tag on a single line.

sitemap A file in a specific format that lists all the pages in a website and may include information about content such as images or video in the pages as well.

skip link A link that targets an id value at the start of the main page content and allows users to bypass navigation.

social media An online tool that provides users with methods for sharing online content and integrating their own comments.

social networking site A website such as Facebook or LinkedIn that enables people to share information about common interests, news, and events with friends, colleagues, and any other people they choose.

specificity A selector's priority relative to other selectors.

spritesheet An image file that contains multiple images used in a web page, which can be downloaded with a single HTTP request.

stack To overlap web page elements using positioning.

stacking context The element containing elements to be stacked using the z-index property.

statement A JavaScript instruction that performs an action.

static layout A layout that specifies a fixed width for web page content.

storyboard In website planning, a sketch that shows the links between the pages in the website.

stream An encoded set of video data.

style rule A line or block of CSS code that specifies the presentation of web page elements.

submit button A button that users can click to submit the data they've entered in a web form.

SVG *See* Scalable Vector Graphics (SVG).

T

ag An HTML code that specifies how user agents should treat an item in a web document.

target document The location, web page, or other document that a link opens.

template A generic website layout that includes a color scheme and element positions, but which uses placeholder images and text.

text area A field that allows users to enter multiple lines of text.

text box A single-line text field in which users can type a small amount of text.

Theora One of four main video codecs in wide use on the web today; developed by the Xiph.org Foundation.

touch icon A custom graphic file that serves as the icon for shortcuts that users create on mobile devices.

transform A change in the appearance of an element in one or more specific ways, applied using the CSS `transform` property.

transition A CSS feature that gradually applies changes to properties in response to user actions over a number of seconds.

tweet A single post on Twitter.

type selector The name of an HTML element used as a selector, which applies associated declarations to every instance of the specified element in a web document.

U

niform resource locator (URL) A standard format for specifying how and where to access a resource on the Internet.

unordered list A list in which the order of list items doesn't matter.

URL *See* uniform resource locator (URL).

user agents Programs and devices that interpret web documents.

V

alidation An automated process of comparing code you've written against the coding standards for the language, such as HTML5 or XHTML, in which it's written.

variable A value that is stored and that you can access with a name that you specify.

vector graphic An electronic representation of an image using geometric shapes.

viewport The imaginary window through which most mobile browsers display web pages.

viewport meta element A meta element with the `name` attribute set to a value of `viewport`, which is used to change a browser's viewport settings.

vocabulary In microdata, a set of terms and definitions that can be used to indicate the semantic value of a specific type of information.

Vorbis One of four main audio codecs in wide use on the web today; developed by the Xiph.org Foundation.

VP8 One of four main video codecs in wide use on the web today; developed by On2, which is owned by Google.

VP9 One of four main video codecs in wide use on the web today; developed by Google.

W

3C *See* World Wide Web consortium (W3C).

WCAG *See* Web Content Accessibility Guidelines (WCAG).

web *See* World Wide Web.

web address *See* uniform resource locator (URL).

Web Content Accessibility Guidelines (WCAG) A widely used reference for implementing web accessibility that is maintained by the World Wide Web Consortium (W3C).

web host A company that provides access to space on a web server for a yearly or monthly fee.

web page A document formatted to be accessible on the web.

web server A computer that is running web server software and that is always connected to the Internet.

web server software Software that makes web documents available over a network to other computers.

WebM A container format commonly used to encode VP8 or VP9 video and Vorbis or Opus audio.

webmaster The person in charge of a website.

website A collection of web pages that is available to anyone with web access.

WebVTT A markup language for creating text tracks to accompany video, including captions and descriptions.

white space Empty space in a layout.

widget Prewritten HTML and/or JavaScript code that enables social media users to provide easy access to their social content from a web page.

wireframe In website planning, a sketch that outlines the components of each page in a website and their places in the layout.

World Wide Web A vast collection of publicly accessible, linked documents written in Hypertext Markup Language and related languages. *Also called* web.

World Wide Web Consortium (W3C) An organization that helps build consensus around changes and additions to HTML5 and publishes descriptions of the current standards.

X

HTML *See* Extensible Hypertext Markup Language (XHTML).

XML *See* Extensible Markup Language (XML).

Index

developer tools, 72, 238–239, 354
device pixels, 239
direct child selector, 64
direct next sibling selector, 64
display property, 146–147, App B–3
div element, 32–33, App A–2
dl element, 206, 207, App A–2
DNS hosts, App C–8, App C–9
DNS servers, App C–8
DOCTYPE declarations, 6, 44
document(s)
  design, 2–3
  HTML. *See* HTML documents
  links within, 154–155
  target, 140
  web, testing on mobile devices, 18
  XHTML, creating, 44–45
Document Object Model (DOM), 352–353
DOM tree, 352, 353
domain name(s), App C–3, App C–8—App C–9
domain name registrars, App C–8, App C–9
domain service providers, App C–9
dots per inch (dpi), 170
downloadable fonts, 110
downloading, Modernizr library, 305
dpi. *See* dots per inch (dpi)
drop-down menus, 276–277
dt element, 206–207, App A–2

E

elements, 6. *See also specific elements*
  accessing using JavaScript, 354–355
em, 85
email harvesters, 145
email value, 269
embedded style sheets, 58–59
embedding social media. *See* social media
emulators, testing layouts, 238–239
encoding, 324
equal operator (===), 367
equal sign (=)
  assignment operator, 356, 366, 367
  attributes, 30
  equal operator (===), 367
  not equal operator (!==), 367
errors. *See also* bugs; debugging
  checking for, App C–2
event(s), 362, 363
event listeners, 362–363
exclamation point (!), not equal operator
  (!==), 367
Extensible Hypertext Markup Language
  (XHTML)
  documents, 44–45
  HTML compared, 7, 45

Extensible Markup Language (XML), 44
  sitemap files, 415
external style sheets, 66–71
  comments, 70–71
  creating, 66–67
  links, 68–69

F

Facebook Like buttons, 382–383
fallback code, using JavaScript, 367
fallback images, 334, 335
fantasy fonts, 111
favicons, 186, 187
feature detection, applying styles based on,
  304–305
feeds, 380
fields, 264
  marking as required, 273
  text, forms. *See* text fields, forms
fieldset(s), 264
fieldset element, 265, 266, App A–2
figcaption element, 178, 179, App A–2
figure element, 176–177, App A–2
file value, 275
finalizing sites, 418–419
:first-child pseudo-class, 246, App B–5
:first-letter pseudo-element, 120,
  App B–5
:first-line pseudo-element, 120, App B–5
:first-of-type pseudo-class, 246, App B–5
fixed positioning, 94–95
Flash Video, 324, 325, 326
float property, 90–91, 92, App B–3
floated content, longer than parent element, 93
fluid layouts, 99
:focus pseudo-class, 270, 299, App B–5
  styling, 150, 151
font(s)
  choosing, 113
  cursive, 111
  custom, 110, 114–115
  downloadable, 110
  fantasy, 111
  monospace, 111
  sans-serif, 110, 111
  serif, 110, 111
  web, 110–111
font families, 110, 111, 112–113
  generic, 110, 111
font properties, 119
font property, 119, App B–3
font stacks, 110, 111
font-family property, 112–113, 119,
  App B–3
font-height property, 119

font-size property, 116, 117, 119, App B–3
font-style property, 118–119, App B–3
font-variant property, 119, App B–3
font-weight property, 119, App B–3
footer element, 35, App A–2
form(s), 263–279
  check boxes, 272–273
  creating, 266–267
  designing, 264–265
  drop-down menus, 276–277
  enabling submission, 278–279
  feedback, 298–299
  option buttons, 274–275
  text fields. *See* text fields, forms
form element, 265, App A–2
formats, web-ready, encoding video, 331
formatting tables with CSS, 216–217
formatting text, 108–127
  bold and italics, 118–119
  colors, 122–123
  custom fonts, 110, 114–115
  font families, 110, 111, 112–113
  font size, 116, 117
  line height, 116, 117
  media queries, 126–127
  pseudo-elements, 120–121
  shadows, 124–125
  web fonts, 110–111
FTP clients, configuring, App C–4—App C–5
function(s), JavaScript, 360–361
function calls, 360

G

generated content, 296–297
generic font families, 110, 111
GIF (Graphics Interchange Format), 170
goals, websites, 2
gradients, 300–301
grandchild elements, 9
grandparent elements, 9
graphics. *See* image(s)
Graphics Interchange Format. *See* GIF
  (Graphics Interchange Format)
greater-than sign (>), character reference, 37

H

h1 through h6 elements, 10–11, 409, App A–2
hamburger menus, 244–245
hand-coding, 6
hash links, 154–155
hash mark (#)
  hash tags, 394
  ID selector, 60
  links, 154